D1287039

9

SAINT ☆ YOUNG MEN

C O N T E N T S

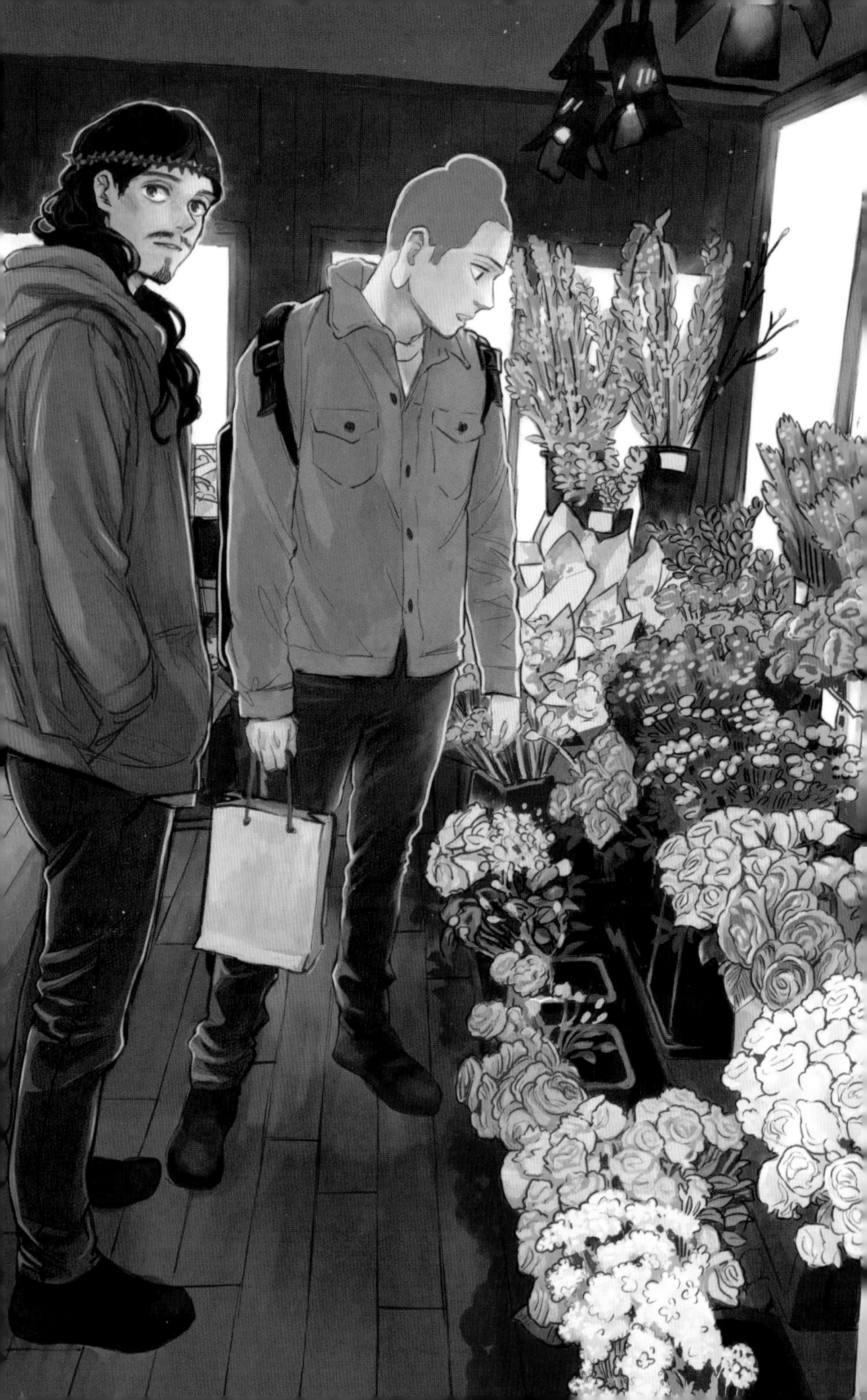

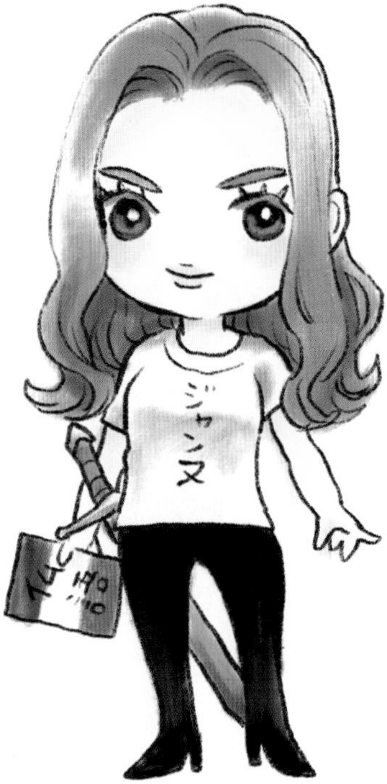
ジャンヌ
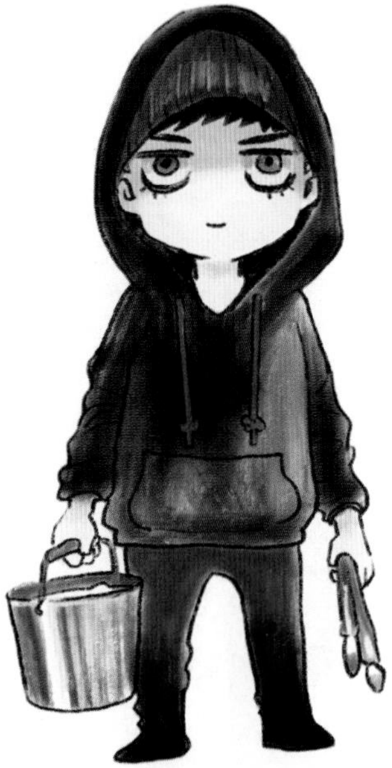

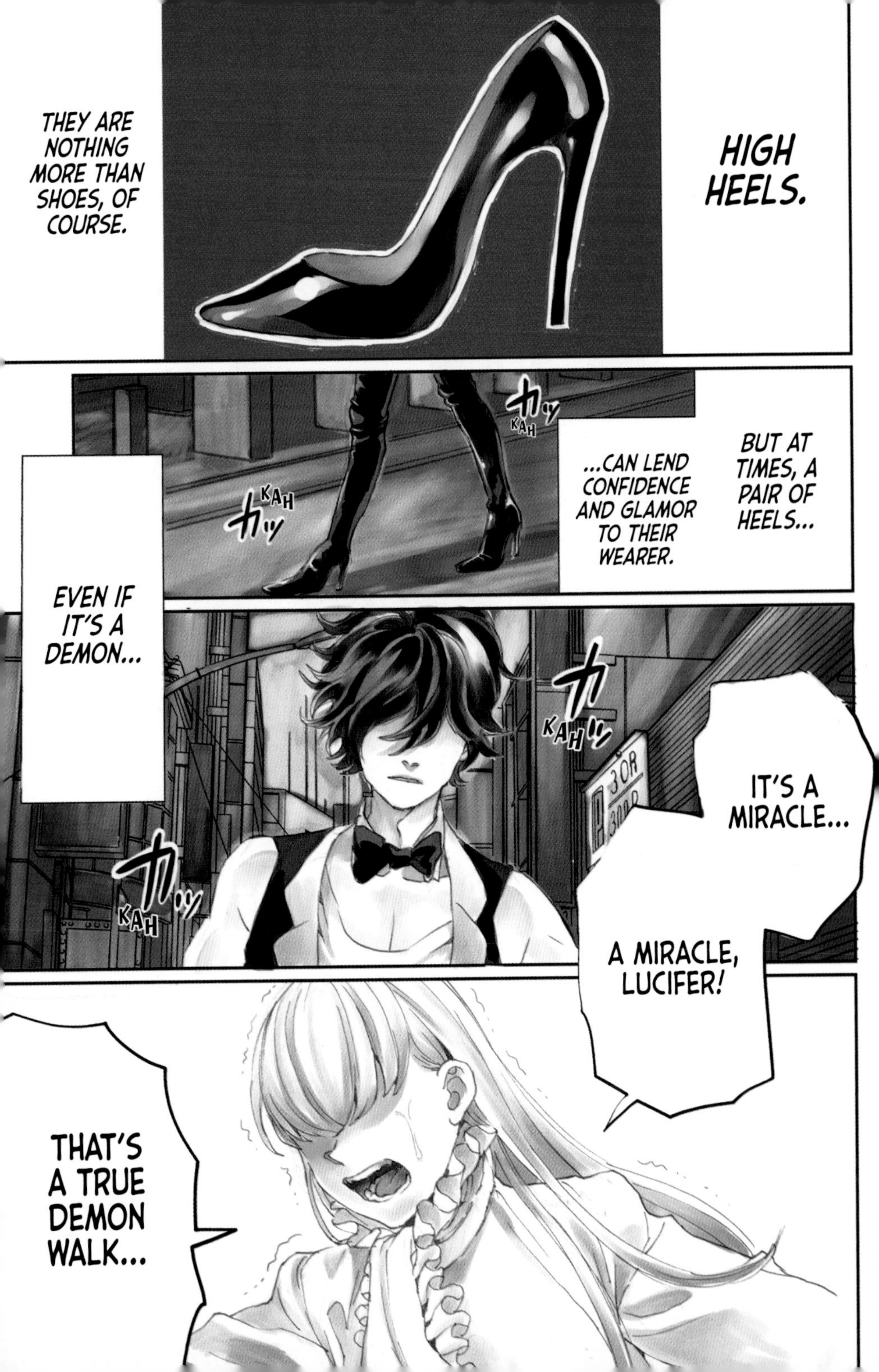
HIGH HEELS.
THEY ARE NOTHING MORE THAN SHOES, OF COURSE.
カッ KAH
BUT AT TIMES, A PAIR OF HEELS...
...CAN LEND CONFIDENCE AND GLAMOR TO THEIR WEARER.
カッ KAH
EVEN IF IT'S A DEMON...
カッ KAH
IT'S A MIRACLE...
A MIRACLE, LUCIFER!
カッ KAH
THAT'S A TRUE DEMON WALK...

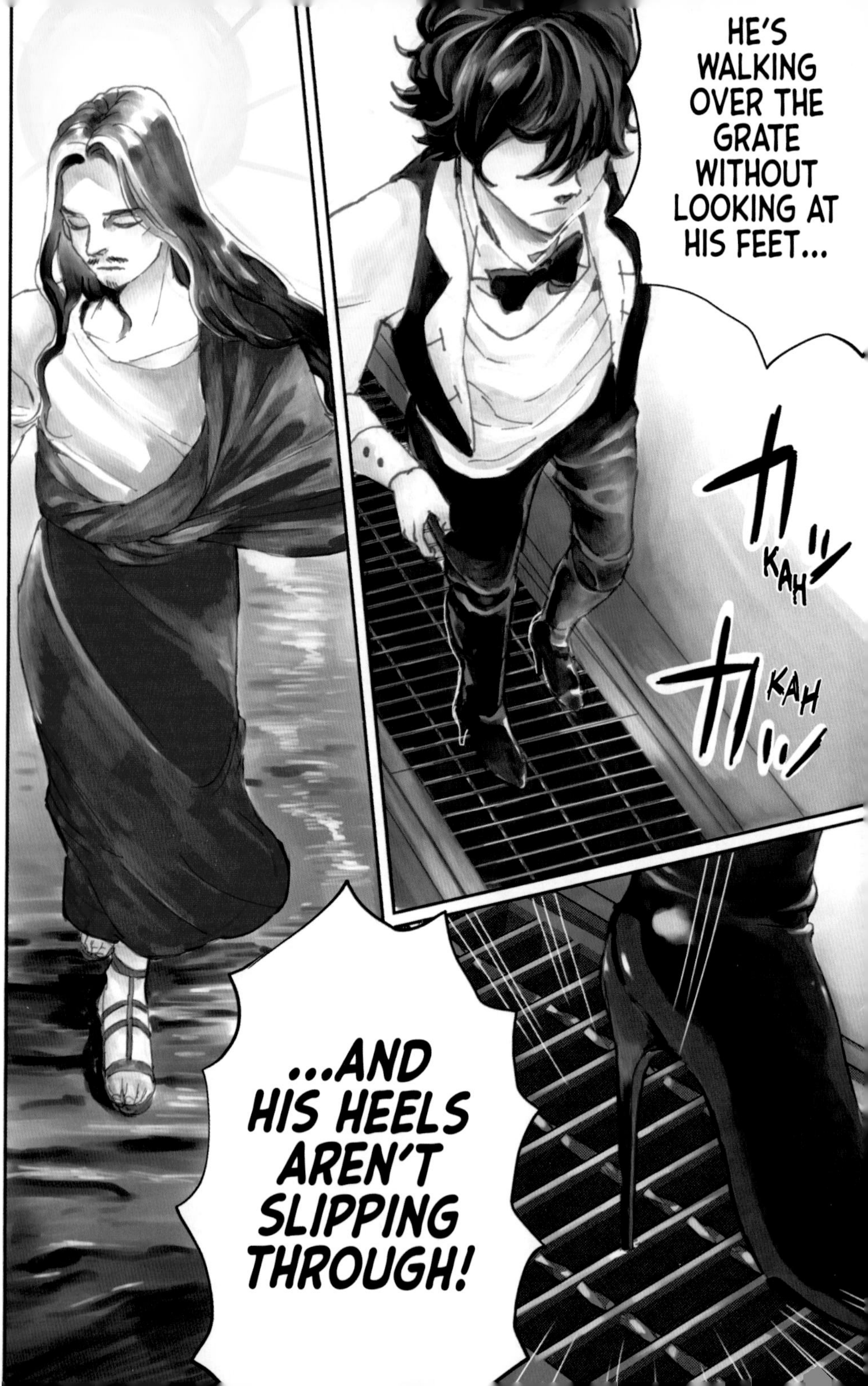
HE'S WALKING OVER THE GRATE WITHOUT LOOKING AT HIS FEET...
カッ
KAH
カッ
KAH
...AND HIS HEELS AREN'T SLIPPING THROUGH!

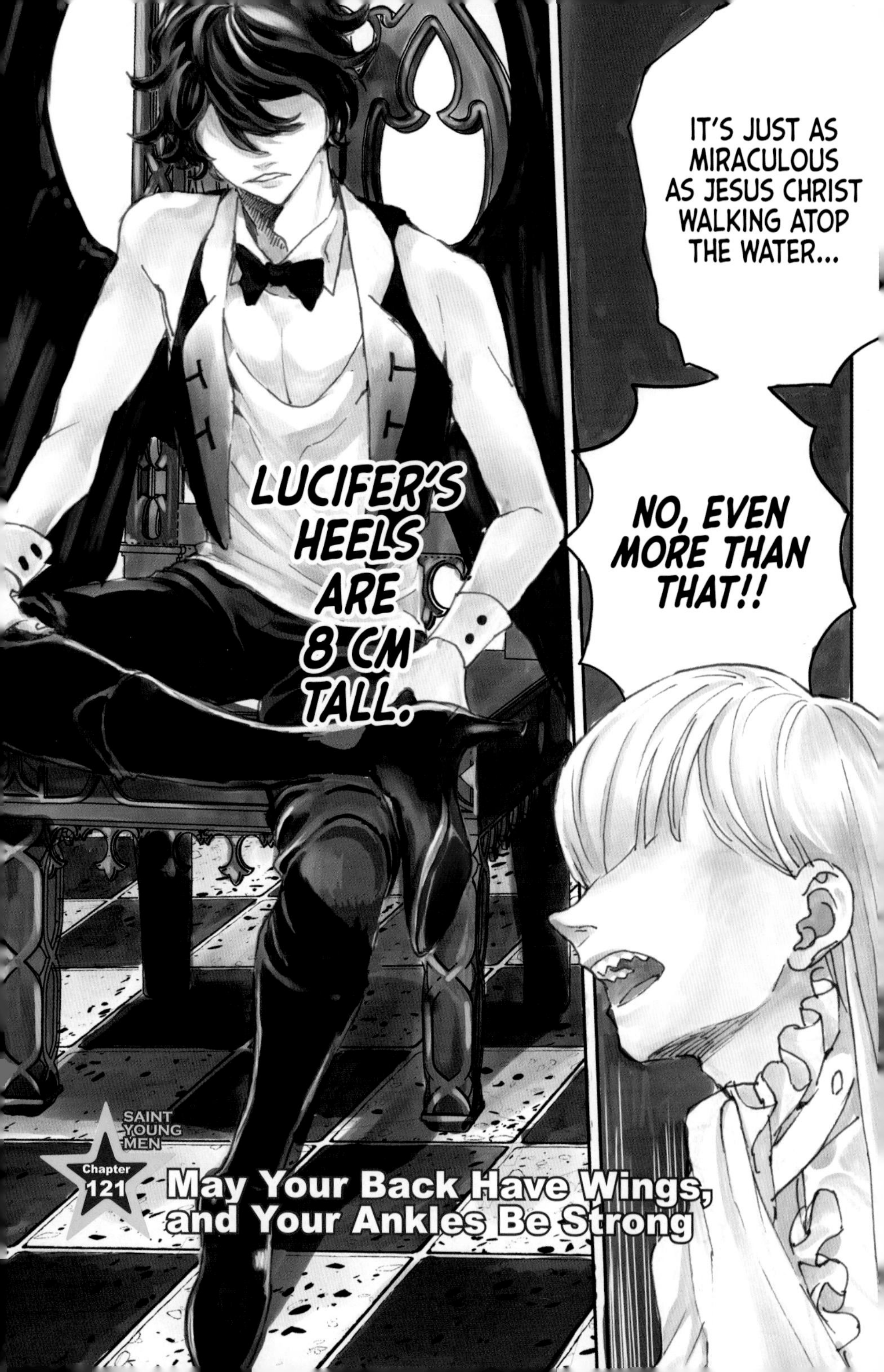
IT'S JUST AS MIRACULOUS AS JESUS CHRIST WALKING ATOP THE WATER...
NO, EVEN MORE THAN THAT!!
LUCIFER'S HEELS ARE 8 CM TALL.
SAINT YOUNG MEN
Chapter 121
May Your Back Have Wings, and Your Ankles Be Strong

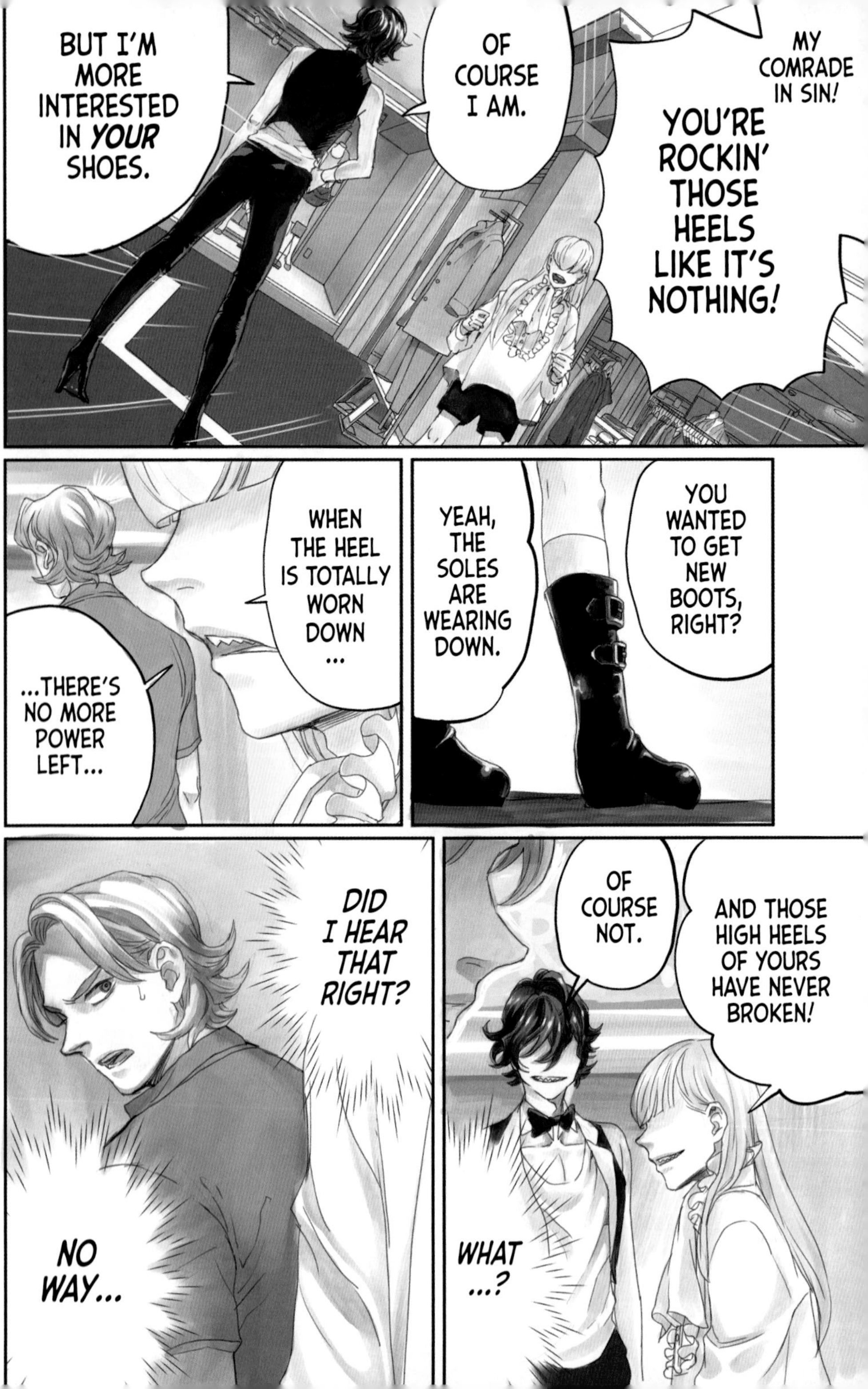
MY COMRADE IN SIN!
YOU'RE ROCKIN' THOSE HEELS LIKE IT'S NOTHING!
OF COURSE I AM.
BUT I'M MORE INTERESTED IN *YOUR* SHOES.
YOU WANTED TO GET NEW BOOTS, RIGHT?
YEAH, THE SOLES ARE WEARING DOWN.
WHEN THE HEEL IS TOTALLY WORN DOWN ...
...THERE'S NO MORE POWER LEFT...
AND THOSE HIGH HEELS OF YOURS HAVE NEVER BROKEN!
OF COURSE NOT.
WHAT ...?
DID I HEAR THAT RIGHT?
NO WAY...

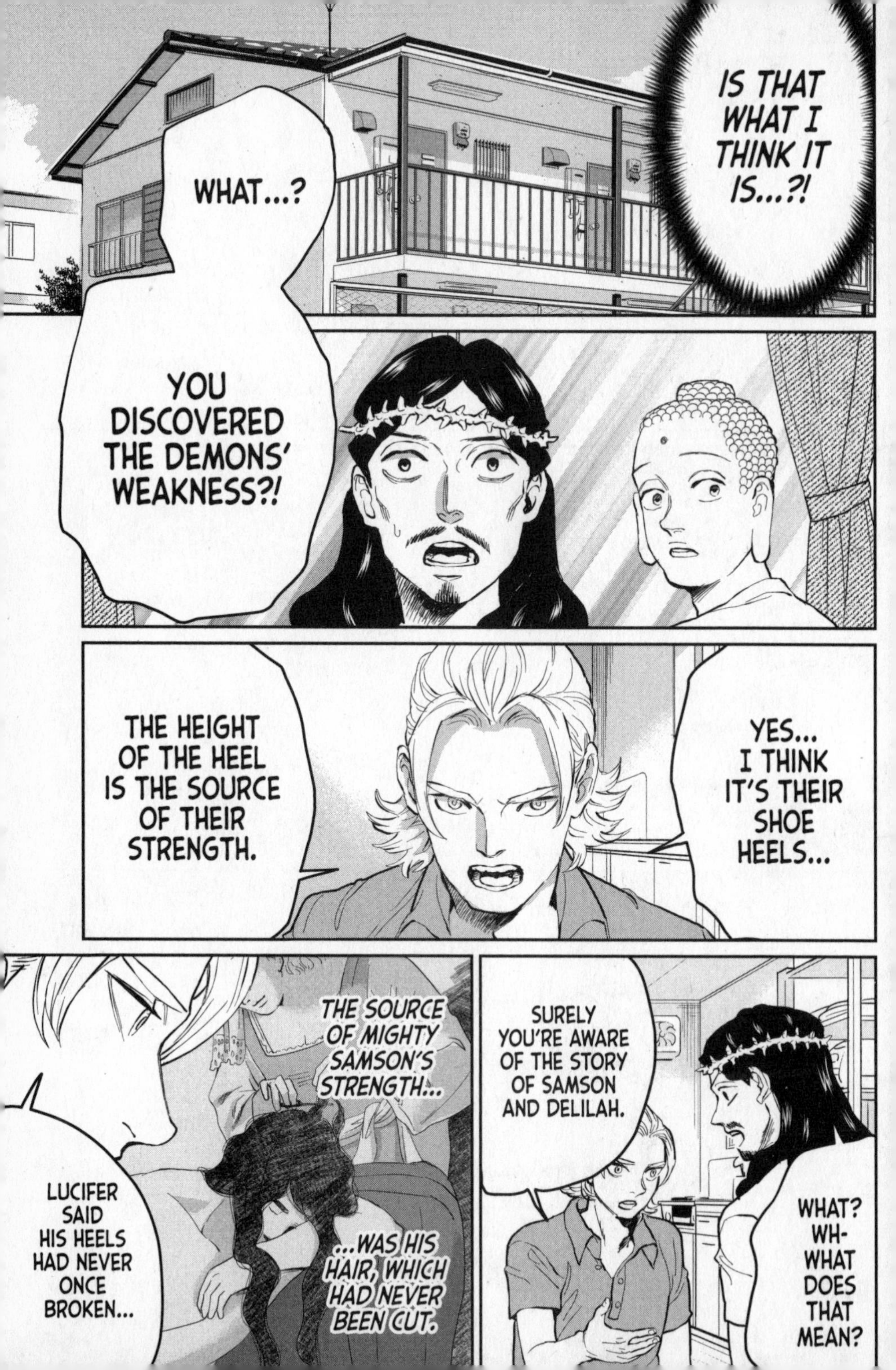
IS THAT WHAT I THINK IT IS...?!
WHAT...?
YOU DISCOVERED THE DEMONS' WEAKNESS?!
YES... I THINK IT'S THEIR SHOE HEELS...
THE HEIGHT OF THE HEEL IS THE SOURCE OF THEIR STRENGTH.
SURELY YOU'RE AWARE OF THE STORY OF SAMSON AND DELILAH.
WHAT? WH-WHAT DOES THAT MEAN?
THE SOURCE OF MIGHTY SAMSON'S STRENGTH...
...WAS HIS HAIR, WHICH HAD NEVER BEEN CUT.
LUCIFER SAID HIS HEELS HAD NEVER ONCE BROKEN...

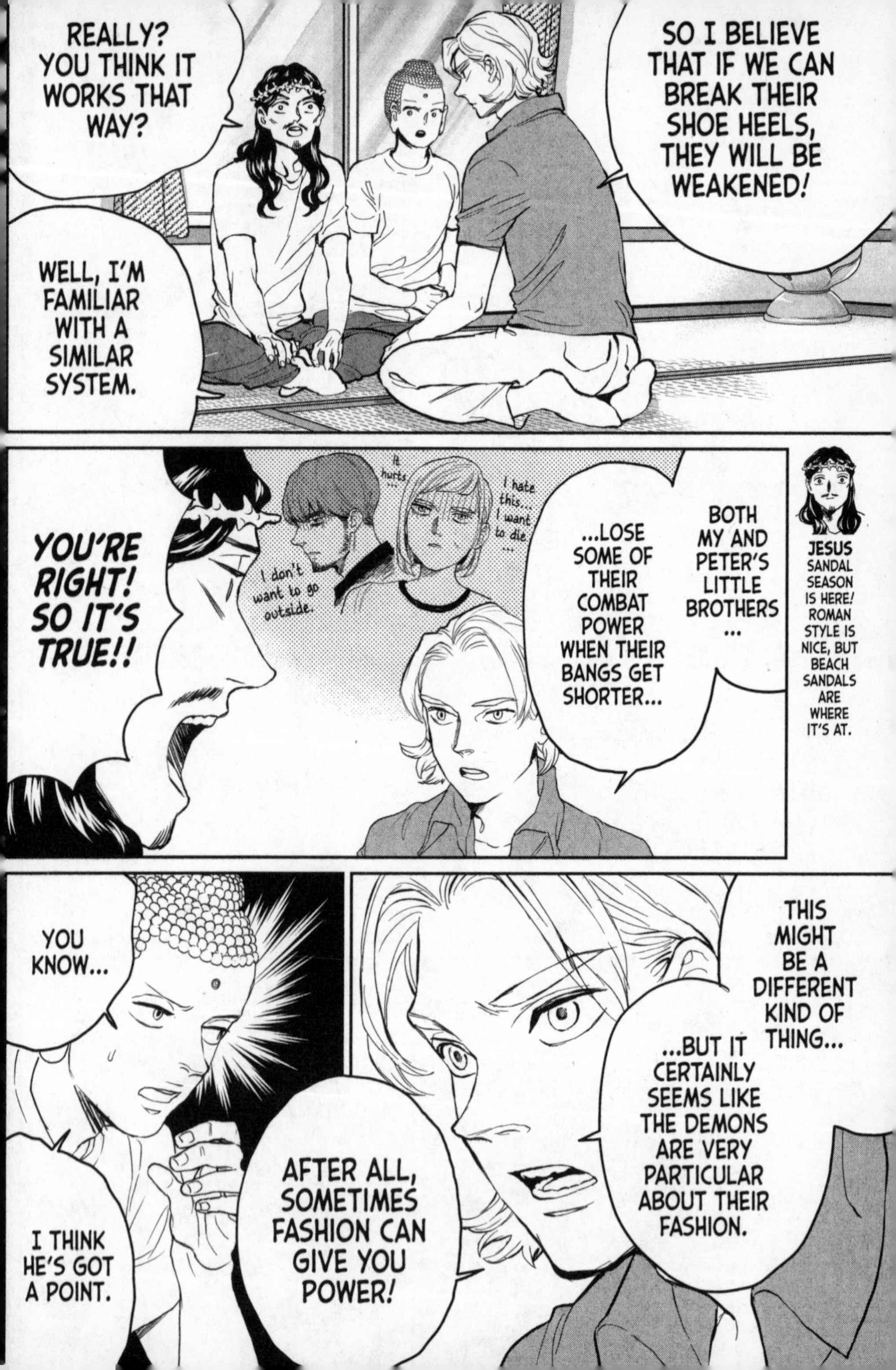
SO I BELIEVE THAT IF WE CAN BREAK THEIR SHOE HEELS, THEY WILL BE WEAKENED!
REALLY? YOU THINK IT WORKS THAT WAY?
WELL, I'M FAMILIAR WITH A SIMILAR SYSTEM.
JESUS SANDAL SEASON IS HERE! ROMAN STYLE IS NICE, BUT BEACH SANDALS ARE WHERE IT'S AT.
BOTH MY AND PETER'S LITTLE BROTHERS...
...LOSE SOME OF THEIR COMBAT POWER WHEN THEIR BANGS GET SHORTER...
I hate this... I want to die...
It hurts...
I don't want to go outside.
YOU'RE RIGHT! SO IT'S TRUE!!
THIS MIGHT BE A DIFFERENT KIND OF THING...
...BUT IT CERTAINLY SEEMS LIKE THE DEMONS ARE VERY PARTICULAR ABOUT THEIR FASHION.
AFTER ALL, SOMETIMES FASHION CAN GIVE YOU POWER!
YOU KNOW...
I THINK HE'S GOT A POINT.

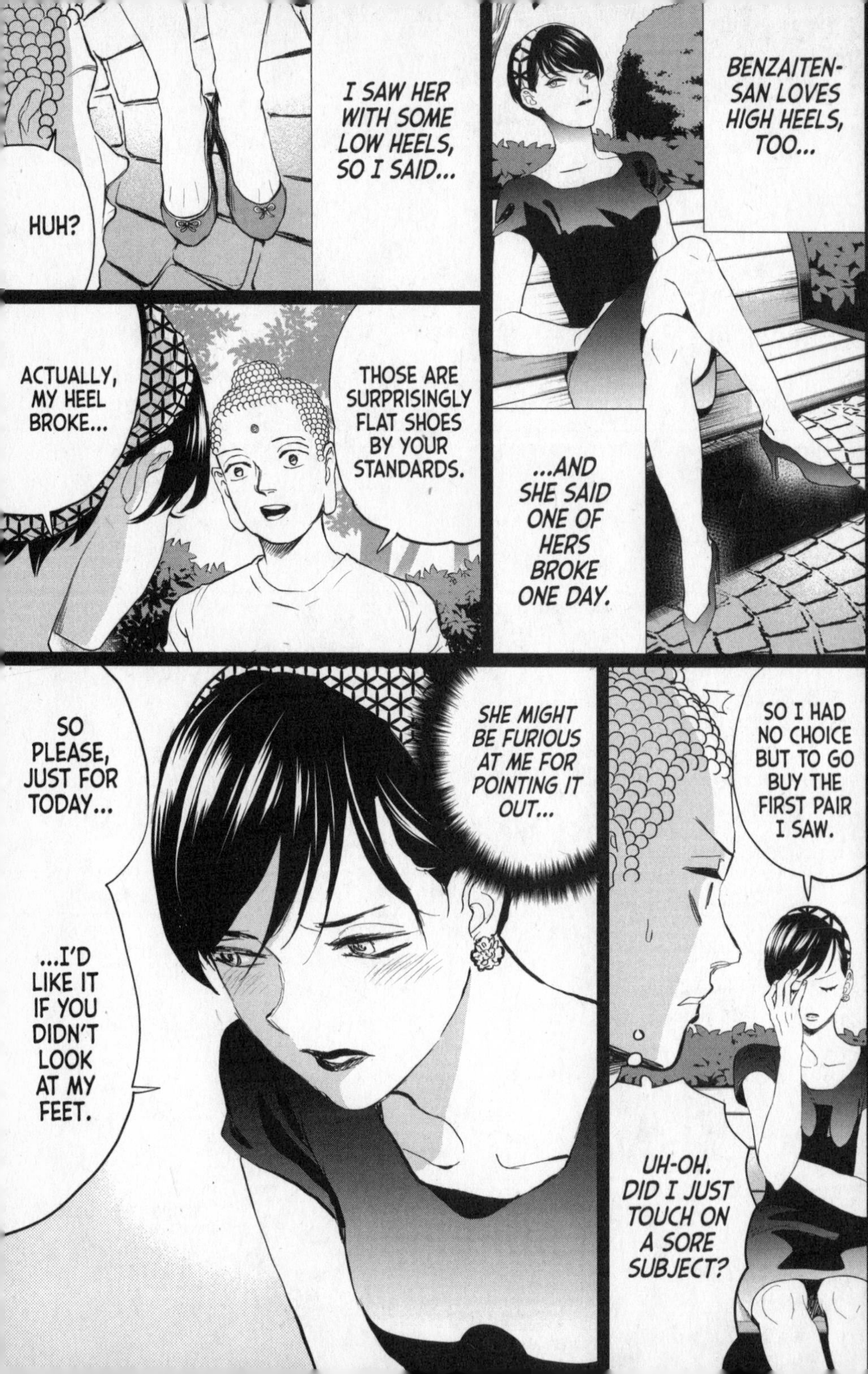
BENZAITEN-SAN LOVES HIGH HEELS, TOO...
...AND SHE SAID ONE OF HERS BROKE ONE DAY.
I SAW HER WITH SOME LOW HEELS, SO I SAID...
HUH?
THOSE ARE SURPRISINGLY FLAT SHOES BY YOUR STANDARDS.
ACTUALLY, MY HEEL BROKE...
SO I HAD NO CHOICE BUT TO GO BUY THE FIRST PAIR I SAW.
UH-OH. DID I JUST TOUCH ON A SORE SUBJECT?
SHE MIGHT BE FURIOUS AT ME FOR POINTING IT OUT...
SO PLEASE, JUST FOR TODAY...
...I'D LIKE IT IF YOU DIDN'T LOOK AT MY FEET.

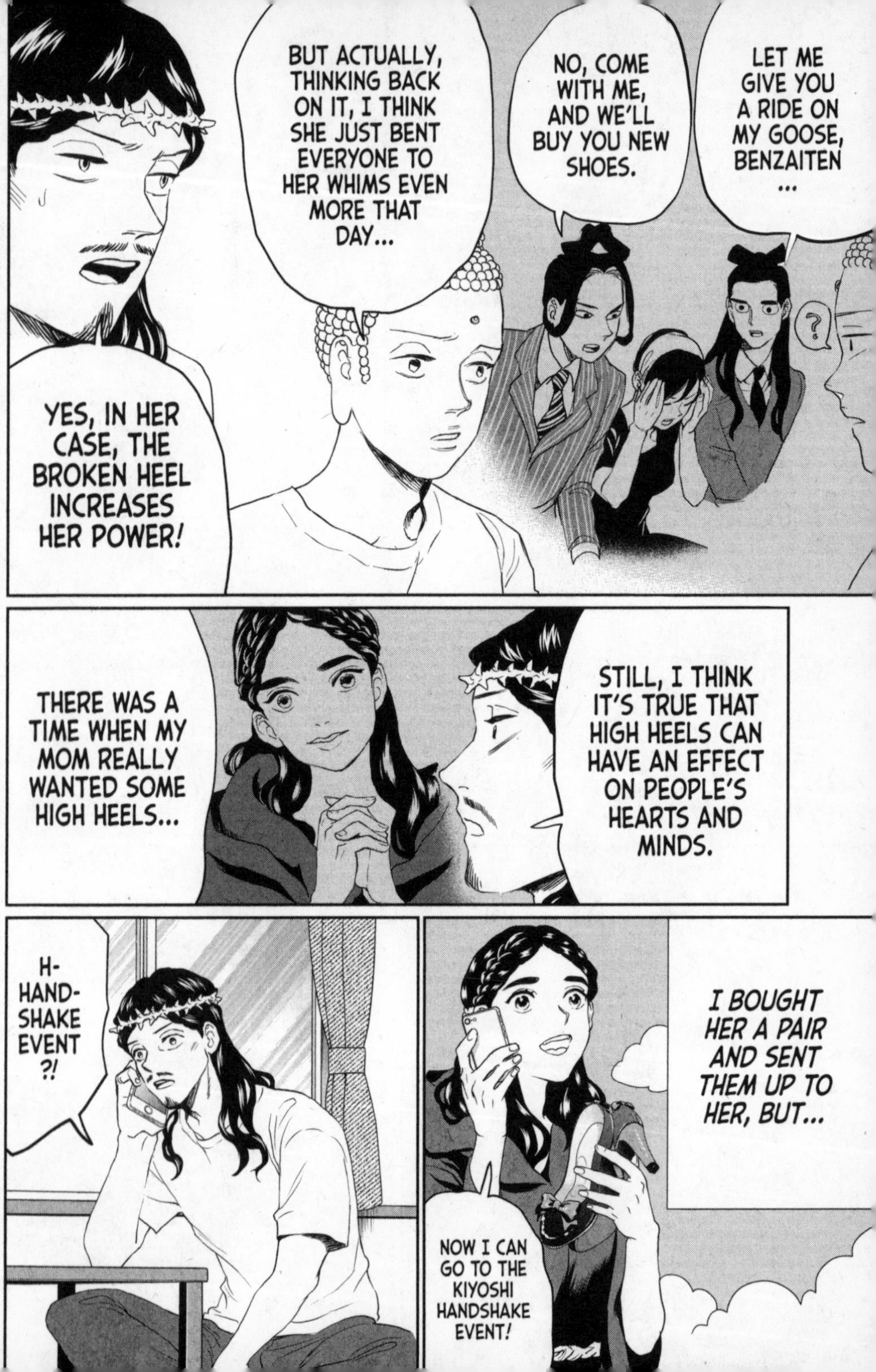
LET ME GIVE YOU A RIDE ON MY GOOSE, BENZAITEN ...
NO, COME WITH ME, AND WE'LL BUY YOU NEW SHOES.
BUT ACTUALLY, THINKING BACK ON IT, I THINK SHE JUST BENT EVERYONE TO HER WHIMS EVEN MORE THAT DAY...
?
YES, IN HER CASE, THE BROKEN HEEL INCREASES HER POWER!
STILL, I THINK IT'S TRUE THAT HIGH HEELS CAN HAVE AN EFFECT ON PEOPLE'S HEARTS AND MINDS.
THERE WAS A TIME WHEN MY MOM REALLY WANTED SOME HIGH HEELS...
I BOUGHT HER A PAIR AND SENT THEM UP TO HER, BUT...
NOW I CAN GO TO THE KIYOSHI HANDSHAKE EVENT!
H-HAND-SHAKE EVENT?!

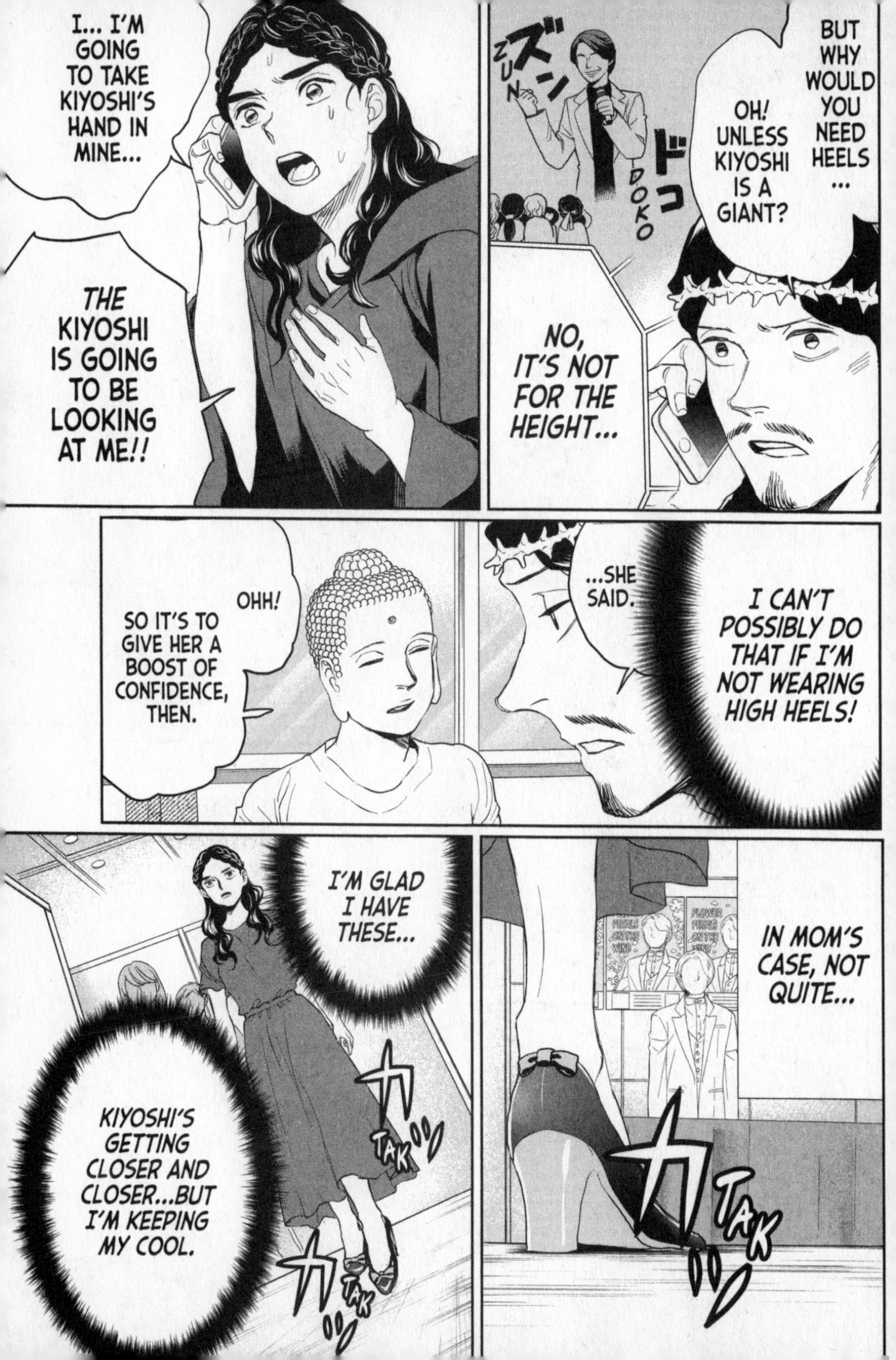
BUT WHY WOULD YOU NEED HEELS ...
OH! UNLESS KIYOSHI IS A GIANT?
ZUN ズン
DOKO ドコ
NO, IT'S NOT FOR THE HEIGHT...
I... I'M GOING TO TAKE KIYOSHI'S HAND IN MINE...
THE KIYOSHI IS GOING TO BE LOOKING AT ME!!
I CAN'T POSSIBLY DO THAT IF I'M NOT WEARING HIGH HEELS!
...SHE SAID.
OHH!
SO IT'S TO GIVE HER A BOOST OF CONFIDENCE, THEN.
IN MOM'S CASE, NOT QUITE...
FLOWER PETALS ON THE WIND
PETALS ON THE WIND
TAK
I'M GLAD I HAVE THESE...
KIYOSHI'S GETTING CLOSER AND CLOSER...BUT I'M KEEPING MY COOL.
TAK
TAK

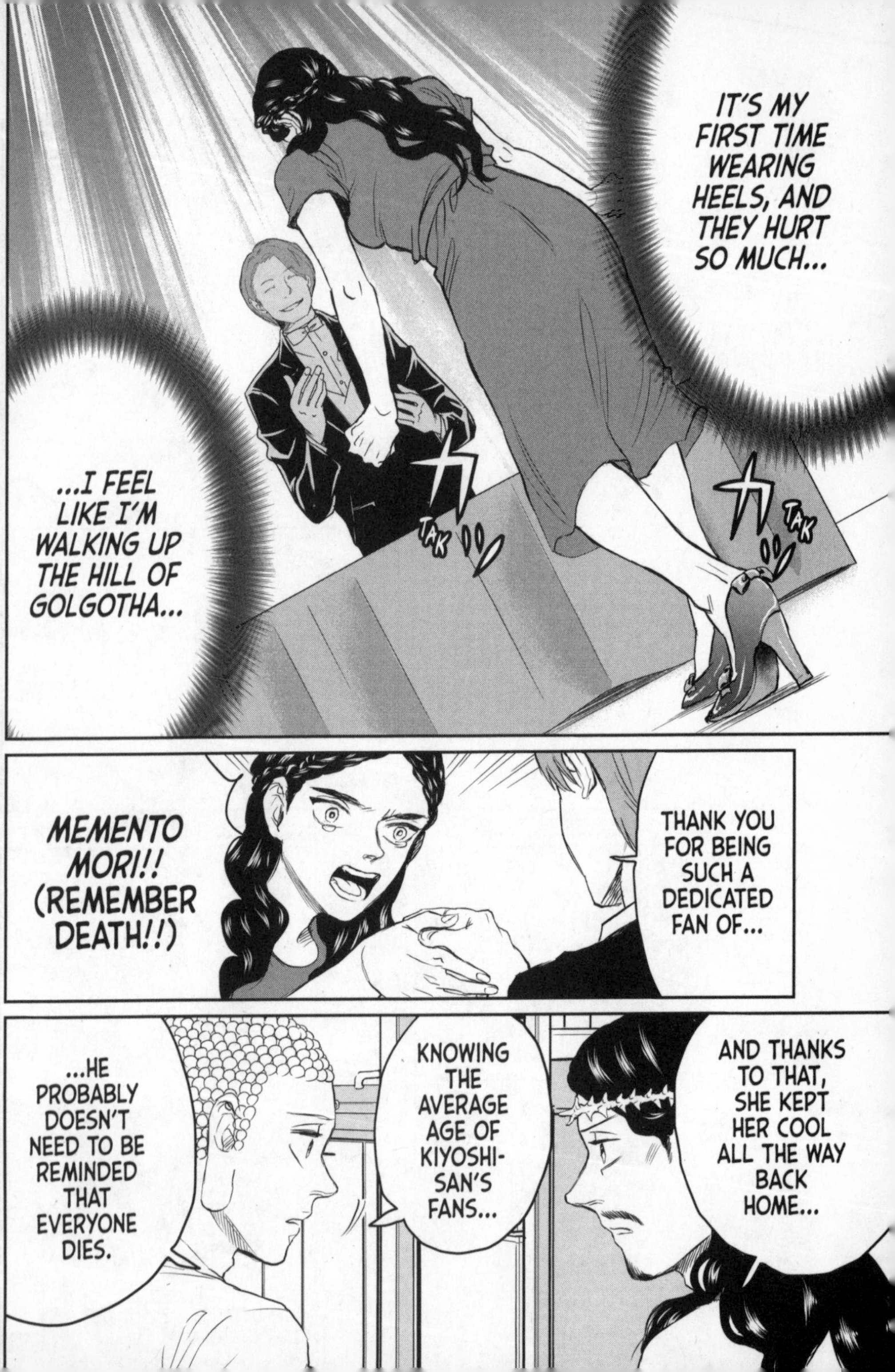
IT'S MY FIRST TIME WEARING HEELS, AND THEY HURT SO MUCH...
TAK
TAK
...I FEEL LIKE I'M WALKING UP THE HILL OF GOLGOTHA...
THANK YOU FOR BEING SUCH A DEDICATED FAN OF...
MEMENTO MORI!! (REMEMBER DEATH!!)
AND THANKS TO THAT, SHE KEPT HER COOL ALL THE WAY BACK HOME...
KNOWING THE AVERAGE AGE OF KIYOSHI-SAN'S FANS...
...HE PROBABLY DOESN'T NEED TO BE REMINDED THAT EVERYONE DIES.

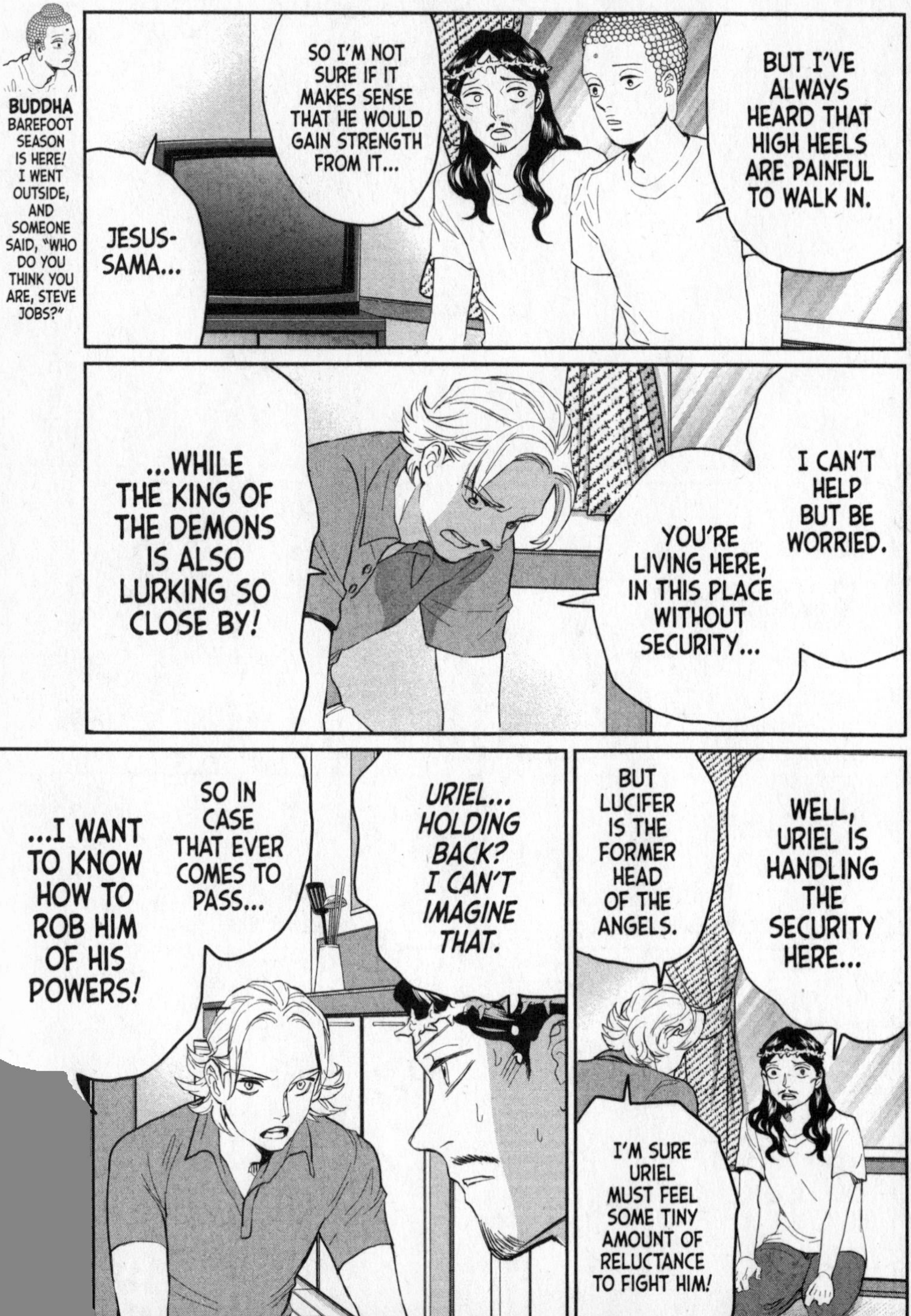
BUT I'VE ALWAYS HEARD THAT HIGH HEELS ARE PAINFUL TO WALK IN.
SO I'M NOT SURE IF IT MAKES SENSE THAT HE WOULD GAIN STRENGTH FROM IT...
JESUS-SAMA...
I CAN'T HELP BUT BE WORRIED.
YOU'RE LIVING HERE, IN THIS PLACE WITHOUT SECURITY...
...WHILE THE KING OF THE DEMONS IS ALSO LURKING SO CLOSE BY!
WELL, URIEL IS HANDLING THE SECURITY HERE...
BUT LUCIFER IS THE FORMER HEAD OF THE ANGELS.
I'M SURE URIEL MUST FEEL SOME TINY AMOUNT OF RELUCTANCE TO FIGHT HIM!
URIEL... HOLDING BACK? I CAN'T IMAGINE THAT.
SO IN CASE THAT EVER COMES TO PASS...
...I WANT TO KNOW HOW TO ROB HIM OF HIS POWERS!
BUDDHA BAREFOOT SEASON IS HERE! I WENT OUTSIDE, AND SOMEONE SAID, "WHO DO YOU THINK YOU ARE, STEVE JOBS?"

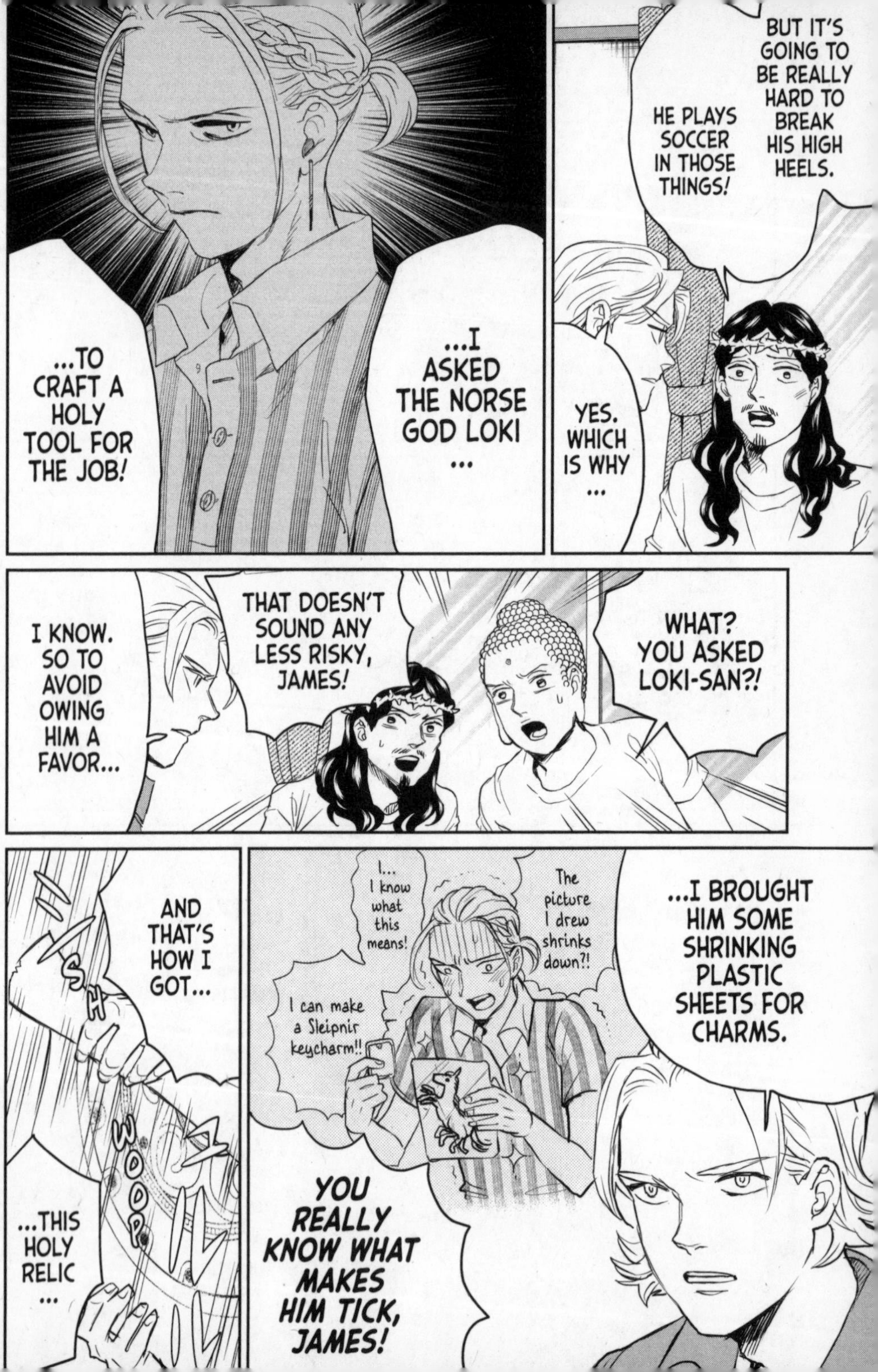
BUT IT'S GOING TO BE REALLY HARD TO BREAK HIS HIGH HEELS.
HE PLAYS SOCCER IN THOSE THINGS!
YES. WHICH IS WHY ...
...I ASKED THE NORSE GOD LOKI ...
...TO CRAFT A HOLY TOOL FOR THE JOB!
WHAT? YOU ASKED LOKI-SAN?!
THAT DOESN'T SOUND ANY LESS RISKY, JAMES!
I KNOW. SO TO AVOID OWING HIM A FAVOR...
...I BROUGHT HIM SOME SHRINKING PLASTIC SHEETS FOR CHARMS.
The picture I drew shrinks down?!
I... I know what this means!
I can make a Sleipnir keycharm!!
YOU REALLY KNOW WHAT MAKES HIM TICK, JAMES!
AND THAT'S HOW I GOT...
SH
WOOP
...THIS HOLY RELIC ...

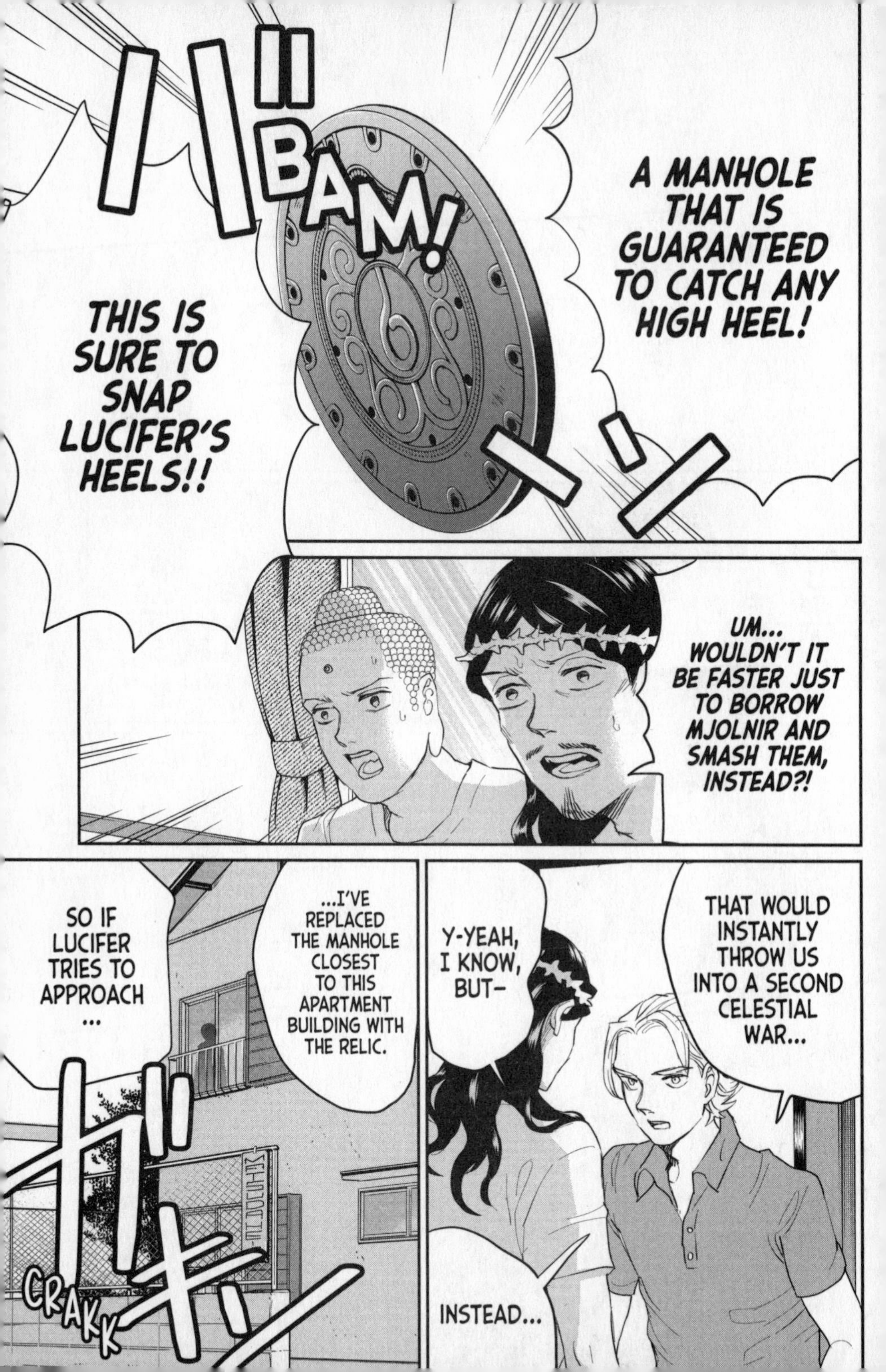
A MANHOLE THAT IS GUARANTEED TO CATCH ANY HIGH HEEL!
BAM!
THIS IS SURE TO SNAP LUCIFER'S HEELS!!
UM... WOULDN'T IT BE FASTER JUST TO BORROW MJOLNIR AND SMASH THEM, INSTEAD?!
THAT WOULD INSTANTLY THROW US INTO A SECOND CELESTIAL WAR...
Y-YEAH, I KNOW, BUT-
INSTEAD...
...I'VE REPLACED THE MANHOLE CLOSEST TO THIS APARTMENT BUILDING WITH THE RELIC.
SO IF LUCIFER TRIES TO APPROACH ...
CRAKK

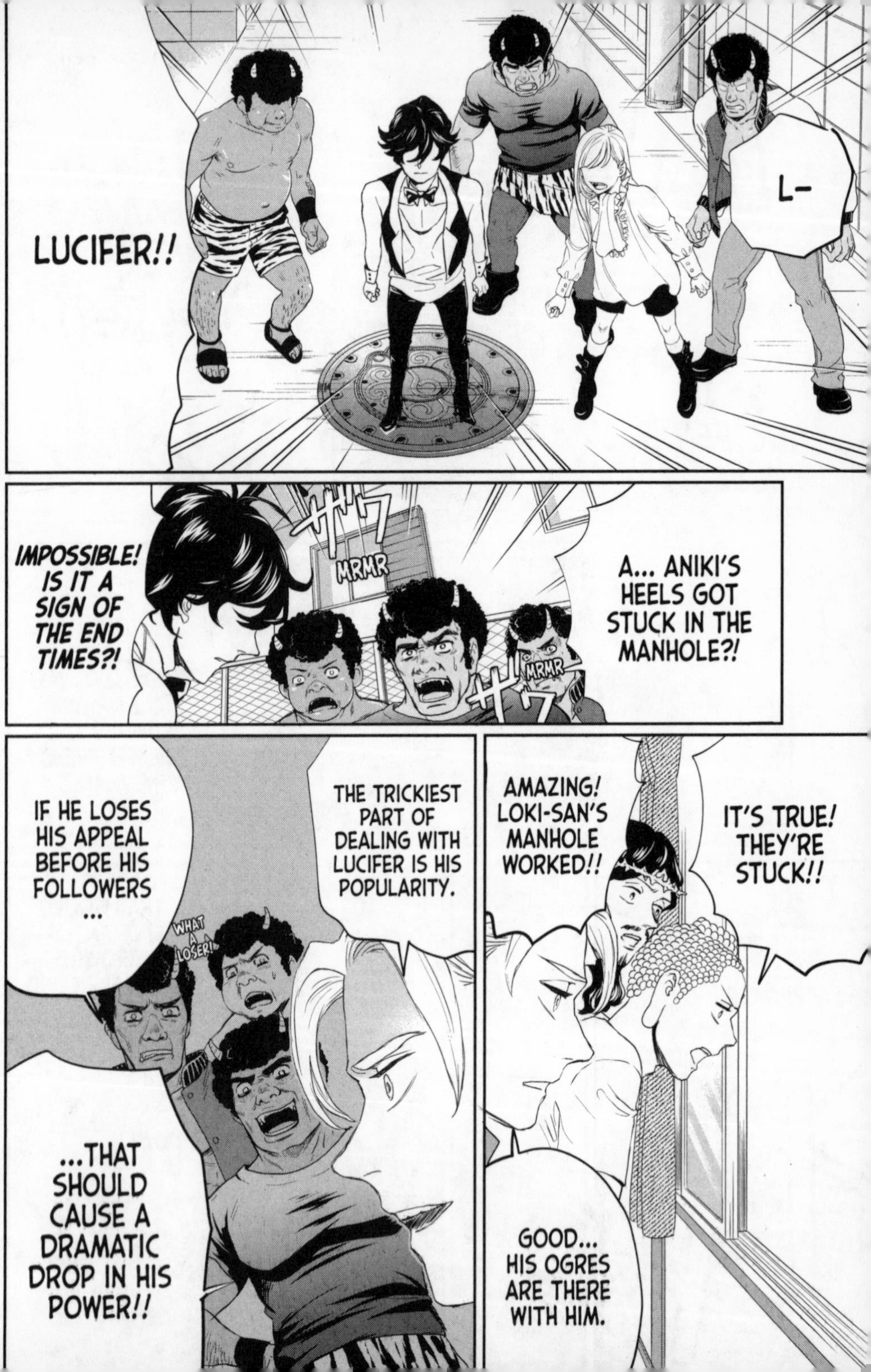
L-
LUCIFER!!
A... ANIKI'S HEELS GOT STUCK IN THE MANHOLE?!
MRMR
MRMR
IMPOSSIBLE! IS IT A SIGN OF THE END TIMES?!
IT'S TRUE! THEY'RE STUCK!!
AMAZING! LOKI-SAN'S MANHOLE WORKED!!
GOOD... HIS OGRES ARE THERE WITH HIM.
THE TRICKIEST PART OF DEALING WITH LUCIFER IS HIS POPULARITY.
IF HE LOSES HIS APPEAL BEFORE HIS FOLLOWERS ...
WHAT A LOSER!
...THAT SHOULD CAUSE A DRAMATIC DROP IN HIS POWER!!

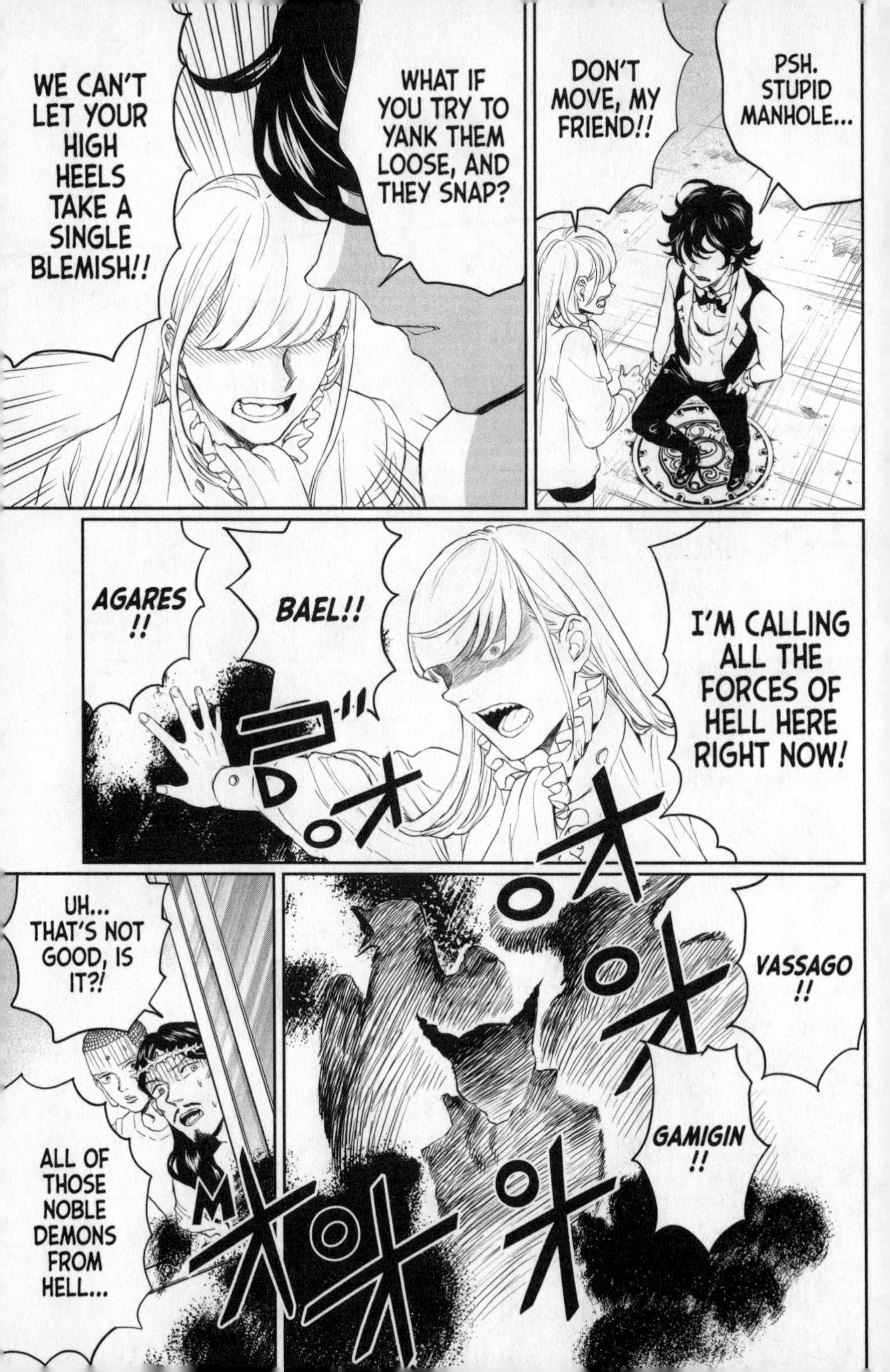
PSH. STUPID MANHOLE...
DON'T MOVE, MY FRIEND!!
WHAT IF YOU TRY TO YANK THEM LOOSE, AND THEY SNAP?
WE CAN'T LET YOUR HIGH HEELS TAKE A SINGLE BLEMISH!!
I'M CALLING ALL THE FORCES OF HELL HERE RIGHT NOW!
BAEL!!
AGARES!!
VASSAGO!!
GAMIGIN!!
UH... THAT'S NOT GOOD, IS IT?!
ALL OF THOSE NOBLE DEMONS FROM HELL...

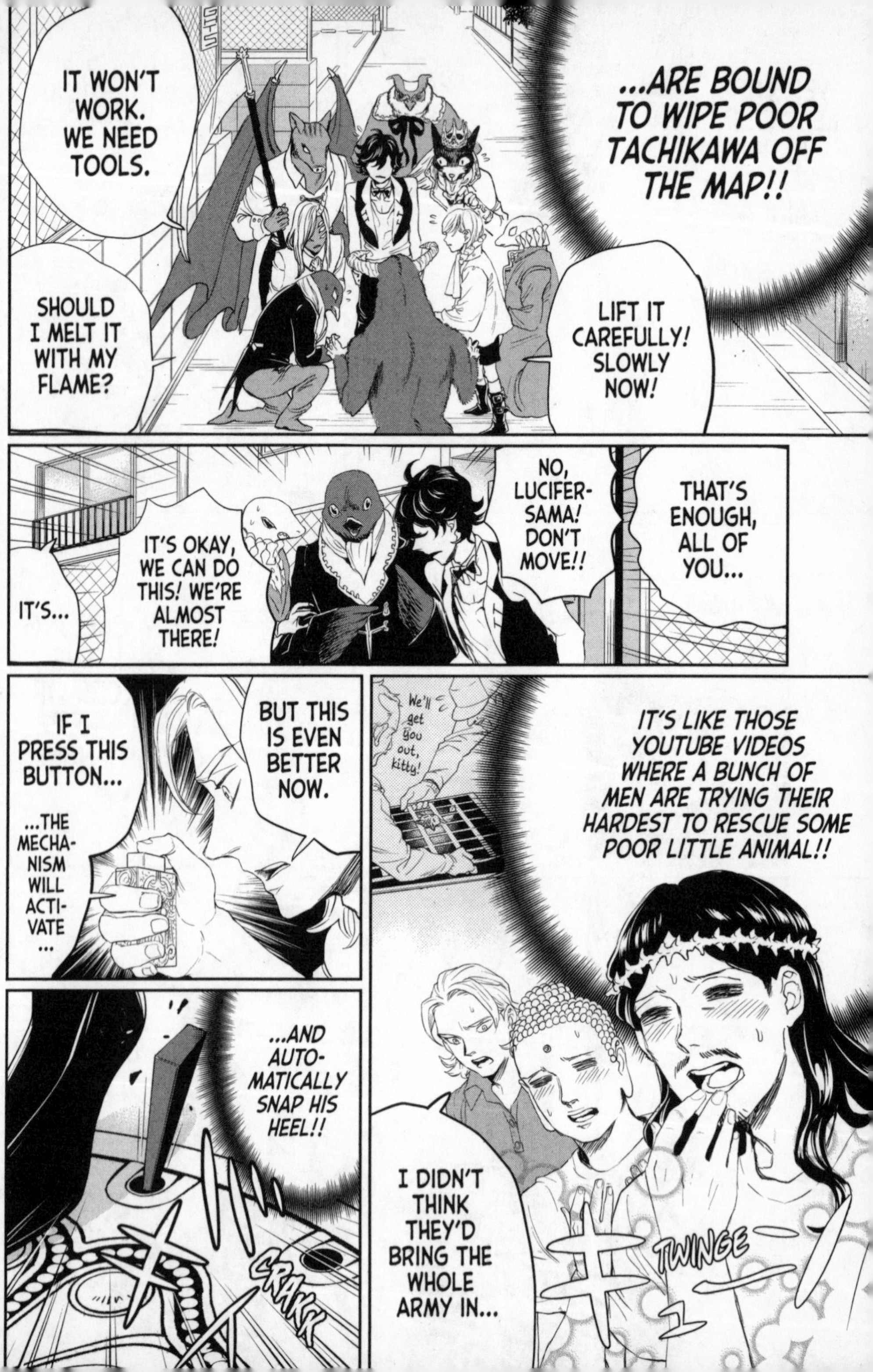
...ARE BOUND TO WIPE POOR TACHIKAWA OFF THE MAP!!
LIFT IT CAREFULLY! SLOWLY NOW!
IT WON'T WORK. WE NEED TOOLS.
SHOULD I MELT IT WITH MY FLAME?
THAT'S ENOUGH, ALL OF YOU...
NO, LUCIFER-SAMA! DON'T MOVE!!
IT'S OKAY, WE CAN DO THIS! WE'RE ALMOST THERE!
IT'S...
IT'S LIKE THOSE YOUTUBE VIDEOS WHERE A BUNCH OF MEN ARE TRYING THEIR HARDEST TO RESCUE SOME POOR LITTLE ANIMAL!!
We'll get you out, kitty!
TWINGE
I DIDN'T THINK THEY'D BRING THE WHOLE ARMY IN...
BUT THIS IS EVEN BETTER NOW.
IF I PRESS THIS BUTTON...
...THE MECHANISM WILL ACTIVATE...
...AND AUTOMATICALLY SNAP HIS HEEL!!
CRAKK

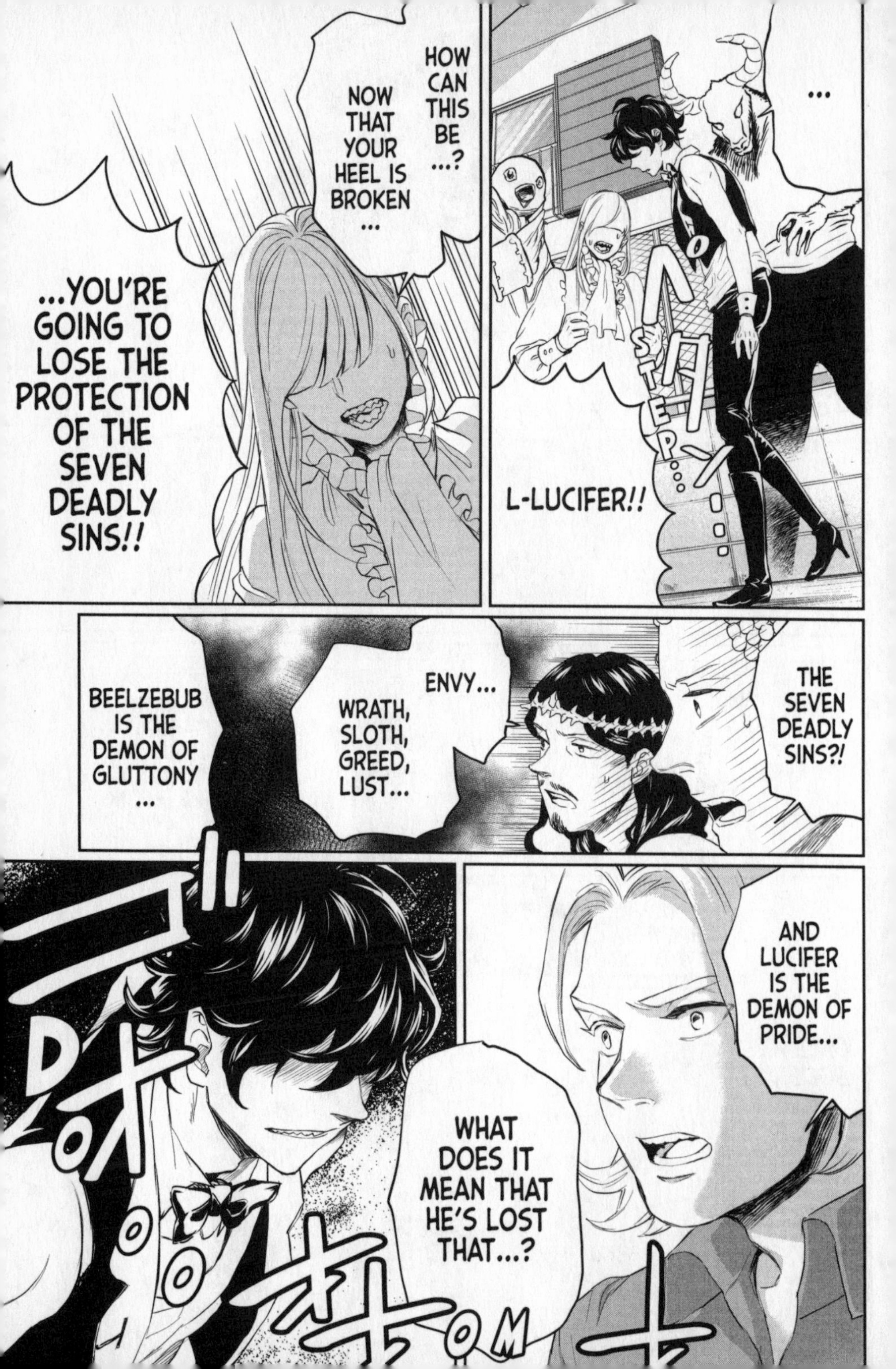
...
L-LUCIFER!!
STEP...
HOW CAN THIS BE ...?
NOW THAT YOUR HEEL IS BROKEN ...
...YOU'RE GOING TO LOSE THE PROTECTION OF THE SEVEN DEADLY SINS!!
THE SEVEN DEADLY SINS?!
ENVY...
WRATH, SLOTH, GREED, LUST...
BEELZEBUB IS THE DEMON OF GLUTTONY ...
AND LUCIFER IS THE DEMON OF PRIDE...
WHAT DOES IT MEAN THAT HE'S LOST THAT...?
DOOOOM

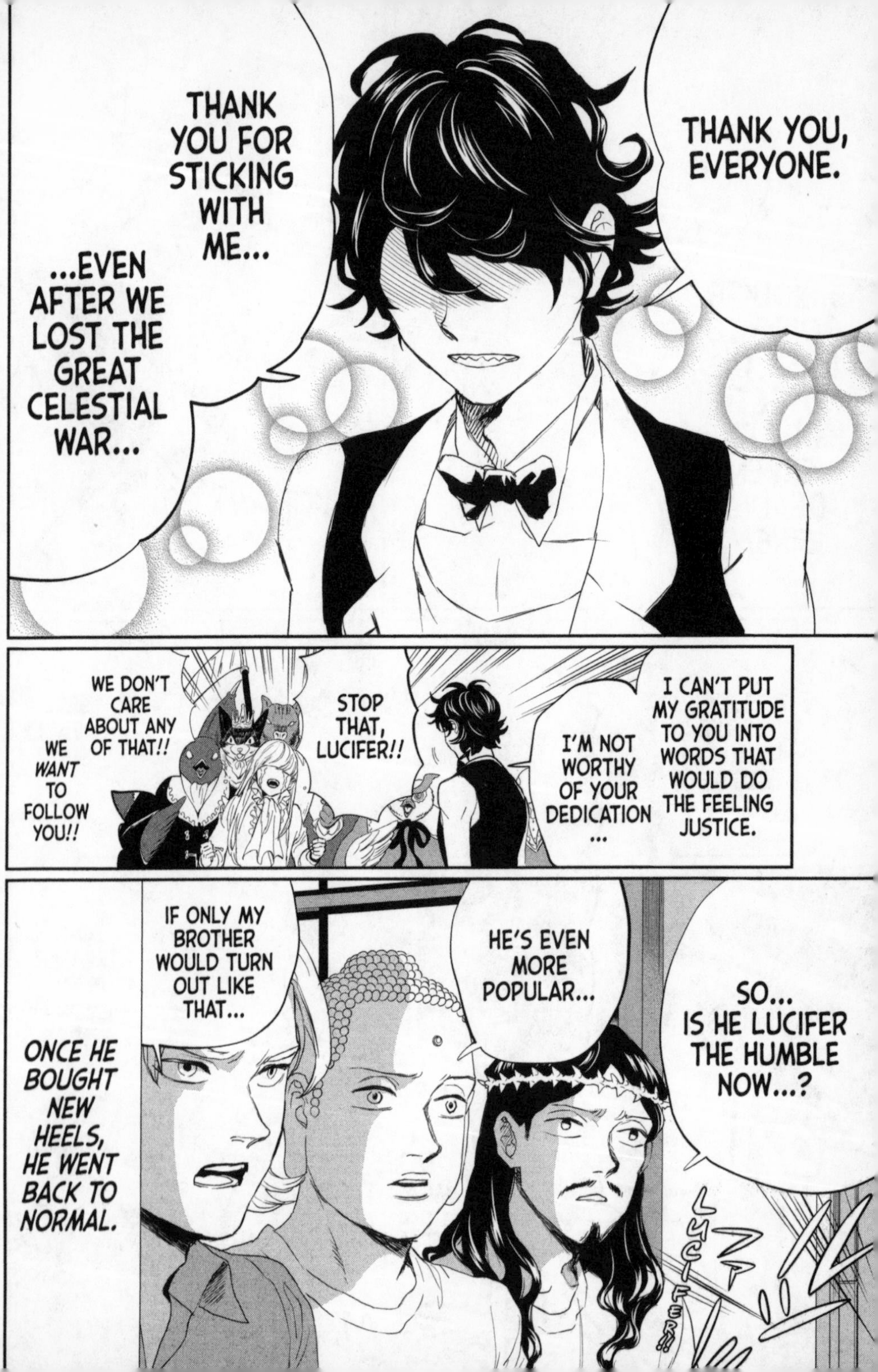
THANK YOU, EVERYONE.
THANK YOU FOR STICKING WITH ME...
...EVEN AFTER WE LOST THE GREAT CELESTIAL WAR...
I CAN'T PUT MY GRATITUDE TO YOU INTO WORDS THAT WOULD DO THE FEELING JUSTICE.
I'M NOT WORTHY OF YOUR DEDICATION ...
STOP THAT, LUCIFER!!
WE DON'T CARE ABOUT ANY OF THAT!!
WE *WANT* TO FOLLOW YOU!!
SO... IS HE LUCIFER THE HUMBLE NOW...?
LUCIFER!!
HE'S EVEN MORE POPULAR...
IF ONLY MY BROTHER WOULD TURN OUT LIKE THAT...
ONCE HE BOUGHT NEW HEELS, HE WENT BACK TO NORMAL.

It...
my Sweet Horse
It is complete !!!
(Loki)

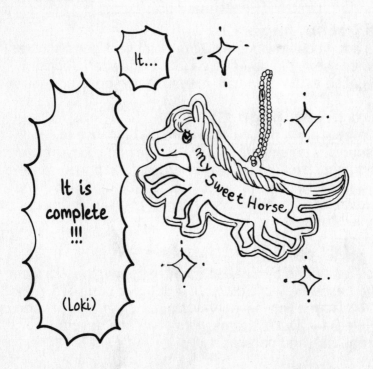

SAINT☆YOUNG MEN

CHAPTER 121 TRANSLATION NOTES

Samson and Delilah, page 9

Samson is a figure mentioned in the Book of Judges. He has long hair that gives him superhuman strength, and is known for his many clashes with his enemies, the Philistines. He famously slew a thousand Philistines with the jawbone of a donkey. His lover Delilah accepts a bribe from the Philistines to find the secret of his strength, which is his uncut hair. After she woos him to sleep, she has his hair cut so that the Philistines can capture him. Eventually Samson is taken to a Philistine temple, where God gives him the strength to knock down the pillars, collapsing the building on everyone inside.

Brahma's goose, page 12

Brahma was adopted into Buddhism from other religions such as Hinduism, where he is the god of creation. He is often depicted riding a bird called a hamsa, which resembles a goose or a swan.

Handshake event, page 12

Handshake events are a particular feature of Japanese show business, especially for singers and idols. They function similarly to autograph signings, except that the reward is getting to shake the hand of the star you're there to see. Jesus's mother, Mary, if you recall, is a big fan of the *enka* singer Kiyoshi Hikawa, and especially his 2002 single "Zundoko-bushi."

Demons, page 19

The demons summoned by Beelzebub all appear in the *Ars Goetia*, a book in *The Lesser Key of Solomon*, a grimoire compiled in the 1600s. The *Ars Goetia* lists seventy-two named demons of various ranks, e.g. King Bael, Duke Agares, with each one described in terms of appearance and personality.

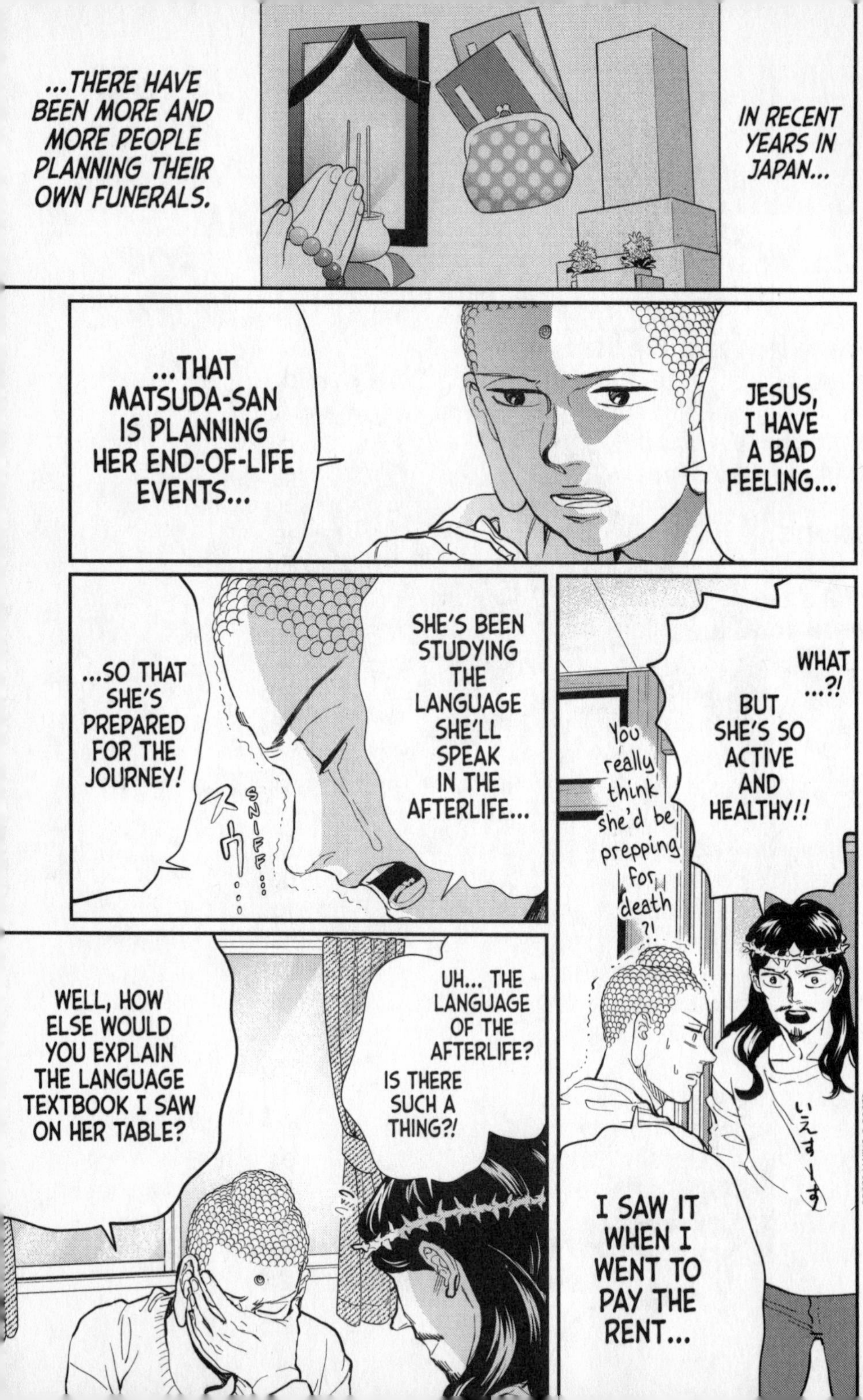
IN RECENT YEARS IN JAPAN...
...THERE HAVE BEEN MORE AND MORE PEOPLE PLANNING THEIR OWN FUNERALS.
JESUS, I HAVE A BAD FEELING...
...THAT MATSUDA-SAN IS PLANNING HER END-OF-LIFE EVENTS...
WHAT...?!
BUT SHE'S SO ACTIVE AND HEALTHY!!
You really think she'd be prepping for death?!
いえすーす
I SAW IT WHEN I WENT TO PAY THE RENT...
SHE'S BEEN STUDYING THE LANGUAGE SHE'LL SPEAK IN THE AFTERLIFE...
...SO THAT SHE'S PREPARED FOR THE JOURNEY!
SNIFF...
スン…
UH... THE LANGUAGE OF THE AFTERLIFE?
IS THERE SUCH A THING?!
WELL, HOW ELSE WOULD YOU EXPLAIN THE LANGUAGE TEXTBOOK I SAW ON HER TABLE?

JESUS'S SHIRT: JESUS

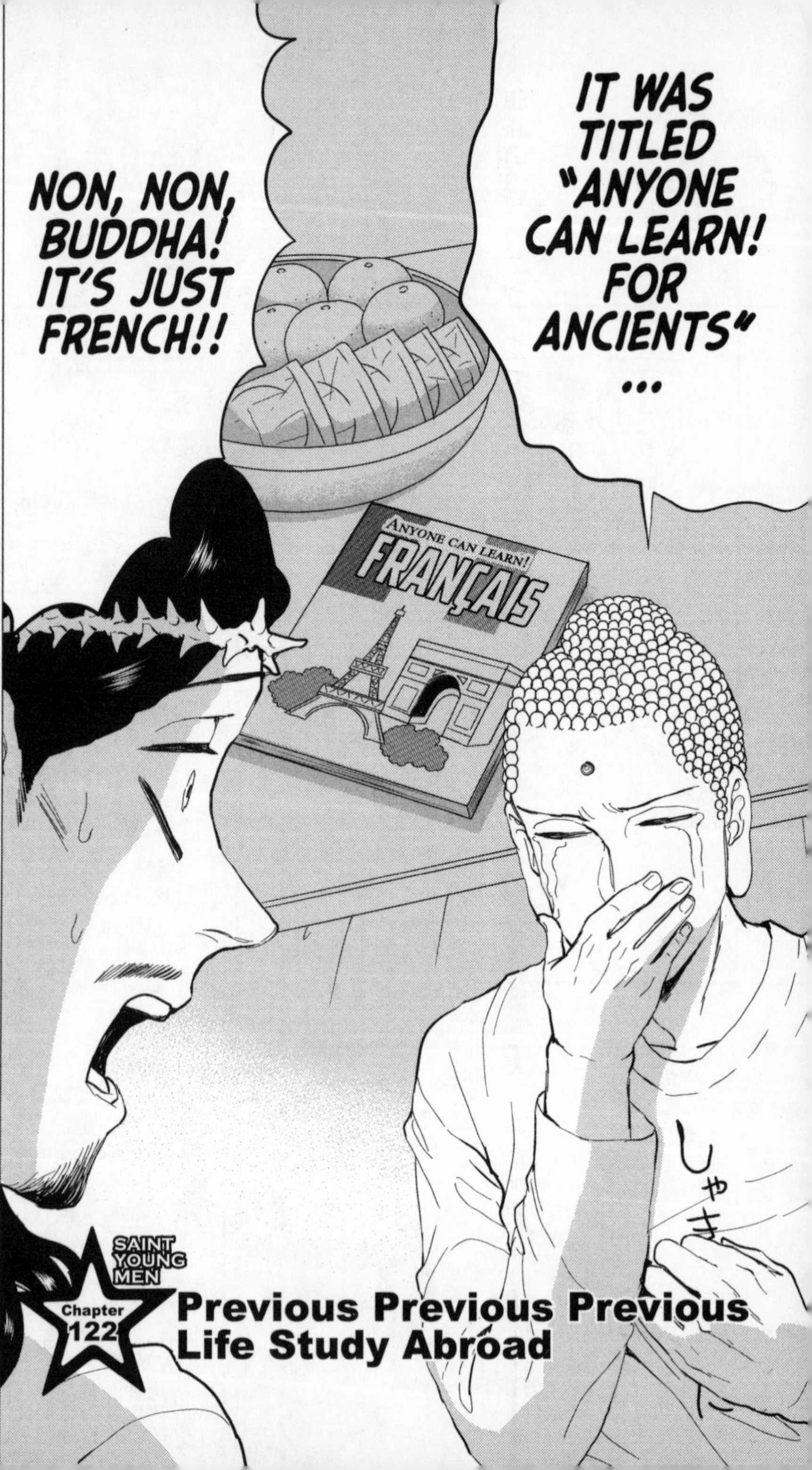
IT WAS TITLED "ANYONE CAN LEARN! FOR ANCIENTS" ...
NON, NON, BUDDHA! IT'S JUST FRENCH!!
ANYONE CAN LEARN!
FRANÇAIS
しゃき
SAINT YOUNG MEN
Chapter 122
Previous Previous Previous Life Study Abroad

IN JAPANESE, THE WORD FOR "FRENCH" ALSO SOUNDS LIKE "WORDS THE BUDDHA SPOKE."

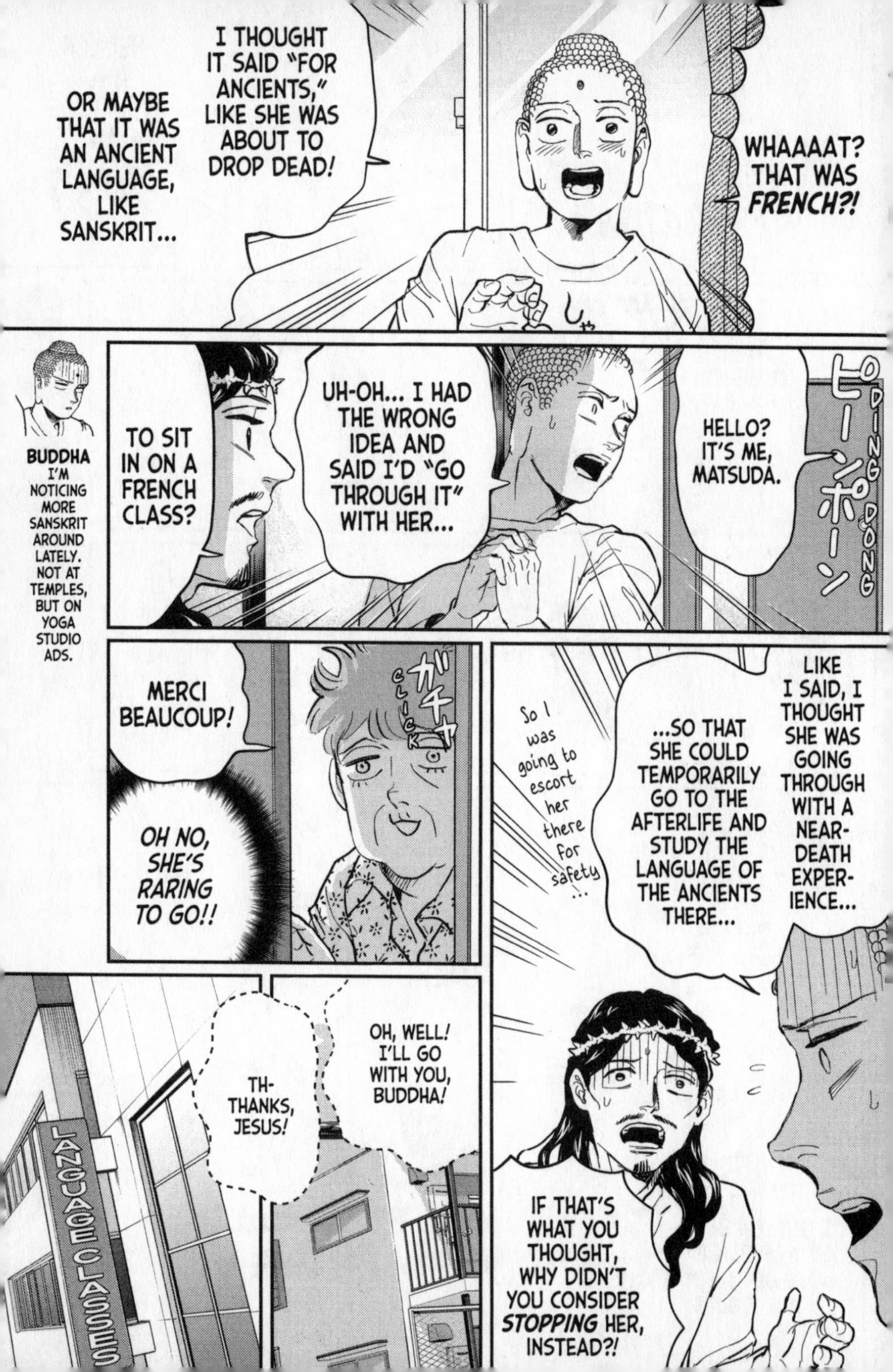
WHAAAAT? THAT WAS FRENCH?!
I THOUGHT IT SAID "FOR ANCIENTS," LIKE SHE WAS ABOUT TO DROP DEAD!
OR MAYBE THAT IT WAS AN ANCIENT LANGUAGE, LIKE SANSKRIT...
ピーンポーン DING DONG
HELLO? IT'S ME, MATSUDA.
UH-OH... I HAD THE WRONG IDEA AND SAID I'D "GO THROUGH IT" WITH HER...
TO SIT IN ON A FRENCH CLASS?
BUDDHA I'M NOTICING MORE SANSKRIT AROUND LATELY. NOT AT TEMPLES, BUT ON YOGA STUDIO ADS.
LIKE I SAID, I THOUGHT SHE WAS GOING THROUGH WITH A NEAR-DEATH EXPER-IENCE...
...SO THAT SHE COULD TEMPORARILY GO TO THE AFTERLIFE AND STUDY THE LANGUAGE OF THE ANCIENTS THERE...
So I was going to escort her there for safety...
IF THAT'S WHAT YOU THOUGHT, WHY DIDN'T YOU CONSIDER STOPPING HER, INSTEAD?!
ガチャ CLICK
MERCI BEAUCOUP!
OH NO, SHE'S RARING TO GO!!
OH, WELL! I'LL GO WITH YOU, BUDDHA!
TH-THANKS, JESUS!
LANGUAGE CLASSES

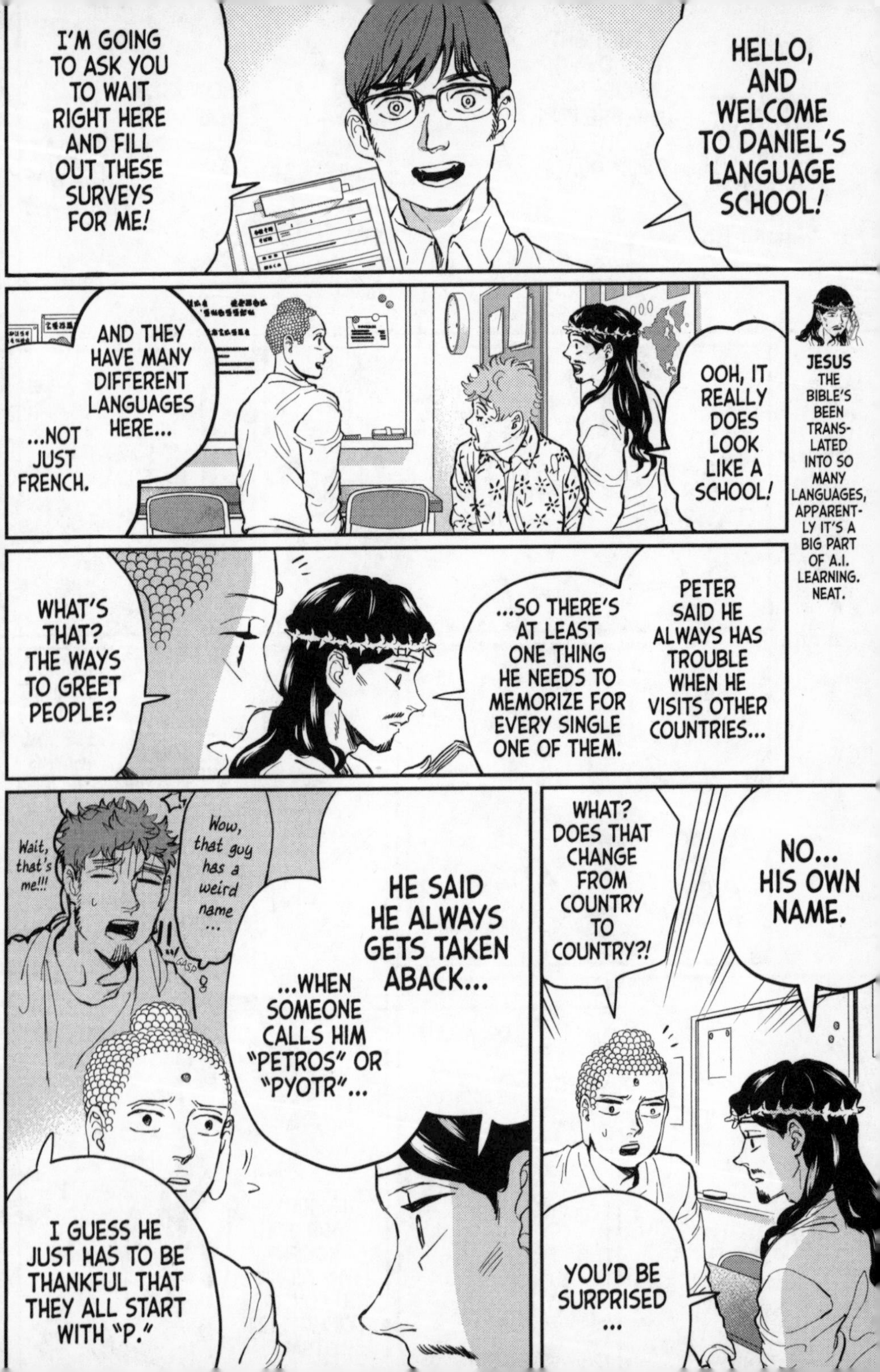
HELLO, AND WELCOME TO DANIEL'S LANGUAGE SCHOOL!
I'M GOING TO ASK YOU TO WAIT RIGHT HERE AND FILL OUT THESE SURVEYS FOR ME!
JESUS THE BIBLE'S BEEN TRANSLATED INTO SO MANY LANGUAGES, APPARENTLY IT'S A BIG PART OF A.I. LEARNING. NEAT.
OOH, IT REALLY DOES LOOK LIKE A SCHOOL!
AND THEY HAVE MANY DIFFERENT LANGUAGES HERE...
...NOT JUST FRENCH.
PETER SAID HE ALWAYS HAS TROUBLE WHEN HE VISITS OTHER COUNTRIES...
...SO THERE'S AT LEAST ONE THING HE NEEDS TO MEMORIZE FOR EVERY SINGLE ONE OF THEM.
WHAT'S THAT? THE WAYS TO GREET PEOPLE?
NO... HIS OWN NAME.
WHAT? DOES THAT CHANGE FROM COUNTRY TO COUNTRY?!
YOU'D BE SURPRISED ...
HE SAID HE ALWAYS GETS TAKEN ABACK...
...WHEN SOMEONE CALLS HIM "PETROS" OR "PYOTR"...
Wow, that guy has a weird name ...
Wait, that's me!!!
GASP
I GUESS HE JUST HAS TO BE THANKFUL THAT THEY ALL START WITH "P."

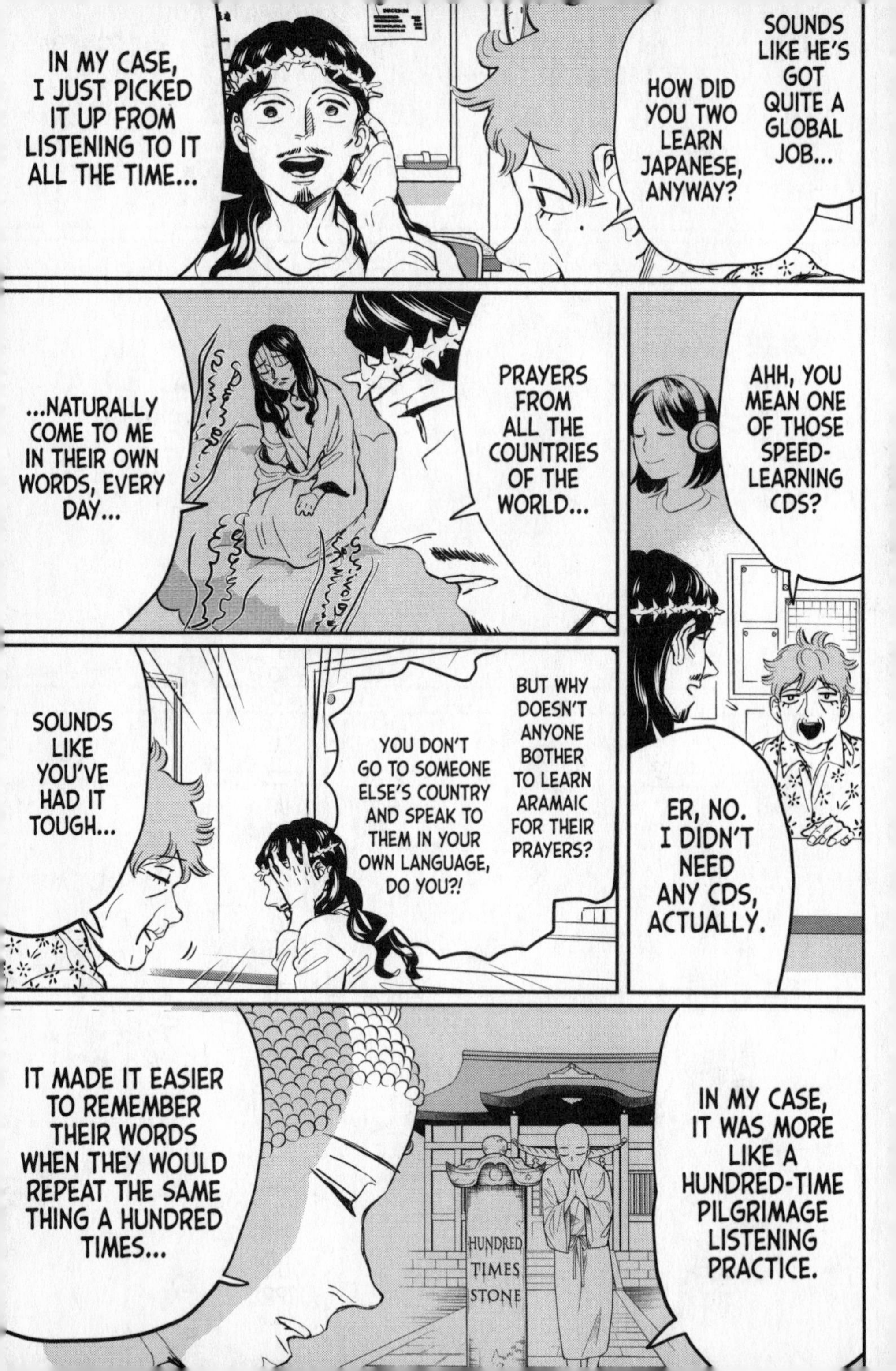

SOUNDS LIKE HE'S GOT QUITE A GLOBAL JOB...
HOW DID YOU TWO LEARN JAPANESE, ANYWAY?
IN MY CASE, I JUST PICKED IT UP FROM LISTENING TO IT ALL THE TIME...
AHH, YOU MEAN ONE OF THOSE SPEED-LEARNING CDS?
ER, NO. I DIDN'T NEED ANY CDS, ACTUALLY.
PRAYERS FROM ALL THE COUNTRIES OF THE WORLD...
...NATURALLY COME TO ME IN THEIR OWN WORDS, EVERY DAY...
BUT WHY DOESN'T ANYONE BOTHER TO LEARN ARAMAIC FOR THEIR PRAYERS?
YOU DON'T GO TO SOMEONE ELSE'S COUNTRY AND SPEAK TO THEM IN YOUR OWN LANGUAGE, DO YOU?!
SOUNDS LIKE YOU'VE HAD IT TOUGH...
IN MY CASE, IT WAS MORE LIKE A HUNDRED-TIME PILGRIMAGE LISTENING PRACTICE.
HUNDRED TIMES STONE
IT MADE IT EASIER TO REMEMBER THEIR WORDS WHEN THEY WOULD REPEAT THE SAME THING A HUNDRED TIMES...

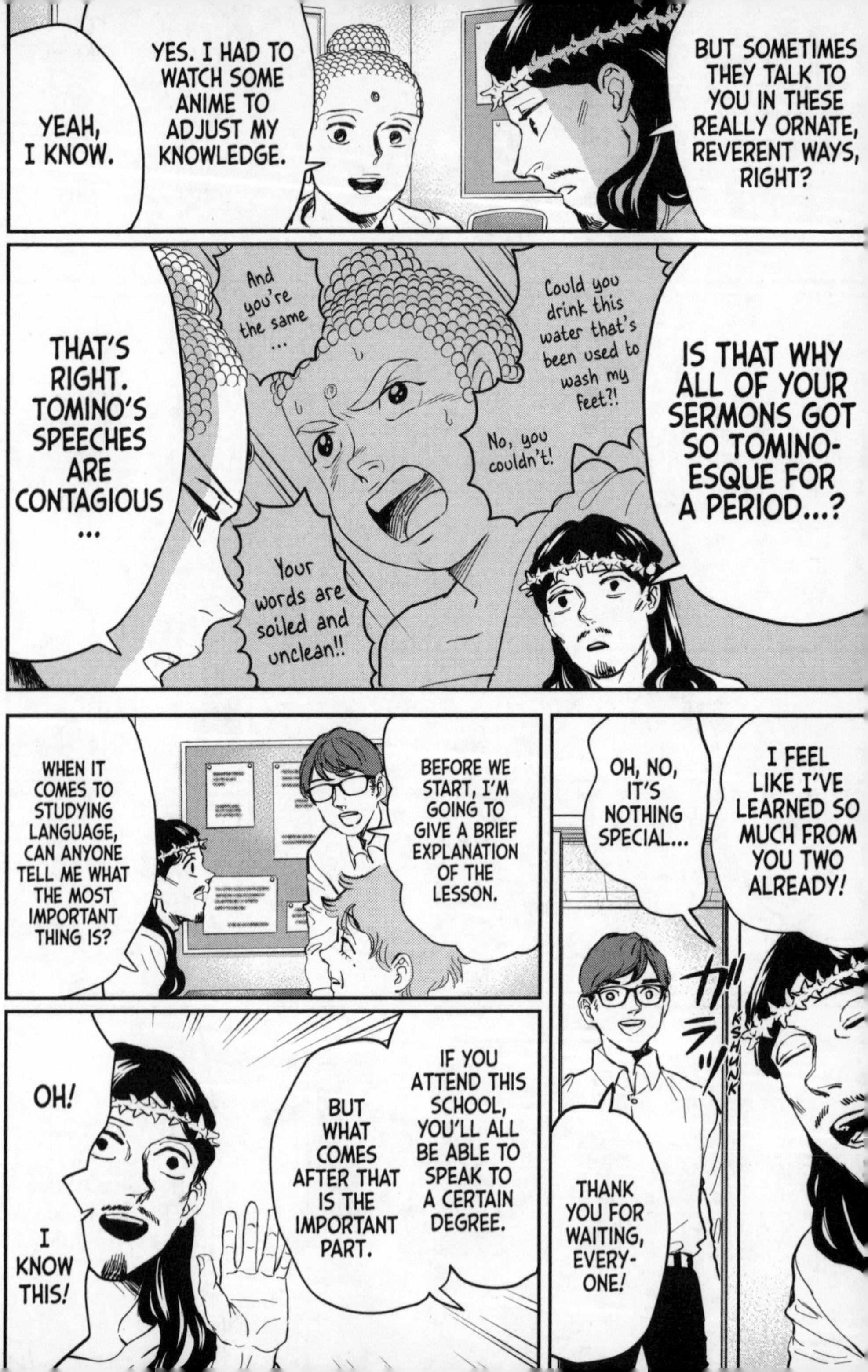
BUT SOMETIMES THEY TALK TO YOU IN THESE REALLY ORNATE, REVERENT WAYS, RIGHT?
YES. I HAD TO WATCH SOME ANIME TO ADJUST MY KNOWLEDGE.
YEAH, I KNOW.
IS THAT WHY ALL OF YOUR SERMONS GOT SO TOMINO-ESQUE FOR A PERIOD...?
Could you drink this water that's been used to wash my feet?!
No, you couldn't!
And you're the same ...
Your words are soiled and unclean!!
THAT'S RIGHT. TOMINO'S SPEECHES ARE CONTAGIOUS ...
I FEEL LIKE I'VE LEARNED SO MUCH FROM YOU TWO ALREADY!
OH, NO, IT'S NOTHING SPECIAL...
KSHUNK
THANK YOU FOR WAITING, EVERYONE!
BEFORE WE START, I'M GOING TO GIVE A BRIEF EXPLANATION OF THE LESSON.
WHEN IT COMES TO STUDYING LANGUAGE, CAN ANYONE TELL ME WHAT THE MOST IMPORTANT THING IS?
IF YOU ATTEND THIS SCHOOL, YOU'LL ALL BE ABLE TO SPEAK TO A CERTAIN DEGREE.
BUT WHAT COMES AFTER THAT IS THE IMPORTANT PART.
OH!
I KNOW THIS!

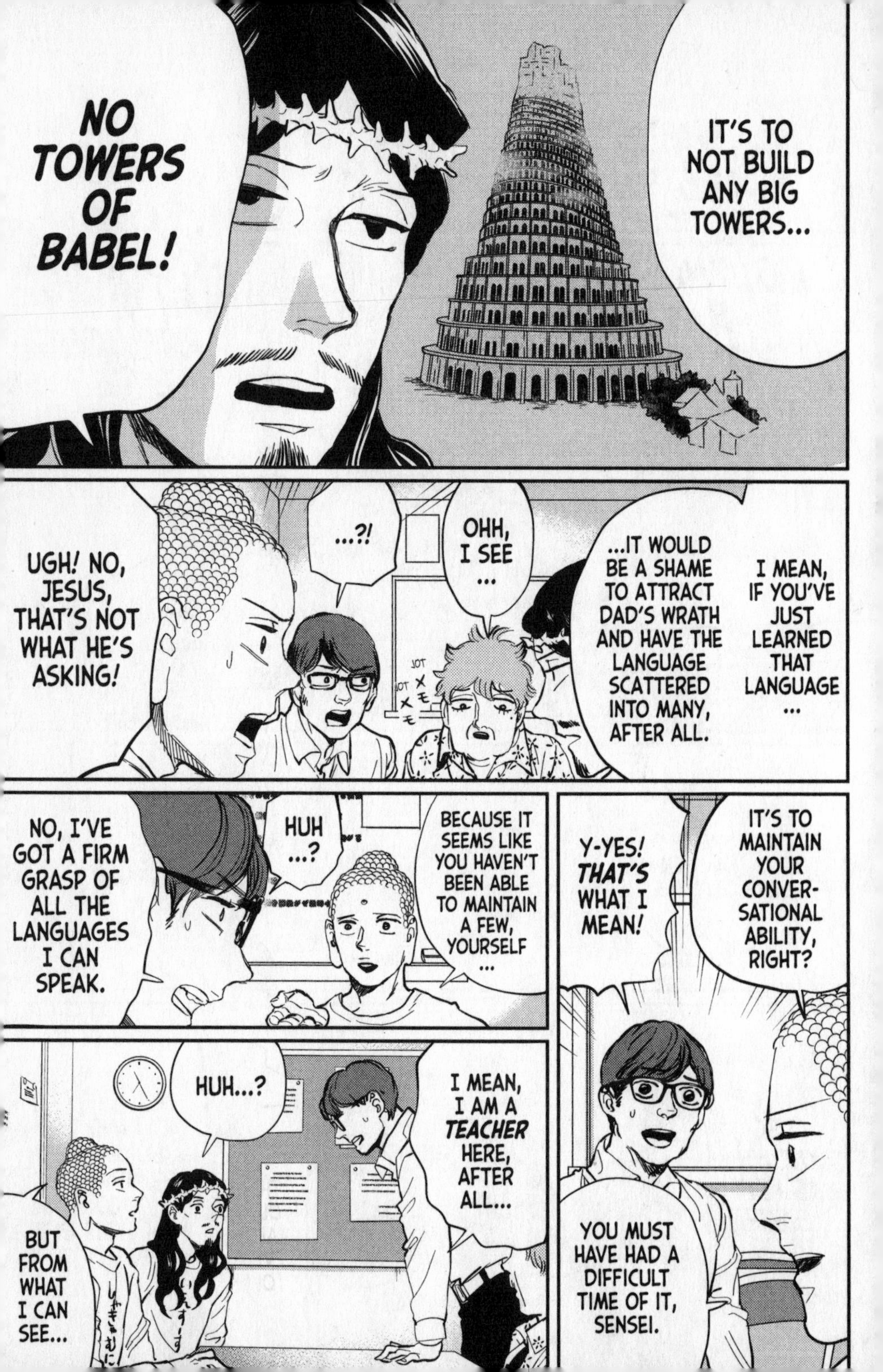
IT'S TO NOT BUILD ANY BIG TOWERS...
NO TOWERS OF BABEL!
I MEAN, IF YOU'VE JUST LEARNED THAT LANGUAGE ...
...IT WOULD BE A SHAME TO ATTRACT DAD'S WRATH AND HAVE THE LANGUAGE SCATTERED INTO MANY, AFTER ALL.
OHH, I SEE ...
JOT メモ JOT メモ
...?!
UGH! NO, JESUS, THAT'S NOT WHAT HE'S ASKING!
IT'S TO MAINTAIN YOUR CONVER-SATIONAL ABILITY, RIGHT?
Y-YES! *THAT'S* WHAT I MEAN!
YOU MUST HAVE HAD A DIFFICULT TIME OF IT, SENSEI.
BECAUSE IT SEEMS LIKE YOU HAVEN'T BEEN ABLE TO MAINTAIN A FEW, YOURSELF ...
HUH ...?
NO, I'VE GOT A FIRM GRASP OF ALL THE LANGUAGES I CAN SPEAK.
I MEAN, I AM A *TEACHER* HERE, AFTER ALL...
HUH...?
BUT FROM WHAT I CAN SEE...

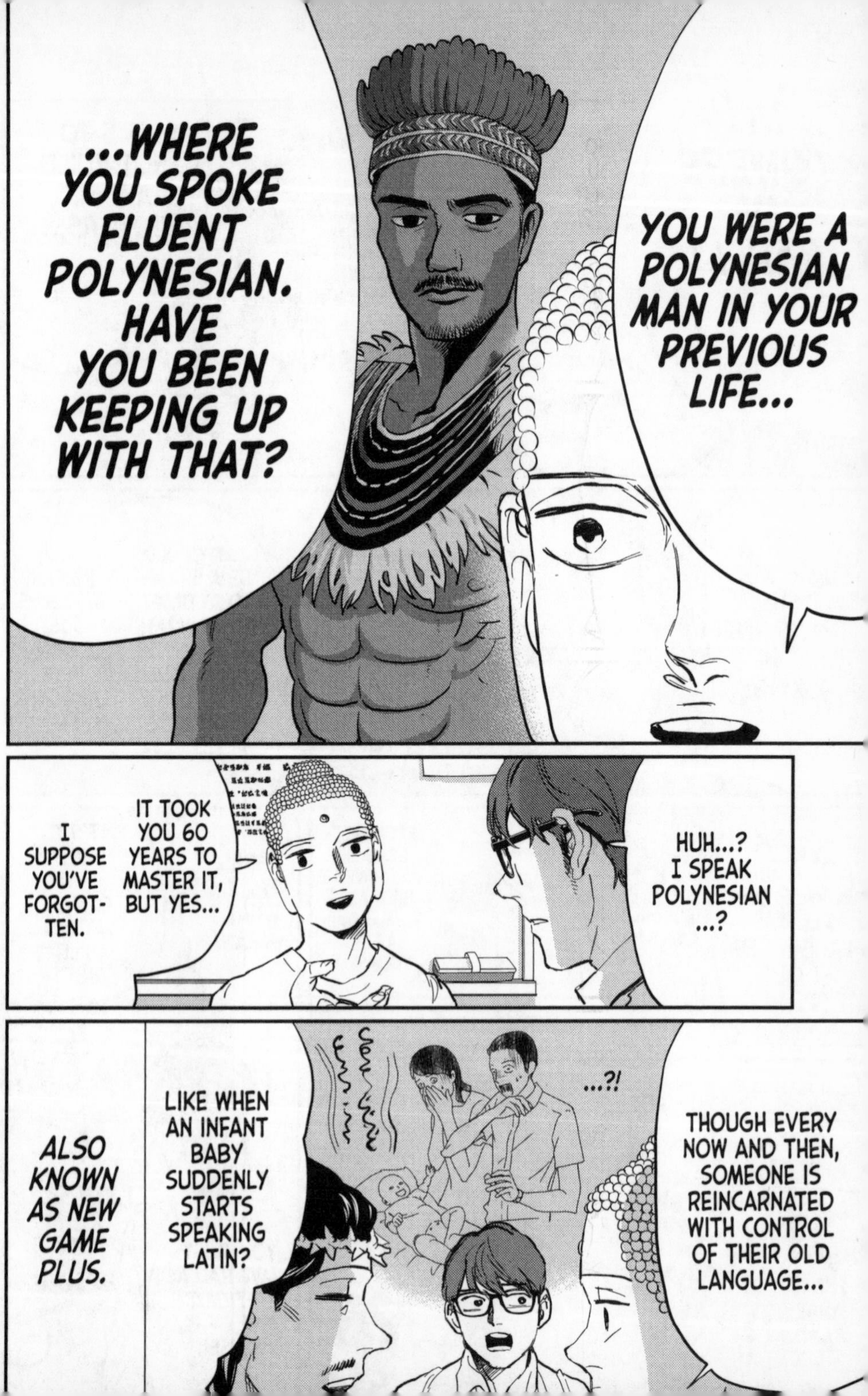
YOU WERE A POLYNESIAN MAN IN YOUR PREVIOUS LIFE...
...WHERE YOU SPOKE FLUENT POLYNESIAN. HAVE YOU BEEN KEEPING UP WITH THAT?
HUH...? I SPEAK POLYNESIAN ...?
IT TOOK YOU 60 YEARS TO MASTER IT, BUT YES...
I SUPPOSE YOU'VE FORGOT-TEN.
THOUGH EVERY NOW AND THEN, SOMEONE IS REINCARNATED WITH CONTROL OF THEIR OLD LANGUAGE...
...?!
LIKE WHEN AN INFANT BABY SUDDENLY STARTS SPEAKING LATIN?
ALSO KNOWN AS NEW GAME PLUS.

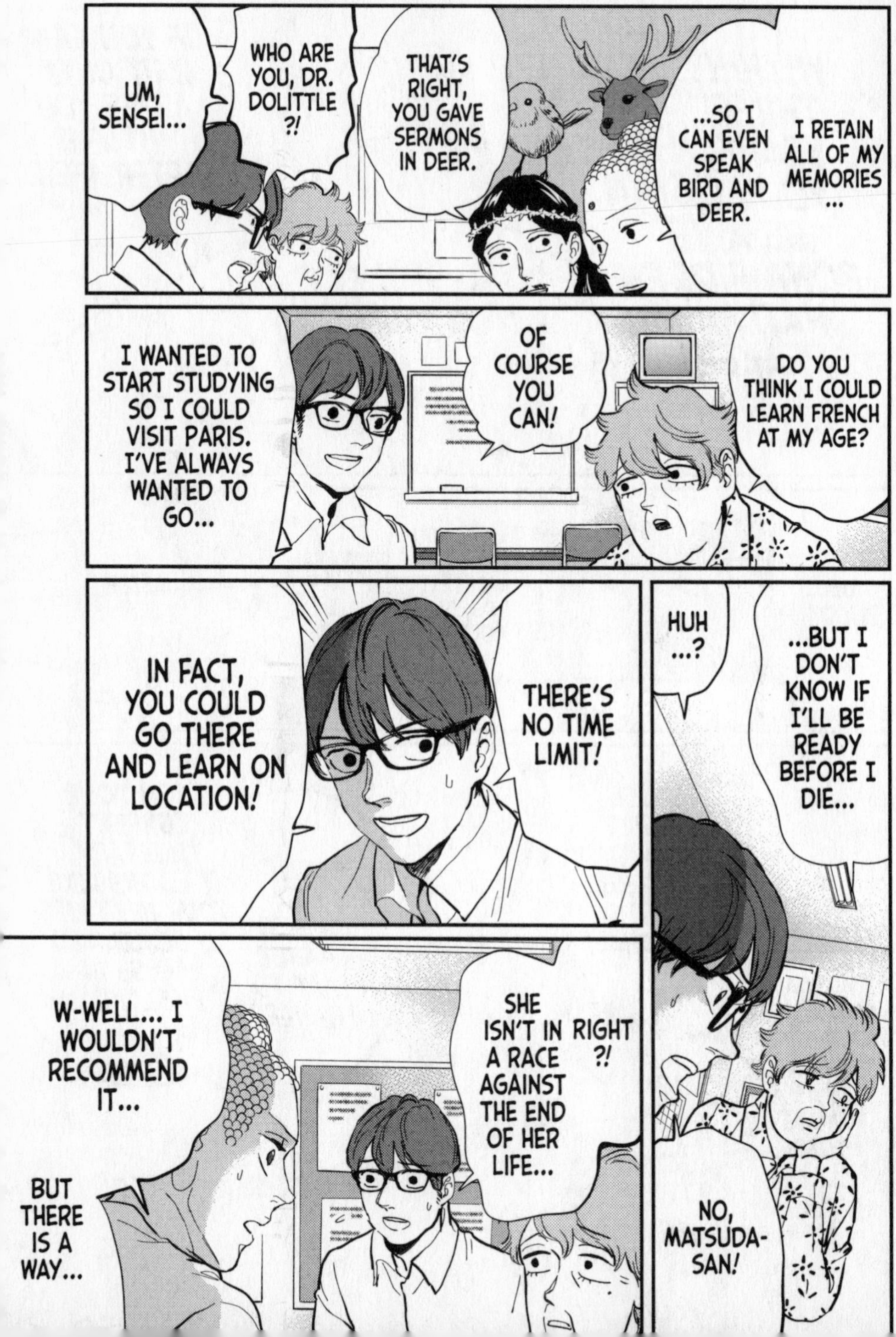
I RETAIN ALL OF MY MEMORIES...
...SO I CAN EVEN SPEAK BIRD AND DEER.
THAT'S RIGHT, YOU GAVE SERMONS IN DEER.
WHO ARE YOU, DR. DOLITTLE?!
UM, SENSEI...
DO YOU THINK I COULD LEARN FRENCH AT MY AGE?
OF COURSE YOU CAN!
I WANTED TO START STUDYING SO I COULD VISIT PARIS. I'VE ALWAYS WANTED TO GO...
...BUT I DON'T KNOW IF I'LL BE READY BEFORE I DIE...
HUH...?
THERE'S NO TIME LIMIT!
IN FACT, YOU COULD GO THERE AND LEARN ON LOCATION!
NO, MATSUDA-SAN!
RIGHT?!
SHE ISN'T IN A RACE AGAINST THE END OF HER LIFE...
W-WELL... I WOULDN'T RECOMMEND IT...
BUT THERE IS A WAY...

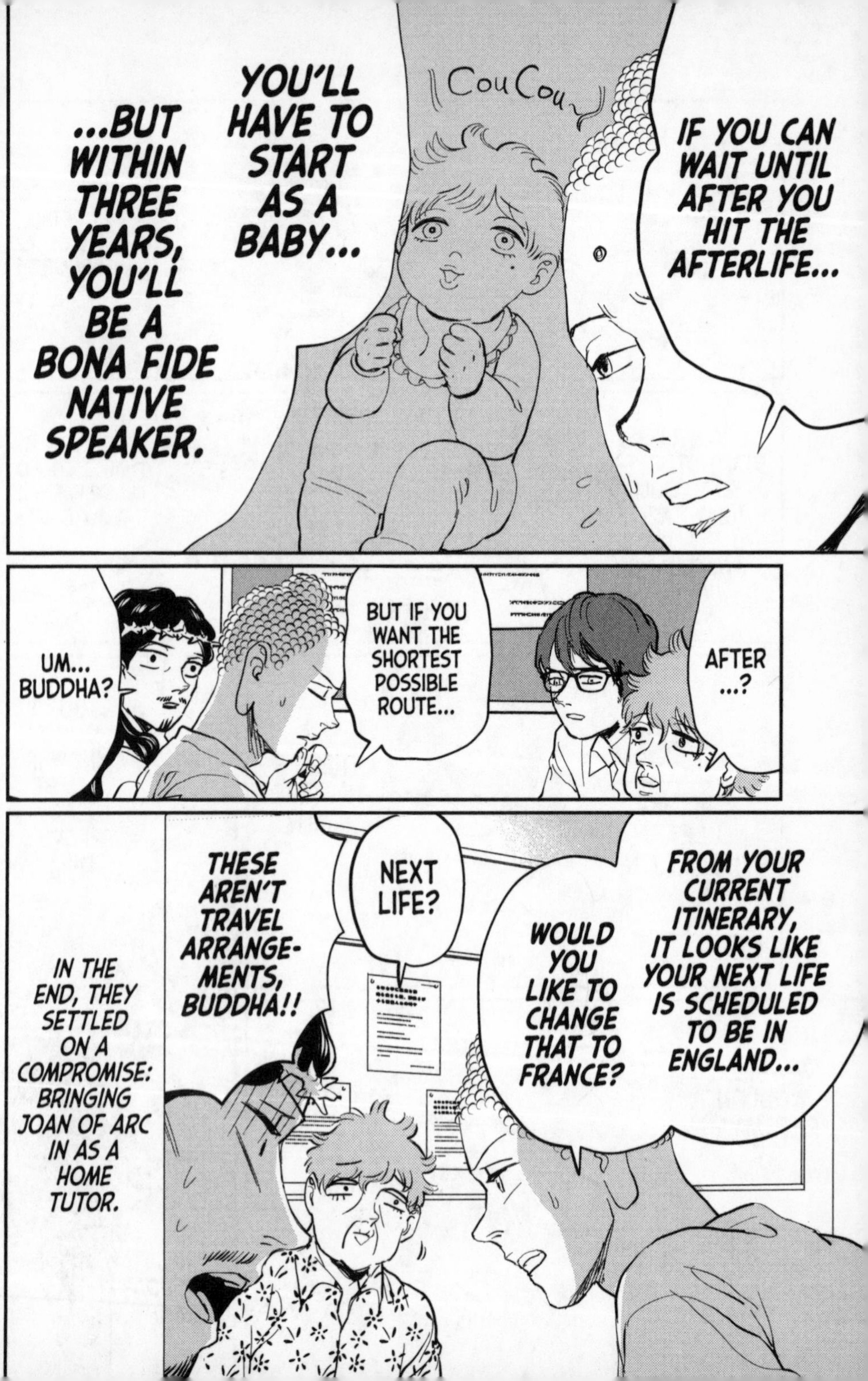
IF YOU CAN WAIT UNTIL AFTER YOU HIT THE AFTERLIFE...
CouCou~
YOU'LL HAVE TO START AS A BABY...
...BUT WITHIN THREE YEARS, YOU'LL BE A BONA FIDE NATIVE SPEAKER.
AFTER ...?
BUT IF YOU WANT THE SHORTEST POSSIBLE ROUTE...
UM... BUDDHA?
FROM YOUR CURRENT ITINERARY, IT LOOKS LIKE YOUR NEXT LIFE IS SCHEDULED TO BE IN ENGLAND...
WOULD YOU LIKE TO CHANGE THAT TO FRANCE?
NEXT LIFE?
THESE AREN'T TRAVEL ARRANGE-MENTS, BUDDHA!!
IN THE END, THEY SETTLED ON A COMPROMISE: BRINGING JOAN OF ARC IN AS A HOME TUTOR.

Matsuda-san
in the
next life

SAINT☆YOUNG MEN

CHAPTER 122 TRANSLATION NOTES

French, Page 26
In addition to simple phonetic *katakana*, which is the preferred modern method of writing foreign names within Japanese, there are traditional kanji used for writing the names of other countries, which was once standard. These kanji are usually based only on sound rather than meaning (using a kanji only to represent a sound divorced of its meaning is called *ateji*) and in the case of France, the most commonly recognized kanji to make the *fu* sound at the start is the kanji for "Buddha" or "dead body." Therefore, in the original Japanese, when Buddha sees the shorthand for "French language" ("Buddha/dead language"), Buddha thinks Matsuda is studying either the "language of the dead," or alternatively, Sanskrit.

Shakyamuni, Page 27
One of Gautama Buddha's titles, meaning "Sage of the Shakyas," after his clan name.

Tomino, page 30
Yoshiyuki Tomino is the creator of the Gundam franchise. He is known for his strong and impassioned writing style, which is known in Japan as "Tomino-bushi," or "Tomino dialect." The dialogue being quoted here is attributed to a story between the Buddha and his son Rahula, in which the Buddha compares a basin of water for washing feet to Rahula's mind, full of lies and filth, as a warning to him to mend his ways and renew his study.

Tower of Babel, page 32
A story that appears in Genesis following the Great Flood, which explains why the world's languages are as numerous as they are. Initially all of humanity spoke the same tongue, until they attempted to build a tower up to Heaven. To punish their hubris, God "confounded" their language so that they could not understand one another and scattered them across the Earth.

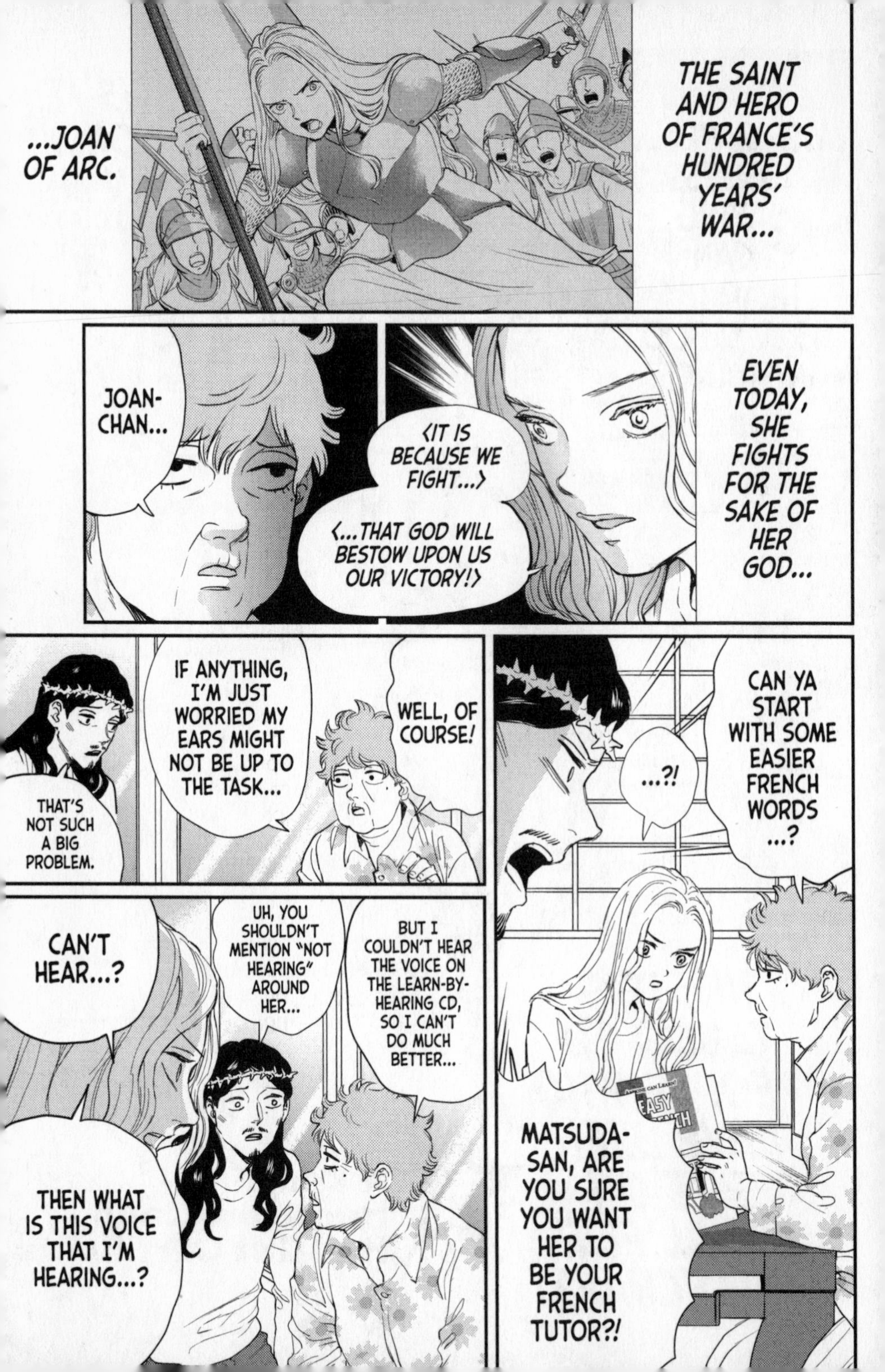
THE SAINT AND HERO OF FRANCE'S HUNDRED YEARS' WAR...
...JOAN OF ARC.
EVEN TODAY, SHE FIGHTS FOR THE SAKE OF HER GOD...
⟨IT IS BECAUSE WE FIGHT...⟩
⟨...THAT GOD WILL BESTOW UPON US OUR VICTORY!⟩
JOAN-CHAN...
CAN YA START WITH SOME EASIER FRENCH WORDS ...?
...?!
MATSUDA-SAN, ARE YOU SURE YOU WANT HER TO BE YOUR FRENCH TUTOR?!
WELL, OF COURSE!
IF ANYTHING, I'M JUST WORRIED MY EARS MIGHT NOT BE UP TO THE TASK...
THAT'S NOT SUCH A BIG PROBLEM.
BUT I COULDN'T HEAR THE VOICE ON THE LEARN-BY-HEARING CD, SO I CAN'T DO MUCH BETTER...
UH, YOU SHOULDN'T MENTION "NOT HEARING" AROUND HER...
CAN'T HEAR...?
THEN WHAT IS THIS VOICE THAT I'M HEARING...?

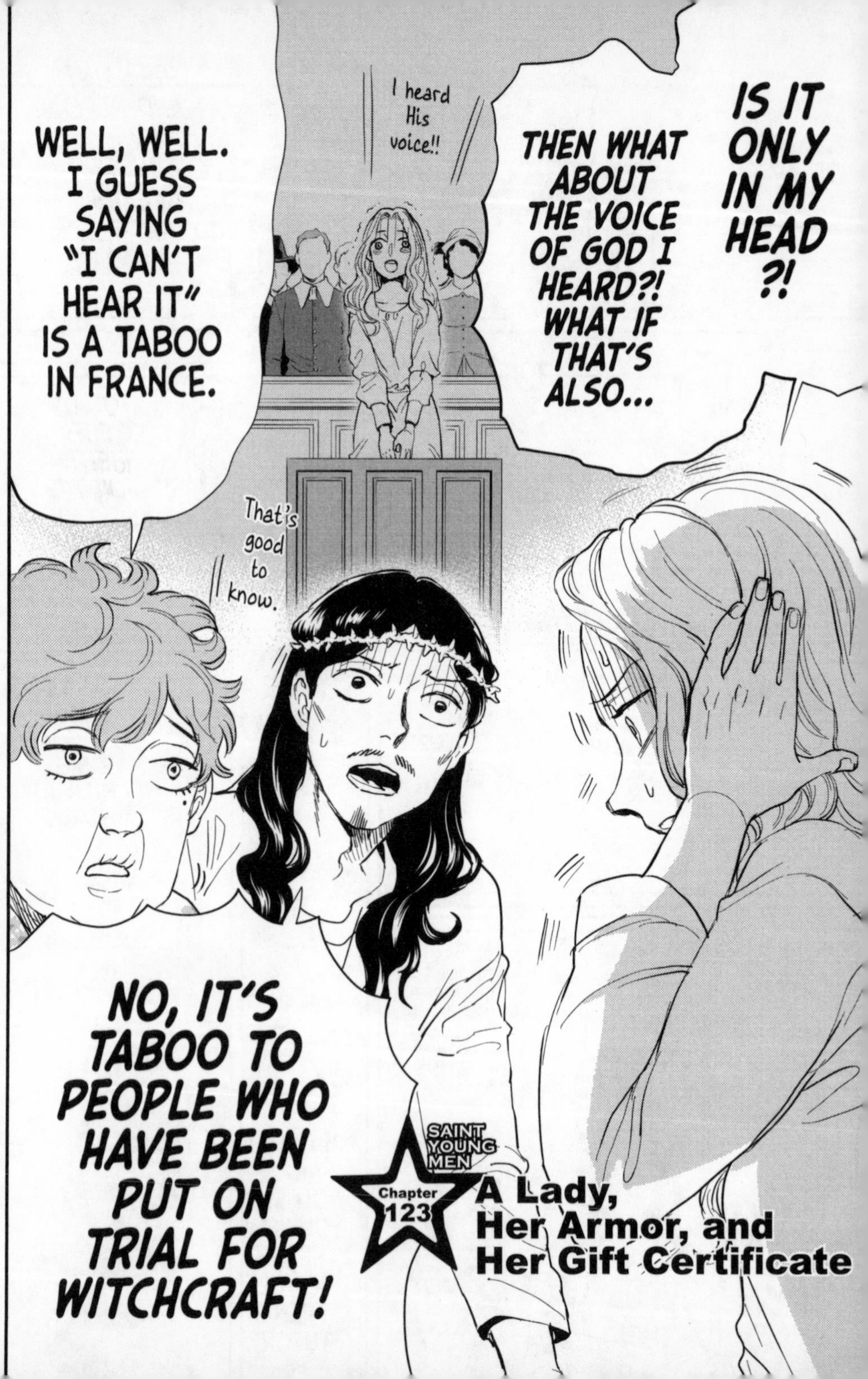
IS IT ONLY IN MY HEAD?!
THEN WHAT ABOUT THE VOICE OF GOD I HEARD?! WHAT IF THAT'S ALSO...
I heard His voice!!
WELL, WELL. I GUESS SAYING "I CAN'T HEAR IT" IS A TABOO IN FRANCE.
That's good to know.
NO, IT'S TABOO TO PEOPLE WHO HAVE BEEN PUT ON TRIAL FOR WITCHCRAFT!
SAINT YOUNG MEN
Chapter 123
A Lady, Her Armor, and Her Gift Certificate

BUDDHA IS THE "OUT-OF-STORE SALES-PERSON" URBAN LEGEND TRUE? IT'S NOT LISTED ON THE MALL MAP. #DEPART-MENTSTORE-BLUES

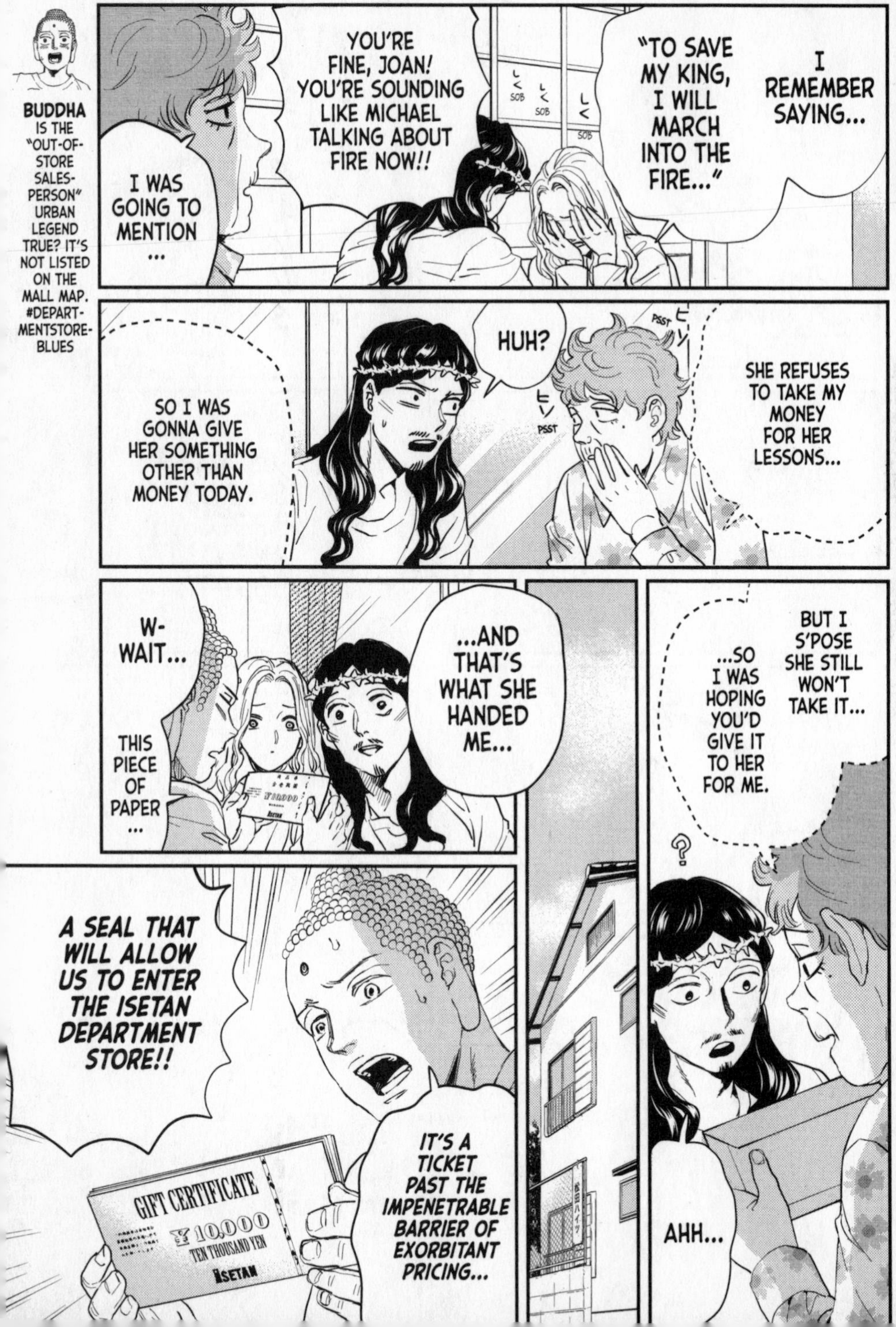
I REMEMBER SAYING...
"TO SAVE MY KING, I WILL MARCH INTO THE FIRE..."
SOB
SOB
SOB
YOU'RE FINE, JOAN! YOU'RE SOUNDING LIKE MICHAEL TALKING ABOUT FIRE NOW!!
I WAS GOING TO MENTION ...
SHE REFUSES TO TAKE MY MONEY FOR HER LESSONS...
PSST
PSST
HUH?
SO I WAS GONNA GIVE HER SOMETHING OTHER THAN MONEY TODAY.
BUT I S'POSE SHE STILL WON'T TAKE IT...
...SO I WAS HOPING YOU'D GIVE IT TO HER FOR ME.
?
AHH...
...AND THAT'S WHAT SHE HANDED ME...
W-WAIT...
THIS PIECE OF PAPER ...
IT'S A TICKET PAST THE IMPENETRABLE BARRIER OF EXORBITANT PRICING...
A SEAL THAT WILL ALLOW US TO ENTER THE ISETAN DEPARTMENT STORE!!
GIFT CERTIFICATE
¥10,000
TEN THOUSAND YEN
ISETAN

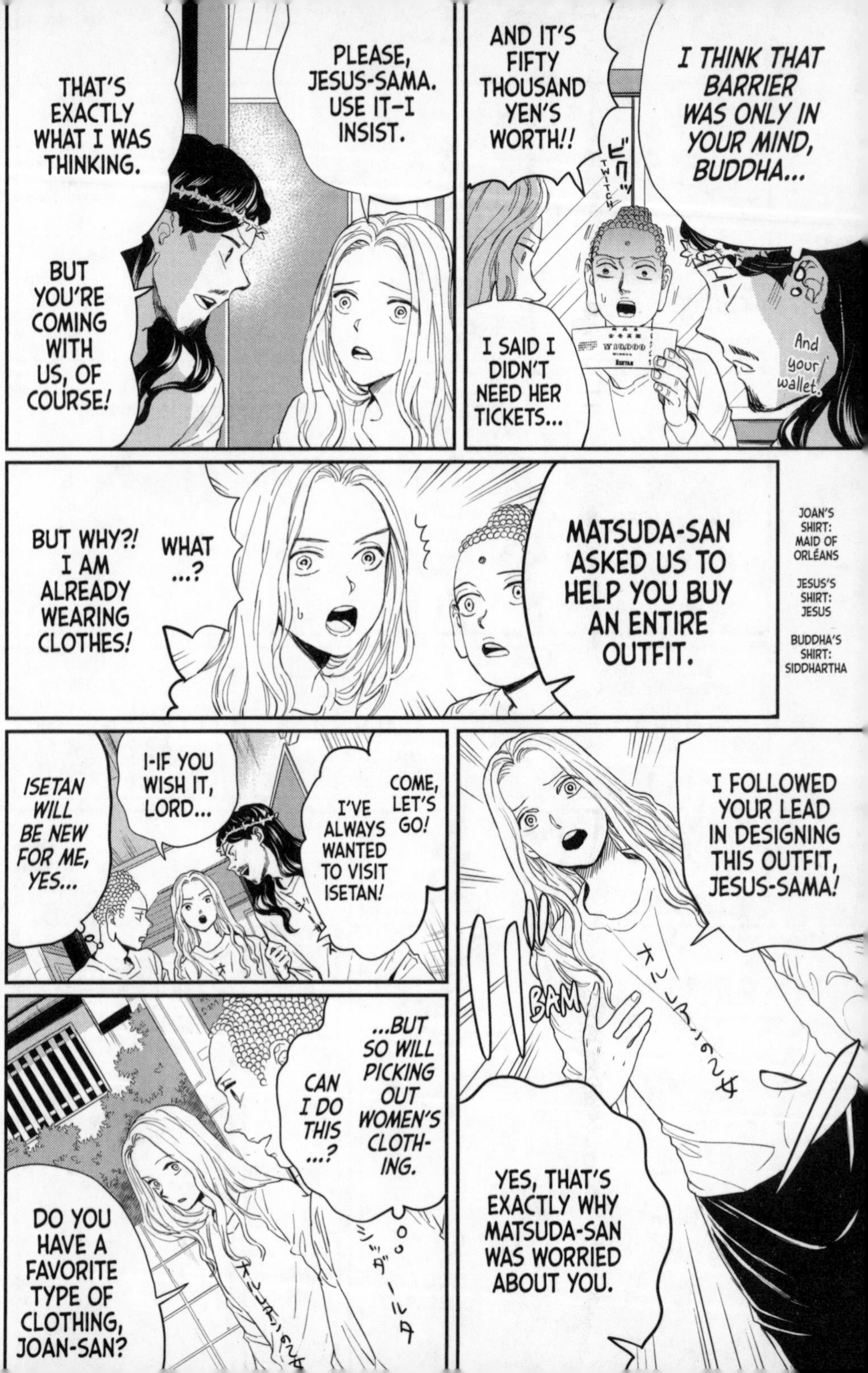
I THINK THAT BARRIER WAS ONLY IN YOUR MIND, BUDDHA...
And your wallet.
AND IT'S FIFTY THOUSAND YEN'S WORTH!!
ビクッ TWITCH
I SAID I DIDN'T NEED HER TICKETS...
PLEASE, JESUS-SAMA. USE IT—I INSIST.
THAT'S EXACTLY WHAT I WAS THINKING.
BUT YOU'RE COMING WITH US, OF COURSE!
MATSUDA-SAN ASKED US TO HELP YOU BUY AN ENTIRE OUTFIT.
WHAT ...?
BUT WHY?! I AM ALREADY WEARING CLOTHES!
I FOLLOWED YOUR LEAD IN DESIGNING THIS OUTFIT, JESUS-SAMA!
BAM
YES, THAT'S EXACTLY WHY MATSUDA-SAN WAS WORRIED ABOUT YOU.
COME, LET'S GO!
I'VE ALWAYS WANTED TO VISIT ISETAN!
I-IF YOU WISH IT, LORD...
ISETAN WILL BE NEW FOR ME, YES...
...BUT SO WILL PICKING OUT WOMEN'S CLOTHING.
CAN I DO THIS ...?
DO YOU HAVE A FAVORITE TYPE OF CLOTHING, JOAN-SAN?

JOAN'S SHIRT: MAID OF ORLÉANS

JESUS'S SHIRT: JESUS

BUDDHA'S SHIRT: SIDDHARTHA

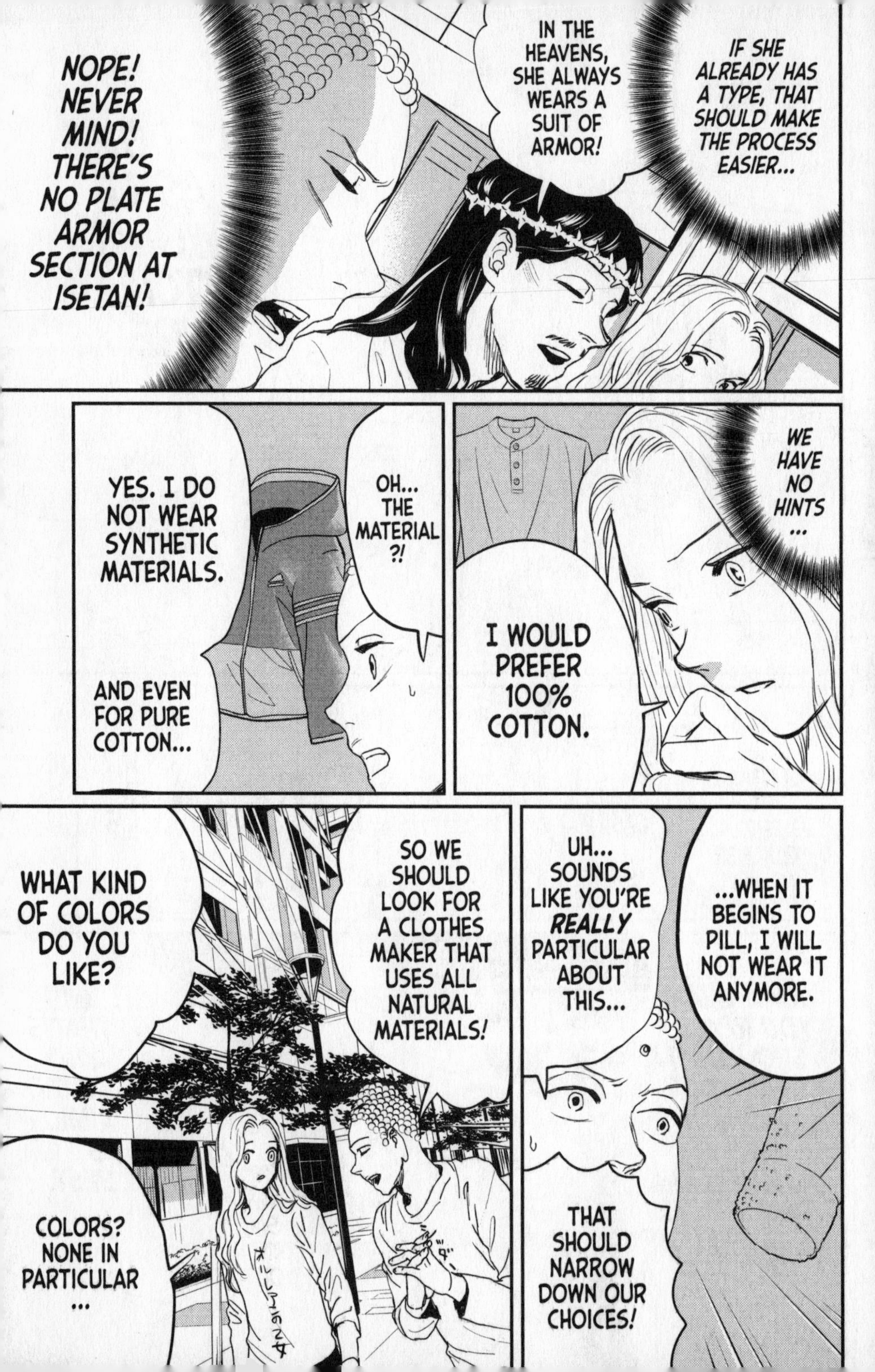
IF SHE ALREADY HAS A TYPE, THAT SHOULD MAKE THE PROCESS EASIER...
IN THE HEAVENS, SHE ALWAYS WEARS A SUIT OF ARMOR!
NOPE! NEVER MIND! THERE'S NO PLATE ARMOR SECTION AT ISETAN!
WE HAVE NO HINTS ...
I WOULD PREFER 100% COTTON.
OH... THE MATERIAL ?!
YES. I DO NOT WEAR SYNTHETIC MATERIALS.
AND EVEN FOR PURE COTTON...
...WHEN IT BEGINS TO PILL, I WILL NOT WEAR IT ANYMORE.
UH... SOUNDS LIKE YOU'RE *REALLY* PARTICULAR ABOUT THIS...
THAT SHOULD NARROW DOWN OUR CHOICES!
SO WE SHOULD LOOK FOR A CLOTHES MAKER THAT USES ALL NATURAL MATERIALS!
WHAT KIND OF COLORS DO YOU LIKE?
COLORS? NONE IN PARTICULAR ...

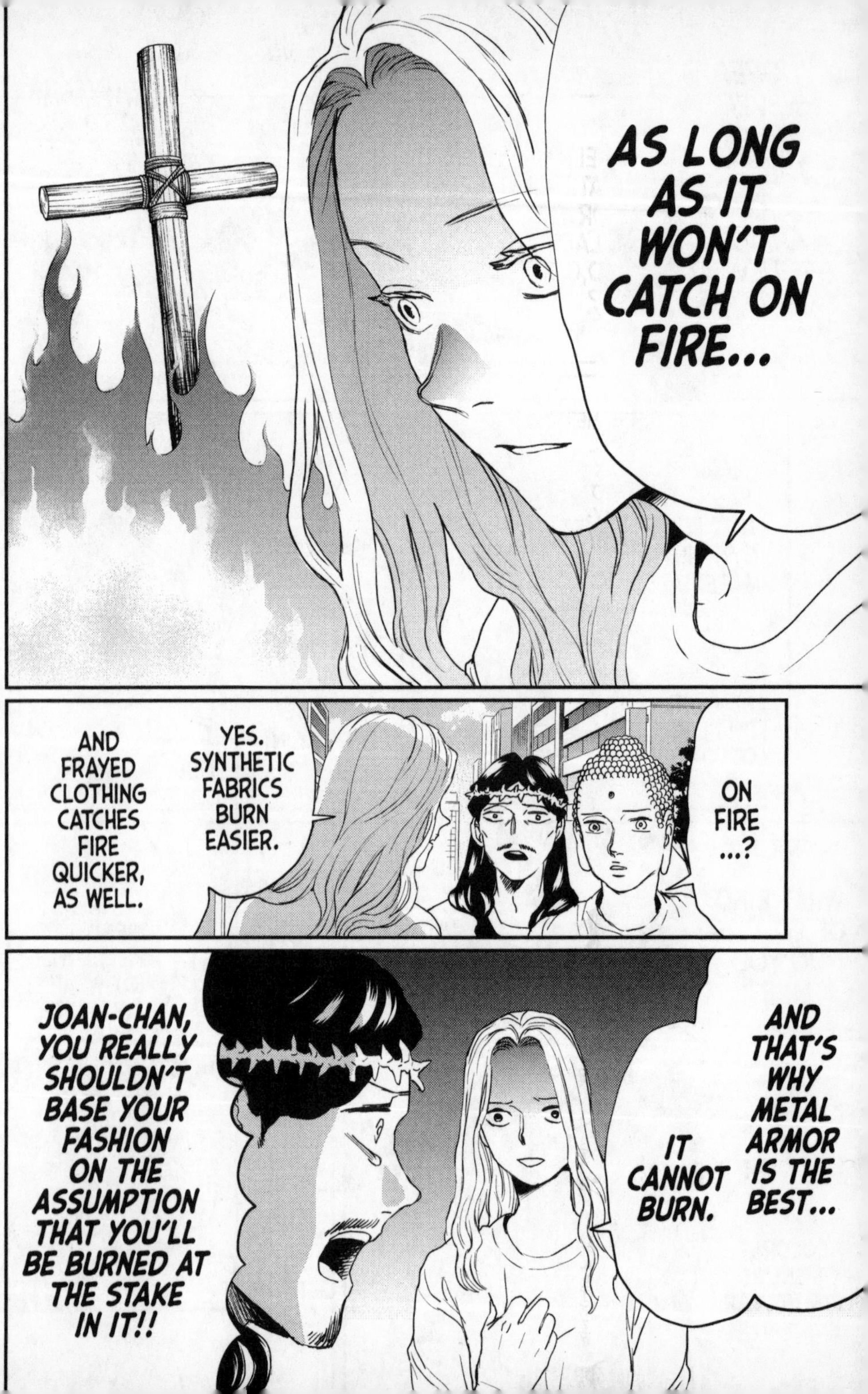
AS LONG AS IT WON'T CATCH ON FIRE...
ON FIRE ...?
YES. SYNTHETIC FABRICS BURN EASIER.
AND FRAYED CLOTHING CATCHES FIRE QUICKER, AS WELL.
AND THAT'S WHY METAL ARMOR IS THE BEST...
IT CANNOT BURN.
JOAN-CHAN, YOU REALLY SHOULDN'T BASE YOUR FASHION ON THE ASSUMPTION THAT YOU'LL BE BURNED AT THE STAKE IN IT!!

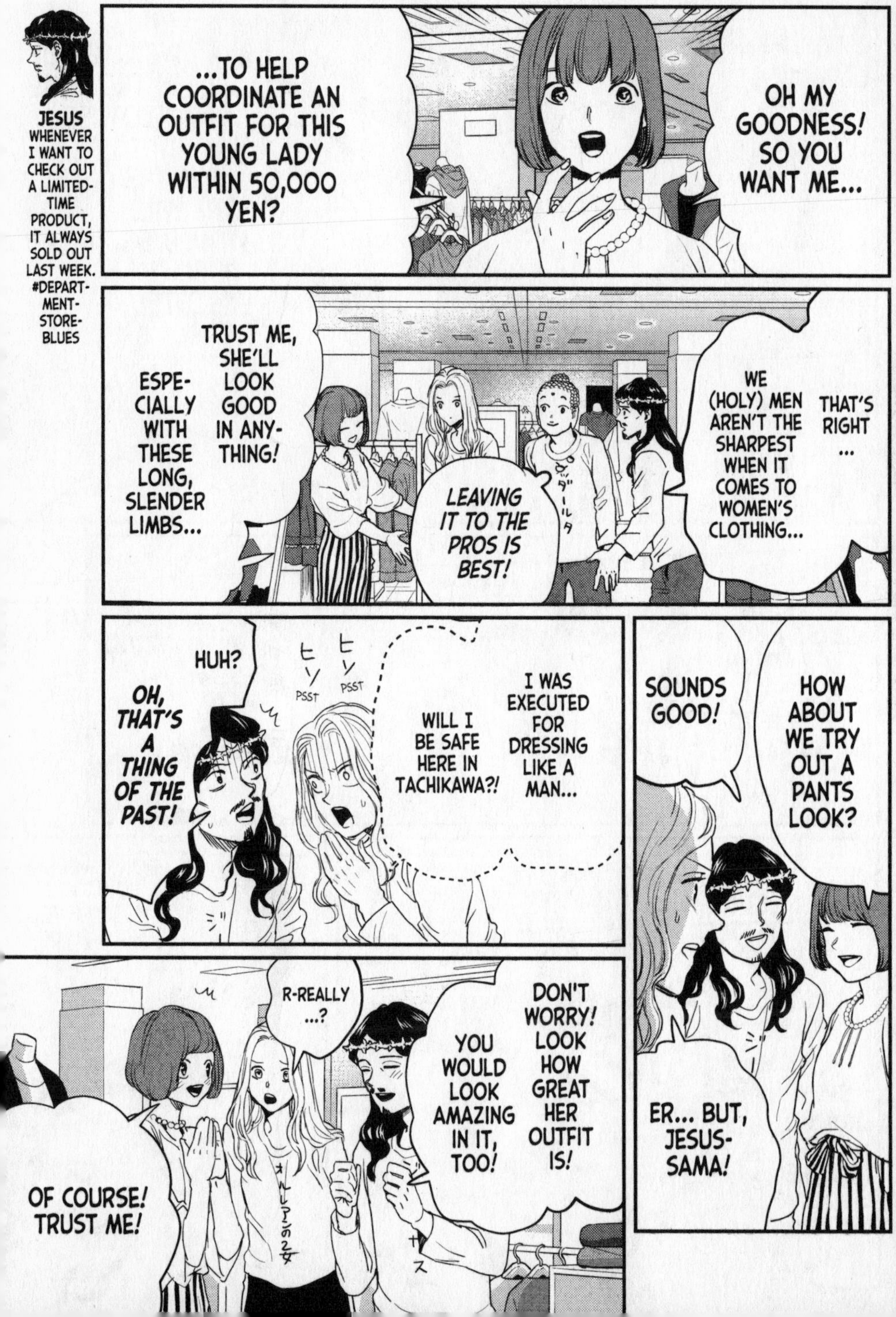
JESUS
WHENEVER I WANT TO CHECK OUT A LIMITED-TIME PRODUCT, IT ALWAYS SOLD OUT LAST WEEK. #DEPARTMENT-STORE-BLUES
OH MY GOODNESS! SO YOU WANT ME...
...TO HELP COORDINATE AN OUTFIT FOR THIS YOUNG LADY WITHIN 50,000 YEN?
THAT'S RIGHT...
WE (HOLY) MEN AREN'T THE SHARPEST WHEN IT COMES TO WOMEN'S CLOTHING...
LEAVING IT TO THE PROS IS BEST!
ダールタ
TRUST ME, SHE'LL LOOK GOOD IN ANYTHING!
ESPECIALLY WITH THESE LONG, SLENDER LIMBS...
HOW ABOUT WE TRY OUT A PANTS LOOK?
SOUNDS GOOD!
ER... BUT, JESUS-SAMA!
I WAS EXECUTED FOR DRESSING LIKE A MAN...
WILL I BE SAFE HERE IN TACHIKAWA?!
ヒソ PSST
ヒソ PSST
HUH?
OH, THAT'S A THING OF THE PAST!
DON'T WORRY! LOOK HOW GREAT HER OUTFIT IS!
YOU WOULD LOOK AMAZING IN IT, TOO!
R-REALLY ...?
OF COURSE! TRUST ME!
オルレアンの乙女
ヤス

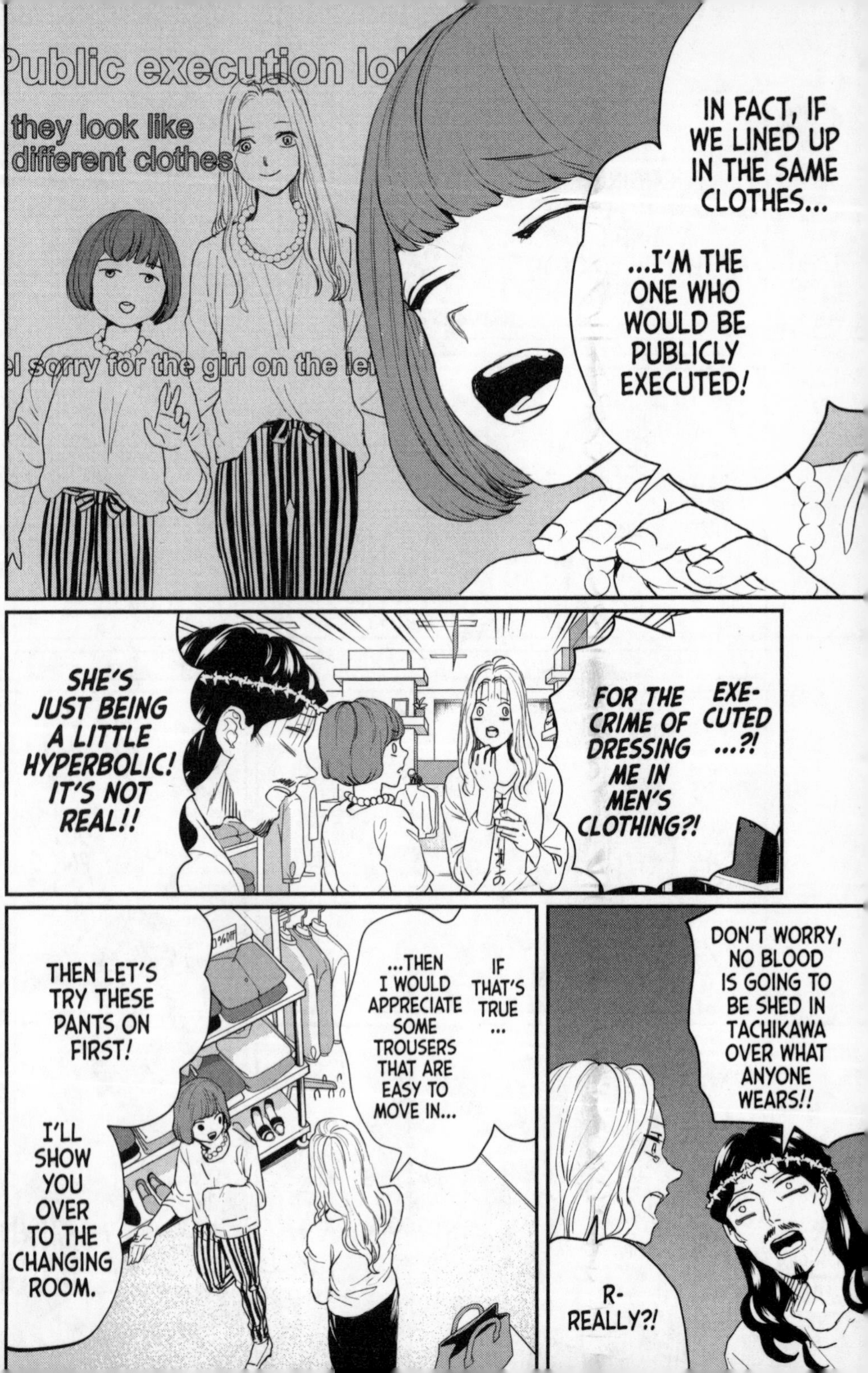
IN FACT, IF WE LINED UP IN THE SAME CLOTHES...
...I'M THE ONE WHO WOULD BE PUBLICLY EXECUTED!
Public execution lo
they look like different clothes
el sorry for the girl on the le
EXE-CUTED ...?!
FOR THE CRIME OF DRESSING ME IN MEN'S CLOTHING?!
SHE'S JUST BEING A LITTLE HYPERBOLIC! IT'S NOT REAL!!
DON'T WORRY, NO BLOOD IS GOING TO BE SHED IN TACHIKAWA OVER WHAT ANYONE WEARS!!
R-REALLY?!
IF THAT'S TRUE ...
...THEN I WOULD APPRECIATE SOME TROUSERS THAT ARE EASY TO MOVE IN...
THEN LET'S TRY THESE PANTS ON FIRST!
I'LL SHOW YOU OVER TO THE CHANGING ROOM.

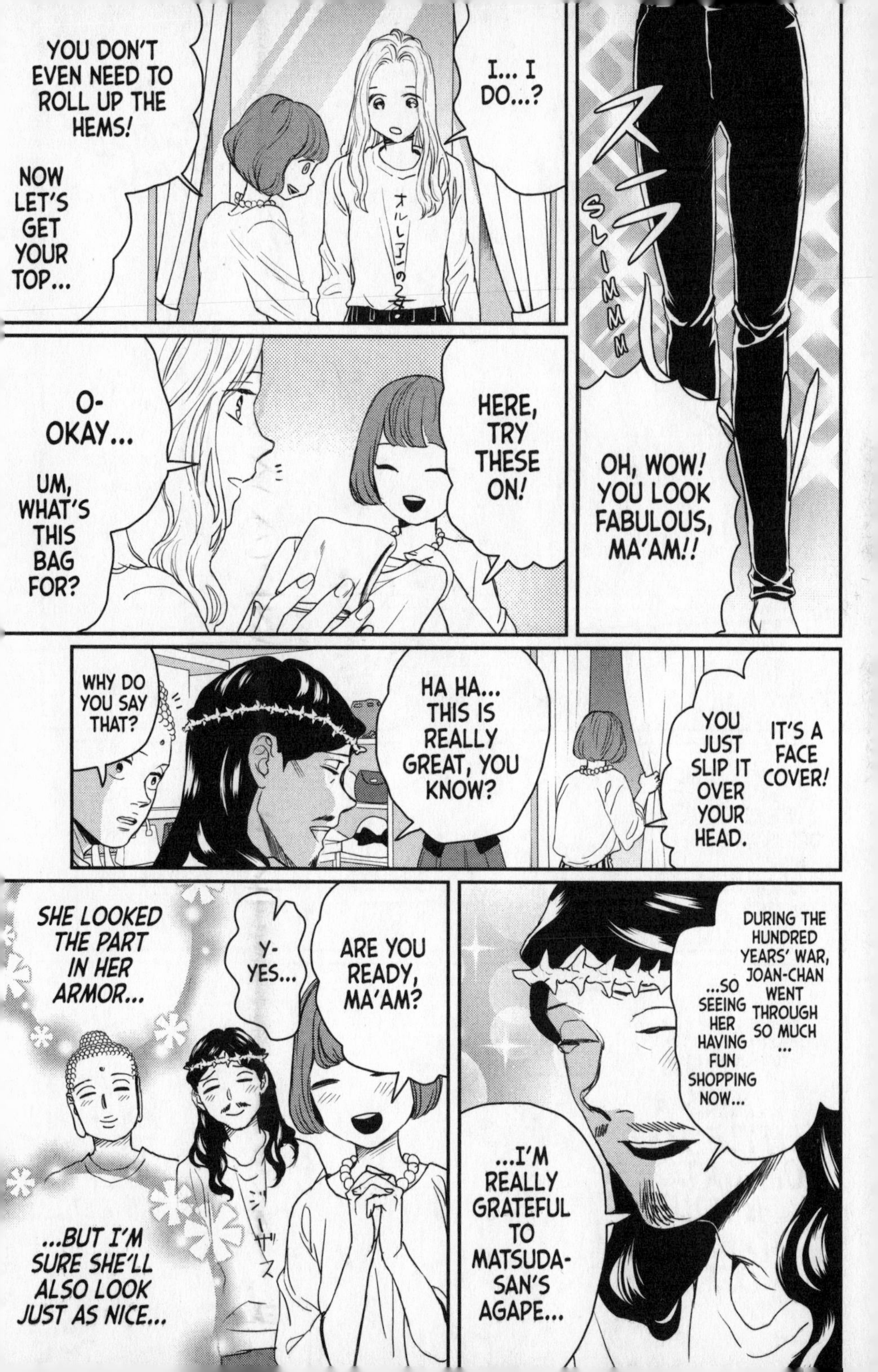
SLIMMM
OH, WOW! YOU LOOK FABULOUS, MA'AM!!
I... I DO...?
YOU DON'T EVEN NEED TO ROLL UP THE HEMS!
NOW LET'S GET YOUR TOP...
HERE, TRY THESE ON!
O-OKAY...
UM, WHAT'S THIS BAG FOR?
IT'S A FACE COVER!
YOU JUST SLIP IT OVER YOUR HEAD.
HA HA... THIS IS REALLY GREAT, YOU KNOW?
WHY DO YOU SAY THAT?
DURING THE HUNDRED YEARS' WAR, JOAN-CHAN WENT THROUGH SO MUCH...
...SO SEEING HER HAVING FUN SHOPPING NOW...
...I'M REALLY GRATEFUL TO MATSUDA-SAN'S AGAPE...
ARE YOU READY, MA'AM?
Y-YES...
SHE LOOKED THE PART IN HER ARMOR...
...BUT I'M SURE SHE'LL ALSO LOOK JUST AS NICE...

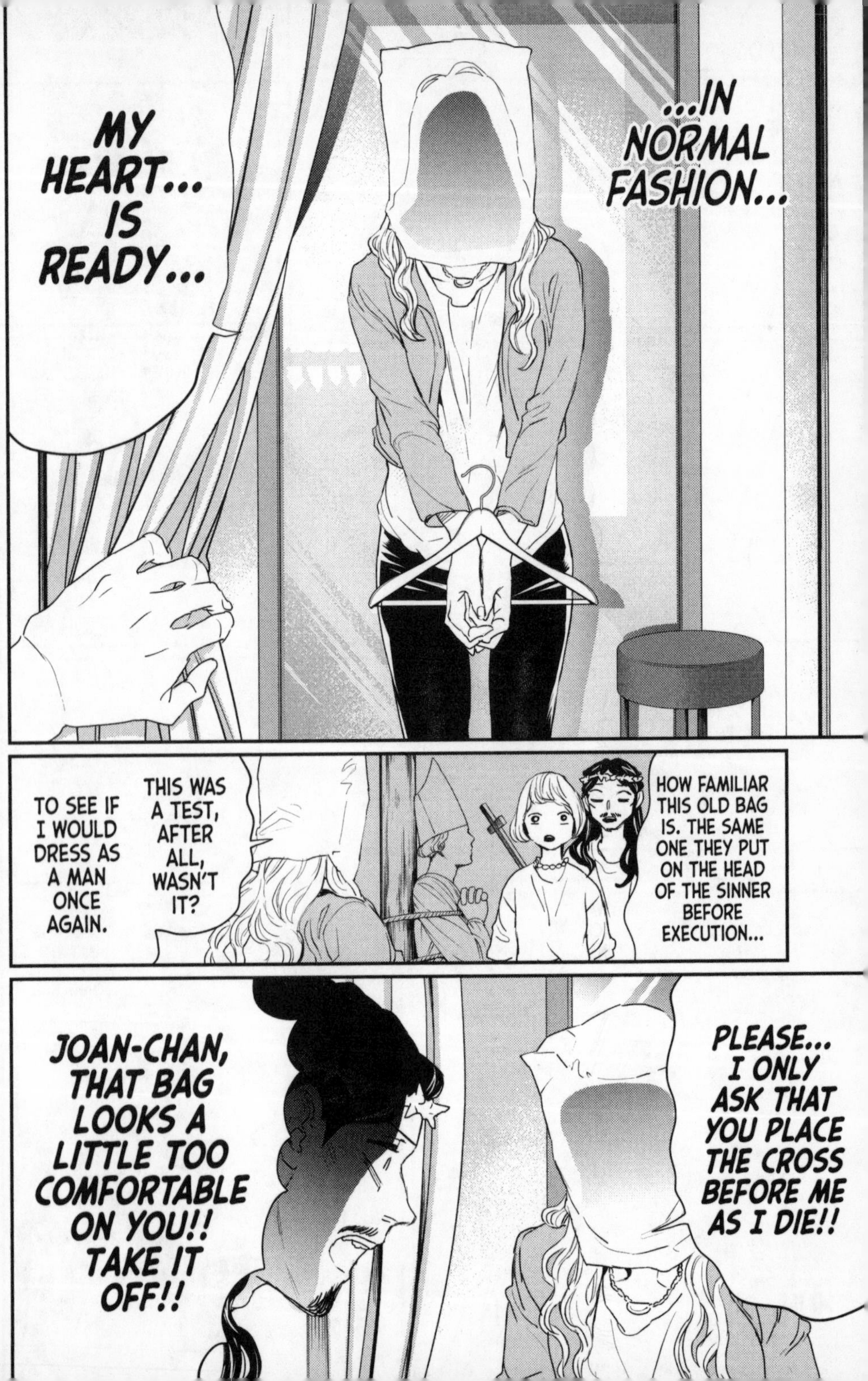
...IN NORMAL FASHION...
MY HEART... IS READY...
HOW FAMILIAR THIS OLD BAG IS. THE SAME ONE THEY PUT ON THE HEAD OF THE SINNER BEFORE EXECUTION...
THIS WAS A TEST, AFTER ALL, WASN'T IT?
TO SEE IF I WOULD DRESS AS A MAN ONCE AGAIN.
PLEASE... I ONLY ASK THAT YOU PLACE THE CROSS BEFORE ME AS I DIE!!
JOAN-CHAN, THAT BAG LOOKS A LITTLE TOO COMFORTABLE ON YOU!! TAKE IT OFF!!

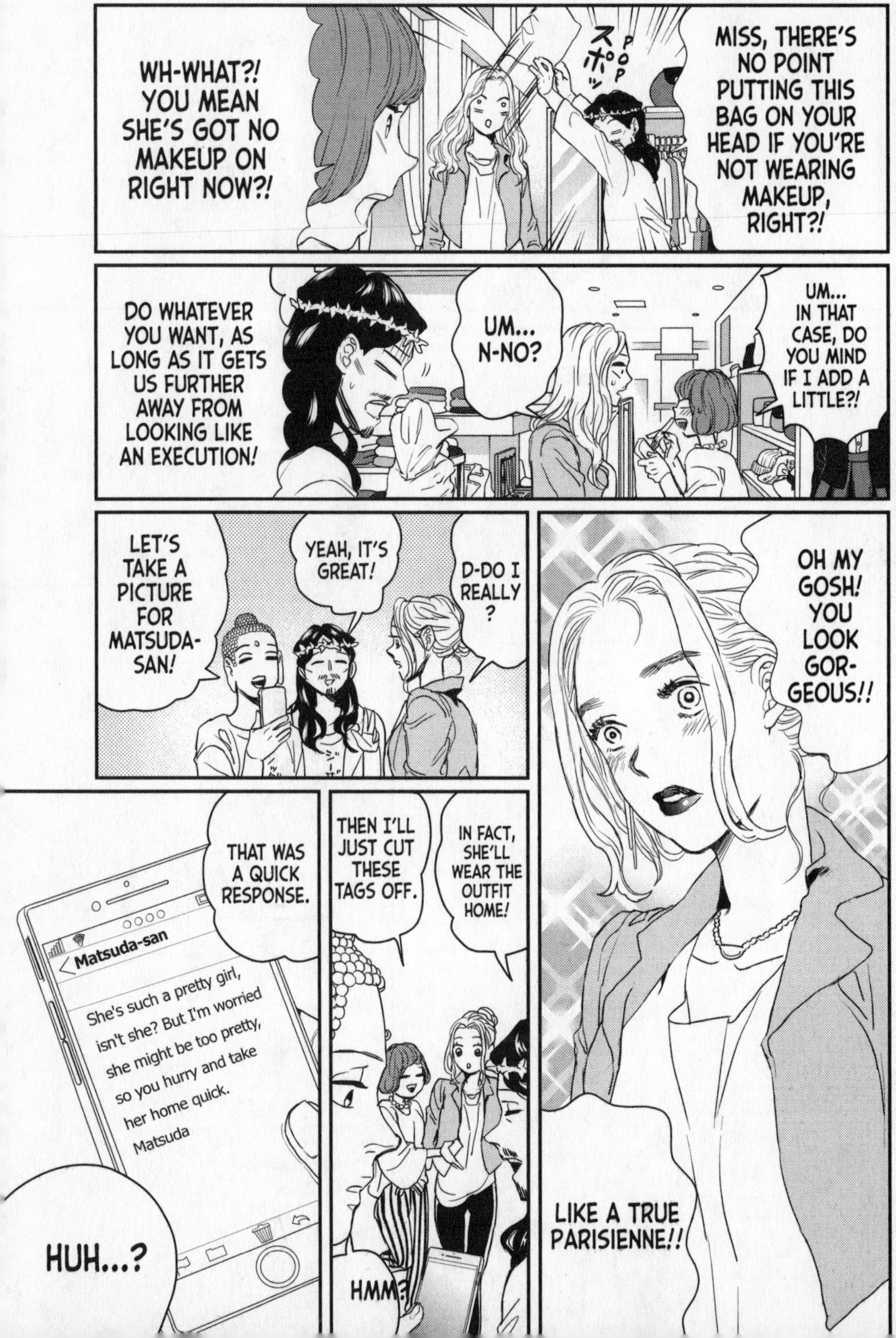
MISS, THERE'S NO POINT PUTTING THIS BAG ON YOUR HEAD IF YOU'RE NOT WEARING MAKEUP, RIGHT?!
スポッ POP
WH-WHAT?! YOU MEAN SHE'S GOT NO MAKEUP ON RIGHT NOW?!
UM... IN THAT CASE, DO YOU MIND IF I ADD A LITTLE?!
UM... N-NO?
DO WHATEVER YOU WANT, AS LONG AS IT GETS US FURTHER AWAY FROM LOOKING LIKE AN EXECUTION!
OH MY GOSH! YOU LOOK GOR-GEOUS!!
LIKE A TRUE PARISIENNE!!
D-DO I REALLY?
YEAH, IT'S GREAT!
LET'S TAKE A PICTURE FOR MATSUDA-SAN!
IN FACT, SHE'LL WEAR THE OUTFIT HOME!
THEN I'LL JUST CUT THESE TAGS OFF.
HMM?
THAT WAS A QUICK RESPONSE.
Matsuda-san
She's such a pretty girl, isn't she? But I'm worried she might be too pretty, so you hurry and take her home quick.
Matsuda
HUH...?

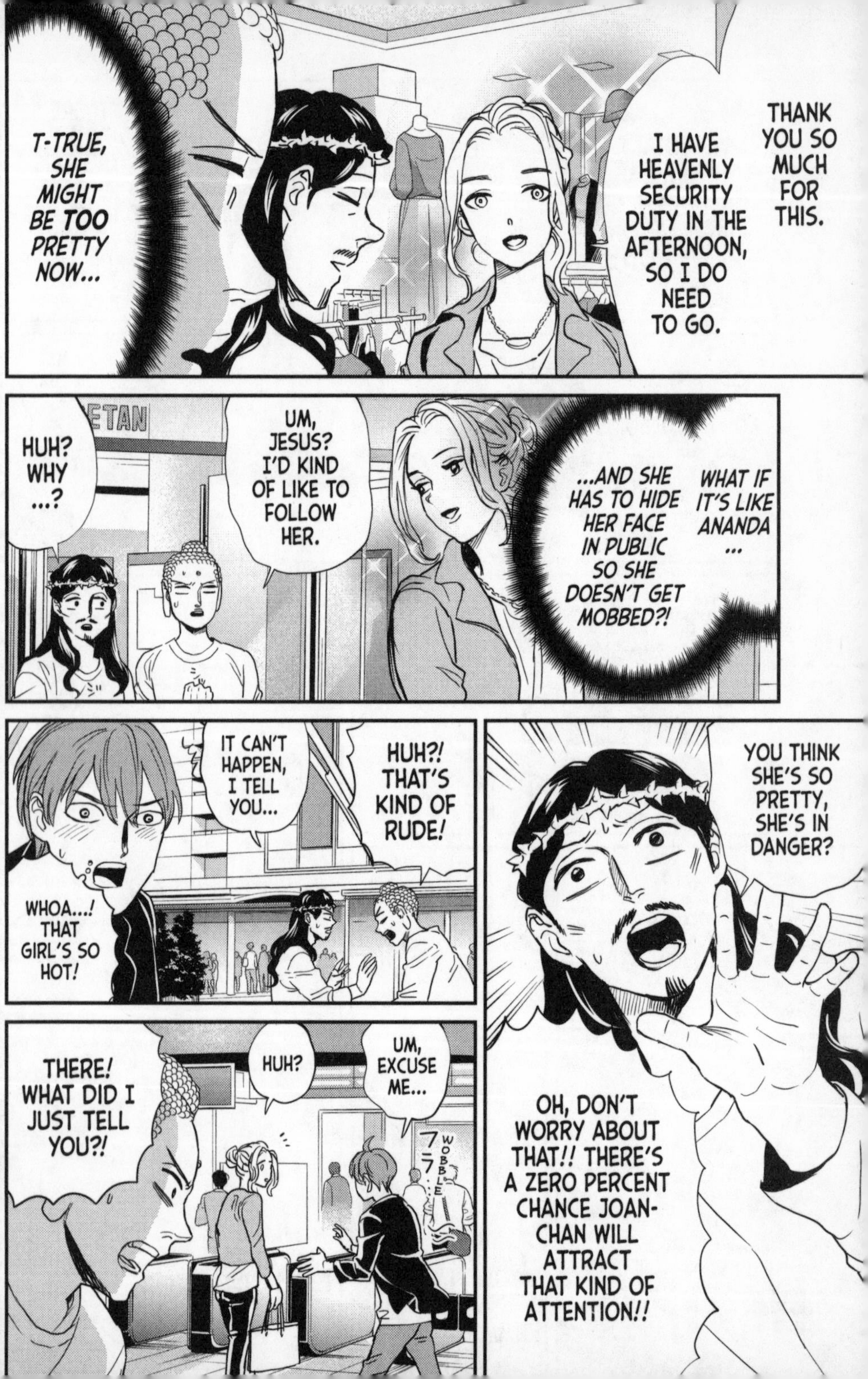
THANK YOU SO MUCH FOR THIS.
I HAVE HEAVENLY SECURITY DUTY IN THE AFTERNOON, SO I DO NEED TO GO.
T-TRUE, SHE MIGHT BE TOO PRETTY NOW...
WHAT IF IT'S LIKE ANANDA...
...AND SHE HAS TO HIDE HER FACE IN PUBLIC SO SHE DOESN'T GET MOBBED?!
UM, JESUS? I'D KIND OF LIKE TO FOLLOW HER.
HUH? WHY...?
YOU THINK SHE'S SO PRETTY, SHE'S IN DANGER?
OH, DON'T WORRY ABOUT THAT!! THERE'S A ZERO PERCENT CHANCE JOAN-CHAN WILL ATTRACT THAT KIND OF ATTENTION!!
HUH?! THAT'S KIND OF RUDE!
IT CAN'T HAPPEN, I TELL YOU...
WHOA...! THAT GIRL'S SO HOT!
UM, EXCUSE ME...
WOBBLE
HUH?
THERE! WHAT DID I JUST TELL YOU?!

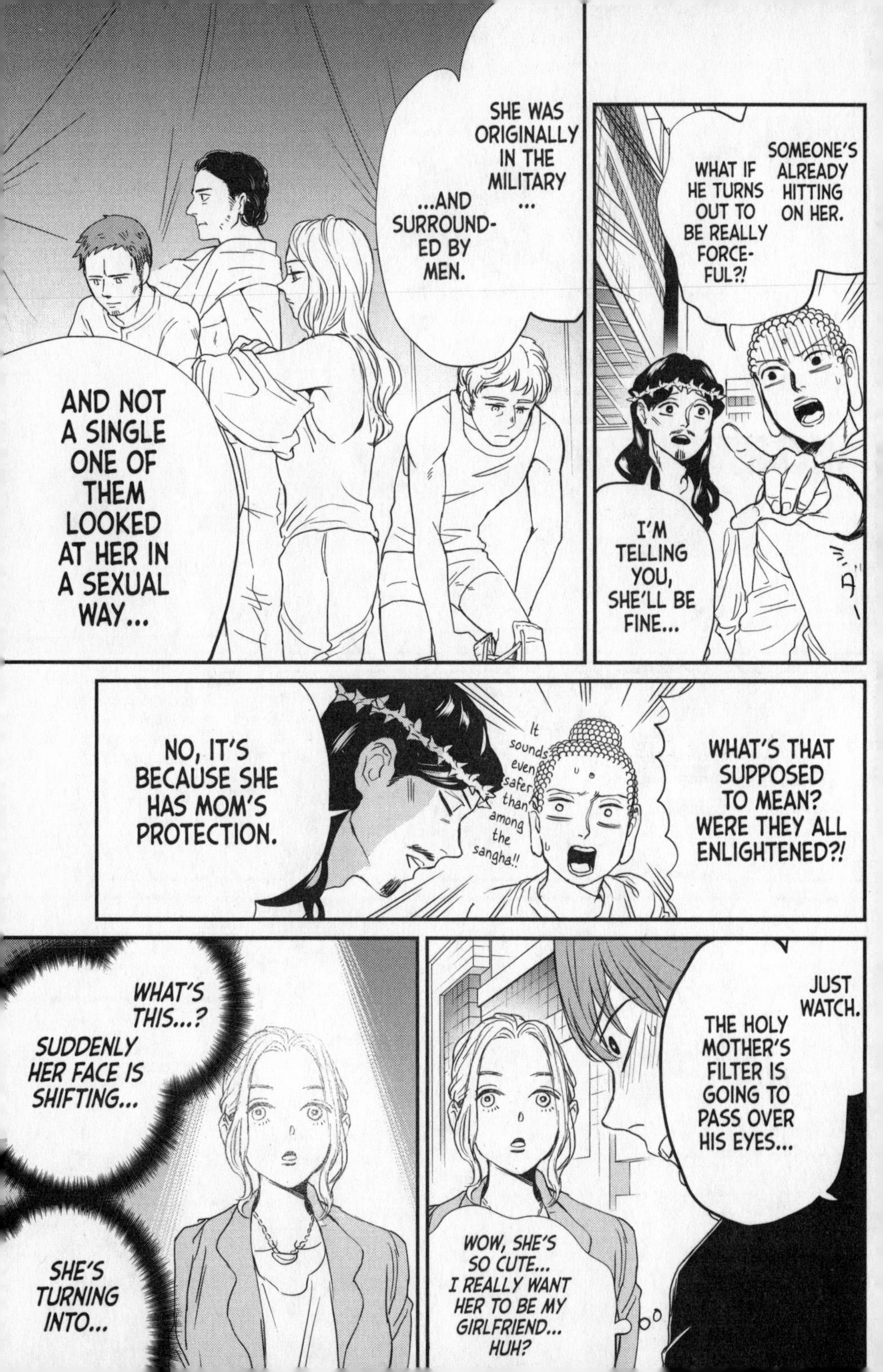
SOMEONE'S ALREADY HITTING ON HER.
WHAT IF HE TURNS OUT TO BE REALLY FORCE-FUL?!
I'M TELLING YOU, SHE'LL BE FINE...
SHE WAS ORIGINALLY IN THE MILITARY ...
...AND SURROUND-ED BY MEN.
AND NOT A SINGLE ONE OF THEM LOOKED AT HER IN A SEXUAL WAY...
WHAT'S THAT SUPPOSED TO MEAN? WERE THEY ALL ENLIGHTENED?!
It sounds even safer than among the sangha!!
NO, IT'S BECAUSE SHE HAS MOM'S PROTECTION.
JUST WATCH.
THE HOLY MOTHER'S FILTER IS GOING TO PASS OVER HIS EYES...
WOW, SHE'S SO CUTE... I REALLY WANT HER TO BE MY GIRLFRIEND... HUH?
WHAT'S THIS...? SUDDENLY HER FACE IS SHIFTING...
SHE'S TURNING INTO...

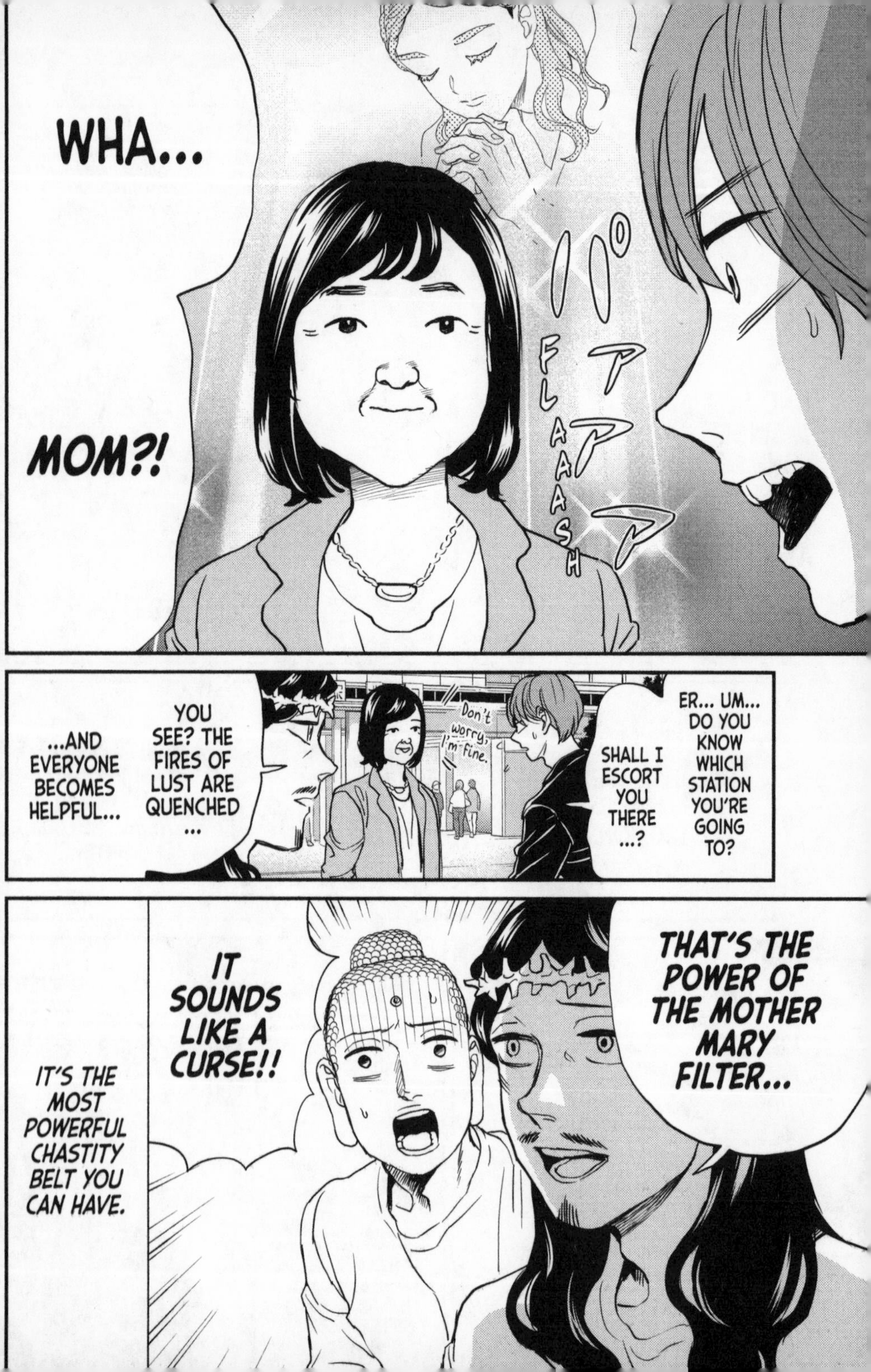
パァァァ
FLAAASH
WHA...
MOM?!
ER... UM... DO YOU KNOW WHICH STATION YOU'RE GOING TO?
SHALL I ESCORT YOU THERE ...?
Don't worry, I'm fine.
YOU SEE? THE FIRES OF LUST ARE QUENCHED ...
...AND EVERYONE BECOMES HELPFUL...
THAT'S THE POWER OF THE MOTHER MARY FILTER...
IT SOUNDS LIKE A CURSE!!
IT'S THE MOST POWERFUL CHASTITY BELT YOU CAN HAVE.

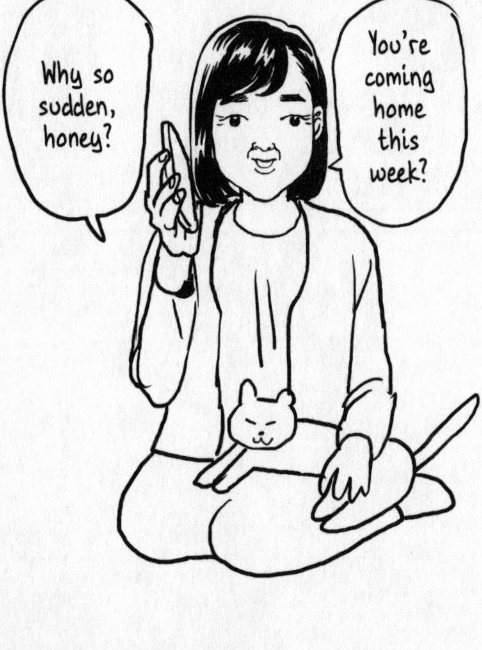
You're coming home this week?
Why so sudden, honey?

SAINT☆YOUNG MEN

CHAPTER 123 TRANSLATION NOTES

Isetan, page 39
Isetan Department Store in Shinjuku is considered one of the premier department stores in Japan.

Sangha, page 49
The Sanskrit word referring to the "spiritual community" of monks and nuns devoted to Buddhism.

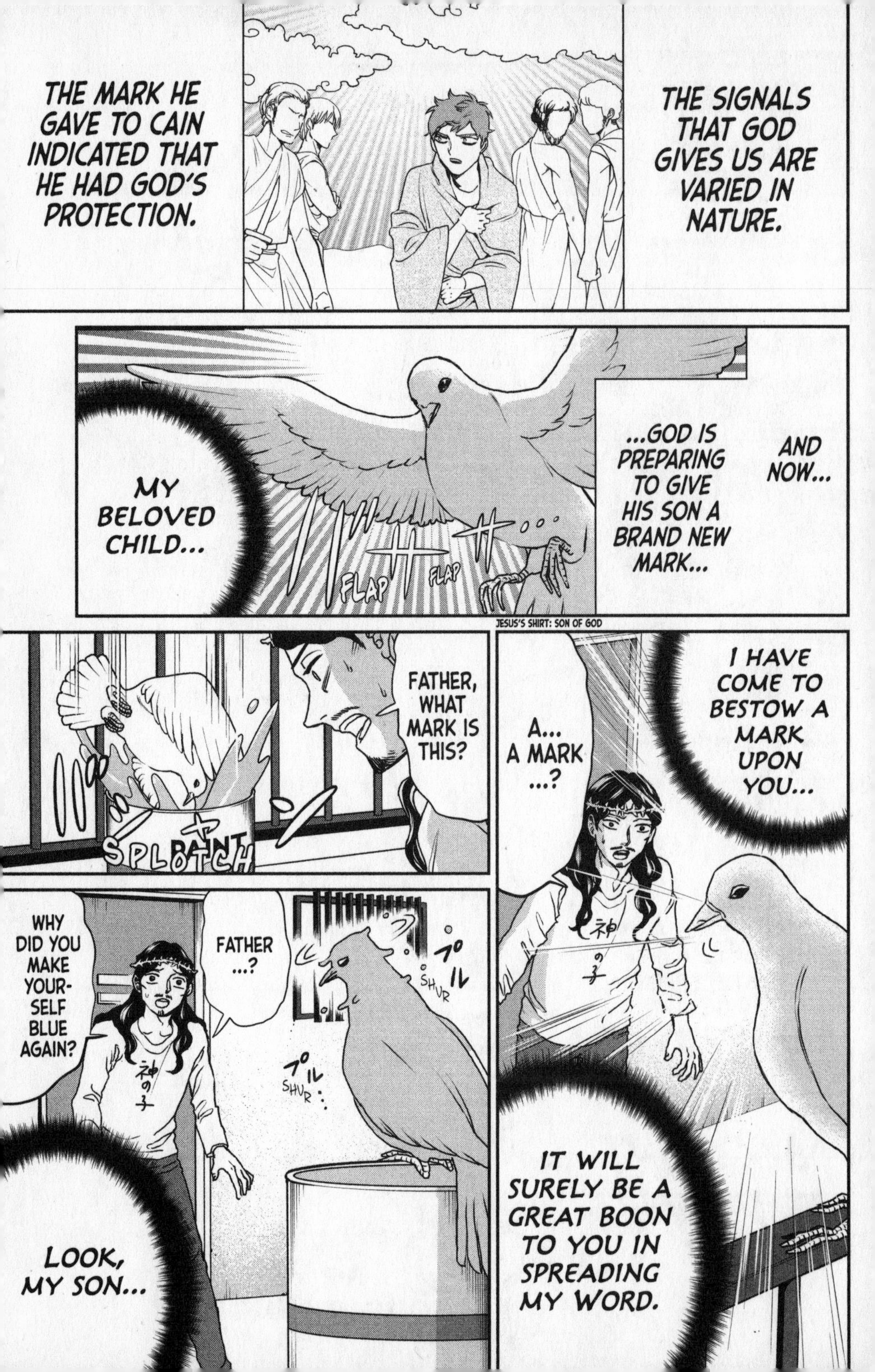
THE SIGNALS THAT GOD GIVES US ARE VARIED IN NATURE.
THE MARK HE GAVE TO CAIN INDICATED THAT HE HAD GOD'S PROTECTION.
AND NOW...
...GOD IS PREPARING TO GIVE HIS SON A BRAND NEW MARK...
MY BELOVED CHILD...
FLAP
FLAP
JESUS'S SHIRT: SON OF GOD
I HAVE COME TO BESTOW A MARK UPON YOU...
A... A MARK ...?
IT WILL SURELY BE A GREAT BOON TO YOU IN SPREADING MY WORD.
FATHER, WHAT MARK IS THIS?
PAINT
SPLOTCH
プル
SHUR
FATHER ...?
WHY DID YOU MAKE YOUR-SELF BLUE AGAIN?
プル
SHUR
LOOK, MY SON...

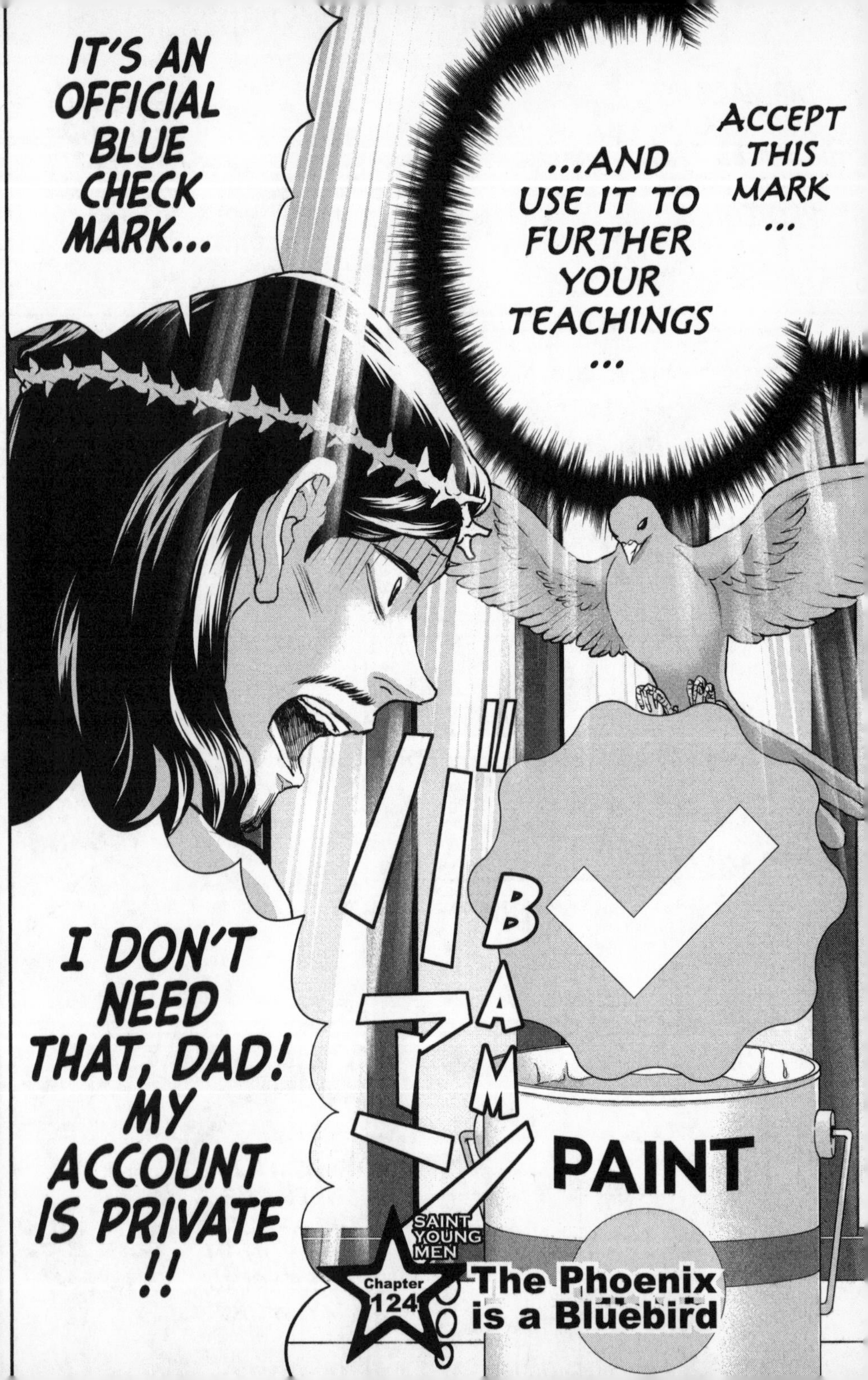
ACCEPT THIS MARK...
...AND USE IT TO FURTHER YOUR TEACHINGS...
IT'S AN OFFICIAL BLUE CHECK MARK...
I DON'T NEED THAT, DAD! MY ACCOUNT IS PRIVATE!!
BAM
PAINT
SAINT YOUNG MEN
Chapter 124
The Phoenix is a Bluebird

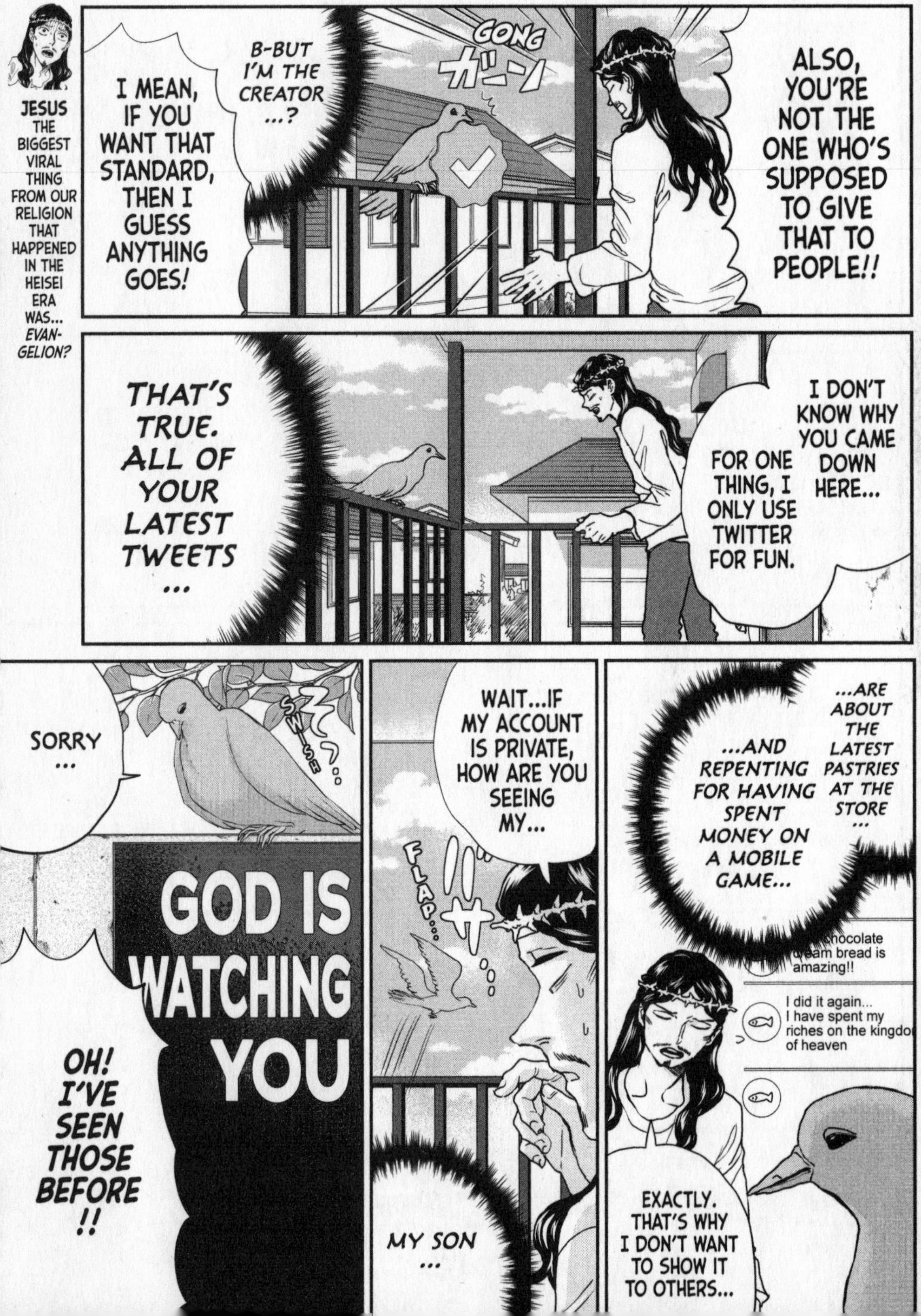
ALSO, YOU'RE NOT THE ONE WHO'S SUPPOSED TO GIVE THAT TO PEOPLE!!
GONG
ガーン
B-BUT I'M THE CREATOR...?
I MEAN, IF YOU WANT THAT STANDARD, THEN I GUESS ANYTHING GOES!
I DON'T KNOW WHY YOU CAME DOWN HERE...
FOR ONE THING, I ONLY USE TWITTER FOR FUN.
THAT'S TRUE. ALL OF YOUR LATEST TWEETS...
...ARE ABOUT THE LATEST PASTRIES AT THE STORE...
...AND REPENTING FOR HAVING SPENT MONEY ON A MOBILE GAME...
chocolate
amazing!!
I did it again... I have spent my riches on the kingdo
of heaven
EXACTLY. THAT'S WHY I DON'T WANT TO SHOW IT TO OTHERS...
WAIT...IF MY ACCOUNT IS PRIVATE, HOW ARE YOU SEEING MY...
FLAP...
サ
MY SON...
SWISH
SORRY...
GOD IS WATCHING YOU
OH! I'VE SEEN THOSE BEFORE!!
JESUS THE BIGGEST VIRAL THING FROM OUR RELIGION THAT HAPPENED IN THE HEISEI ERA WAS... EVANGELION?

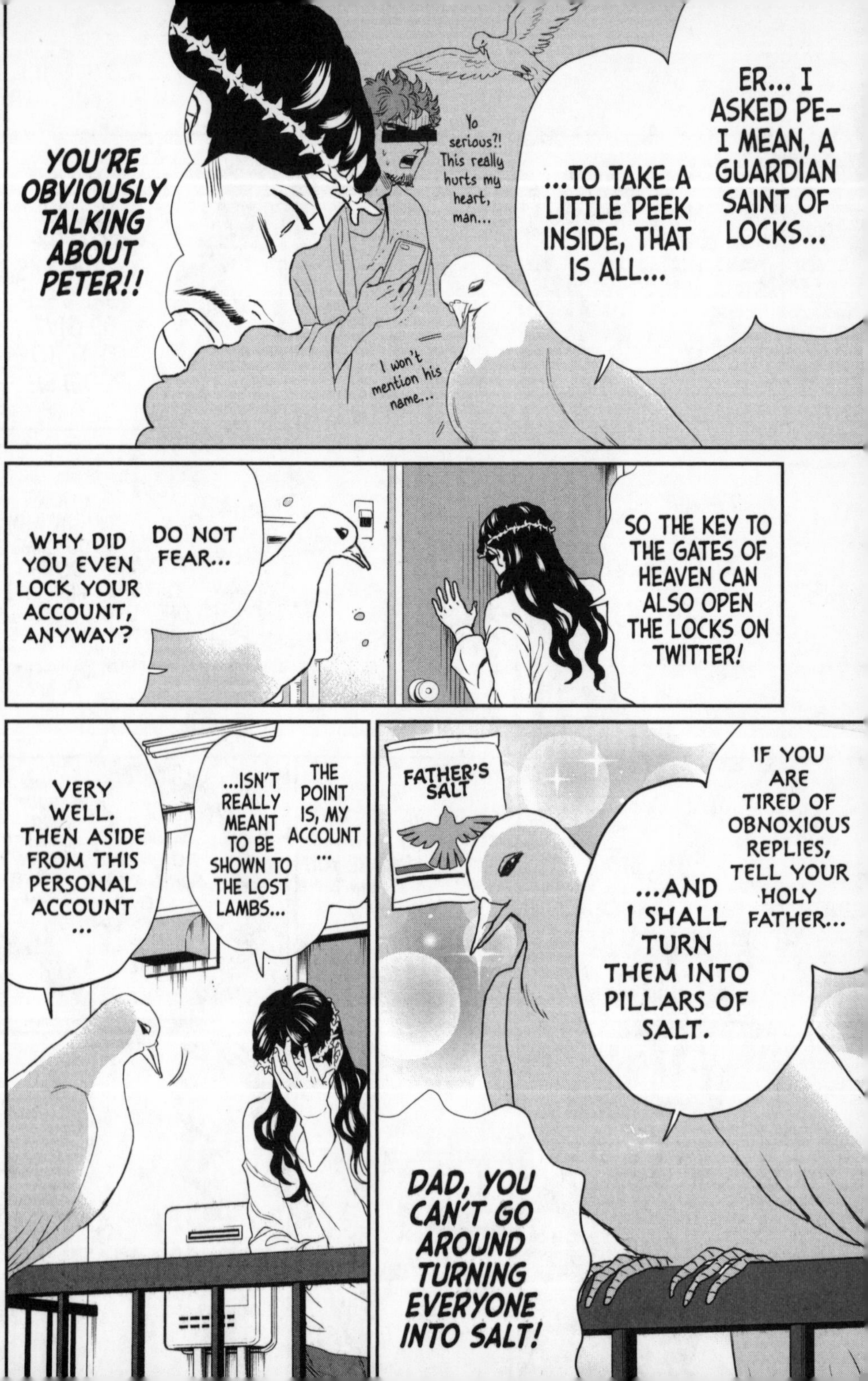
ER... I ASKED PE— I MEAN, A GUARDIAN SAINT OF LOCKS...
...TO TAKE A LITTLE PEEK INSIDE, THAT IS ALL...
Yo serious?! This really hurts my heart, man...
I won't mention his name...
YOU'RE OBVIOUSLY TALKING ABOUT PETER!!
SO THE KEY TO THE GATES OF HEAVEN CAN ALSO OPEN THE LOCKS ON TWITTER!
DO NOT FEAR...
WHY DID YOU EVEN LOCK YOUR ACCOUNT, ANYWAY?
IF YOU ARE TIRED OF OBNOXIOUS REPLIES, TELL YOUR HOLY FATHER...
...AND I SHALL TURN THEM INTO PILLARS OF SALT.
FATHER'S SALT
DAD, YOU CAN'T GO AROUND TURNING EVERYONE INTO SALT!
THE POINT IS, MY ACCOUNT ...
...ISN'T REALLY MEANT TO BE SHOWN TO THE LOST LAMBS...
VERY WELL. THEN ASIDE FROM THIS PERSONAL ACCOUNT ...

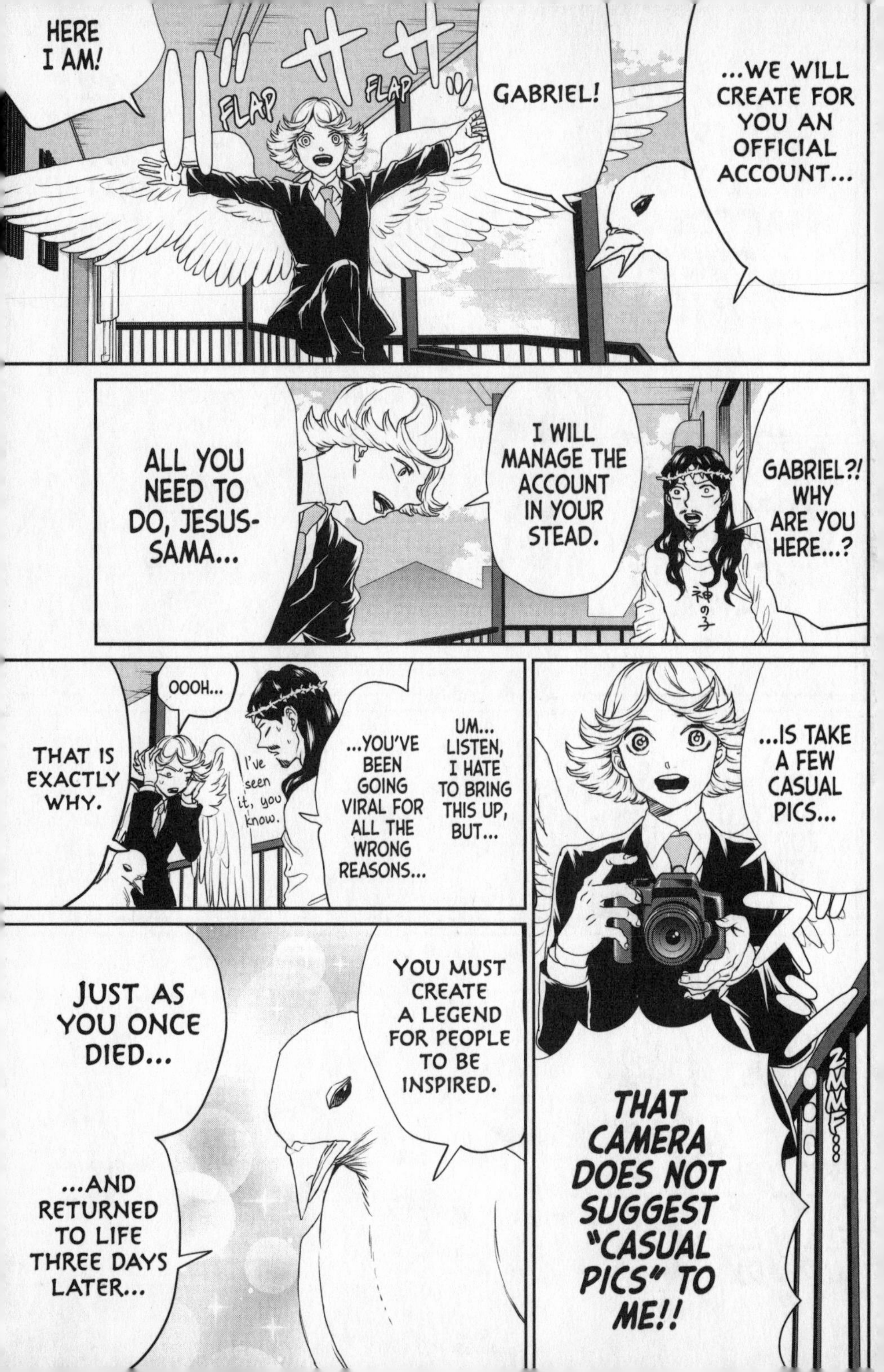
...WE WILL CREATE FOR YOU AN OFFICIAL ACCOUNT...
GABRIEL!
FLAP FLAP
HERE I AM!
GABRIEL?! WHY ARE YOU HERE...?
神の子
I WILL MANAGE THE ACCOUNT IN YOUR STEAD.
ALL YOU NEED TO DO, JESUS-SAMA...
...IS TAKE A FEW CASUAL PICS...
ZMMF...
THAT CAMERA DOES NOT SUGGEST "CASUAL PICS" TO ME!!
UM... LISTEN, I HATE TO BRING THIS UP, BUT...
...YOU'VE BEEN GOING VIRAL FOR ALL THE WRONG REASONS...
OOOH...
I've seen it, you know.
THAT IS EXACTLY WHY.
YOU MUST CREATE A LEGEND FOR PEOPLE TO BE INSPIRED.
JUST AS YOU ONCE DIED...
...AND RETURNED TO LIFE THREE DAYS LATER...

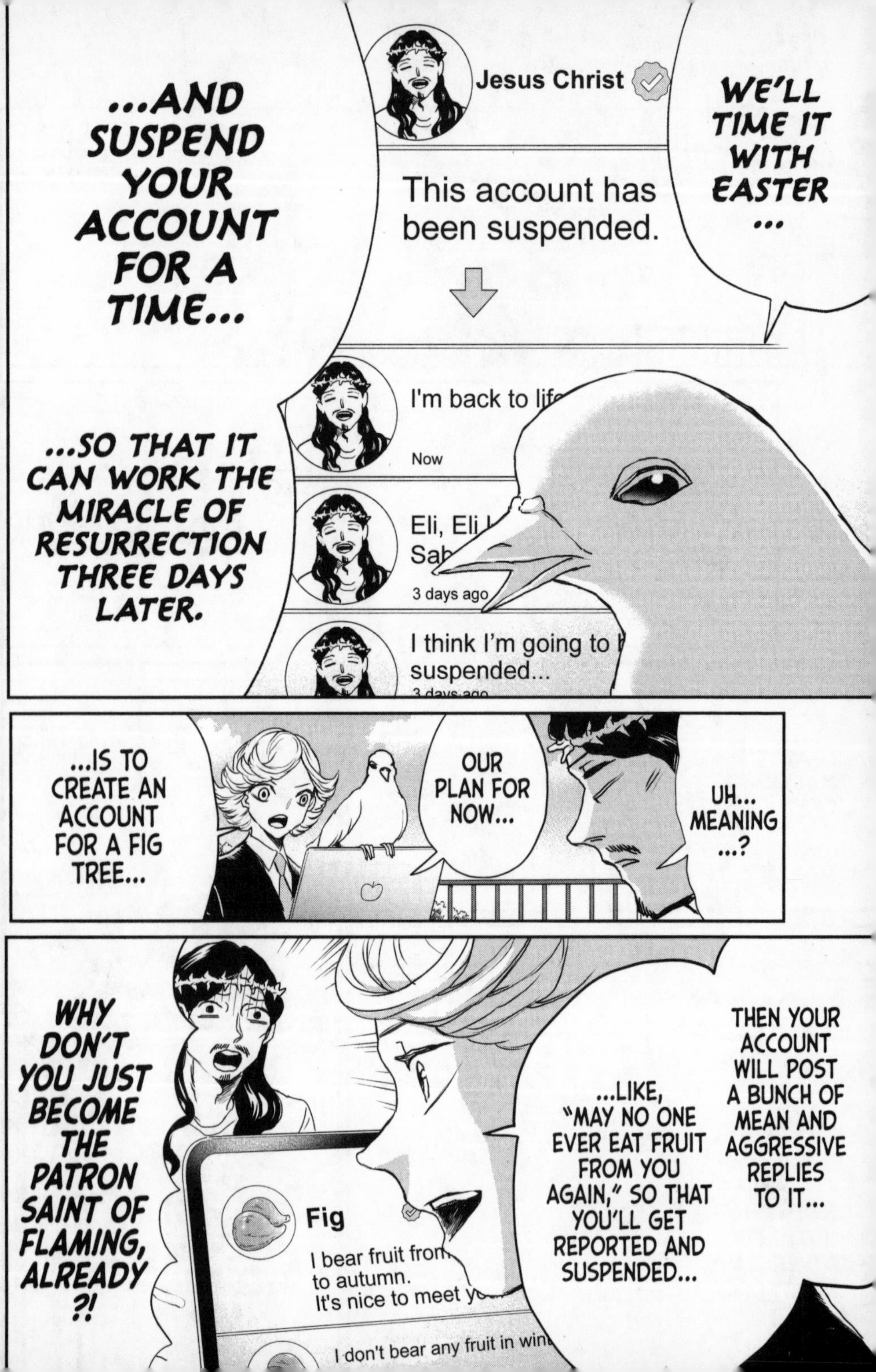
WE'LL TIME IT WITH EASTER...
Jesus Christ
This account has been suspended.
I'm back to lif
Now
Eli, Eli
Sab
3 days ago
I think I'm going to b
suspended...
...AND SUSPEND YOUR ACCOUNT FOR A TIME...
...SO THAT IT CAN WORK THE MIRACLE OF RESURRECTION THREE DAYS LATER.
UH... MEANING...?
OUR PLAN FOR NOW...
...IS TO CREATE AN ACCOUNT FOR A FIG TREE...
THEN YOUR ACCOUNT WILL POST A BUNCH OF MEAN AND AGGRESSIVE REPLIES TO IT...
...LIKE, "MAY NO ONE EVER EAT FRUIT FROM YOU AGAIN," SO THAT YOU'LL GET REPORTED AND SUSPENDED...
Fig
I bear fruit from
to autumn.
It's nice to meet y
I don't bear any fruit in win
WHY DON'T YOU JUST BECOME THE PATRON SAINT OF FLAMING, ALREADY?!

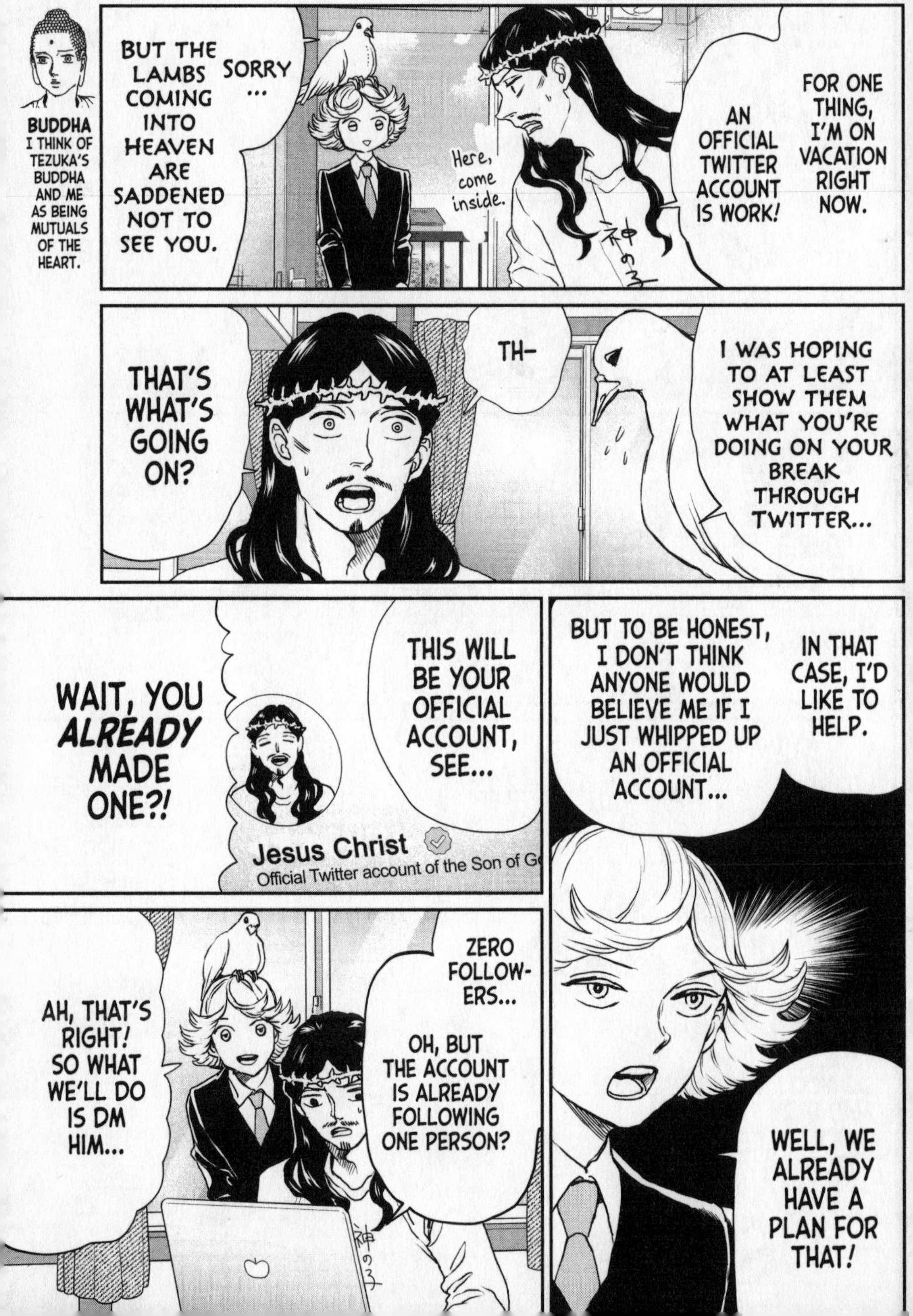
BUDDHA
I THINK OF TEZUKA'S BUDDHA AND ME AS BEING MUTUALS OF THE HEART.
FOR ONE THING, I'M ON VACATION RIGHT NOW.
AN OFFICIAL TWITTER ACCOUNT IS WORK!
Here, come inside.
SORRY...
BUT THE LAMBS COMING INTO HEAVEN ARE SADDENED NOT TO SEE YOU.
I WAS HOPING TO AT LEAST SHOW THEM WHAT YOU'RE DOING ON YOUR BREAK THROUGH TWITTER...
TH-
THAT'S WHAT'S GOING ON?
IN THAT CASE, I'D LIKE TO HELP.
BUT TO BE HONEST, I DON'T THINK ANYONE WOULD BELIEVE ME IF I JUST WHIPPED UP AN OFFICIAL ACCOUNT...
WELL, WE ALREADY HAVE A PLAN FOR THAT!
THIS WILL BE YOUR OFFICIAL ACCOUNT, SEE...
Jesus Christ
Official Twitter account of the Son of G
WAIT, YOU *ALREADY* MADE ONE?!
ZERO FOLLOW-ERS...
OH, BUT THE ACCOUNT IS ALREADY FOLLOWING ONE PERSON?
AH, THAT'S RIGHT! SO WHAT WE'LL DO IS DM HIM...

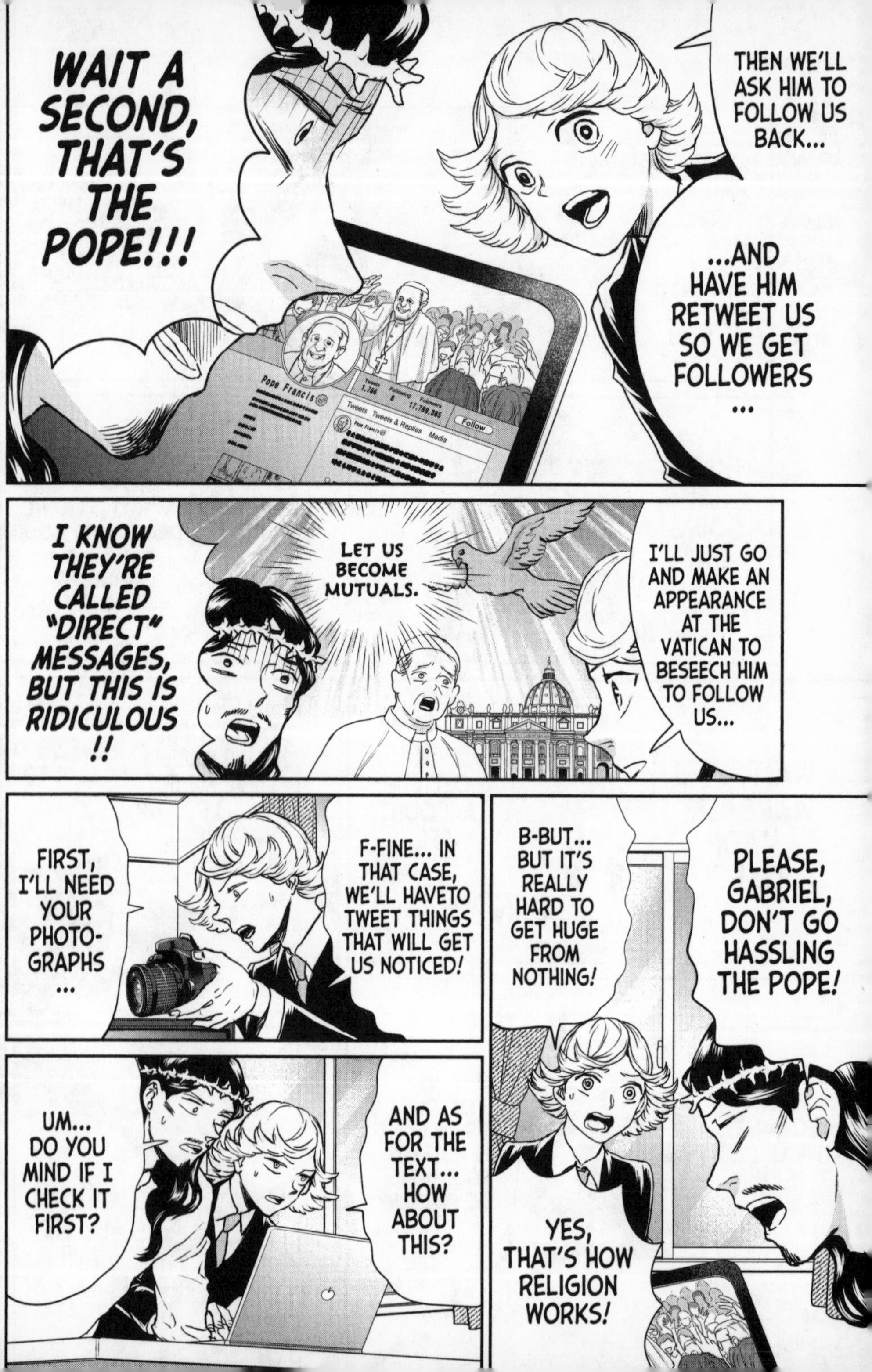
THEN WE'LL ASK HIM TO FOLLOW US BACK...
...AND HAVE HIM RETWEET US SO WE GET FOLLOWERS ...
WAIT A SECOND, THAT'S THE POPE!!!
Pope Francis
Tweets Tweets & Replies Media
Follow
I'LL JUST GO AND MAKE AN APPEARANCE AT THE VATICAN TO BESEECH HIM TO FOLLOW US...
LET US BECOME MUTUALS.
I KNOW THEY'RE CALLED "DIRECT" MESSAGES, BUT THIS IS RIDICULOUS !!
PLEASE, GABRIEL, DON'T GO HASSLING THE POPE!
B-BUT... BUT IT'S REALLY HARD TO GET HUGE FROM NOTHING!
YES, THAT'S HOW RELIGION WORKS!
F-FINE... IN THAT CASE, WE'LL HAVETO TWEET THINGS THAT WILL GET US NOTICED!
FIRST, I'LL NEED YOUR PHOTOGRAPHS ...
AND AS FOR THE TEXT... HOW ABOUT THIS?
UM... DO YOU MIND IF I CHECK IT FIRST?

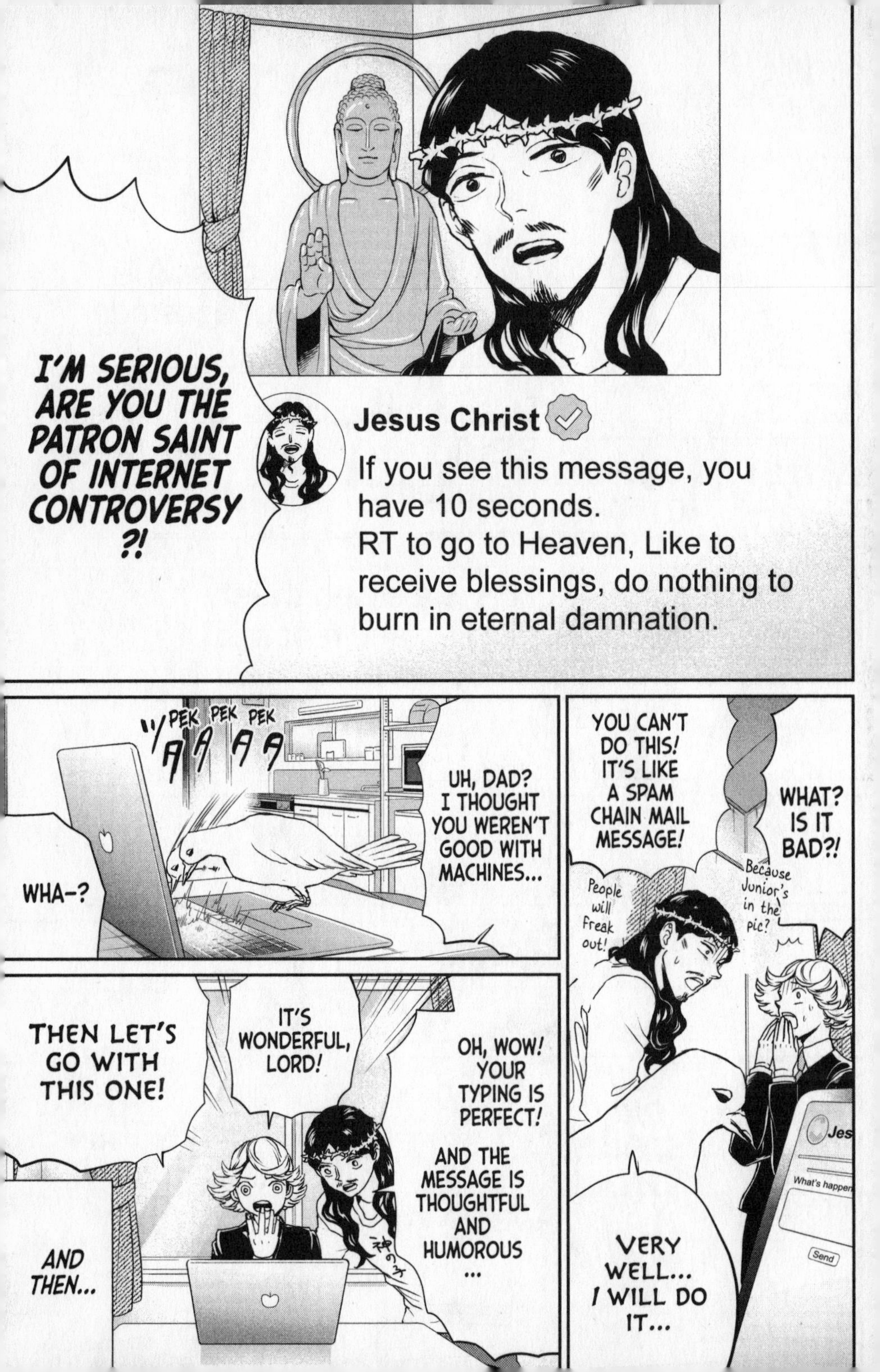
Jesus Christ
If you see this message, you have 10 seconds.
RT to go to Heaven, Like to receive blessings, do nothing to burn in eternal damnation.
I'M SERIOUS, ARE YOU THE PATRON SAINT OF INTERNET CONTROVERSY?!
WHAT? IS IT BAD?!
Because Junior's in the pic?
YOU CAN'T DO THIS! IT'S LIKE A SPAM CHAIN MAIL MESSAGE!
People will freak out!
Send
VERY WELL... I WILL DO IT...
UH, DAD? I THOUGHT YOU WEREN'T GOOD WITH MACHINES...
PEK PEK PEK
WHA-?
OH, WOW! YOUR TYPING IS PERFECT!
AND THE MESSAGE IS THOUGHTFUL AND HUMOROUS...
IT'S WONDERFUL, LORD!
神の子
THEN LET'S GO WITH THIS ONE!
AND THEN...

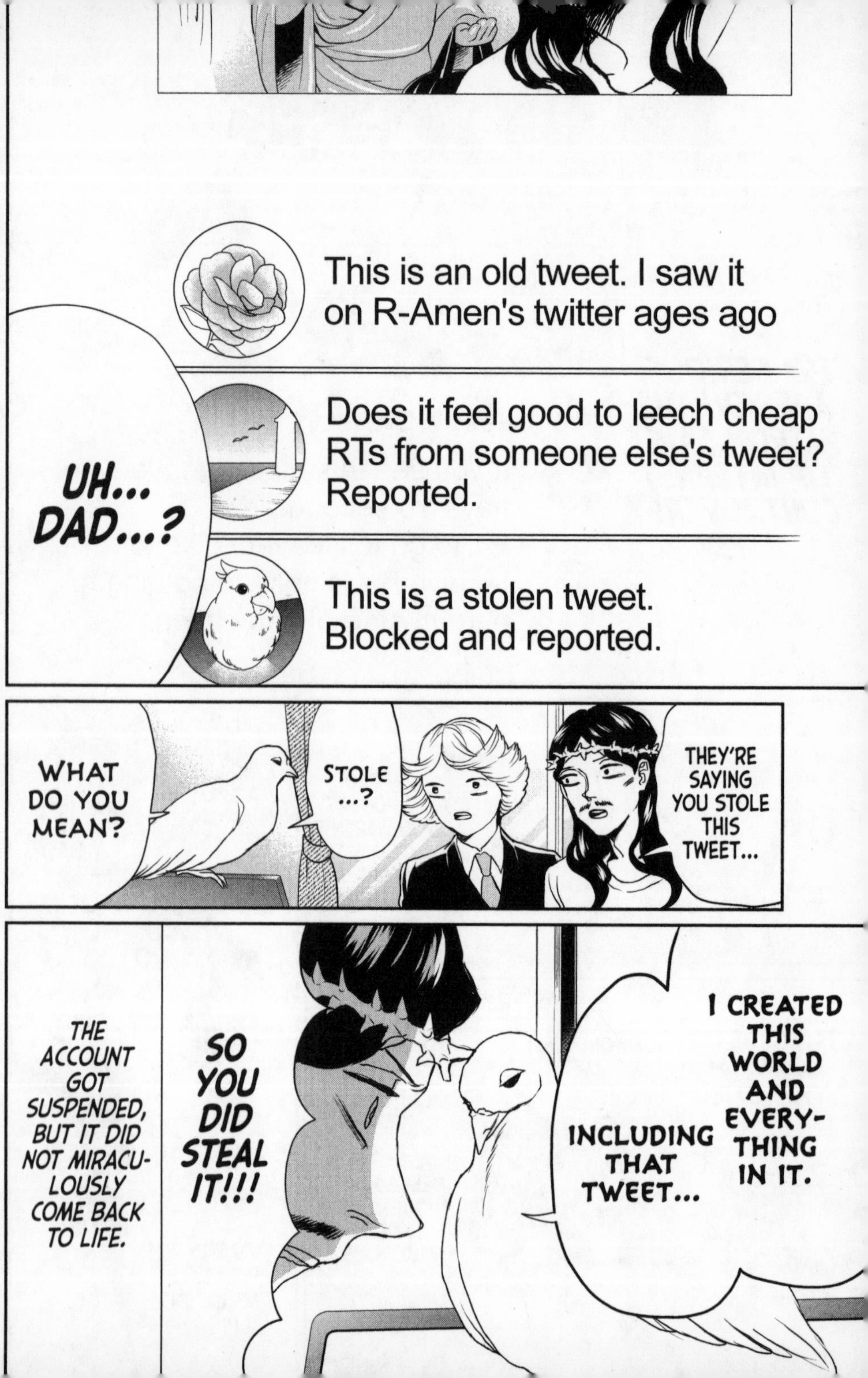
This is an old tweet. I saw it on R-Amen's twitter ages ago
Does it feel good to leech cheap RTs from someone else's tweet? Reported.
This is a stolen tweet. Blocked and reported.
UH... DAD...?
THEY'RE SAYING YOU STOLE THIS TWEET...
STOLE ...?
WHAT DO YOU MEAN?
I CREATED THIS WORLD AND EVERY-THING IN IT.
INCLUDING THAT TWEET...
SO YOU DID STEAL IT!!!
THE ACCOUNT GOT SUSPENDED, BUT IT DID NOT MIRACU-LOUSLY COME BACK TO LIFE.

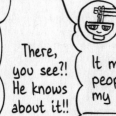

R-Amen
It makes me so happy that people continue to rip off my old tweets
Lol, tell em king
Everything you say is Kannon
Will they never learn?
There, you see?! He knows about it!!

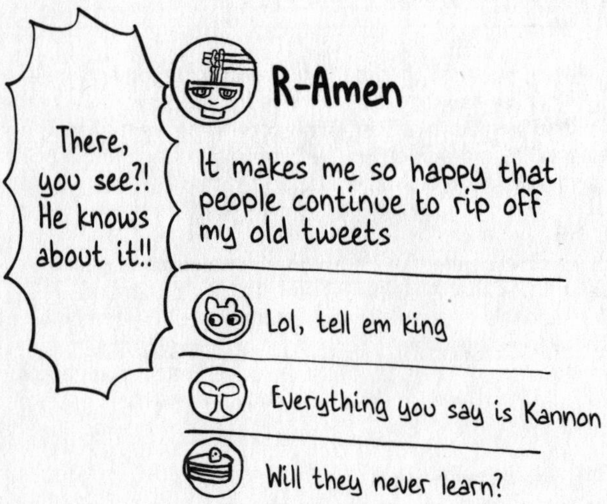

SAINT☆YOUNG MEN

CHAPTER 124 TRANSLATION NOTES

Mark of Cain, page 53
A phenomenon mentioned in the Book of Genesis, following Cain's murder of his brother Abel. When Cain is fearful that he will be killed after his banishment, God says that "anyone who kills Cain will suffer vengeance seven times over," and places a "mark" upon him to ensure he is safe, although the nature of that mark is not clear.

Heisei, page 55
Heisei is the name of the era corresponding to the reign of Emperor Akihito, which began in 1989. Era names in Japan, especially once they have ended, come to embody a kind of generational memory for the populace. The Showa era prior to Heisei, for example, is the "old-fashioned" time or "good old days" encompassing the hard post-war years and ending with the economic bubble of the 1980s, while Heisei might come to be associated with the Lost Decade of recession and the boom of anime's popularity worldwide. This chapter was published at a time when Akihito's abdication was upcoming; the Reiwa era began in May 2019.

Signs, page 55
A common sight (not everywhere, but enough to be noticeable) in Japan is simple black signs with white and yellow Japanese text on them featuring basic Christian slogans on them like "Christ died for your sins" or "Think about your eternal soul." These are created and displayed by a group called the Biblical Distribution Co-op, and there are possibly up to half a million of them in Japan.

Pillars of salt, page 56
In the Book of Genesis, Lot was the nephew of Abraham, the patriarch of the "Abrahamic religions" (Judaism, Christianity, Islam). The cities of Sodom and Gomorrah were destroyed in Genesis as a result of wickedness; Lot welcomed angels into his home in Sodom, where they urged him to flee the city before its destruction, and not look back. But in the process of fleeing, Lot's wife looked back in apparent longing at the life they were leaving behind, and was instantly turned into a pillar of salt.

The cursing of the fig tree, page 58
In the Gospel of Mark, there is a mention of a barren fig tree that Jesus curses, saying, "May no one ever eat fruit from you again." This comes just before the incident in which he drives the money-lenders from the temple, and the disciples later discover that the fig tree has died. This is seen as a message that a temple that is not righteous is doomed to be barren and not bear the fruit of holy work.

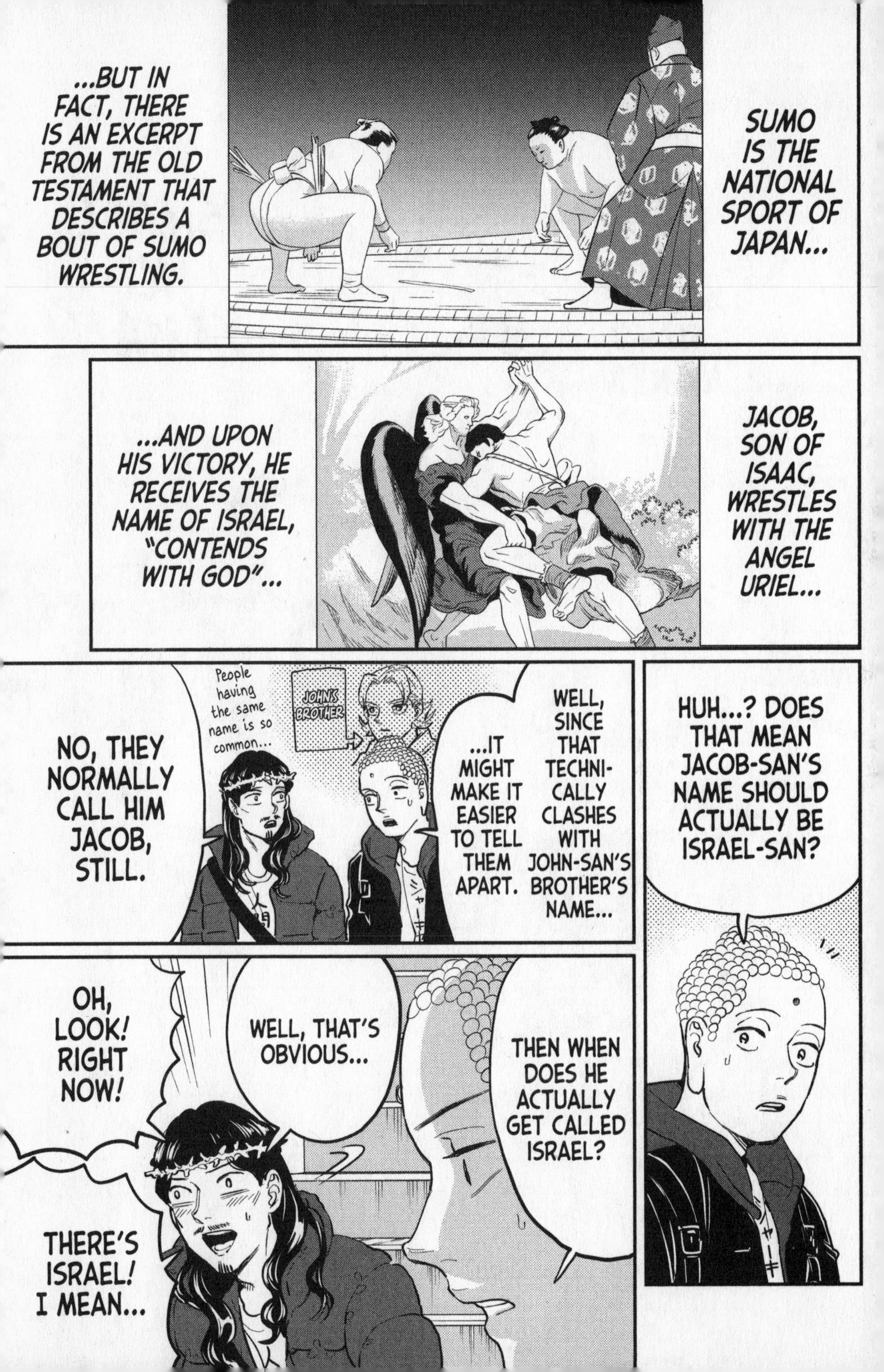
SUMO IS THE NATIONAL SPORT OF JAPAN...
...BUT IN FACT, THERE IS AN EXCERPT FROM THE OLD TESTAMENT THAT DESCRIBES A BOUT OF SUMO WRESTLING.
JACOB, SON OF ISAAC, WRESTLES WITH THE ANGEL URIEL...
...AND UPON HIS VICTORY, HE RECEIVES THE NAME OF ISRAEL, "CONTENDS WITH GOD"...
HUH...? DOES THAT MEAN JACOB-SAN'S NAME SHOULD ACTUALLY BE ISRAEL-SAN?
WELL, SINCE THAT TECHNI-CALLY CLASHES WITH JOHN-SAN'S BROTHER'S NAME...
...IT MIGHT MAKE IT EASIER TO TELL THEM APART.
JOHN'S BROTHER
People having the same name is so common...
NO, THEY NORMALLY CALL HIM JACOB, STILL.
THEN WHEN DOES HE ACTUALLY GET CALLED ISRAEL?
WELL, THAT'S OBVIOUS...
OH, LOOK! RIGHT NOW!
THERE'S ISRAEL! I MEAN...

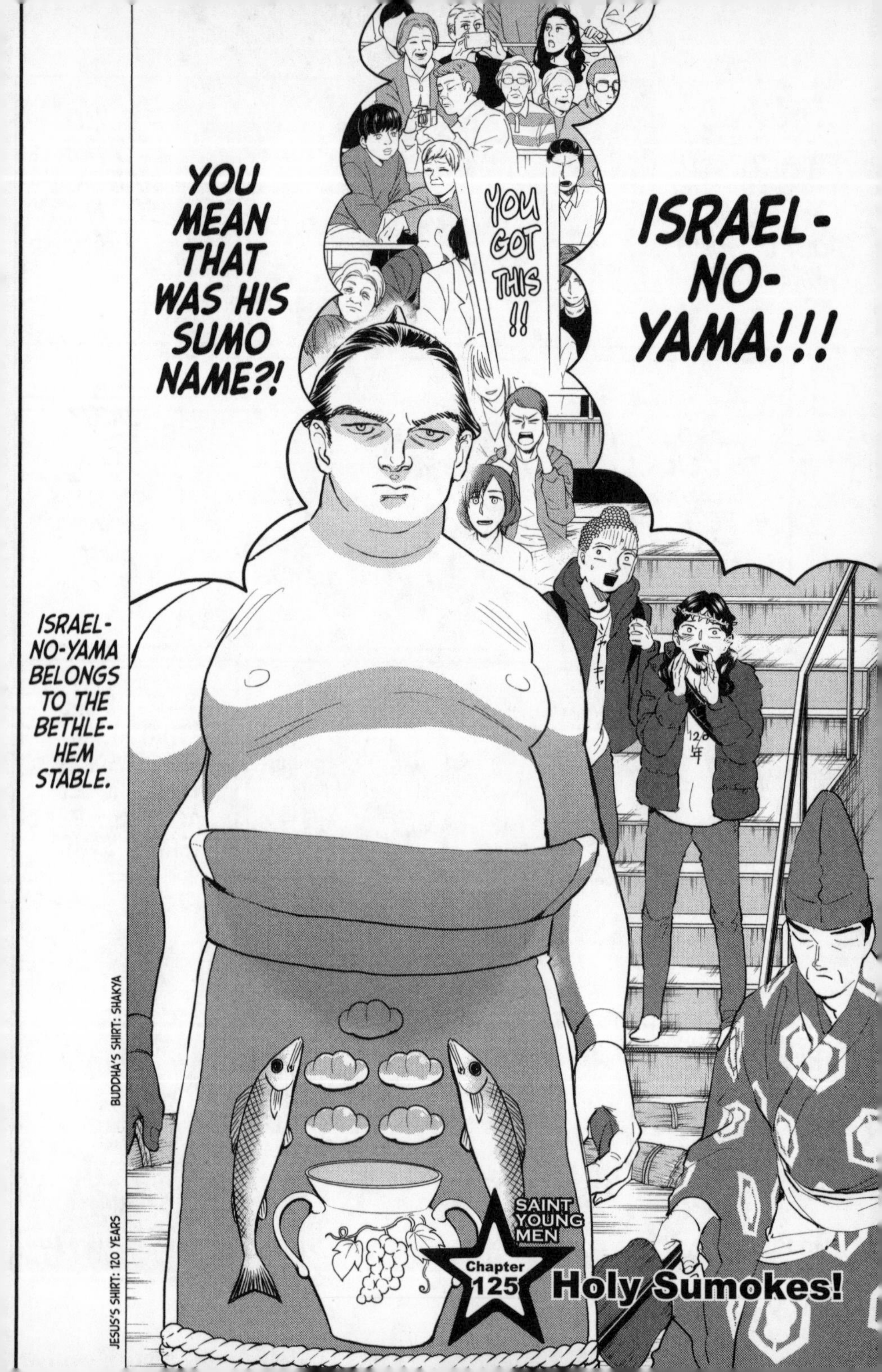
ISRAEL-NO-YAMA!!!
YOU GOT THIS!!
YOU MEAN THAT WAS HIS SUMO NAME?!
ISRAEL-NO-YAMA BELONGS TO THE BETHLEHEM STABLE.
SAINT YOUNG MEN
Chapter 125
Holy Sumokes!
BUDDHA'S SHIRT: SHAKYA
JESUS'S SHIRT: 120 YEARS

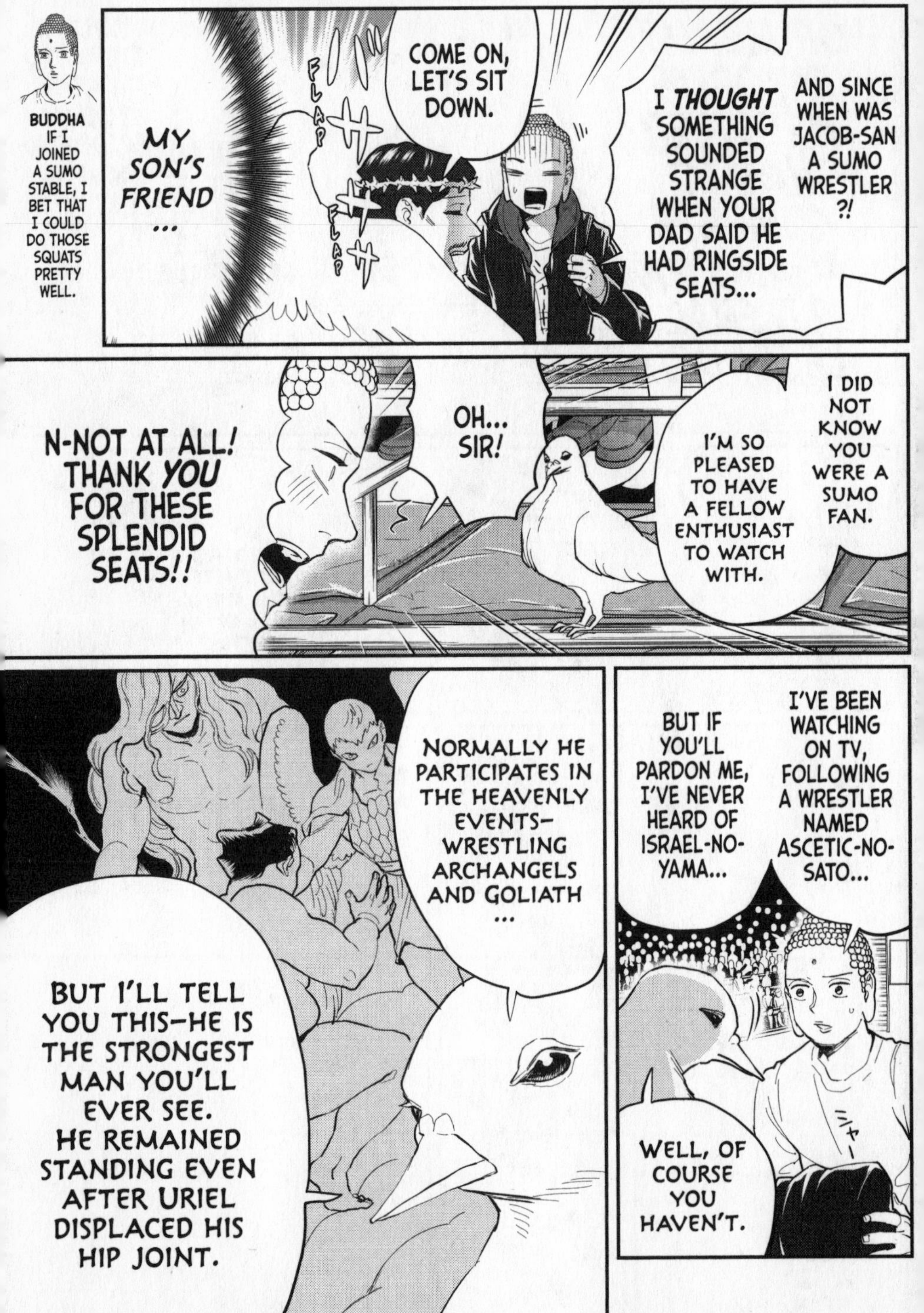
AND SINCE WHEN WAS JACOB-SAN A SUMO WRESTLER?!
I *THOUGHT* SOMETHING SOUNDED STRANGE WHEN YOUR DAD SAID HE HAD RINGSIDE SEATS...
COME ON, LET'S SIT DOWN.
FLAP
FLAP
MY SON'S FRIEND...
BUDDHA IF I JOINED A SUMO STABLE, I BET THAT I COULD DO THOSE SQUATS PRETTY WELL.
I DID NOT KNOW YOU WERE A SUMO FAN.
I'M SO PLEASED TO HAVE A FELLOW ENTHUSIAST TO WATCH WITH.
OH... SIR!
N-NOT AT ALL! THANK *YOU* FOR THESE SPLENDID SEATS!!
I'VE BEEN WATCHING ON TV, FOLLOWING A WRESTLER NAMED ASCETIC-NO-SATO...
BUT IF YOU'LL PARDON ME, I'VE NEVER HEARD OF ISRAEL-NO-YAMA...
WELL, OF COURSE YOU HAVEN'T.
NORMALLY HE PARTICIPATES IN THE HEAVENLY EVENTS—WRESTLING ARCHANGELS AND GOLIATH...
BUT I'LL TELL YOU THIS—HE IS THE STRONGEST MAN YOU'LL EVER SEE. HE REMAINED STANDING EVEN AFTER URIEL DISPLACED HIS HIP JOINT.

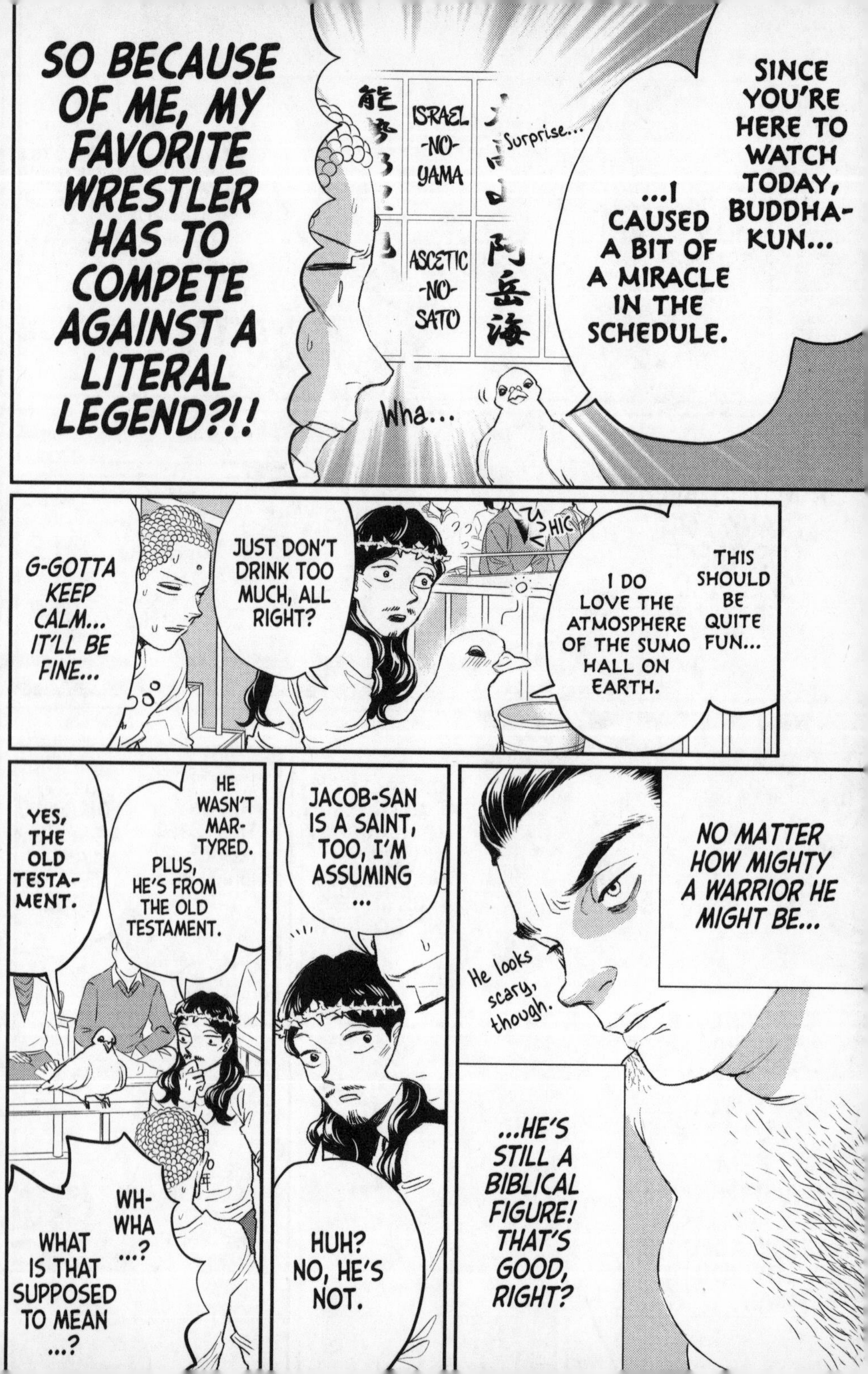
SINCE YOU'RE HERE TO WATCH TODAY, BUDDHA-KUN...
...I CAUSED A BIT OF A MIRACLE IN THE SCHEDULE.
Surprise...
ISRAEL -NO- YAMA
ASCETIC -NO- SATO
Wha...
SO BECAUSE OF ME, MY FAVORITE WRESTLER HAS TO COMPETE AGAINST A LITERAL LEGEND?!!
THIS SHOULD BE QUITE FUN...
I DO LOVE THE ATMOSPHERE OF THE SUMO HALL ON EARTH.
HIC
JUST DON'T DRINK TOO MUCH, ALL RIGHT?
G-GOTTA KEEP CALM... IT'LL BE FINE...
NO MATTER HOW MIGHTY A WARRIOR HE MIGHT BE...
He looks scary, though.
...HE'S STILL A BIBLICAL FIGURE! THAT'S GOOD, RIGHT?
JACOB-SAN IS A SAINT, TOO, I'M ASSUMING...
HUH? NO, HE'S NOT.
HE WASN'T MAR-TYRED.
PLUS, HE'S FROM THE OLD TESTAMENT.
YES, THE OLD TESTA-MENT.
WH-WHA...?
WHAT IS THAT SUPPOSED TO MEAN...?

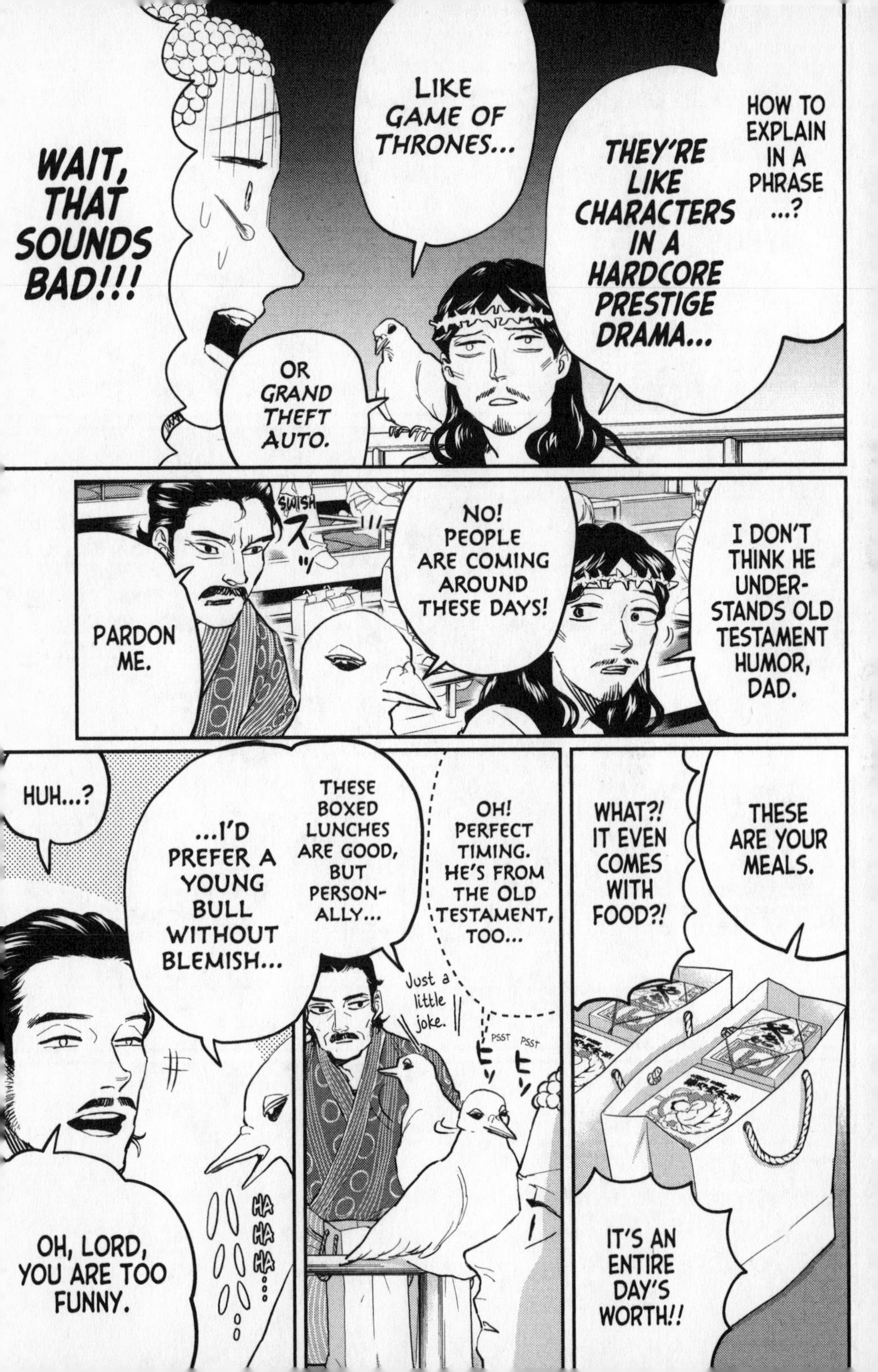

HOW TO EXPLAIN IN A PHRASE ...?
THEY'RE LIKE CHARACTERS IN A HARDCORE PRESTIGE DRAMA...
LIKE GAME OF THRONES...
OR GRAND THEFT AUTO.
WAIT, THAT SOUNDS BAD!!!
I DON'T THINK HE UNDER-STANDS OLD TESTAMENT HUMOR, DAD.
NO! PEOPLE ARE COMING AROUND THESE DAYS!
SWISH
PARDON ME.
THESE ARE YOUR MEALS.
WHAT?! IT EVEN COMES WITH FOOD?!
IT'S AN ENTIRE DAY'S WORTH!!
OH! PERFECT TIMING. HE'S FROM THE OLD TESTAMENT, TOO...
PSST PSST
THESE BOXED LUNCHES ARE GOOD, BUT PERSON-ALLY...
...I'D PREFER A YOUNG BULL WITHOUT BLEMISH...
Just a little joke.
HUH...?
HA HA HA...
OH, LORD, YOU ARE TOO FUNNY.

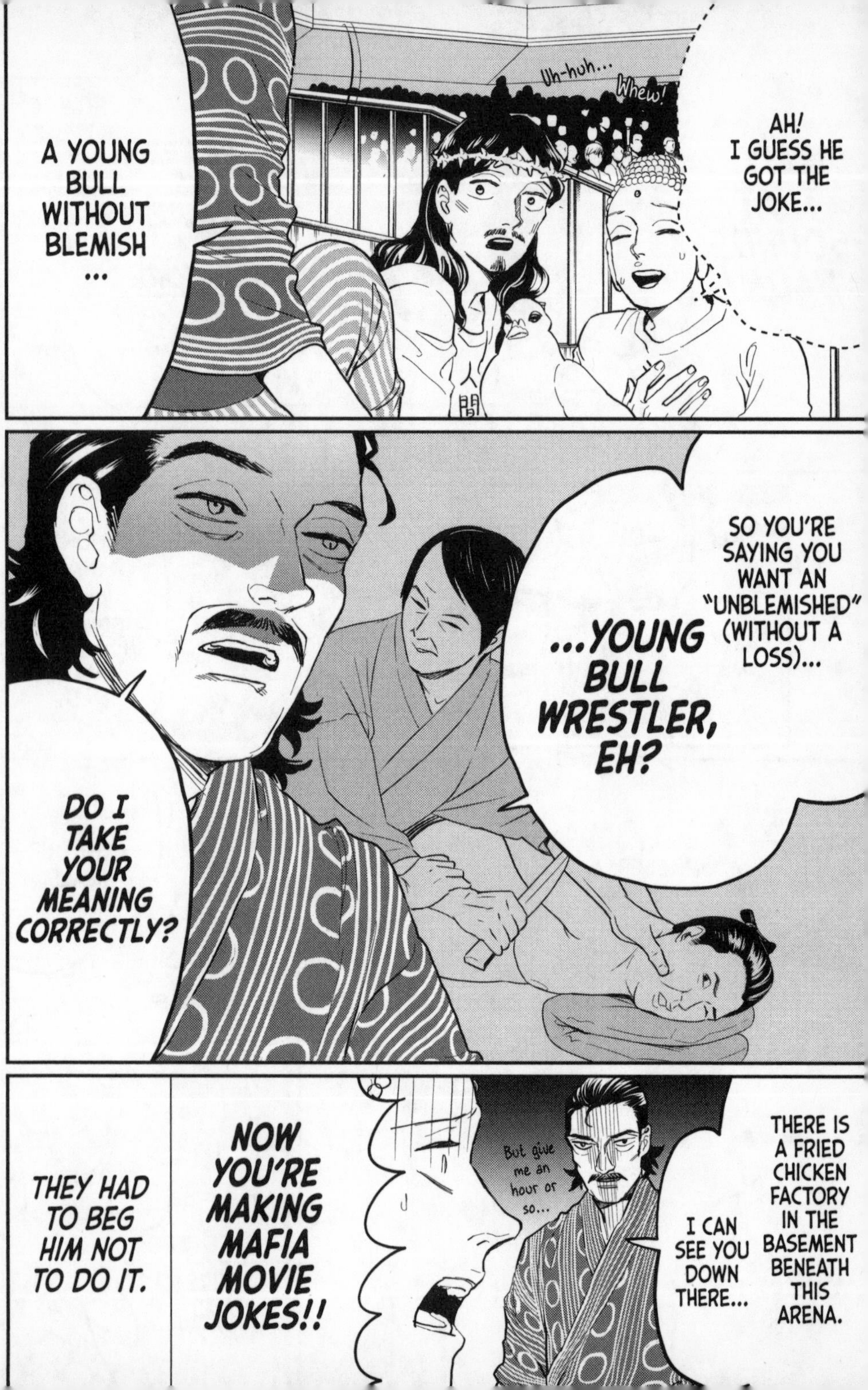
AH! I GUESS HE GOT THE JOKE...
Whew!
Uh-huh...
A YOUNG BULL WITHOUT BLEMISH ...
SO YOU'RE SAYING YOU WANT AN "UNBLEMISHED" (WITHOUT A LOSS)...
...YOUNG BULL WRESTLER, EH?
DO I TAKE YOUR MEANING CORRECTLY?
THERE IS A FRIED CHICKEN FACTORY IN THE BASEMENT BENEATH THIS ARENA.
I CAN SEE YOU DOWN THERE...
But give me an hour or so...
NOW YOU'RE MAKING MAFIA MOVIE JOKES!!
THEY HAD TO BEG HIM NOT TO DO IT.

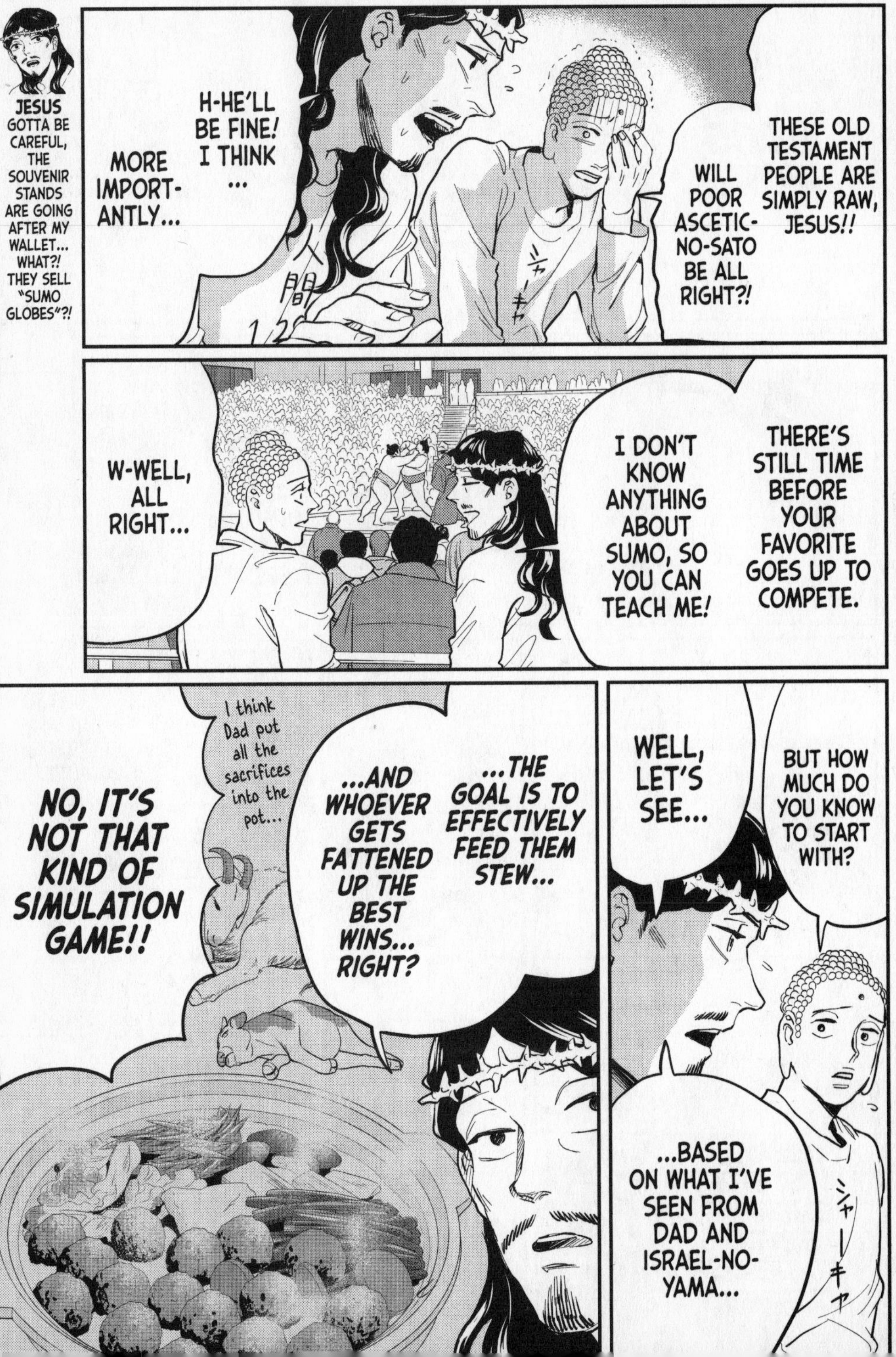
JESUS
GOTTA BE CAREFUL, THE SOUVENIR STANDS ARE GOING AFTER MY WALLET... WHAT?! THEY SELL "SUMO GLOBES"?!
THESE OLD TESTAMENT PEOPLE ARE SIMPLY RAW, JESUS!!
WILL POOR ASCETIC-NO-SATO BE ALL RIGHT?!
シャーキャ
H-HE'LL BE FINE! I THINK ...
MORE IMPORT-ANTLY...
THERE'S STILL TIME BEFORE YOUR FAVORITE GOES UP TO COMPETE.
I DON'T KNOW ANYTHING ABOUT SUMO, SO YOU CAN TEACH ME!
W-WELL, ALL RIGHT...
BUT HOW MUCH DO YOU KNOW TO START WITH?
WELL, LET'S SEE...
...BASED ON WHAT I'VE SEEN FROM DAD AND ISRAEL-NO-YAMA...
シャーキャ
...THE GOAL IS TO EFFECTIVELY FEED THEM STEW...
...AND WHOEVER GETS FATTENED UP THE BEST WINS... RIGHT?
I think Dad put all the sacrifices into the pot...
NO, IT'S NOT THAT KIND OF SIMULATION GAME!!

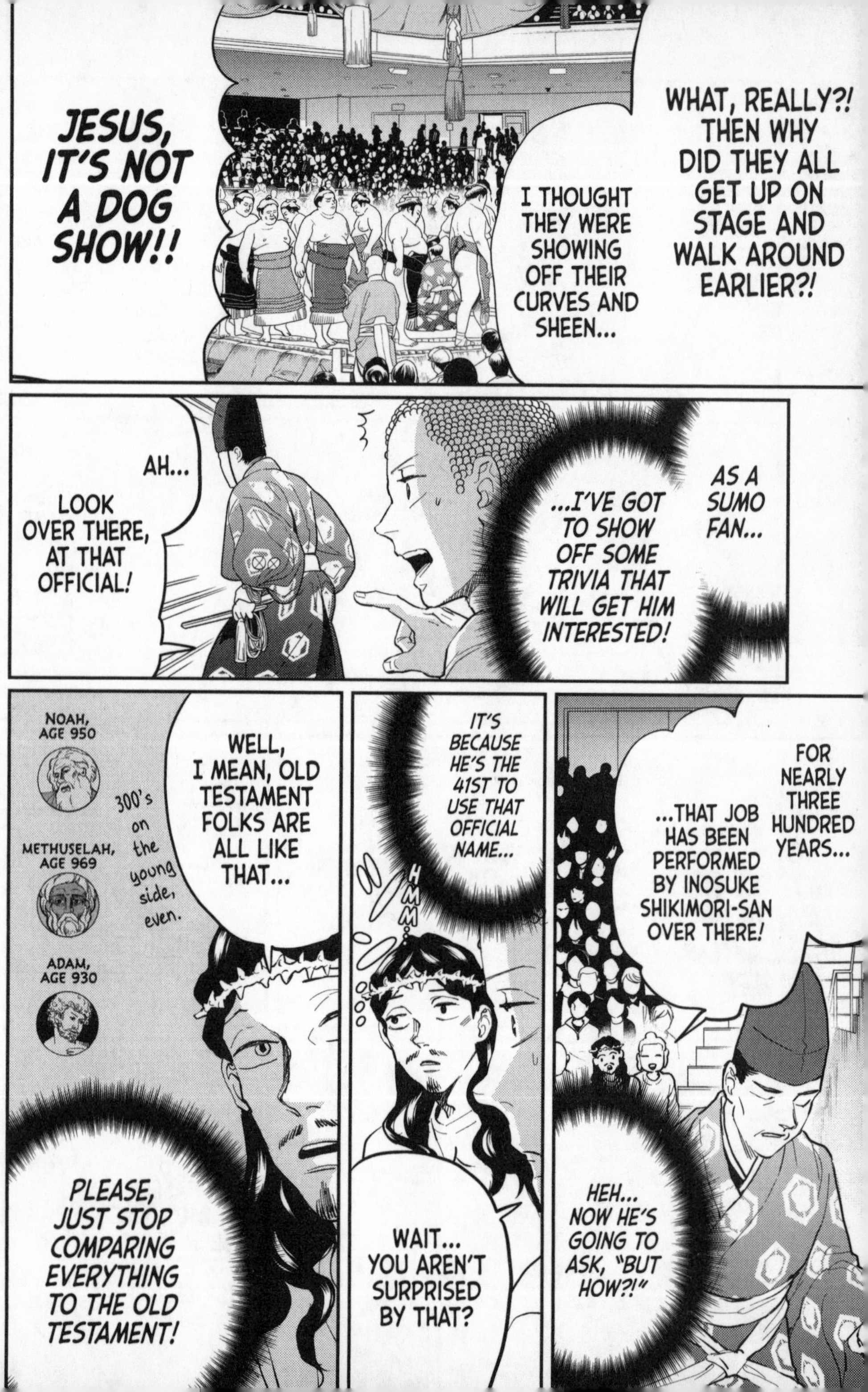
WHAT, REALLY?! THEN WHY DID THEY ALL GET UP ON STAGE AND WALK AROUND EARLIER?!
I THOUGHT THEY WERE SHOWING OFF THEIR CURVES AND SHEEN...
JESUS, IT'S NOT A DOG SHOW!!
AS A SUMO FAN...
...I'VE GOT TO SHOW OFF SOME TRIVIA THAT WILL GET HIM INTERESTED!
AH...
LOOK OVER THERE, AT THAT OFFICIAL!
FOR NEARLY THREE HUNDRED YEARS...
...THAT JOB HAS BEEN PERFORMED BY INOSUKE SHIKIMORI-SAN OVER THERE!
HEH... NOW HE'S GOING TO ASK, "BUT HOW?!"
IT'S BECAUSE HE'S THE 41ST TO USE THAT OFFICIAL NAME...
HMM
WAIT... YOU AREN'T SURPRISED BY THAT?
WELL, I MEAN, OLD TESTAMENT FOLKS ARE ALL LIKE THAT...
NOAH, AGE 950
300's on the young side, even.
METHUSELAH, AGE 969
ADAM, AGE 930
PLEASE, JUST STOP COMPARING EVERYTHING TO THE OLD TESTAMENT!

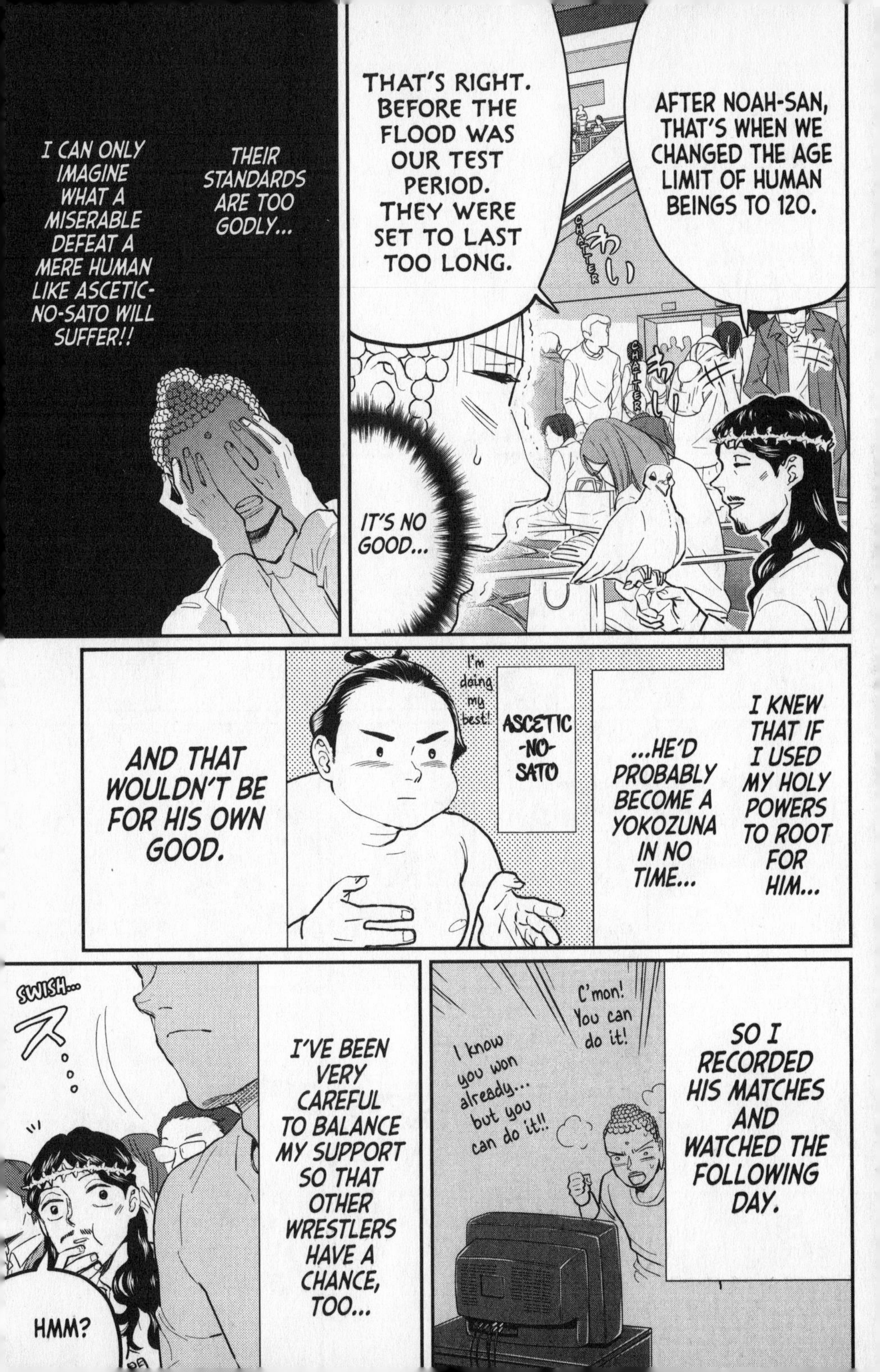
AFTER NOAH-SAN, THAT'S WHEN WE CHANGED THE AGE LIMIT OF HUMAN BEINGS TO 120.
THAT'S RIGHT. BEFORE THE FLOOD WAS OUR TEST PERIOD. THEY WERE SET TO LAST TOO LONG.
CHATTER
CHATTER
IT'S NO GOOD...
THEIR STANDARDS ARE TOO GODLY...
I CAN ONLY IMAGINE WHAT A MISERABLE DEFEAT A MERE HUMAN LIKE ASCETIC-NO-SATO WILL SUFFER!!
I KNEW THAT IF I USED MY HOLY POWERS TO ROOT FOR HIM...
...HE'D PROBABLY BECOME A YOKOZUNA IN NO TIME...
ASCETIC-NO-SATO
I'm doing my best!
AND THAT WOULDN'T BE FOR HIS OWN GOOD.
SO I RECORDED HIS MATCHES AND WATCHED THE FOLLOWING DAY.
C'mon! You can do it!
I know you won already... but you can do it!!
I'VE BEEN VERY CAREFUL TO BALANCE MY SUPPORT SO THAT OTHER WRESTLERS HAVE A CHANCE, TOO...
SWISH...
HMM?

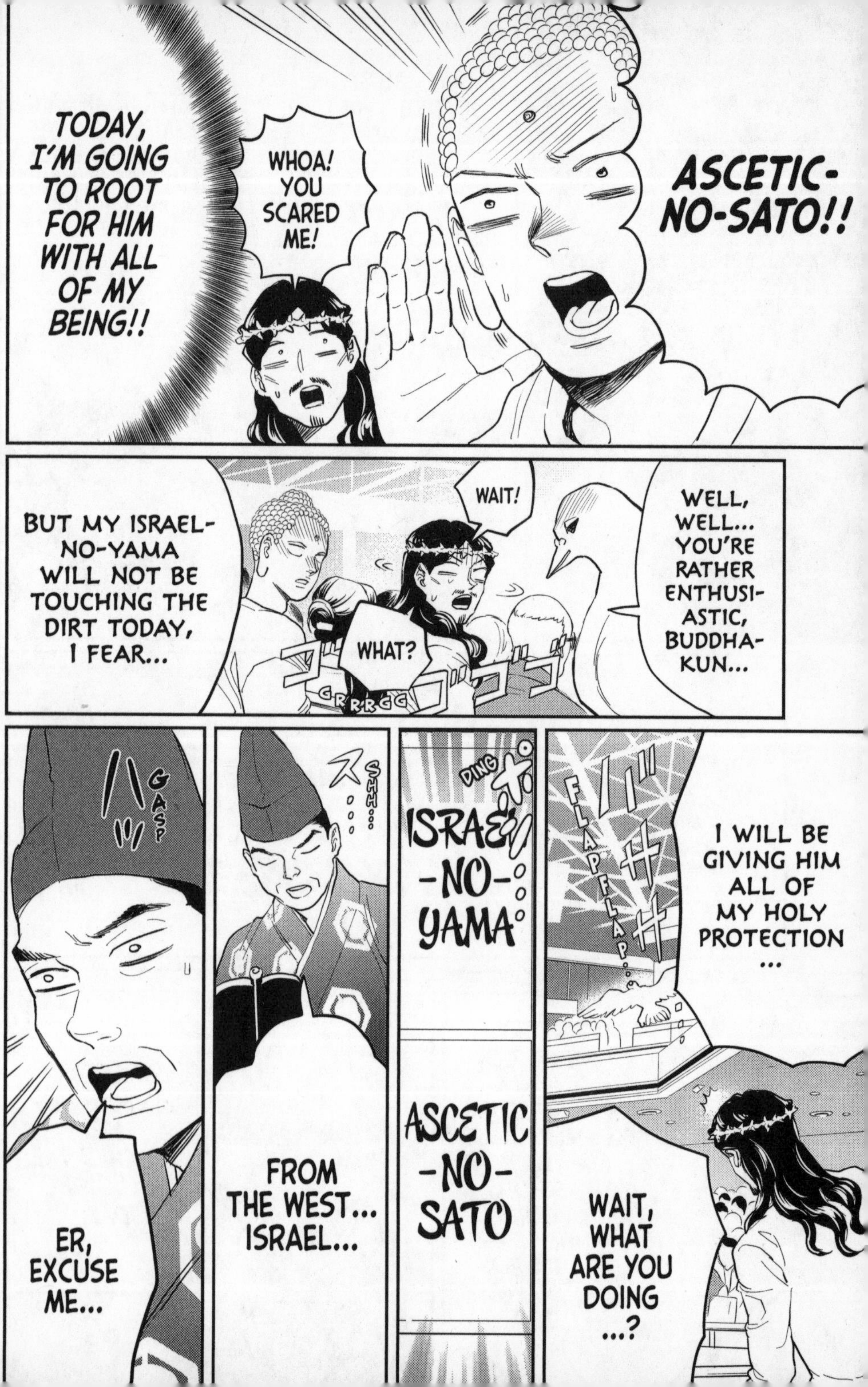
ASCETIC-NO-SATO!!
WHOA! YOU SCARED ME!
TODAY, I'M GOING TO ROOT FOR HIM WITH ALL OF MY BEING!!
WELL, WELL... YOU'RE RATHER ENTHUSI-ASTIC, BUDDHA-KUN...
WAIT!
WHAT?
GRRRGG
BUT MY ISRAEL-NO-YAMA WILL NOT BE TOUCHING THE DIRT TODAY, I FEAR...
I WILL BE GIVING HIM ALL OF MY HOLY PROTECTION ...
FLAPFLAP...
WAIT, WHAT ARE YOU DOING ...?
DING
ISRAE -NO- YAMA
ASCETIC -NO- SATO
SHHH...
FROM THE WEST... ISRAEL...
GASP
ER, EXCUSE ME...

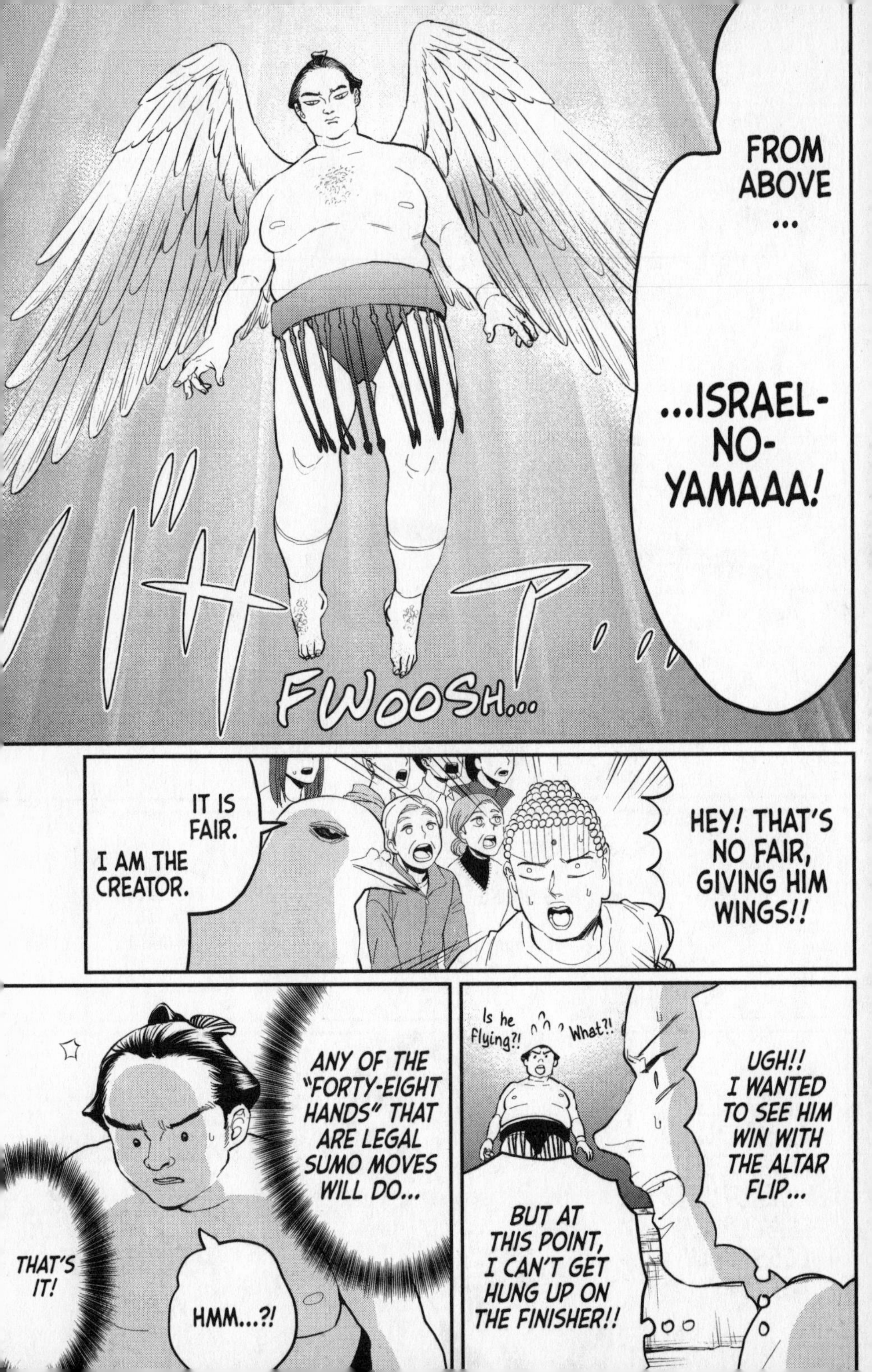
FROM ABOVE ...
...ISRAEL-NO-YAMAAA!
FWOOSH...
HEY! THAT'S NO FAIR, GIVING HIM WINGS!!
IT IS FAIR. I AM THE CREATOR.
UGH!! I WANTED TO SEE HIM WIN WITH THE ALTAR FLIP...
What?!
Is he flying?!
BUT AT THIS POINT, I CAN'T GET HUNG UP ON THE FINISHER!!
ANY OF THE "FORTY-EIGHT HANDS" THAT ARE LEGAL SUMO MOVES WILL DO...
HMM...?!
THAT'S IT!

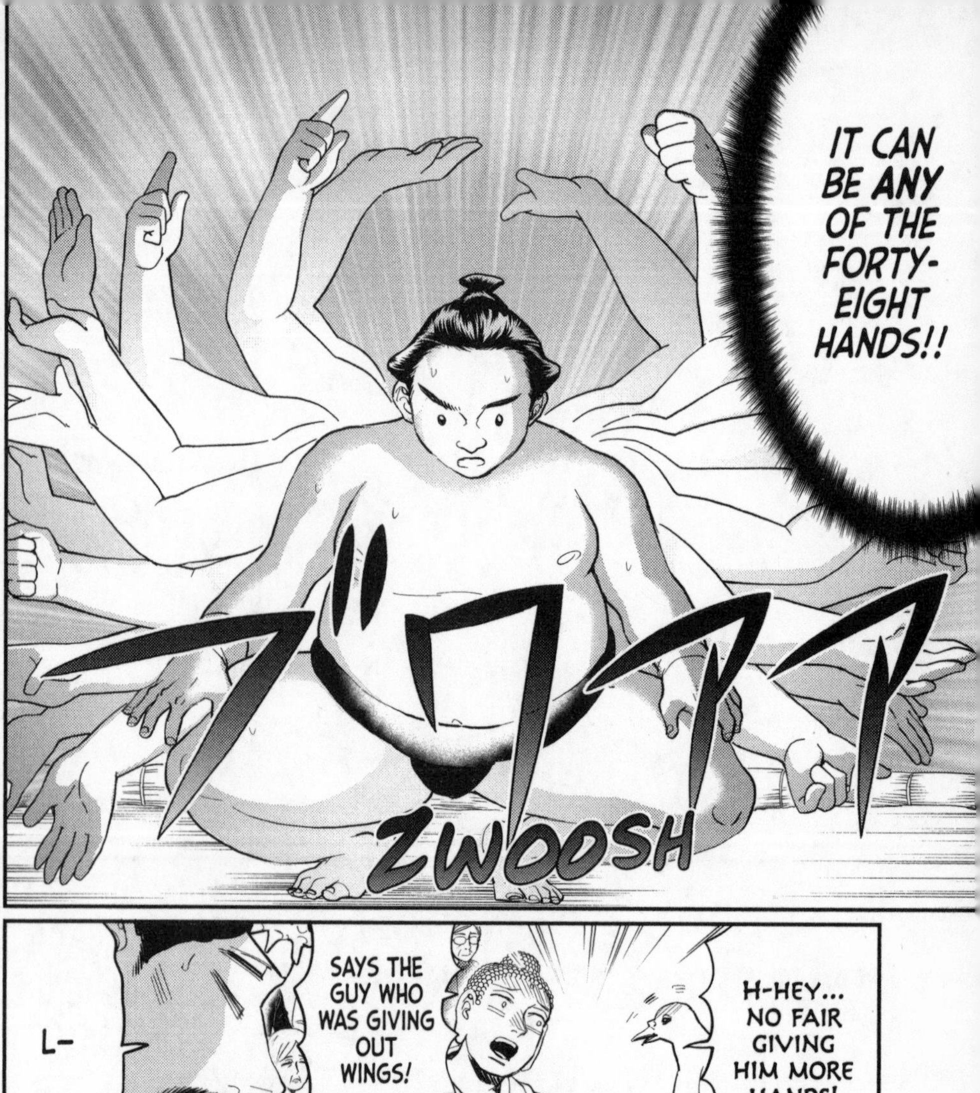
IT CAN BE ANY OF THE FORTY-EIGHT HANDS!!
ブワアア
ZWOOSH

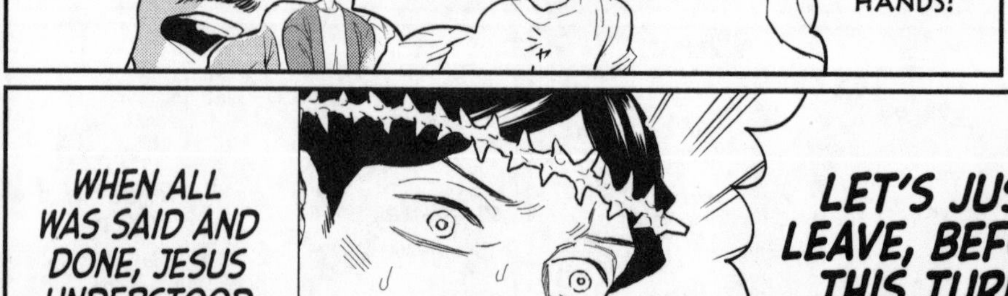
H-HEY... NO FAIR GIVING HIM MORE HANDS!
SAYS THE GUY WHO WAS GIVING OUT WINGS!
L-

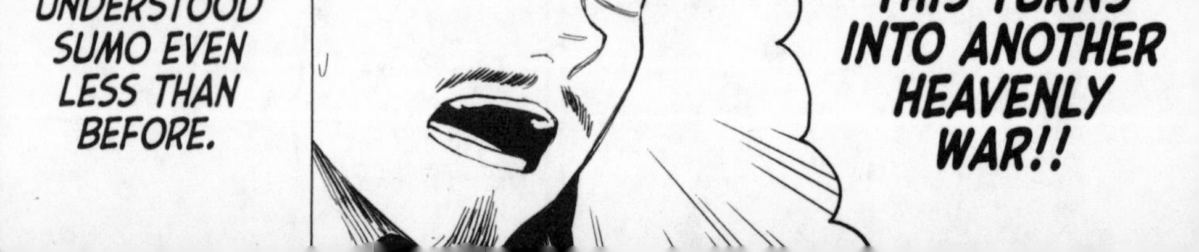
LET'S JUST LEAVE, BEFORE THIS TURNS INTO ANOTHER HEAVENLY WAR!!
WHEN ALL WAS SAID AND DONE, JESUS UNDERSTOOD SUMO EVEN LESS THAN BEFORE.

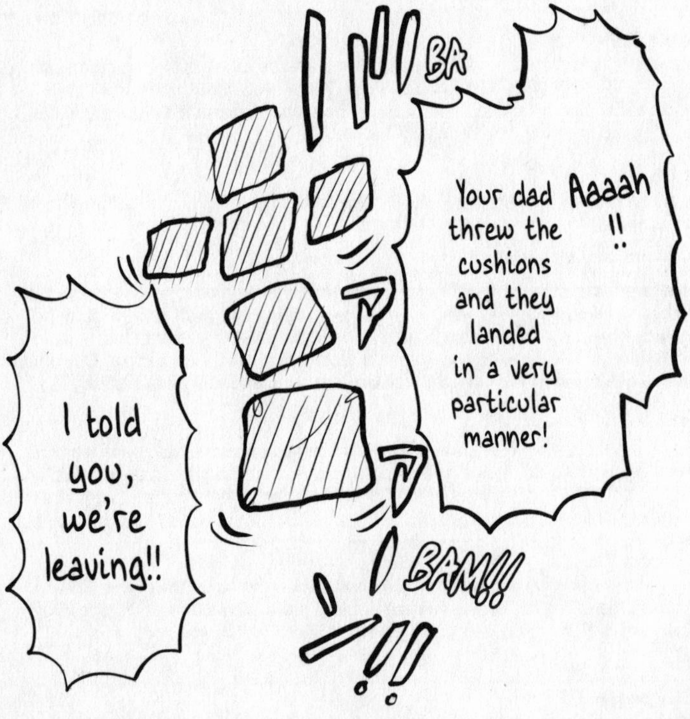
BA
Aaaah!!
Your dad threw the cushions and they landed in a very particular manner!
I told you, we're leaving!!
BAM!!

CHAPTER 125 TRANSLATION NOTES

Jacob wrestling the angel, page 65
Jacob wrestling with the angel is an event that takes place starting in Genesis 32:22. In it, Jacob (son of Isaac, not to be confused with the disciple James, see below) wrestles with a "man" until dawn. When the man does not win, he touches Jacob's hip and pulls it out of joint. Jacob says, "I will not let go unless you bless me," and the man says, "Your name shall be Israel, for you have striven with God and prevailed." While the nature of the man is not identified, most theories claim he is an angel or God himself.

Jacob/James, page 65
The disciple of Jesus known as James in English (or James the Greater), brother of John, was actually named Jacob. Through a series of complex linguistic shifts, from Latin Iacobus to Iacomus to the French Jammes, it became Anglicized as James. Other European forms derive from this as well, like the Italian Giacomo, while the Spanish took the "Iaco" sound and added "saint" to make Santiago or "Diego" for short.

Sumo names, page 66
A sumo wrestler's ring name is called a *shikona*. A wrestler starts at a *heya*, or stable, an organization where sumo wrestlers train and are developed for competition. There are various rules on when a *shikona* is adopted and how it should be styled, and these may change depending on the particular stable. Many are initially derived from the wrestler's birth name.

120 years, page 66
In Genesis 6:3, God is quoted as saying, "My spirit shall not abide in man for ever, for that he also is flesh; therefore shall his days be a hundred and twenty years."

Goliath, page 67
When the people of Israel were at war with the Philistines, the Philistines' greatest hero Goliath challenged them to a one-on-one duel. Goliath was a very large and powerful man, and most of the Israelites were afraid to face him. It was little David, who was only there to bring food to his older brothers, who accepted Goliath's challenge, having faith that God would deliver his people. David used a sling to throw a stone at Goliath, which hit him right between the eyes and killed him instantly.

Chanko, page 71
Chanko, or *chankonabe*, is a hot pot stew that is traditionally eaten by sumo wrestlers because of its ability to add bulk. While there isn't a strict recipe, the idea is to have as much protein as possible and be served in huge amounts, so there is usually some kind of chicken, fish, beef, and tofu, as well as vegetables.

Referee names, page 72
Sumo judges, or *gyôji*, also take ceremonial names, which change depending on their rank. The highest rank of *gyôji* is called the *tate-gyôji*, of which there are two professional names, Shonosuke Kimura and Inosuke Shikimori, which are passed along as each official retires and another is promoted.

Forty-eight hands, page 75
The standard, accepted moves of sumo wrestling are known by the term "forty-eight hands" (*shijuhatte*). This term arose not from a specific number of techniques, but because the number forty-eight was an auspicious and "numerous" one in the past. Therefore, it started as a description of the "many techniques" that a sumo wrestler has, not specifically forty-eight of them. Additionally, the word "hand" in Japanese has many meanings, including combat techniques, and a "move" in a board game like chess or go.

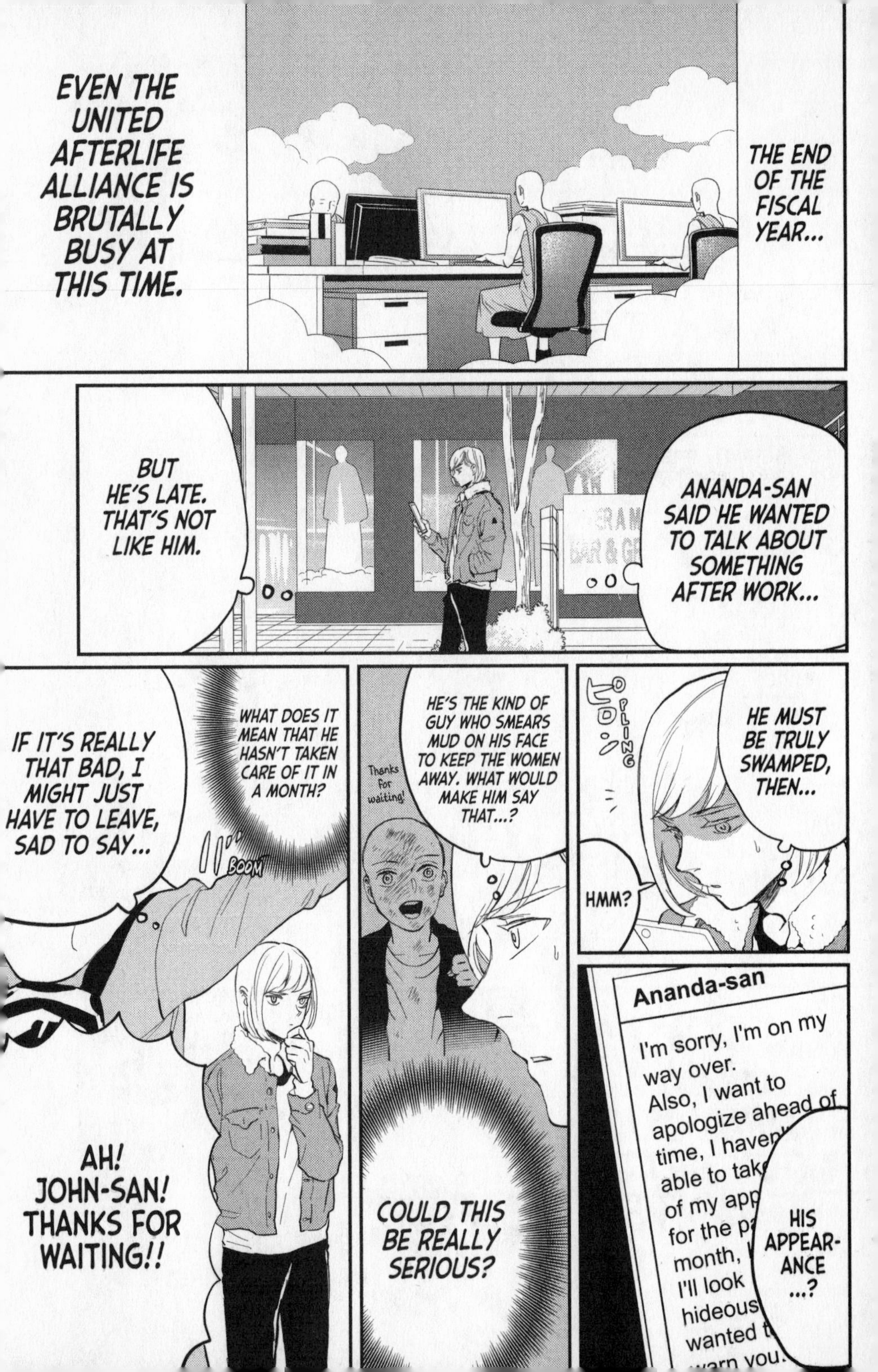
THE END OF THE FISCAL YEAR...
EVEN THE UNITED AFTERLIFE ALLIANCE IS BRUTALLY BUSY AT THIS TIME.
ANANDA-SAN SAID HE WANTED TO TALK ABOUT SOMETHING AFTER WORK...
BUT HE'S LATE. THAT'S NOT LIKE HIM.
PLING
HE MUST BE TRULY SWAMPED, THEN...
HMM?
Ananda-san
I'm sorry, I'm on my way over.
Also, I want to apologize ahead of time, I haven
able to tak
of my app
for the pa
month, I
I'll look
hideous
wanted t
warn you.
HIS APPEARANCE...?
HE'S THE KIND OF GUY WHO SMEARS MUD ON HIS FACE TO KEEP THE WOMEN AWAY. WHAT WOULD MAKE HIM SAY THAT...?
Thanks for waiting!
COULD THIS BE REALLY SERIOUS?
WHAT DOES IT MEAN THAT HE HASN'T TAKEN CARE OF IT IN A MONTH?
IF IT'S REALLY THAT BAD, I MIGHT JUST HAVE TO LEAVE, SAD TO SAY...
BOOM
AH! JOHN-SAN! THANKS FOR WAITING!!

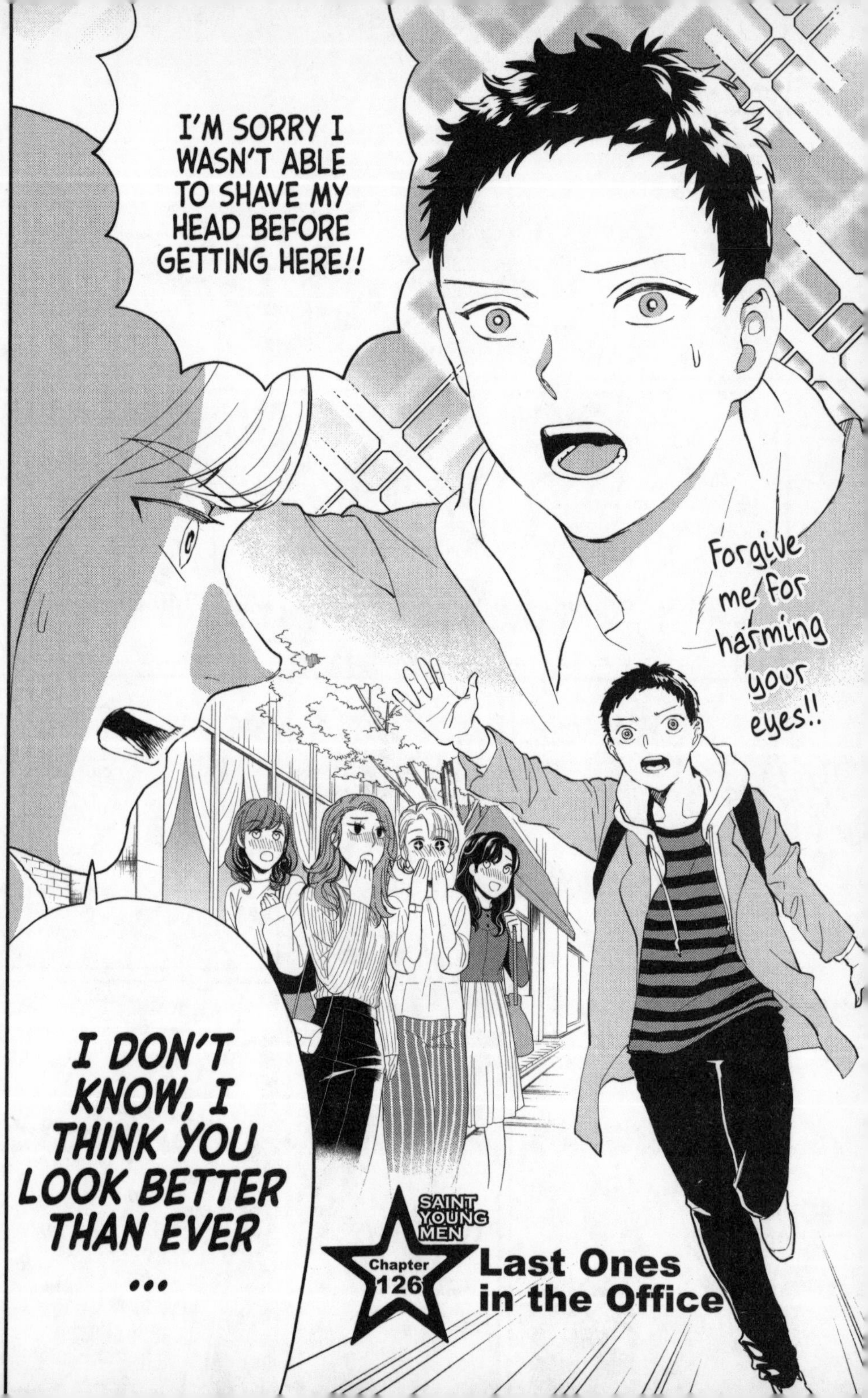
I'M SORRY I WASN'T ABLE TO SHAVE MY HEAD BEFORE GETTING HERE!!
Forgive me for harming your eyes!!
I DON'T KNOW, I THINK YOU LOOK BETTER THAN EVER ...
SAINT YOUNG MEN
Chapter 126
Last Ones in the Office

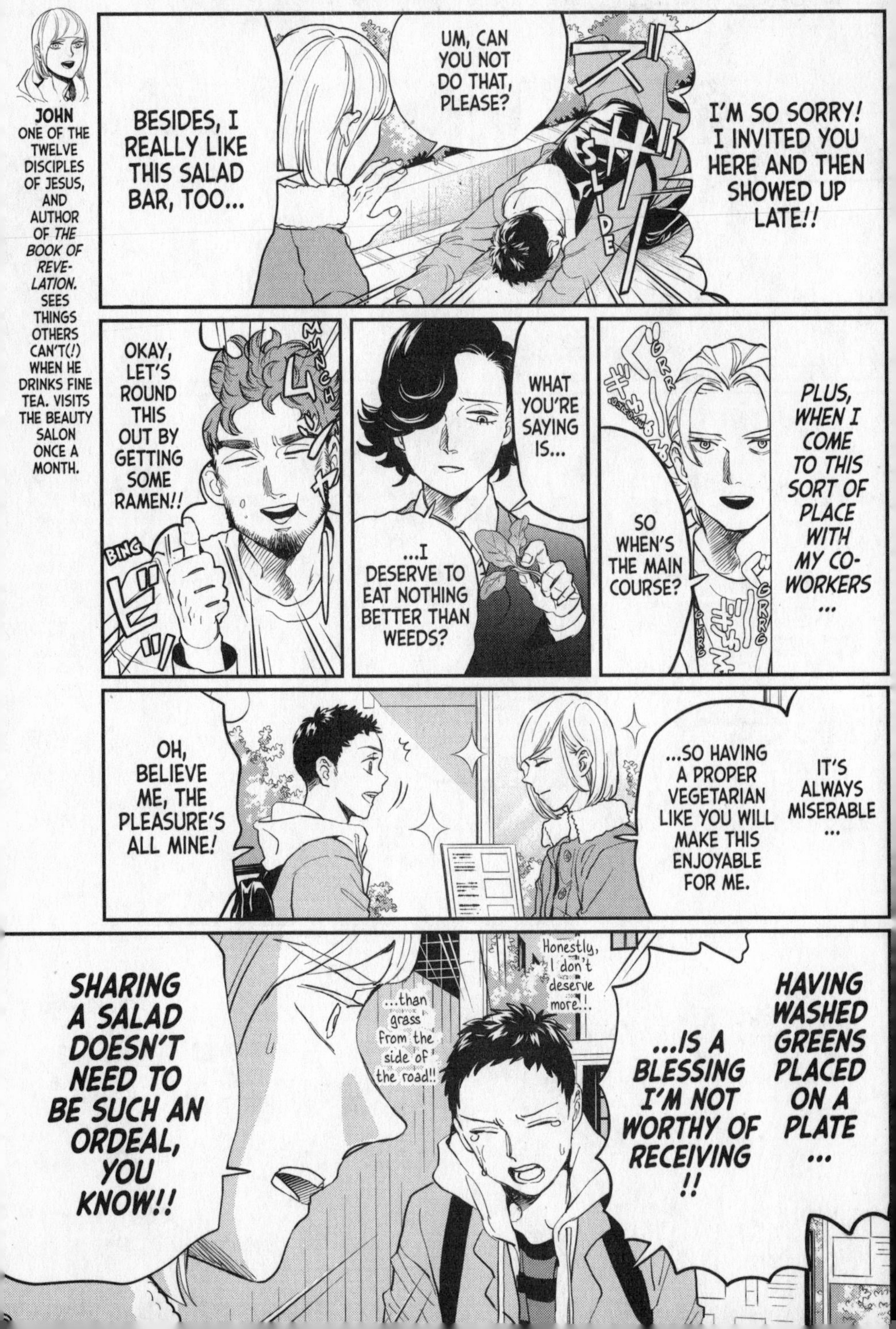
I'M SO SORRY! I INVITED YOU HERE AND THEN SHOWED UP LATE!!
SLIDE
UM, CAN YOU NOT DO THAT, PLEASE?
BESIDES, I REALLY LIKE THIS SALAD BAR, TOO...
PLUS, WHEN I COME TO THIS SORT OF PLACE WITH MY CO-WORKERS ...
SO WHEN'S THE MAIN COURSE?
WHAT YOU'RE SAYING IS...
...I DESERVE TO EAT NOTHING BETTER THAN WEEDS?
MUNCH
OKAY, LET'S ROUND THIS OUT BY GETTING SOME RAMEN!!
BING
IT'S ALWAYS MISERABLE ...
...SO HAVING A PROPER VEGETARIAN LIKE YOU WILL MAKE THIS ENJOYABLE FOR ME.
OH, BELIEVE ME, THE PLEASURE'S ALL MINE!
HAVING WASHED GREENS PLACED ON A PLATE ...
...IS A BLESSING I'M NOT WORTHY OF RECEIVING !!
Honestly, I don't deserve more...!
...than grass from the side of the road!!
SHARING A SALAD DOESN'T NEED TO BE SUCH AN ORDEAL, YOU KNOW!!
JOHN
ONE OF THE TWELVE DISCIPLES OF JESUS, AND AUTHOR OF THE BOOK OF REVELATION. SEES THINGS OTHERS CAN'T(!) WHEN HE DRINKS FINE TEA. VISITS THE BEAUTY SALON ONCE A MONTH.

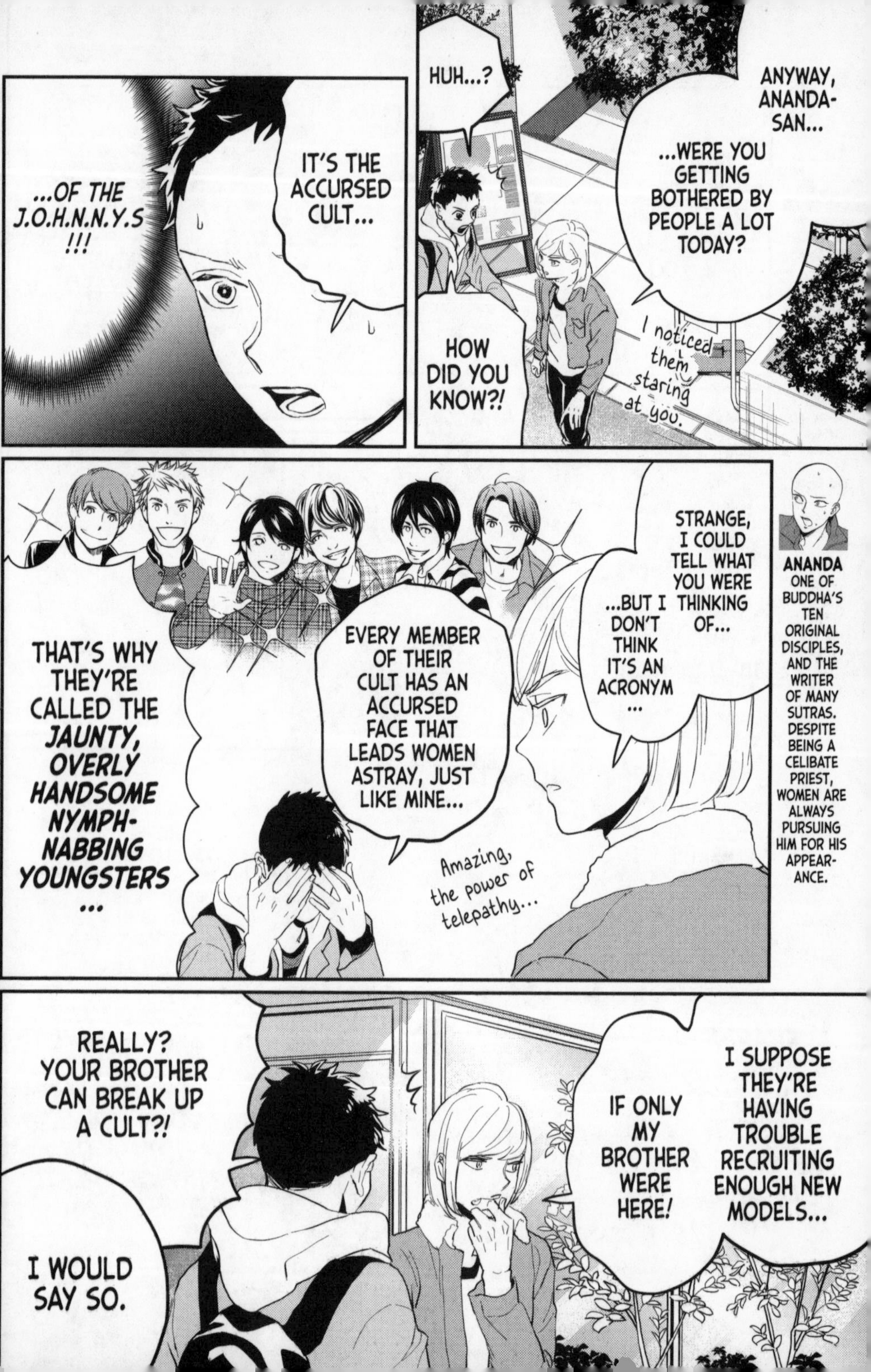
HUH...?
ANYWAY, ANANDA-SAN...
...WERE YOU GETTING BOTHERED BY PEOPLE A LOT TODAY?
I noticed them staring at you.
HOW DID YOU KNOW?!
IT'S THE ACCURSED CULT...
...OF THE J.O.H.N.N.Y.S !!!
ANANDA ONE OF BUDDHA'S TEN ORIGINAL DISCIPLES, AND THE WRITER OF MANY SUTRAS. DESPITE BEING A CELIBATE PRIEST, WOMEN ARE ALWAYS PURSUING HIM FOR HIS APPEAR-ANCE.
STRANGE, I COULD TELL WHAT YOU WERE THINKING OF...
...BUT I DON'T THINK IT'S AN ACRONYM...
EVERY MEMBER OF THEIR CULT HAS AN ACCURSED FACE THAT LEADS WOMEN ASTRAY, JUST LIKE MINE...
Amazing, the power of telepathy...
THAT'S WHY THEY'RE CALLED THE *JAUNTY, OVERLY HANDSOME NYMPH-NABBING YOUNGSTERS*...
I SUPPOSE THEY'RE HAVING TROUBLE RECRUITING ENOUGH NEW MODELS...
IF ONLY MY BROTHER WERE HERE!
REALLY? YOUR BROTHER CAN BREAK UP A CULT?!
I WOULD SAY SO.

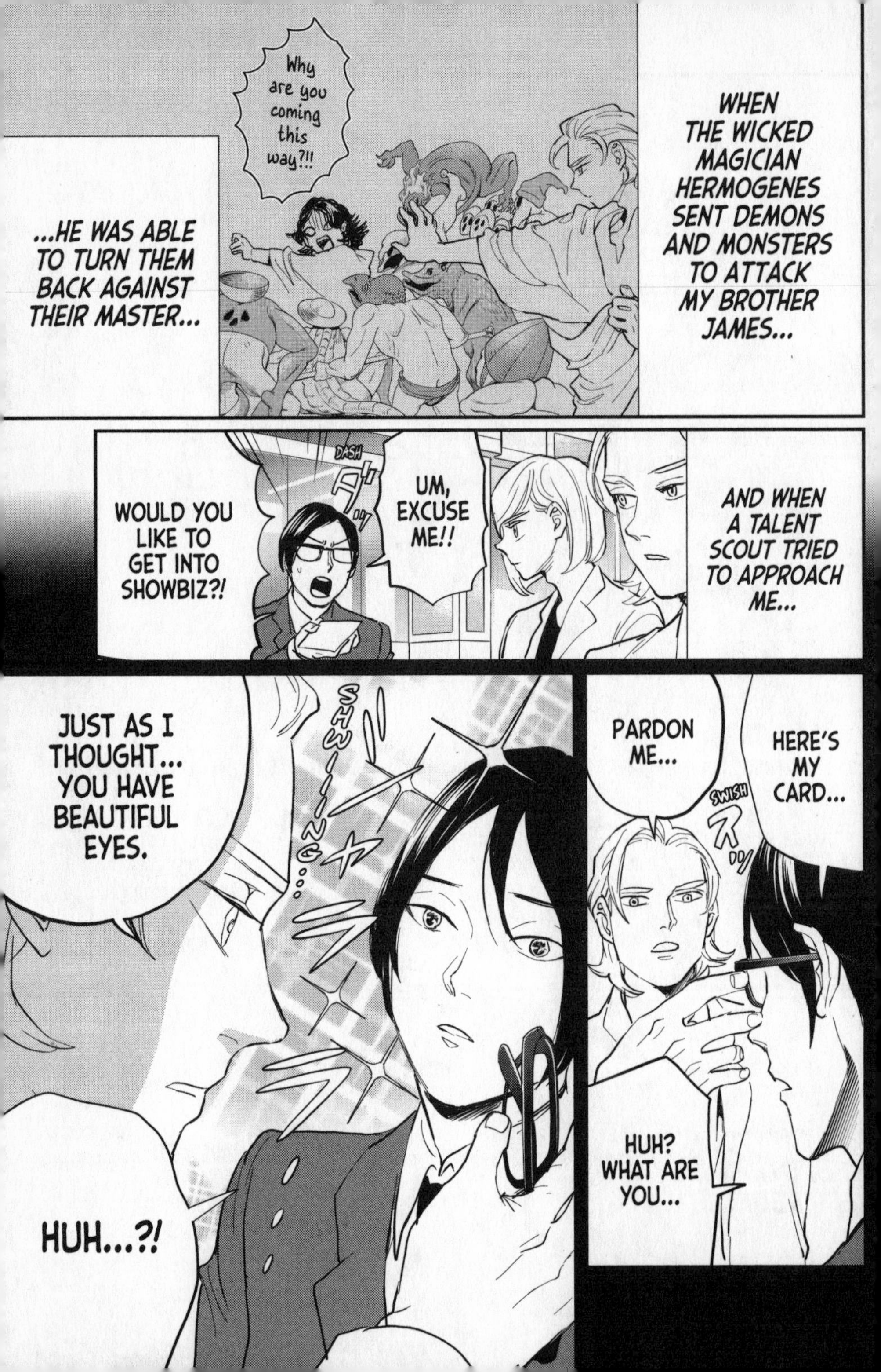
WHEN THE WICKED MAGICIAN HERMOGENES SENT DEMONS AND MONSTERS TO ATTACK MY BROTHER JAMES...
Why are you coming this way?!!
...HE WAS ABLE TO TURN THEM BACK AGAINST THEIR MASTER...
AND WHEN A TALENT SCOUT TRIED TO APPROACH ME...
UM, EXCUSE ME!!
DASH
WOULD YOU LIKE TO GET INTO SHOWBIZ?!
HERE'S MY CARD...
PARDON ME...
SWISH
HUH? WHAT ARE YOU...
SHWIIING...
JUST AS I THOUGHT... YOU HAVE BEAUTIFUL EYES.
HUH...?!

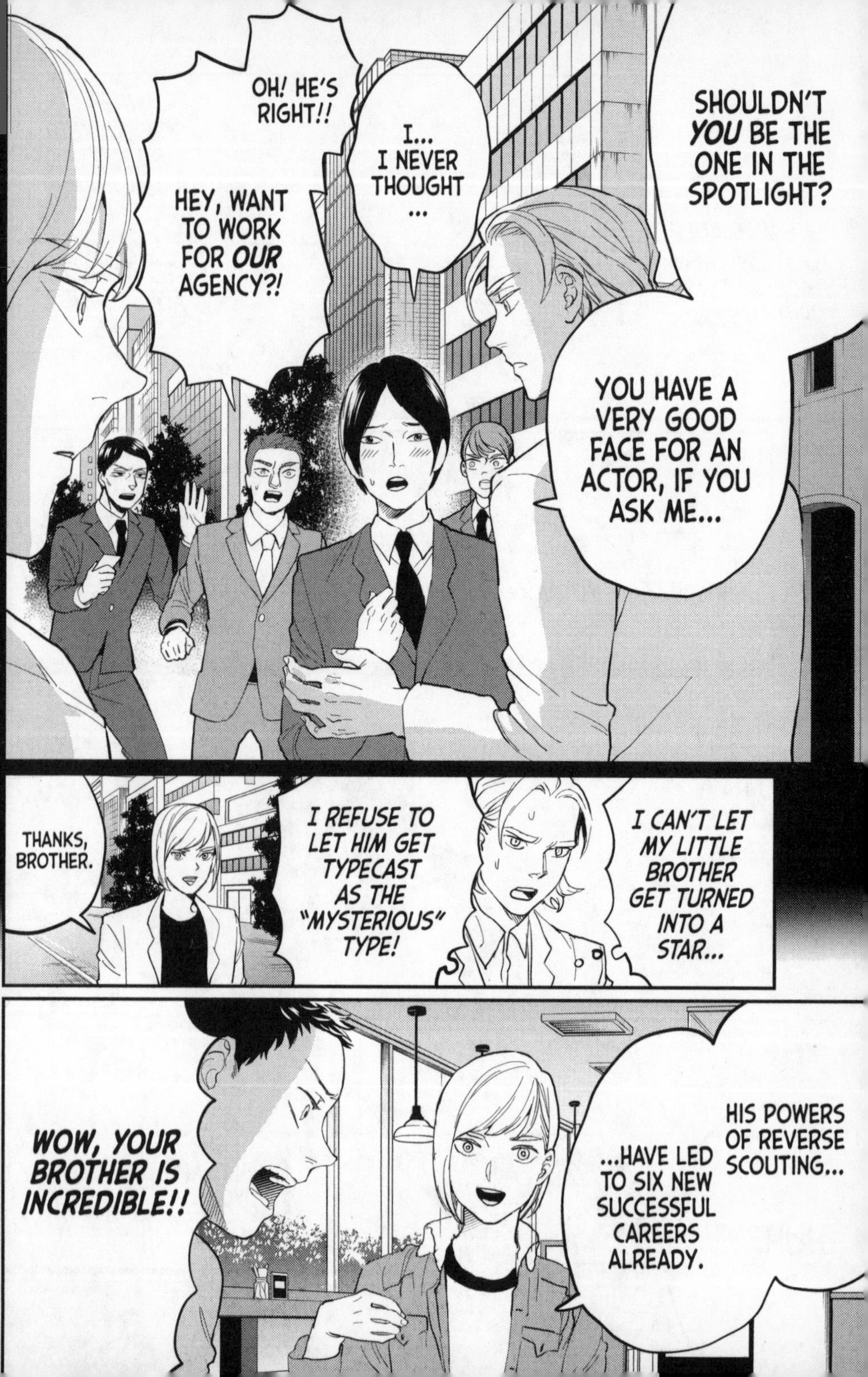
SHOULDN'T *YOU* BE THE ONE IN THE SPOTLIGHT?
YOU HAVE A VERY GOOD FACE FOR AN ACTOR, IF YOU ASK ME...
I... I NEVER THOUGHT...
OH! HE'S RIGHT!!
HEY, WANT TO WORK FOR *OUR* AGENCY?!
I CAN'T LET MY LITTLE BROTHER GET TURNED INTO A STAR...
I REFUSE TO LET HIM GET TYPECAST AS THE "MYSTERIOUS" TYPE!
THANKS, BROTHER.
HIS POWERS OF REVERSE SCOUTING...
...HAVE LED TO SIX NEW SUCCESSFUL CAREERS ALREADY.
WOW, YOUR BROTHER IS INCREDIBLE!!

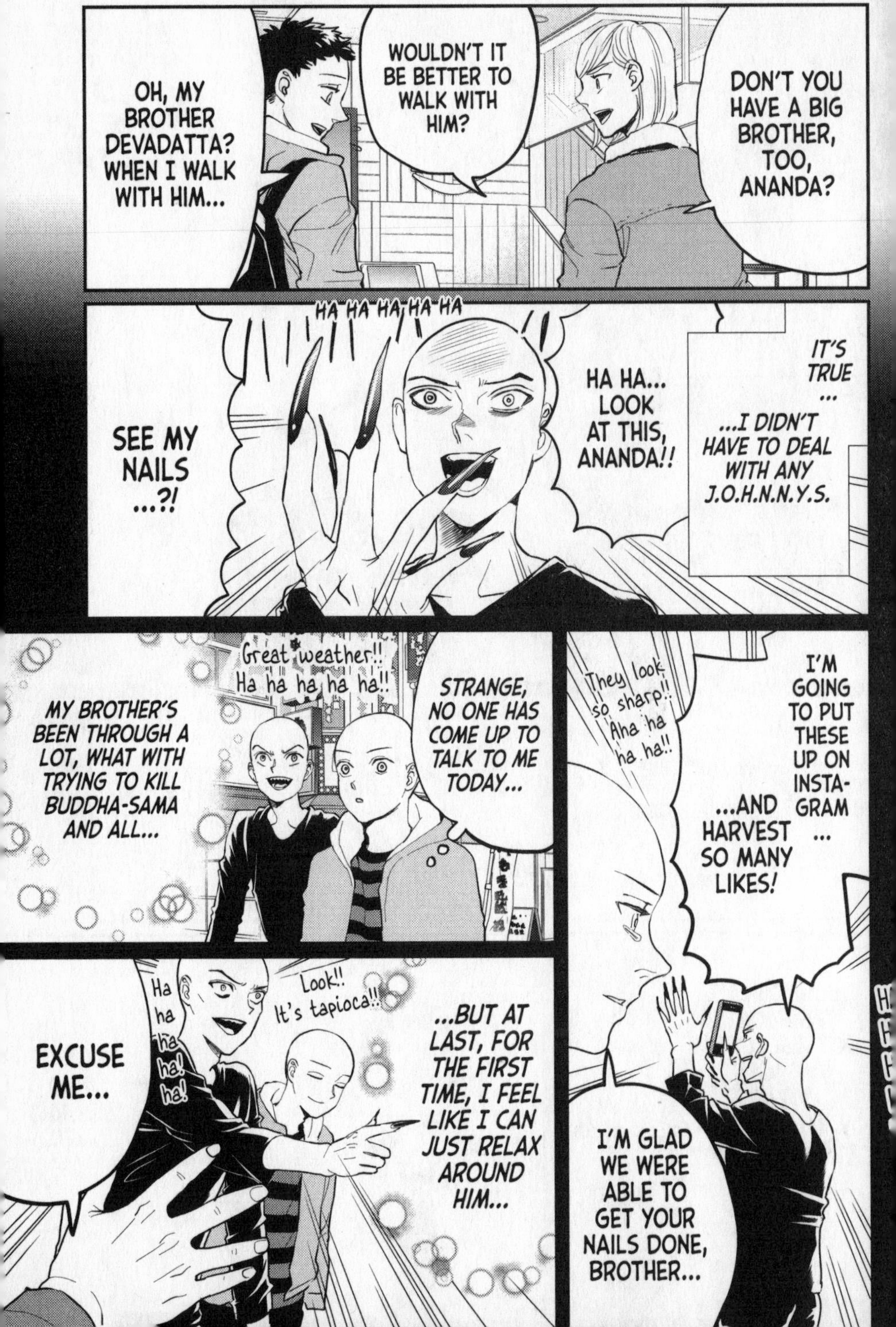
DON'T YOU HAVE A BIG BROTHER, TOO, ANANDA?
WOULDN'T IT BE BETTER TO WALK WITH HIM?
OH, MY BROTHER DEVADATTA? WHEN I WALK WITH HIM...
IT'S TRUE... ...I DIDN'T HAVE TO DEAL WITH ANY J.O.H.N.N.Y.S.
HA HA HA HA HA
HA HA... LOOK AT THIS, ANANDA!!
SEE MY NAILS...?!
I'M GOING TO PUT THESE UP ON INSTA-GRAM...
They look so sharp!! Aha ha ha ha!!
...AND HARVEST SO MANY LIKES!
I'M GLAD WE WERE ABLE TO GET YOUR NAILS DONE, BROTHER...
STRANGE, NO ONE HAS COME UP TO TALK TO ME TODAY...
Great weather!! Ha ha ha ha ha!!
MY BROTHER'S BEEN THROUGH A LOT, WHAT WITH TRYING TO KILL BUDDHA-SAMA AND ALL...
...BUT AT LAST, FOR THE FIRST TIME, I FEEL LIKE I CAN JUST RELAX AROUND HIM...
Look!! It's tapioca!!
Ha ha ha ha! ha!
EXCUSE ME...

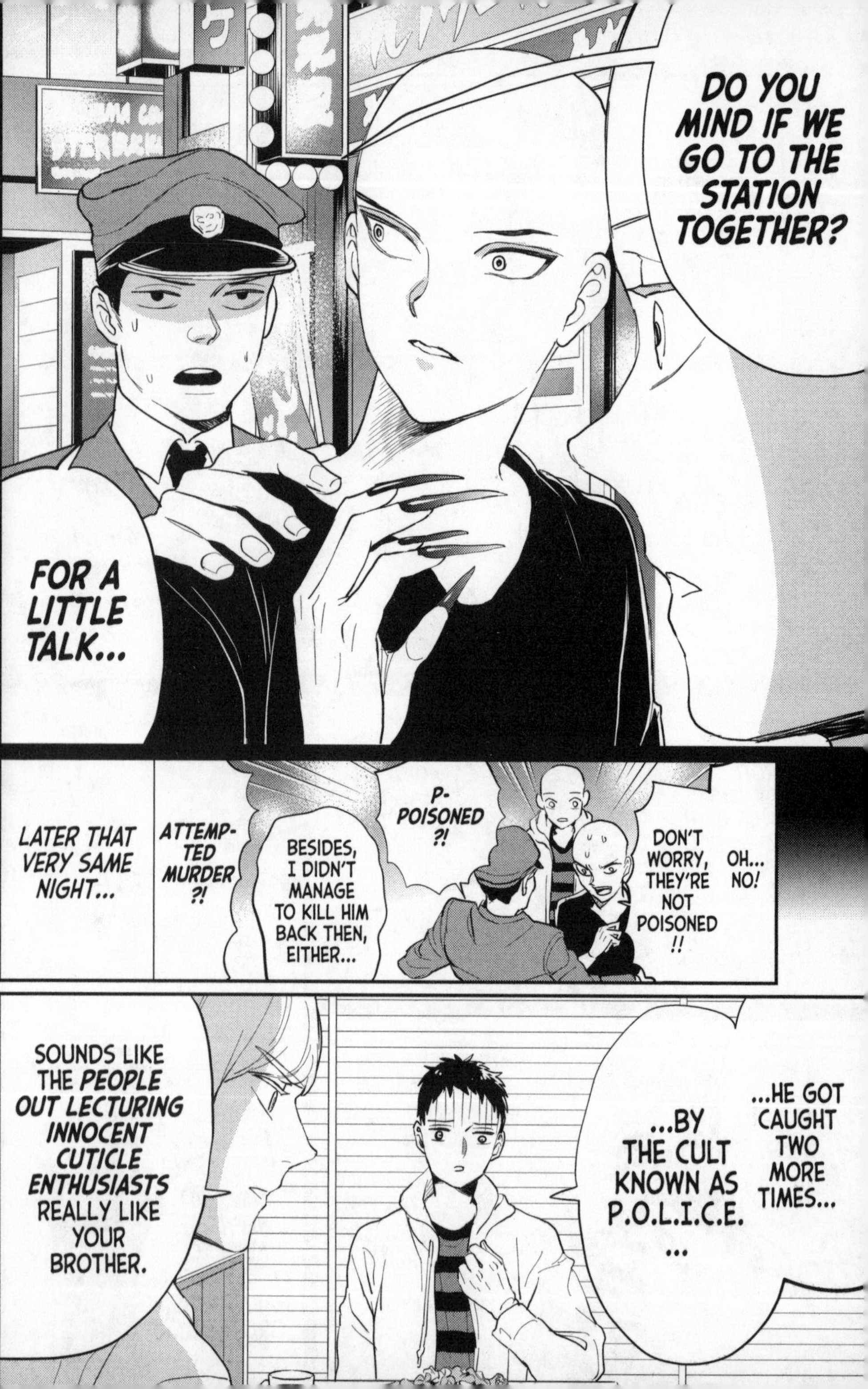
DO YOU MIND IF WE GO TO THE STATION TOGETHER?
FOR A LITTLE TALK...
LATER THAT VERY SAME NIGHT...
OH... NO!
DON'T WORRY, THEY'RE NOT POISONED !!
P-POISONED ?!
BESIDES, I DIDN'T MANAGE TO KILL HIM BACK THEN, EITHER...
ATTEMPTED MURDER ?!
...HE GOT CAUGHT TWO MORE TIMES...
...BY THE CULT KNOWN AS P.O.L.I.C.E. ...
SOUNDS LIKE THE PEOPLE OUT LECTURING INNOCENT CUTICLE ENTHUSIASTS REALLY LIKE YOUR BROTHER.

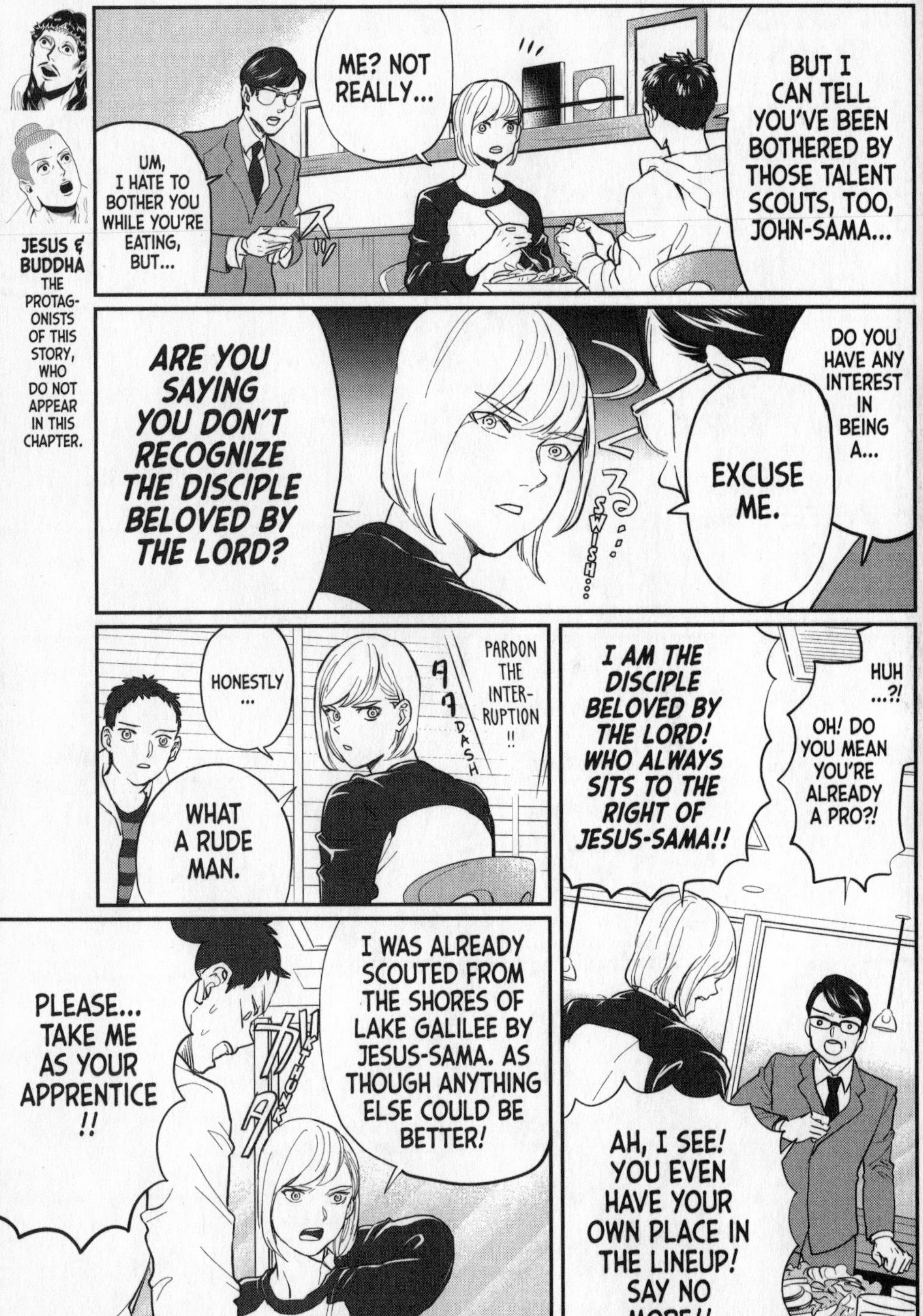
JESUS & BUDDHA THE PROTAGONISTS OF THIS STORY, WHO DO NOT APPEAR IN THIS CHAPTER.
BUT I CAN TELL YOU'VE BEEN BOTHERED BY THOSE TALENT SCOUTS, TOO, JOHN-SAMA...
ME? NOT REALLY...
UM, I HATE TO BOTHER YOU WHILE YOU'RE EATING, BUT...
DO YOU HAVE ANY INTEREST IN BEING A...
EXCUSE ME.
SWISH...
ARE YOU SAYING YOU DON'T RECOGNIZE THE DISCIPLE BELOVED BY THE LORD?
HUH ...?!
OH! DO YOU MEAN YOU'RE ALREADY A PRO?!
I AM THE DISCIPLE BELOVED BY THE LORD! WHO ALWAYS SITS TO THE RIGHT OF JESUS-SAMA!!
PARDON THE INTERRUPTION !!
DASH
HONESTLY ...
WHAT A RUDE MAN.
AH, I SEE! YOU EVEN HAVE YOUR OWN PLACE IN THE LINEUP! SAY NO MORE!!
I WAS ALREADY SCOUTED FROM THE SHORES OF LAKE GALILEE BY JESUS-SAMA. AS THOUGH ANYTHING ELSE COULD BE BETTER!
PLEASE... TAKE ME AS YOUR APPRENTICE !!

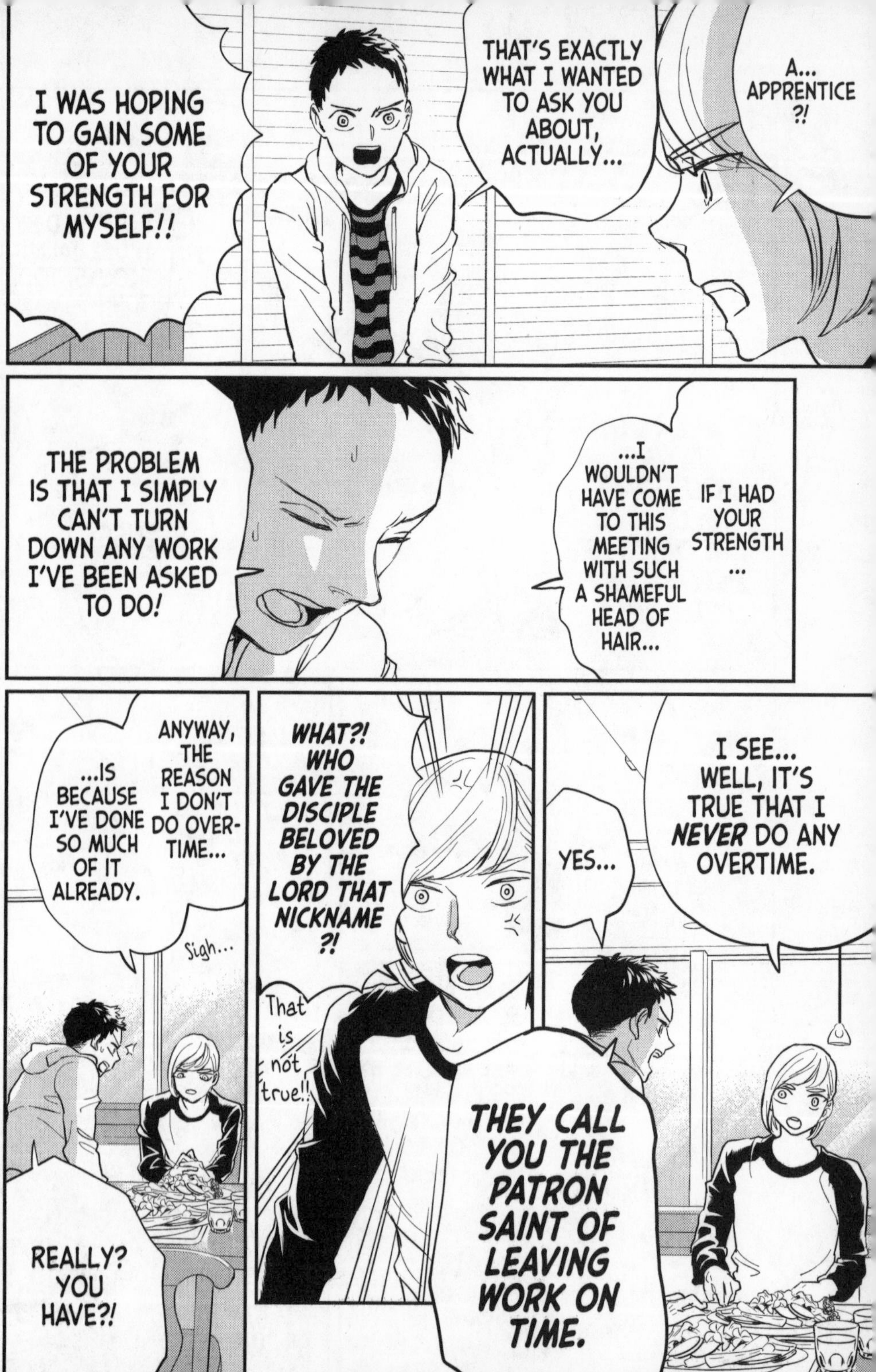
A... APPRENTICE?!
THAT'S EXACTLY WHAT I WANTED TO ASK YOU ABOUT, ACTUALLY...
I WAS HOPING TO GAIN SOME OF YOUR STRENGTH FOR MYSELF!!
IF I HAD YOUR STRENGTH...
...I WOULDN'T HAVE COME TO THIS MEETING WITH SUCH A SHAMEFUL HEAD OF HAIR...
THE PROBLEM IS THAT I SIMPLY CAN'T TURN DOWN ANY WORK I'VE BEEN ASKED TO DO!
I SEE... WELL, IT'S TRUE THAT I *NEVER* DO ANY OVERTIME.
YES...
THEY CALL YOU THE PATRON SAINT OF LEAVING WORK ON TIME.
WHAT?! WHO GAVE THE DISCIPLE BELOVED BY THE LORD THAT NICKNAME?!
That is not true!!
ANYWAY, THE REASON I DON'T DO OVER-TIME...
...IS BECAUSE I'VE DONE SO MUCH OF IT ALREADY.
Sigh...
REALLY? YOU HAVE?!

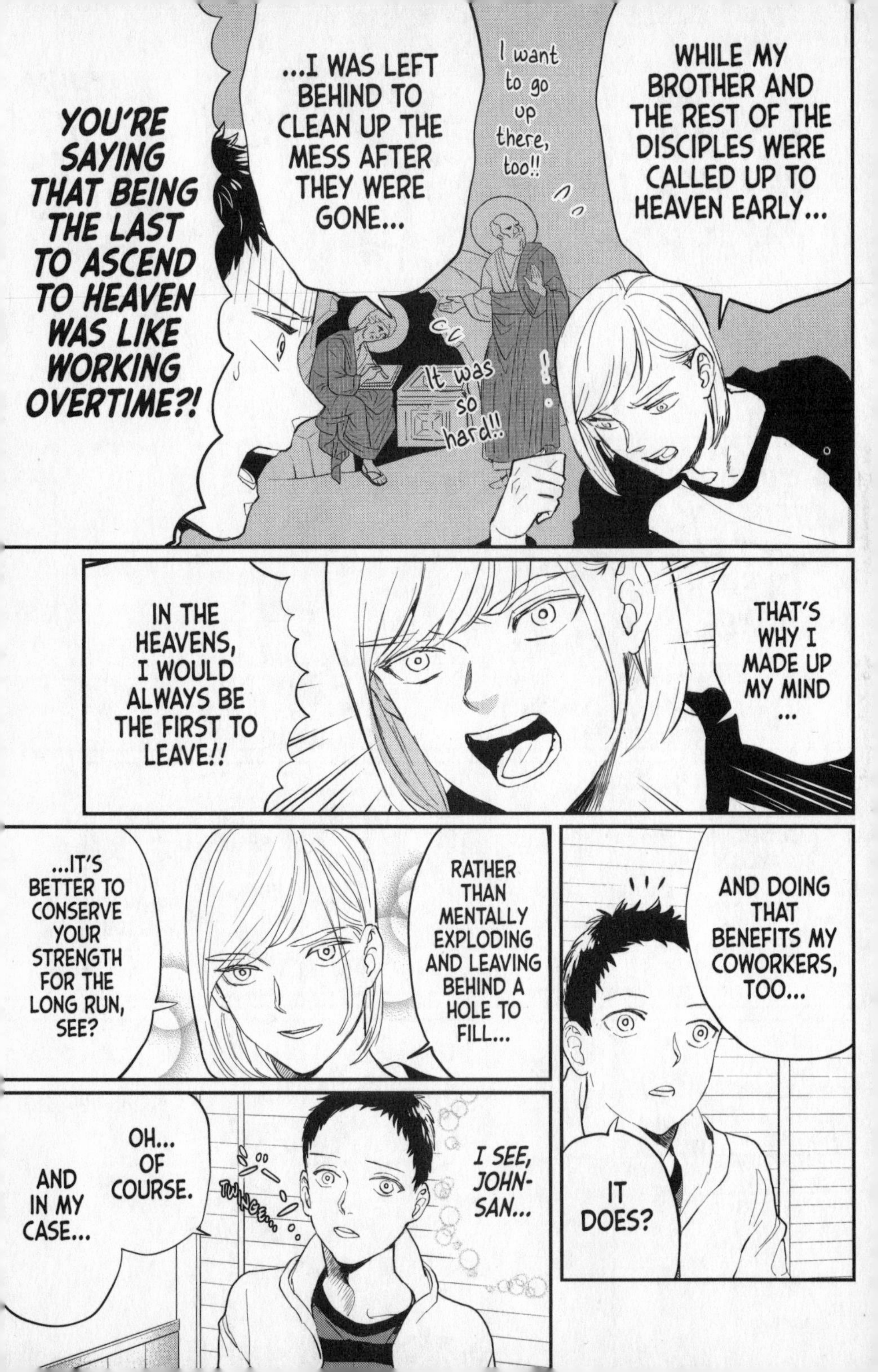
WHILE MY BROTHER AND THE REST OF THE DISCIPLES WERE CALLED UP TO HEAVEN EARLY...
I want to go up there, too!!
...I WAS LEFT BEHIND TO CLEAN UP THE MESS AFTER THEY WERE GONE...
It was so hard!!
YOU'RE SAYING THAT BEING THE LAST TO ASCEND TO HEAVEN WAS LIKE WORKING OVERTIME?!
THAT'S WHY I MADE UP MY MIND...
IN THE HEAVENS, I WOULD ALWAYS BE THE FIRST TO LEAVE!!
AND DOING THAT BENEFITS MY COWORKERS, TOO...
IT DOES?
RATHER THAN MENTALLY EXPLODING AND LEAVING BEHIND A HOLE TO FILL...
...IT'S BETTER TO CONSERVE YOUR STRENGTH FOR THE LONG RUN, SEE?
I SEE, JOHN-SAN...
TWINGE...
OH... OF COURSE.
AND IN MY CASE...

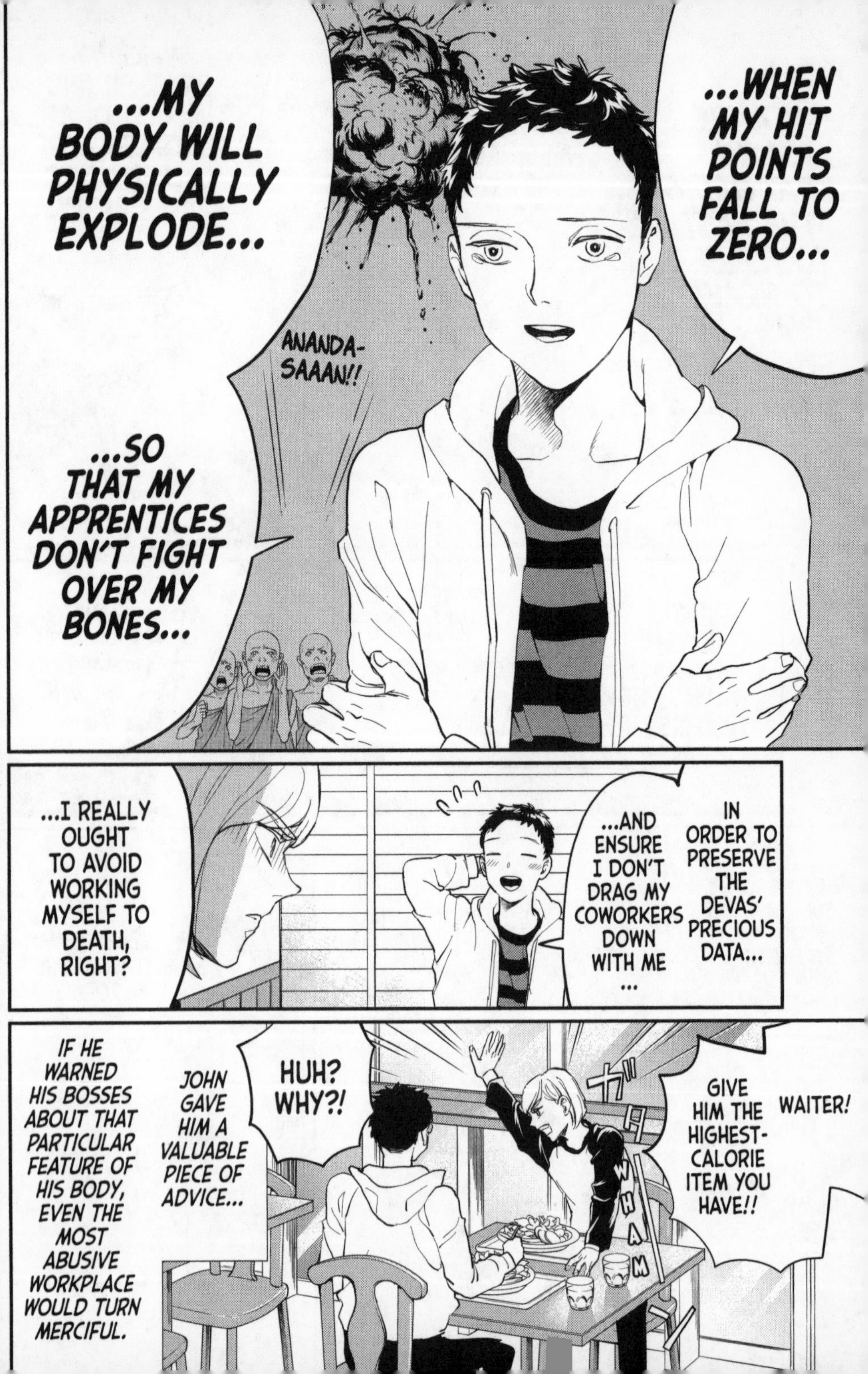
...WHEN MY HIT POINTS FALL TO ZERO...
...MY BODY WILL PHYSICALLY EXPLODE...
ANANDA-SAAAN!!
...SO THAT MY APPRENTICES DON'T FIGHT OVER MY BONES...
IN ORDER TO PRESERVE THE DEVAS' PRECIOUS DATA...
...AND ENSURE I DON'T DRAG MY COWORKERS DOWN WITH ME...
...I REALLY OUGHT TO AVOID WORKING MYSELF TO DEATH, RIGHT?
WAITER!
GIVE HIM THE HIGHEST-CALORIE ITEM YOU HAVE!!
WHAM
HUH? WHY?!
JOHN GAVE HIM A VALUABLE PIECE OF ADVICE...
IF HE WARNED HIS BOSSES ABOUT THAT PARTICULAR FEATURE OF HIS BODY, EVEN THE MOST ABUSIVE WORKPLACE WOULD TURN MERCIFUL.

Card for the Patron Saint of Leaving Work on Time

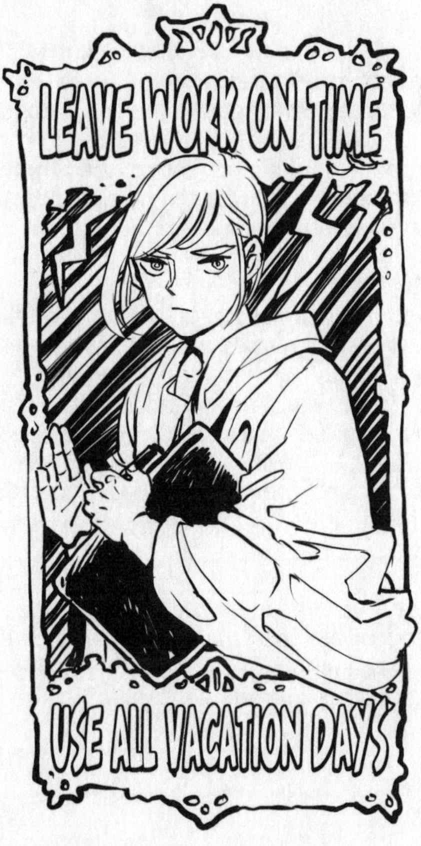
LEAVE WORK ON TIME
USE ALL VACATION DAYS

SAINT ☆ YOUNG MEN

CHAPTER 126 TRANSLATION NOTE

Johnny's, page 82

Johnny & Associates (typically just called "Johnny's") is a talent agency that specializes in producing handsome male entertainers, especially singers and models. Their classically handsome style is known colloquially as *Johnnys-kei* or "Johnny's style." In the original Japanese joke, Ananda envisioned their name with homophonic kanji that meant "a group with cursed faces that even cause wicked urges in nuns."

Hermogenes, page 83

A magician described in *The Golden Legend,* a medieval collection of legends and stories, many of which featured figures from the Bible. In the story of Hermogenes, he was asked by the Pharisees to expose James's heretical doctrine. He summoned demons to imprison James, but they could not harm him because of the protection of God. James then threw Hermogenes's book of magic into the sea and spared the magician's life. From that point on, Hermogenes lived a pious life in fear of God.

Devadatta's nails, page 85

Devadatta was a disciple of the Buddha's who was eager to succeed him and become a leader of the community. In his jealousy of the Buddha, he tried twice to have an elephant "accidentally" kill him, and failing that, tried to recruit his own followers. Eventually he was taken to the Buddha to be punished for his various crimes, and he pretended to repent, but dipped his hand in poison and tried to scratch the Buddha's foot. The Buddha pushed him away, at which point the ground opened up and Devadatta was swallowed in the flames that sprang out of the Earth.

Ananda's death, page 90

According to some sources, when Ananda was in his old age and close to death, there were several sides vying for his body so that the parts could be collected as relics. Supposedly, he managed to levitate his body as it died over the river, so that it split into equal pieces for the waiting parties on either riverbank.

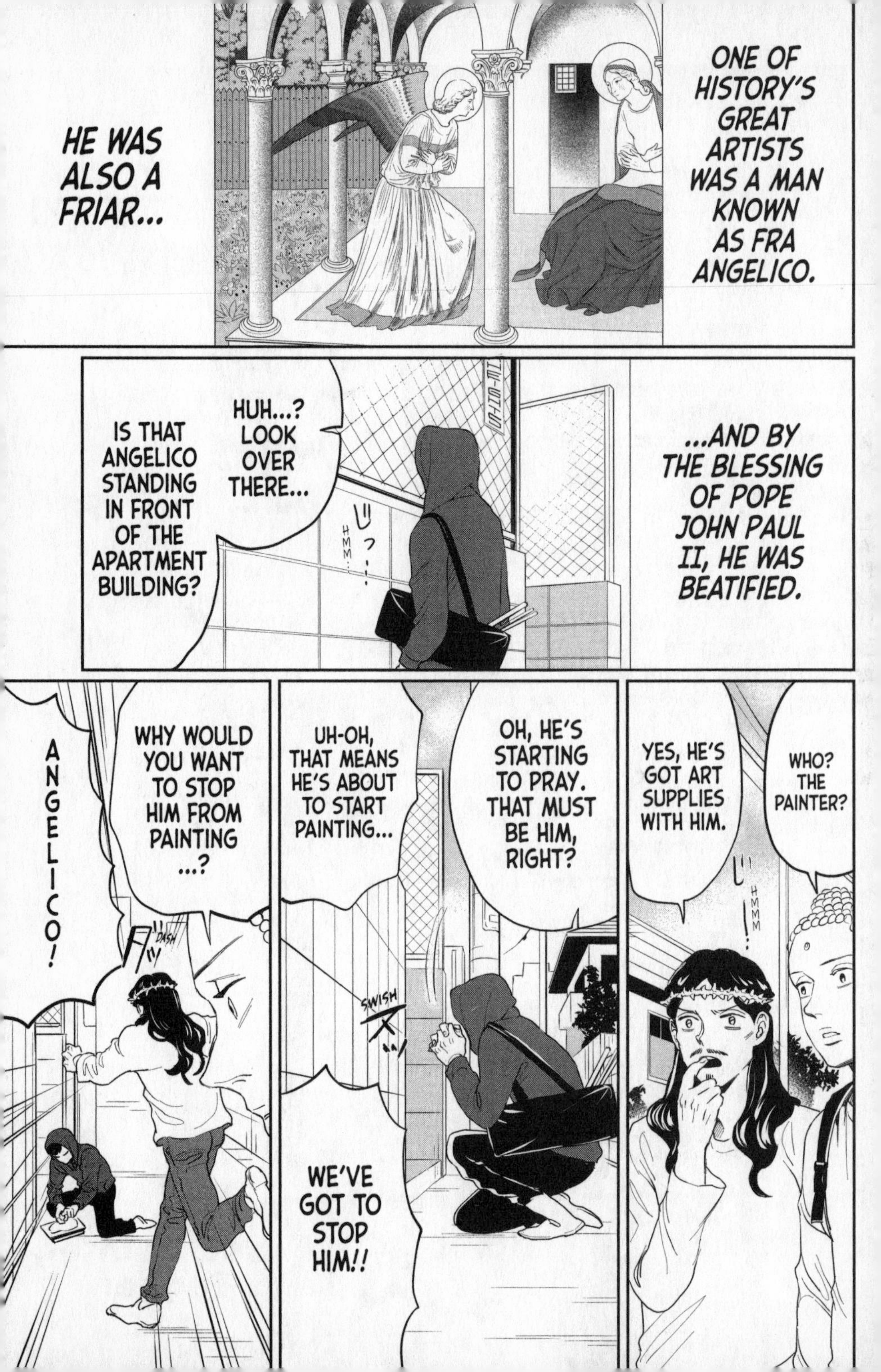
ONE OF HISTORY'S GREAT ARTISTS WAS A MAN KNOWN AS FRA ANGELICO.
HE WAS ALSO A FRIAR...
...AND BY THE BLESSING OF POPE JOHN PAUL II, HE WAS BEATIFIED.
HMM...
HUH...? LOOK OVER THERE...
IS THAT ANGELICO STANDING IN FRONT OF THE APARTMENT BUILDING?
WHO? THE PAINTER?
YES, HE'S GOT ART SUPPLIES WITH HIM.
HMMM
OH, HE'S STARTING TO PRAY. THAT MUST BE HIM, RIGHT?
UH-OH, THAT MEANS HE'S ABOUT TO START PAINTING...
SWISH
WE'VE GOT TO STOP HIM!!
WHY WOULD YOU WANT TO STOP HIM FROM PAINTING ...?
ANGELICO!
DASH

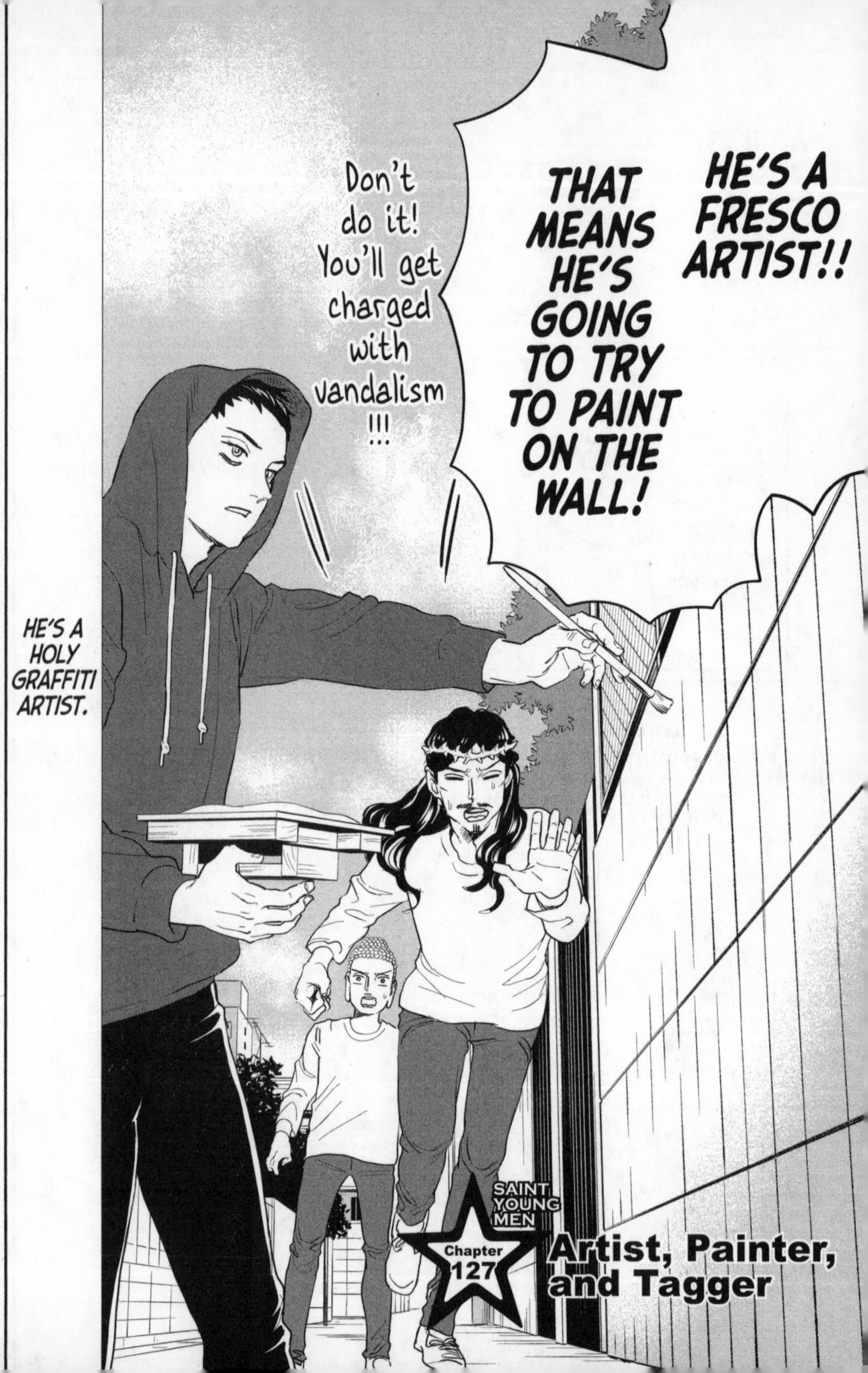
HE'S A FRESCO ARTIST!!
THAT MEANS HE'S GOING TO TRY TO PAINT ON THE WALL!
Don't do it! You'll get charged with vandalism!!!
HE'S A HOLY GRAFFITI ARTIST.
SAINT YOUNG MEN
Chapter 127
Artist, Painter, and Tagger

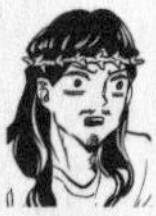

JESUS
IF YOU MAKE A FRAME WITH YOUR THUMBS AND INDEX FINGERS, IT LOOKS LIKE THE MOUTHS OF THE ONION SQUAD.

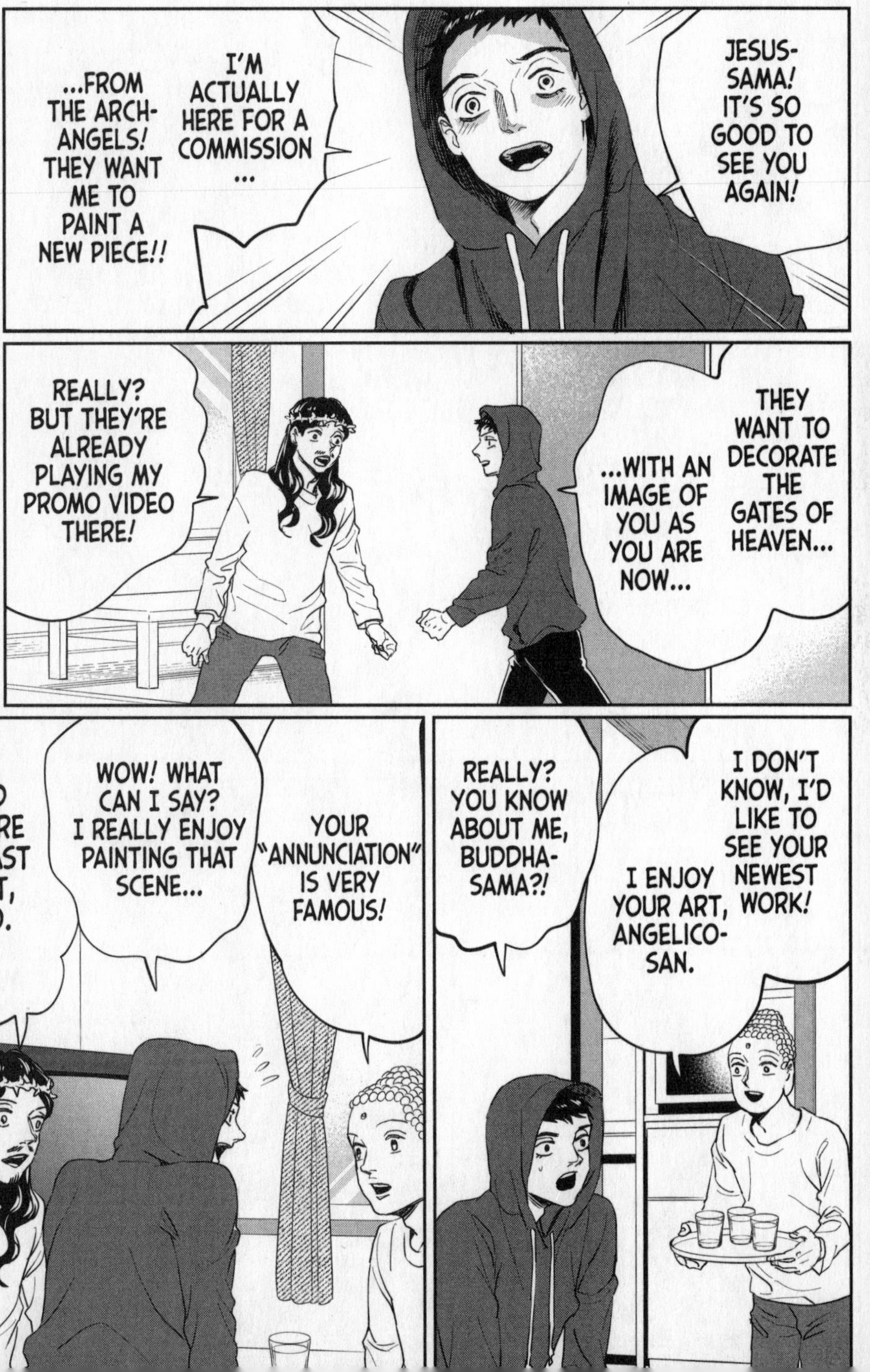
JESUS-SAMA! IT'S SO GOOD TO SEE YOU AGAIN!
I'M ACTUALLY HERE FOR A COMMISSION ...
...FROM THE ARCH-ANGELS! THEY WANT ME TO PAINT A NEW PIECE!!
THEY WANT TO DECORATE THE GATES OF HEAVEN...
...WITH AN IMAGE OF YOU AS YOU ARE NOW...
REALLY? BUT THEY'RE ALREADY PLAYING MY PROMO VIDEO THERE!
I DON'T KNOW, I'D LIKE TO SEE YOUR NEWEST WORK!
I ENJOY YOUR ART, ANGELICO-SAN.
REALLY? YOU KNOW ABOUT ME, BUDDHA-SAMA?!
YOUR "ANNUNCIATION" IS VERY FAMOUS!
WOW! WHAT CAN I SAY? I REALLY ENJOY PAINTING THAT SCENE...
AND YOU'RE SO FAST AT IT, TOO.

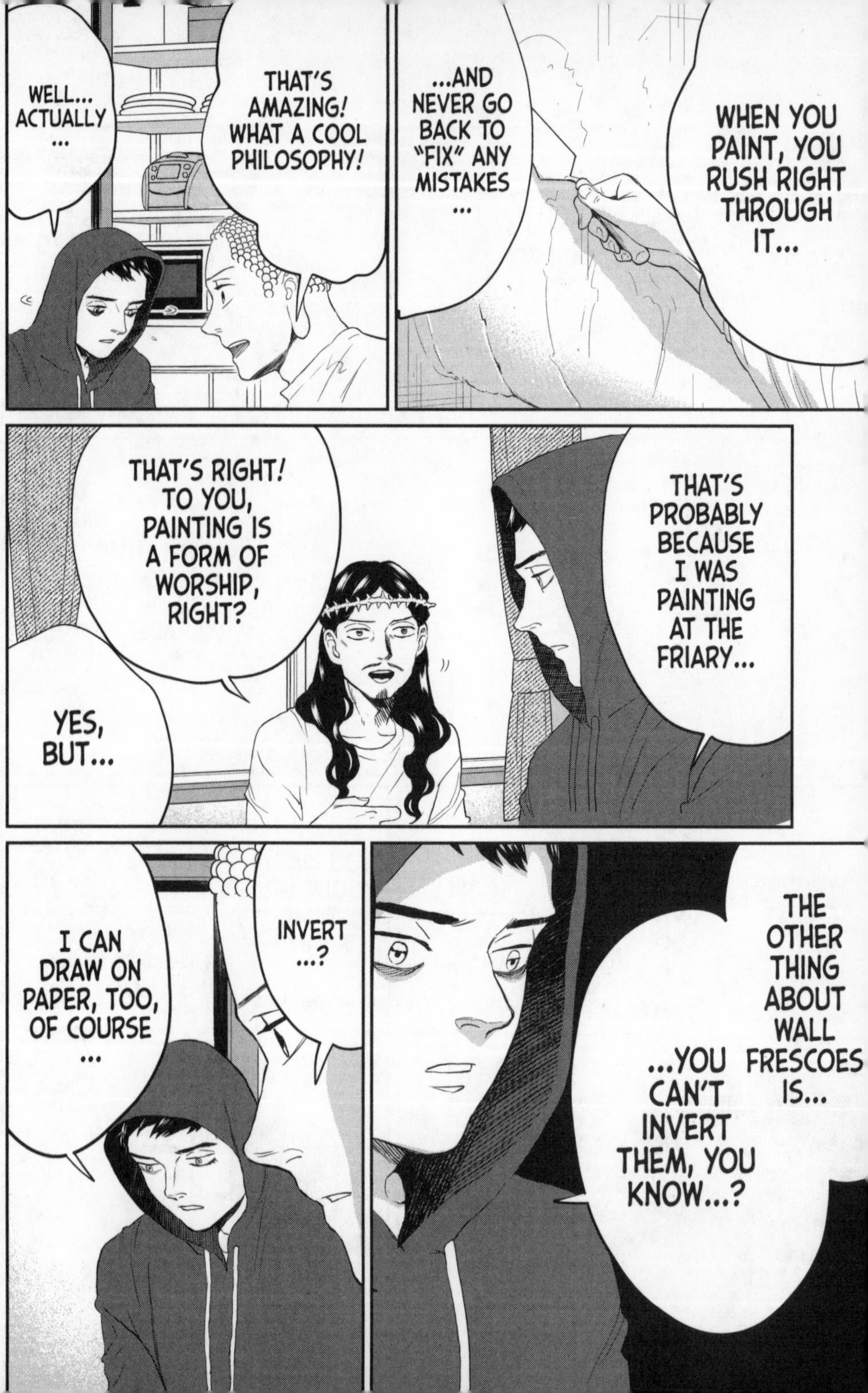
WHEN YOU PAINT, YOU RUSH RIGHT THROUGH IT...
...AND NEVER GO BACK TO "FIX" ANY MISTAKES...
THAT'S AMAZING! WHAT A COOL PHILOSOPHY!
WELL... ACTUALLY...
THAT'S PROBABLY BECAUSE I WAS PAINTING AT THE FRIARY...
THAT'S RIGHT! TO YOU, PAINTING IS A FORM OF WORSHIP, RIGHT?
YES, BUT...
THE OTHER THING ABOUT WALL FRESCOES IS...
...YOU CAN'T INVERT THEM, YOU KNOW...?
INVERT...?
I CAN DRAW ON PAPER, TOO, OF COURSE...

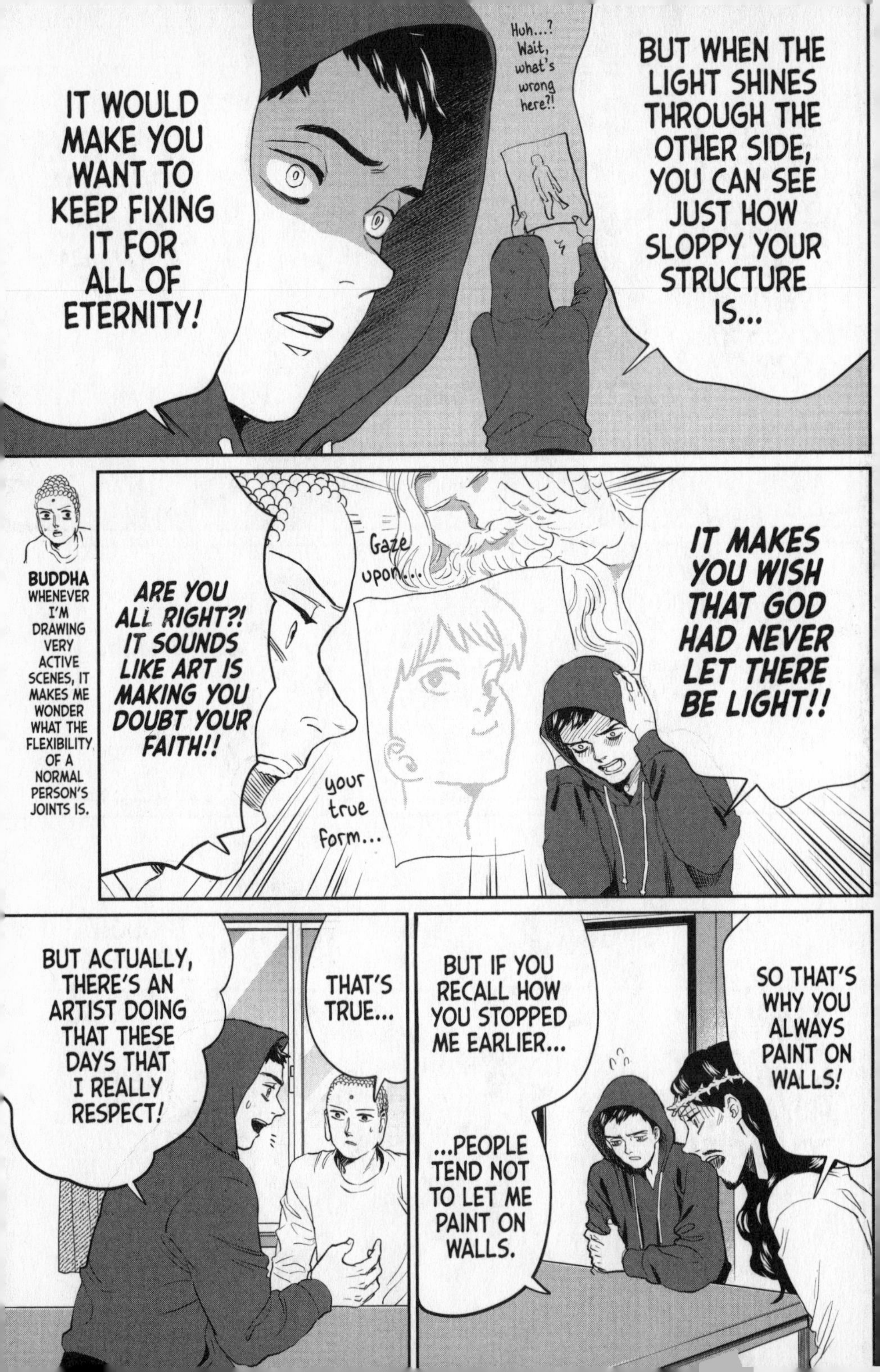
BUT WHEN THE LIGHT SHINES THROUGH THE OTHER SIDE, YOU CAN SEE JUST HOW SLOPPY YOUR STRUCTURE IS...
Huh...? Wait, what's wrong here?!
IT WOULD MAKE YOU WANT TO KEEP FIXING IT FOR ALL OF ETERNITY!
IT MAKES YOU WISH THAT GOD HAD NEVER LET THERE BE LIGHT!!
Gaze upon...
your true form...
ARE YOU ALL RIGHT?! IT SOUNDS LIKE ART IS MAKING YOU DOUBT YOUR FAITH!!
BUDDHA
WHENEVER I'M DRAWING VERY ACTIVE SCENES, IT MAKES ME WONDER WHAT THE FLEXIBILITY OF A NORMAL PERSON'S JOINTS IS.
SO THAT'S WHY YOU ALWAYS PAINT ON WALLS!
BUT IF YOU RECALL HOW YOU STOPPED ME EARLIER...
...PEOPLE TEND NOT TO LET ME PAINT ON WALLS.
THAT'S TRUE...
BUT ACTUALLY, THERE'S AN ARTIST DOING THAT THESE DAYS THAT I REALLY RESPECT!

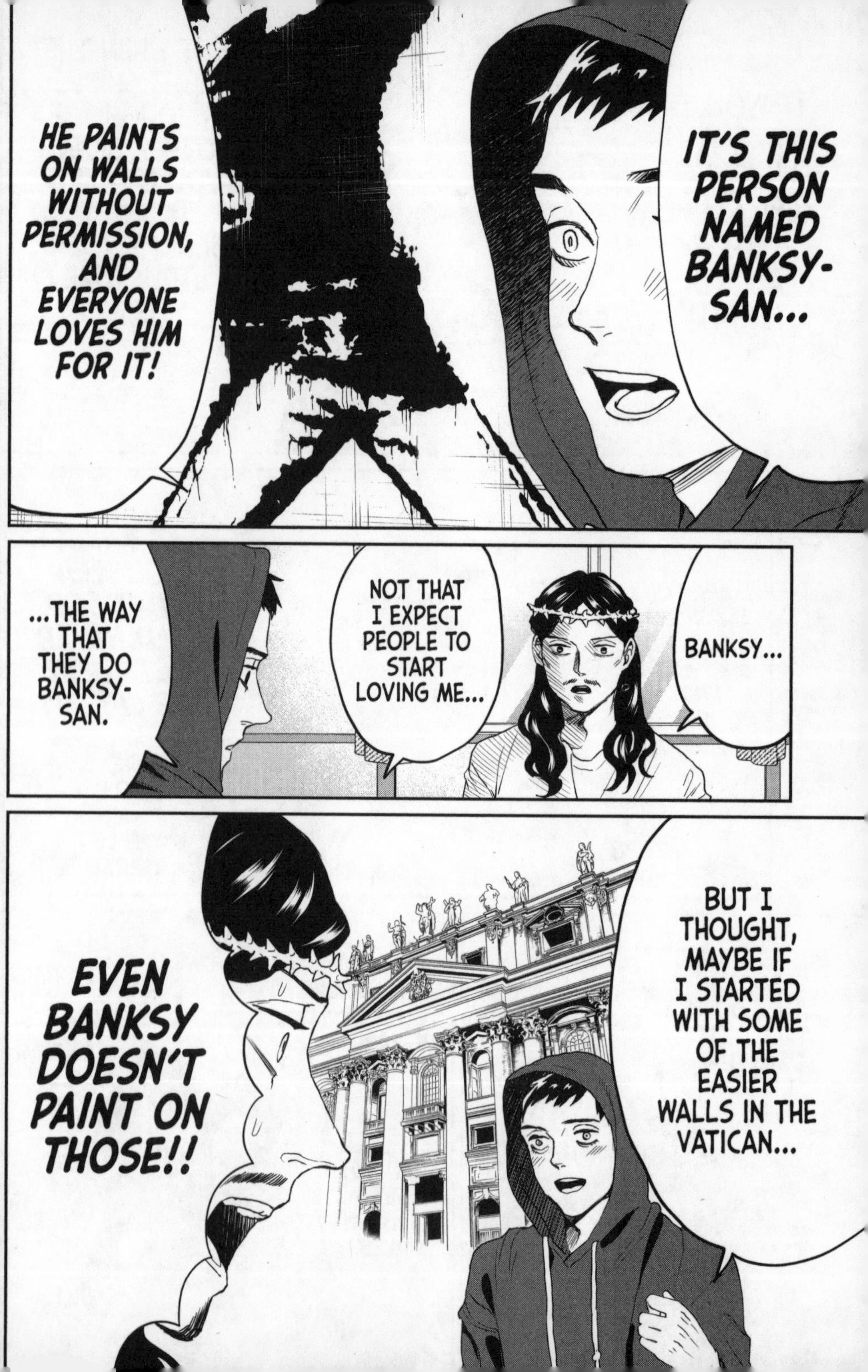
IT'S THIS PERSON NAMED BANKSY-SAN...
HE PAINTS ON WALLS WITHOUT PERMISSION, AND EVERYONE LOVES HIM FOR IT!
BANKSY...
NOT THAT I EXPECT PEOPLE TO START LOVING ME...
...THE WAY THAT THEY DO BANKSY-SAN.
BUT I THOUGHT, MAYBE IF I STARTED WITH SOME OF THE EASIER WALLS IN THE VATICAN...
EVEN BANKSY DOESN'T PAINT ON THOSE!!

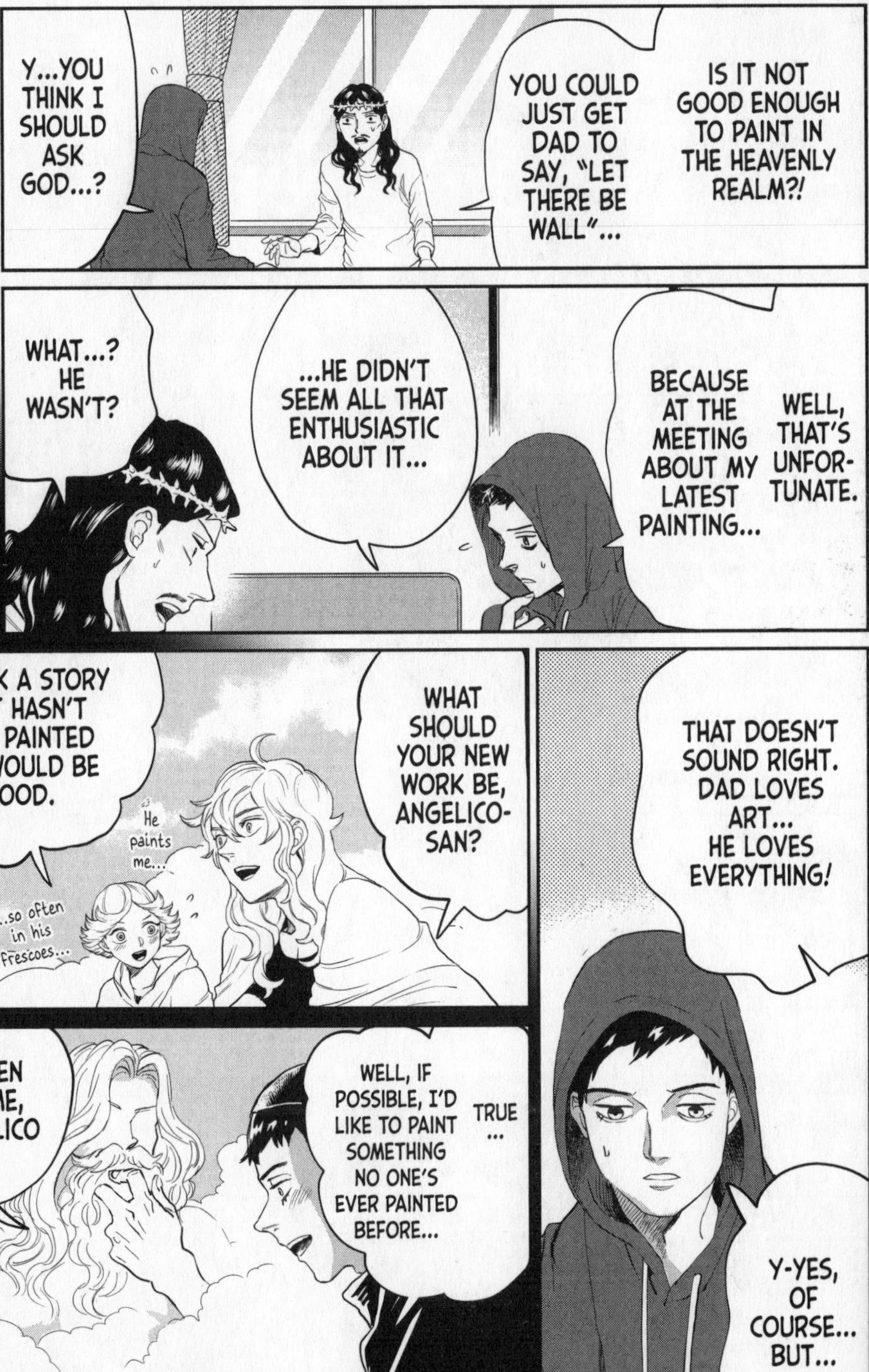
IS IT NOT GOOD ENOUGH TO PAINT IN THE HEAVENLY REALM?!
YOU COULD JUST GET DAD TO SAY, "LET THERE BE WALL"...
Y...YOU THINK I SHOULD ASK GOD...?
WELL, THAT'S UNFORTUNATE.
BECAUSE AT THE MEETING ABOUT MY LATEST PAINTING...
...HE DIDN'T SEEM ALL THAT ENTHUSIASTIC ABOUT IT...
WHAT...? HE WASN'T?
THAT DOESN'T SOUND RIGHT. DAD LOVES ART... HE LOVES EVERYTHING!
Y-YES, OF COURSE... BUT...
WHAT SHOULD YOUR NEW WORK BE, ANGELICO-SAN?
I THINK A STORY THAT HASN'T BEEN PAINTED YET WOULD BE GOOD.
He paints me...
...so often in his Frescoes...
TRUE...
WELL, IF POSSIBLE, I'D LIKE TO PAINT SOMETHING NO ONE'S EVER PAINTED BEFORE...
LISTEN TO ME, ANGELICO...

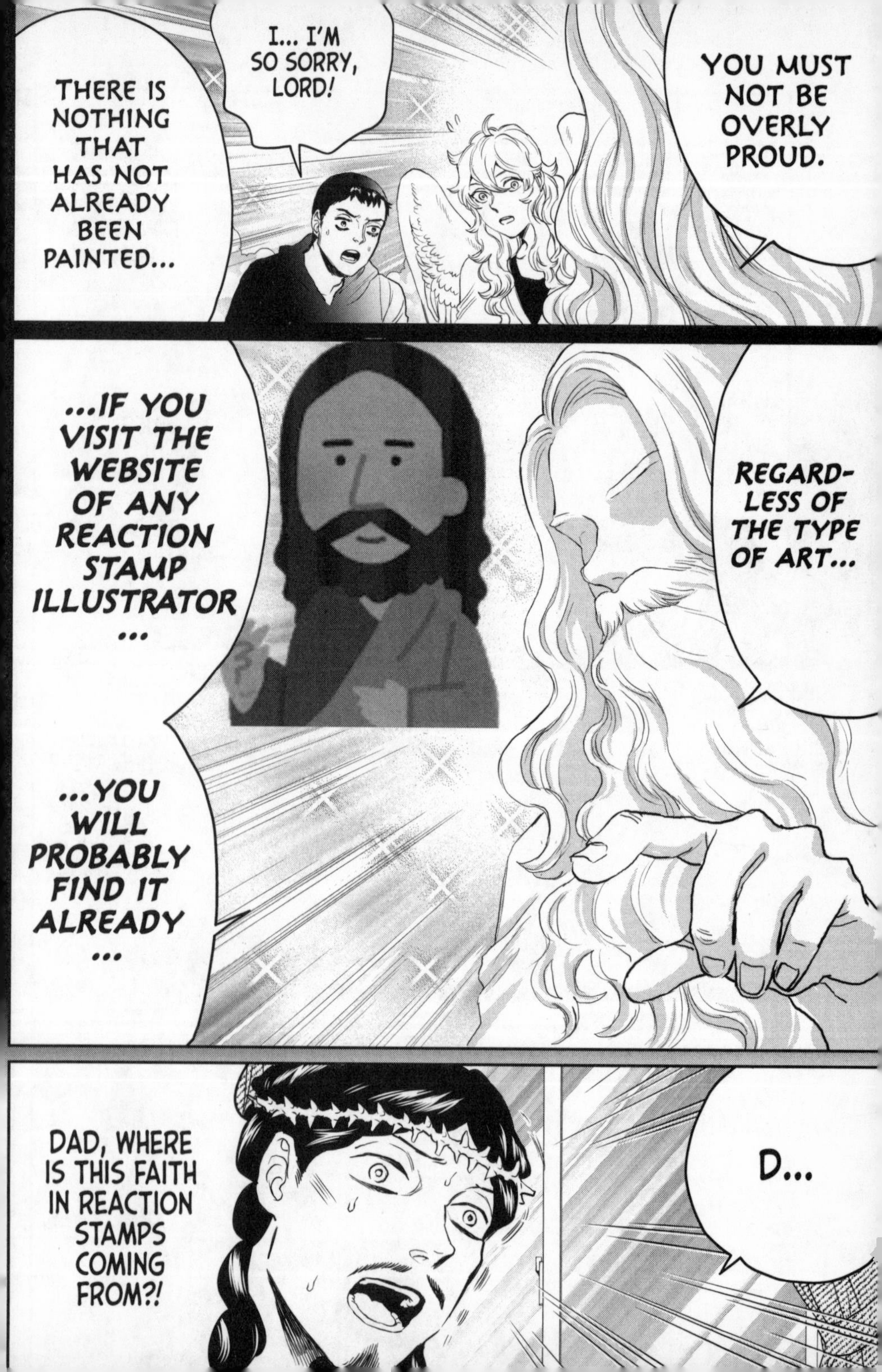
YOU MUST NOT BE OVERLY PROUD.
I... I'M SO SORRY, LORD!
THERE IS NOTHING THAT HAS NOT ALREADY BEEN PAINTED...
REGARD-LESS OF THE TYPE OF ART...
...IF YOU VISIT THE WEBSITE OF ANY REACTION STAMP ILLUSTRATOR...
...YOU WILL PROBABLY FIND IT ALREADY...
D...
DAD, WHERE IS THIS FAITH IN REACTION STAMPS COMING FROM?!

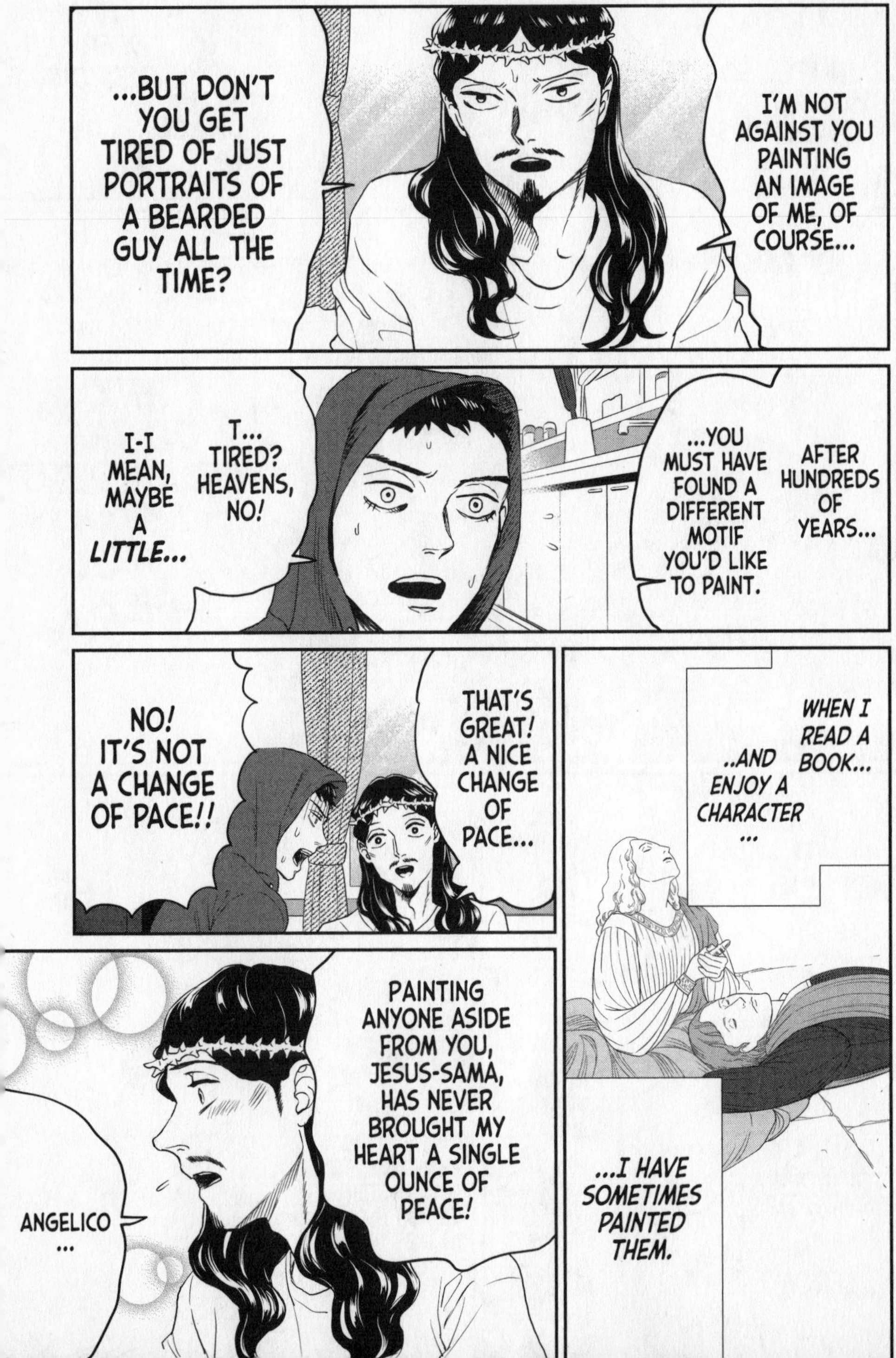
I'M NOT AGAINST YOU PAINTING AN IMAGE OF ME, OF COURSE...
...BUT DON'T YOU GET TIRED OF JUST PORTRAITS OF A BEARDED GUY ALL THE TIME?
AFTER HUNDREDS OF YEARS...
...YOU MUST HAVE FOUND A DIFFERENT MOTIF YOU'D LIKE TO PAINT.
T... TIRED? HEAVENS, NO!
I-I MEAN, MAYBE A *LITTLE...*
WHEN I READ A BOOK...
..AND ENJOY A CHARACTER ...
...I HAVE SOMETIMES PAINTED THEM.
THAT'S GREAT! A NICE CHANGE OF PACE...
NO! IT'S NOT A CHANGE OF PACE!!
PAINTING ANYONE ASIDE FROM YOU, JESUS-SAMA, HAS NEVER BROUGHT MY HEART A SINGLE OUNCE OF PEACE!
ANGELICO ...

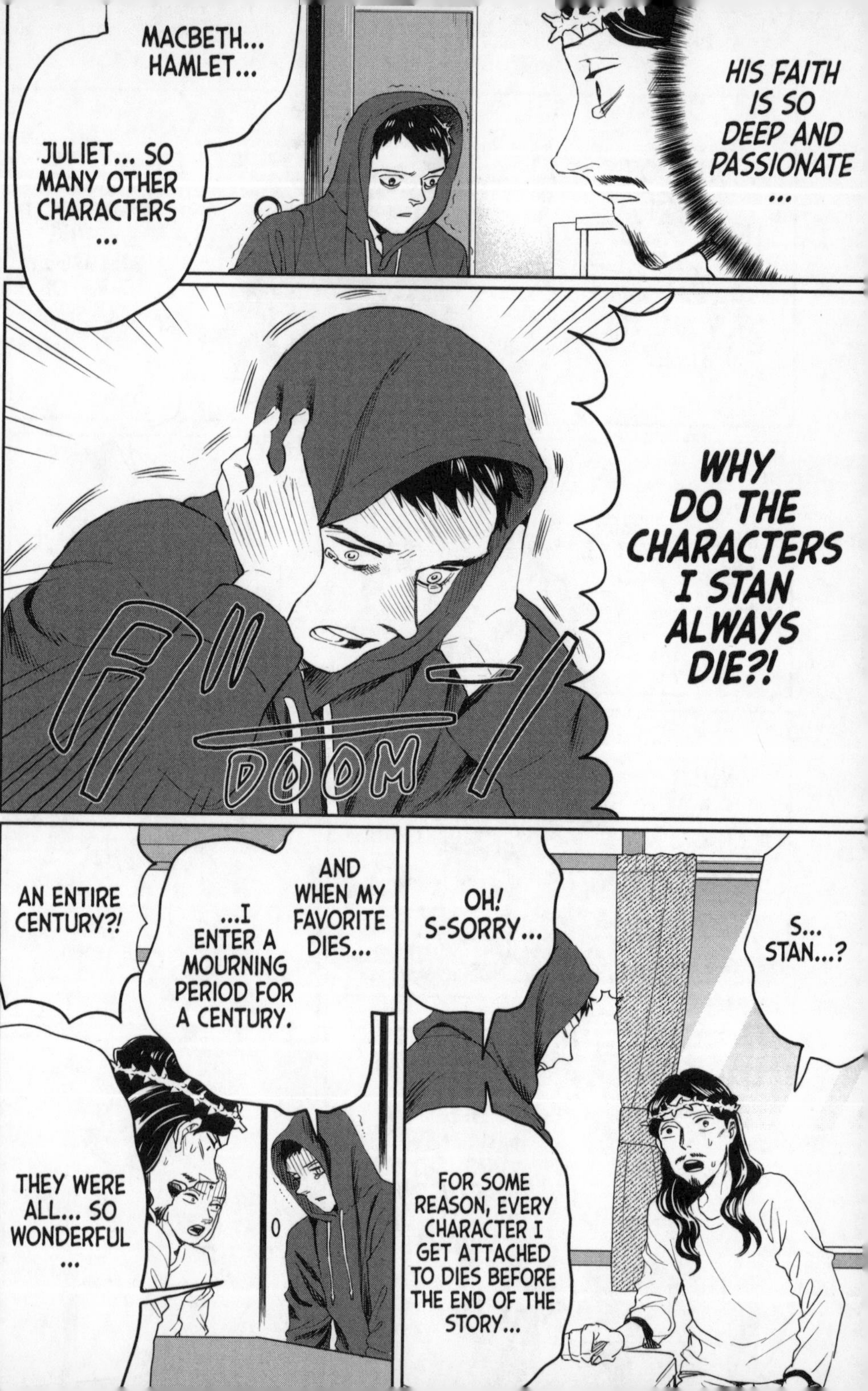
HIS FAITH IS SO DEEP AND PASSIONATE ...
MACBETH... HAMLET...
JULIET... SO MANY OTHER CHARACTERS ...
WHY DO THE CHARACTERS I STAN ALWAYS DIE?!
DOOM
S... STAN...?
OH! S-SORRY...
FOR SOME REASON, EVERY CHARACTER I GET ATTACHED TO DIES BEFORE THE END OF THE STORY...
AND WHEN MY FAVORITE DIES...
...I ENTER A MOURNING PERIOD FOR A CENTURY.
AN ENTIRE CENTURY?!
THEY WERE ALL... SO WONDERFUL ...

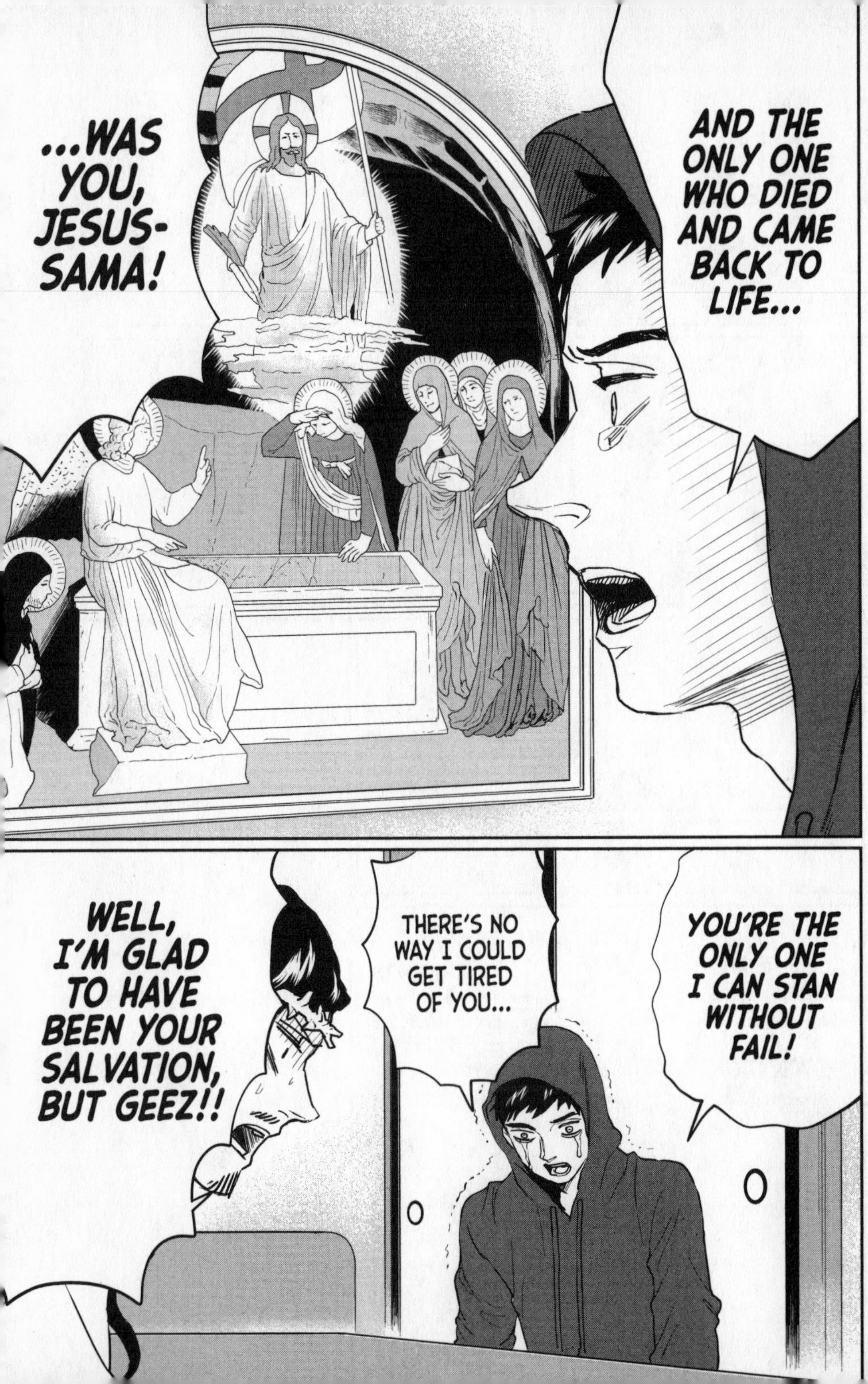
AND THE ONLY ONE WHO DIED AND CAME BACK TO LIFE...
...WAS YOU, JESUS-SAMA!
YOU'RE THE ONLY ONE I CAN STAN WITHOUT FAIL!
THERE'S NO WAY I COULD GET TIRED OF YOU...
WELL, I'M GLAD TO HAVE BEEN YOUR SALVATION, BUT GEEZ!!

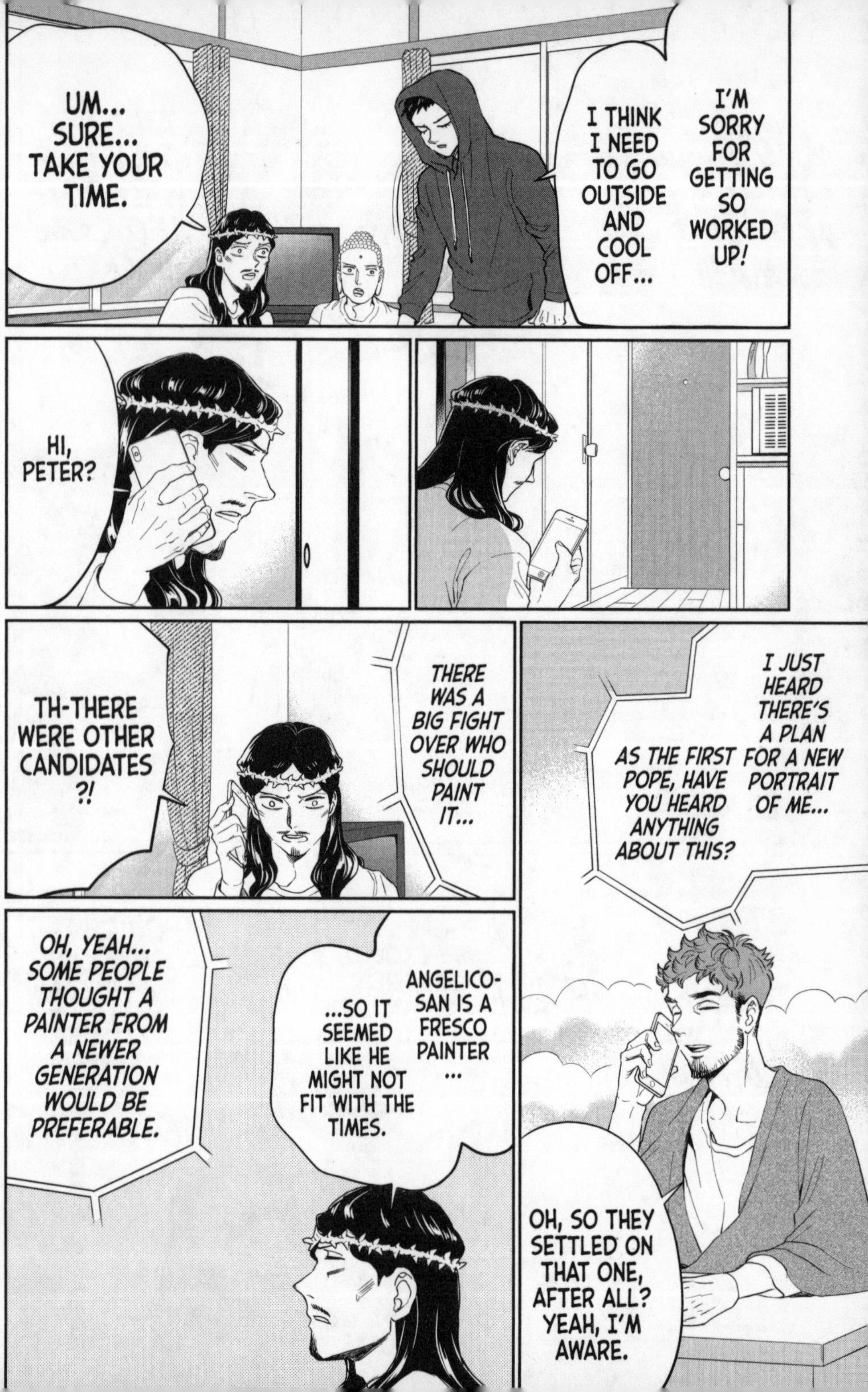
I'M SORRY FOR GETTING SO WORKED UP!
I THINK I NEED TO GO OUTSIDE AND COOL OFF...
UM... SURE... TAKE YOUR TIME.
HI, PETER?
I JUST HEARD THERE'S A PLAN FOR A NEW PORTRAIT OF ME...
AS THE FIRST POPE, HAVE YOU HEARD ANYTHING ABOUT THIS?
OH, SO THEY SETTLED ON THAT ONE, AFTER ALL? YEAH, I'M AWARE.
THERE WAS A BIG FIGHT OVER WHO SHOULD PAINT IT...
TH-THERE WERE OTHER CANDIDATES ?!
ANGELICO-SAN IS A FRESCO PAINTER ...
...SO IT SEEMED LIKE HE MIGHT NOT FIT WITH THE TIMES.
OH, YEAH... SOME PEOPLE THOUGHT A PAINTER FROM A NEWER GENERATION WOULD BE PREFERABLE.

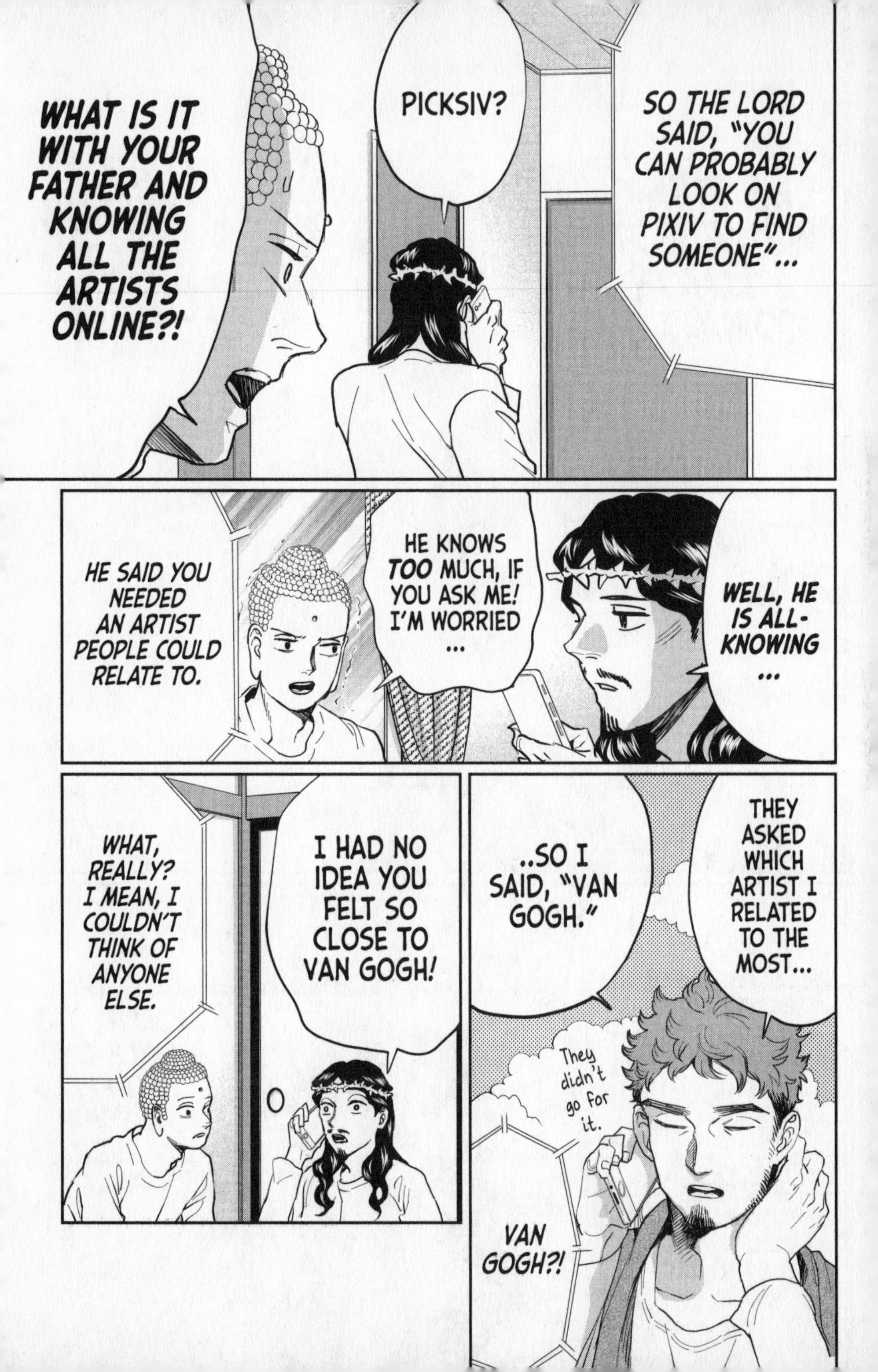
SO THE LORD SAID, "YOU CAN PROBABLY LOOK ON PIXIV TO FIND SOMEONE"...
PICKSIV?
WHAT IS IT WITH YOUR FATHER AND KNOWING ALL THE ARTISTS ONLINE?!
WELL, HE IS ALL-KNOWING ...
HE KNOWS TOO MUCH, IF YOU ASK ME! I'M WORRIED ...
HE SAID YOU NEEDED AN ARTIST PEOPLE COULD RELATE TO.
THEY ASKED WHICH ARTIST I RELATED TO THE MOST...
..SO I SAID, "VAN GOGH."
They didn't go for it.
VAN GOGH?!
I HAD NO IDEA YOU FELT SO CLOSE TO VAN GOGH!
WHAT, REALLY? I MEAN, I COULDN'T THINK OF ANYONE ELSE.

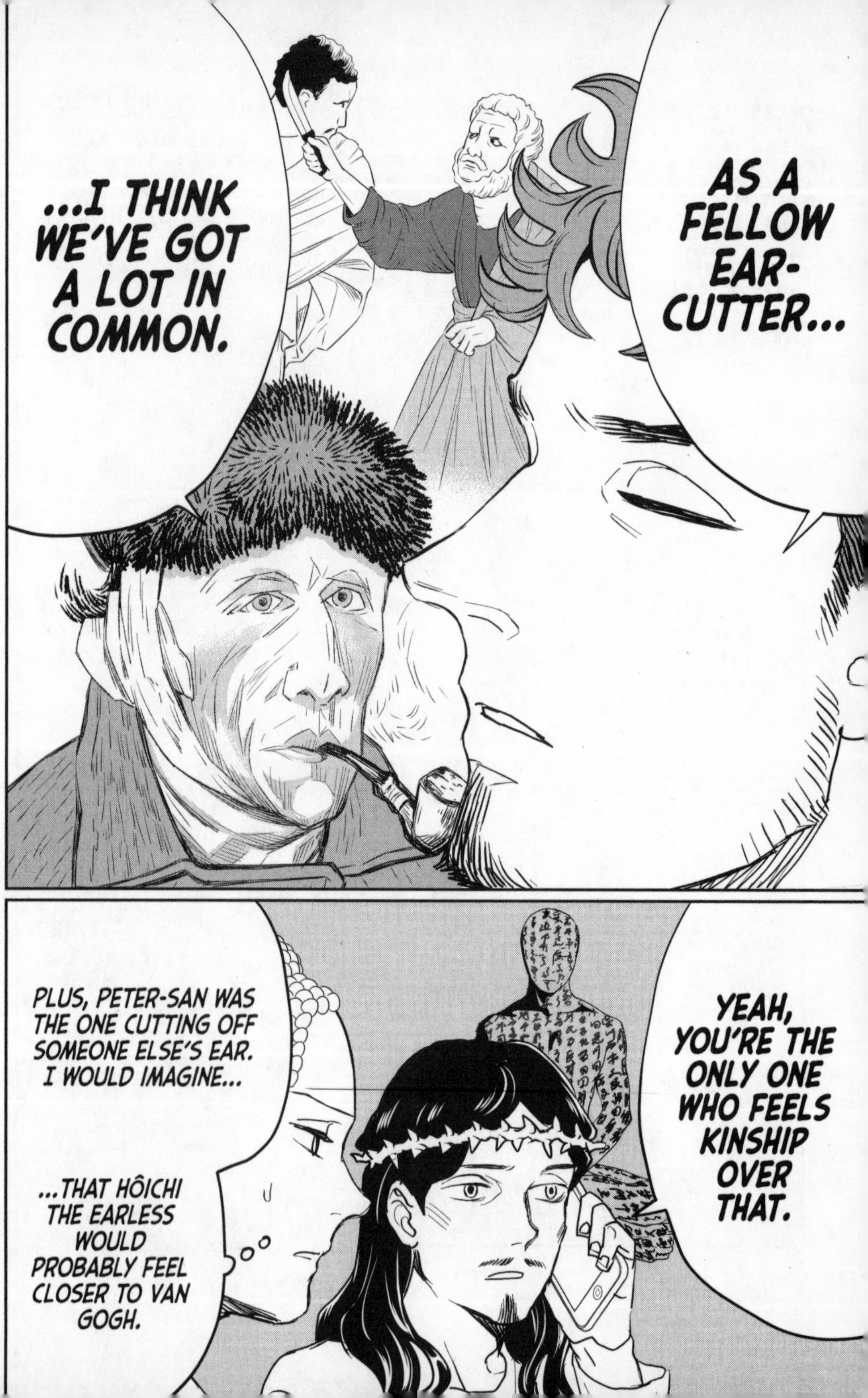
AS A FELLOW EAR-CUTTER...
...I THINK WE'VE GOT A LOT IN COMMON.
YEAH, YOU'RE THE ONLY ONE WHO FEELS KINSHIP OVER THAT.
PLUS, PETER-SAN WAS THE ONE CUTTING OFF SOMEONE ELSE'S EAR. I WOULD IMAGINE...
...THAT HÔICHI THE EARLESS WOULD PROBABLY FEEL CLOSER TO VAN GOGH.

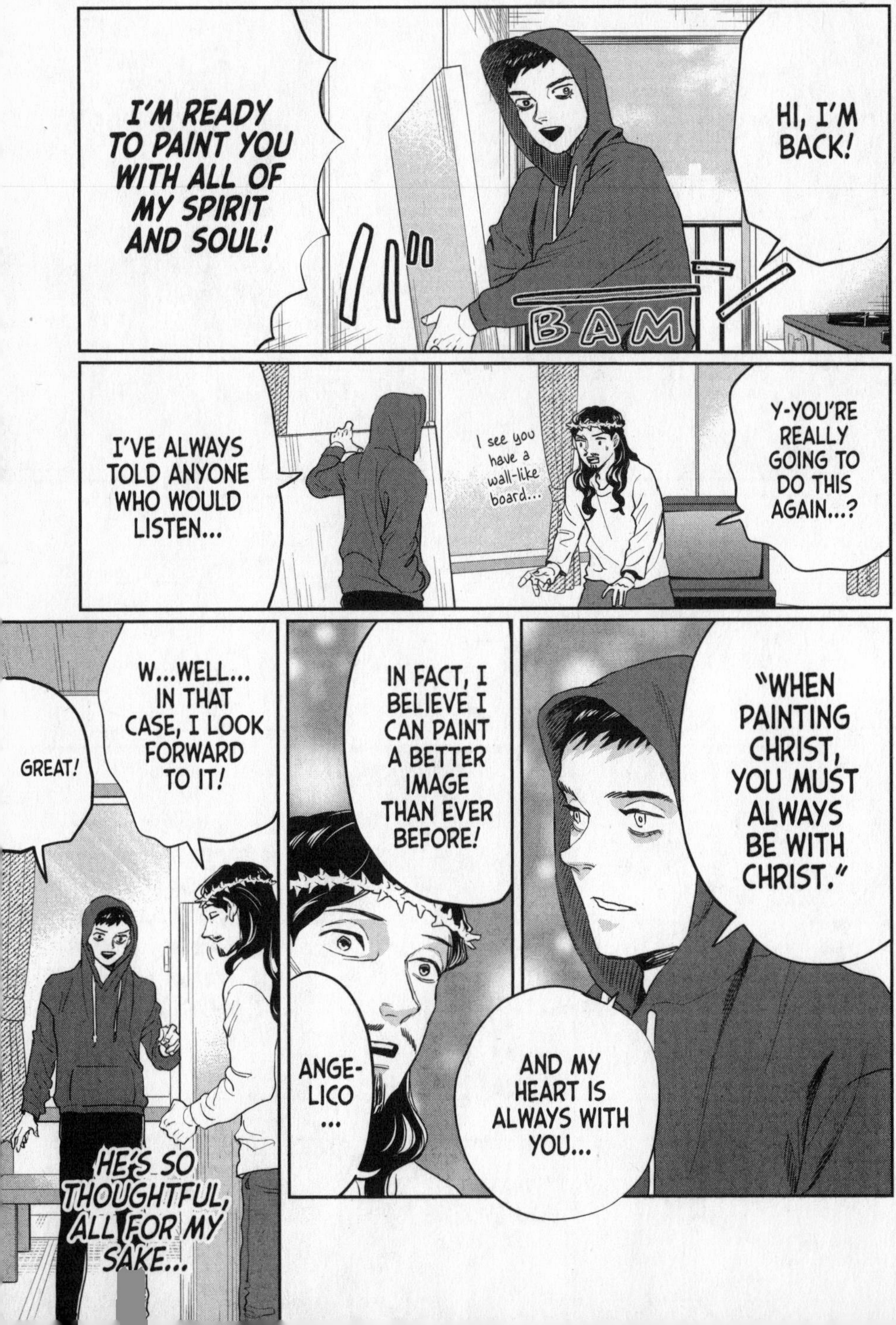

HI, I'M BACK!
BAM
I'M READY TO PAINT YOU WITH ALL OF MY SPIRIT AND SOUL!
Y-YOU'RE REALLY GOING TO DO THIS AGAIN...?
I see you have a wall-like board...
I'VE ALWAYS TOLD ANYONE WHO WOULD LISTEN...
"WHEN PAINTING CHRIST, YOU MUST ALWAYS BE WITH CHRIST."
AND MY HEART IS ALWAYS WITH YOU...
IN FACT, I BELIEVE I CAN PAINT A BETTER IMAGE THAN EVER BEFORE!
ANGE-LICO ...
W...WELL... IN THAT CASE, I LOOK FORWARD TO IT!
GREAT!
HE'S SO THOUGHTFUL, ALL FOR MY SAKE...

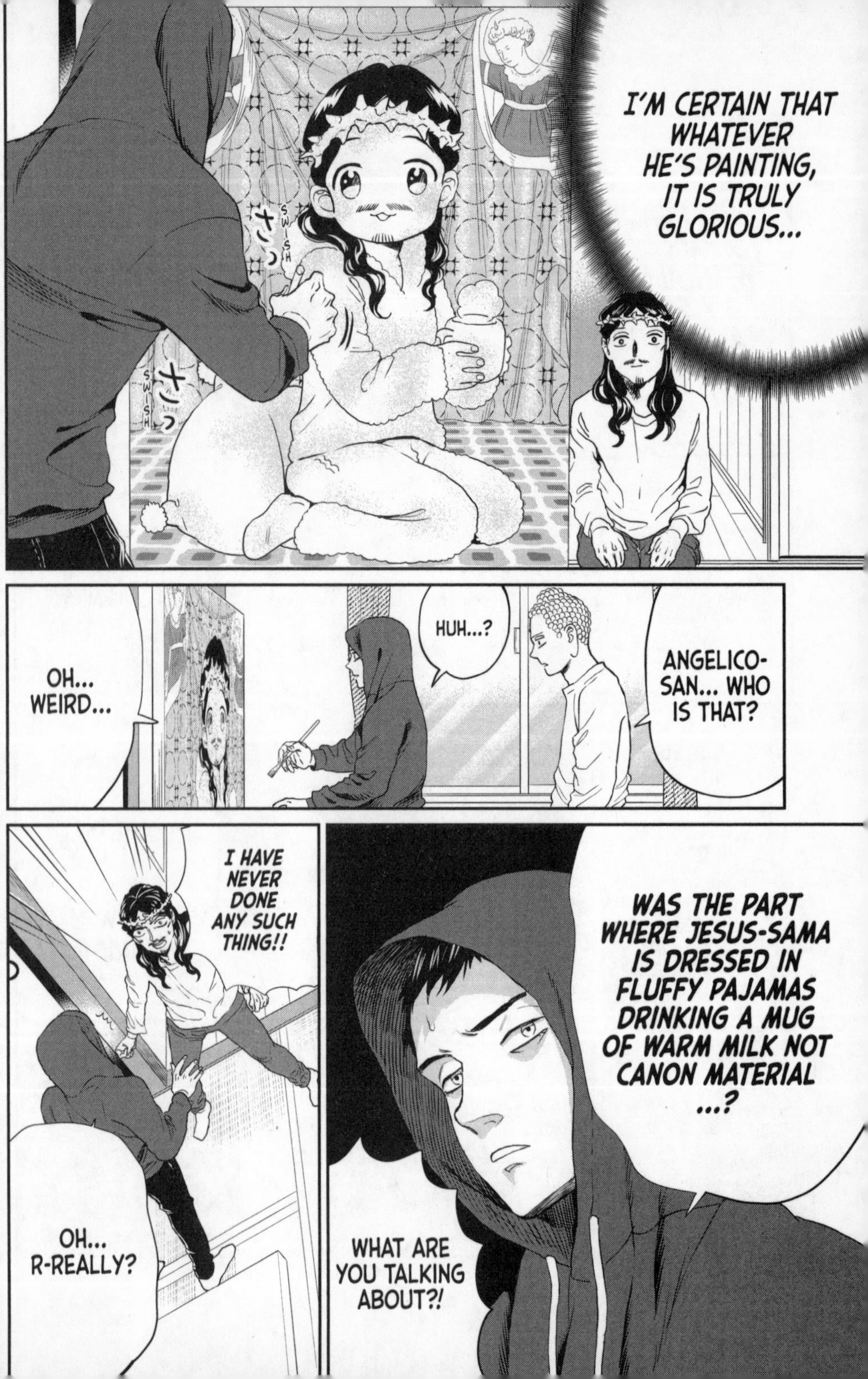
I'M CERTAIN THAT WHATEVER HE'S PAINTING, IT IS TRULY GLORIOUS...
SWISH
SWISH
ANGELICO-SAN... WHO IS THAT?
HUH...?
OH... WEIRD...
WAS THE PART WHERE JESUS-SAMA IS DRESSED IN FLUFFY PAJAMAS DRINKING A MUG OF WARM MILK NOT CANON MATERIAL ...?
WHAT ARE YOU TALKING ABOUT?!
I HAVE NEVER DONE ANY SUCH THING!!
OH... R-REALLY?

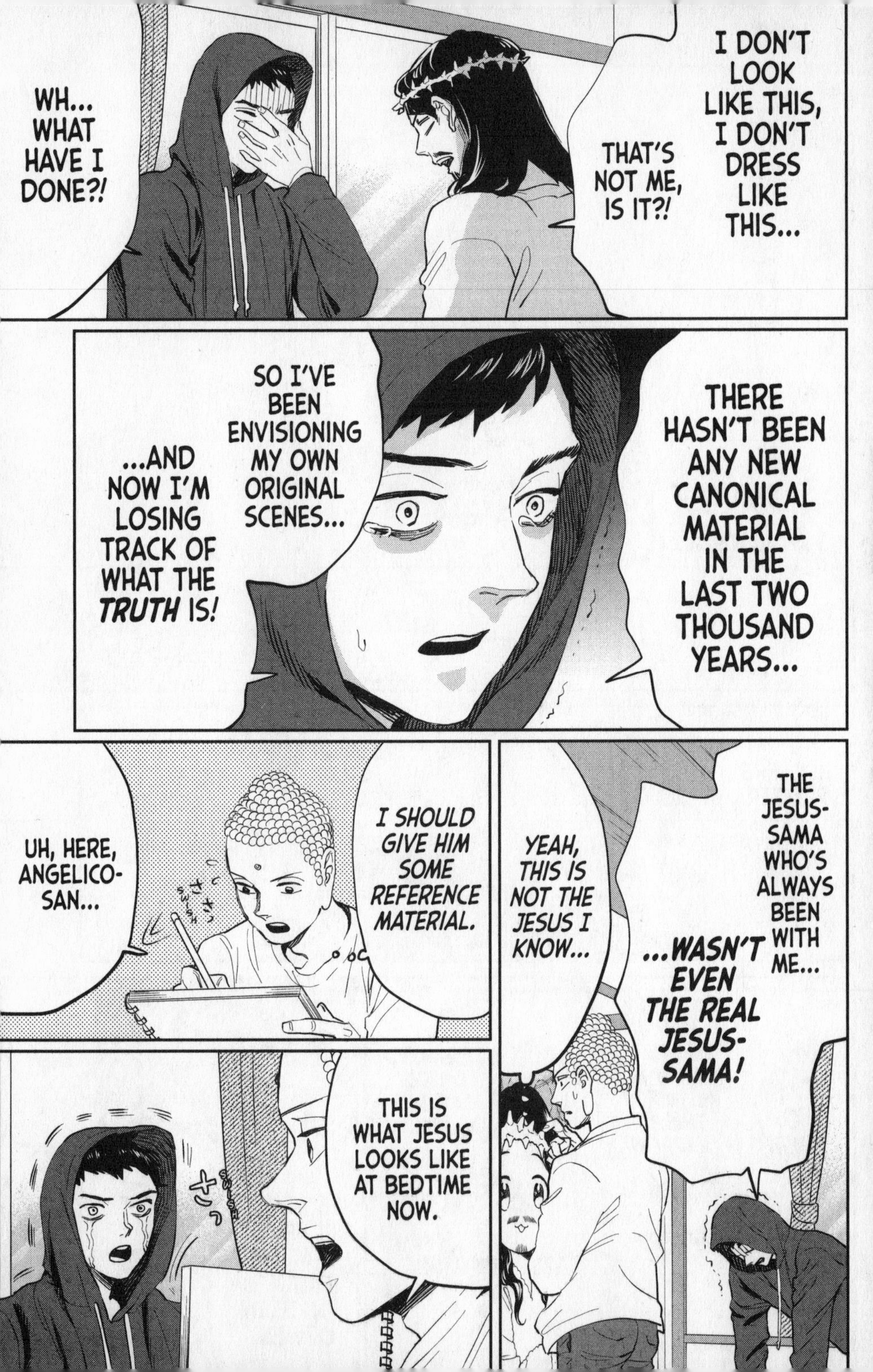
I DON'T LOOK LIKE THIS, I DON'T DRESS LIKE THIS...
THAT'S NOT ME, IS IT?!
WH... WHAT HAVE I DONE?!
THERE HASN'T BEEN ANY NEW CANONICAL MATERIAL IN THE LAST TWO THOUSAND YEARS...
SO I'VE BEEN ENVISIONING MY OWN ORIGINAL SCENES...
...AND NOW I'M LOSING TRACK OF WHAT THE *TRUTH* IS!
THE JESUS-SAMA WHO'S ALWAYS BEEN WITH ME...
...WASN'T EVEN THE REAL JESUS-SAMA!
YEAH, THIS IS NOT THE JESUS I KNOW...
I SHOULD GIVE HIM SOME REFERENCE MATERIAL.
UH, HERE, ANGELICO-SAN...
THIS IS WHAT JESUS LOOKS LIKE AT BEDTIME NOW.

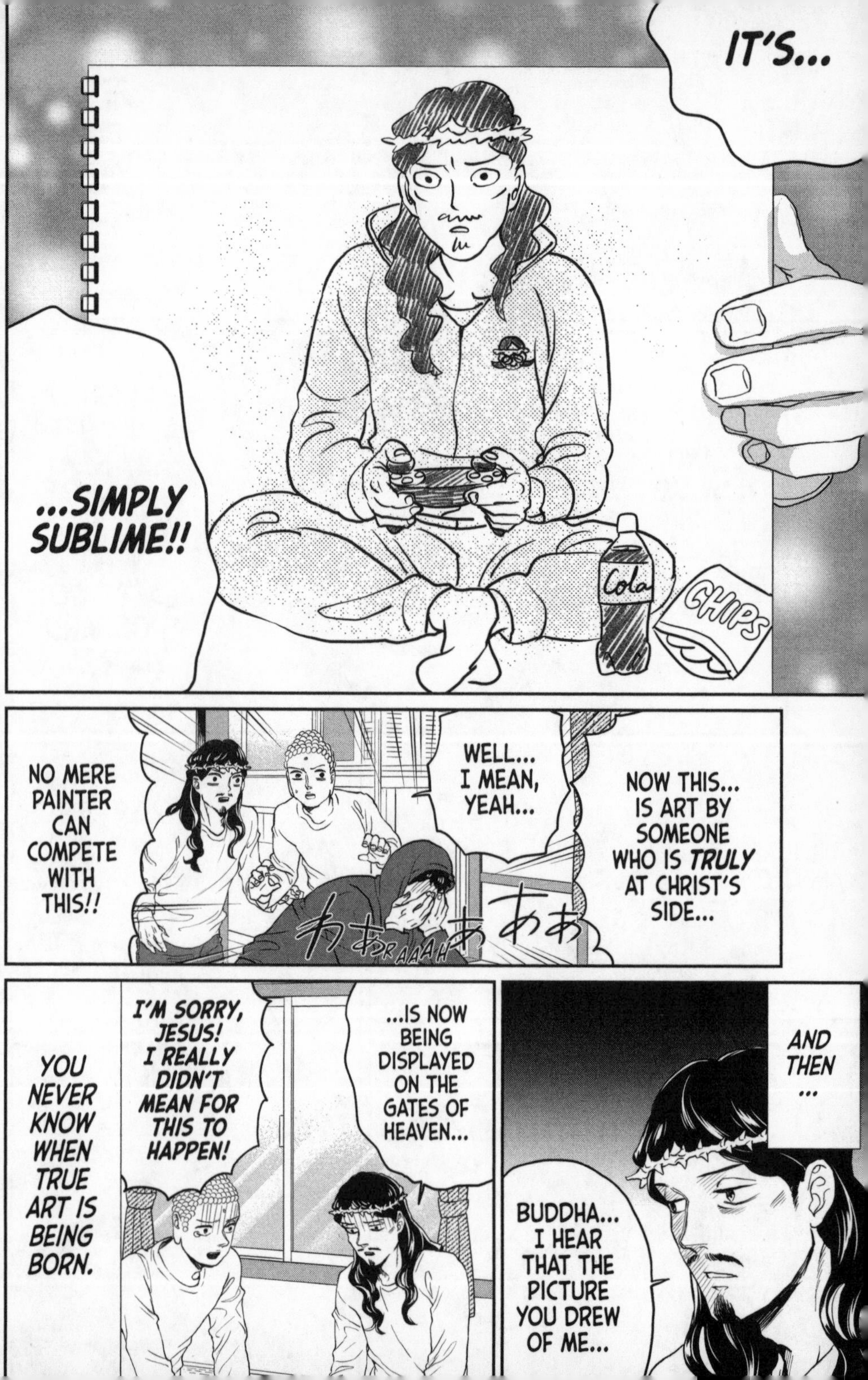
IT'S...
...SIMPLY SUBLIME!!
Cola
CHIPS
NOW THIS... IS ART BY SOMEONE WHO IS *TRULY* AT CHRIST'S SIDE...
WELL... I MEAN, YEAH...
NO MERE PAINTER CAN COMPETE WITH THIS!!
ああ RAAAAH あああ
AND THEN ...
BUDDHA... I HEAR THAT THE PICTURE YOU DREW OF ME...
...IS NOW BEING DISPLAYED ON THE GATES OF HEAVEN...
I'M SORRY, JESUS! I REALLY DIDN'T MEAN FOR THIS TO HAPPEN!
YOU NEVER KNOW WHEN TRUE ART IS BEING BORN.

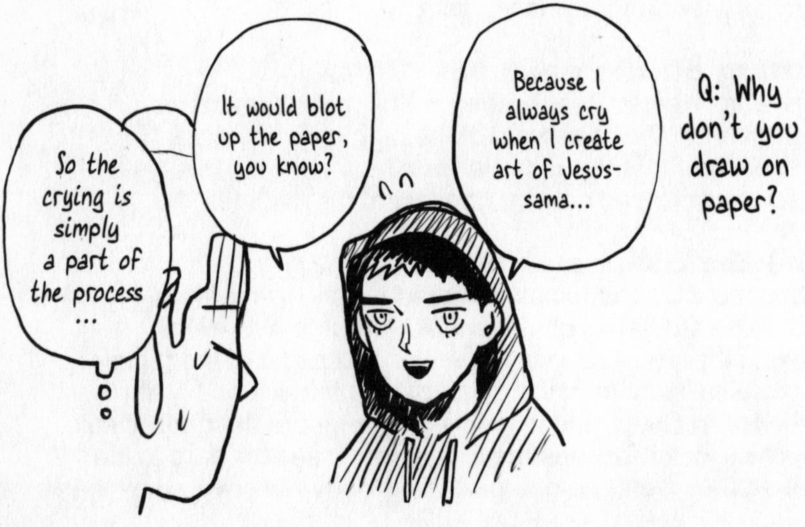
Q: Why don't you draw on paper?
Because I always cry when I create art of Jesus-sama...
It would blot up the paper, you know?
So the crying is simply a part of the process ...

CHAPTER 127 TRANSLATION NOTES

Fra Angelico, page 94

An Italian friar from the 14th and 15th centuries who was renowned for the many frescoes he painted, especially on his own friary in Florence. His most frequent subjects were the Annunciation (when Gabriel came to tell the Virgin Mary she was pregnant) and the Last Judgment of mankind.

Onion Squad, page 95

The name of a bodyguard squad for the title character of the long-running shoujo comedy manga *Patalliro!* They are described as extremely handsome, and must wear an identical disguise of molded hair, glasses, and a large, diamond-shaped mouth.

Pixiv, page 105

A Japanese website for uploading personal art. It is used widely, especially by amateur and *dôjinshi* artists.

Peter cutting off the ear, page 106

When Jesus was arrested, the Gospels mention that one of his disciples cut the ear off of a servant of the high priest of Israel. in John, it is mentioned that this disciple was Peter. In Luke, it says that Jesus healed the wounded servant, the last of his miracles.

Hôichi the Earless, page 106

A folklore tale about a blind minstrel named Hôichi. When he is approached by a samurai--a ghost, unbeknownst to him--Hôichi ends up playing his biwa lute in a cemetery. The priest of the temple decides to protect Hôichi from the ghost by painting his body with the kanji from the Heart Sutra, and instructs him to ignore the ghost's call. When it returns, Hôichi survives the ordeal, but loses his ears to the ghost, because they were the one part of his body not covered by the sutra kanji.

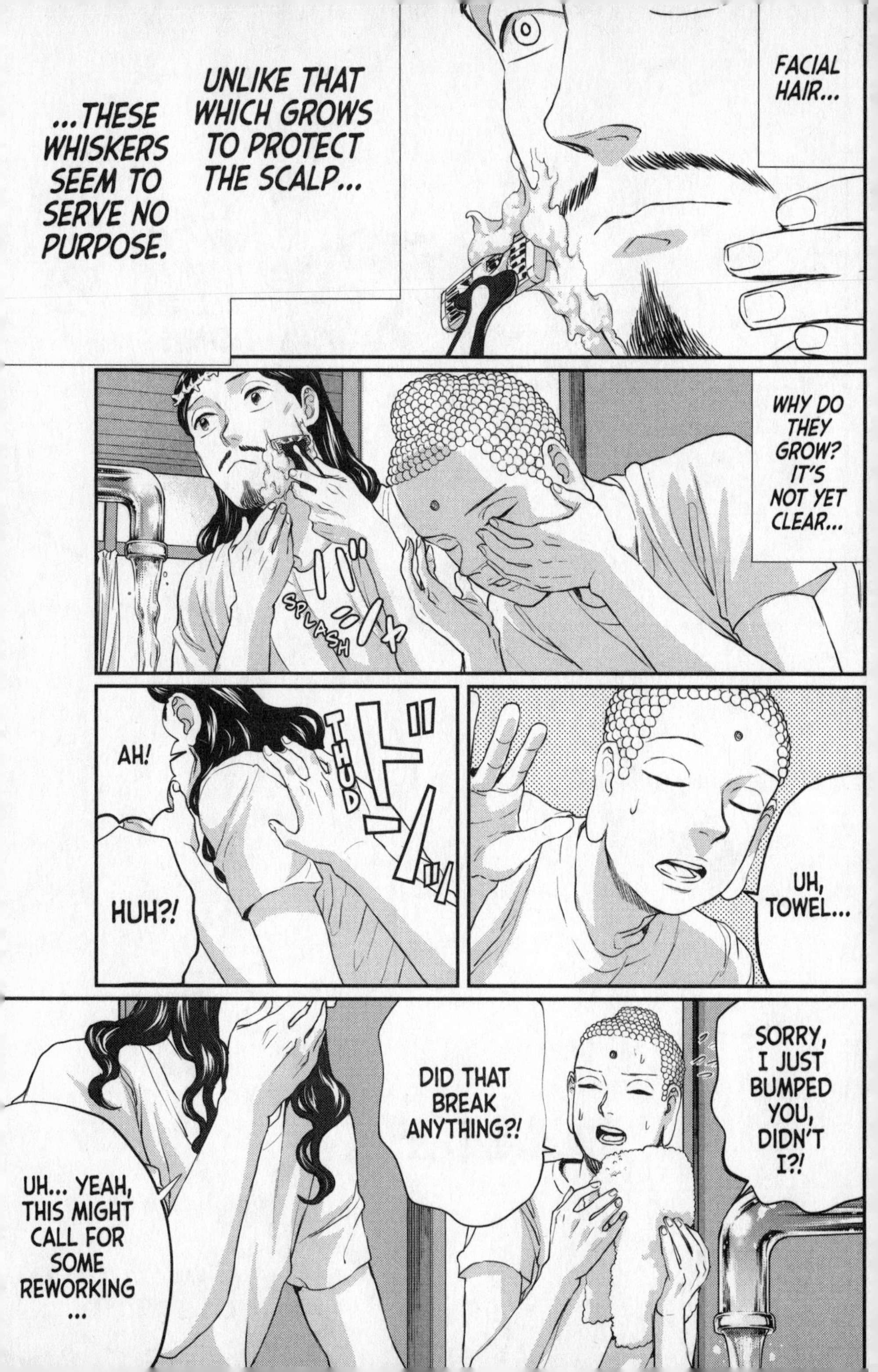
FACIAL HAIR...
UNLIKE THAT WHICH GROWS TO PROTECT THE SCALP...
...THESE WHISKERS SEEM TO SERVE NO PURPOSE.
WHY DO THEY GROW? IT'S NOT YET CLEAR...
SPLASH
UH, TOWEL...
THUD
AH!
HUH?!
SORRY, I JUST BUMPED YOU, DIDN'T I?!
DID THAT BREAK ANYTHING?!
UH... YEAH, THIS MIGHT CALL FOR SOME REWORKING ...

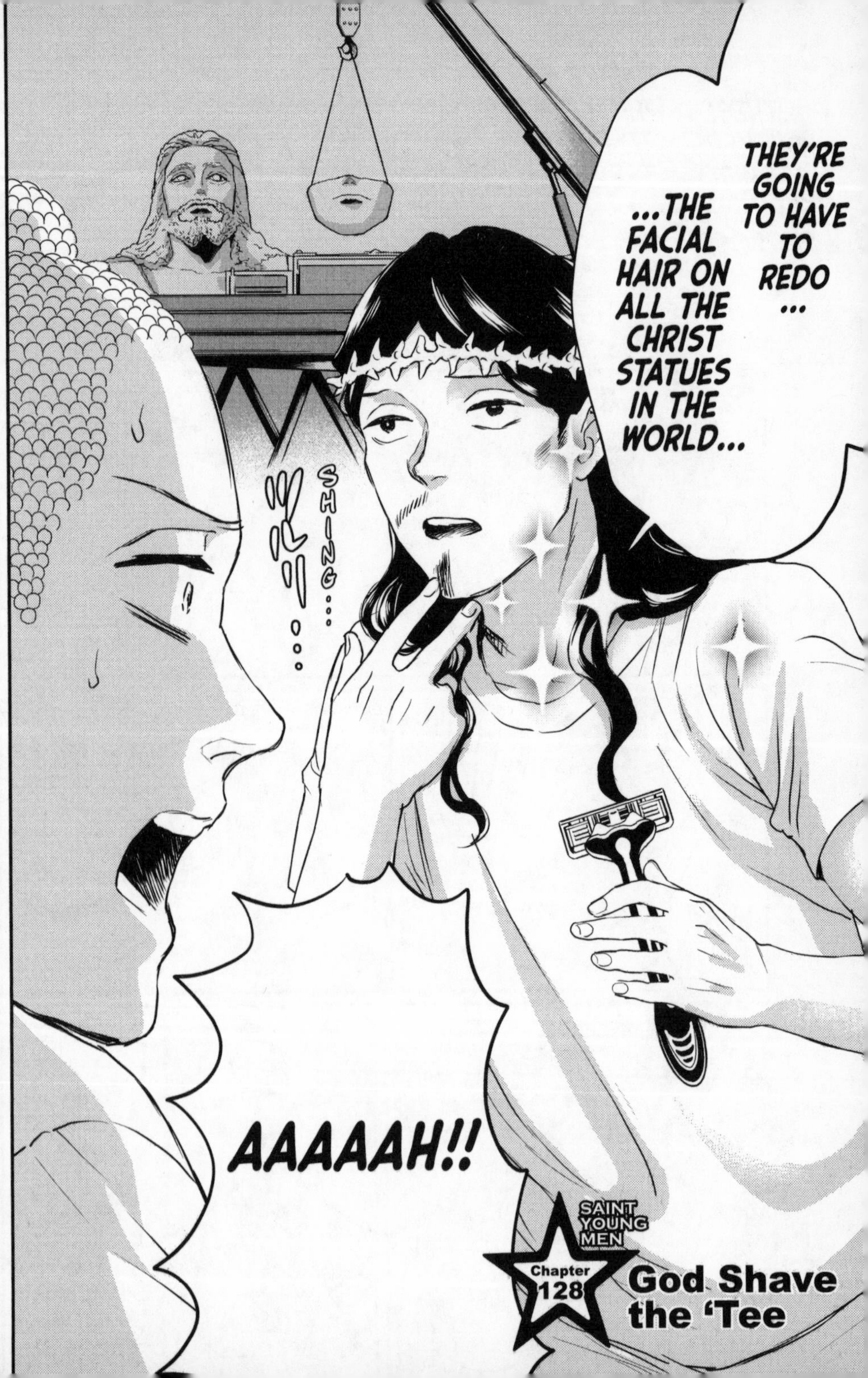

THEY'RE GOING TO HAVE TO REDO... ...THE FACIAL HAIR ON ALL THE CHRIST STATUES IN THE WORLD...
SHING...
AAAAAH!!
SAINT YOUNG MEN
Chapter 128
God Shave the 'Tee

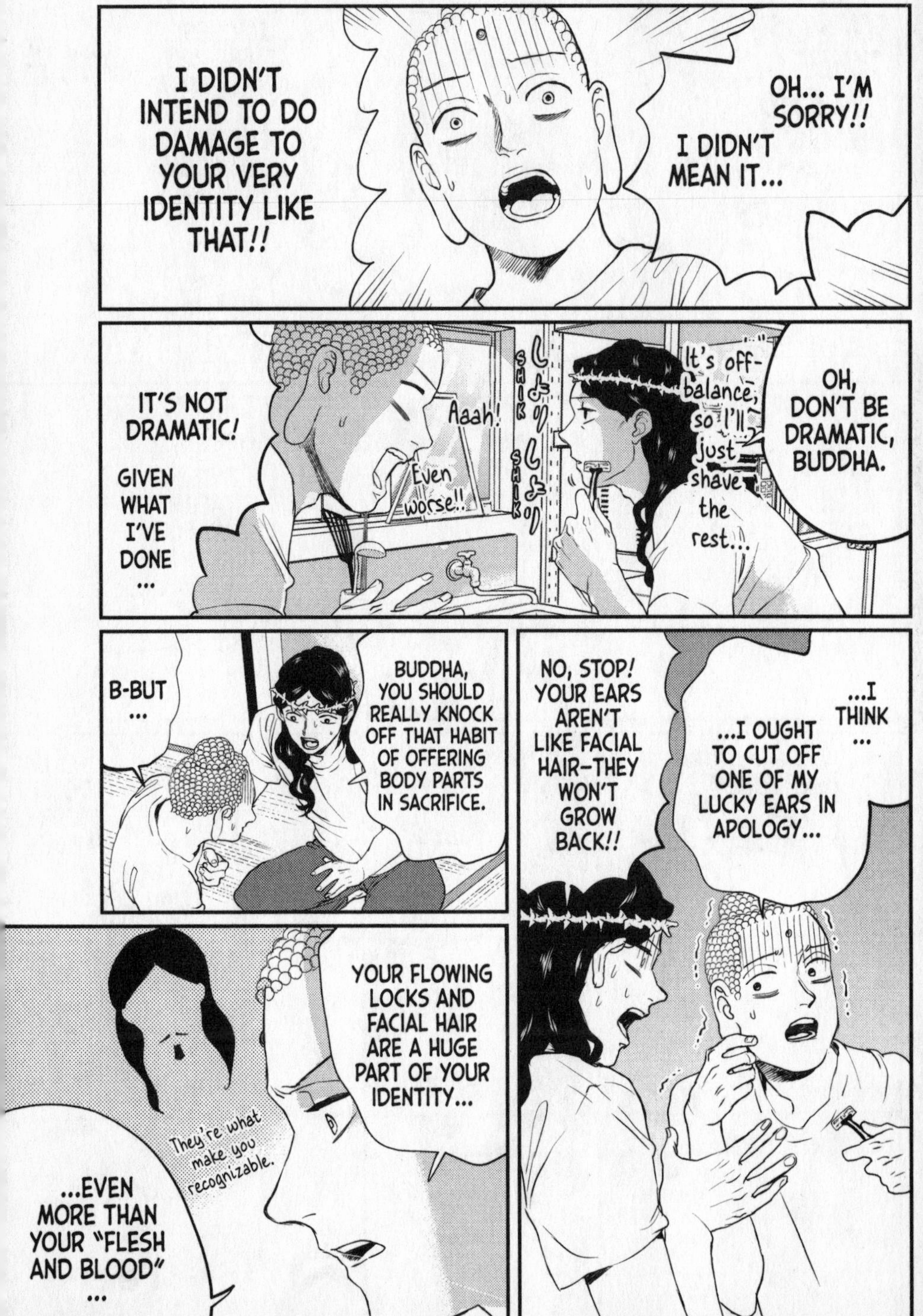
OH... I'M SORRY!!
I DIDN'T MEAN IT...
I DIDN'T INTEND TO DO DAMAGE TO YOUR VERY IDENTITY LIKE THAT!!
OH, DON'T BE DRAMATIC, BUDDHA.
...It's off-balance, so I'll just shave the rest...
SHIK
SHIK
Aaah!
Even worse!!
IT'S NOT DRAMATIC!
GIVEN WHAT I'VE DONE...
...I THINK...
...I OUGHT TO CUT OFF ONE OF MY LUCKY EARS IN APOLOGY...
NO, STOP! YOUR EARS AREN'T LIKE FACIAL HAIR—THEY WON'T GROW BACK!!
BUDDHA, YOU SHOULD REALLY KNOCK OFF THAT HABIT OF OFFERING BODY PARTS IN SACRIFICE.
B-BUT...
YOUR FLOWING LOCKS AND FACIAL HAIR ARE A HUGE PART OF YOUR IDENTITY...
They're what make you recognizable.
...EVEN MORE THAN YOUR "FLESH AND BLOOD"...

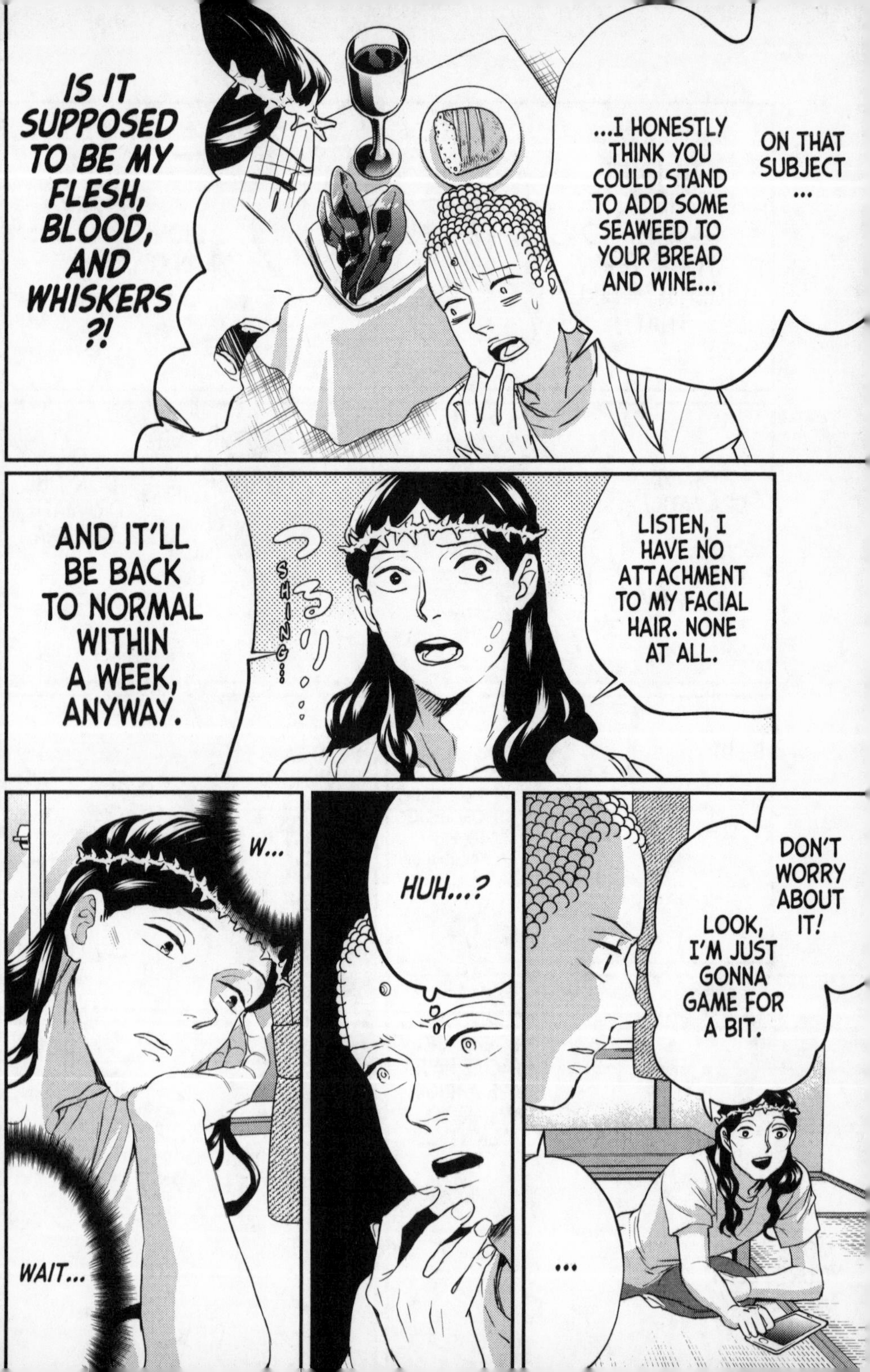
ON THAT SUBJECT...
...I HONESTLY THINK YOU COULD STAND TO ADD SOME SEAWEED TO YOUR BREAD AND WINE...
IS IT SUPPOSED TO BE MY FLESH, BLOOD, AND WHISKERS?!
LISTEN, I HAVE NO ATTACHMENT TO MY FACIAL HAIR. NONE AT ALL.
つるり
SHING...
AND IT'LL BE BACK TO NORMAL WITHIN A WEEK, ANYWAY.
DON'T WORRY ABOUT IT!
LOOK, I'M JUST GONNA GAME FOR A BIT.
...
HUH...?
W...
WAIT...

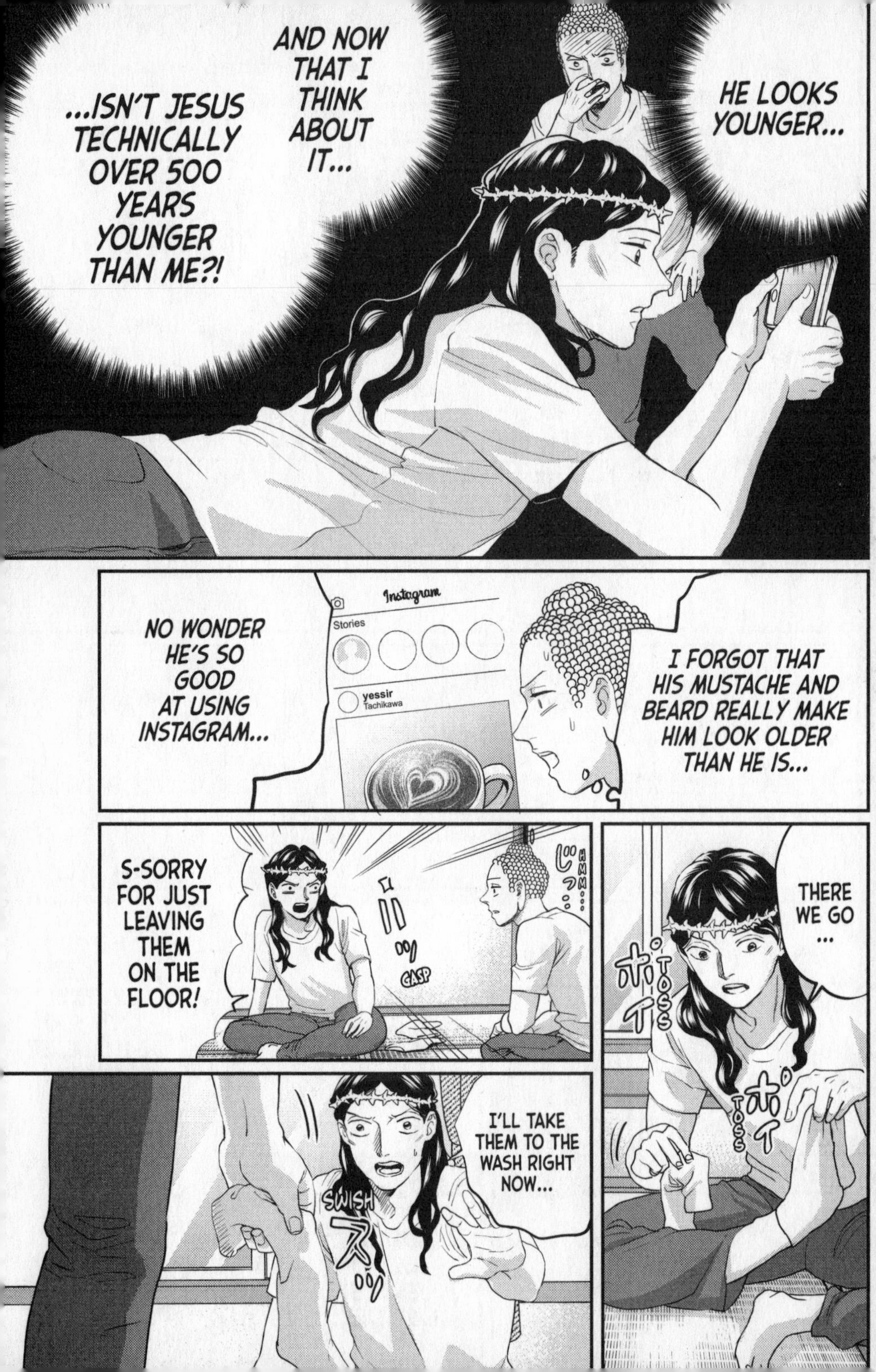
HE LOOKS YOUNGER...
AND NOW THAT I THINK ABOUT IT...
...ISN'T JESUS TECHNICALLY OVER 500 YEARS YOUNGER THAN ME?!
I FORGOT THAT HIS MUSTACHE AND BEARD REALLY MAKE HIM LOOK OLDER THAN HE IS...
Instagram
Stories
yessir
Tachikawa
NO WONDER HE'S SO GOOD AT USING INSTAGRAM...
THERE WE GO ...
ホイ TOSS
ホイ TOSS
じっ… HMMM...
GASP
S-SORRY FOR JUST LEAVING THEM ON THE FLOOR!
I'LL TAKE THEM TO THE WASH RIGHT NOW...
ス SWISH

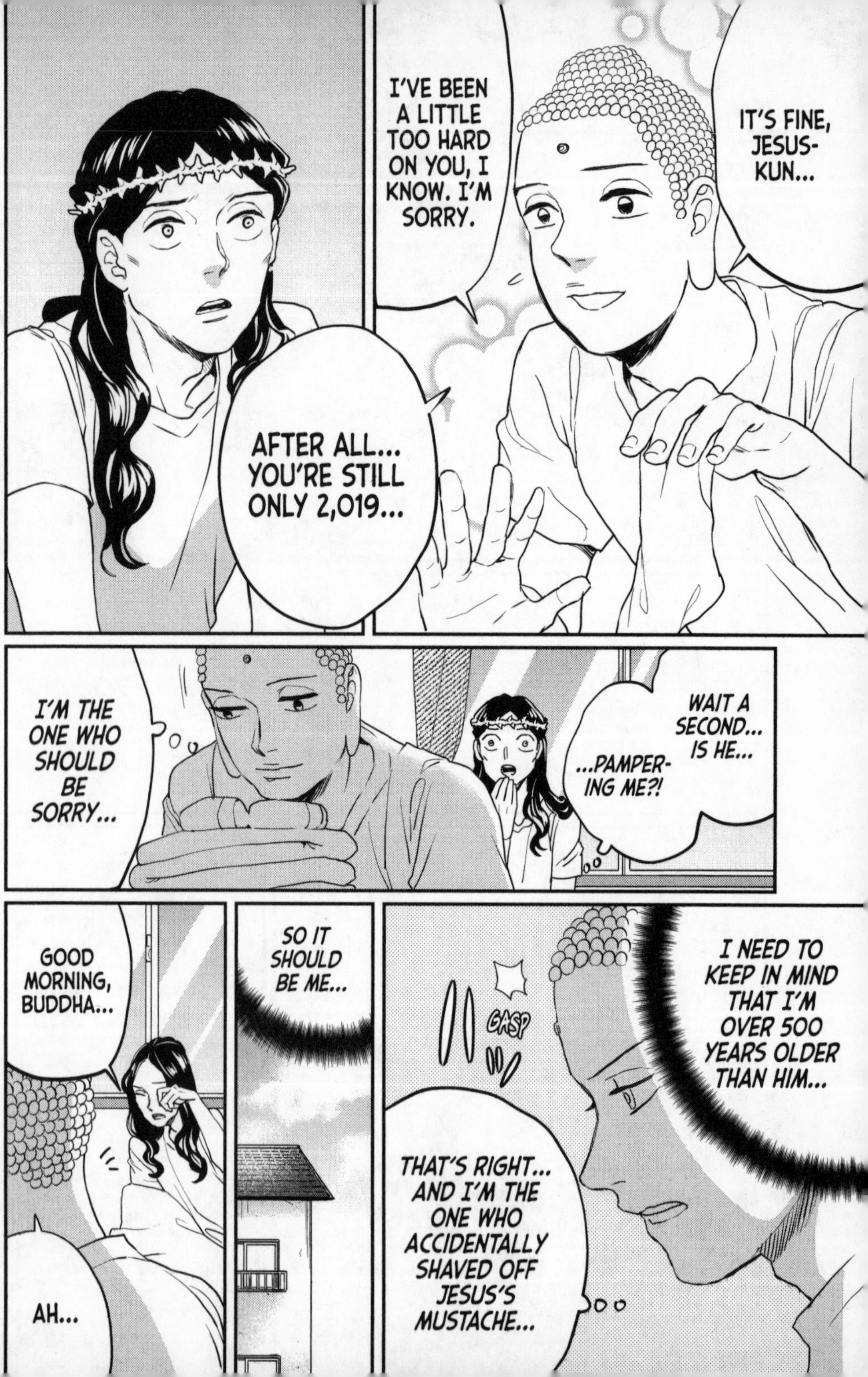
IT'S FINE, JESUS-KUN...
I'VE BEEN A LITTLE TOO HARD ON YOU, I KNOW. I'M SORRY.
AFTER ALL... YOU'RE STILL ONLY 2,019...
WAIT A SECOND... IS HE...
...PAMPER-ING ME?!
I'M THE ONE WHO SHOULD BE SORRY...
I NEED TO KEEP IN MIND THAT I'M OVER 500 YEARS OLDER THAN HIM...
GASP
THAT'S RIGHT... AND I'M THE ONE WHO ACCIDENTALLY SHAVED OFF JESUS'S MUSTACHE...
SO IT SHOULD BE ME...
GOOD MORNING, BUDDHA...
AH...

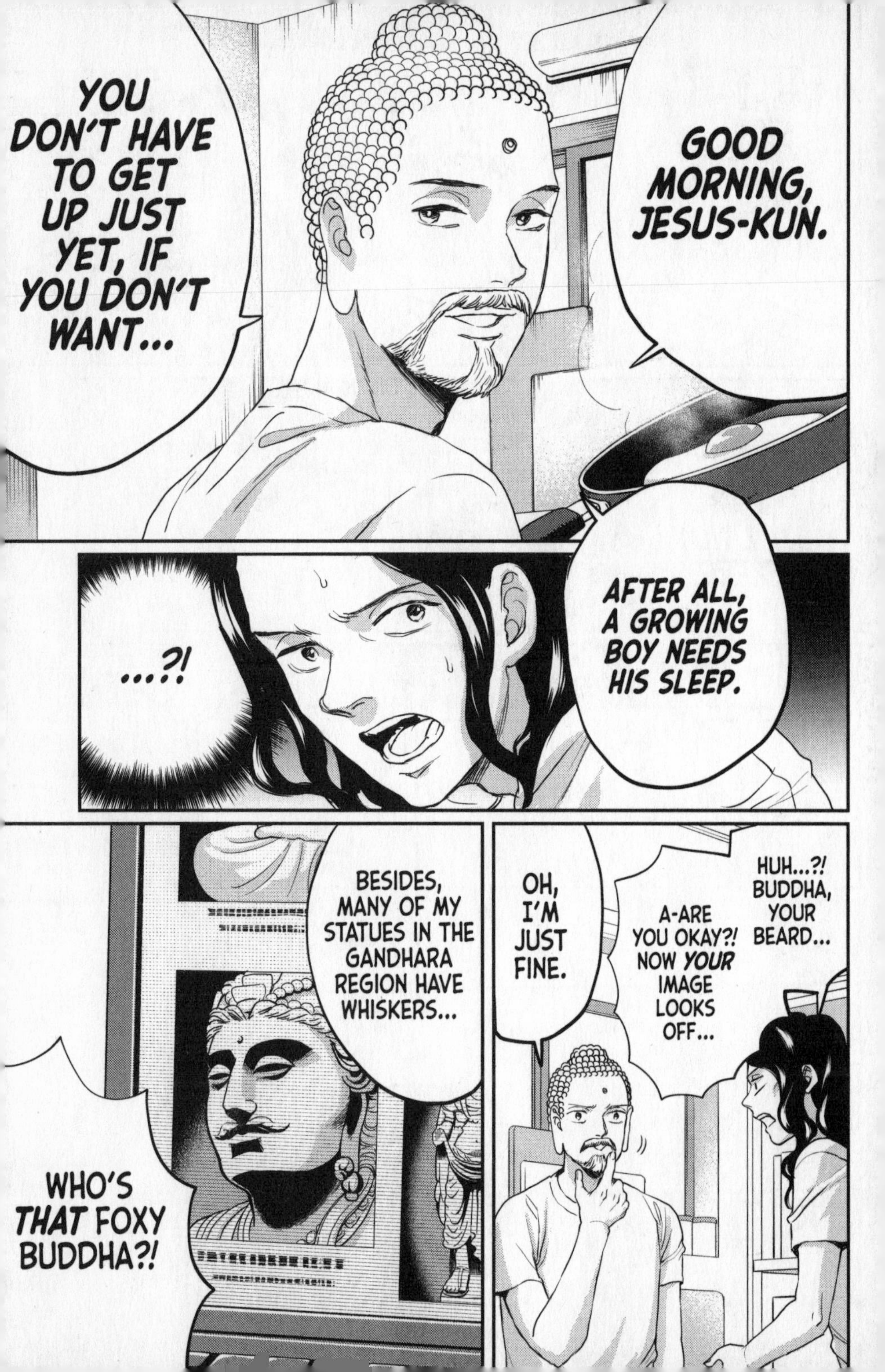
GOOD MORNING, JESUS-KUN.
YOU DON'T HAVE TO GET UP JUST YET, IF YOU DON'T WANT...
AFTER ALL, A GROWING BOY NEEDS HIS SLEEP.
...?!
HUH...?! BUDDHA, YOUR BEARD...
A-ARE YOU OKAY?! NOW *YOUR* IMAGE LOOKS OFF...
OH, I'M JUST FINE.
BESIDES, MANY OF MY STATUES IN THE GANDHARA REGION HAVE WHISKERS...
WHO'S *THAT* FOXY BUDDHA?!

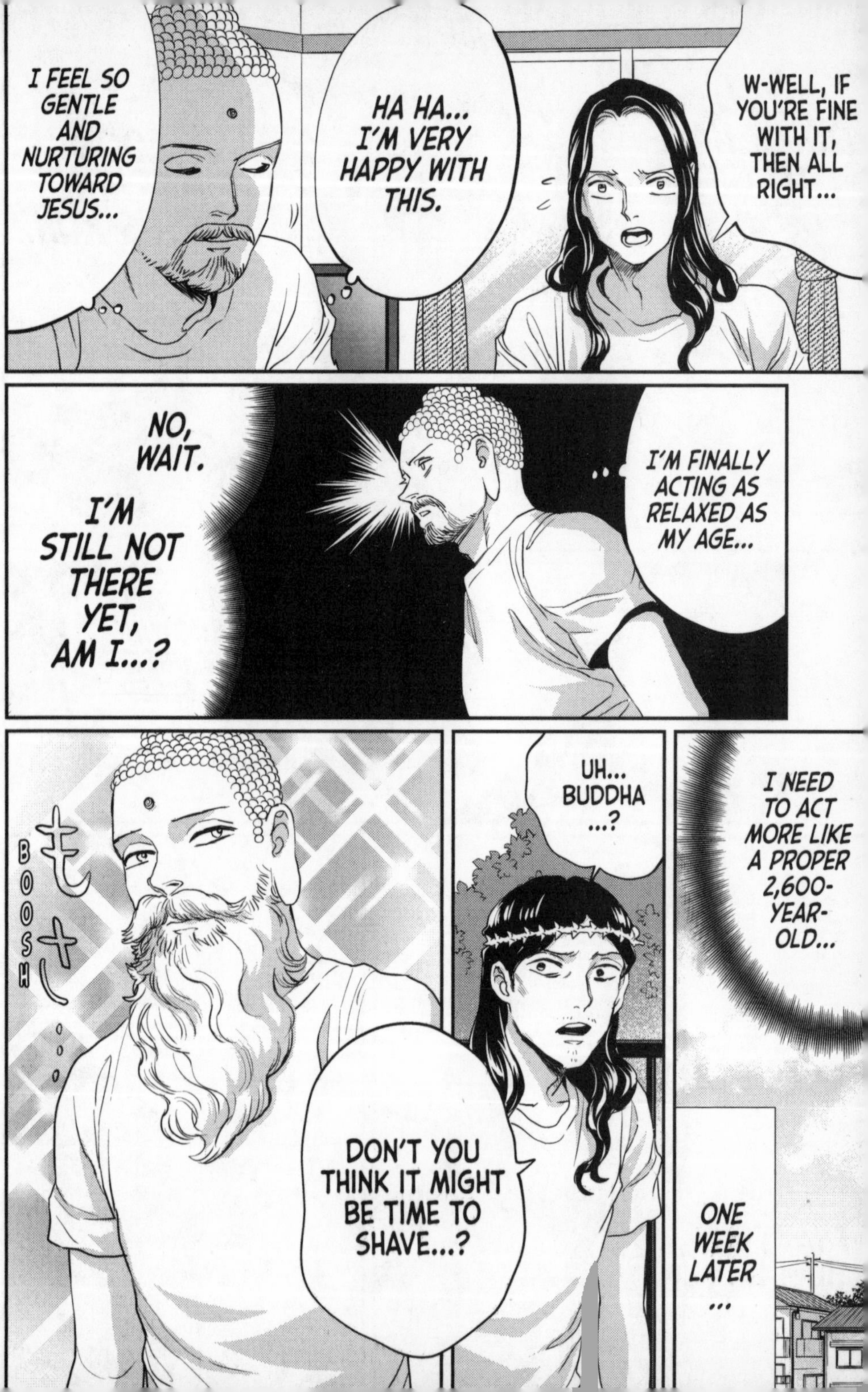
W-WELL, IF YOU'RE FINE WITH IT, THEN ALL RIGHT...
HA HA... I'M VERY HAPPY WITH THIS.
I FEEL SO GENTLE AND NURTURING TOWARD JESUS...
I'M FINALLY ACTING AS RELAXED AS MY AGE...
NO, WAIT.
I'M STILL NOT THERE YET, AM I...?
I NEED TO ACT MORE LIKE A PROPER 2,600-YEAR-OLD...
ONE WEEK LATER ...
UH... BUDDHA ...?
BOOSH
DON'T YOU THINK IT MIGHT BE TIME TO SHAVE...?

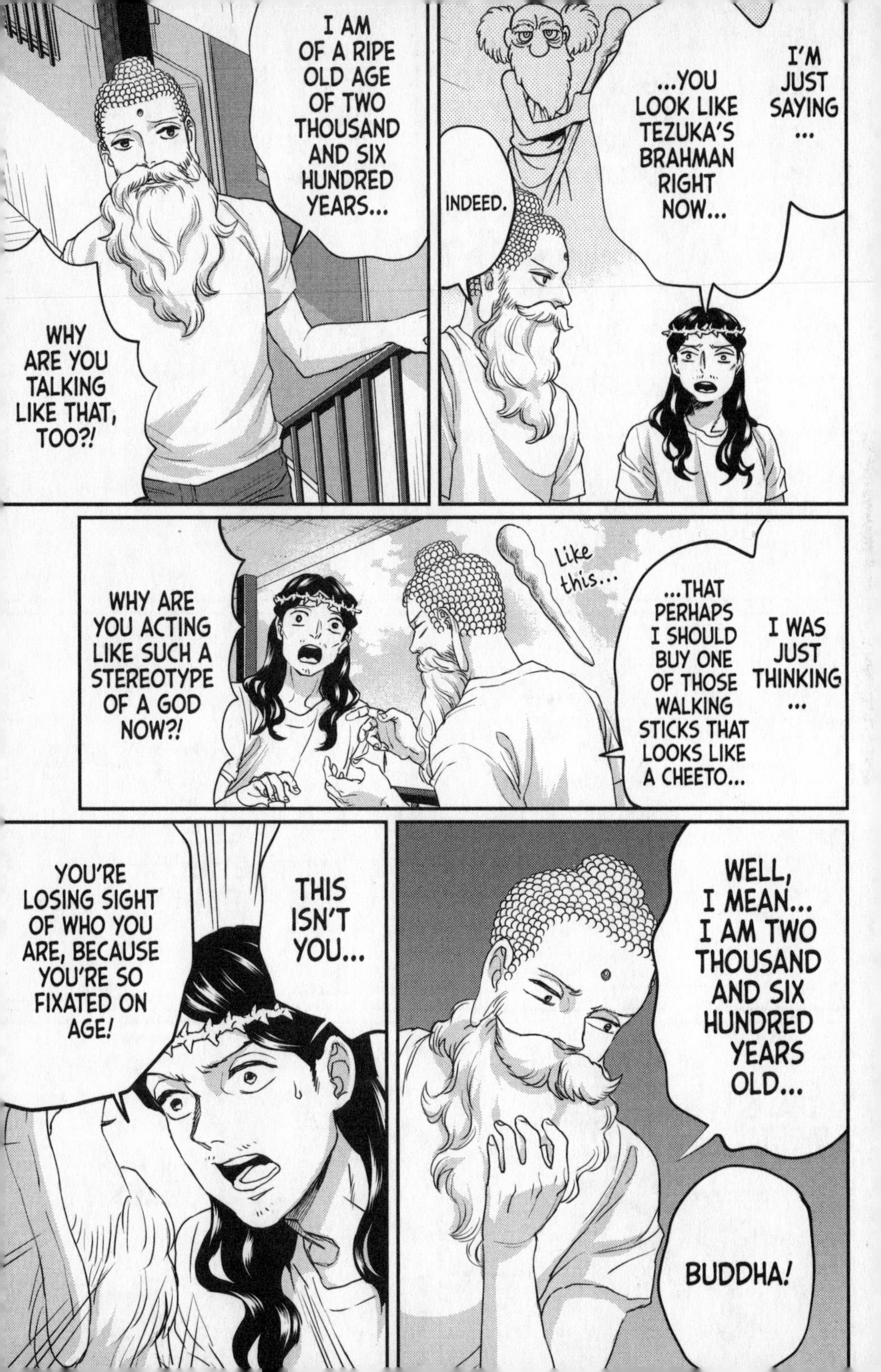
I'M JUST SAYING ...
...YOU LOOK LIKE TEZUKA'S BRAHMAN RIGHT NOW...
INDEED.
I AM OF A RIPE OLD AGE OF TWO THOUSAND AND SIX HUNDRED YEARS...
WHY ARE YOU TALKING LIKE THAT, TOO?!
I WAS JUST THINKING ...
...THAT PERHAPS I SHOULD BUY ONE OF THOSE WALKING STICKS THAT LOOKS LIKE A CHEETO...
Like this...
WHY ARE YOU ACTING LIKE SUCH A STEREOTYPE OF A GOD NOW?!
WELL, I MEAN... I AM TWO THOUSAND AND SIX HUNDRED YEARS OLD...
BUDDHA!
THIS ISN'T YOU...
YOU'RE LOSING SIGHT OF WHO YOU ARE, BECAUSE YOU'RE SO FIXATED ON AGE!

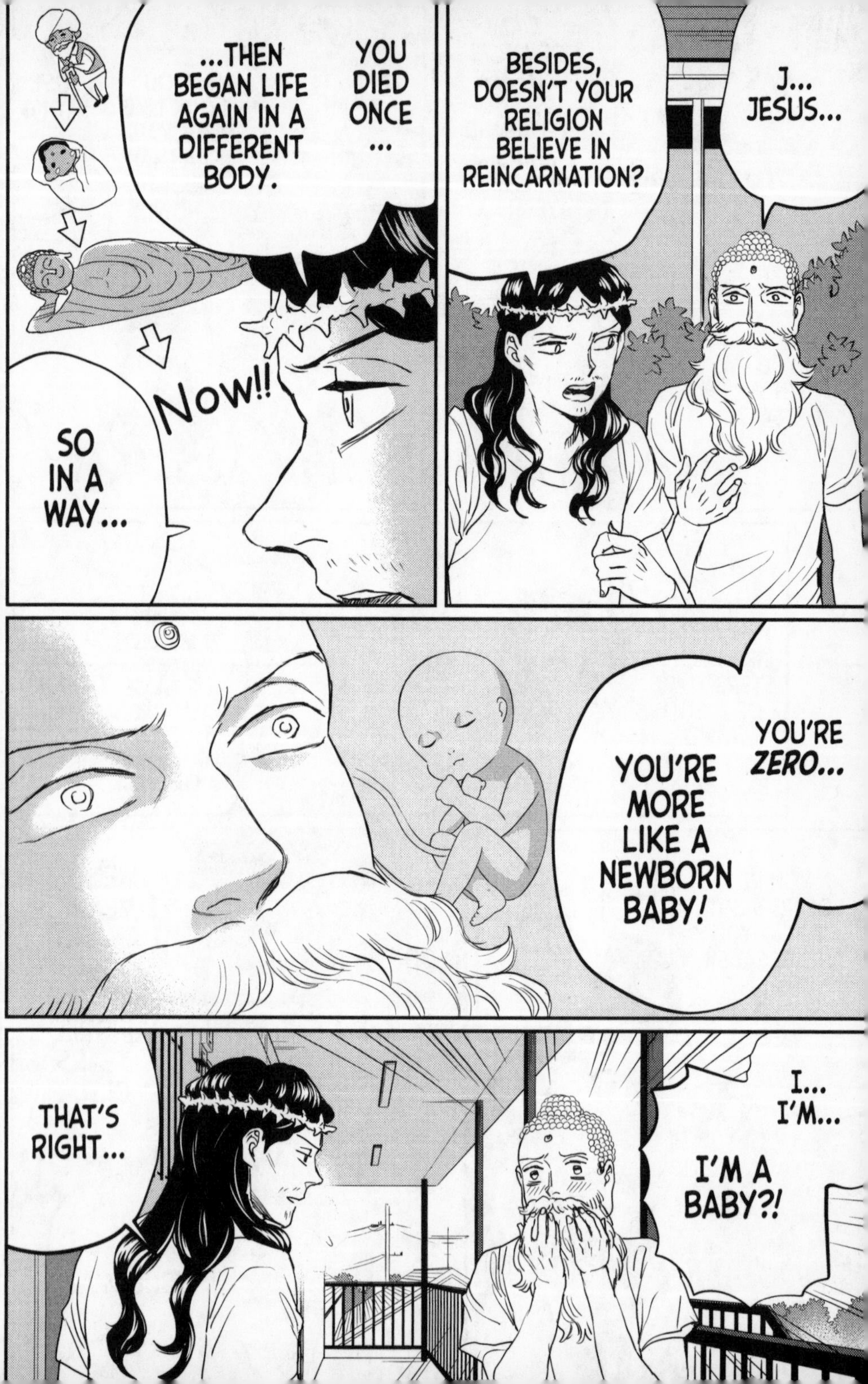
J... JESUS...
BESIDES, DOESN'T YOUR RELIGION BELIEVE IN REINCARNATION?
YOU DIED ONCE ...
...THEN BEGAN LIFE AGAIN IN A DIFFERENT BODY.
NOW!!
SO IN A WAY...
YOU'RE ZERO...
YOU'RE MORE LIKE A NEWBORN BABY!
I... I'M...
I'M A BABY?!
THAT'S RIGHT...

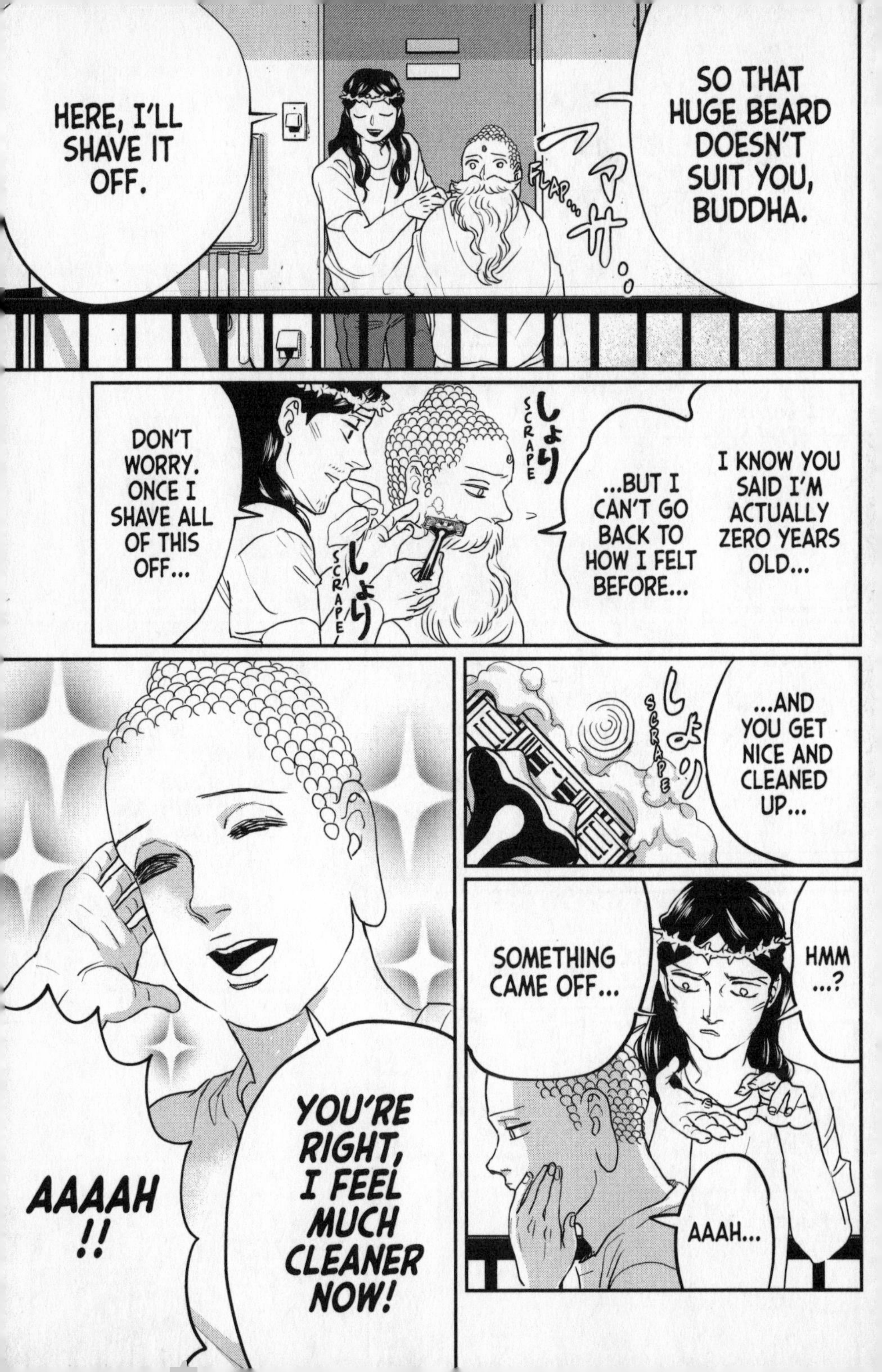
SO THAT HUGE BEARD DOESN'T SUIT YOU, BUDDHA.
ファサ
FLAP...
HERE, I'LL SHAVE IT OFF.
I KNOW YOU SAID I'M ACTUALLY ZERO YEARS OLD...
...BUT I CAN'T GO BACK TO HOW I FELT BEFORE...
しょり
SCRAPE
DON'T WORRY. ONCE I SHAVE ALL OF THIS OFF...
しょり
SCRAPE
...AND YOU GET NICE AND CLEANED UP...
しょり
SCRAPE
HMM ...?
SOMETHING CAME OFF...
AAAH...
YOU'RE RIGHT, I FEEL MUCH CLEANER NOW!
AAAAH !!

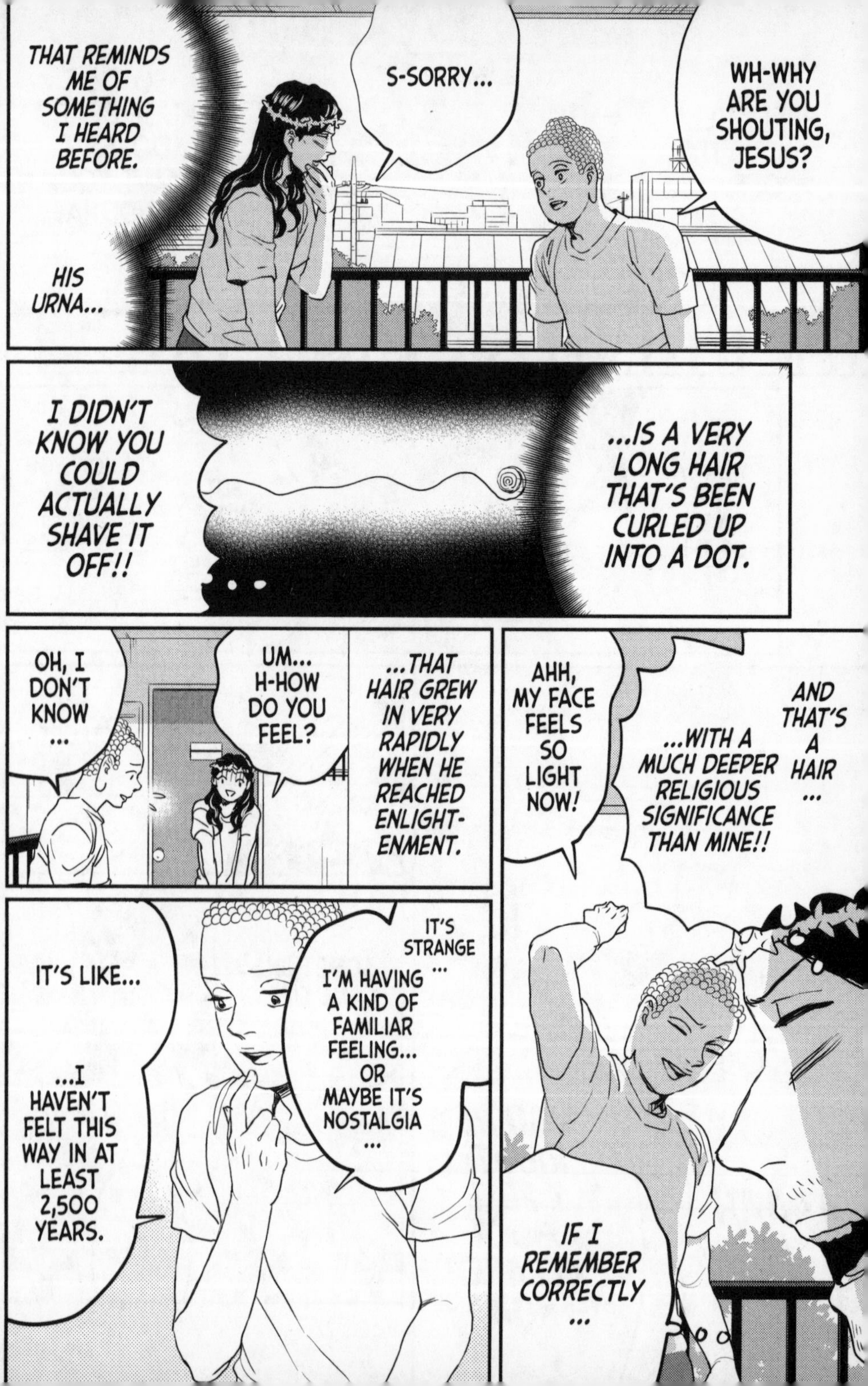
WH-WHY ARE YOU SHOUTING, JESUS?
S-SORRY...
THAT REMINDS ME OF SOMETHING I HEARD BEFORE.
HIS URNA...
...IS A VERY LONG HAIR THAT'S BEEN CURLED UP INTO A DOT.
I DIDN'T KNOW YOU COULD ACTUALLY SHAVE IT OFF!!
...
AND THAT'S A HAIR...
...WITH A MUCH DEEPER RELIGIOUS SIGNIFICANCE THAN MINE!!
AHH, MY FACE FEELS SO LIGHT NOW!
IF I REMEMBER CORRECTLY...
...THAT HAIR GREW IN VERY RAPIDLY WHEN HE REACHED ENLIGHTENMENT.
UM... H-HOW DO YOU FEEL?
OH, I DON'T KNOW...
IT'S STRANGE...
I'M HAVING A KIND OF FAMILIAR FEELING... OR MAYBE IT'S NOSTALGIA...
IT'S LIKE...
...I HAVEN'T FELT THIS WAY IN AT LEAST 2,500 YEARS.

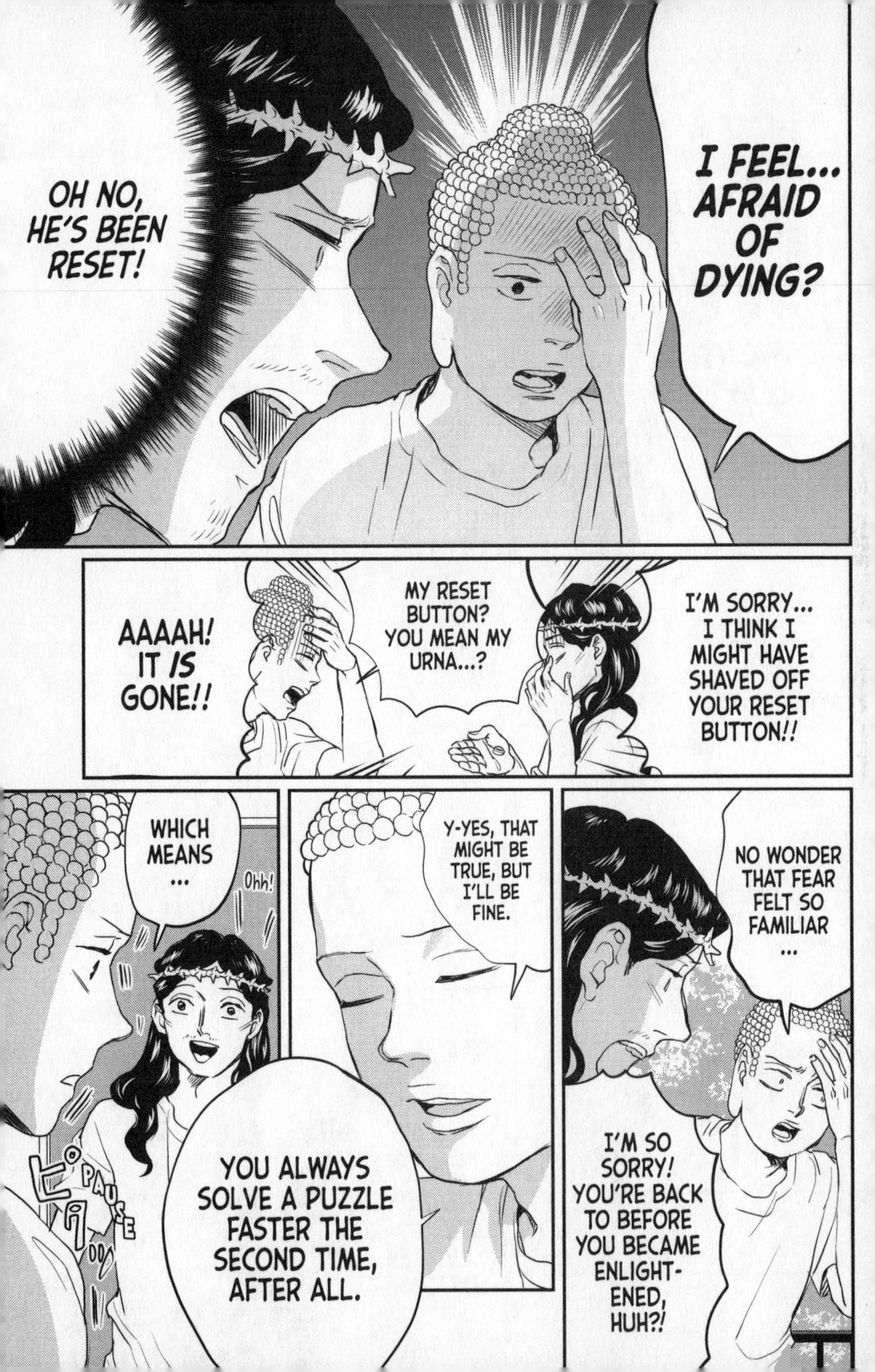
I FEEL... AFRAID OF DYING?
OH NO, HE'S BEEN RESET!
I'M SORRY... I THINK I MIGHT HAVE SHAVED OFF YOUR RESET BUTTON!!
MY RESET BUTTON? YOU MEAN MY URNA...?
AAAAH! IT *IS* GONE!!
NO WONDER THAT FEAR FELT SO FAMILIAR ...
I'M SO SORRY! YOU'RE BACK TO BEFORE YOU BECAME ENLIGHT-ENED, HUH?!
Y-YES, THAT MIGHT BE TRUE, BUT I'LL BE FINE.
YOU ALWAYS SOLVE A PUZZLE FASTER THE SECOND TIME, AFTER ALL.
WHICH MEANS ...
Ohh!
PAUSE

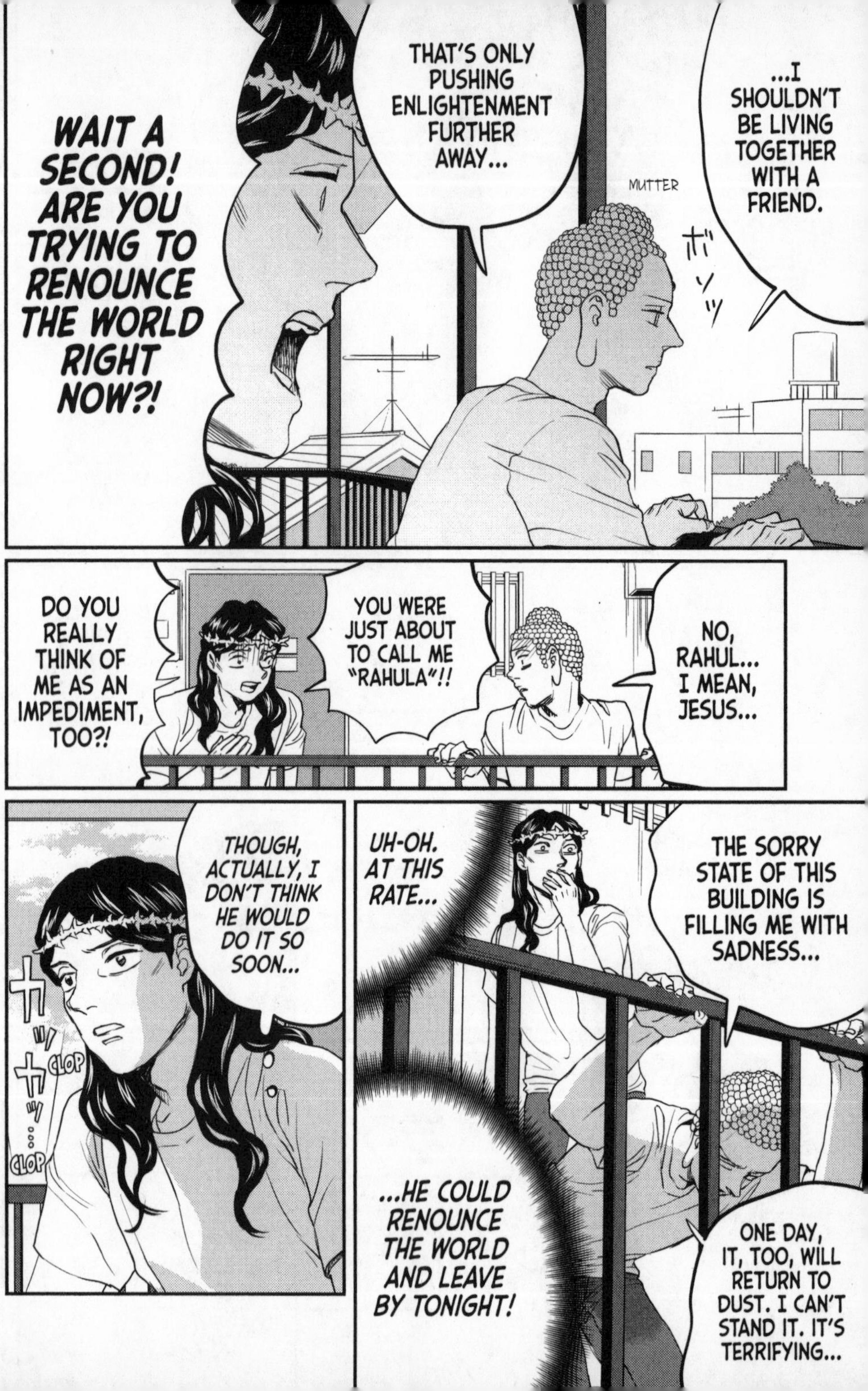
...I SHOULDN'T BE LIVING TOGETHER WITH A FRIEND.
MUTTER
ボソッ
THAT'S ONLY PUSHING ENLIGHTENMENT FURTHER AWAY...
WAIT A SECOND! ARE YOU TRYING TO RENOUNCE THE WORLD RIGHT NOW?!
NO, RAHUL... I MEAN, JESUS...
YOU WERE JUST ABOUT TO CALL ME "RAHULA"!!
DO YOU REALLY THINK OF ME AS AN IMPEDIMENT, TOO?!
THE SORRY STATE OF THIS BUILDING IS FILLING ME WITH SADNESS...
UH-OH. AT THIS RATE...
ONE DAY, IT, TOO, WILL RETURN TO DUST. I CAN'T STAND IT. IT'S TERRIFYING...
...HE COULD RENOUNCE THE WORLD AND LEAVE BY TONIGHT!
THOUGH, ACTUALLY, I DON'T THINK HE WOULD DO IT SO SOON...
カッ
CLOP
カッ...
CLOP

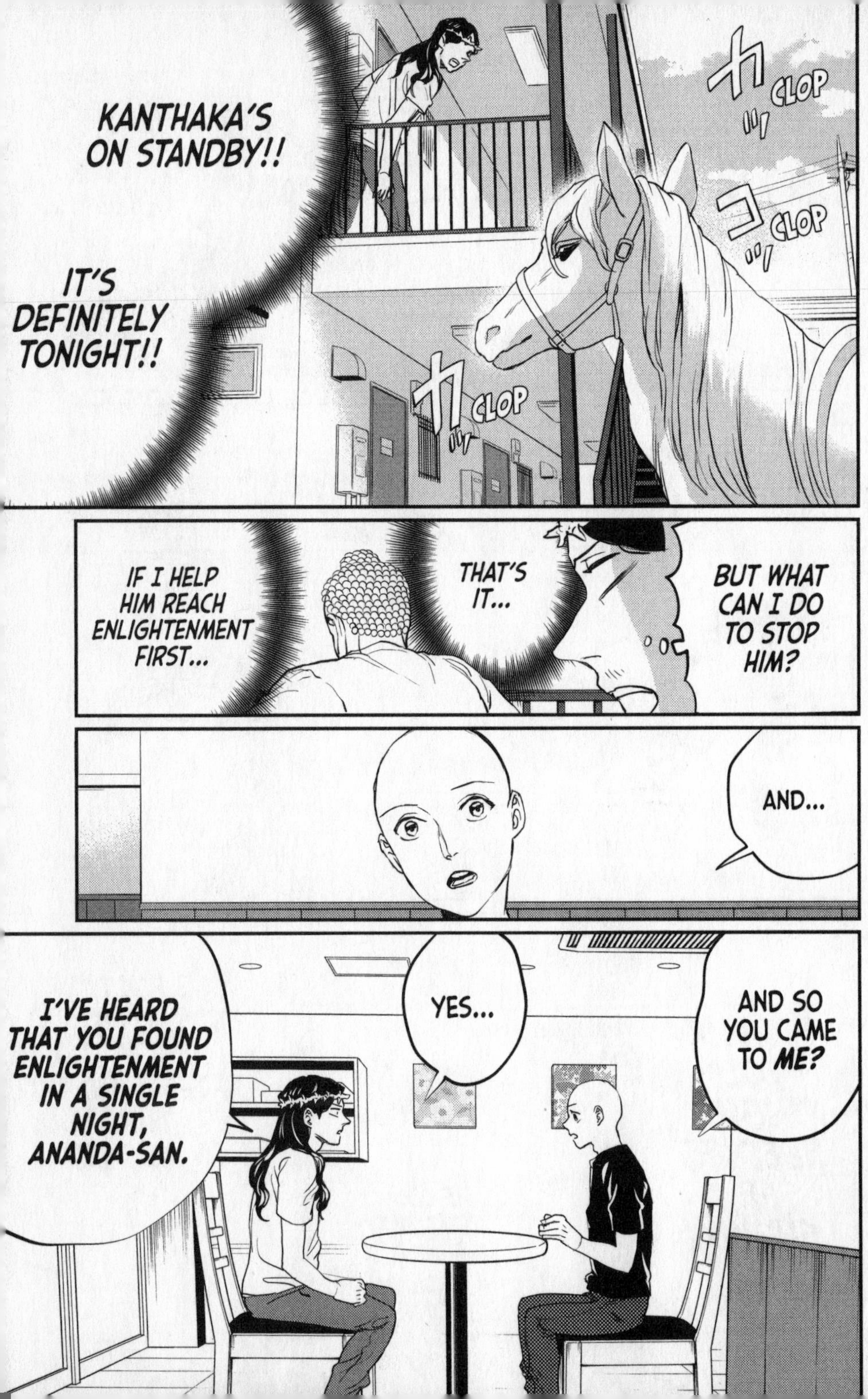
CLOP
KANTHAKA'S ON STANDBY!!
CLOP
IT'S DEFINITELY TONIGHT!!
CLOP
BUT WHAT CAN I DO TO STOP HIM?
THAT'S IT...
IF I HELP HIM REACH ENLIGHTENMENT FIRST...
AND...
AND SO YOU CAME TO *ME*?
YES...
I'VE HEARD THAT YOU FOUND ENLIGHTENMENT IN A SINGLE NIGHT, ANANDA-SAN.

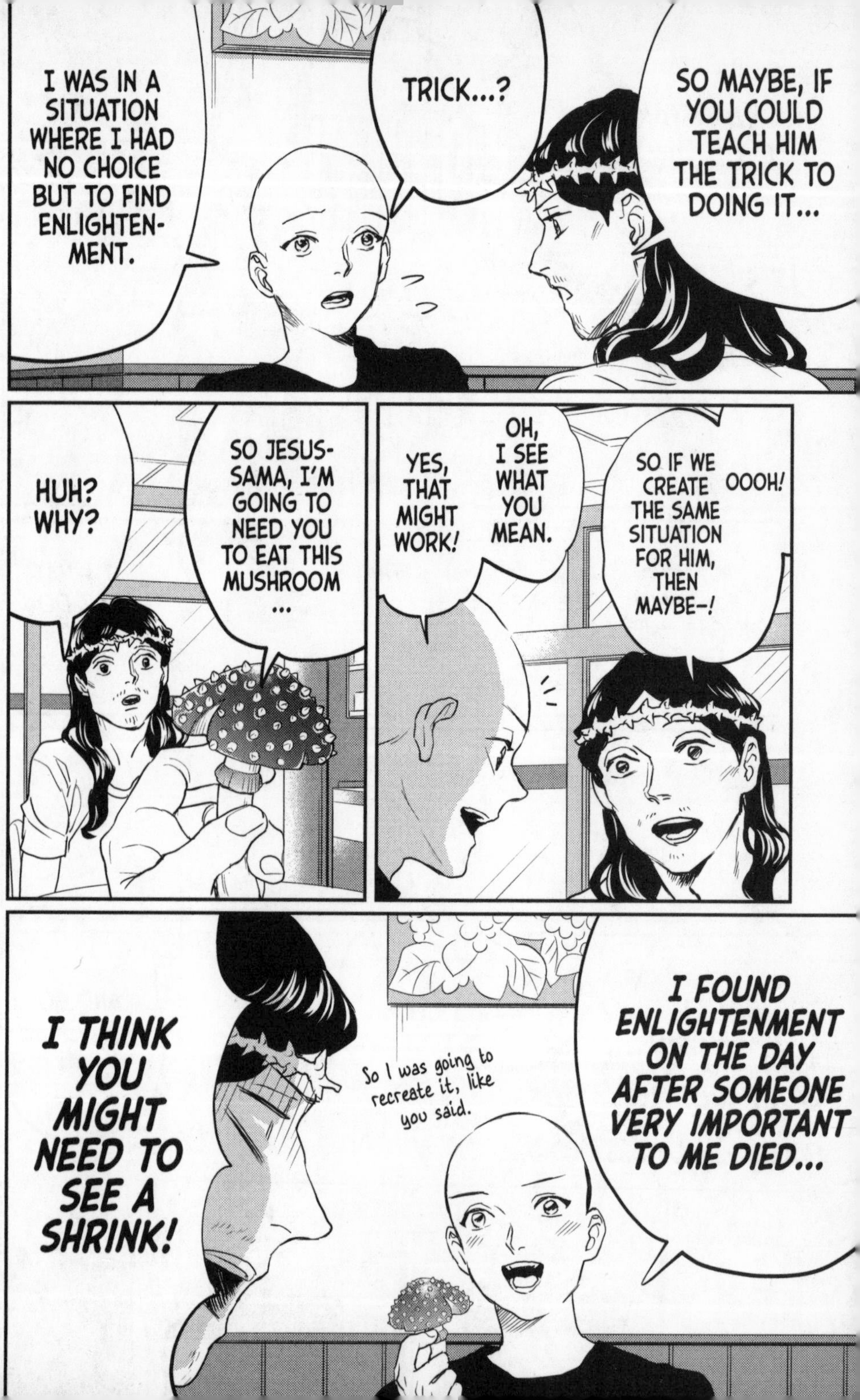
SO MAYBE, IF YOU COULD TEACH HIM THE TRICK TO DOING IT...
TRICK...?
I WAS IN A SITUATION WHERE I HAD NO CHOICE BUT TO FIND ENLIGHTEN-MENT.
OOOH!
SO IF WE CREATE THE SAME SITUATION FOR HIM, THEN MAYBE-!
OH, I SEE WHAT YOU MEAN.
YES, THAT MIGHT WORK!
SO JESUS-SAMA, I'M GOING TO NEED YOU TO EAT THIS MUSHROOM ...
HUH? WHY?
I FOUND ENLIGHTENMENT ON THE DAY AFTER SOMEONE VERY IMPORTANT TO ME DIED...
So I was going to recreate it, like you said.
I THINK YOU MIGHT NEED TO SEE A SHRINK!

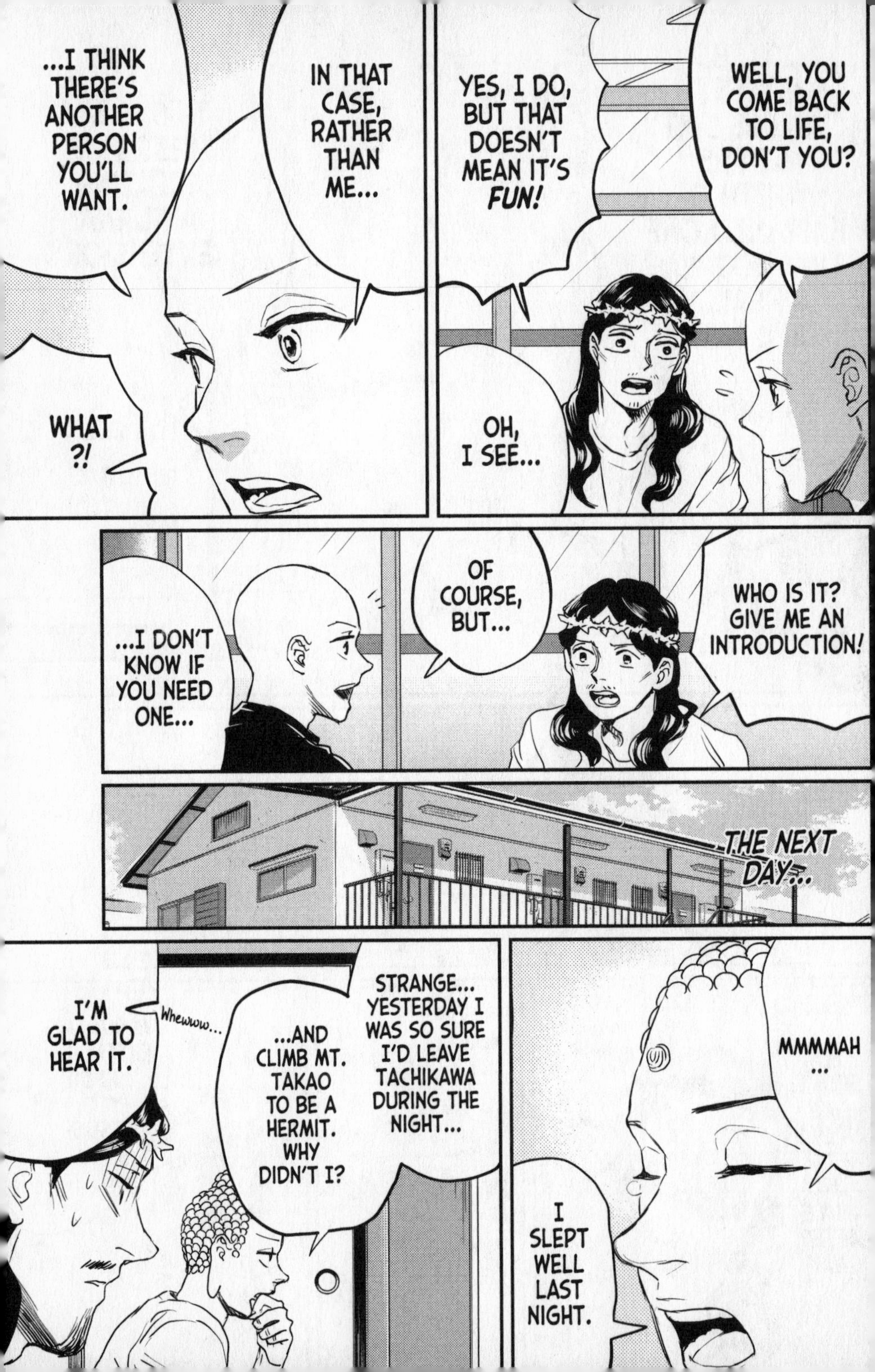
WELL, YOU COME BACK TO LIFE, DON'T YOU?
YES, I DO, BUT THAT DOESN'T MEAN IT'S *FUN!*
OH, I SEE...
IN THAT CASE, RATHER THAN ME...
...I THINK THERE'S ANOTHER PERSON YOU'LL WANT.
WHAT?!
WHO IS IT? GIVE ME AN INTRODUCTION!
OF COURSE, BUT...
...I DON'T KNOW IF YOU NEED ONE...
THE NEXT DAY...
MMMMAH...
I SLEPT WELL LAST NIGHT.
STRANGE... YESTERDAY I WAS SO SURE I'D LEAVE TACHIKAWA DURING THE NIGHT...
...AND CLIMB MT. TAKAO TO BE A HERMIT. WHY DIDN'T I?
Whewww...
I'M GLAD TO HEAR IT.

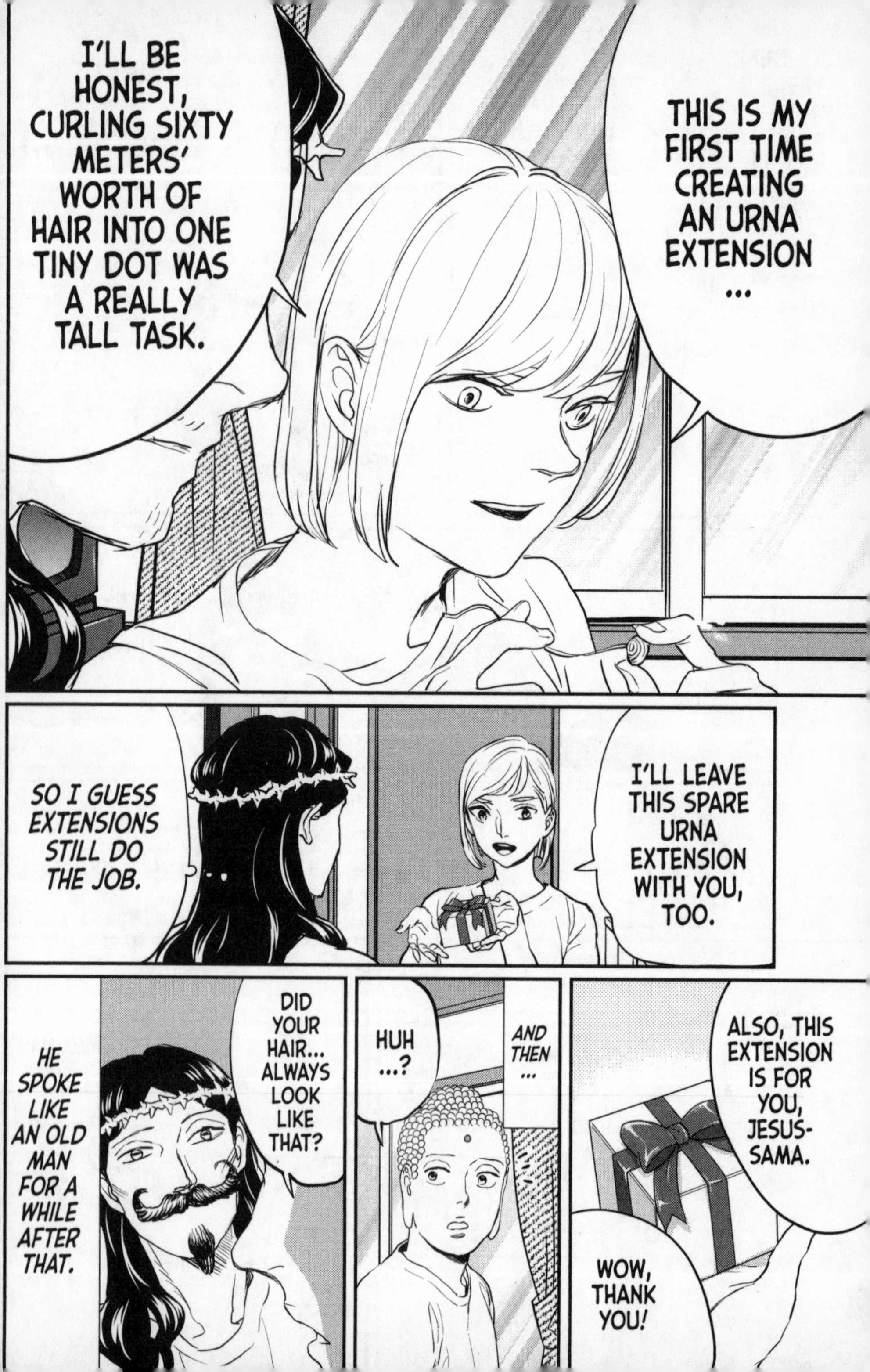
THIS IS MY FIRST TIME CREATING AN URNA EXTENSION ...
I'LL BE HONEST, CURLING SIXTY METERS' WORTH OF HAIR INTO ONE TINY DOT WAS A REALLY TALL TASK.
I'LL LEAVE THIS SPARE URNA EXTENSION WITH YOU, TOO.
SO I GUESS EXTENSIONS STILL DO THE JOB.
ALSO, THIS EXTENSION IS FOR YOU, JESUS-SAMA.
WOW, THANK YOU!
AND THEN ...
HUH ...?
DID YOUR HAIR... ALWAYS LOOK LIKE THAT?
HE SPOKE LIKE AN OLD MAN FOR A WHILE AFTER THAT.

Tsk...

CHAPTER 128 TRANSLATION NOTES

Gandhara, page 119
A region at the foot of the Himalayas in northwest India and northeast Pakistan today. Gandhara is known for its historical style of art, which is highly influenced by Greek customs in the first several centuries AD, and thus bears a distinct difference from Buddhist styles further east in Asia.

Brahman, page 122
In Hinduism, Brahman is the conceptual ultimate truth of the universe, the binding element that ties all of existence together. While Buddhism rejects the concept of Brahman, within the Osamu Tezuka Buddha manga, the character Brahman, who appears as a wizened old man, is a godlike being who guides the Buddha on his path.

Urna, page 124
The dot on Buddha's forehead is a symbolic representation of his third eye, which gives him vision beyond the mundane world into the realm of the divine. It's called a *byakugô*, meaning "white hair," because it's considered a long, swirled hair.

Ananda's enlightenment, page 128
Ananda is often presented as a foil to the Buddha, because of his comparative difficulties in finding enlightenment. The day after the Buddha's death, the First Council was gathered with 500 monks, 499 of whom had reached enlightenment, with only Ananda being of a lesser rank. Humiliated by his inability, Ananda stopped in his attempts briefly to rest, at which point he became enlightened and was able to join the council.

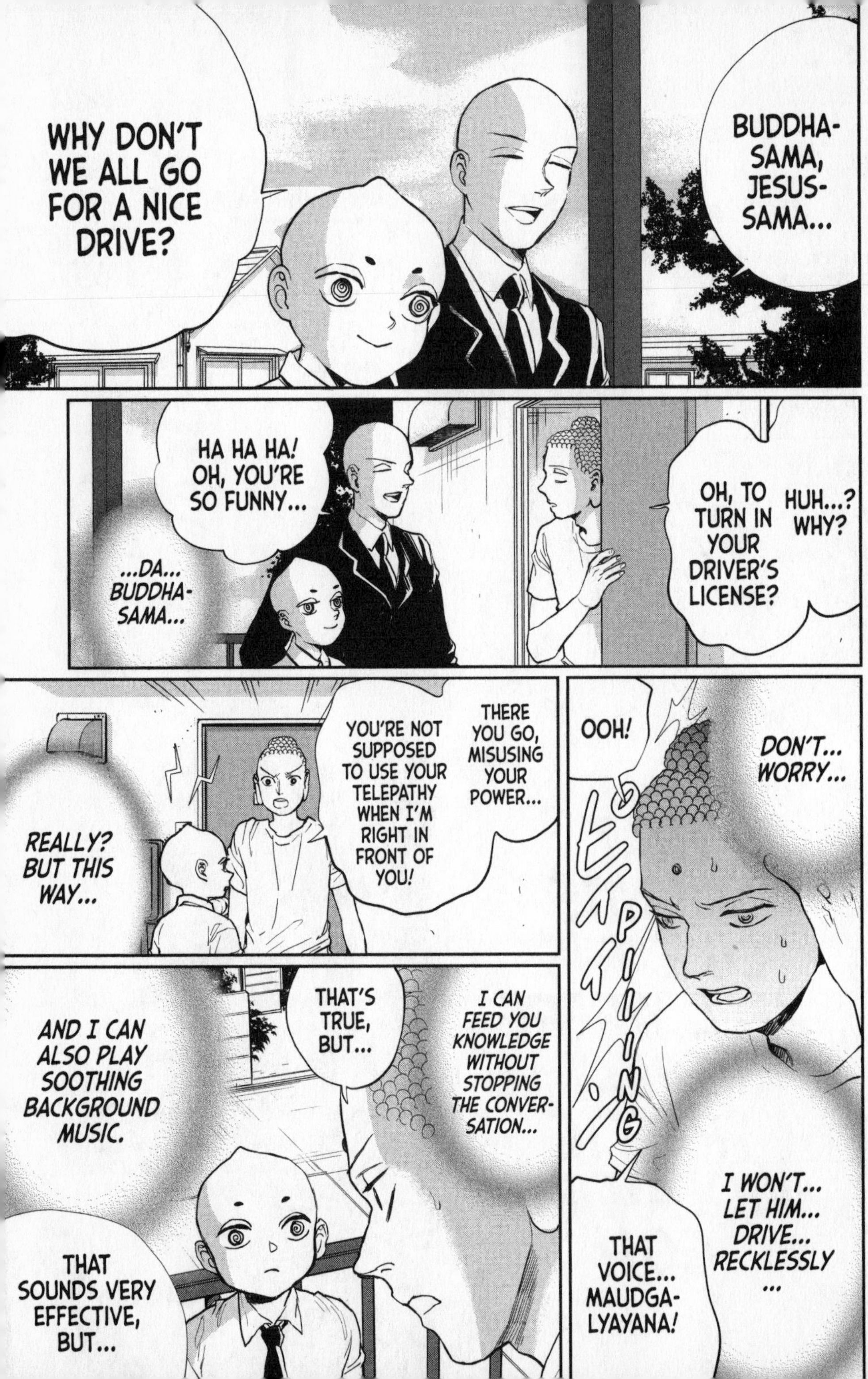
BUDDHA-SAMA, JESUS-SAMA...
WHY DON'T WE ALL GO FOR A NICE DRIVE?
HUH...? WHY?
OH, TO TURN IN YOUR DRIVER'S LICENSE?
HA HA HA! OH, YOU'RE SO FUNNY...
...DA... BUDDHA-SAMA...
DON'T... WORRY...
OOH!
PIIING
I WON'T... LET HIM... DRIVE... RECKLESSLY...
THAT VOICE... MAUDGALYAYANA!
THERE YOU GO, MISUSING YOUR POWER...
YOU'RE NOT SUPPOSED TO USE YOUR TELEPATHY WHEN I'M RIGHT IN FRONT OF YOU!
REALLY? BUT THIS WAY...
I CAN FEED YOU KNOWLEDGE WITHOUT STOPPING THE CONVER-SATION...
THAT'S TRUE, BUT...
AND I CAN ALSO PLAY SOOTHING BACKGROUND MUSIC.
THAT SOUNDS VERY EFFECTIVE, BUT...

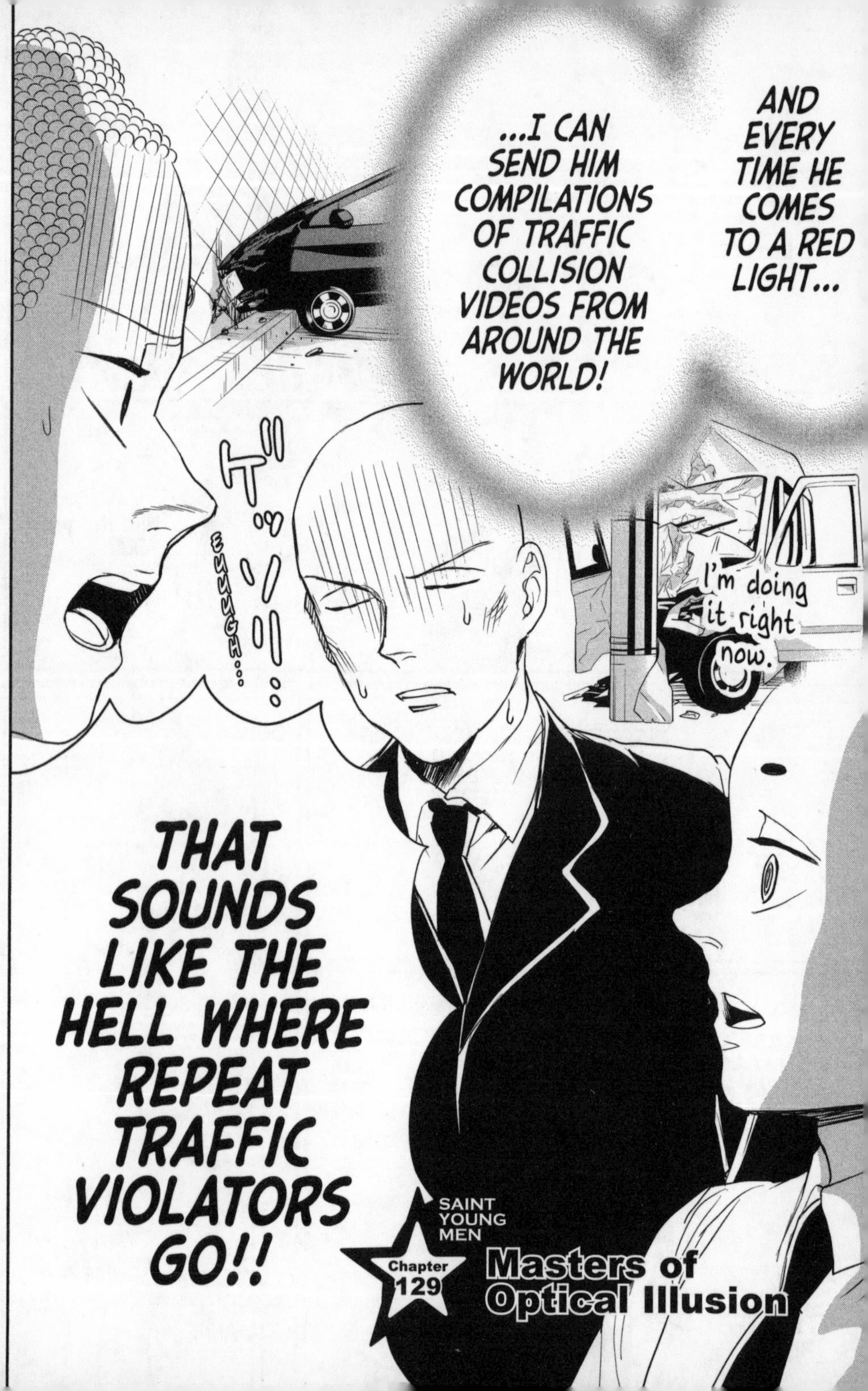
AND EVERY TIME HE COMES TO A RED LIGHT...
...I CAN SEND HIM COMPILATIONS OF TRAFFIC COLLISION VIDEOS FROM AROUND THE WORLD!
I'm doing it right now.
EUUUGH...
THAT SOUNDS LIKE THE HELL WHERE REPEAT TRAFFIC VIOLATORS GO!!
SAINT YOUNG MEN
Chapter 129
Masters of Optical Illusion

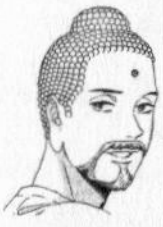

BUDDHA
MY FAVORITE FIREWORKS ARE THE CHRYSANTHEMUM AND THE PEONY. I LOVE THE DELICATE ARTISTRY OF A BURSTING FIREWORK!

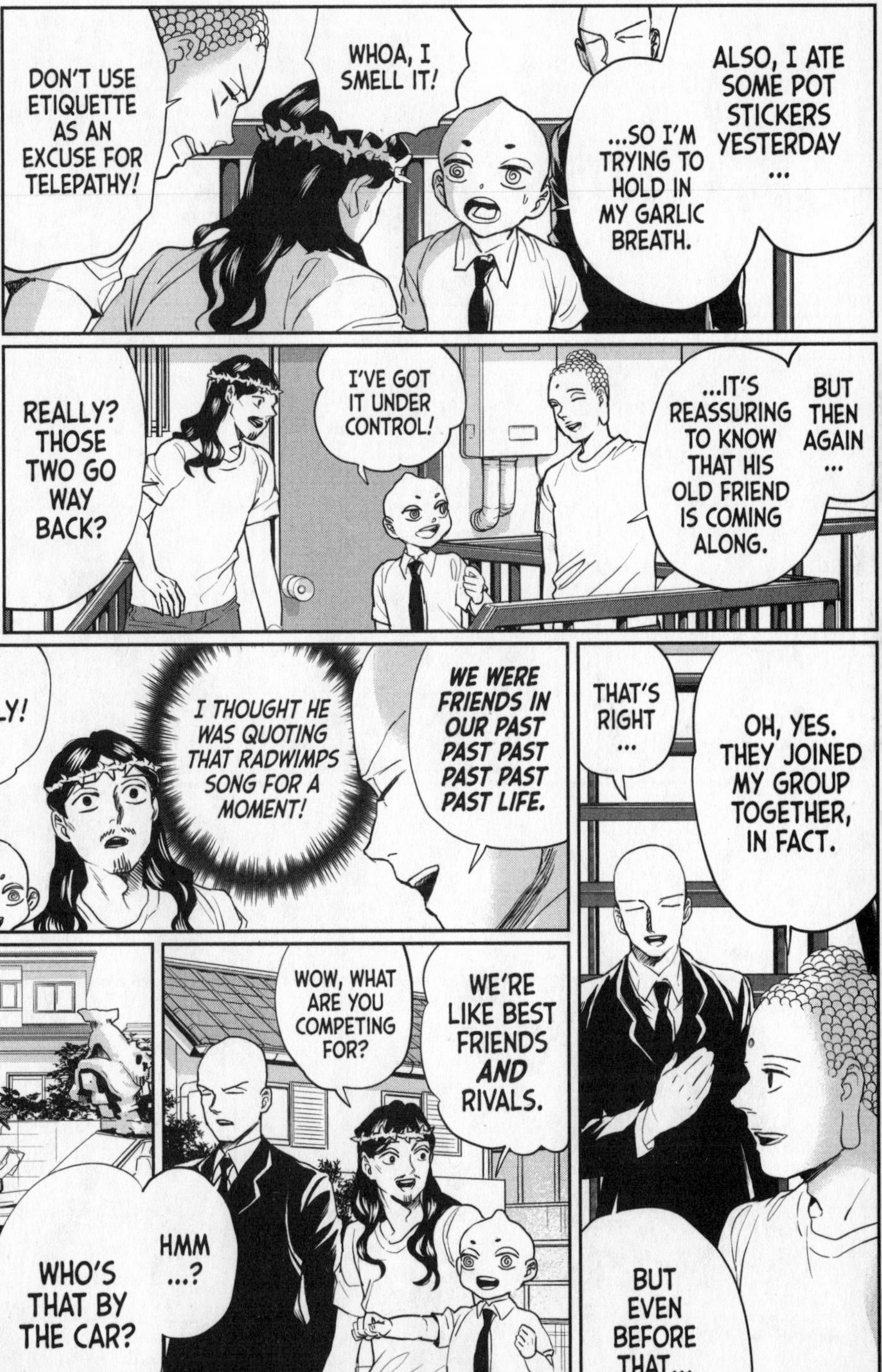
ALSO, I ATE SOME POT STICKERS YESTERDAY ...
...SO I'M TRYING TO HOLD IN MY GARLIC BREATH.
WHOA, I SMELL IT!
DON'T USE ETIQUETTE AS AN EXCUSE FOR TELEPATHY!
BUT THEN AGAIN ...
...IT'S REASSURING TO KNOW THAT HIS OLD FRIEND IS COMING ALONG.
I'VE GOT IT UNDER CONTROL!
REALLY? THOSE TWO GO WAY BACK?
OH, YES. THEY JOINED MY GROUP TOGETHER, IN FACT.
THAT'S RIGHT ...
BUT EVEN BEFORE THAT...
WE WERE FRIENDS IN OUR PAST PAST PAST PAST PAST LIFE.
I THOUGHT HE WAS QUOTING THAT RADWIMPS SONG FOR A MOMENT!
EXACTLY!
WE'RE LIKE BEST FRIENDS AND RIVALS.
WOW, WHAT ARE YOU COMPETING FOR?
HMM ...?
WHO'S THAT BY THE CAR?

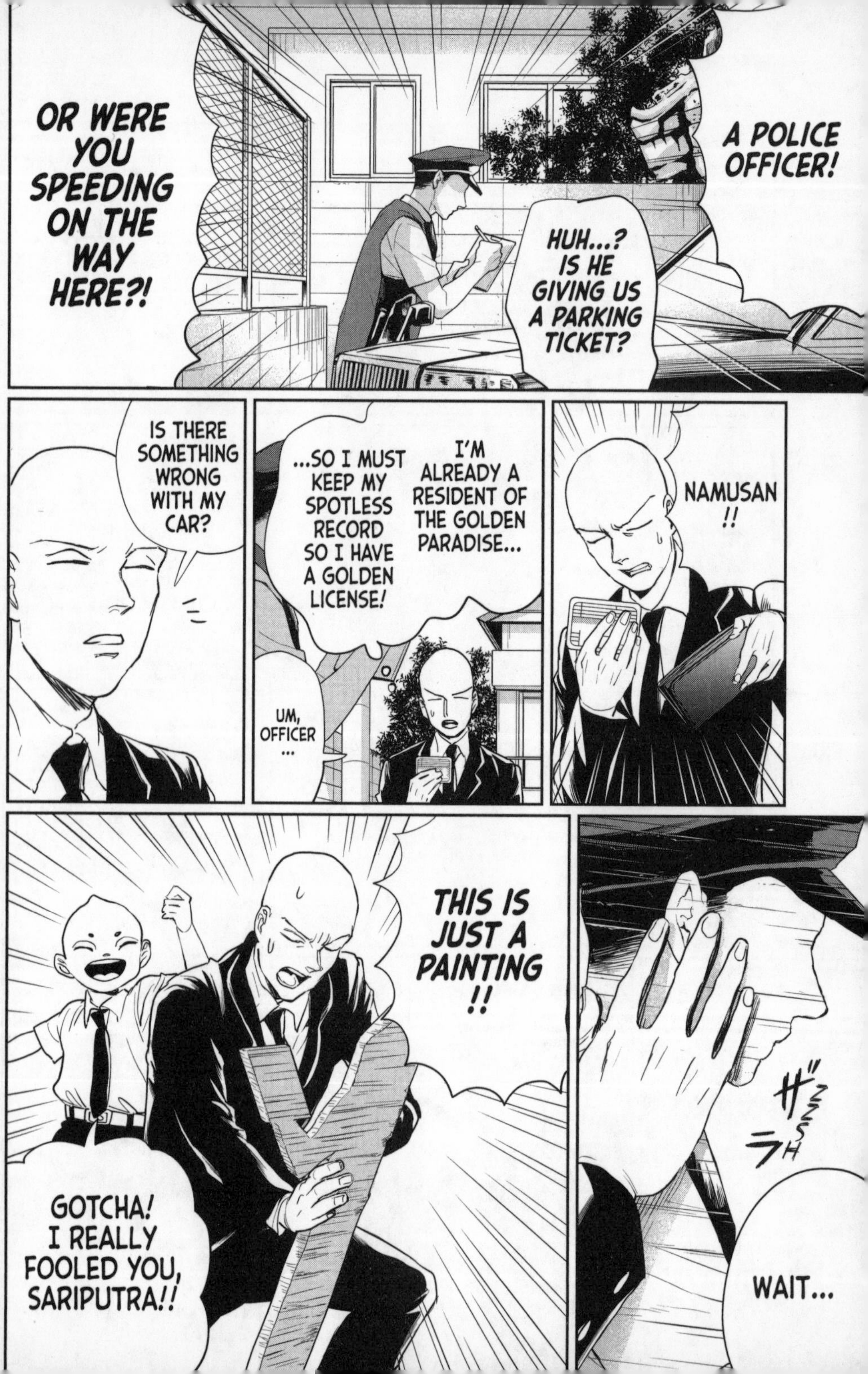
A POLICE OFFICER!
HUH...? IS HE GIVING US A PARKING TICKET?
OR WERE YOU SPEEDING ON THE WAY HERE?!
NAMUSAN!!
I'M ALREADY A RESIDENT OF THE GOLDEN PARADISE...
...SO I MUST KEEP MY SPOTLESS RECORD SO I HAVE A GOLDEN LICENSE!
UM, OFFICER...
IS THERE SOMETHING WRONG WITH MY CAR?
ザラ ZZSH
WAIT...
THIS IS JUST A PAINTING!!
GOTCHA! I REALLY FOOLED YOU, SARIPUTRA!!

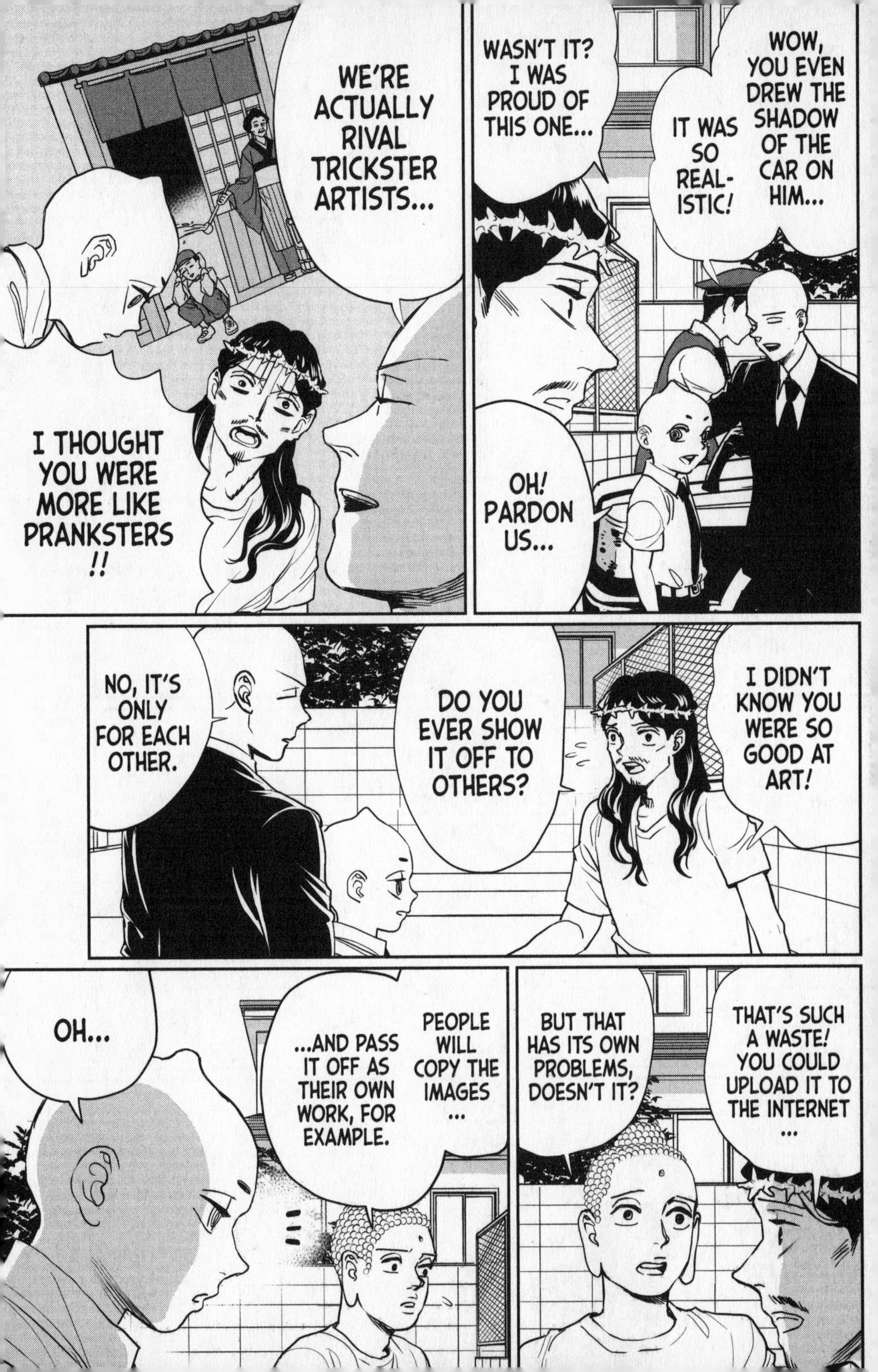
WOW, YOU EVEN DREW THE SHADOW OF THE CAR ON HIM...
IT WAS SO REAL-ISTIC!
WASN'T IT? I WAS PROUD OF THIS ONE...
OH! PARDON US...
WE'RE ACTUALLY RIVAL TRICKSTER ARTISTS...
I THOUGHT YOU WERE MORE LIKE PRANKSTERS!!
I DIDN'T KNOW YOU WERE SO GOOD AT ART!
DO YOU EVER SHOW IT OFF TO OTHERS?
NO, IT'S ONLY FOR EACH OTHER.
THAT'S SUCH A WASTE! YOU COULD UPLOAD IT TO THE INTERNET...
BUT THAT HAS ITS OWN PROBLEMS, DOESN'T IT?
PEOPLE WILL COPY THE IMAGES...
...AND PASS IT OFF AS THEIR OWN WORK, FOR EXAMPLE.
OH...

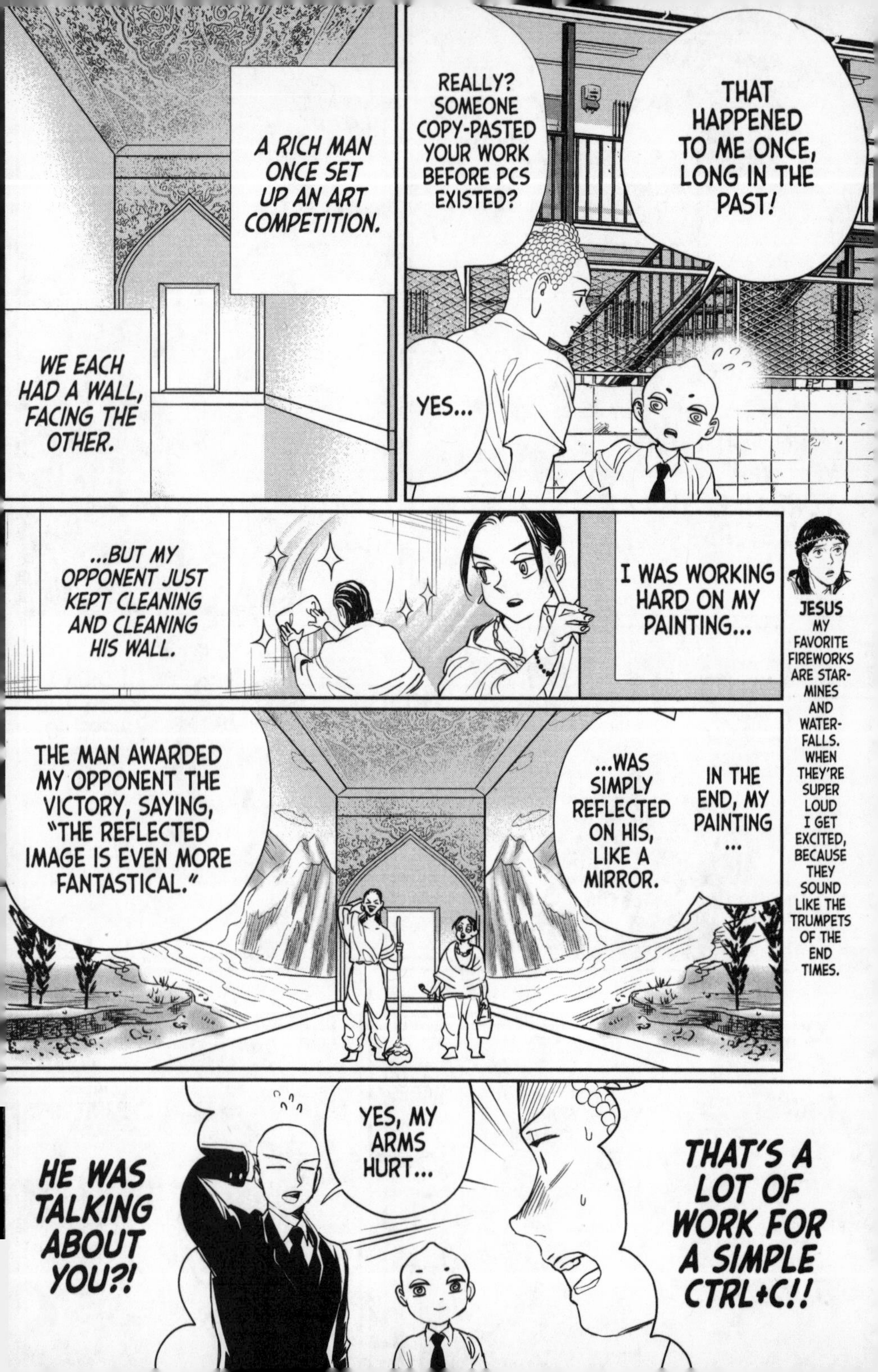
THAT HAPPENED TO ME ONCE, LONG IN THE PAST!
REALLY? SOMEONE COPY-PASTED YOUR WORK BEFORE PCS EXISTED?
YES...
A RICH MAN ONCE SET UP AN ART COMPETITION.
WE EACH HAD A WALL, FACING THE OTHER.
I WAS WORKING HARD ON MY PAINTING...
...BUT MY OPPONENT JUST KEPT CLEANING AND CLEANING HIS WALL.
IN THE END, MY PAINTING ...
...WAS SIMPLY REFLECTED ON HIS, LIKE A MIRROR.
THE MAN AWARDED MY OPPONENT THE VICTORY, SAYING, "THE REFLECTED IMAGE IS EVEN MORE FANTASTICAL."
THAT'S A LOT OF WORK FOR A SIMPLE CTRL+C!!
YES, MY ARMS HURT...
HE WAS TALKING ABOUT YOU?!
JESUS
MY FAVORITE FIREWORKS ARE STAR-MINES AND WATER-FALLS. WHEN THEY'RE SUPER LOUD I GET EXCITED, BECAUSE THEY SOUND LIKE THE TRUMPETS OF THE END TIMES.

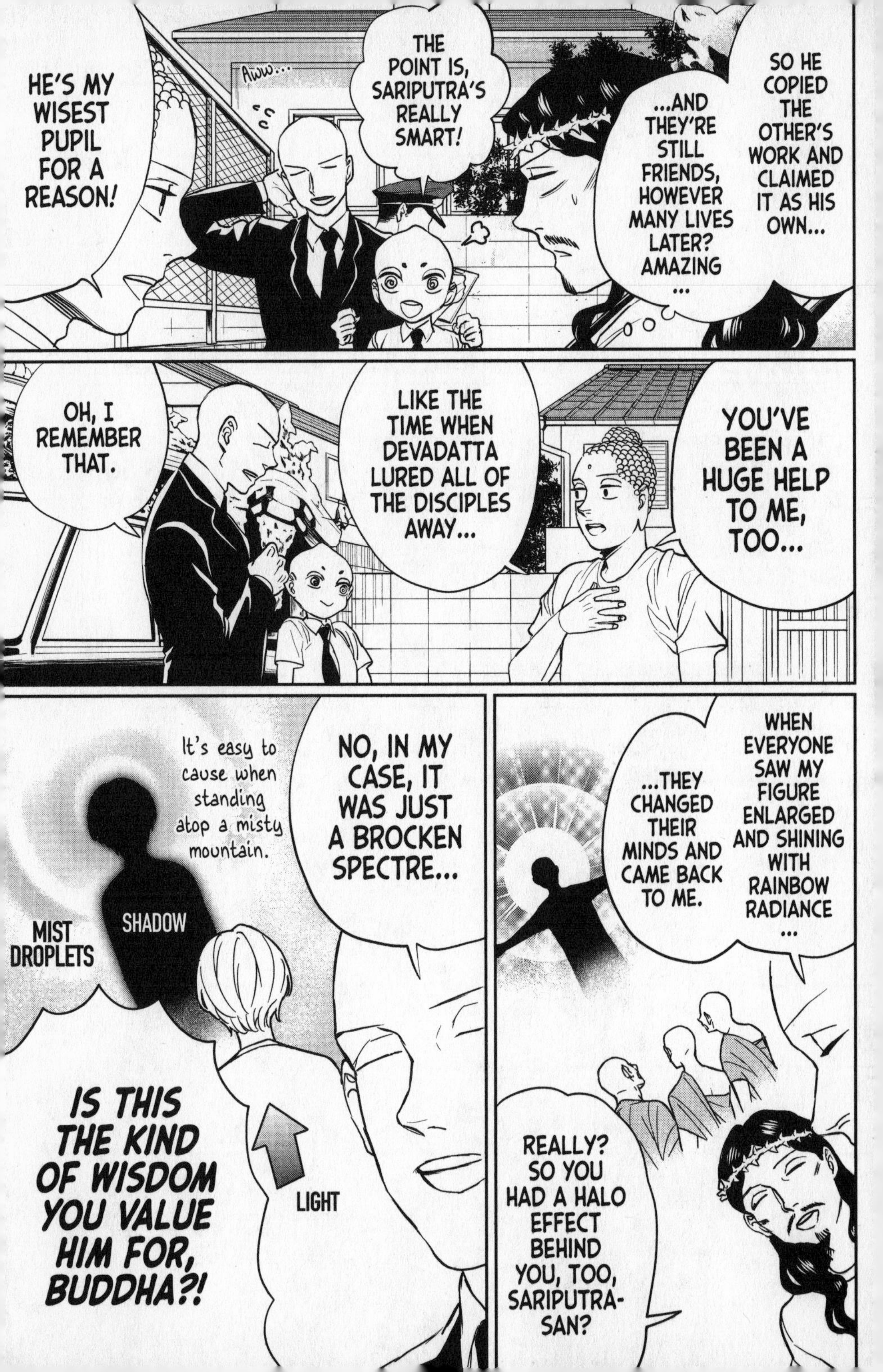
SO HE COPIED THE OTHER'S WORK AND CLAIMED IT AS HIS OWN...
...AND THEY'RE STILL FRIENDS, HOWEVER MANY LIVES LATER? AMAZING...
THE POINT IS, SARIPUTRA'S REALLY SMART!
Awww...
HE'S MY WISEST PUPIL FOR A REASON!
YOU'VE BEEN A HUGE HELP TO ME, TOO...
LIKE THE TIME WHEN DEVADATTA LURED ALL OF THE DISCIPLES AWAY...
OH, I REMEMBER THAT.
WHEN EVERYONE SAW MY FIGURE ENLARGED AND SHINING WITH RAINBOW RADIANCE...
...THEY CHANGED THEIR MINDS AND CAME BACK TO ME.
REALLY? SO YOU HAD A HALO EFFECT BEHIND YOU, TOO, SARIPUTRA-SAN?
NO, IN MY CASE, IT WAS JUST A BROCKEN SPECTRE...
It's easy to cause when standing atop a misty mountain.
SHADOW
MIST DROPLETS
LIGHT
IS THIS THE KIND OF WISDOM YOU VALUE HIM FOR, BUDDHA?!

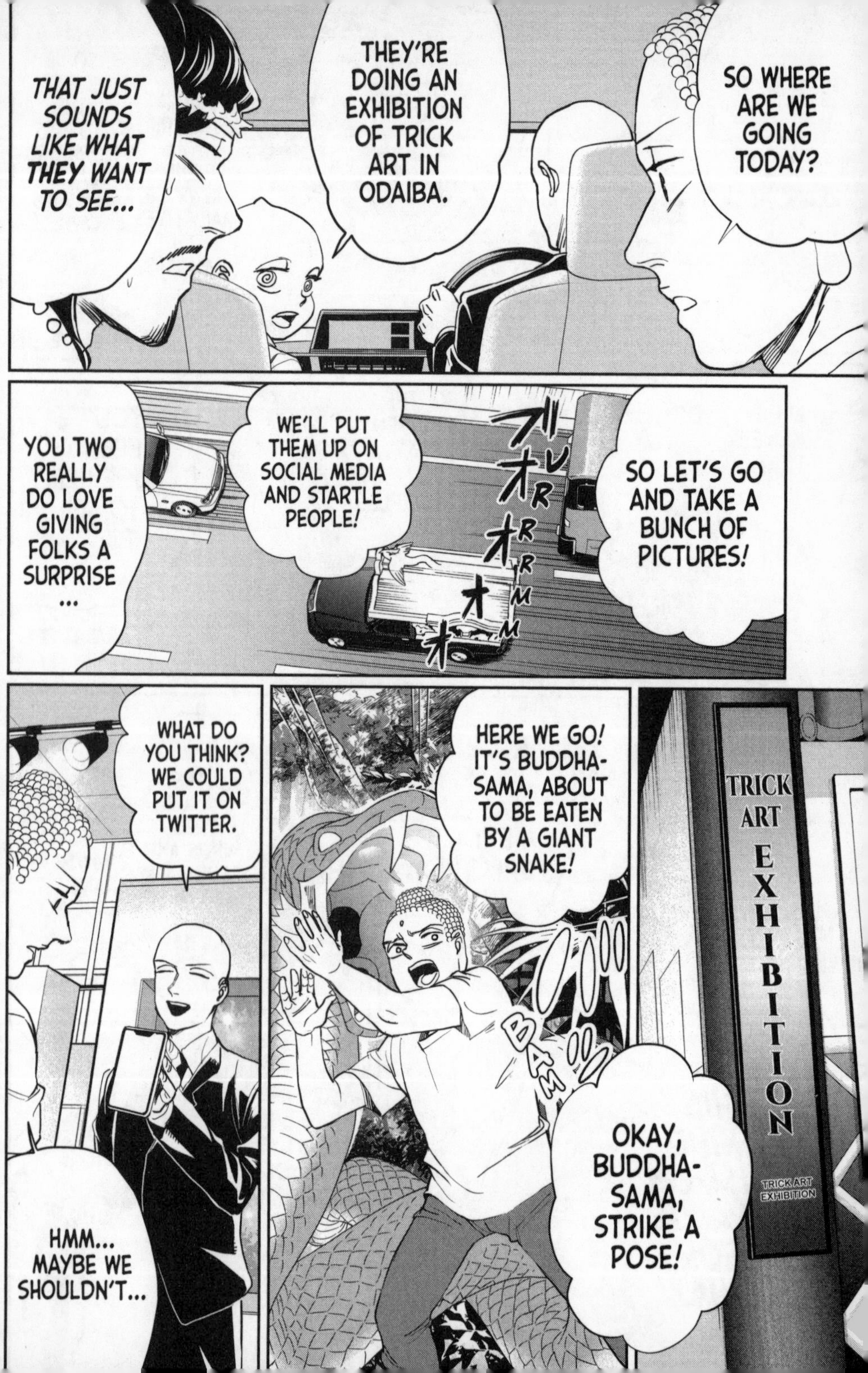
SO WHERE ARE WE GOING TODAY?
THEY'RE DOING AN EXHIBITION OF TRICK ART IN ODAIBA.
THAT JUST SOUNDS LIKE WHAT THEY WANT TO SEE...
SO LET'S GO AND TAKE A BUNCH OF PICTURES!
VRRRMM
WE'LL PUT THEM UP ON SOCIAL MEDIA AND STARTLE PEOPLE!
YOU TWO REALLY DO LOVE GIVING FOLKS A SURPRISE...
TRICK ART EXHIBITION
TRICK ART EXHIBITION
OKAY, BUDDHA-SAMA, STRIKE A POSE!
BAM
HERE WE GO! IT'S BUDDHA-SAMA, ABOUT TO BE EATEN BY A GIANT SNAKE!
WHAT DO YOU THINK? WE COULD PUT IT ON TWITTER.
HMM... MAYBE WE SHOULDN'T...

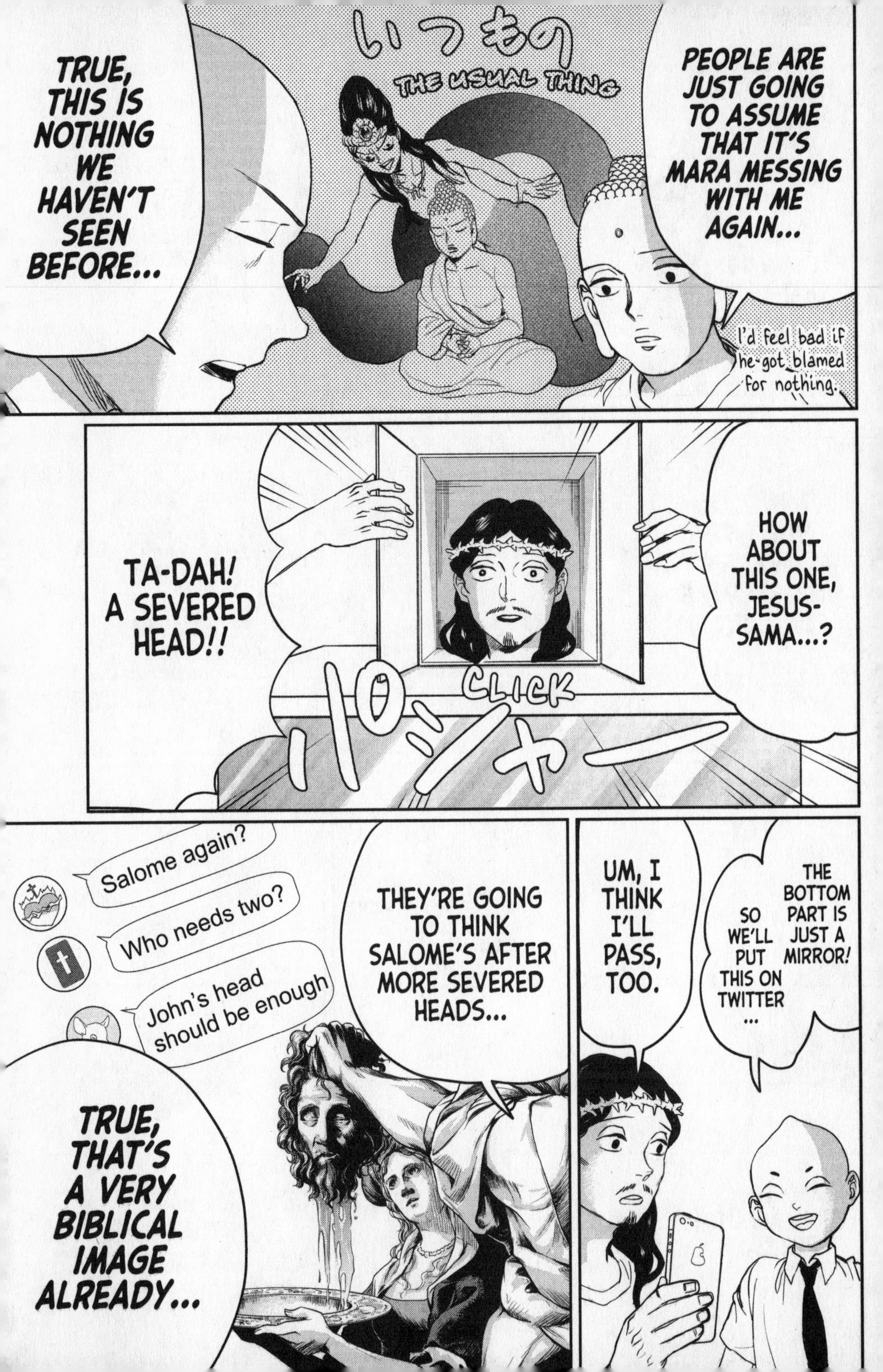
PEOPLE ARE JUST GOING TO ASSUME THAT IT'S MARA MESSING WITH ME AGAIN...
I'd feel bad if he got blamed for nothing.
いつもの
THE USUAL THING
TRUE, THIS IS NOTHING WE HAVEN'T SEEN BEFORE...
HOW ABOUT THIS ONE, JESUS-SAMA...?
パシャー
CLICK
TA-DAH! A SEVERED HEAD!!
THE BOTTOM PART IS JUST A MIRROR!
SO WE'LL PUT THIS ON TWITTER ...
UM, I THINK I'LL PASS, TOO.
THEY'RE GOING TO THINK SALOME'S AFTER MORE SEVERED HEADS...
Salome again?
Who needs two?
John's head should be enough
TRUE, THAT'S A VERY BIBLICAL IMAGE ALREADY...

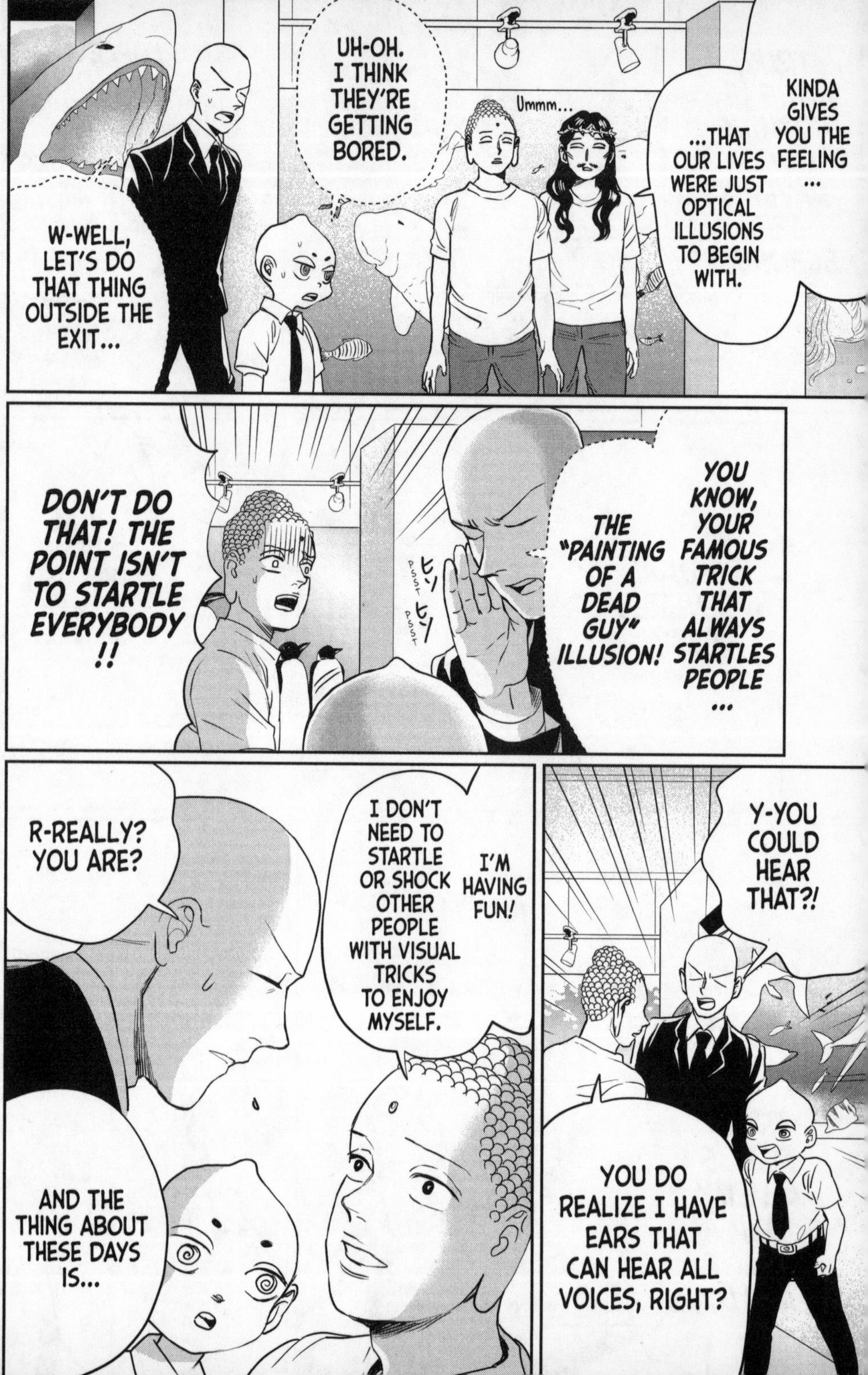
KINDA GIVES YOU THE FEELING ...
...THAT OUR LIVES WERE JUST OPTICAL ILLUSIONS TO BEGIN WITH.
Ummm...
UH-OH. I THINK THEY'RE GETTING BORED.
W-WELL, LET'S DO THAT THING OUTSIDE THE EXIT...
YOU KNOW, YOUR FAMOUS TRICK THAT ALWAYS STARTLES PEOPLE ...
THE "PAINTING OF A DEAD GUY" ILLUSION!
ヒソ PSSST
ヒソ PSSST
DON'T DO THAT! THE POINT ISN'T TO STARTLE EVERYBODY !!
Y-YOU COULD HEAR THAT?!
YOU DO REALIZE I HAVE EARS THAT CAN HEAR ALL VOICES, RIGHT?
I'M HAVING FUN!
I DON'T NEED TO STARTLE OR SHOCK OTHER PEOPLE WITH VISUAL TRICKS TO ENJOY MYSELF.
R-REALLY? YOU ARE?
AND THE THING ABOUT THESE DAYS IS...

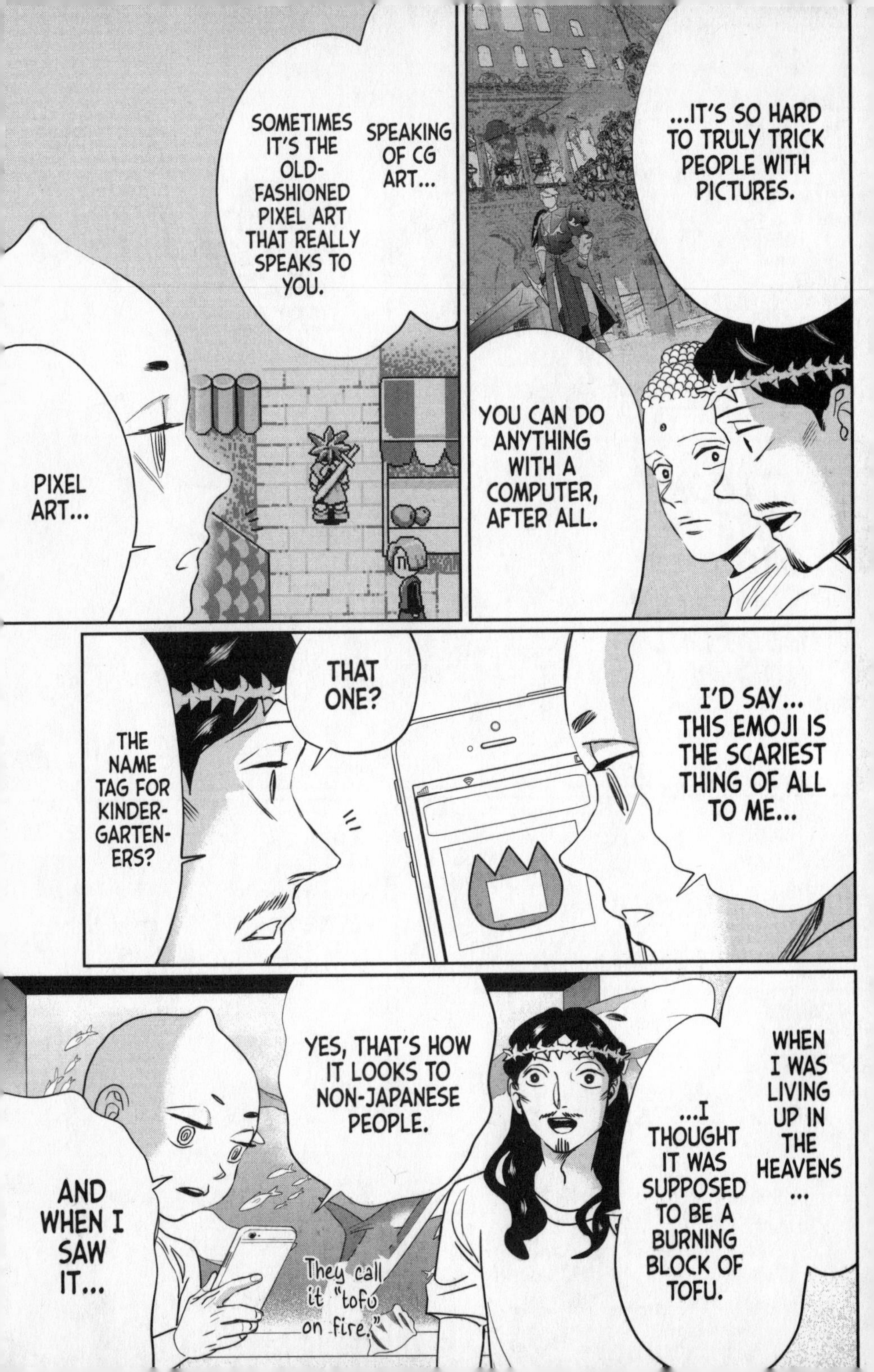
...IT'S SO HARD TO TRULY TRICK PEOPLE WITH PICTURES.
YOU CAN DO ANYTHING WITH A COMPUTER, AFTER ALL.
SPEAKING OF CG ART...
SOMETIMES IT'S THE OLD-FASHIONED PIXEL ART THAT REALLY SPEAKS TO YOU.
PIXEL ART...
I'D SAY... THIS EMOJI IS THE SCARIEST THING OF ALL TO ME...
THAT ONE?
THE NAME TAG FOR KINDER-GARTEN-ERS?
WHEN I WAS LIVING UP IN THE HEAVENS...
...I THOUGHT IT WAS SUPPOSED TO BE A BURNING BLOCK OF TOFU.
YES, THAT'S HOW IT LOOKS TO NON-JAPANESE PEOPLE.
They call it "tofu on fire."
AND WHEN I SAW IT...

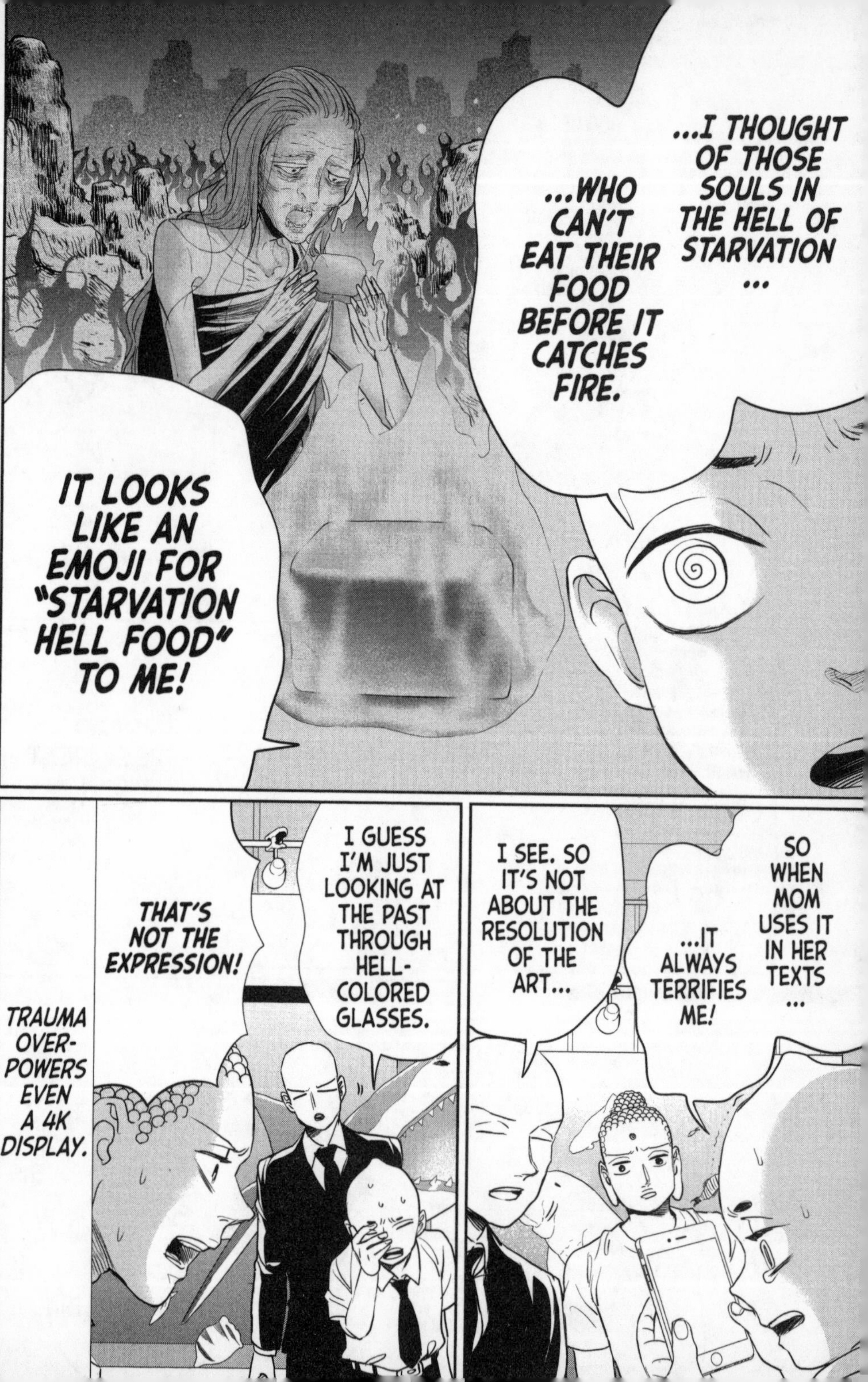
...I THOUGHT OF THOSE SOULS IN THE HELL OF STARVATION ...
...WHO CAN'T EAT THEIR FOOD BEFORE IT CATCHES FIRE.
IT LOOKS LIKE AN EMOJI FOR "STARVATION HELL FOOD" TO ME!
SO WHEN MOM USES IT IN HER TEXTS ...
...IT ALWAYS TERRIFIES ME!
I SEE. SO IT'S NOT ABOUT THE RESOLUTION OF THE ART...
I GUESS I'M JUST LOOKING AT THE PAST THROUGH HELL-COLORED GLASSES.
THAT'S NOT THE EXPRESSION!
TRAUMA OVER-POWERS EVEN A 4K DISPLAY.

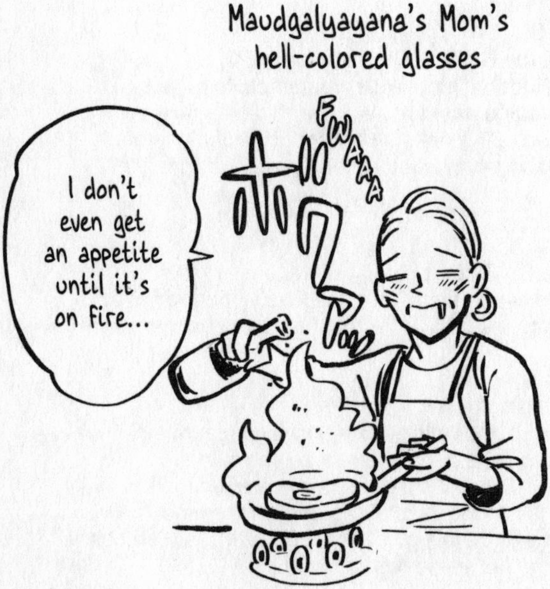
Maudgalyayana's Mom's
hell-colored glasses
FWAAA
I don't even get an appetite until it's on fire...

CHAPTER 129 TRANSLATION NOTES

Radwimps, page 135
A popular Japanese rock band that grew to prominence in the late 2000s. They provided the soundtrack to the hit animated film *Your Name,* which included the single "Zenzenzense" ("Past Past Past Life").

Namusan, page 136
Namusan is an abbreviation of *namusanpô,* which literally means "I take refuge in the Three Jewels," the Buddha, Dharma (teachings), and Sangha (the spiritual community). In modern Japanese, it is a phrase used when something goes unexpectedly wrong or is shocking.

Gold license, page 136
New drivers in Japan have a driver's license with a green strip in the middle for their initial licensed period, which lasts three years. Upon renewing, you receive a standard blue license, which is then renewed every three years. If you received no infractions on your record in the previous period, you will receive a golden license, instead, which only needs to be renewed every five years, and may offer benefits like reduced costs on certain business services, hotels, etc.

Devadatta's schism, page 139
Devadatta, who was a cousin to Gautama Buddha and later a pupil of his teachings, was known for his antagonism to the Buddha and frequent attempts to have him killed or overthrown. One of these sabotage attempts was a would-be schism within the Buddha's followers. Devadatta lured 500 monks away, and it was only through the clever thinking of Sariputra and Maudgalyayana that they were convinced to return.

Salome, page 141
There are two Salomes who appear in the Bible, but this reference is to the stepdaughter of Herod, who convinced him to have John the Baptist beheaded on the urging of her mother. The story is the inspiration for much subsequent art, such as Oscar Wilde's play *Salome.*

Maudgalyayana's mother, page 144
There is a tale about Maudgalyayana's mother after death, in which Maudgalyayana attempts to find her where she has been reborn, only to realize she is in the starvation or "hungry ghost" hell, in which souls with poor karma are damned to feel ravenous hunger. He attempts to send her food through an ancestral shrine, but it burns up before she can eat it. With the Buddha's guidance, however, his meritous actions are transferred to her, ascending her to Heaven instead.

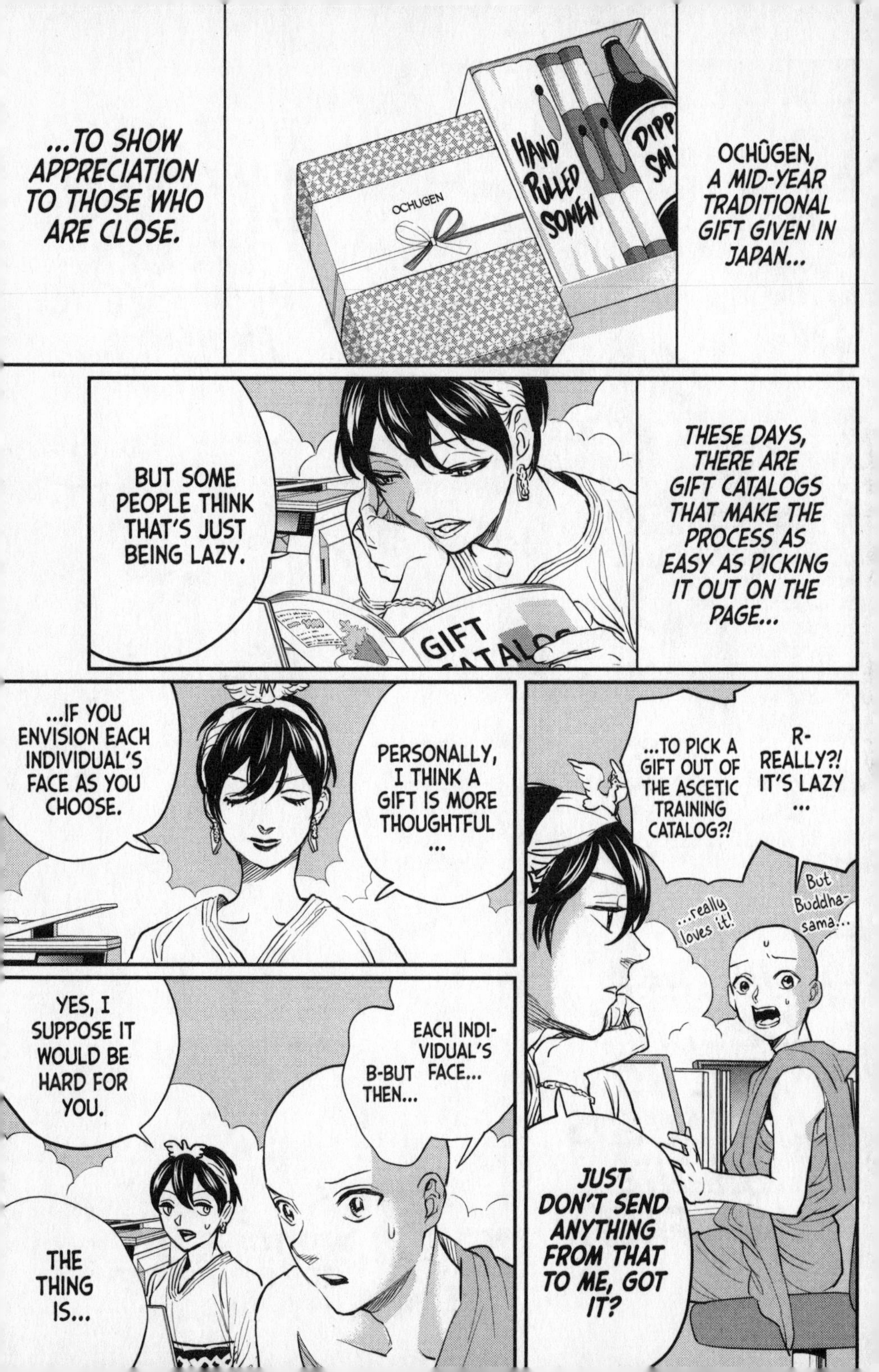

OCHÛGEN, A MID-YEAR TRADITIONAL GIFT GIVEN IN JAPAN...
HAND PULLED SOMEN
OCHUGEN
...TO SHOW APPRECIATION TO THOSE WHO ARE CLOSE.
THESE DAYS, THERE ARE GIFT CATALOGS THAT MAKE THE PROCESS AS EASY AS PICKING IT OUT ON THE PAGE...
BUT SOME PEOPLE THINK THAT'S JUST BEING LAZY.
GIFT
R- REALLY?! IT'S LAZY ...
...TO PICK A GIFT OUT OF THE ASCETIC TRAINING CATALOG?!
But Buddha-sama...
...really loves it!
JUST DON'T SEND ANYTHING FROM THAT TO ME, GOT IT?
PERSONALLY, I THINK A GIFT IS MORE THOUGHTFUL ...
...IF YOU ENVISION EACH INDIVIDUAL'S FACE AS YOU CHOOSE.
EACH INDI-VIDUAL'S FACE...
B-BUT THEN...
YES, I SUPPOSE IT WOULD BE HARD FOR YOU.
THE THING IS...

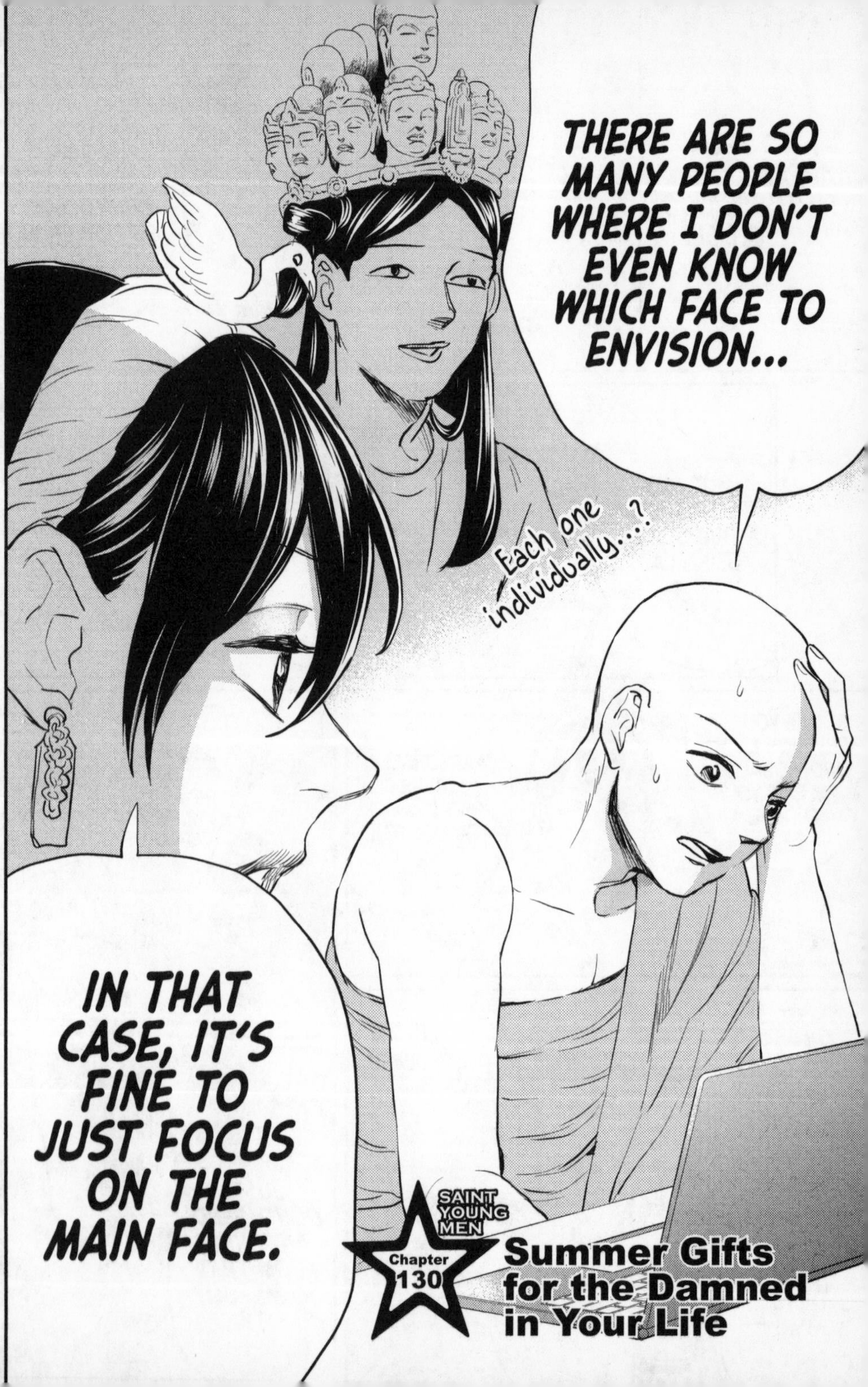
THERE ARE SO MANY PEOPLE WHERE I DON'T EVEN KNOW WHICH FACE TO ENVISION...
Each one individually...?
IN THAT CASE, IT'S FINE TO JUST FOCUS ON THE MAIN FACE.
SAINT YOUNG MEN
Chapter 130
Summer Gifts for the Damned in Your Life

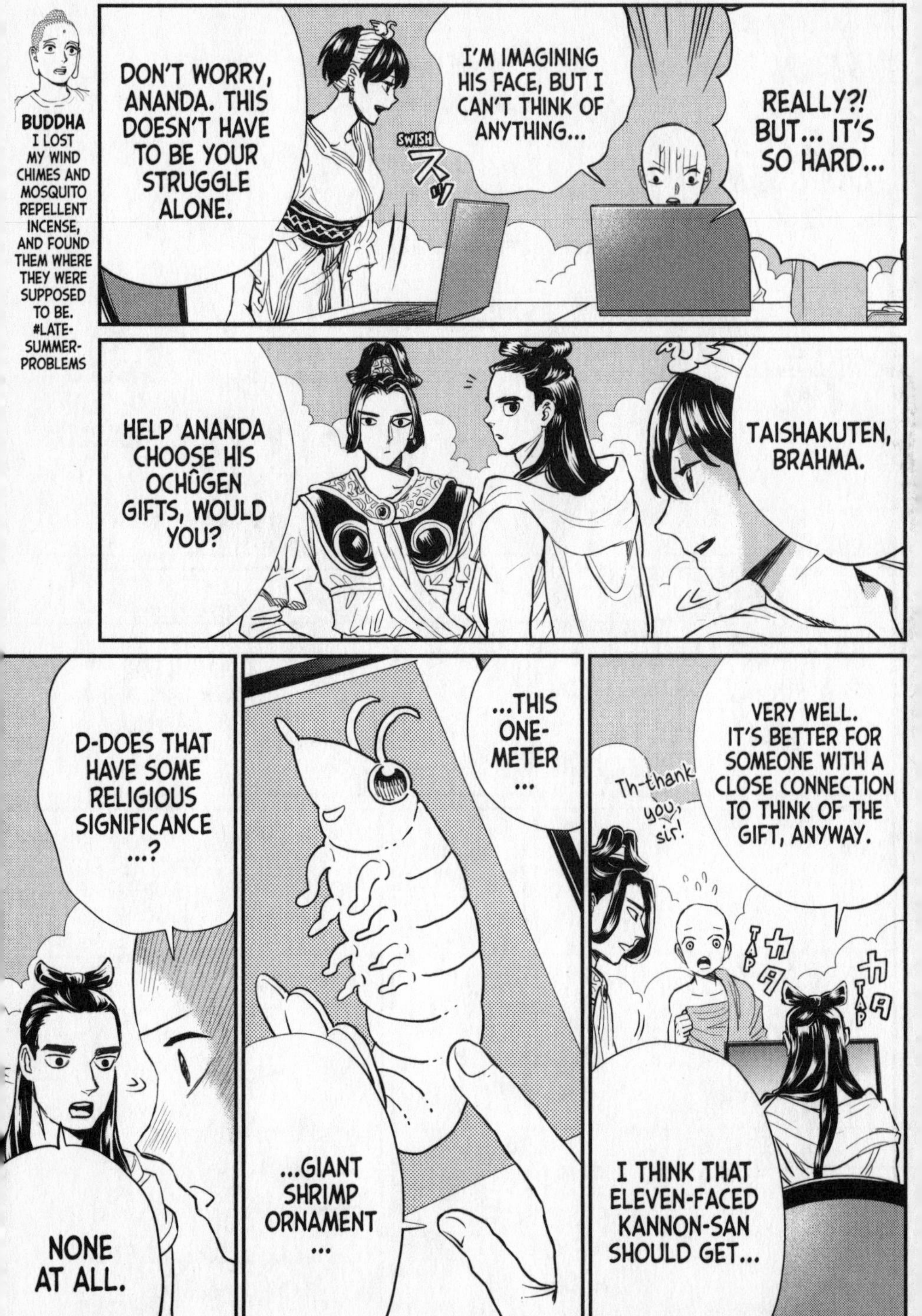
REALLY?! BUT... IT'S SO HARD...
I'M IMAGINING HIS FACE, BUT I CAN'T THINK OF ANYTHING...
SWISH
DON'T WORRY, ANANDA. THIS DOESN'T HAVE TO BE YOUR STRUGGLE ALONE.
TAISHAKUTEN, BRAHMA.
HELP ANANDA CHOOSE HIS OCHÛGEN GIFTS, WOULD YOU?
VERY WELL. IT'S BETTER FOR SOMEONE WITH A CLOSE CONNECTION TO THINK OF THE GIFT, ANYWAY.
Th-thank you, sir!
TAP
TAP
I THINK THAT ELEVEN-FACED KANNON-SAN SHOULD GET...
...THIS ONE-METER...
...GIANT SHRIMP ORNAMENT...
D-DOES THAT HAVE SOME RELIGIOUS SIGNIFICANCE...?
NONE AT ALL.
BUDDHA
I LOST MY WIND CHIMES AND MOSQUITO REPELLENT INCENSE, AND FOUND THEM WHERE THEY WERE SUPPOSED TO BE. #LATE-SUMMER-PROBLEMS

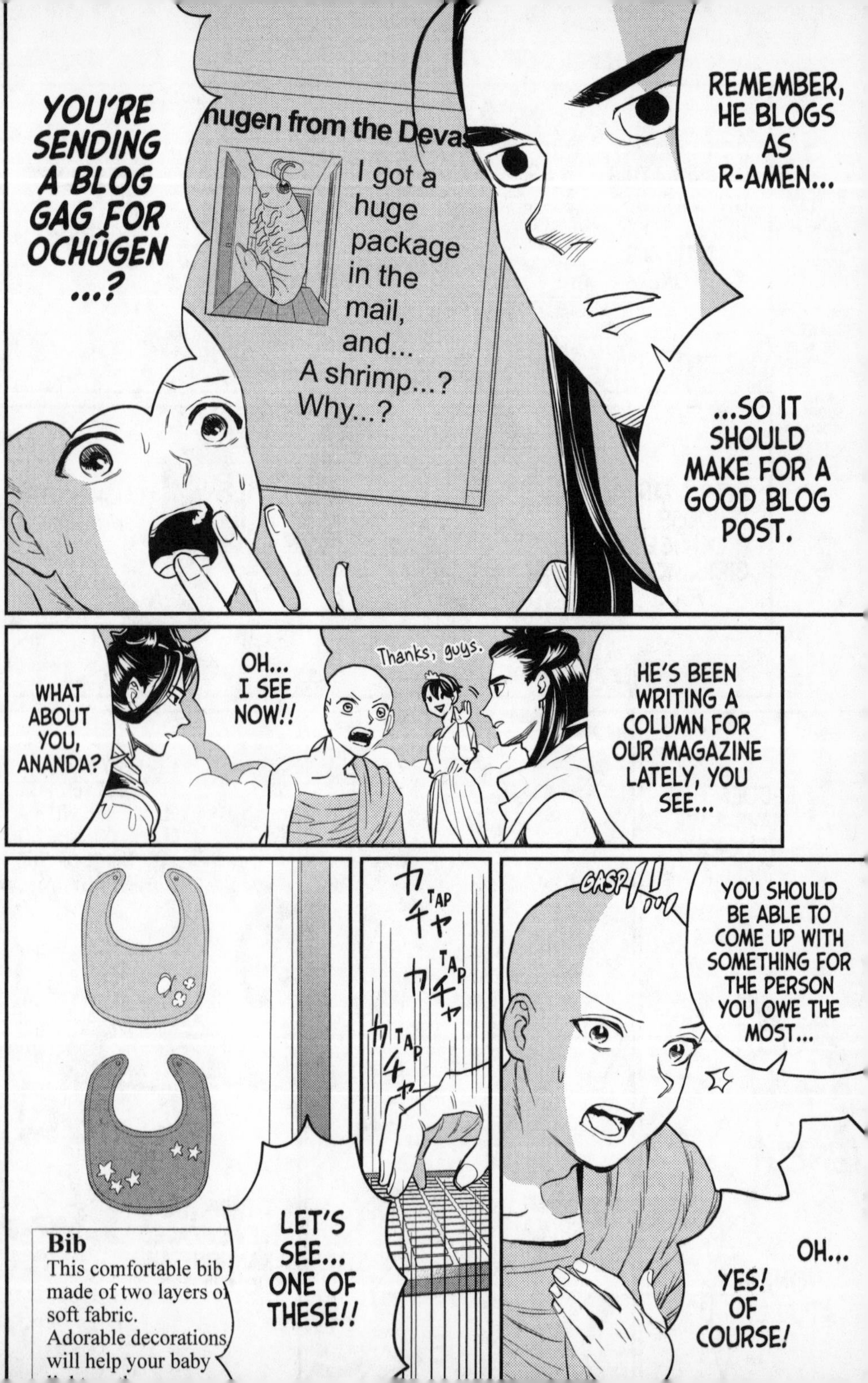
REMEMBER, HE BLOGS AS R-AMEN...
YOU'RE SENDING A BLOG GAG FOR OCHÛGEN ...?
hugen from the Devas
I got a huge package in the mail, and... A shrimp...? Why...?
...SO IT SHOULD MAKE FOR A GOOD BLOG POST.
HE'S BEEN WRITING A COLUMN FOR OUR MAGAZINE LATELY, YOU SEE...
Thanks, guys.
OH... I SEE NOW!!
WHAT ABOUT YOU, ANANDA?
GASP
YOU SHOULD BE ABLE TO COME UP WITH SOMETHING FOR THE PERSON YOU OWE THE MOST...
OH...
YES! OF COURSE!
カチャ TAP
カチャ TAP
カチャ TAP
LET'S SEE... ONE OF THESE!!
Bib
This comfortable bib i
made of two layers o
soft fabric.
Adorable decorations
will help your baby

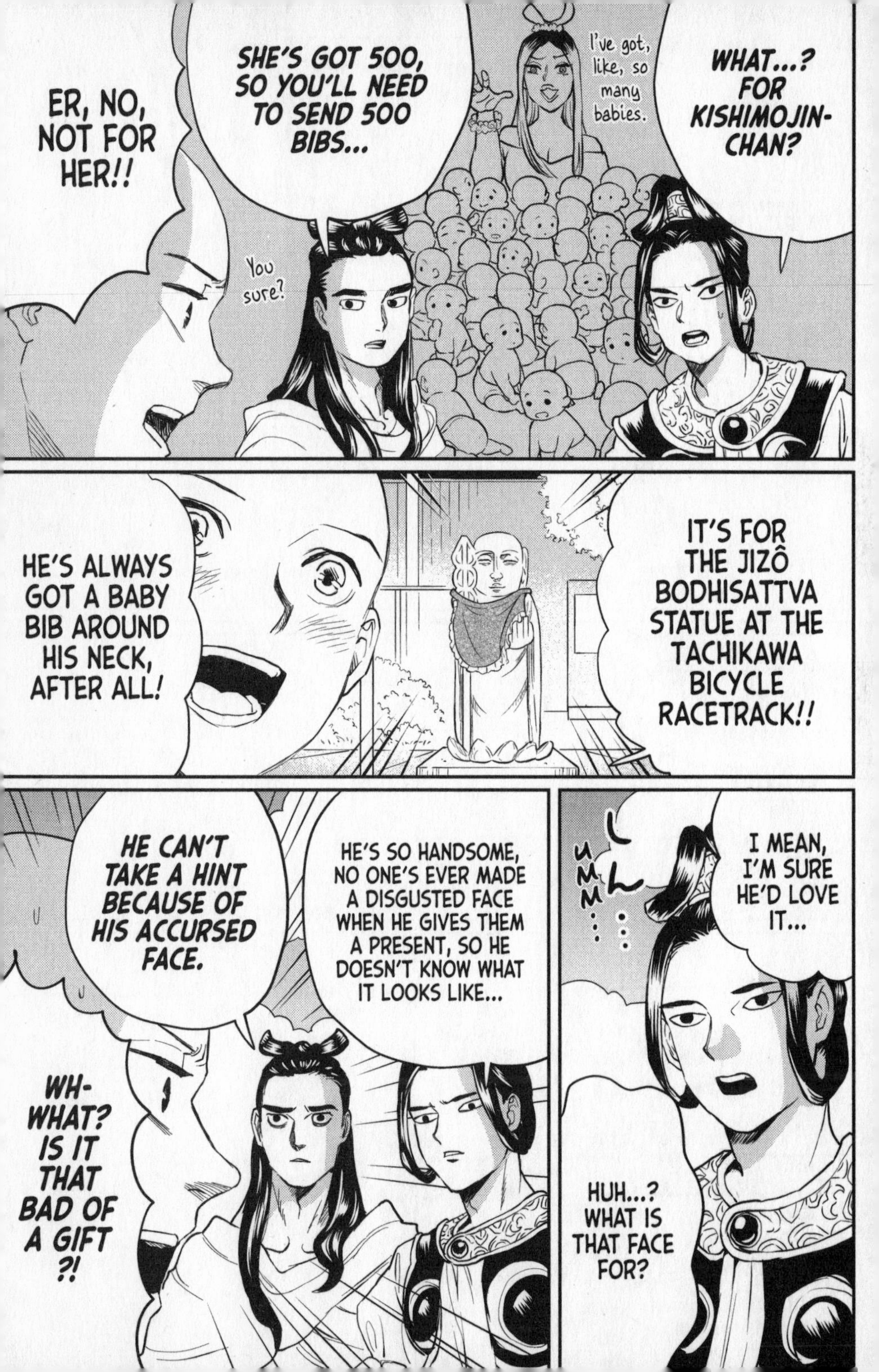
WHAT...? FOR KISHIMOJIN-CHAN?
I've got, like, so many babies.
SHE'S GOT 500, SO YOU'LL NEED TO SEND 500 BIBS...
ER, NO, NOT FOR HER!!
You sure?
IT'S FOR THE JIZÔ BODHISATTVA STATUE AT THE TACHIKAWA BICYCLE RACETRACK!!
HE'S ALWAYS GOT A BABY BIB AROUND HIS NECK, AFTER ALL!
I MEAN, I'M SURE HE'D LOVE IT...
UMM...
HUH...? WHAT IS THAT FACE FOR?
HE'S SO HANDSOME, NO ONE'S EVER MADE A DISGUSTED FACE WHEN HE GIVES THEM A PRESENT, SO HE DOESN'T KNOW WHAT IT LOOKS LIKE...
HE CAN'T TAKE A HINT BECAUSE OF HIS ACCURSED FACE.
WH-WHAT? IS IT THAT BAD OF A GIFT?!

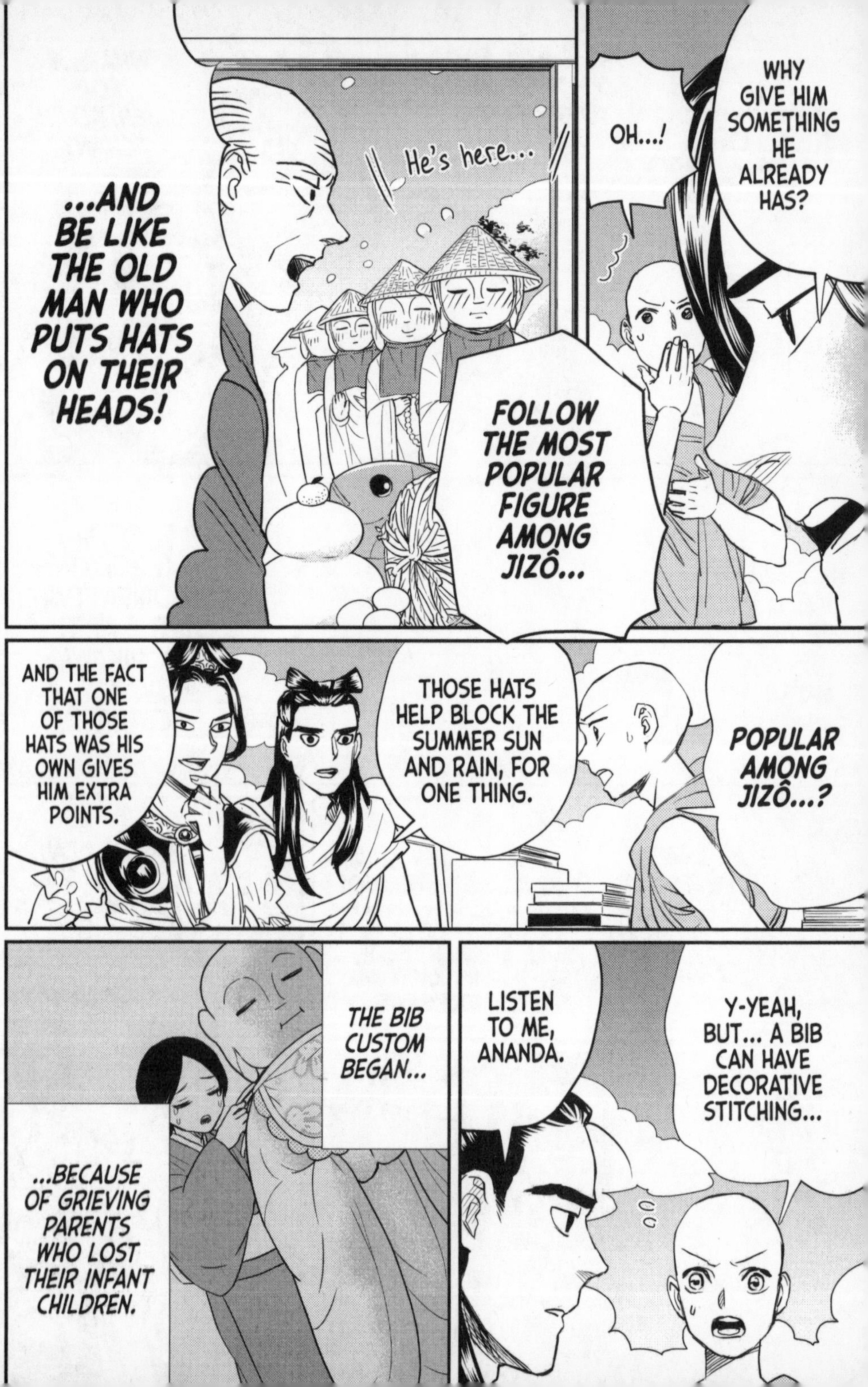
WHY GIVE HIM SOMETHING HE ALREADY HAS?
OH...!
He's here...
FOLLOW THE MOST POPULAR FIGURE AMONG JIZÔ...
...AND BE LIKE THE OLD MAN WHO PUTS HATS ON THEIR HEADS!
POPULAR AMONG JIZÔ...?
THOSE HATS HELP BLOCK THE SUMMER SUN AND RAIN, FOR ONE THING.
AND THE FACT THAT ONE OF THOSE HATS WAS HIS OWN GIVES HIM EXTRA POINTS.
Y-YEAH, BUT... A BIB CAN HAVE DECORATIVE STITCHING...
LISTEN TO ME, ANANDA.
THE BIB CUSTOM BEGAN...
...BECAUSE OF GRIEVING PARENTS WHO LOST THEIR INFANT CHILDREN.

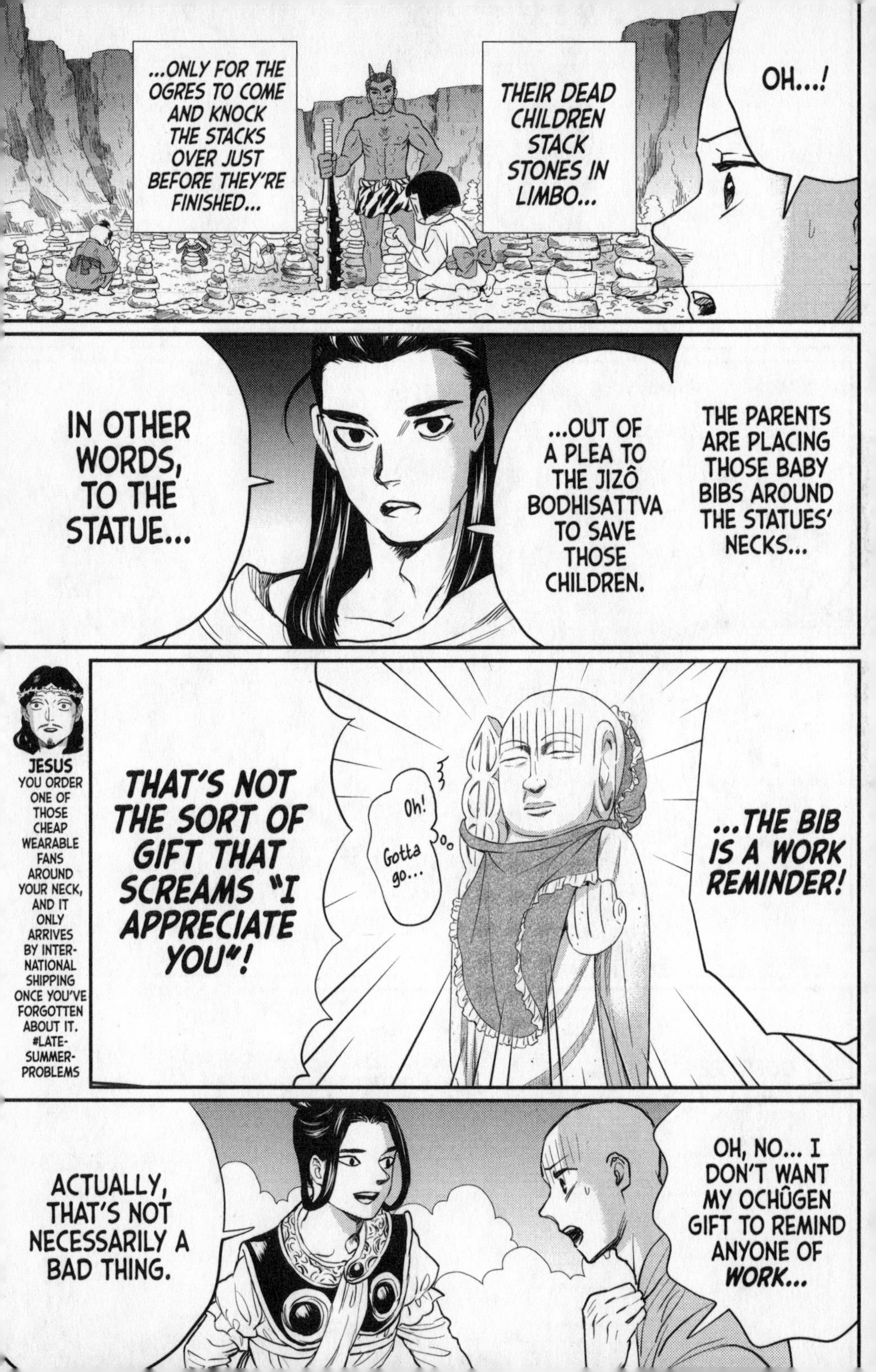
OH...!
THEIR DEAD CHILDREN STACK STONES IN LIMBO...
...ONLY FOR THE OGRES TO COME AND KNOCK THE STACKS OVER JUST BEFORE THEY'RE FINISHED...
THE PARENTS ARE PLACING THOSE BABY BIBS AROUND THE STATUES' NECKS...
...OUT OF A PLEA TO THE JIZÔ BODHISATTVA TO SAVE THOSE CHILDREN.
IN OTHER WORDS, TO THE STATUE...
...THE BIB IS A WORK REMINDER!
Oh!
Gotta go...
THAT'S NOT THE SORT OF GIFT THAT SCREAMS "I APPRECIATE YOU"!
JESUS
YOU ORDER ONE OF THOSE CHEAP WEARABLE FANS AROUND YOUR NECK, AND IT ONLY ARRIVES BY INTERNATIONAL SHIPPING ONCE YOU'VE FORGOTTEN ABOUT IT. #LATE-SUMMER-PROBLEMS
OH, NO... I DON'T WANT MY OCHÛGEN GIFT TO REMIND ANYONE OF WORK...
ACTUALLY, THAT'S NOT NECESSARILY A BAD THING.

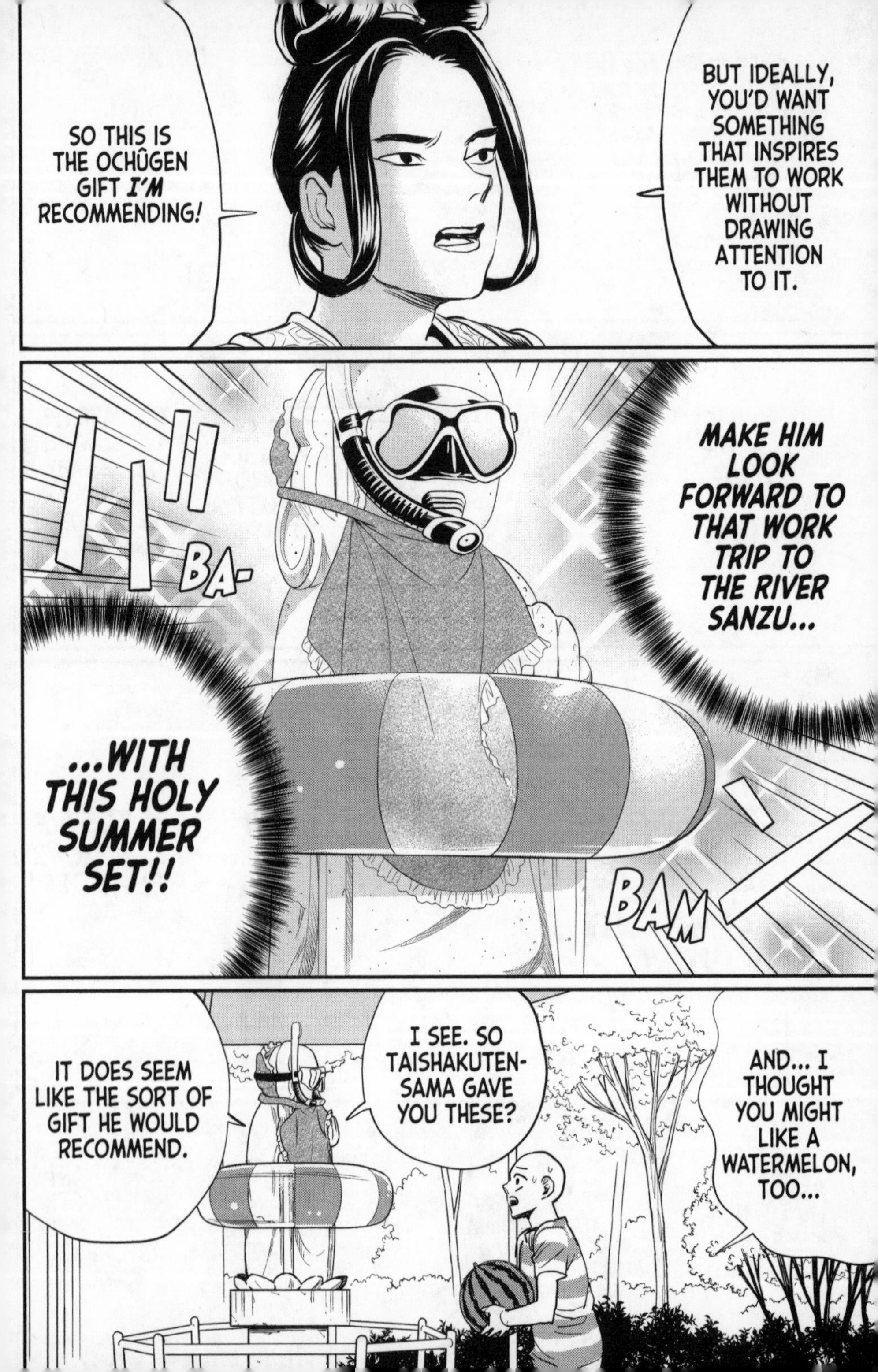
BUT IDEALLY, YOU'D WANT SOMETHING THAT INSPIRES THEM TO WORK WITHOUT DRAWING ATTENTION TO IT.
SO THIS IS THE OCHÛGEN GIFT *I'M* RECOMMENDING!
MAKE HIM LOOK FORWARD TO THAT WORK TRIP TO THE RIVER SANZU...
BA-
...WITH THIS HOLY SUMMER SET!!
BAM
AND... I THOUGHT YOU MIGHT LIKE A WATERMELON, TOO...
I SEE. SO TAISHAKUTEN-SAMA GAVE YOU THESE?
IT DOES SEEM LIKE THE SORT OF GIFT HE WOULD RECOMMEND.

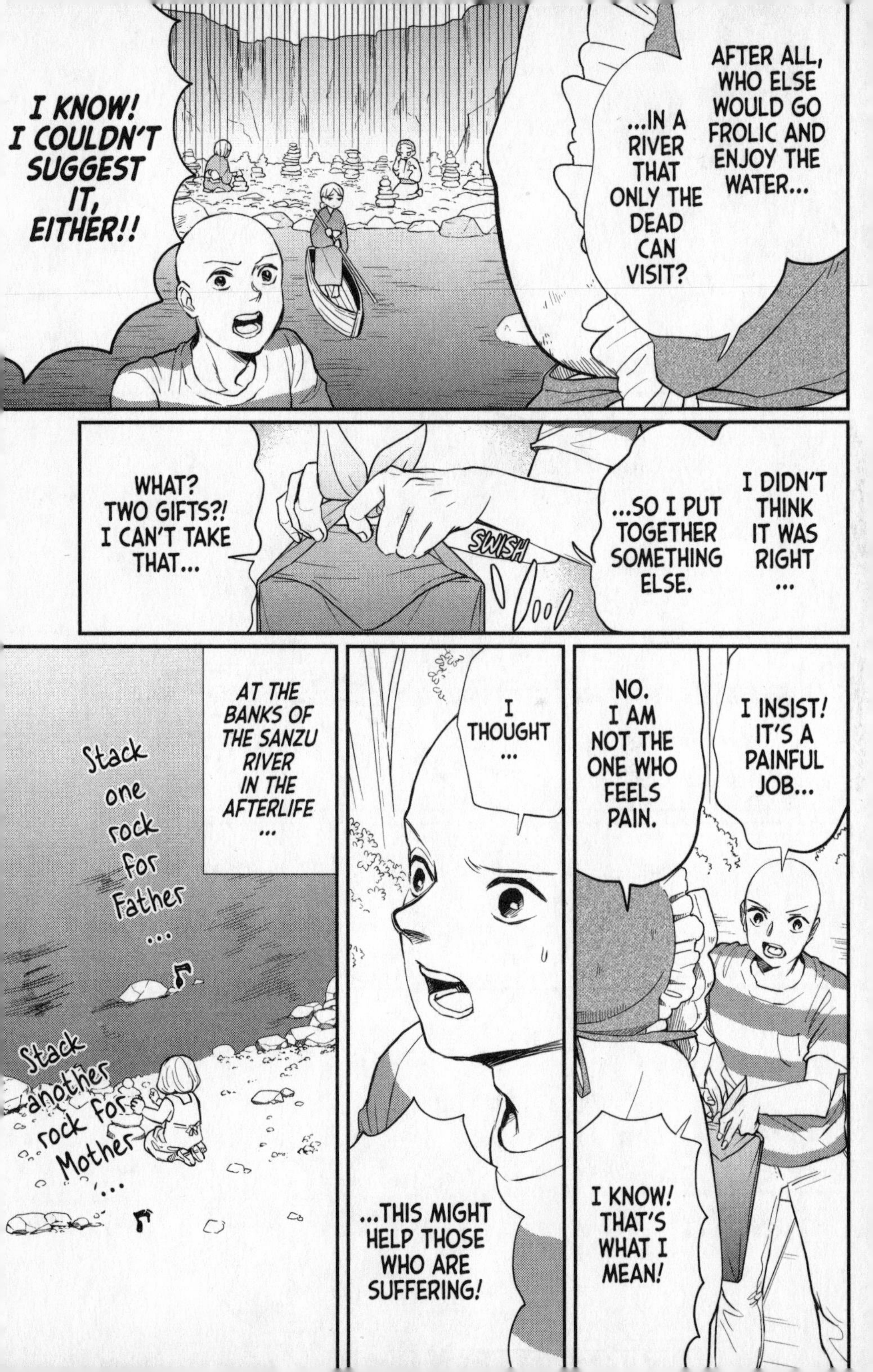
AFTER ALL, WHO ELSE WOULD GO FROLIC AND ENJOY THE WATER...
...IN A RIVER THAT ONLY THE DEAD CAN VISIT?
I KNOW! I COULDN'T SUGGEST IT, EITHER!!
I DIDN'T THINK IT WAS RIGHT...
...SO I PUT TOGETHER SOMETHING ELSE.
SWISH
WHAT? TWO GIFTS?! I CAN'T TAKE THAT...
I INSIST! IT'S A PAINFUL JOB...
NO. I AM NOT THE ONE WHO FEELS PAIN.
I KNOW! THAT'S WHAT I MEAN!
I THOUGHT...
...THIS MIGHT HELP THOSE WHO ARE SUFFERING!
AT THE BANKS OF THE SANZU RIVER IN THE AFTERLIFE...
Stack one rock for Father...
Stack another rock for Mother...

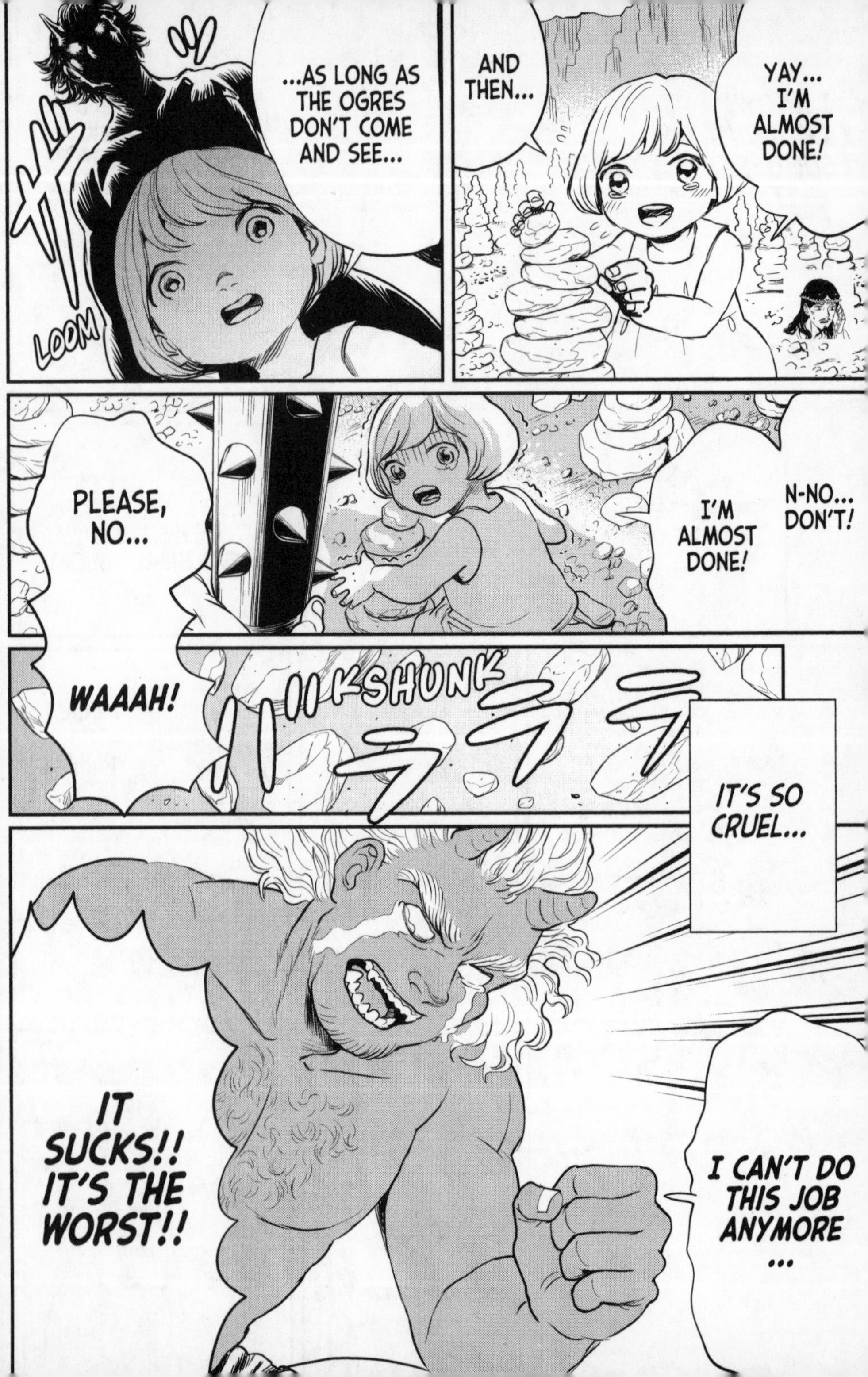
YAY... I'M ALMOST DONE!
AND THEN...
...AS LONG AS THE OGRES DON'T COME AND SEE...
LOOM
N-NO... DON'T!
I'M ALMOST DONE!
PLEASE, NO...
KSHUNK
WAAAH!
IT'S SO CRUEL...
I CAN'T DO THIS JOB ANYMORE ...
IT SUCKS!! IT'S THE WORST!!

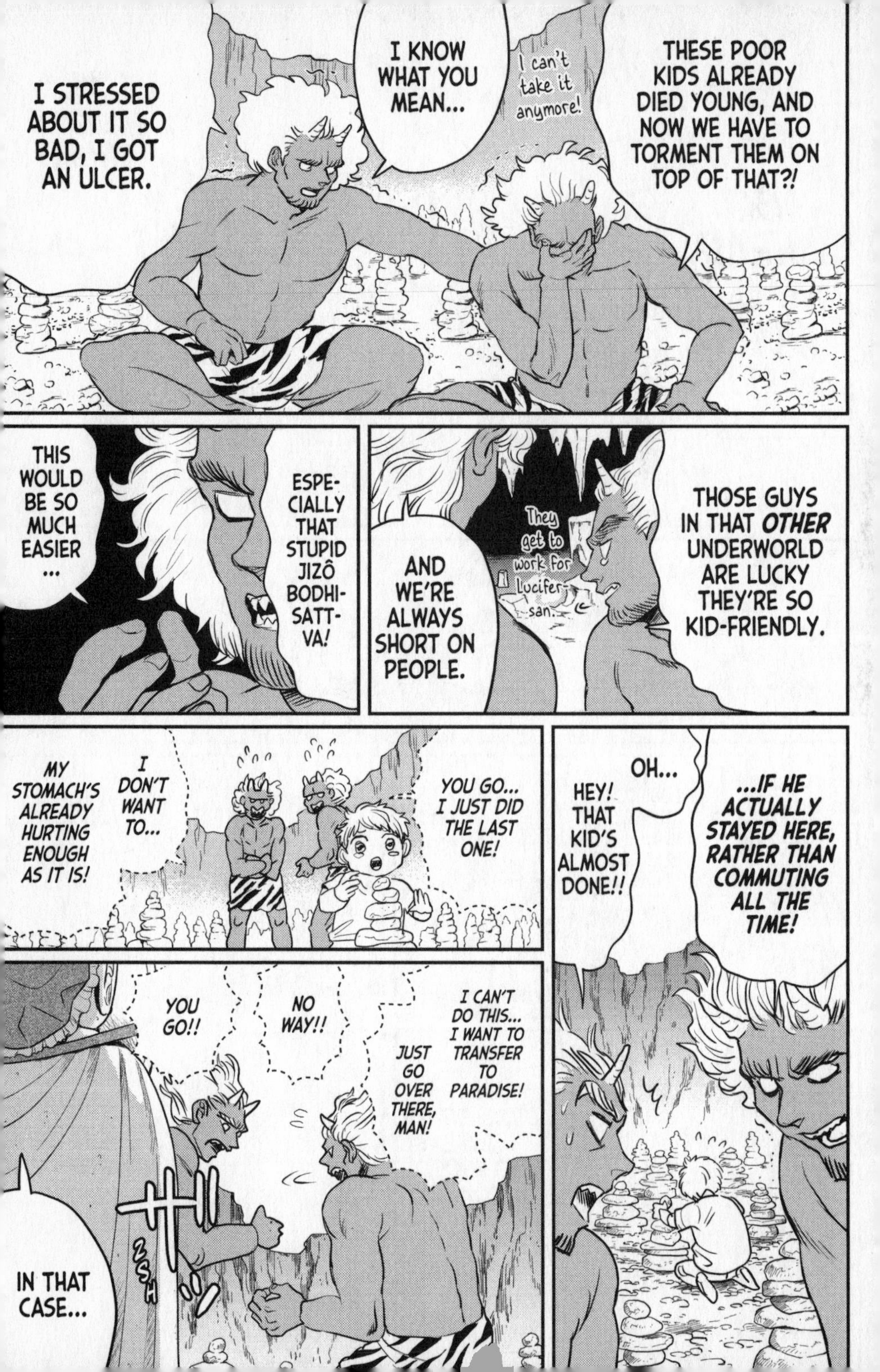
THESE POOR KIDS ALREADY DIED YOUNG, AND NOW WE HAVE TO TORMENT THEM ON TOP OF THAT?!
I can't take it anymore!
I KNOW WHAT YOU MEAN...
I STRESSED ABOUT IT SO BAD, I GOT AN ULCER.
THOSE GUYS IN THAT *OTHER* UNDERWORLD ARE LUCKY THEY'RE SO KID-FRIENDLY.
They get to work for Lucifer-san.
AND WE'RE ALWAYS SHORT ON PEOPLE.
ESPE-CIALLY THAT STUPID JIZÔ BODHI-SATT-VA!
THIS WOULD BE SO MUCH EASIER...
...IF HE ACTUALLY STAYED HERE, RATHER THAN COMMUTING ALL THE TIME!
OH...
HEY! THAT KID'S ALMOST DONE!!
YOU GO... I JUST DID THE LAST ONE!
I DON'T WANT TO...
MY STOMACH'S ALREADY HURTING ENOUGH AS IT IS!
I CAN'T DO THIS... I WANT TO TRANSFER TO PARADISE!
JUST GO OVER THERE, MAN!
NO WAY!!
YOU GO!!
ZSH
IN THAT CASE...

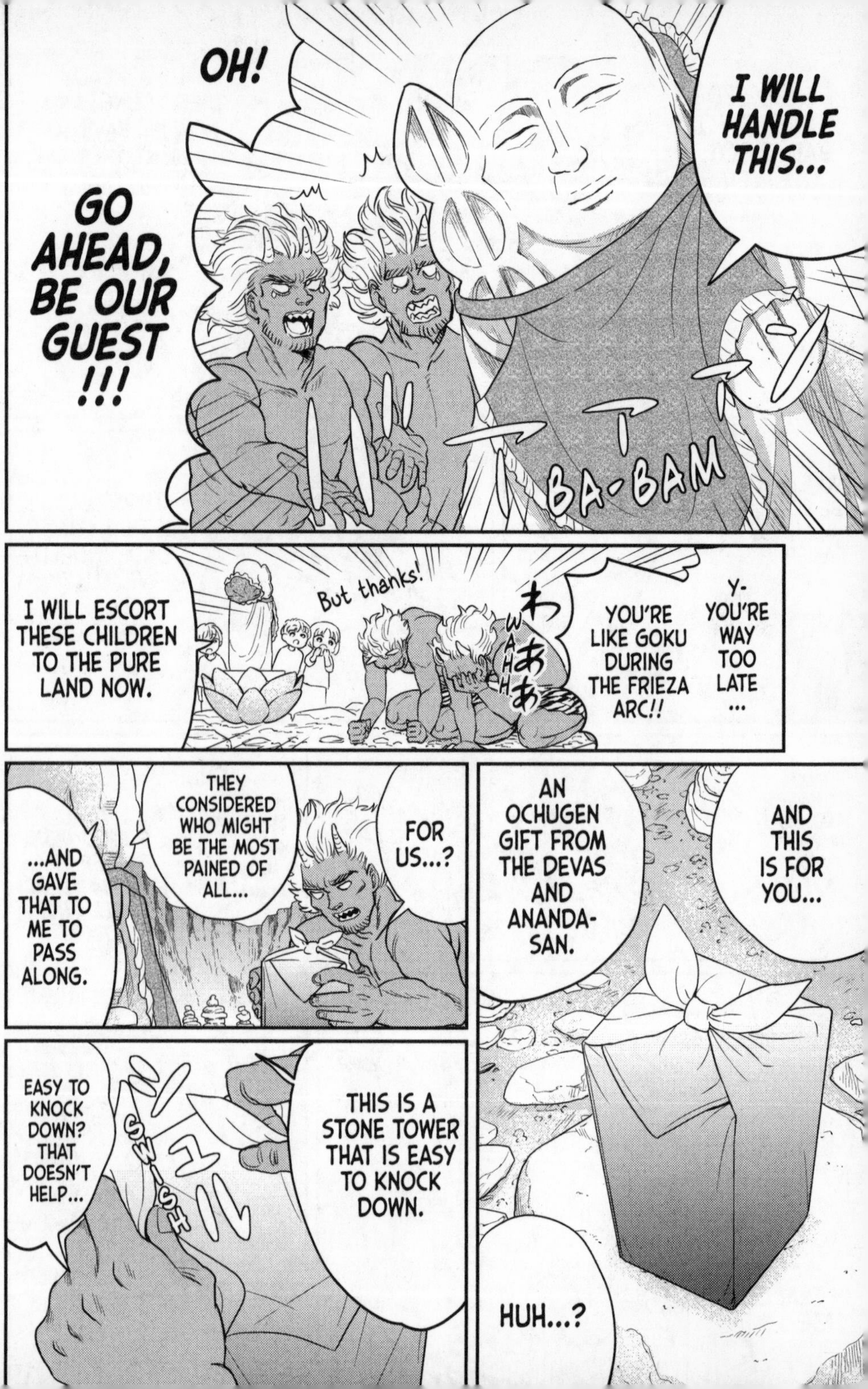
I WILL HANDLE THIS...
OH!
GO AHEAD, BE OUR GUEST!!!
BA-BAM
Y-YOU'RE WAY TOO LATE...
YOU'RE LIKE GOKU DURING THE FRIEZA ARC!!
WAHH
But thanks!
I WILL ESCORT THESE CHILDREN TO THE PURE LAND NOW.
AND THIS IS FOR YOU...
AN OCHUGEN GIFT FROM THE DEVAS AND ANANDA-SAN.
HUH...?
FOR US...?
THEY CONSIDERED WHO MIGHT BE THE MOST PAINED OF ALL...
...AND GAVE THAT TO ME TO PASS ALONG.
THIS IS A STONE TOWER THAT IS EASY TO KNOCK DOWN.
SWISH
EASY TO KNOCK DOWN? THAT DOESN'T HELP...

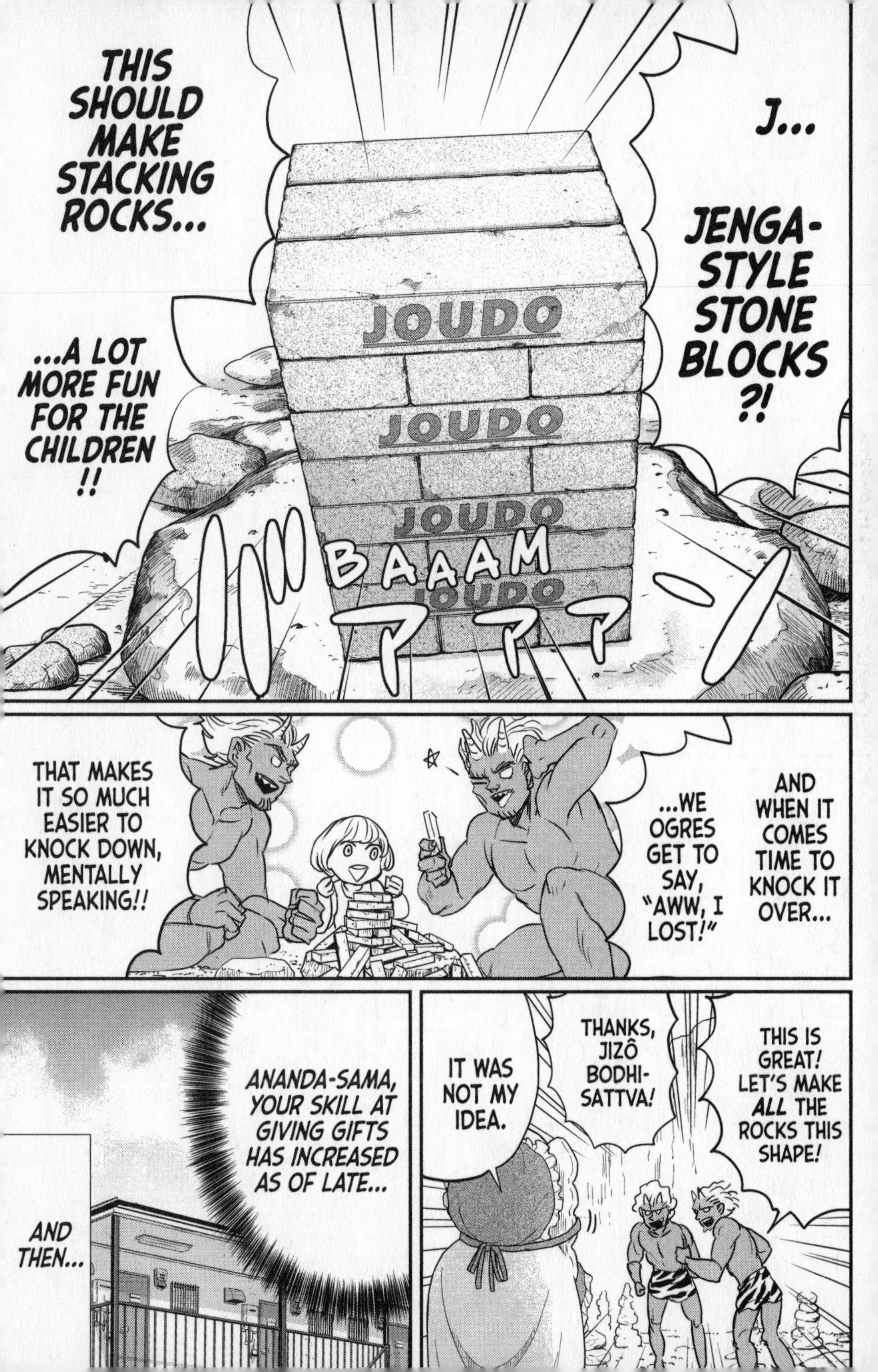
J...
JENGA-STYLE STONE BLOCKS?!
THIS SHOULD MAKE STACKING ROCKS...
...A LOT MORE FUN FOR THE CHILDREN!!
JOUDO
JOUDO
JOUDO
BAAAM
AND WHEN IT COMES TIME TO KNOCK IT OVER...
...WE OGRES GET TO SAY, "AWW, I LOST!"
THAT MAKES IT SO MUCH EASIER TO KNOCK DOWN, MENTALLY SPEAKING!!
THIS IS GREAT! LET'S MAKE *ALL* THE ROCKS THIS SHAPE!
THANKS, JIZÔ BODHI-SATTVA!
IT WAS NOT MY IDEA.
ANANDA-SAMA, YOUR SKILL AT GIVING GIFTS HAS INCREASED AS OF LATE...
AND THEN...

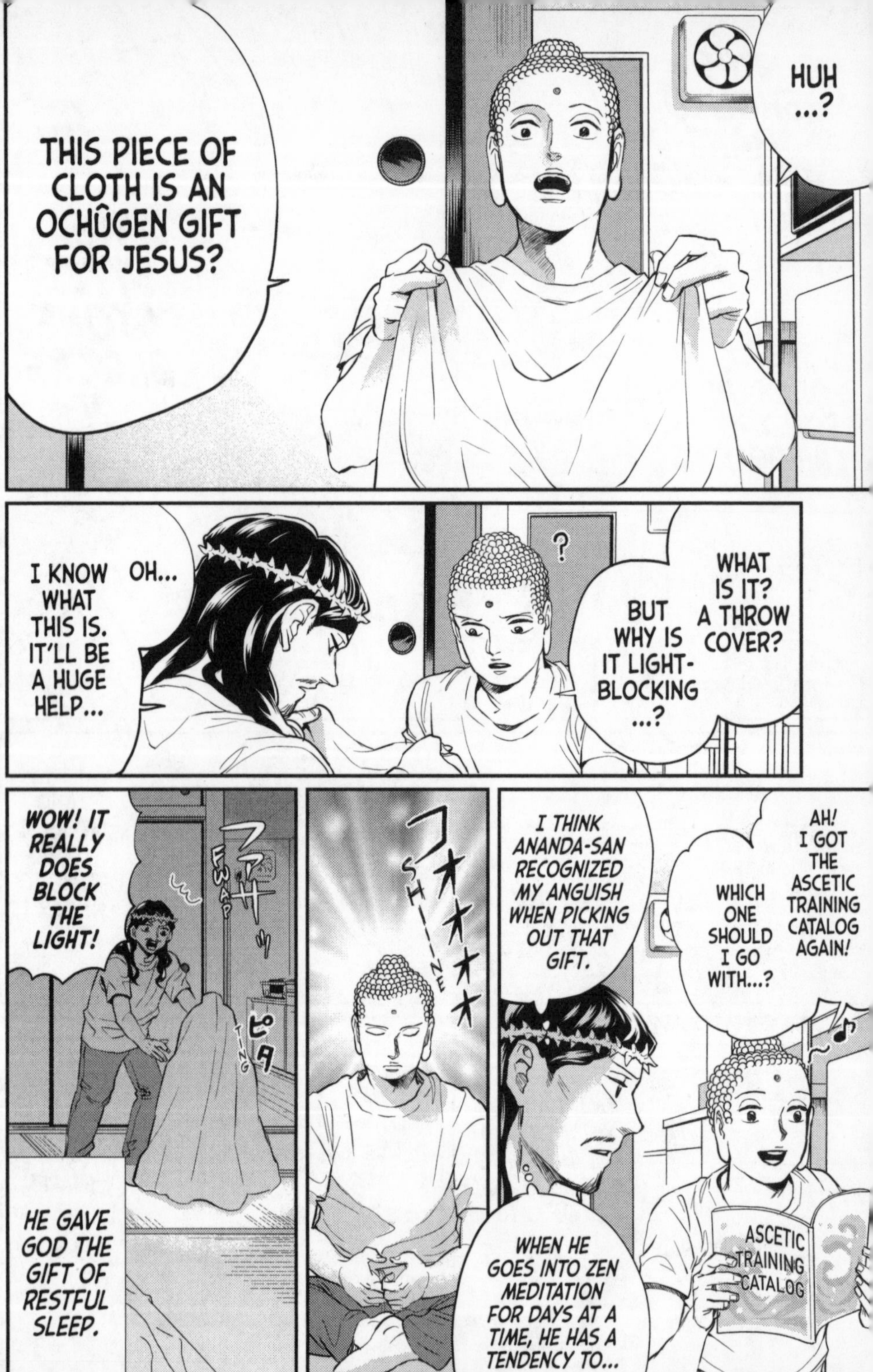
HUH ...?
THIS PIECE OF CLOTH IS AN OCHÛGEN GIFT FOR JESUS?
?
WHAT IS IT? A THROW COVER?
BUT WHY IS IT LIGHT-BLOCKING ...?
OH...
I KNOW WHAT THIS IS. IT'LL BE A HUGE HELP...
AH! I GOT THE ASCETIC TRAINING CATALOG AGAIN!
WHICH ONE SHOULD I GO WITH...?
I THINK ANANDA-SAN RECOGNIZED MY ANGUISH WHEN PICKING OUT THAT GIFT.
ASCETIC TRAINING CATALOG
WHEN HE GOES INTO ZEN MEDITATION FOR DAYS AT A TIME, HE HAS A TENDENCY TO...
SHINE
WOW! IT REALLY DOES BLOCK THE LIGHT!
ファサッ
FWAP
ピタ
TING
HE GAVE GOD THE GIFT OF RESTFUL SLEEP.

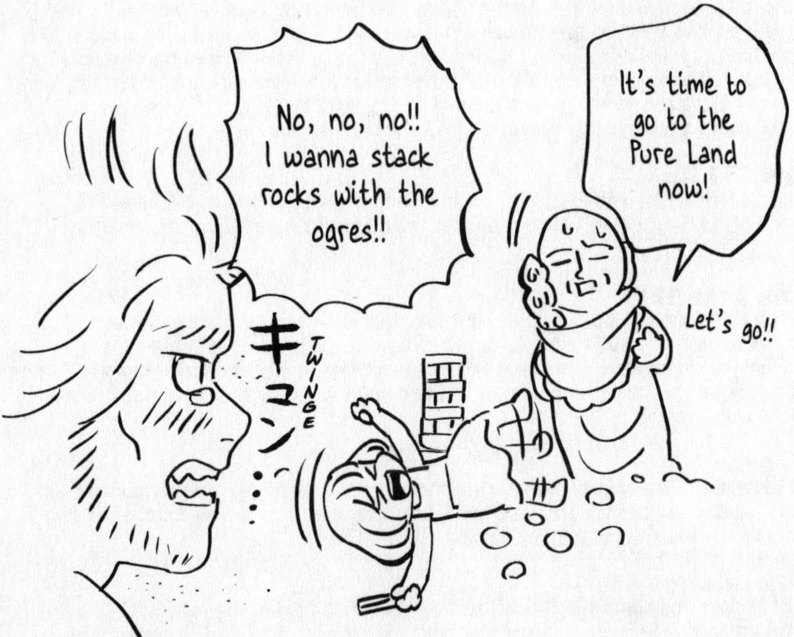
It's time to go to the Pure Land now!
Let's go!!
No, no, no!! I wanna stack rocks with the ogres!!
キュン
TWINGE

SAINT☆YOUNG MEN

CHAPTER 130 TRANSLATION NOTES

Sômen, page 147

A type of thin noodle made with wheat flour; it can be offered in both hand-cut and hand-pulled varieties for a slightly different texture. While it can be eaten in a hot soup similar to ramen or udon, sômen is typically enjoyed cold in the summertime, and dipped in a broth called *tsuyu*.

Kishimojin, page 151

Kishimojin, also known as Hariti, is both a demon and protector of children as a guardian deity in Buddhism. She is originally described as a *rakshasi*, or a kind of man-eating demon. The legend says that she had many children of her own, but killed the children of others to feed them. In order to help, the Buddha hid her youngest child to show her the pain of "losing" a child. After that point, she swore only to eat pomegranates and became a protector of all children and pregnant women.

Jizô, page 151

In general terms, it refers to small stone statues seen on roadsides and near graveyards. Jizô was a bodhisattva who is considered a protector of children, especially deceased or stillborn children. Therefore, the statues are often seen adorned in baby bibs and other baby-related offerings. The most well-known folklore story revolves around their *kasa* straw hats, however. An old man who wove the hats to sell at the end of the year was unable to sell his stock due to an incoming blizzard, and headed home without enough money to buy *mochi* rice cakes for the new year. Then he spotted a line of Jizô statues with snow piled atop their heads. He decided to place the hats atop their heads to protect them from the snow, and had to give his own hat to the last one. After returning home empty-handed, he and his wife awoke in the middle of the night when they heard the sound of a great bounty of food, gold coins, and such being placed on their doorstep, with the sight of the retreating statues in the distance.

Sanzu, page 154

The "Limbo" for children is also known as the "Sanzu riverbed" (*Sai no kawara*) because it exists on the side of the Sanzu river, which separates the realm of the living from the realm of the dead.

Watermelon, page 154

While watermelon is of course popular to eat in the summertime, it also factors into some traditional summer games. Similar to a piñata or the "pin the tail on the donkey" game, there is a custom of bringing a watermelon to the beach (or other outdoor venue), then blindfolding a player holding a stick and spinning them around, to see if they can swing down in the right spot to break open the watermelon.

Pure Land, page 158

The term for the realm of a Buddha or bodhisattva. It is sought as a kind of paradise, but also as an ideal place to practice the dharma away from the distractions of the world. In Japanese this word is *jôdo* (or *joudo*, as seen on the game blocks).

Goku vs. Frieza, page 158

One of the most climactic battles in the *Dragon Ball* manga/anime happens between Goku and the villain Frieza. While it's not particularly unique within the series to have Goku delayed while a villain defeats or kills the good guys, the Frieza fight is particularly noteworthy for how long it takes Goku to return to battle, and how many characters are taken out in the meantime.

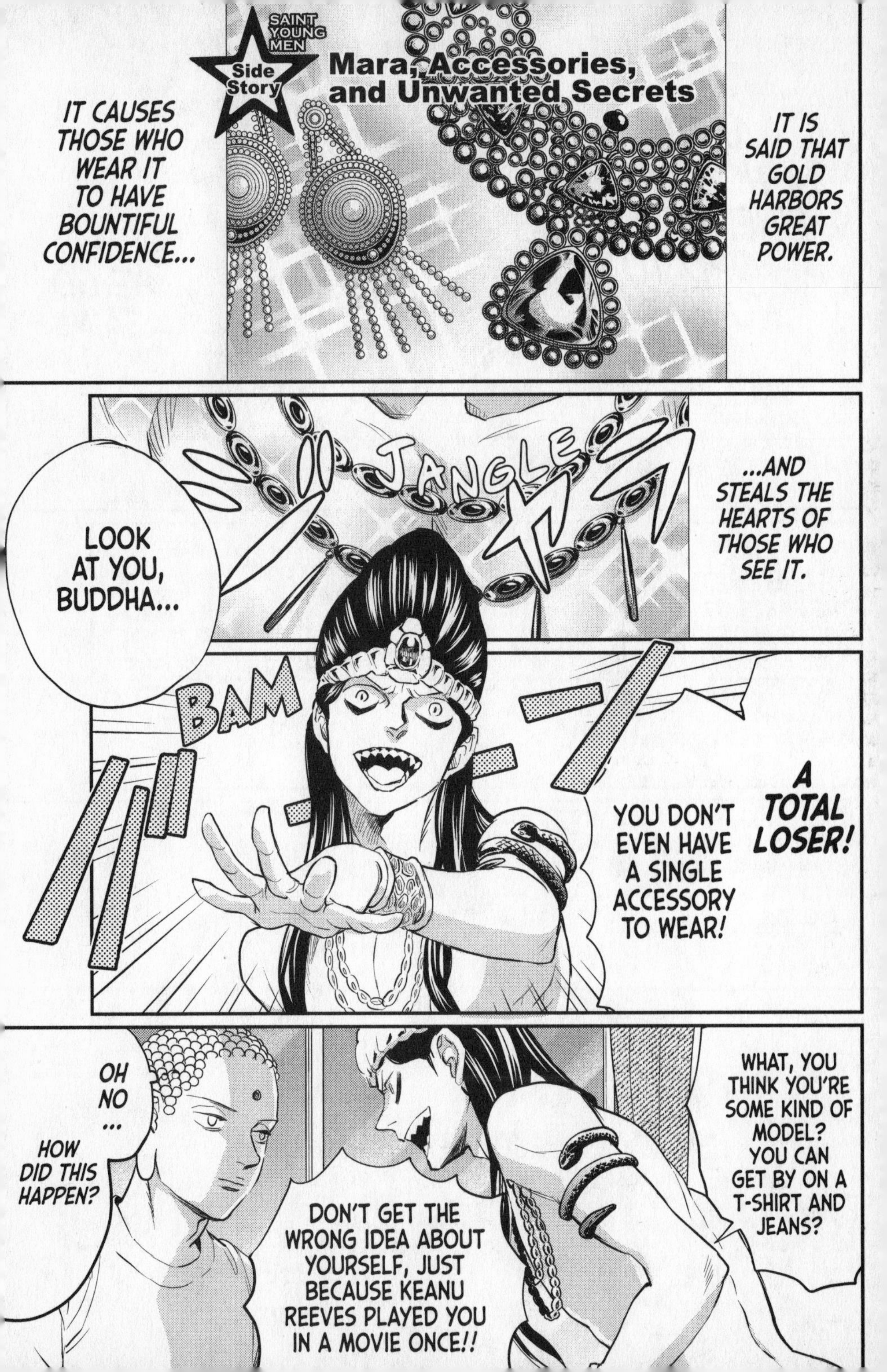
SAINT YOUNG MEN
Side Story
Mara, Accessories, and Unwanted Secrets
IT IS SAID THAT GOLD HARBORS GREAT POWER.
IT CAUSES THOSE WHO WEAR IT TO HAVE BOUNTIFUL CONFIDENCE...
...AND STEALS THE HEARTS OF THOSE WHO SEE IT.
JANGLE
LOOK AT YOU, BUDDHA...
BAM
A TOTAL LOSER!
YOU DON'T EVEN HAVE A SINGLE ACCESSORY TO WEAR!
WHAT, YOU THINK YOU'RE SOME KIND OF MODEL? YOU CAN GET BY ON A T-SHIRT AND JEANS?
DON'T GET THE WRONG IDEA ABOUT YOURSELF, JUST BECAUSE KEANU REEVES PLAYED YOU IN A MOVIE ONCE!!
OH NO...
HOW DID THIS HAPPEN?

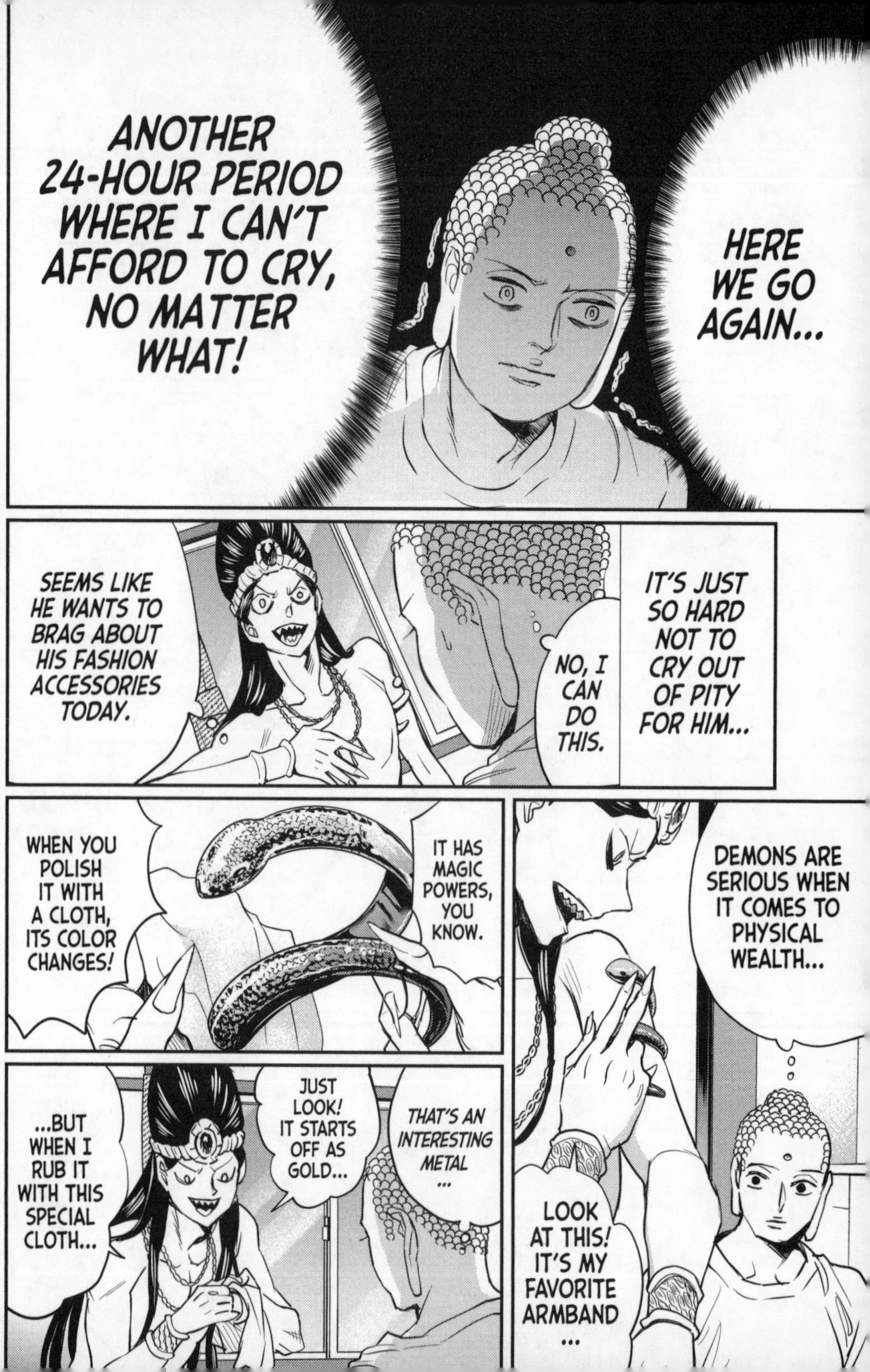
HERE WE GO AGAIN...
ANOTHER 24-HOUR PERIOD WHERE I CAN'T AFFORD TO CRY, NO MATTER WHAT!
IT'S JUST SO HARD NOT TO CRY OUT OF PITY FOR HIM...
NO, I CAN DO THIS.
SEEMS LIKE HE WANTS TO BRAG ABOUT HIS FASHION ACCESSORIES TODAY.
DEMONS ARE SERIOUS WHEN IT COMES TO PHYSICAL WEALTH...
LOOK AT THIS! IT'S MY FAVORITE ARMBAND ...
IT HAS MAGIC POWERS, YOU KNOW.
WHEN YOU POLISH IT WITH A CLOTH, ITS COLOR CHANGES!
THAT'S AN INTERESTING METAL ...
JUST LOOK! IT STARTS OFF AS GOLD...
...BUT WHEN I RUB IT WITH THIS SPECIAL CLOTH...

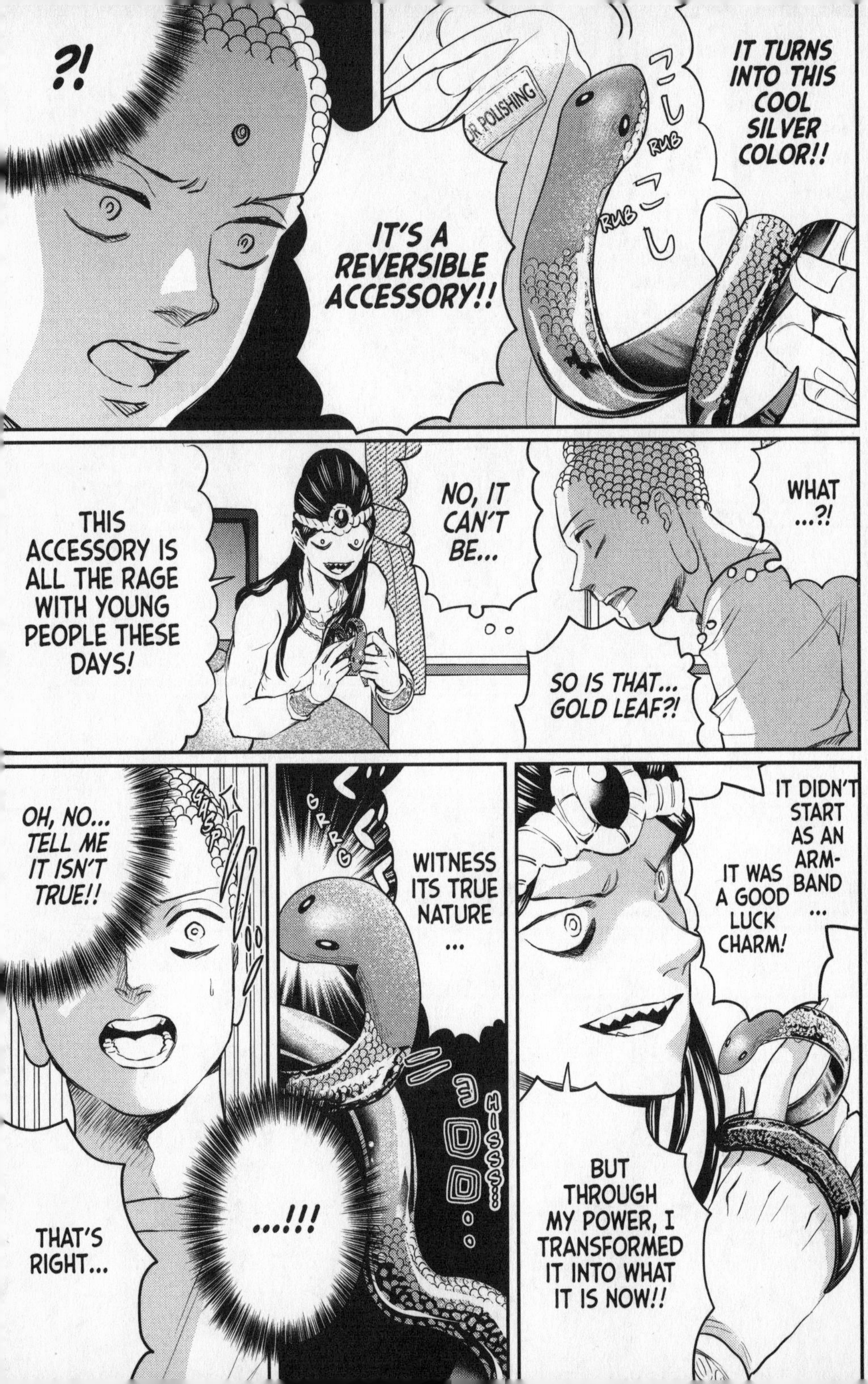
IT TURNS INTO THIS COOL SILVER COLOR!!
こし RUB
こし RUB
こし
OR POLISHING
IT'S A REVERSIBLE ACCESSORY!!
?!
WHAT ...?!
NO, IT CAN'T BE...
SO IS THAT... GOLD LEAF?!
THIS ACCESSORY IS ALL THE RAGE WITH YOUNG PEOPLE THESE DAYS!
IT DIDN'T START AS AN ARM-BAND ...
IT WAS A GOOD LUCK CHARM!
BUT THROUGH MY POWER, I TRANSFORMED IT INTO WHAT IT IS NOW!!
GRRR
WITNESS ITS TRUE NATURE ...
HISSS...
...!!!
OH, NO... TELL ME IT ISN'T TRUE!!
GASP
THAT'S RIGHT...

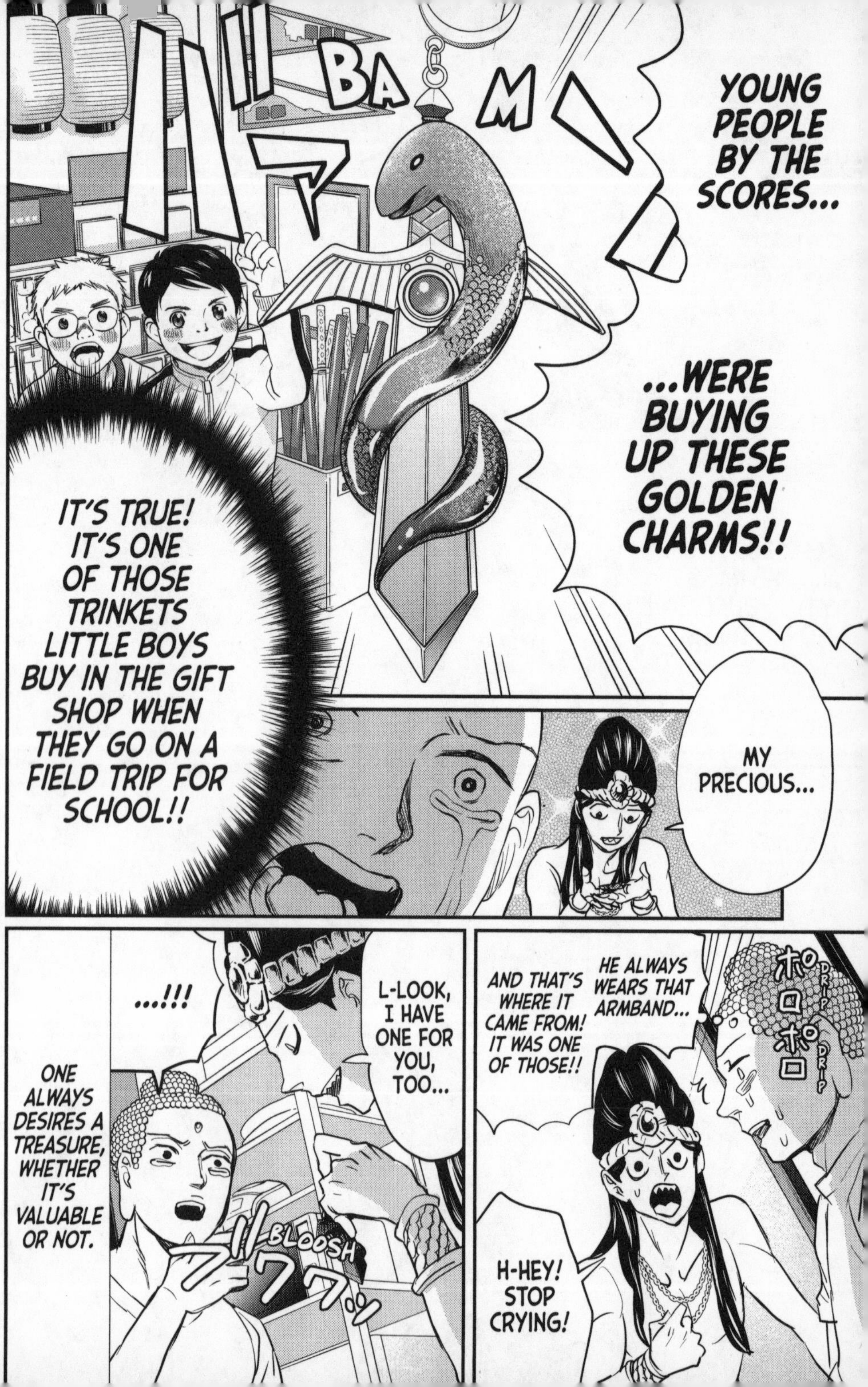
BAM
YOUNG PEOPLE BY THE SCORES...
...WERE BUYING UP THESE GOLDEN CHARMS!!
IT'S TRUE! IT'S ONE OF THOSE TRINKETS LITTLE BOYS BUY IN THE GIFT SHOP WHEN THEY GO ON A FIELD TRIP FOR SCHOOL!!
MY PRECIOUS...
HE ALWAYS WEARS THAT ARMBAND...
AND THAT'S WHERE IT CAME FROM! IT WAS ONE OF THOSE!!
DRIP DRIP
H-HEY! STOP CRYING!
L-LOOK, I HAVE ONE FOR YOU, TOO...
...!!!
ONE ALWAYS DESIRES A TREASURE, WHETHER IT'S VALUABLE OR NOT.
BLOOSH

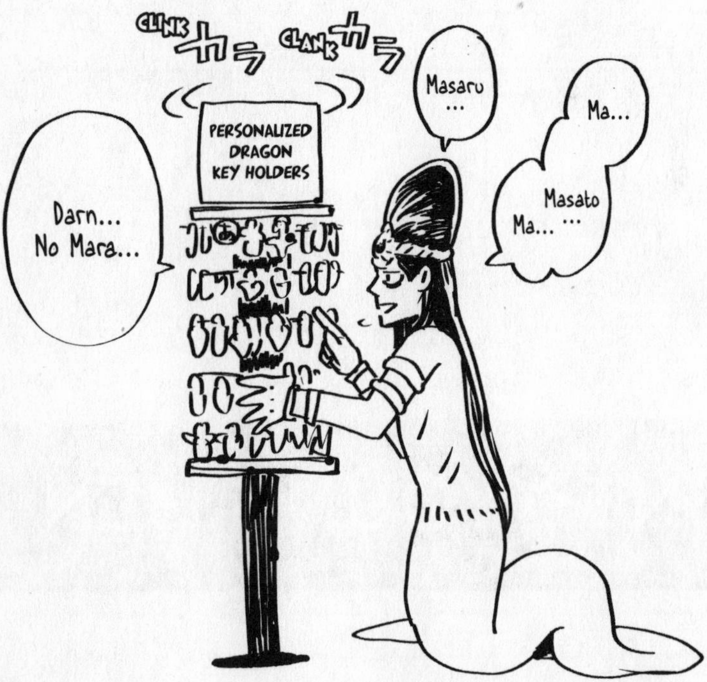
Ma...
Masato ...
Ma...
Masaru ...
CLANK カラ
CLINK カラ
PERSONALIZED DRAGON KEY HOLDERS
Darn... No Mara...

SAINT☆YOUNG MEN

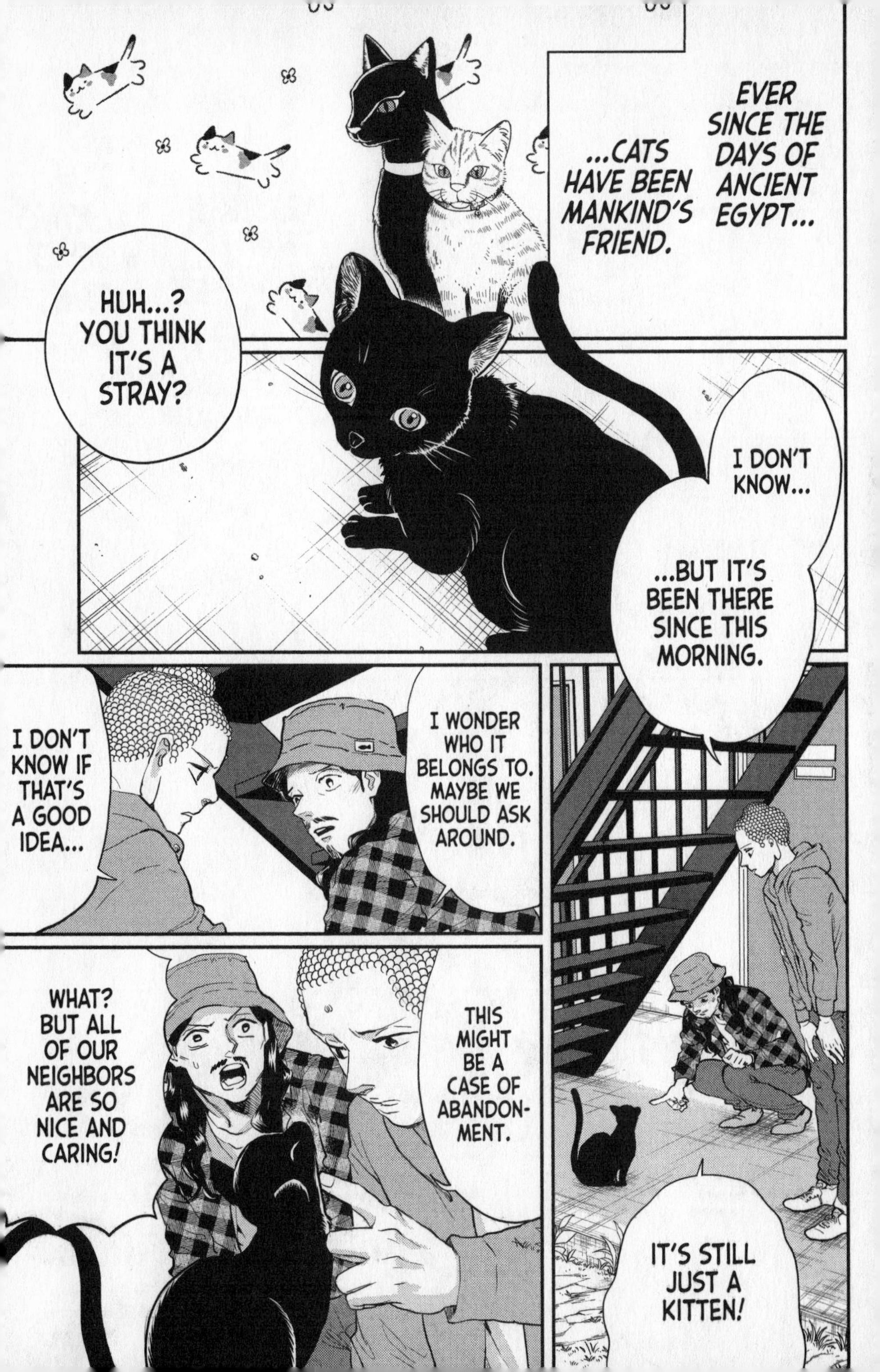
EVER SINCE THE DAYS OF ANCIENT EGYPT...
...CATS HAVE BEEN MANKIND'S FRIEND.
HUH...? YOU THINK IT'S A STRAY?
I DON'T KNOW...
...BUT IT'S BEEN THERE SINCE THIS MORNING.
IT'S STILL JUST A KITTEN!
I WONDER WHO IT BELONGS TO. MAYBE WE SHOULD ASK AROUND.
I DON'T KNOW IF THAT'S A GOOD IDEA...
THIS MIGHT BE A CASE OF ABANDONMENT.
WHAT? BUT ALL OF OUR NEIGHBORS ARE SO NICE AND CARING!

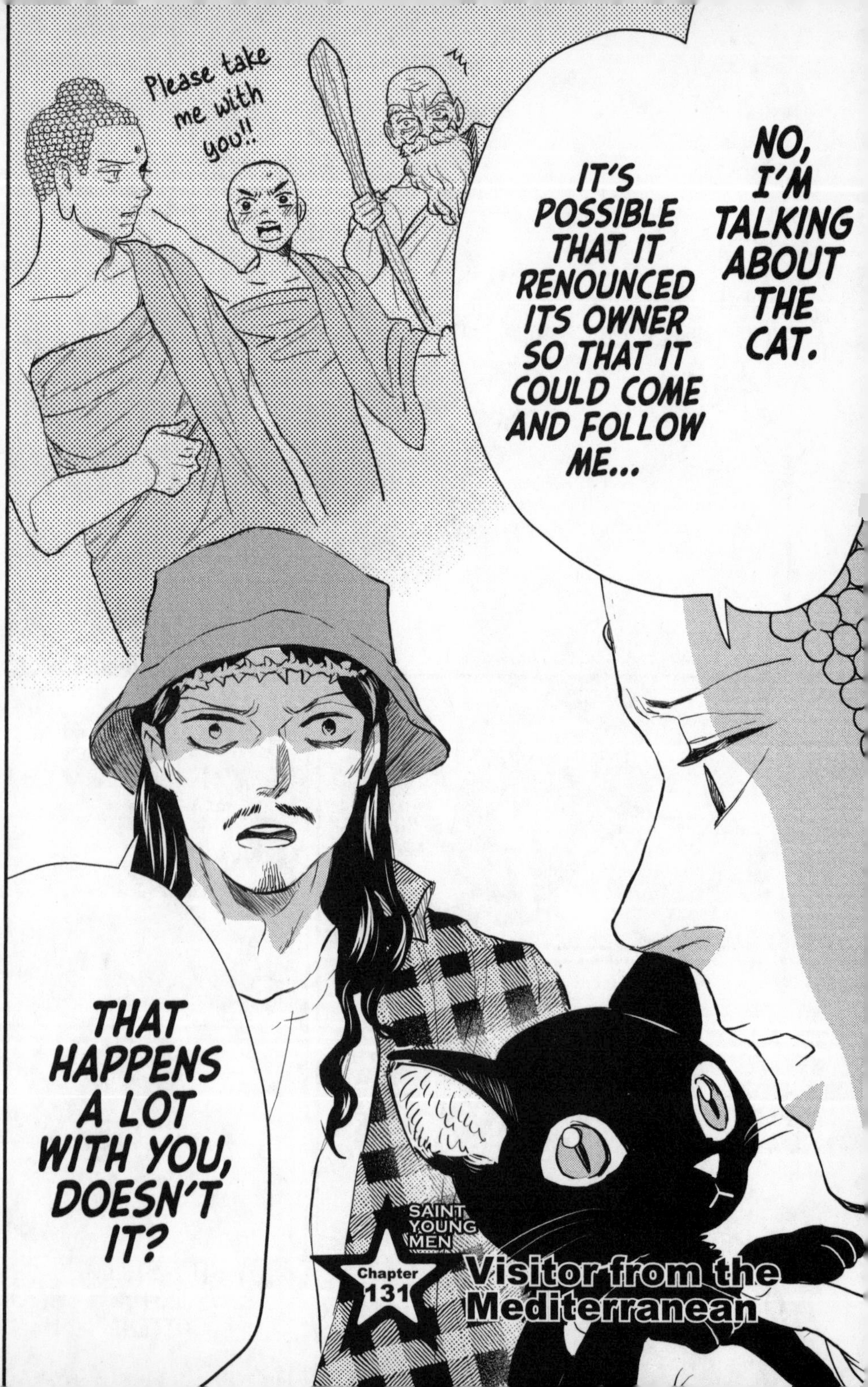
NO, I'M TALKING ABOUT THE CAT.
IT'S POSSIBLE THAT IT RENOUNCED ITS OWNER SO THAT IT COULD COME AND FOLLOW ME...
Please take me with you!!
THAT HAPPENS A LOT WITH YOU, DOESN'T IT?
SAINT YOUNG MEN
Chapter 131
Visitor from the Mediterranean

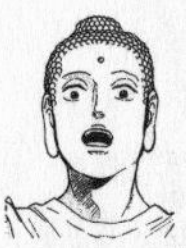

BUDDHA
3 <- THE SYMBOL OF AN APPROACHING CAT.

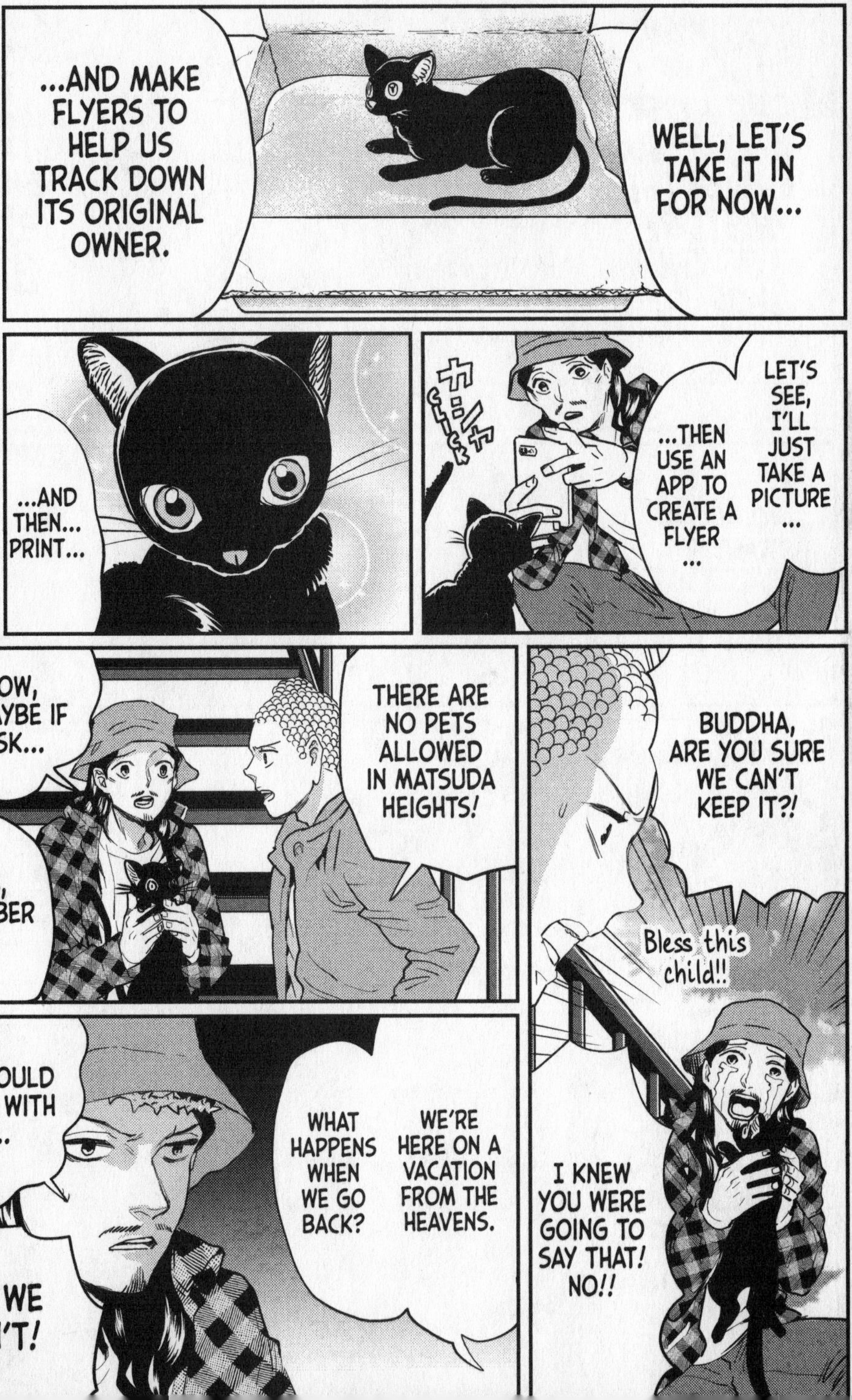

WELL, LET'S TAKE IT IN FOR NOW...
...AND MAKE FLYERS TO HELP US TRACK DOWN ITS ORIGINAL OWNER.
LET'S SEE, I'LL JUST TAKE A PICTURE...
...THEN USE AN APP TO CREATE A FLYER...
カシャ CLICK
...AND THEN... PRINT...
BUDDHA, ARE YOU SURE WE CAN'T KEEP IT?!
Bless this child!!
I KNEW YOU WERE GOING TO SAY THAT! NO!!
THERE ARE NO PETS ALLOWED IN MATSUDA HEIGHTS!
I KNOW, BUT MAYBE IF WE ASK...
PLUS, REMEMBER...
WE'RE HERE ON A VACATION FROM THE HEAVENS.
WHAT HAPPENS WHEN WE GO BACK?
W-WE COULD TAKE IT WITH US...
NO, WE CAN'T!

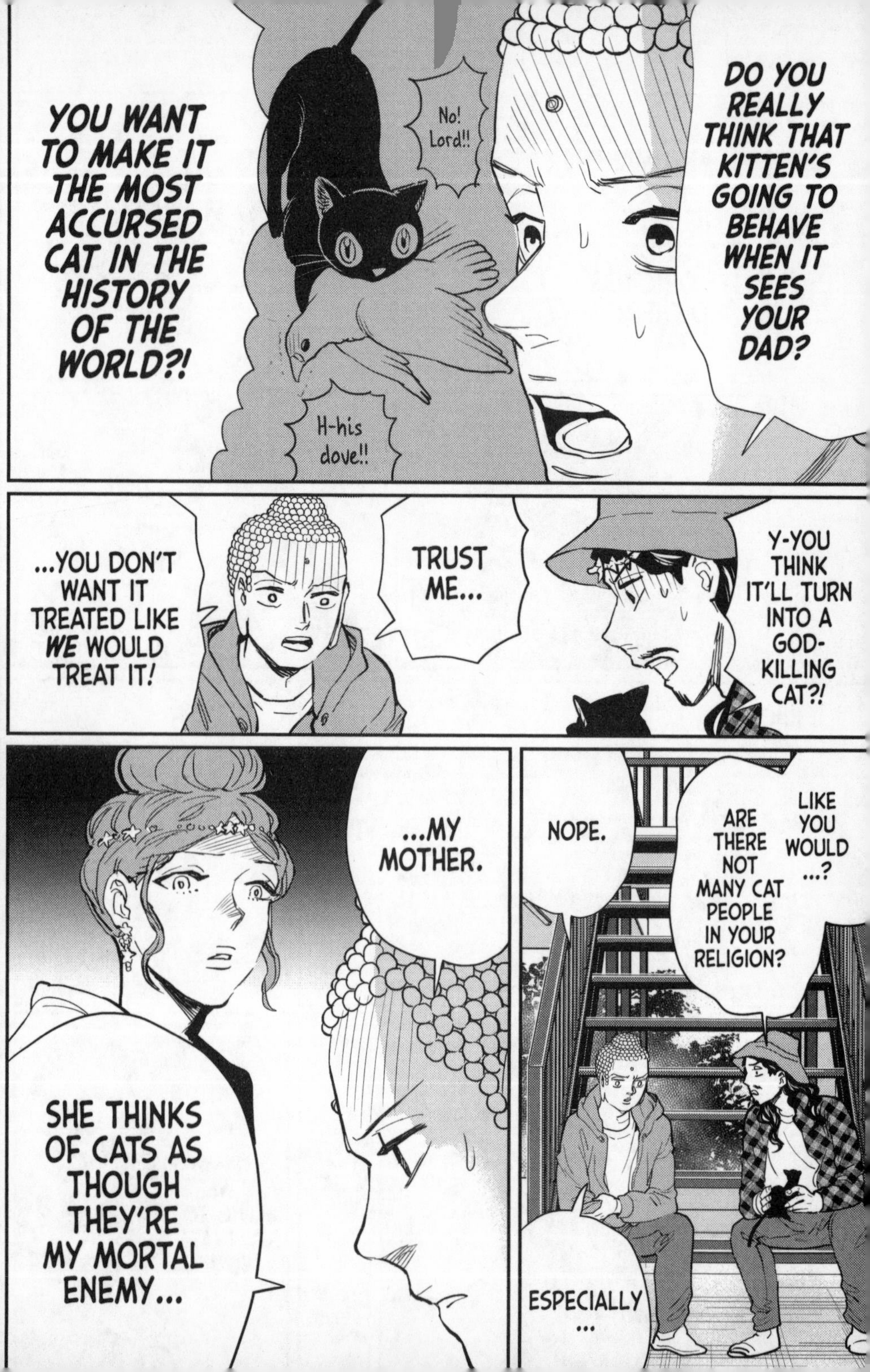
DO YOU REALLY THINK THAT KITTEN'S GOING TO BEHAVE WHEN IT SEES YOUR DAD?
No! Lord!!
YOU WANT TO MAKE IT THE MOST ACCURSED CAT IN THE HISTORY OF THE WORLD?!
H-his dove!!
Y-YOU THINK IT'LL TURN INTO A GOD-KILLING CAT?!
TRUST ME...
...YOU DON'T WANT IT TREATED LIKE *WE* WOULD TREAT IT!
LIKE YOU WOULD ...?
ARE THERE NOT MANY CAT PEOPLE IN YOUR RELIGION?
NOPE.
ESPECIALLY ...
...MY MOTHER.
SHE THINKS OF CATS AS THOUGH THEY'RE MY MORTAL ENEMY...

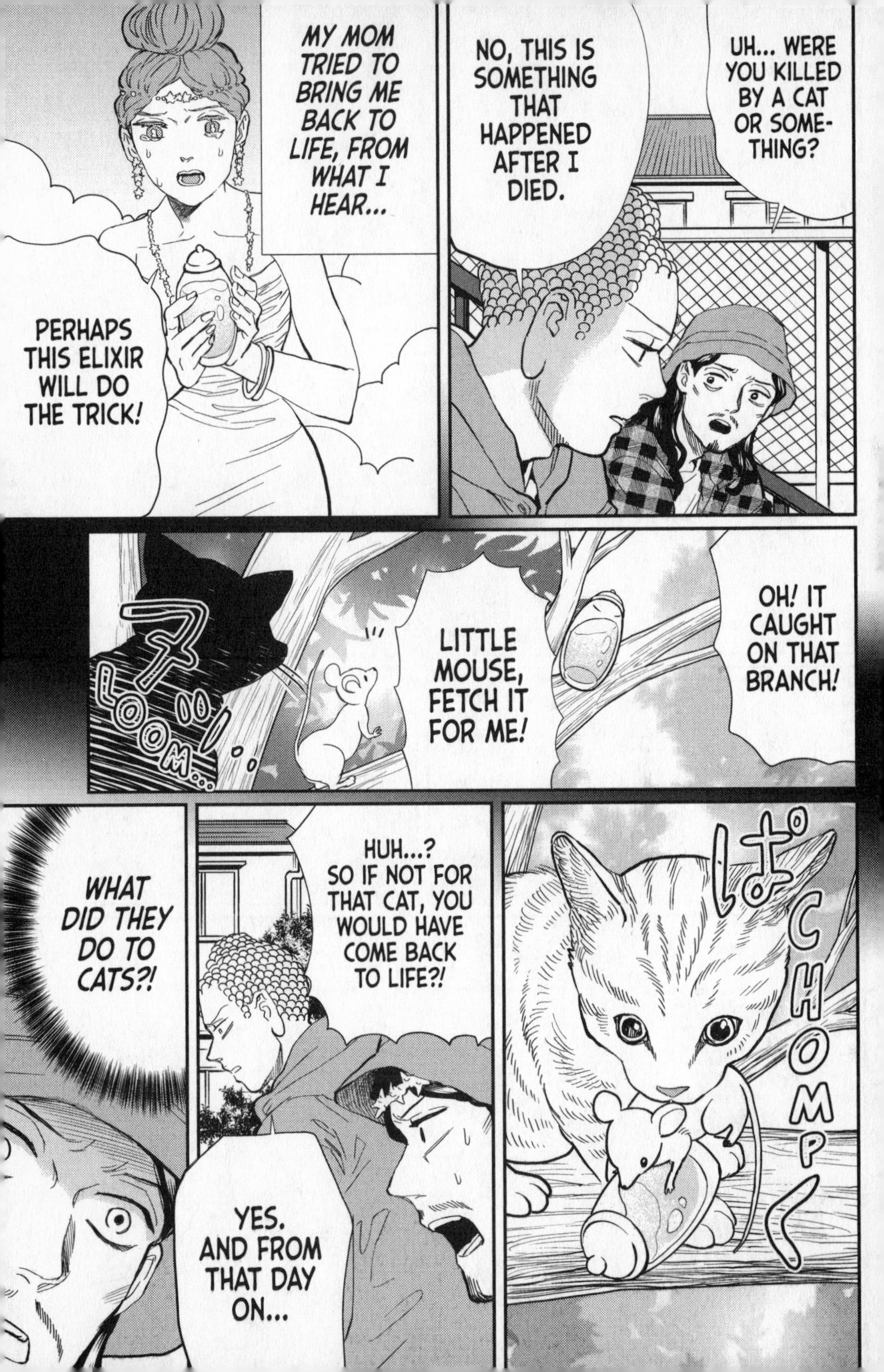
UH... WERE YOU KILLED BY A CAT OR SOME-THING?
NO, THIS IS SOMETHING THAT HAPPENED AFTER I DIED.
MY MOM TRIED TO BRING ME BACK TO LIFE, FROM WHAT I HEAR...
PERHAPS THIS ELIXIR WILL DO THE TRICK!
OH! IT CAUGHT ON THAT BRANCH!
LITTLE MOUSE, FETCH IT FOR ME!
フLOOM...
ぱく
CHOMP
HUH...? SO IF NOT FOR THAT CAT, YOU WOULD HAVE COME BACK TO LIFE?!
YES. AND FROM THAT DAY ON...
WHAT DID THEY DO TO CATS?!

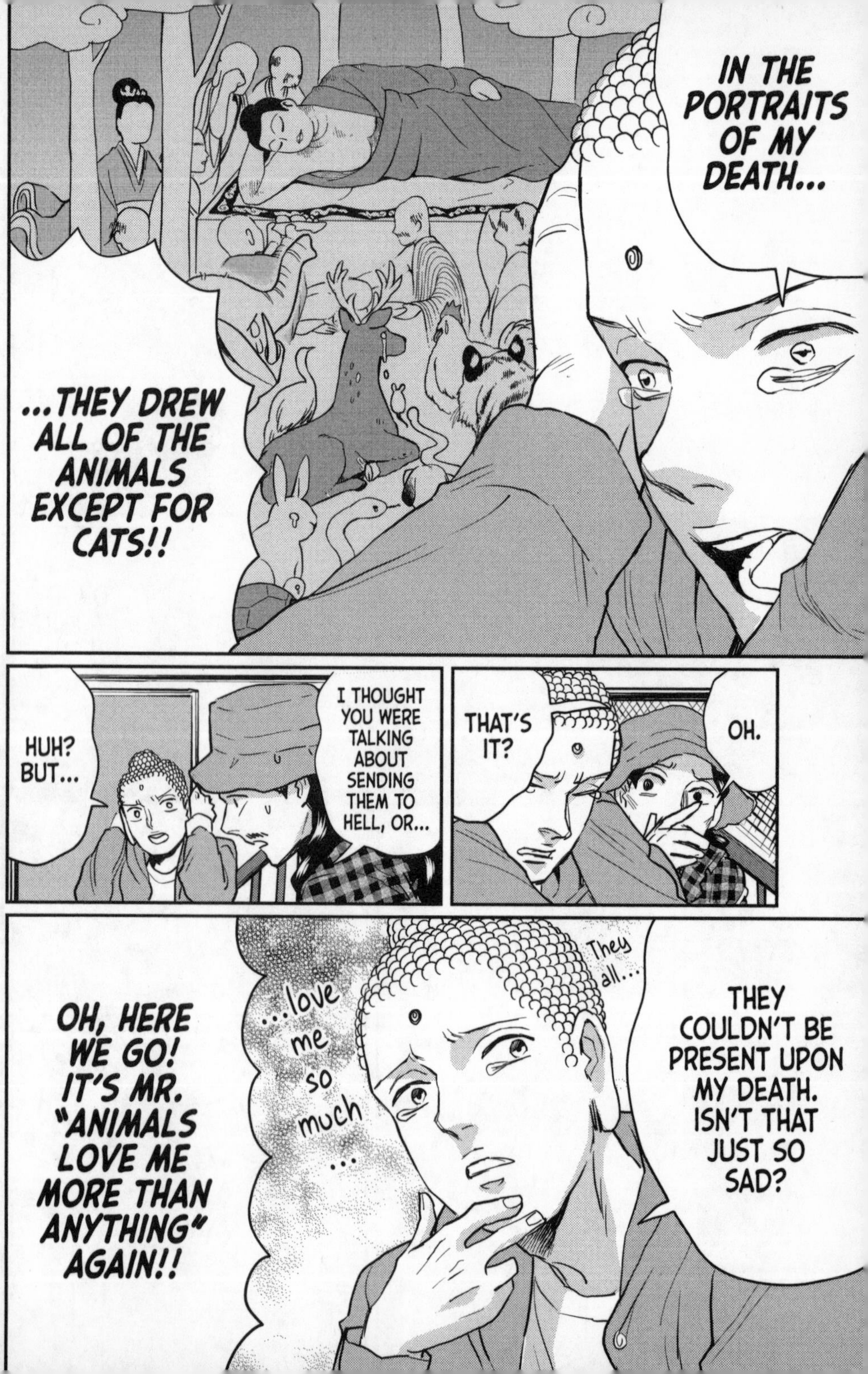
IN THE PORTRAITS OF MY DEATH...
...THEY DREW ALL OF THE ANIMALS EXCEPT FOR CATS!!
OH.
THAT'S IT?
I THOUGHT YOU WERE TALKING ABOUT SENDING THEM TO HELL, OR...
HUH? BUT...
THEY COULDN'T BE PRESENT UPON MY DEATH. ISN'T THAT JUST SO SAD?
They all...
...love me so much...
OH, HERE WE GO! IT'S MR. "ANIMALS LOVE ME MORE THAN ANYTHING" AGAIN!!

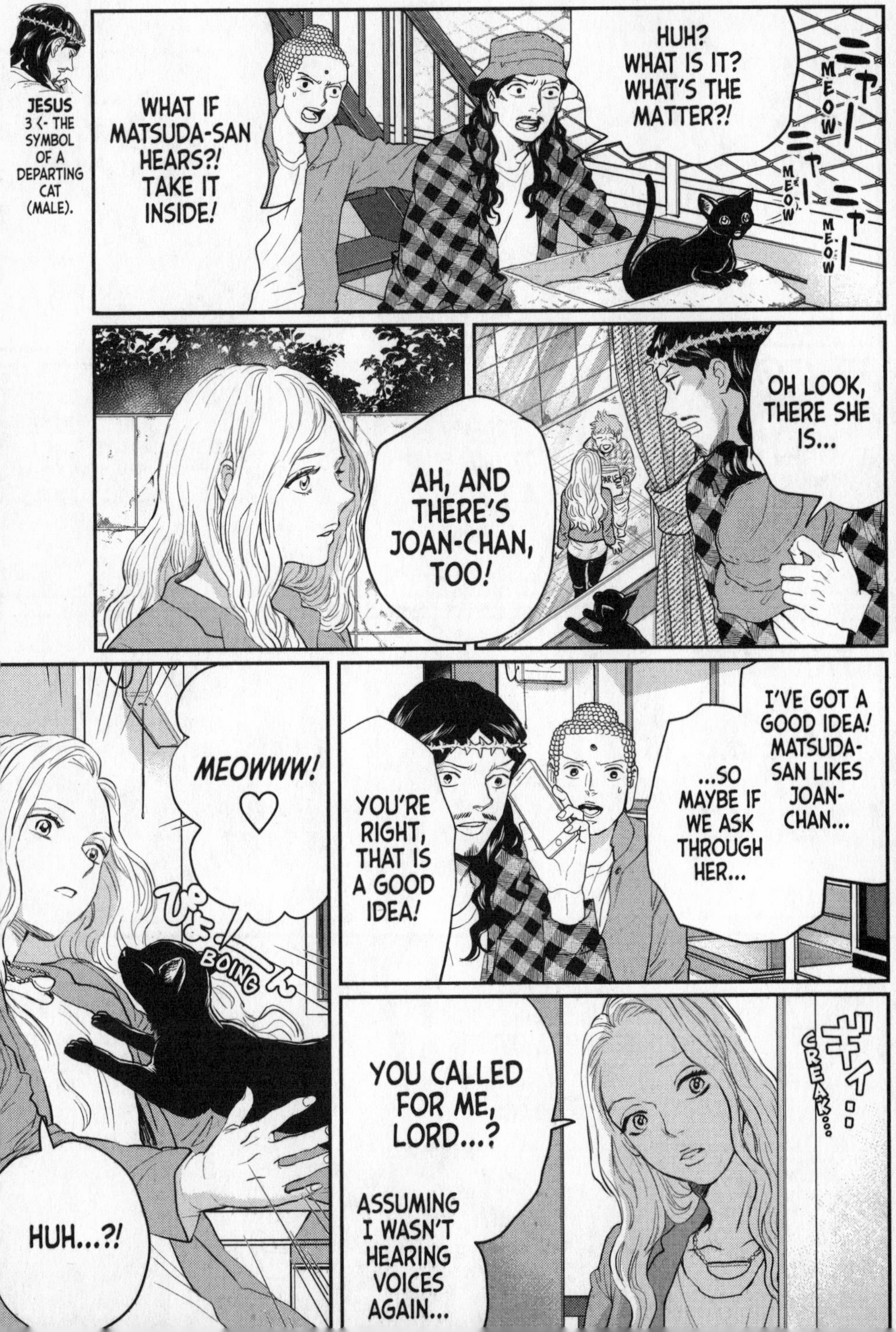
ニャー
MEOW
ニャー
MEOW
ニャー
MEOW
HUH? WHAT IS IT? WHAT'S THE MATTER?!
WHAT IF MATSUDA-SAN HEARS?! TAKE IT INSIDE!
JESUS
3 <- THE SYMBOL OF A DEPARTING CAT (MALE).
OH LOOK, THERE SHE IS...
AH, AND THERE'S JOAN-CHAN, TOO!
I'VE GOT A GOOD IDEA! MATSUDA-SAN LIKES JOAN-CHAN...
...SO MAYBE IF WE ASK THROUGH HER...
YOU'RE RIGHT, THAT IS A GOOD IDEA!
ギイ..
CREAK...
YOU CALLED FOR ME, LORD...?
ASSUMING I WASN'T HEARING VOICES AGAIN...
MEOWWW! ♡
ぴょーん
BOING
HUH...?!

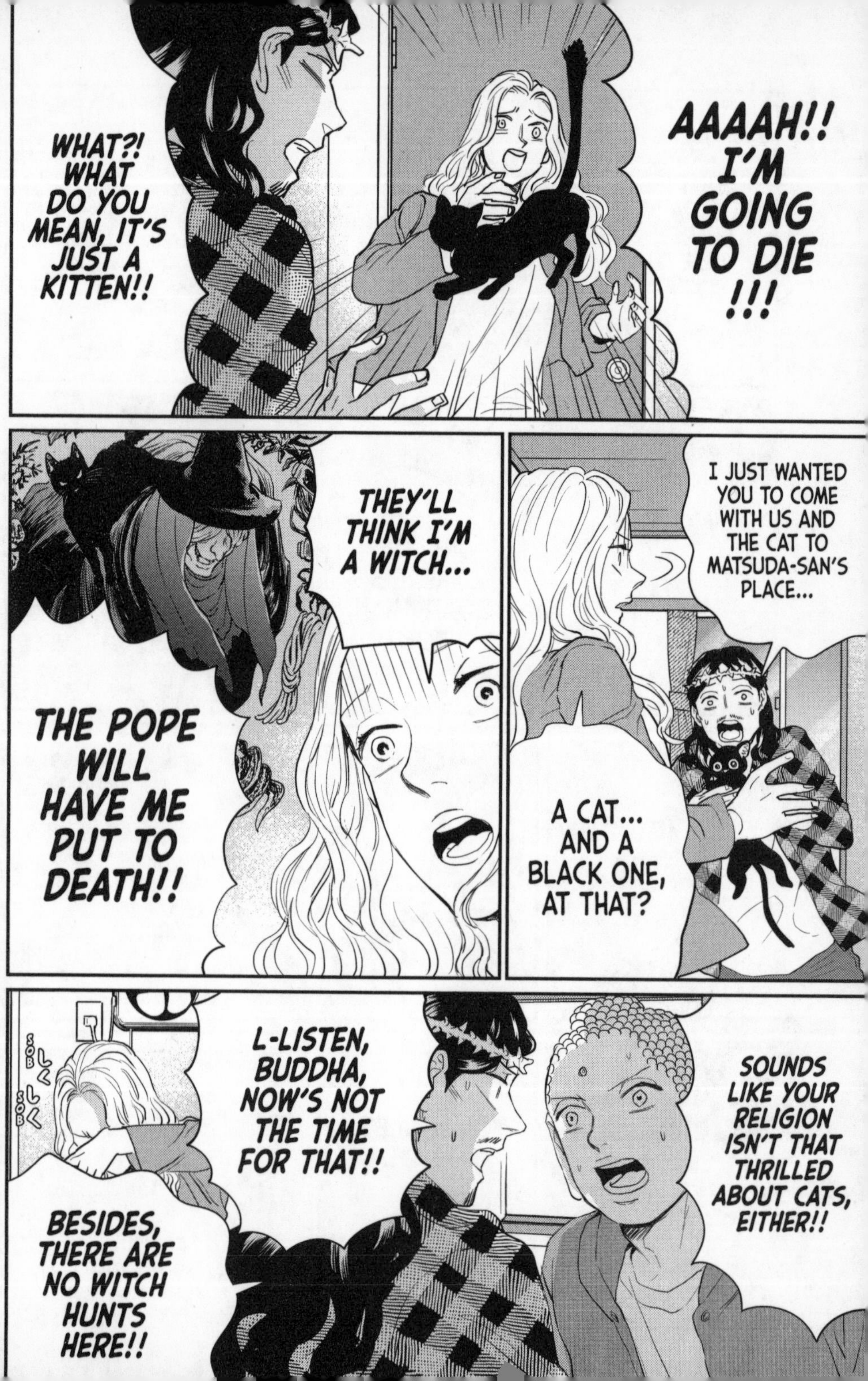
AAAAH!! I'M GOING TO DIE !!!
WHAT?! WHAT DO YOU MEAN, IT'S JUST A KITTEN!!
I JUST WANTED YOU TO COME WITH US AND THE CAT TO MATSUDA-SAN'S PLACE...
A CAT... AND A BLACK ONE, AT THAT?
THEY'LL THINK I'M A WITCH...
THE POPE WILL HAVE ME PUT TO DEATH!!
SOUNDS LIKE YOUR RELIGION ISN'T THAT THRILLED ABOUT CATS, EITHER!!
L-LISTEN, BUDDHA, NOW'S NOT THE TIME FOR THAT!!
しく SOB
しく SOB
BESIDES, THERE ARE NO WITCH HUNTS HERE!!

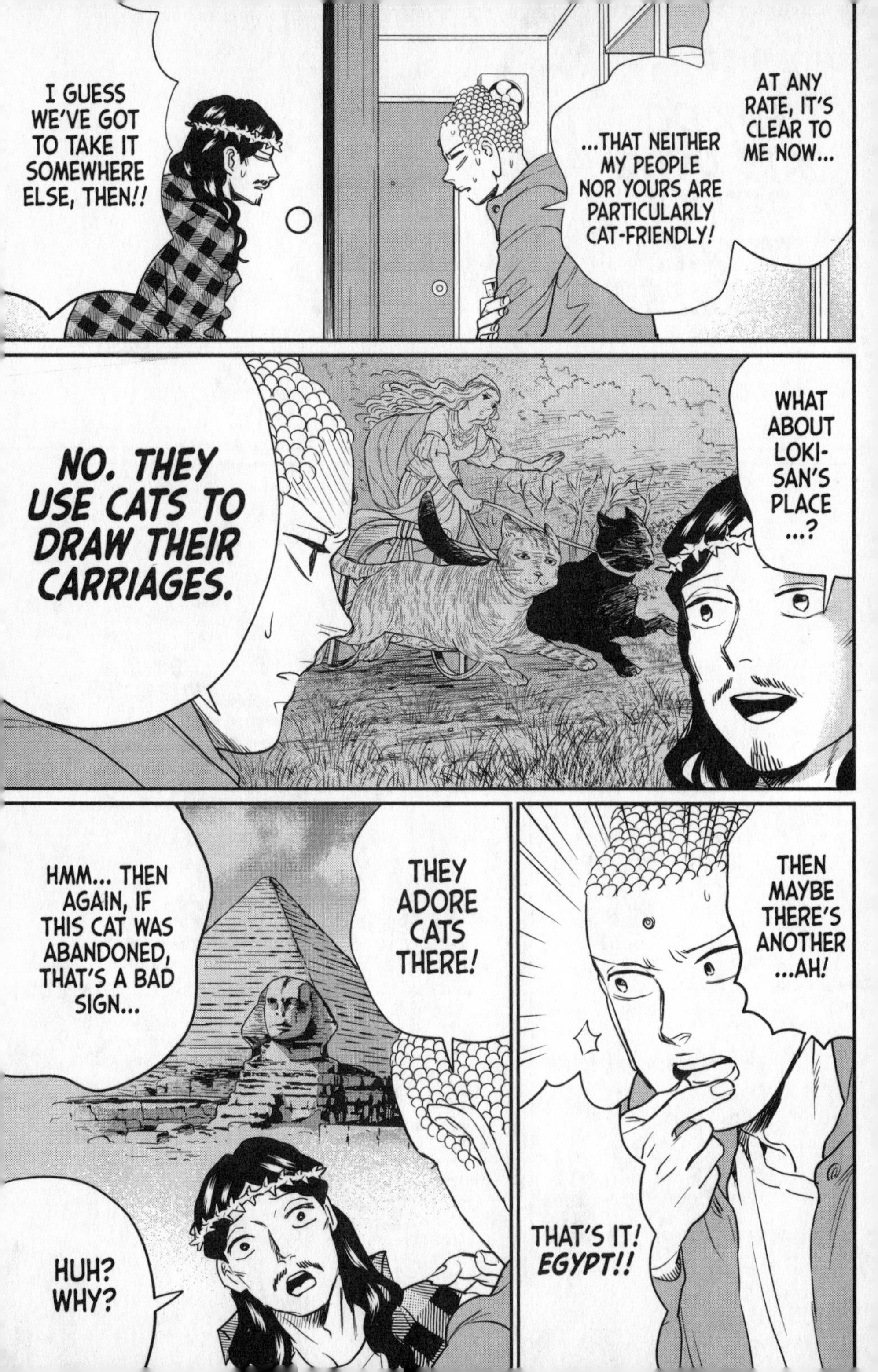
AT ANY RATE, IT'S CLEAR TO ME NOW...
...THAT NEITHER MY PEOPLE NOR YOURS ARE PARTICULARLY CAT-FRIENDLY!
I GUESS WE'VE GOT TO TAKE IT SOMEWHERE ELSE, THEN!!
WHAT ABOUT LOKI-SAN'S PLACE ...?
NO. THEY USE CATS TO DRAW THEIR CARRIAGES.
THEN MAYBE THERE'S ANOTHER ...AH!
THAT'S IT! EGYPT!!
THEY ADORE CATS THERE!
HMM... THEN AGAIN, IF THIS CAT WAS ABANDONED, THAT'S A BAD SIGN...
HUH? WHY?

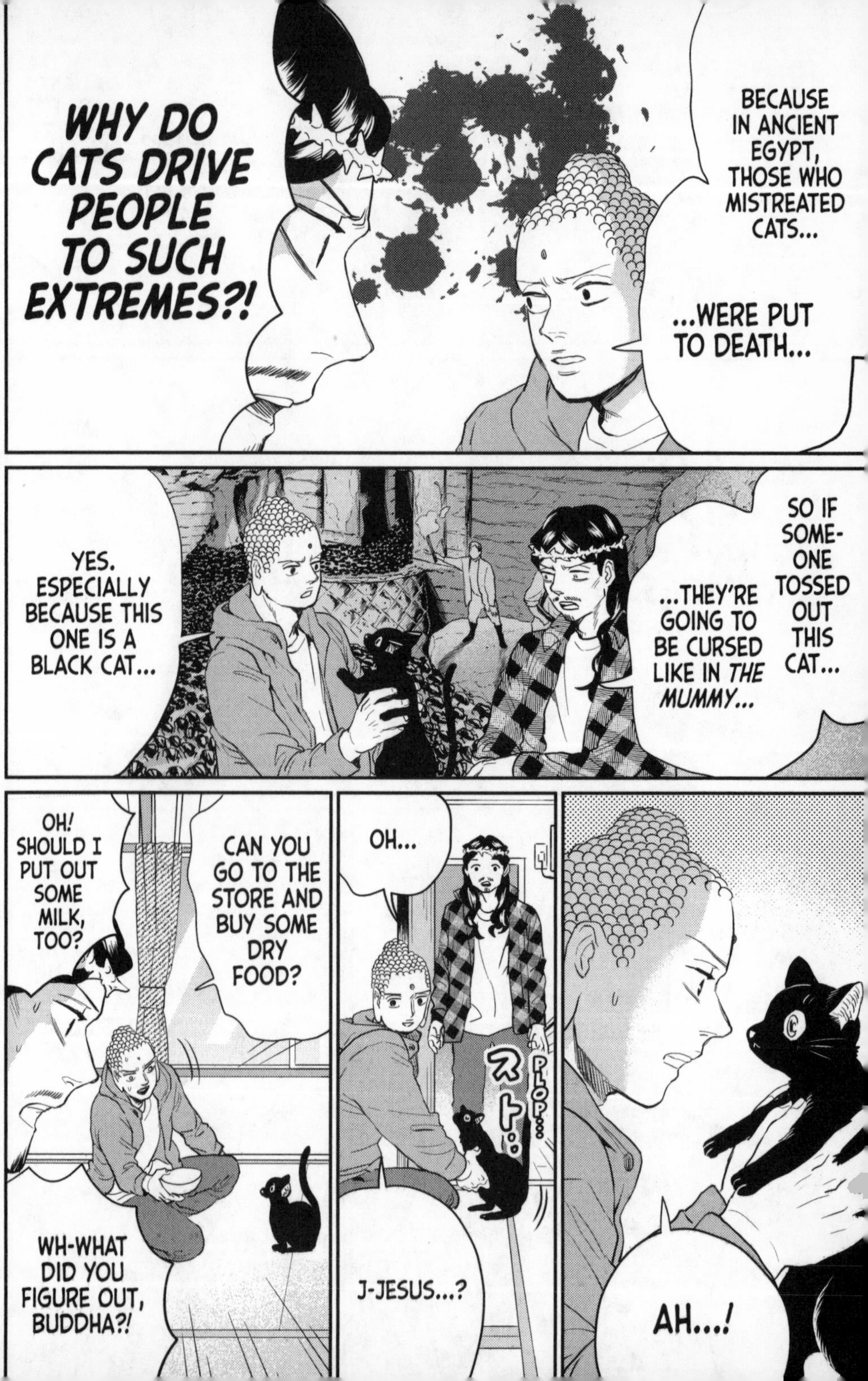
BECAUSE IN ANCIENT EGYPT, THOSE WHO MISTREATED CATS...
...WERE PUT TO DEATH...
WHY DO CATS DRIVE PEOPLE TO SUCH EXTREMES?!
SO IF SOMEONE TOSSED OUT THIS CAT...
...THEY'RE GOING TO BE CURSED LIKE IN *THE MUMMY*...
YES. ESPECIALLY BECAUSE THIS ONE IS A BLACK CAT...
AH...!
OH...
スト。。
PLOP...
J-JESUS...?
CAN YOU GO TO THE STORE AND BUY SOME DRY FOOD?
OH! SHOULD I PUT OUT SOME MILK, TOO?
WH-WHAT DID YOU FIGURE OUT, BUDDHA?!

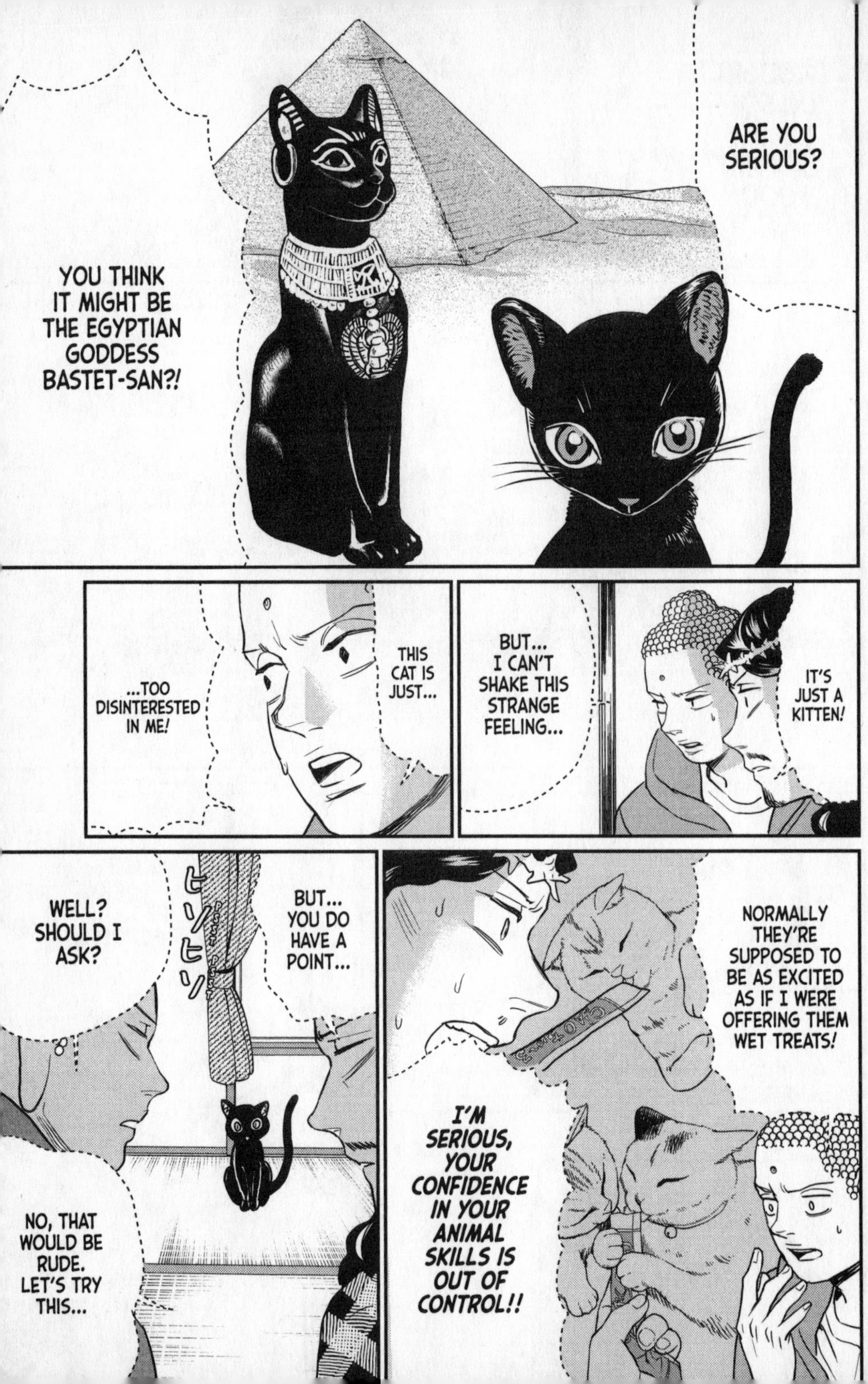
ARE YOU SERIOUS?
YOU THINK IT MIGHT BE THE EGYPTIAN GODDESS BASTET-SAN?!
IT'S JUST A KITTEN!
BUT... I CAN'T SHAKE THIS STRANGE FEELING...
THIS CAT IS JUST...
...TOO DISINTERESTED IN ME!
NORMALLY THEY'RE SUPPOSED TO BE AS EXCITED AS IF I WERE OFFERING THEM WET TREATS!
I'M SERIOUS, YOUR CONFIDENCE IN YOUR ANIMAL SKILLS IS OUT OF CONTROL!!
ヒソヒソ
BUT... YOU DO HAVE A POINT...
WELL? SHOULD I ASK?
NO, THAT WOULD BE RUDE. LET'S TRY THIS...

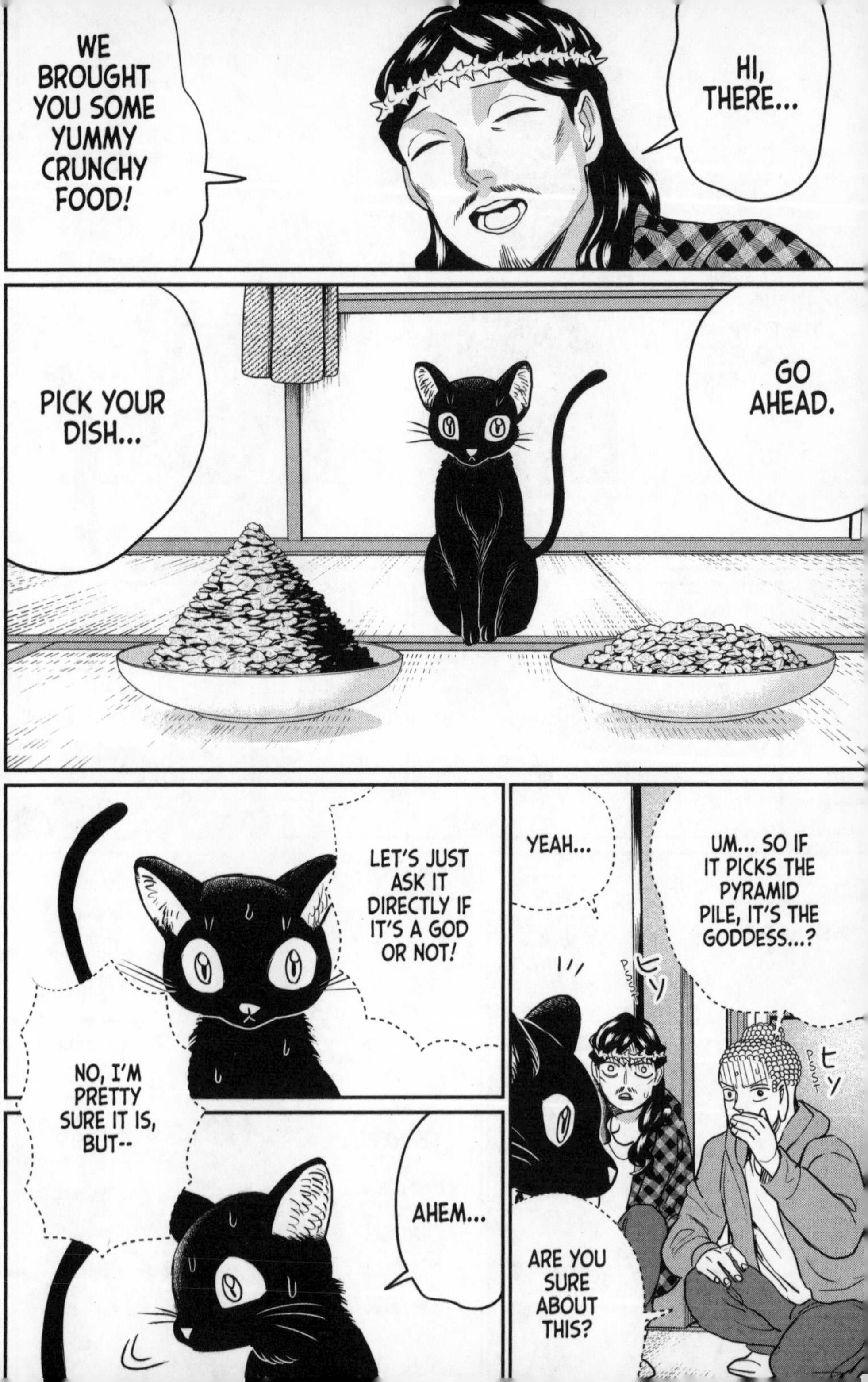
HI, THERE...
WE BROUGHT YOU SOME YUMMY CRUNCHY FOOD!
GO AHEAD.
PICK YOUR DISH...
UM... SO IF IT PICKS THE PYRAMID PILE, IT'S THE GODDESS...?
YEAH...
ヒソ PSSST
ヒソ PSSST
ARE YOU SURE ABOUT THIS?
LET'S JUST ASK IT DIRECTLY IF IT'S A GOD OR NOT!
NO, I'M PRETTY SURE IT IS, BUT--
AHEM...

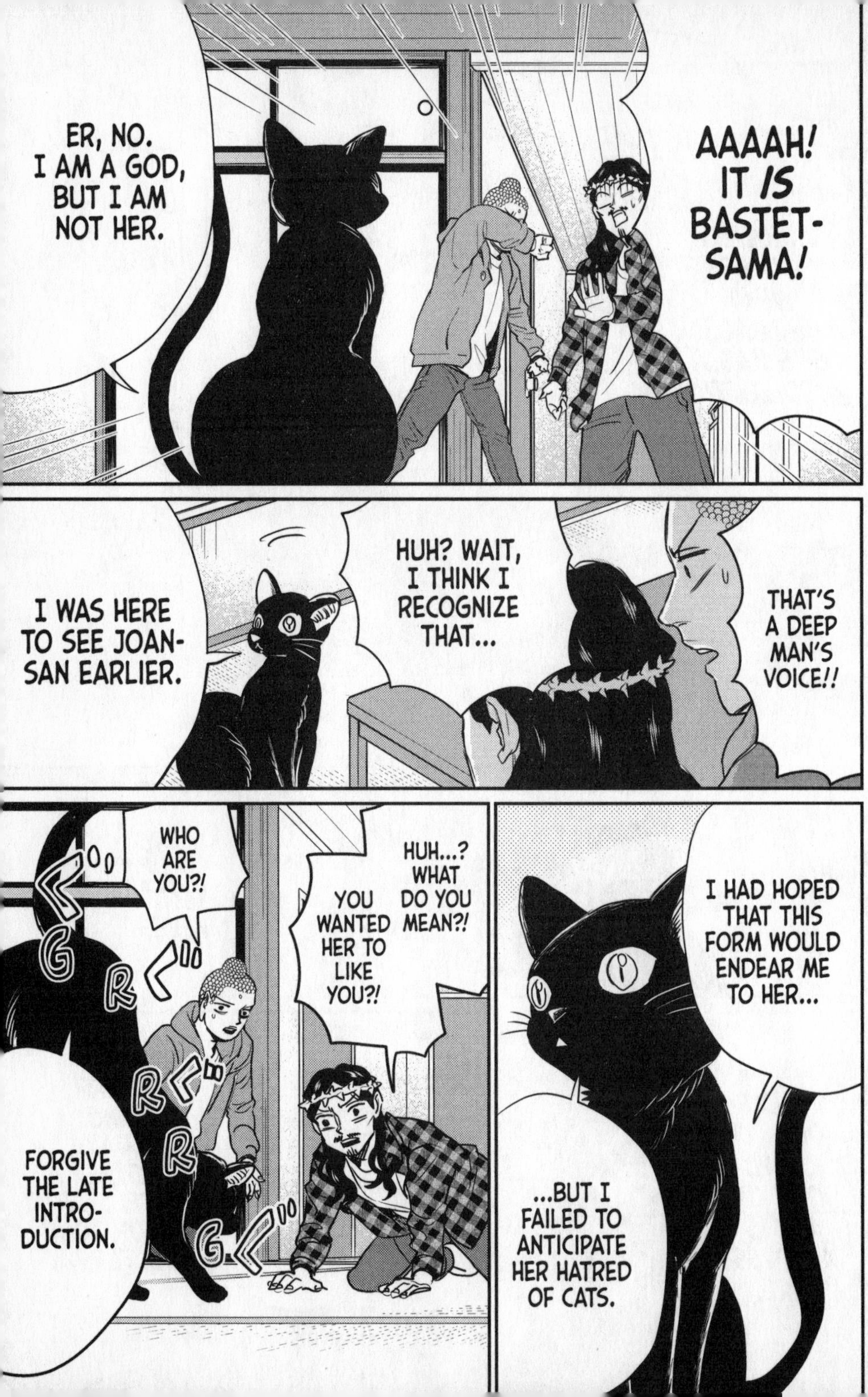
AAAAH! IT *IS* BASTET-SAMA!
ER, NO. I AM A GOD, BUT I AM NOT HER.
THAT'S A DEEP MAN'S VOICE!!
HUH? WAIT, I THINK I RECOGNIZE THAT...
I WAS HERE TO SEE JOAN-SAN EARLIER.
I HAD HOPED THAT THIS FORM WOULD ENDEAR ME TO HER...
...BUT I FAILED TO ANTICIPATE HER HATRED OF CATS.
HUH...? WHAT DO YOU MEAN?!
YOU WANTED HER TO LIKE YOU?!
WHO ARE YOU?!
GRRRRG
FORGIVE THE LATE INTRO-DUCTION.

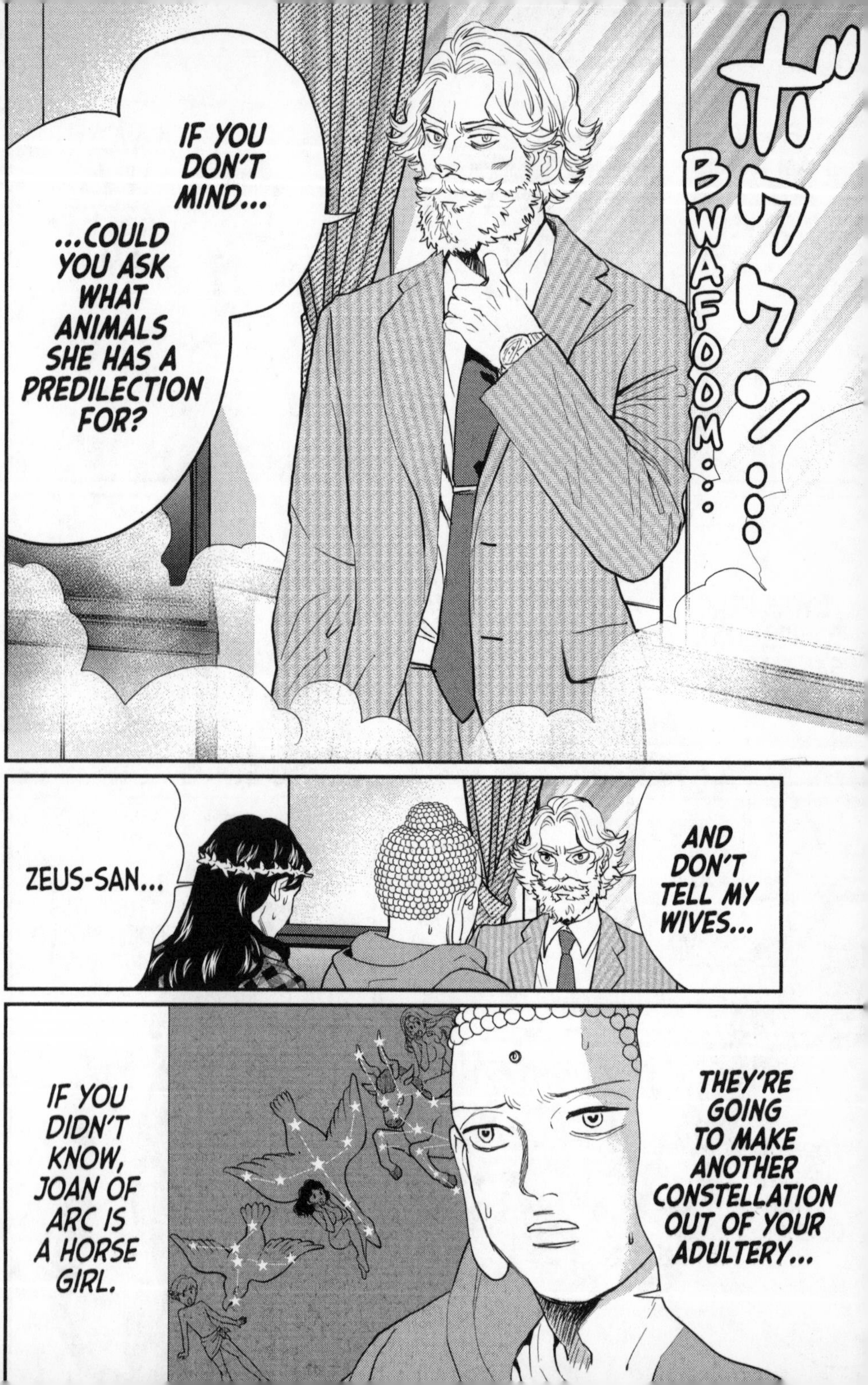
BWAFOOOM...
IF YOU DON'T MIND... ...COULD YOU ASK WHAT ANIMALS SHE HAS A PREDILECTION FOR?
AND DON'T TELL MY WIVES...
ZEUS-SAN...
THEY'RE GOING TO MAKE ANOTHER CONSTELLATION OUT OF YOUR ADULTERY...
IF YOU DIDN'T KNOW, JOAN OF ARC IS A HORSE GIRL.

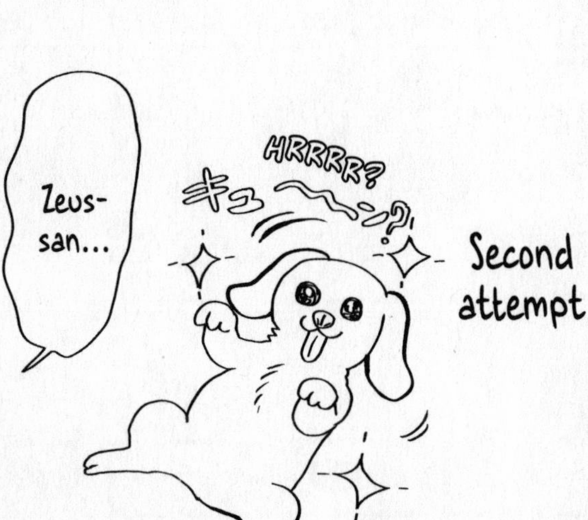
Second attempt
HRRRR?
キュ〜ン?!
Zeus-san...

CHAPTER 131 TRANSLATION NOTES

Norse carriage, page 177
The Norse goddess Freyja (or Freya) is often described as riding in a chariot pulled by two cats that accompany her constantly.

Bastet, page 179
The cat-headed goddess from Egyptian mythology. She was the goddess of the home, women, childbirth, and cats, among other things.

Wet treats, page 179
The brand shown in this panel is Ciao's "Chu-ru" tube-packet cat treats, which have a variety of cat-friendly flavors that can be licked right from the tube.

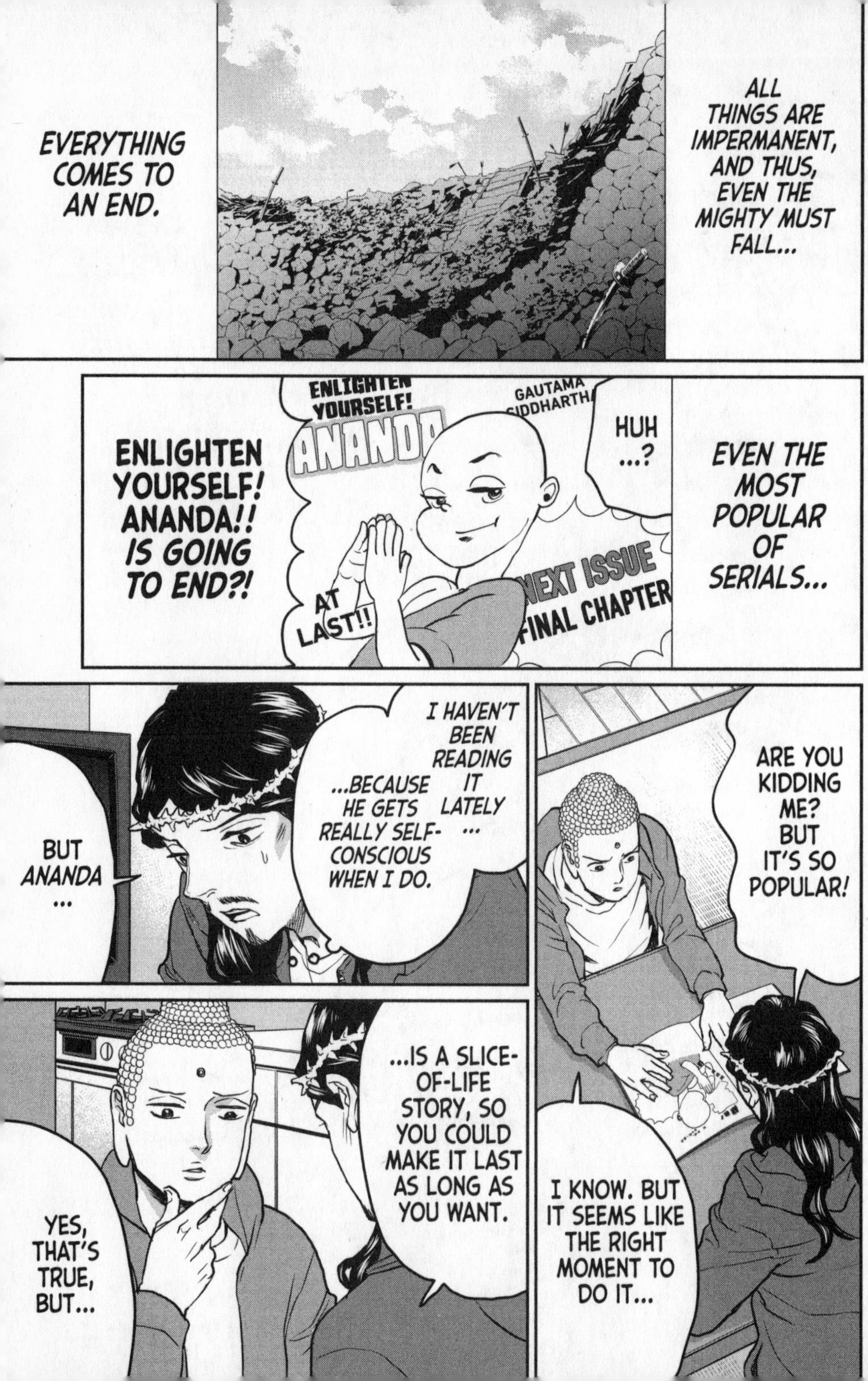
ALL THINGS ARE IMPERMANENT, AND THUS, EVEN THE MIGHTY MUST FALL...
EVERYTHING COMES TO AN END.
EVEN THE MOST POPULAR OF SERIALS...
HUH ...?
GAUTAMA SIDDHARTHA
ENLIGHTEN YOURSELF! ANANDA
NEXT ISSUE FINAL CHAPTER
AT LAST!!
ENLIGHTEN YOURSELF! ANANDA!! IS GOING TO END?!
ARE YOU KIDDING ME? BUT IT'S SO POPULAR!
I KNOW. BUT IT SEEMS LIKE THE RIGHT MOMENT TO DO IT...
I HAVEN'T BEEN READING IT LATELY ...
...BECAUSE HE GETS REALLY SELF-CONSCIOUS WHEN I DO.
BUT ANANDA ...
...IS A SLICE-OF-LIFE STORY, SO YOU COULD MAKE IT LAST AS LONG AS YOU WANT.
YES, THAT'S TRUE, BUT...

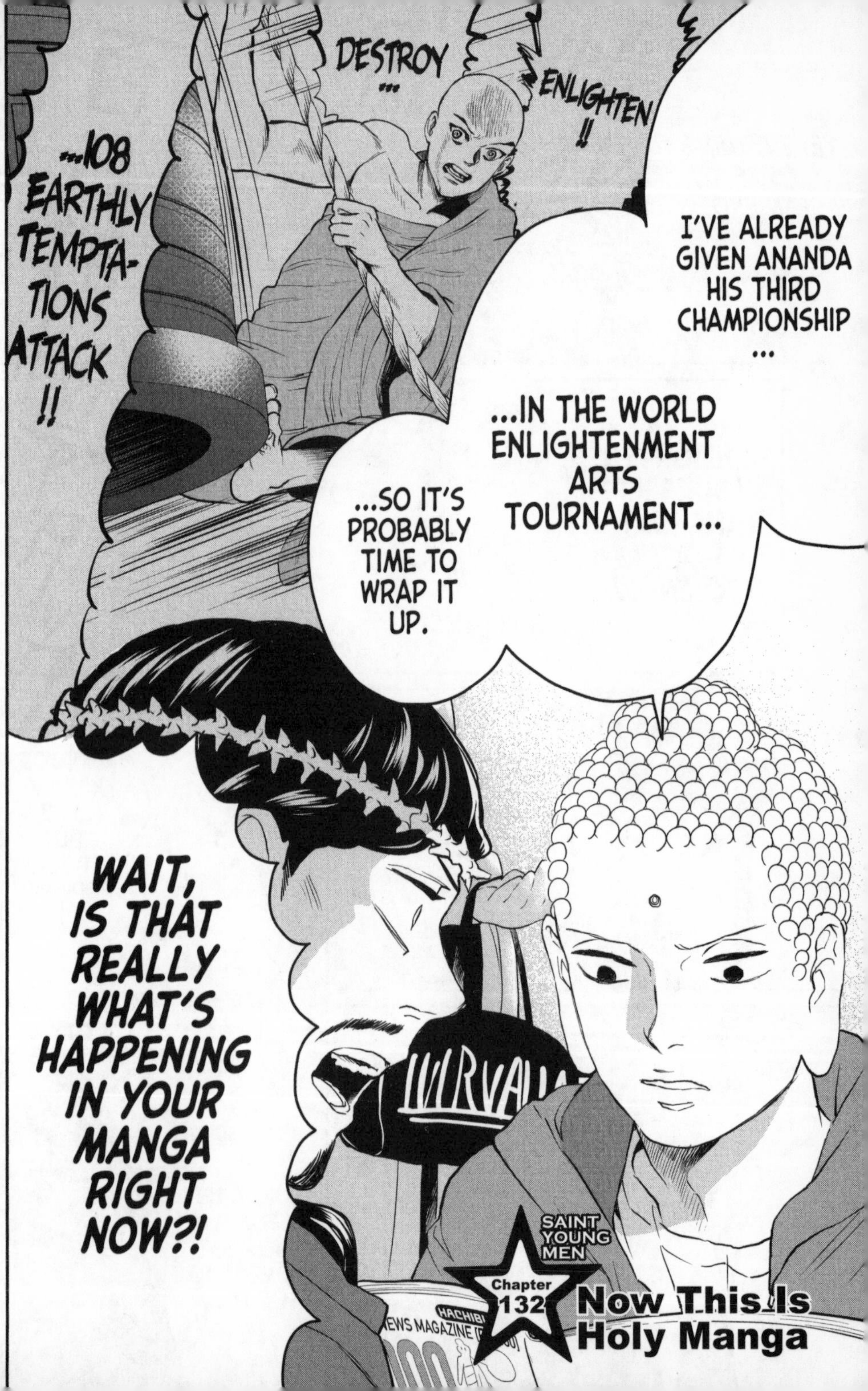
DESTROY ...
ENLIGHTEN !!
...108 EARTHLY TEMPTA-TIONS ATTACK !!
I'VE ALREADY GIVEN ANANDA HIS THIRD CHAMPIONSHIP ...
...IN THE WORLD ENLIGHTENMENT ARTS TOURNAMENT...
...SO IT'S PROBABLY TIME TO WRAP IT UP.
WAIT, IS THAT REALLY WHAT'S HAPPENING IN YOUR MANGA RIGHT NOW?!
SAINT YOUNG MEN
Chapter 132
Now This Is Holy Manga
NEWS MAGAZINE

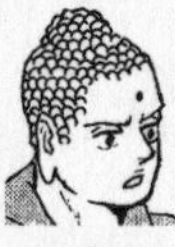

BUDDHA
WHEN YOU LOOK AT VOLUME ONE AND THINK, "DID IT REALLY LOOK LIKE THIS?" BUT IT SOON FEELS NORMAL AGAIN. #LONG-SERIES-PROBLEMS

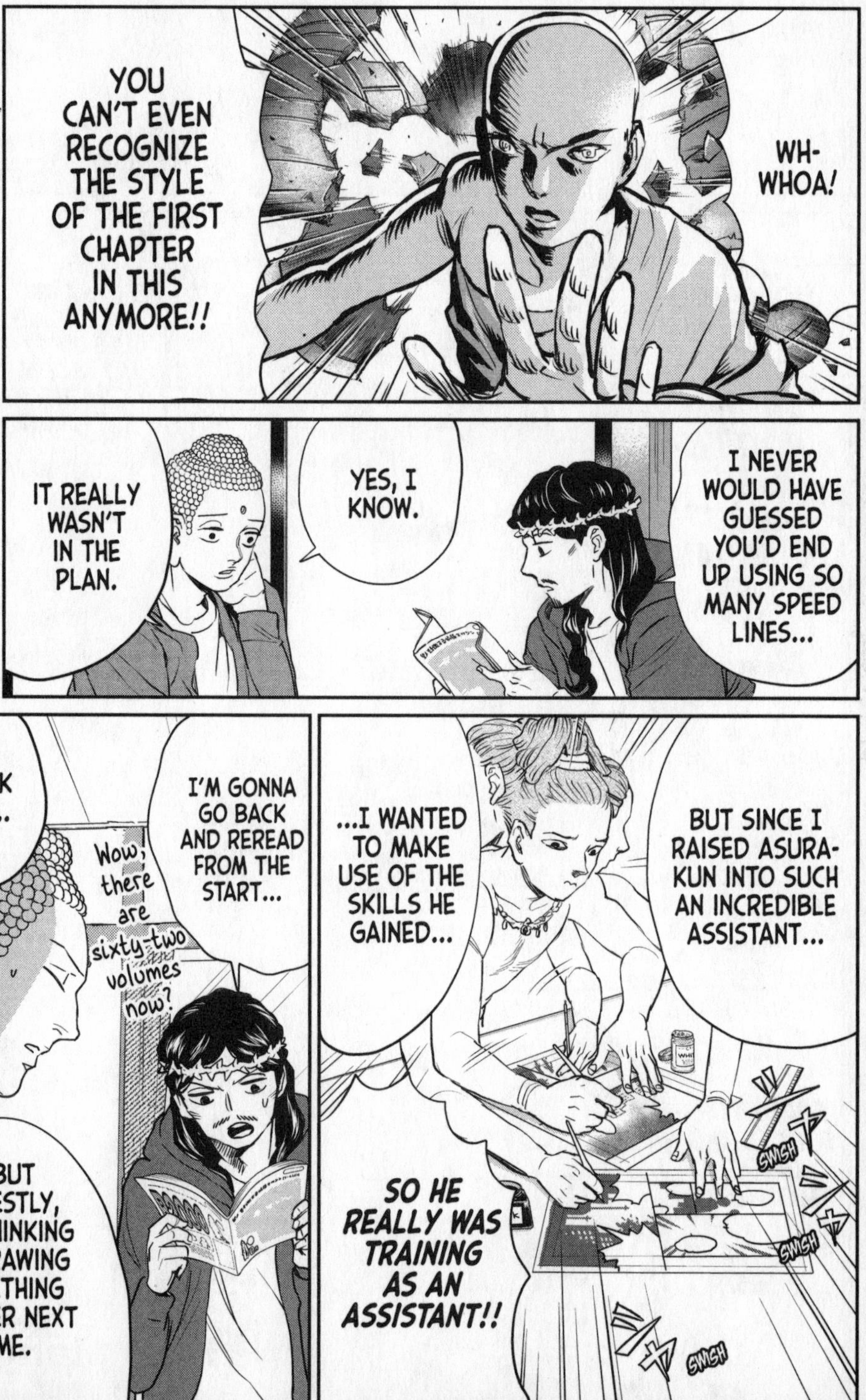
WH-WHOA!
YOU CAN'T EVEN RECOGNIZE THE STYLE OF THE FIRST CHAPTER IN THIS ANYMORE!!
I NEVER WOULD HAVE GUESSED YOU'D END UP USING SO MANY SPEED LINES...
YES, I KNOW.
IT REALLY WASN'T IN THE PLAN.
BUT SINCE I RAISED ASURA-KUN INTO SUCH AN INCREDIBLE ASSISTANT...
...I WANTED TO MAKE USE OF THE SKILLS HE GAINED...
SWISH
SWISH
SO HE REALLY WAS TRAINING AS AN ASSISTANT!!
SWISH
I'M GONNA GO BACK AND REREAD FROM THE START...
Wow, there are sixty-two volumes now?
THANK YOU...
...BUT HONESTLY, I'M THINKING OF DRAWING SOMETHING LIGHTER NEXT TIME.

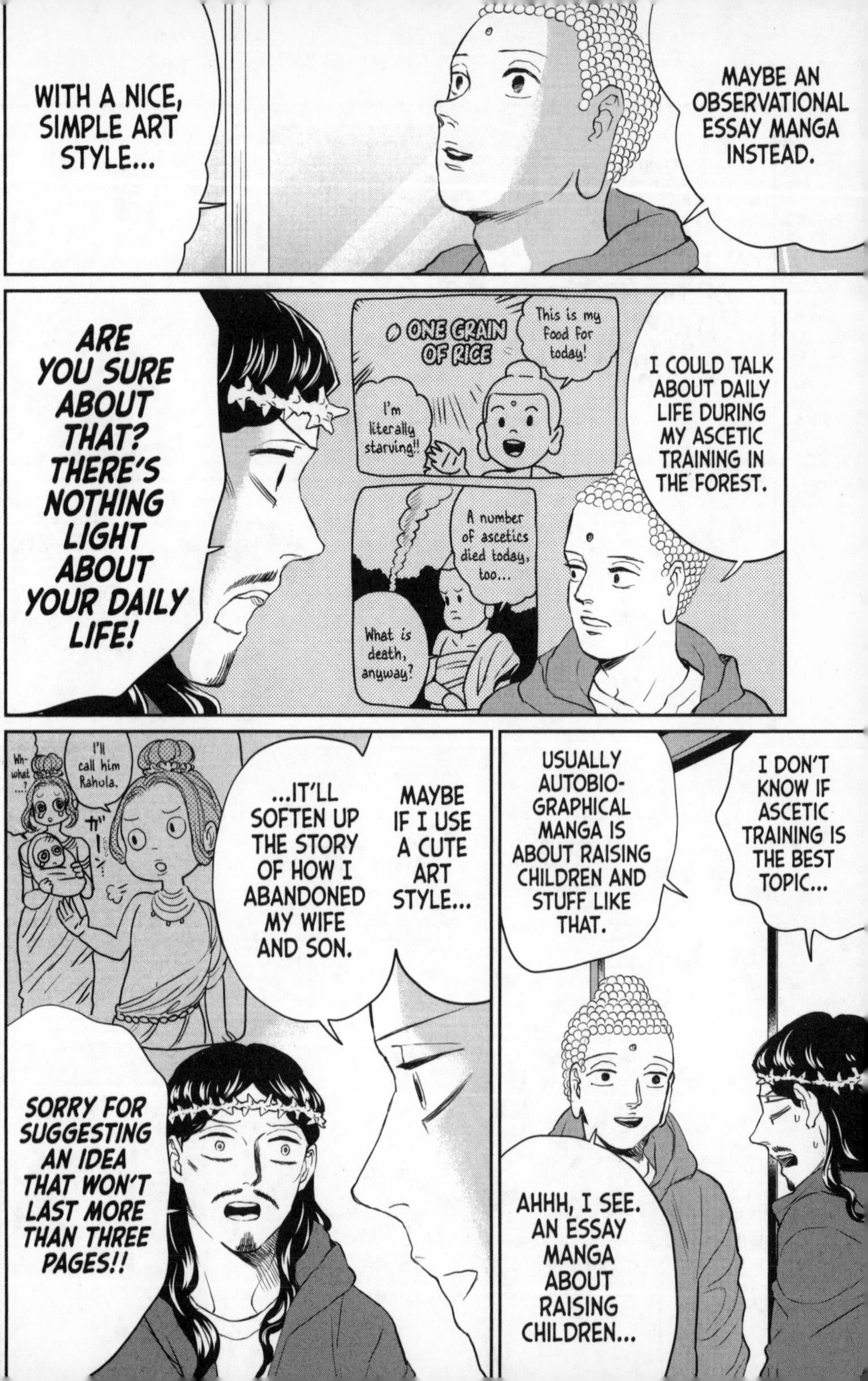
MAYBE AN OBSERVATIONAL ESSAY MANGA INSTEAD.
WITH A NICE, SIMPLE ART STYLE...
I COULD TALK ABOUT DAILY LIFE DURING MY ASCETIC TRAINING IN THE FOREST.
ONE GRAIN OF RICE
This is my food for today!
I'm literally starving!!
A number of ascetics died today, too...
What is death, anyway?
ARE YOU SURE ABOUT THAT? THERE'S NOTHING LIGHT ABOUT YOUR DAILY LIFE!
I DON'T KNOW IF ASCETIC TRAINING IS THE BEST TOPIC...
USUALLY AUTOBIO-GRAPHICAL MANGA IS ABOUT RAISING CHILDREN AND STUFF LIKE THAT.
AHHH, I SEE. AN ESSAY MANGA ABOUT RAISING CHILDREN...
MAYBE IF I USE A CUTE ART STYLE...
...IT'LL SOFTEN UP THE STORY OF HOW I ABANDONED MY WIFE AND SON.
I'll call him Rahula.
Wh-what...?
SORRY FOR SUGGESTING AN IDEA THAT WON'T LAST MORE THAN THREE PAGES!!

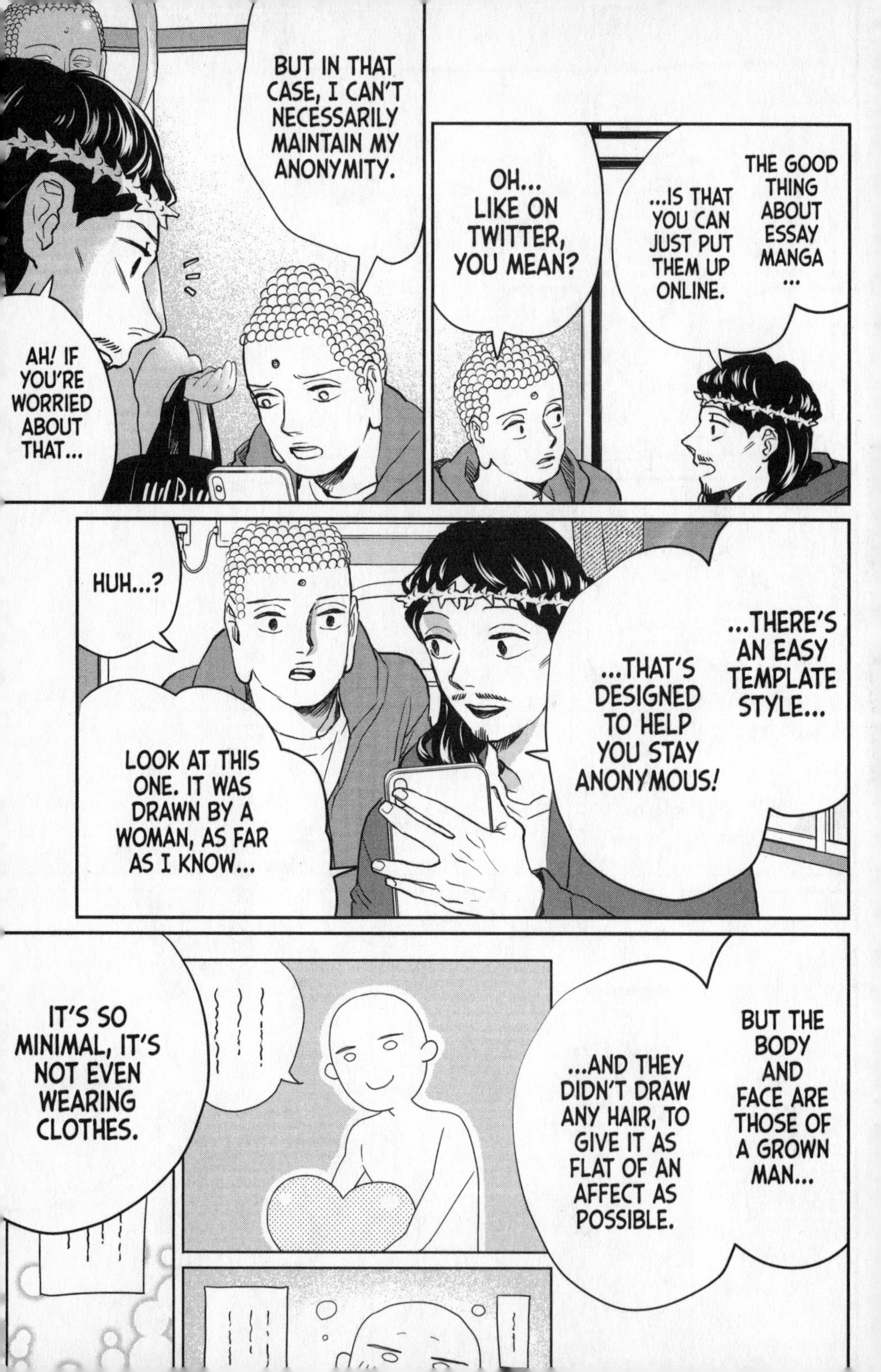
THE GOOD THING ABOUT ESSAY MANGA ...
...IS THAT YOU CAN JUST PUT THEM UP ONLINE.
OH... LIKE ON TWITTER, YOU MEAN?
BUT IN THAT CASE, I CAN'T NECESSARILY MAINTAIN MY ANONYMITY.
AH! IF YOU'RE WORRIED ABOUT THAT...
...THERE'S AN EASY TEMPLATE STYLE...
...THAT'S DESIGNED TO HELP YOU STAY ANONYMOUS!
HUH...?
LOOK AT THIS ONE. IT WAS DRAWN BY A WOMAN, AS FAR AS I KNOW...
BUT THE BODY AND FACE ARE THOSE OF A GROWN MAN...
...AND THEY DIDN'T DRAW ANY HAIR, TO GIVE IT AS FLAT OF AN AFFECT AS POSSIBLE.
IT'S SO MINIMAL, IT'S NOT EVEN WEARING CLOTHES.

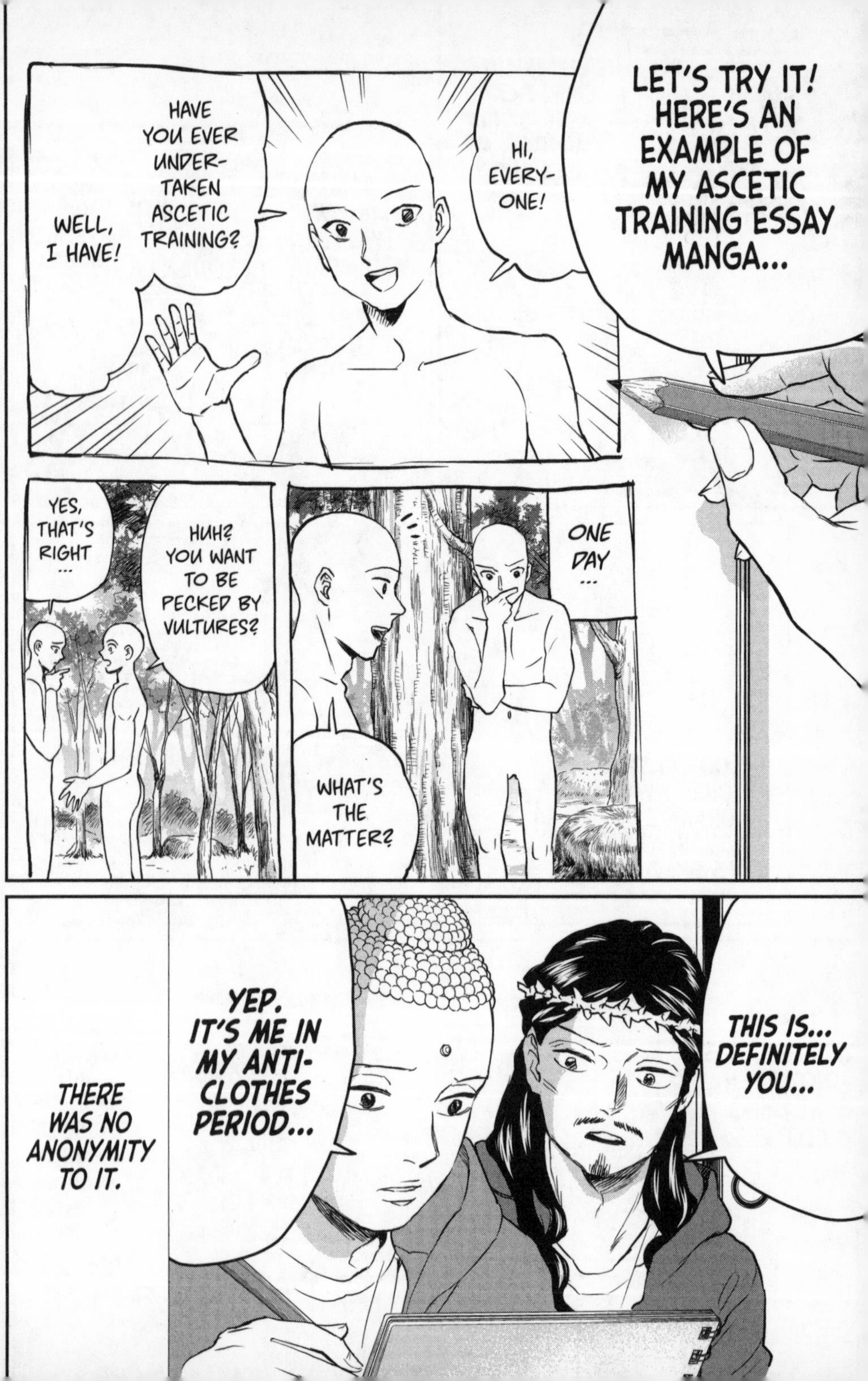
LET'S TRY IT! HERE'S AN EXAMPLE OF MY ASCETIC TRAINING ESSAY MANGA...
HI, EVERY-ONE!
HAVE YOU EVER UNDER-TAKEN ASCETIC TRAINING?
WELL, I HAVE!
ONE DAY ...
WHAT'S THE MATTER?
HUH? YOU WANT TO BE PECKED BY VULTURES?
YES, THAT'S RIGHT ...
THIS IS... DEFINITELY YOU...
YEP. IT'S ME IN MY ANTI-CLOTHES PERIOD...
THERE WAS NO ANONYMITY TO IT.

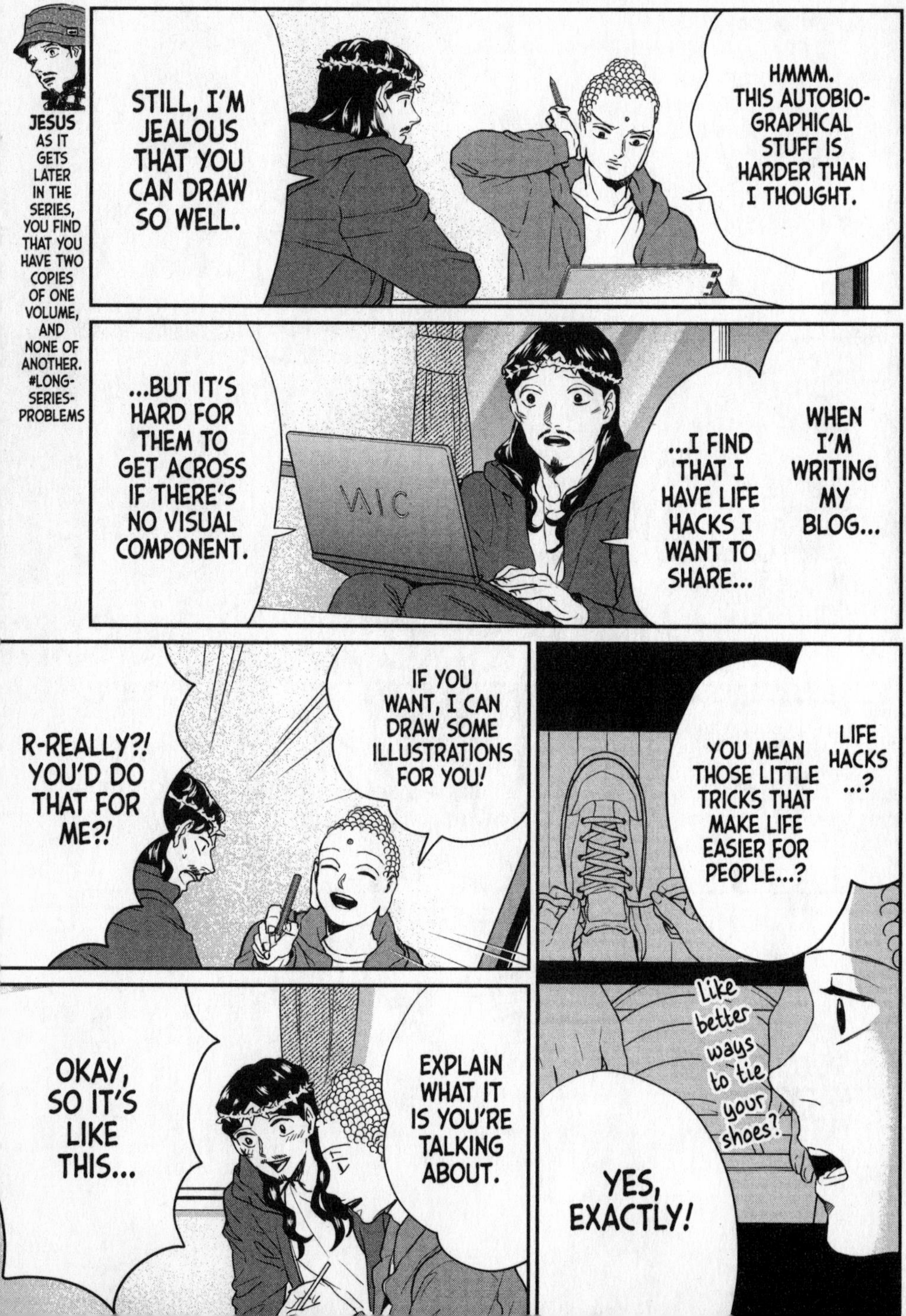
JESUS AS IT GETS LATER IN THE SERIES, YOU FIND THAT YOU HAVE TWO COPIES OF ONE VOLUME, AND NONE OF ANOTHER. #LONG-SERIES-PROBLEMS
HMMM. THIS AUTOBIOGRAPHICAL STUFF IS HARDER THAN I THOUGHT.
STILL, I'M JEALOUS THAT YOU CAN DRAW SO WELL.
WHEN I'M WRITING MY BLOG...
...I FIND THAT I HAVE LIFE HACKS I WANT TO SHARE...
...BUT IT'S HARD FOR THEM TO GET ACROSS IF THERE'S NO VISUAL COMPONENT.
LIFE HACKS ...?
YOU MEAN THOSE LITTLE TRICKS THAT MAKE LIFE EASIER FOR PEOPLE...?
Like better ways to tie your shoes?
YES, EXACTLY!
IF YOU WANT, I CAN DRAW SOME ILLUSTRATIONS FOR YOU!
R-REALLY?! YOU'D DO THAT FOR ME?!
EXPLAIN WHAT IT IS YOU'RE TALKING ABOUT.
OKAY, SO IT'S LIKE THIS...

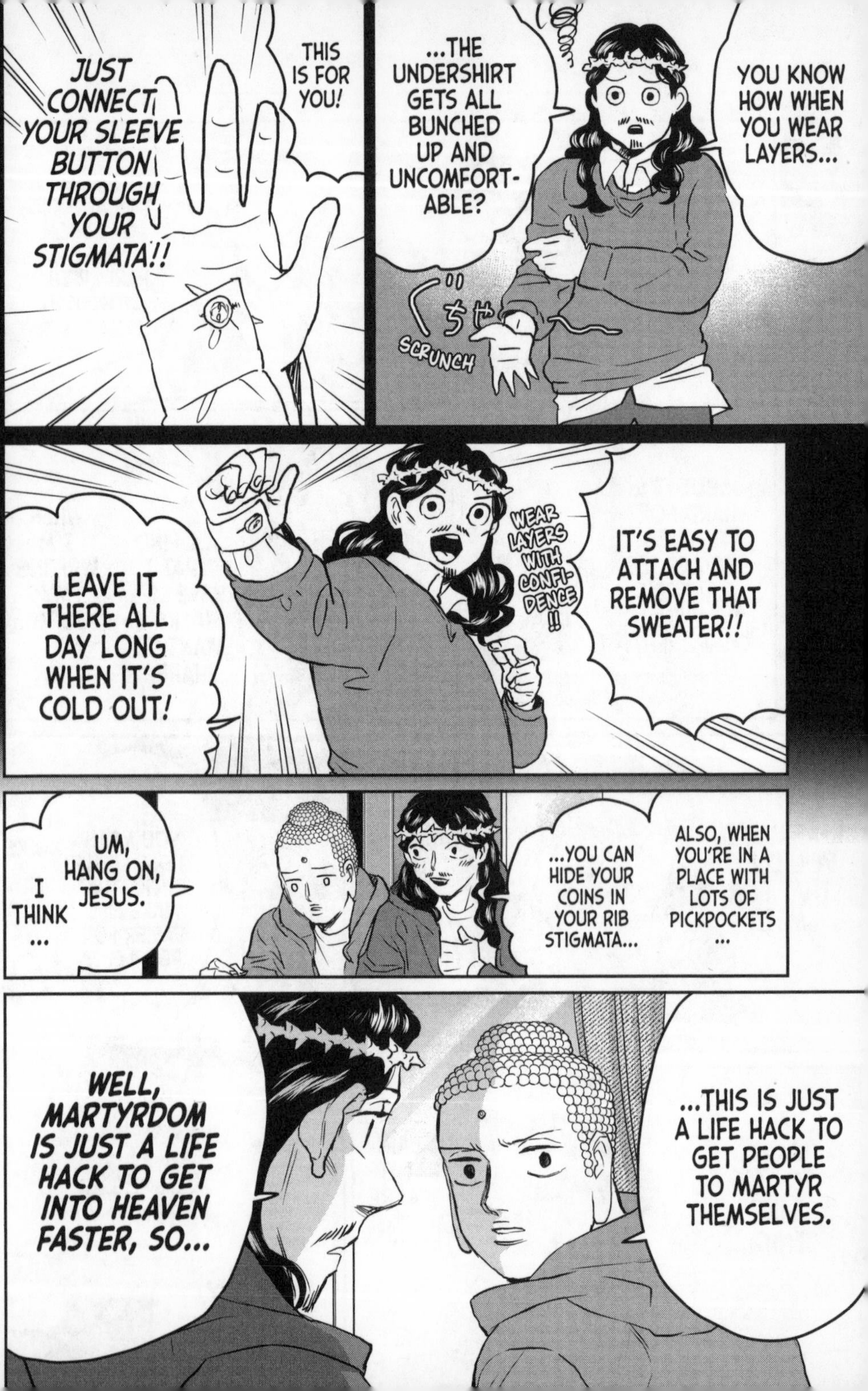
YOU KNOW HOW WHEN YOU WEAR LAYERS...
...THE UNDERSHIRT GETS ALL BUNCHED UP AND UNCOMFORT-ABLE?
ぐちゃ
SCRUNCH
THIS IS FOR YOU!
JUST CONNECT YOUR SLEEVE BUTTON THROUGH YOUR STIGMATA!!
IT'S EASY TO ATTACH AND REMOVE THAT SWEATER!!
WEAR LAYERS WITH CONFI-DENCE!!
LEAVE IT THERE ALL DAY LONG WHEN IT'S COLD OUT!
ALSO, WHEN YOU'RE IN A PLACE WITH LOTS OF PICKPOCKETS ...
...YOU CAN HIDE YOUR COINS IN YOUR RIB STIGMATA...
UM, HANG ON, JESUS.
I THINK ...
...THIS IS JUST A LIFE HACK TO GET PEOPLE TO MARTYR THEMSELVES.
WELL, MARTYRDOM IS JUST A LIFE HACK TO GET INTO HEAVEN FASTER, SO...

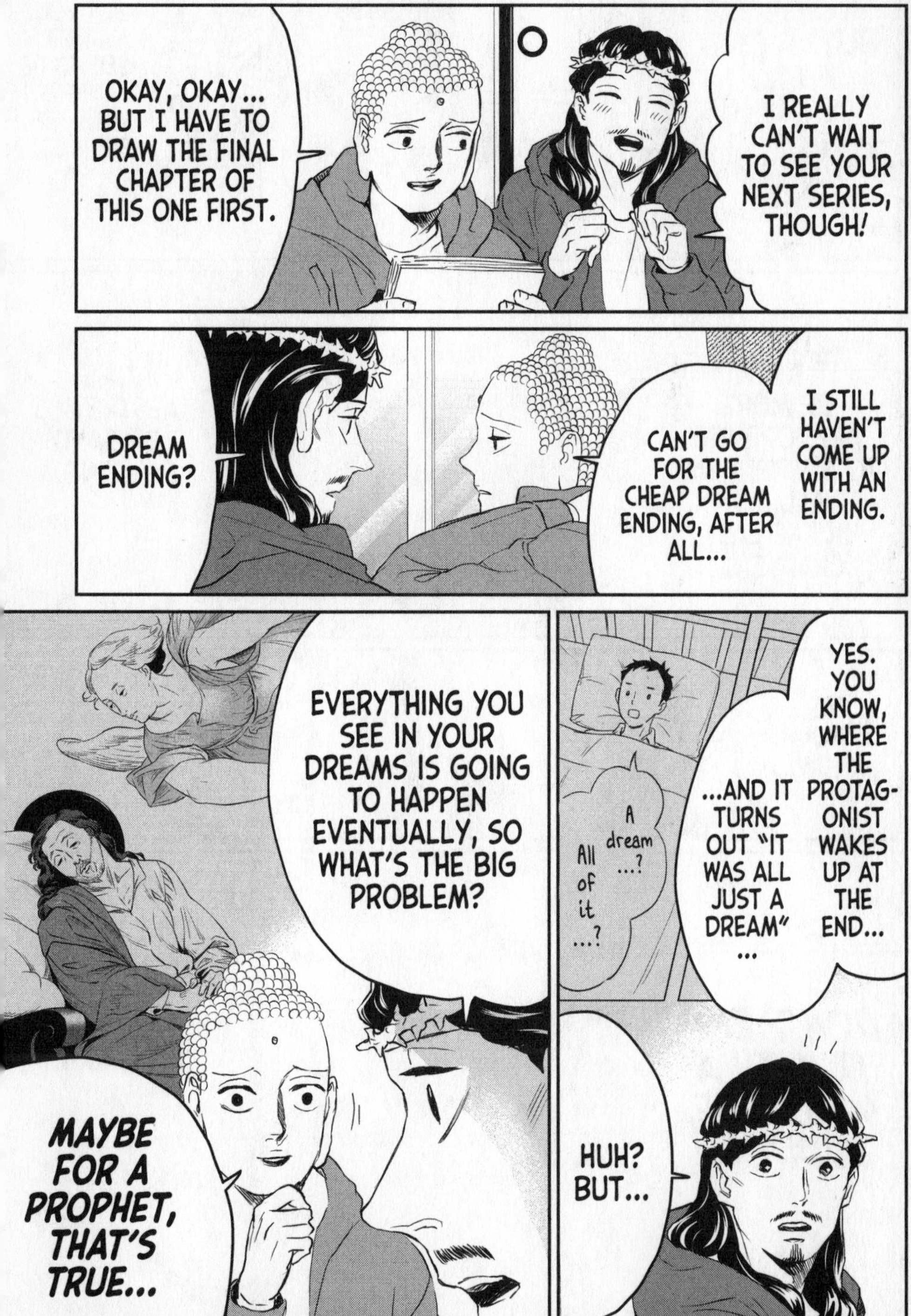
I REALLY CAN'T WAIT TO SEE YOUR NEXT SERIES, THOUGH!
OKAY, OKAY... BUT I HAVE TO DRAW THE FINAL CHAPTER OF THIS ONE FIRST.
I STILL HAVEN'T COME UP WITH AN ENDING.
CAN'T GO FOR THE CHEAP DREAM ENDING, AFTER ALL...
DREAM ENDING?
YES. YOU KNOW, WHERE THE PROTAG-ONIST WAKES UP AT THE END...
...AND IT TURNS OUT "IT WAS ALL JUST A DREAM"...
A dream ...?
All of it ...?
HUH? BUT...
EVERYTHING YOU SEE IN YOUR DREAMS IS GOING TO HAPPEN EVENTUALLY, SO WHAT'S THE BIG PROBLEM?
MAYBE FOR A PROPHET, THAT'S TRUE...

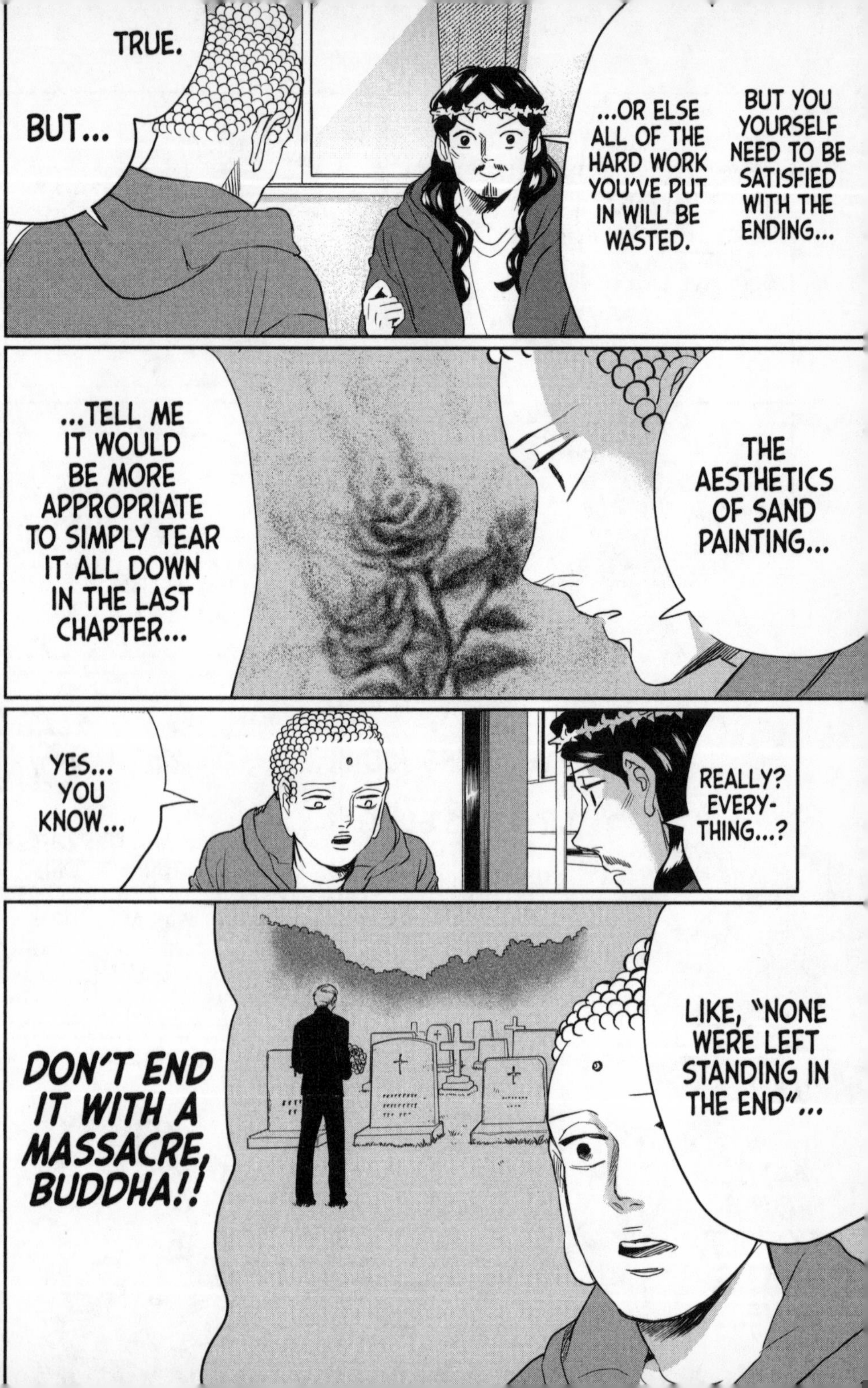
BUT YOU YOURSELF NEED TO BE SATISFIED WITH THE ENDING...
...OR ELSE ALL OF THE HARD WORK YOU'VE PUT IN WILL BE WASTED.
TRUE.
BUT...
THE AESTHETICS OF SAND PAINTING...
...TELL ME IT WOULD BE MORE APPROPRIATE TO SIMPLY TEAR IT ALL DOWN IN THE LAST CHAPTER...
REALLY? EVERY-THING...?
YES... YOU KNOW...
LIKE, "NONE WERE LEFT STANDING IN THE END"...
DON'T END IT WITH A MASSACRE, BUDDHA!!

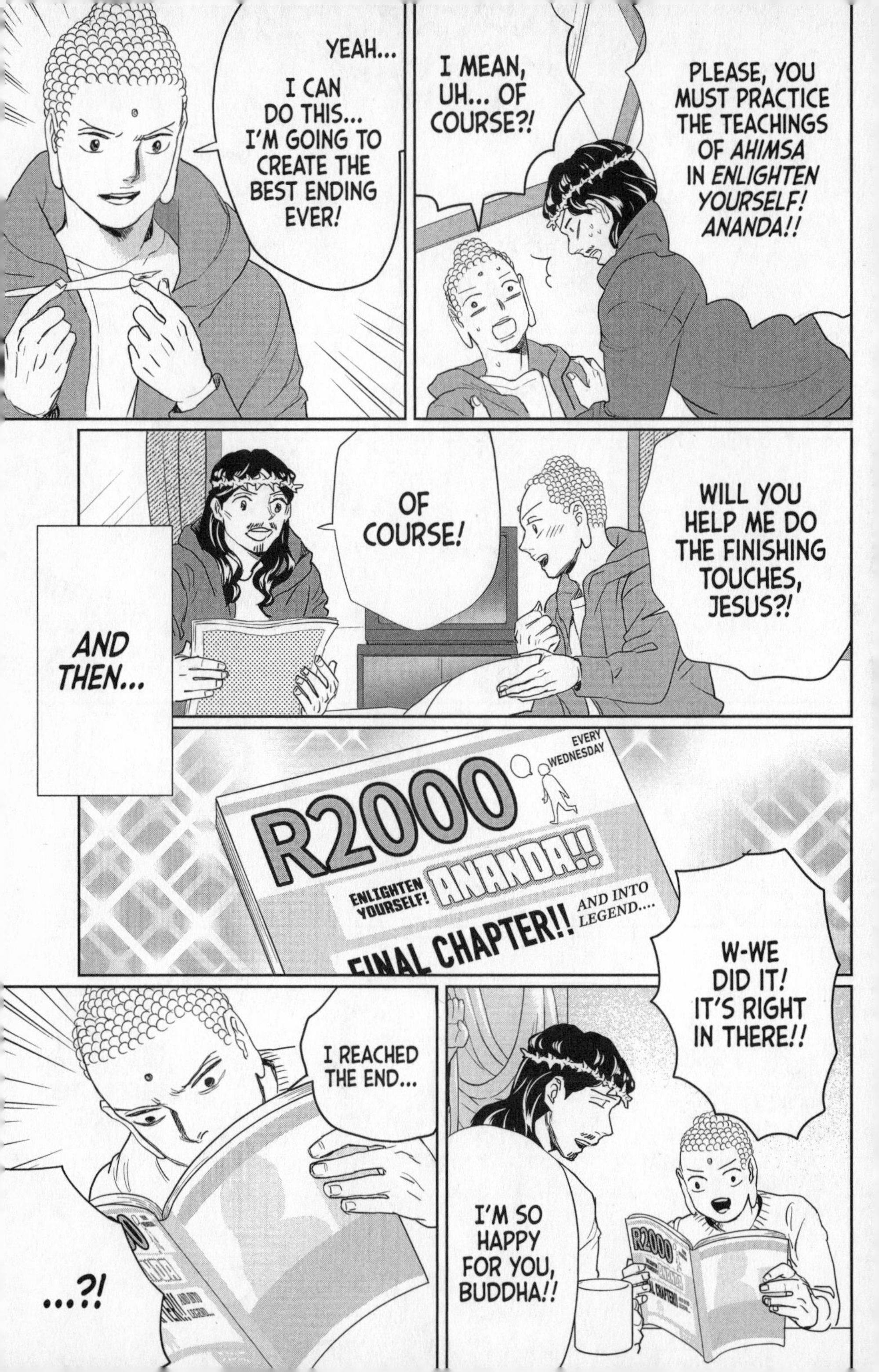
PLEASE, YOU MUST PRACTICE THE TEACHINGS OF *AHIMSA* IN *ENLIGHTEN YOURSELF! ANANDA!!*
I MEAN, UH... OF COURSE?!
YEAH...
I CAN DO THIS... I'M GOING TO CREATE THE BEST ENDING EVER!
WILL YOU HELP ME DO THE FINISHING TOUCHES, JESUS?!
OF COURSE!
AND THEN...
EVERY WEDNESDAY
R2000
ENLIGHTEN YOURSELF!
ANANDA!!
FINAL CHAPTER!!
AND INTO LEGEND....
W-WE DID IT! IT'S RIGHT IN THERE!!
I'M SO HAPPY FOR YOU, BUDDHA!!
I REACHED THE END...
...?!

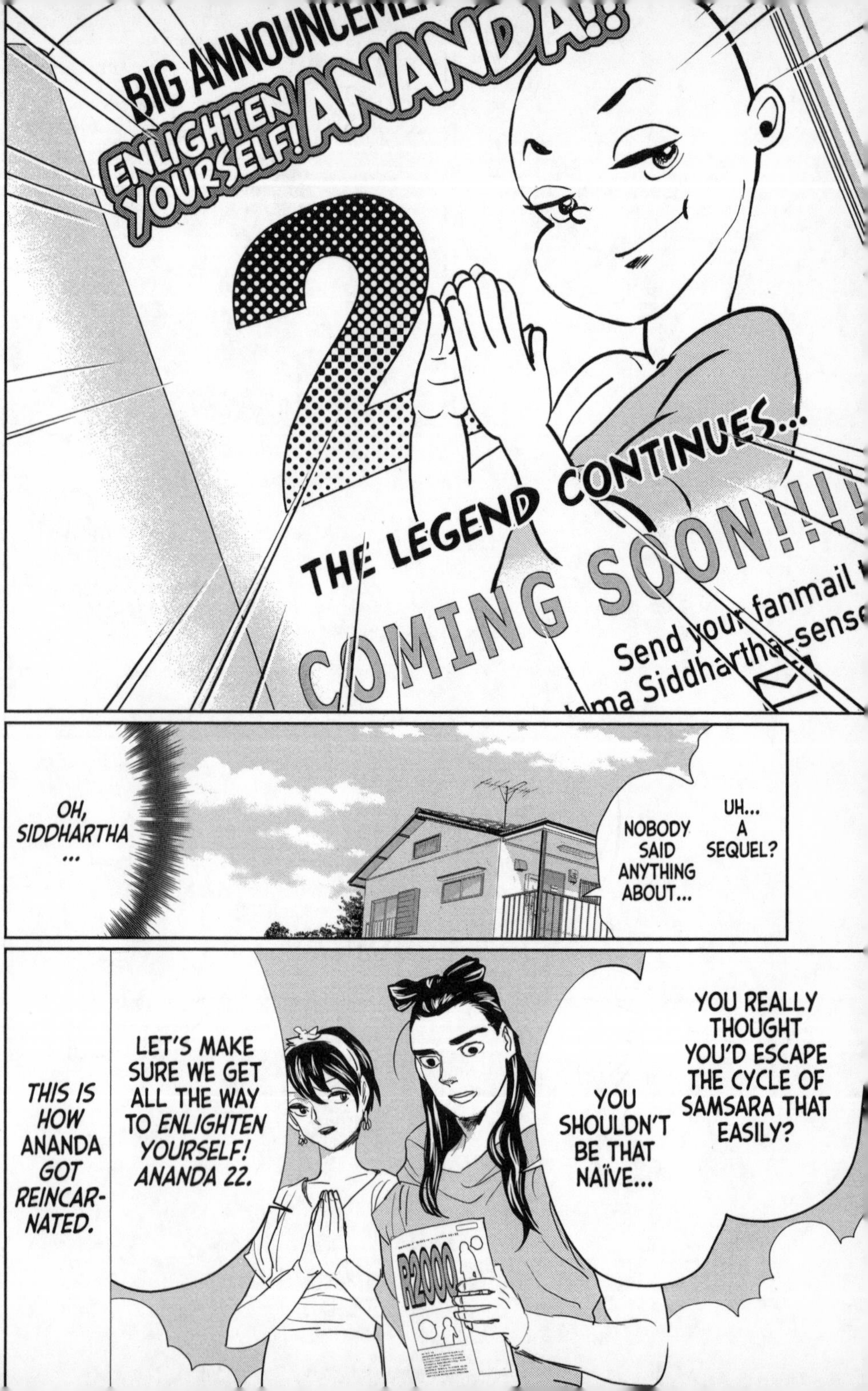
ENLIGHTEN YOURSELF! ANANDA!!
2
THE LEGEND CONTINUES...
COMING SOON!!!!
UH... A SEQUEL?
NOBODY SAID ANYTHING ABOUT...
OH, SIDDHARTHA...
YOU REALLY THOUGHT YOU'D ESCAPE THE CYCLE OF SAMSARA THAT EASILY?
YOU SHOULDN'T BE THAT NAÏVE...
R2000
LET'S MAKE SURE WE GET ALL THE WAY TO *ENLIGHTEN YOURSELF! ANANDA 22.*
THIS IS HOW ANANDA GOT REINCARNATED.

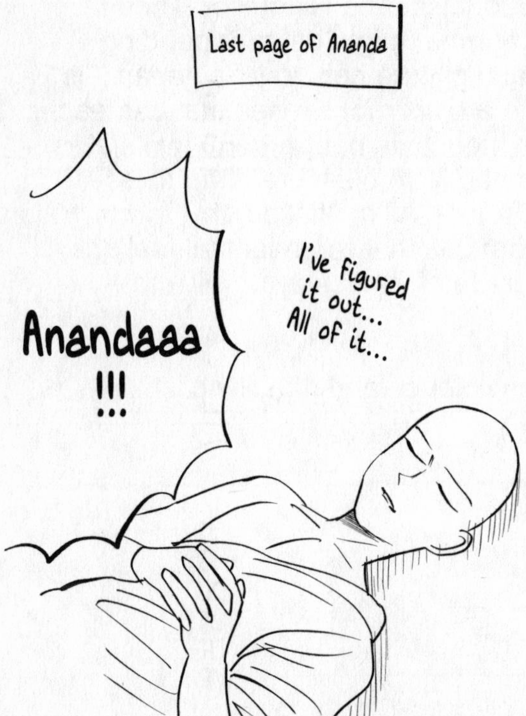
Last page of Ananda
I've figured it out... All of it...
Anandaaa!!!

SAINT☆YOUNG MEN

CHAPTER 132 TRANSLATION NOTES

World Enlightenment Arts Tournament, page 186
A parody of the World Martial Arts Tournament, or *Tenkaichi Budôkai,* from the *Dragon Ball* manga and anime. As shown in the manga here, the *Dragon Ball* tournament happens several times over the course of the story.

108 Earthly Temptations, page 186
The number 108 appears in many sacred contexts throughout Dharmic religions such as Buddhism and Hinduism. Though the methods of deriving the number might differ depending on the school of Buddhism and culture behind it, in Japan it is generally accepted that there are six root senses that can each have three aspects (positive, negative, neutral) and two states of being attached to or detached from pleasure, then three worlds of past, present, and future. All multiplied, this forms 108 distinct temptations or attachments that represent all feelings that keep one rooted to the cycle of Samsara.

Ahimsa, Page 195
The Buddhist principle of nonviolence and nonkilling.

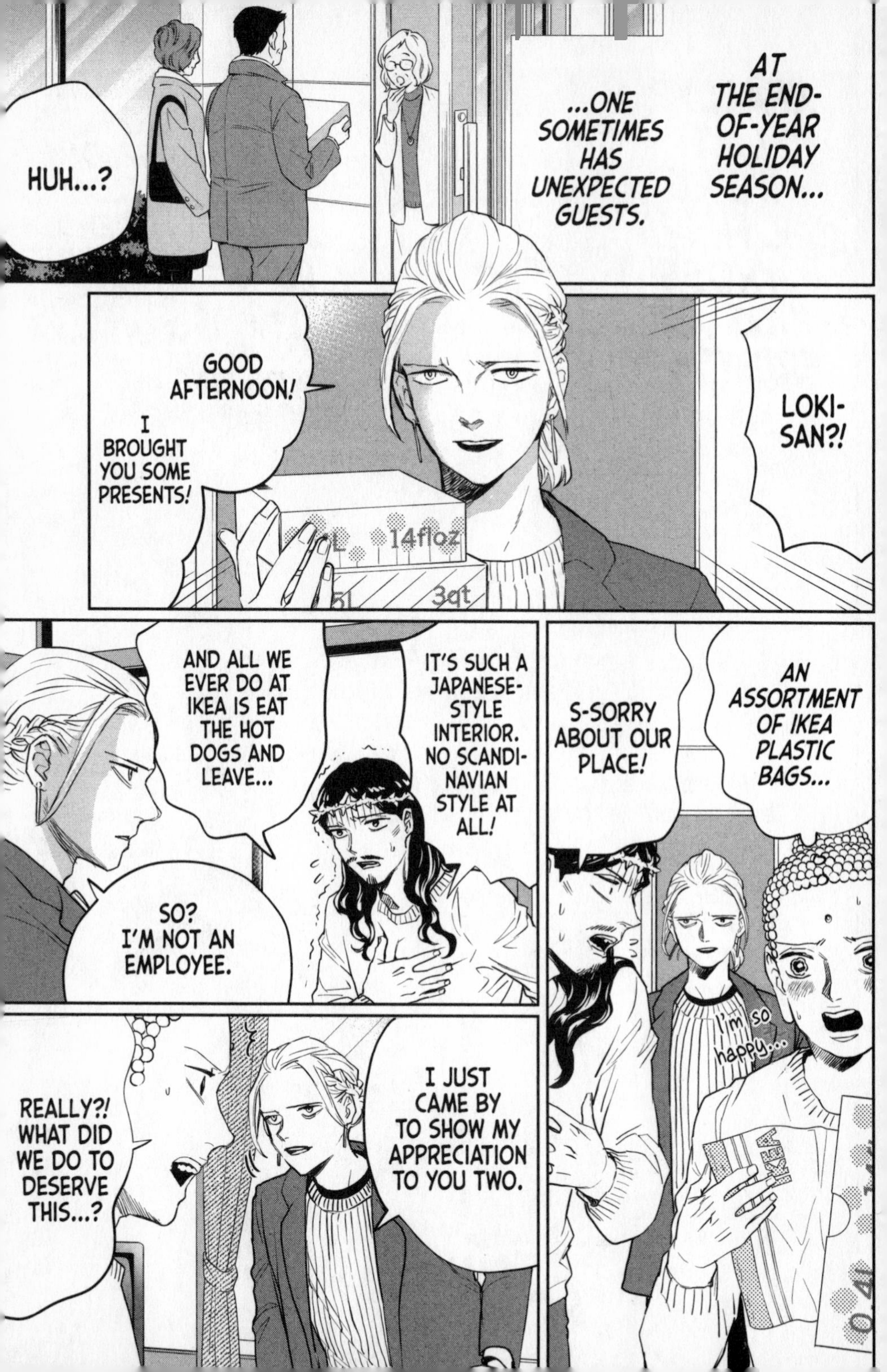
AT THE END-OF-YEAR HOLIDAY SEASON...
...ONE SOMETIMES HAS UNEXPECTED GUESTS.
HUH...?
LOKI-SAN?!
GOOD AFTERNOON!
I BROUGHT YOU SOME PRESENTS!
14floz
3qt
AN ASSORTMENT OF IKEA PLASTIC BAGS...
S-SORRY ABOUT OUR PLACE!
I'm so happy...
IT'S SUCH A JAPANESE-STYLE INTERIOR. NO SCANDINAVIAN STYLE AT ALL!
AND ALL WE EVER DO AT IKEA IS EAT THE HOT DOGS AND LEAVE...
SO? I'M NOT AN EMPLOYEE.
I JUST CAME BY TO SHOW MY APPRECIATION TO YOU TWO.
REALLY?! WHAT DID WE DO TO DESERVE THIS...?

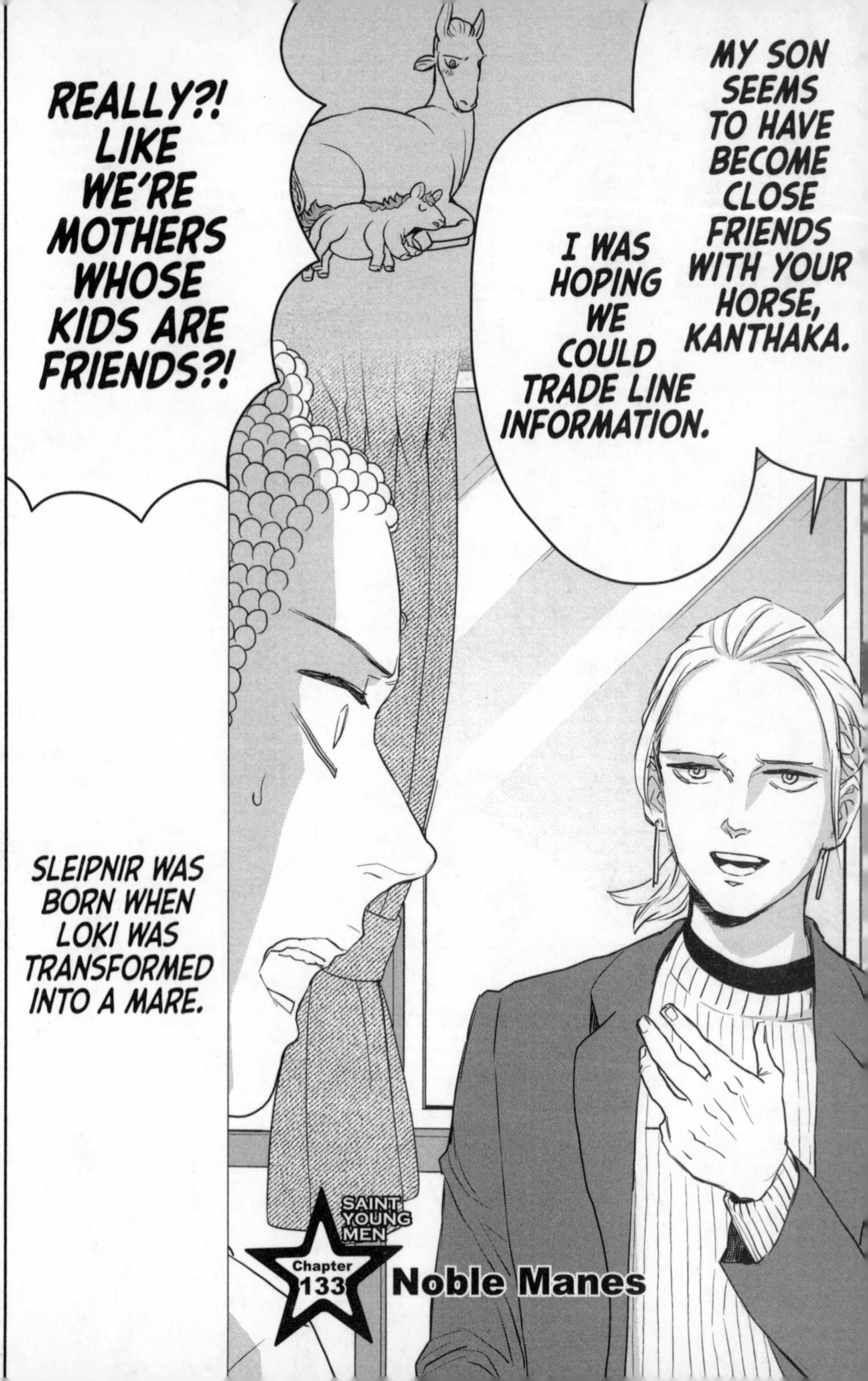
MY SON SEEMS TO HAVE BECOME CLOSE FRIENDS WITH YOUR HORSE, KANTHAKA.
I WAS HOPING WE COULD TRADE LINE INFORMATION.
REALLY?! LIKE WE'RE MOTHERS WHOSE KIDS ARE FRIENDS?!
SLEIPNIR WAS BORN WHEN LOKI WAS TRANSFORMED INTO A MARE.
SAINT YOUNG MEN
Chapter 133
Noble Manes

BUDDHA
PEOPLE THINK THE SAYING COMPARING A HORSE TO THE UPS AND DOWNS OF LIFE COMES FROM BUDDHIST TEACHINGS, BUT IT ACTUALLY COMES FROM CHINA.

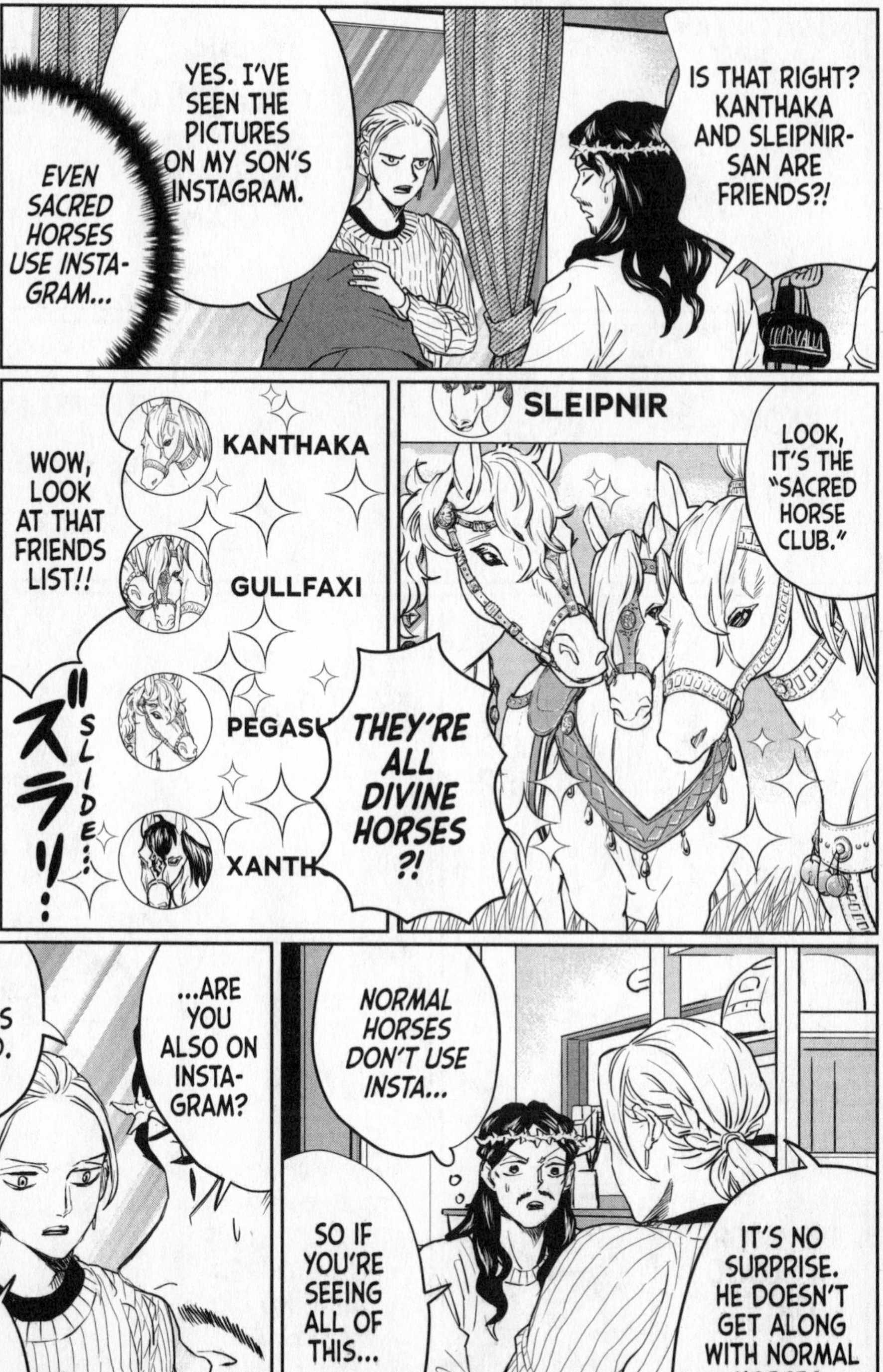
IS THAT RIGHT? KANTHAKA AND SLEIPNIR-SAN ARE FRIENDS?!
YES. I'VE SEEN THE PICTURES ON MY SON'S INSTAGRAM.
EVEN SACRED HORSES USE INSTA-GRAM...
LOOK, IT'S THE "SACRED HORSE CLUB."
SLEIPNIR
THEY'RE ALL DIVINE HORSES?!
KANTHAKA
GULLFAXI
PEGASU
XANTH
WOW, LOOK AT THAT FRIENDS LIST!!
ズラリ SLIDE...
IT'S NO SURPRISE. HE DOESN'T GET ALONG WITH NORMAL HORSES.
NORMAL HORSES DON'T USE INSTA...
SO IF YOU'RE SEEING ALL OF THIS...
...ARE YOU ALSO ON INSTA-GRAM?
NO. IT'S STUPID.
BUT...

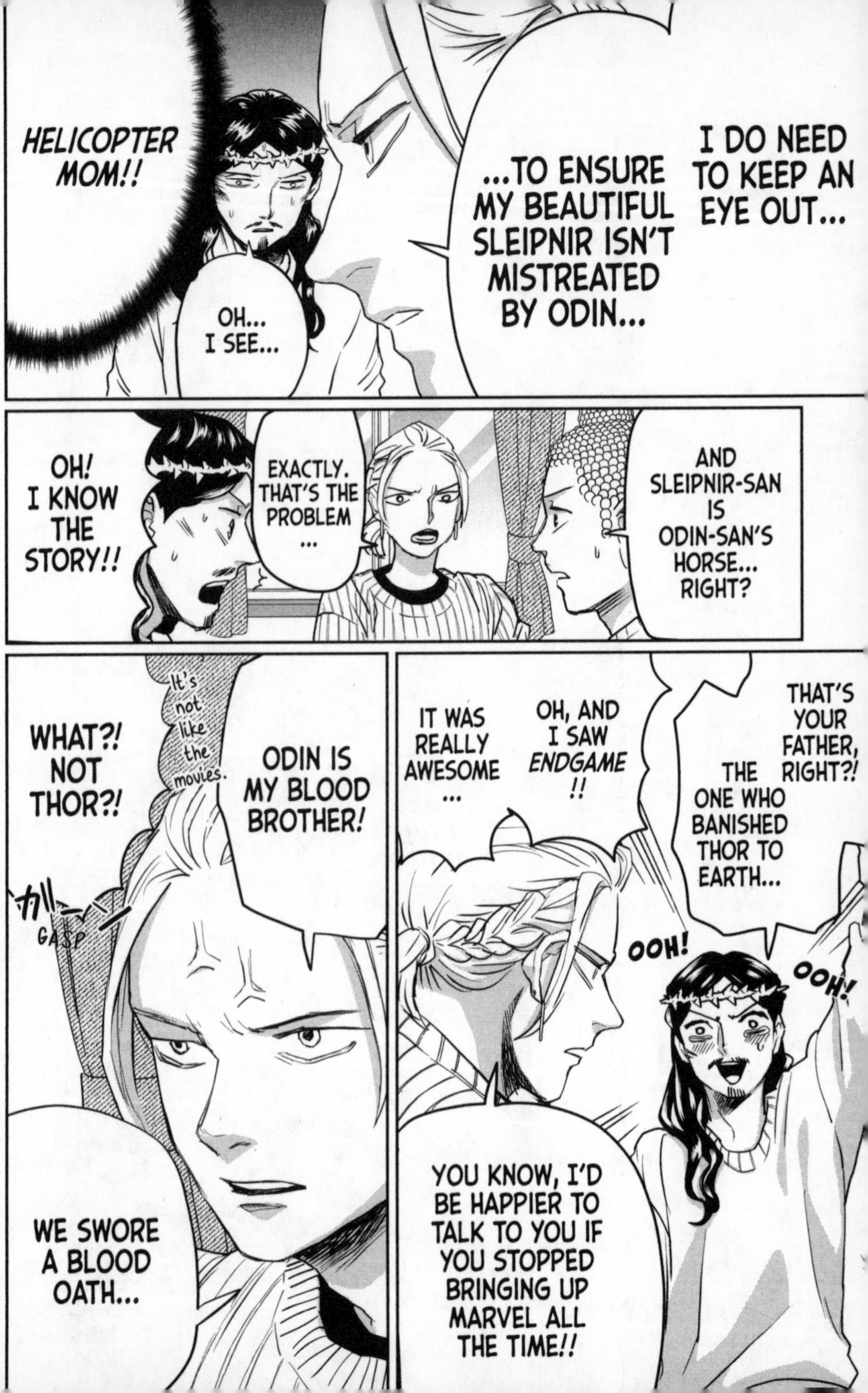
I DO NEED TO KEEP AN EYE OUT...
...TO ENSURE MY BEAUTIFUL SLEIPNIR ISN'T MISTREATED BY ODIN...
OH... I SEE...
HELICOPTER MOM!!
AND SLEIPNIR-SAN IS ODIN-SAN'S HORSE... RIGHT?
EXACTLY. THAT'S THE PROBLEM ...
OH! I KNOW THE STORY!!
THAT'S YOUR FATHER, RIGHT?!
THE ONE WHO BANISHED THOR TO EARTH...
OH, AND I SAW *ENDGAME* !!
IT WAS REALLY AWESOME ...
OOH!
OOH!
YOU KNOW, I'D BE HAPPIER TO TALK TO YOU IF YOU STOPPED BRINGING UP MARVEL ALL THE TIME!!
ODIN IS MY BLOOD BROTHER!
It's not like the movies.
WHAT?! NOT THOR?!
カッ
GASP
WE SWORE A BLOOD OATH...

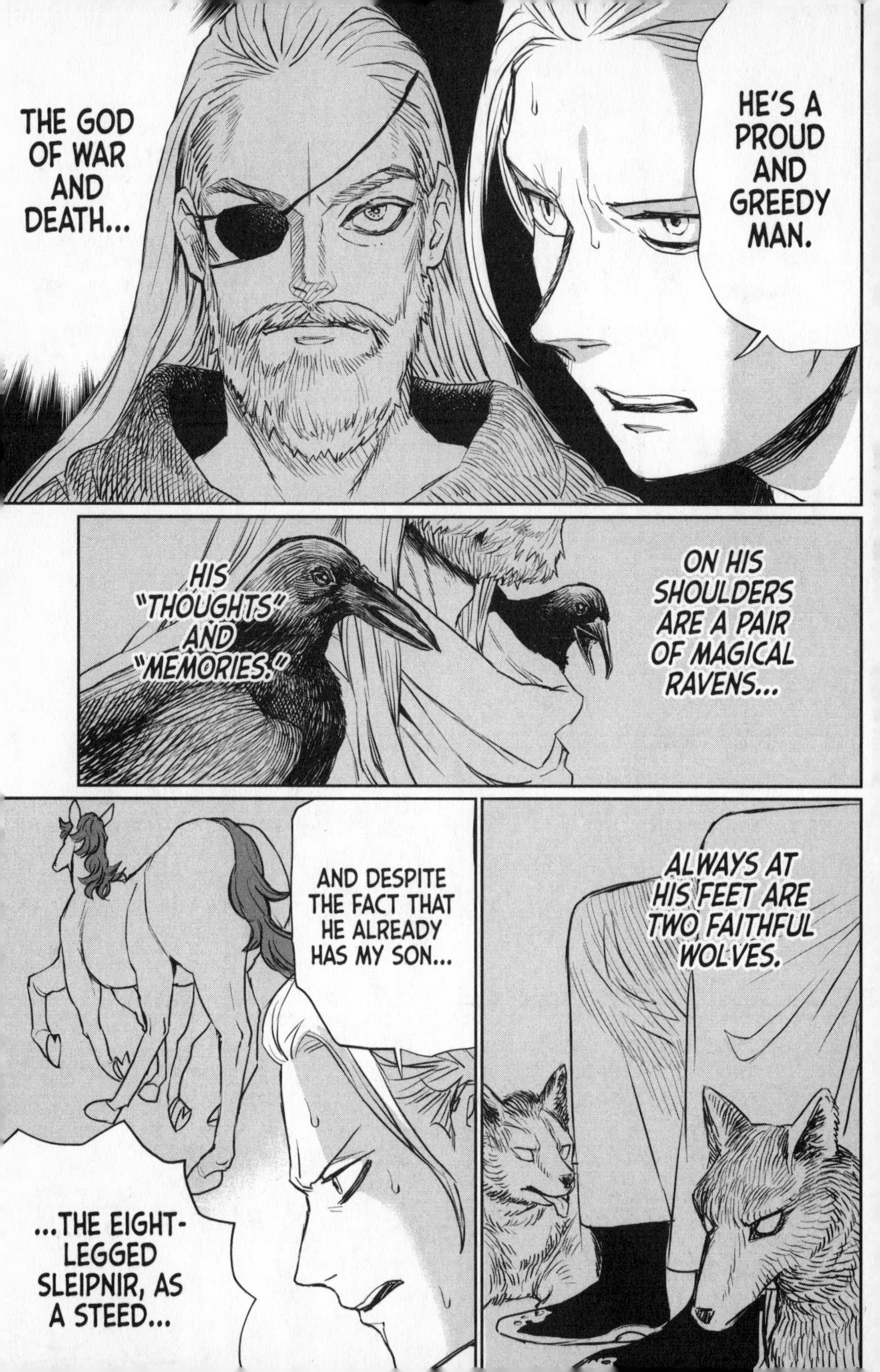
HE'S A PROUD AND GREEDY MAN.
THE GOD OF WAR AND DEATH...
ON HIS SHOULDERS ARE A PAIR OF MAGICAL RAVENS...
HIS "THOUGHTS" AND "MEMORIES."
ALWAYS AT HIS FEET ARE TWO FAITHFUL WOLVES.
AND DESPITE THE FACT THAT HE ALREADY HAS MY SON...
...THE EIGHT-LEGGED SLEIPNIR, AS A STEED...

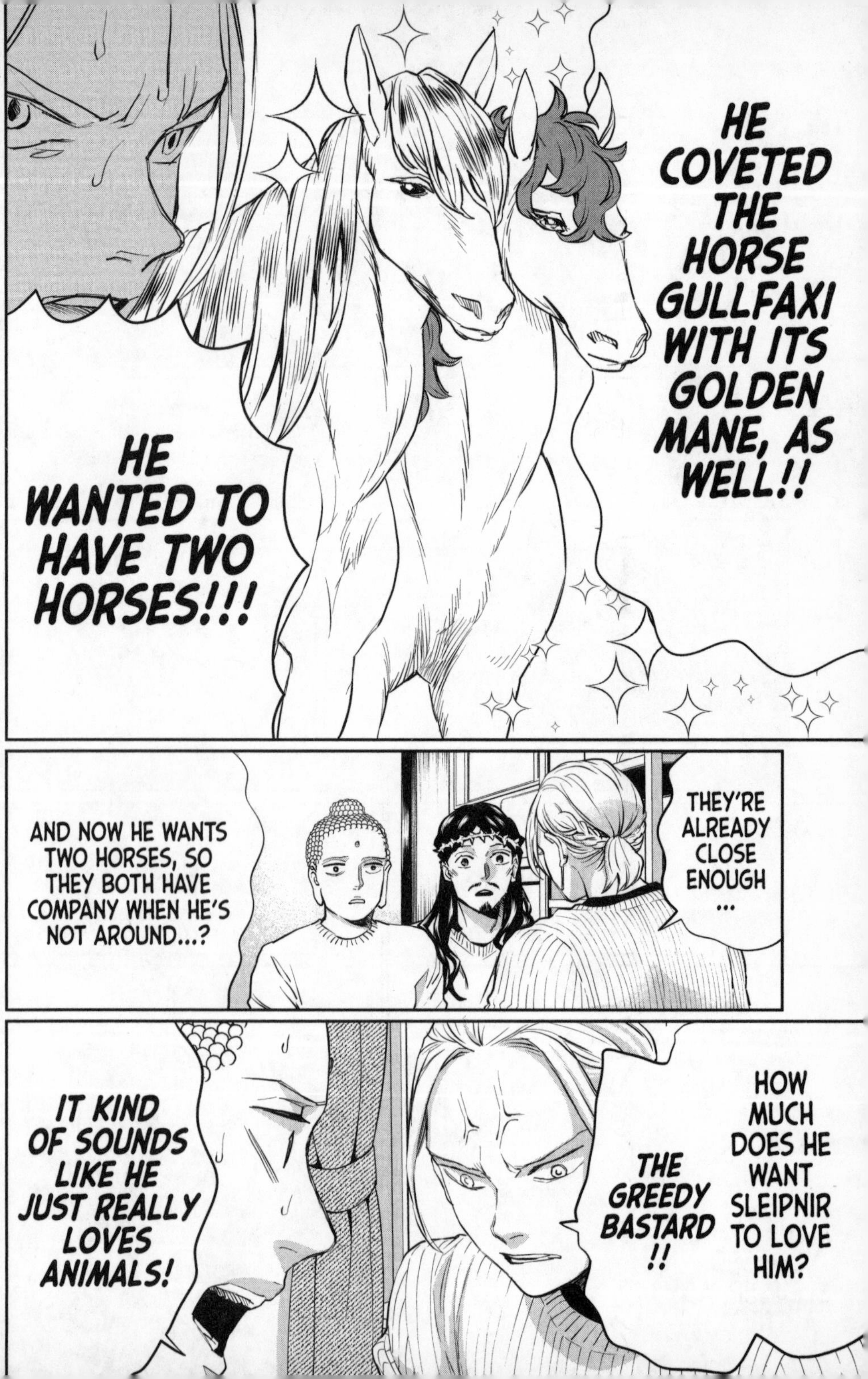
HE COVETED THE HORSE GULLFAXI WITH ITS GOLDEN MANE, AS WELL!!
HE WANTED TO HAVE TWO HORSES!!!
THEY'RE ALREADY CLOSE ENOUGH ...
AND NOW HE WANTS TWO HORSES, SO THEY BOTH HAVE COMPANY WHEN HE'S NOT AROUND...?
HOW MUCH DOES HE WANT SLEIPNIR TO LOVE HIM?
THE GREEDY BASTARD !!
IT KIND OF SOUNDS LIKE HE JUST REALLY LOVES ANIMALS!

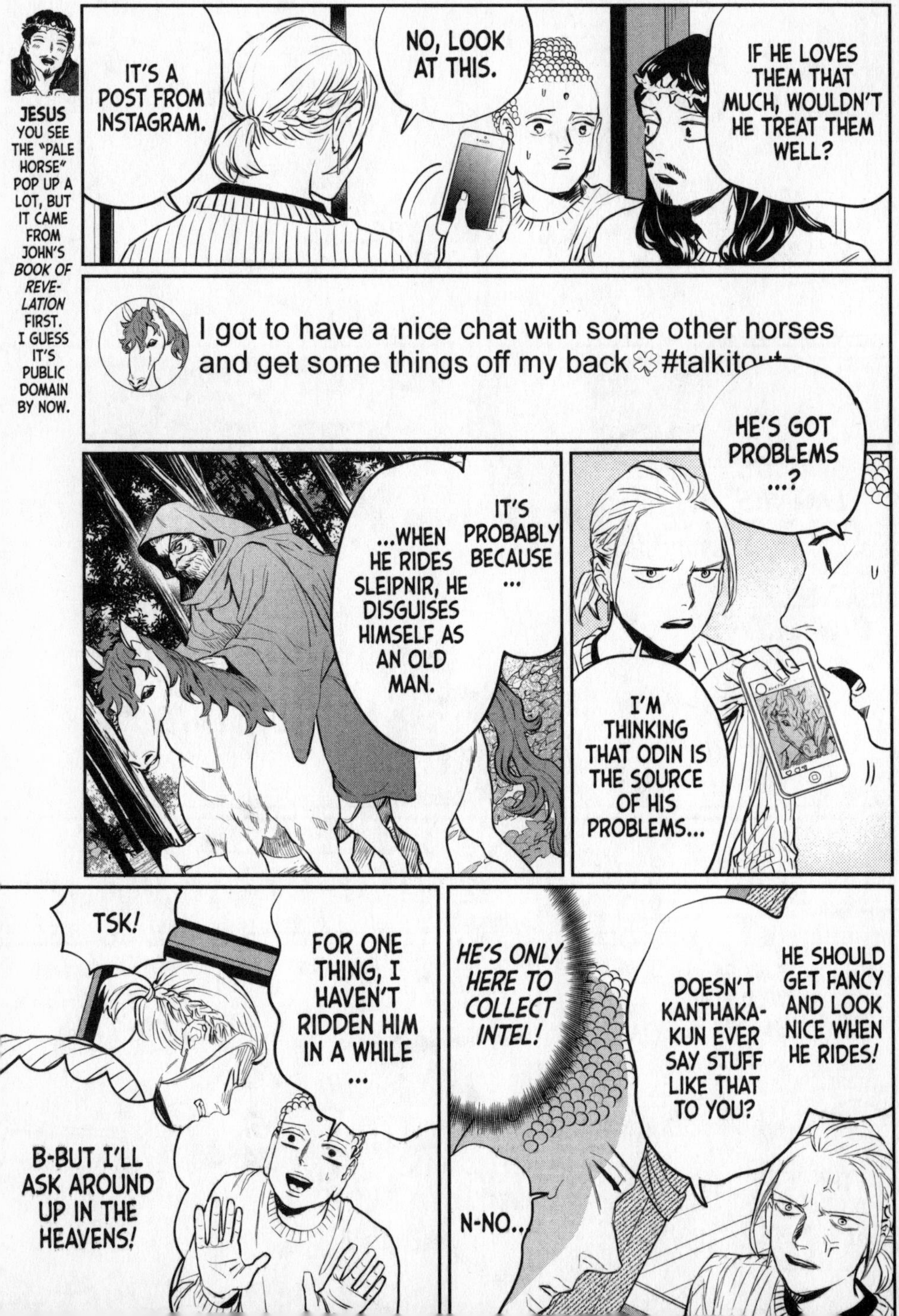
JESUS
YOU SEE THE "PALE HORSE" POP UP A LOT, BUT IT CAME FROM JOHN'S *BOOK OF REVELATION* FIRST. I GUESS IT'S PUBLIC DOMAIN BY NOW.
IF HE LOVES THEM THAT MUCH, WOULDN'T HE TREAT THEM WELL?
NO, LOOK AT THIS.
IT'S A POST FROM INSTAGRAM.
I got to have a nice chat with some other horses and get some things off my back #talkitout
HE'S GOT PROBLEMS ...?
I'M THINKING THAT ODIN IS THE SOURCE OF HIS PROBLEMS...
IT'S PROBABLY BECAUSE ...
...WHEN HE RIDES SLEIPNIR, HE DISGUISES HIMSELF AS AN OLD MAN.
HE SHOULD GET FANCY AND LOOK NICE WHEN HE RIDES!
DOESN'T KANTHAKA-KUN EVER SAY STUFF LIKE THAT TO YOU?
HE'S ONLY HERE TO COLLECT INTEL!
N-NO...
FOR ONE THING, I HAVEN'T RIDDEN HIM IN A WHILE ...
TSK!
B-BUT I'LL ASK AROUND UP IN THE HEAVENS!

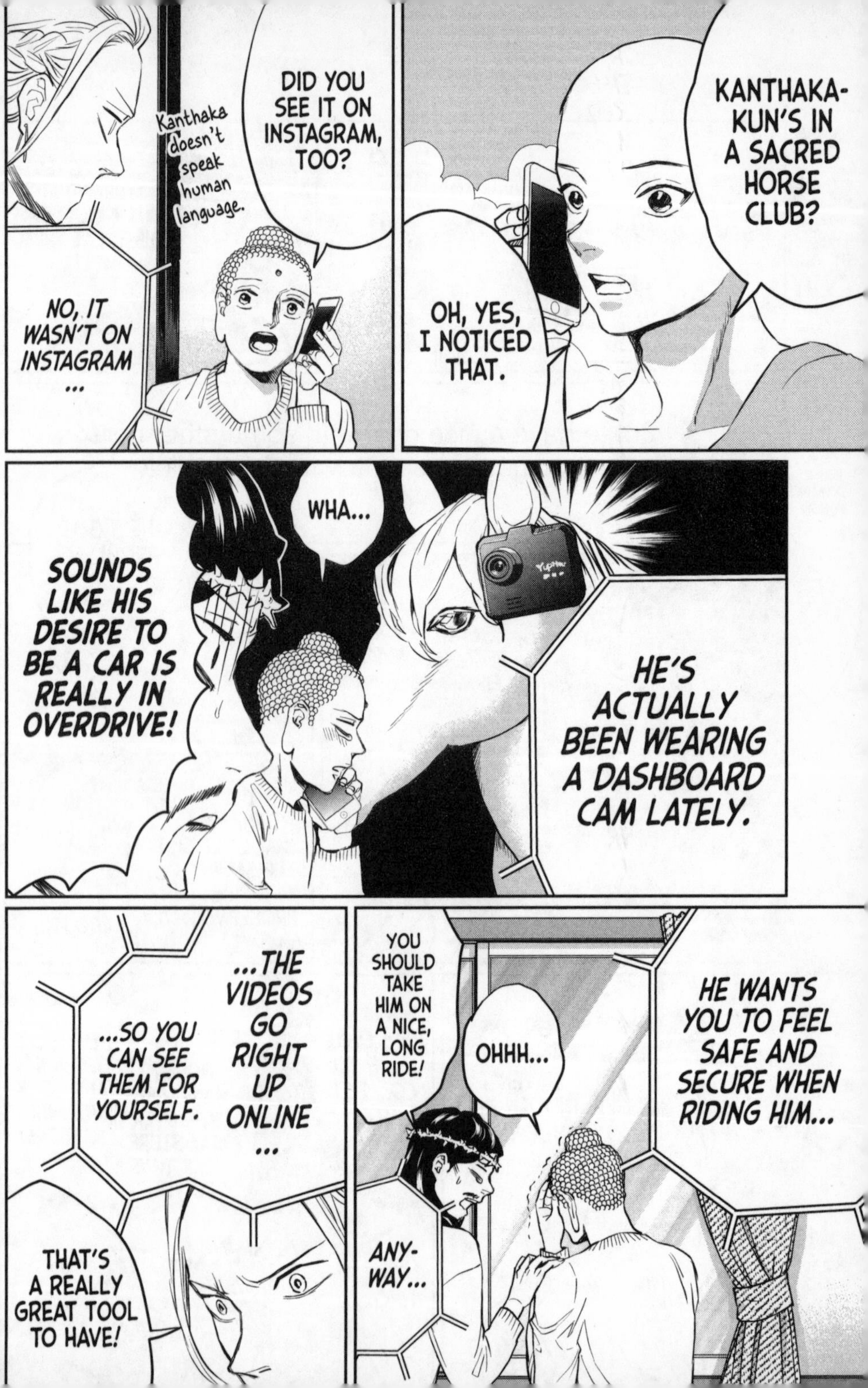
KANTHAKA-KUN'S IN A SACRED HORSE CLUB?
OH, YES, I NOTICED THAT.
DID YOU SEE IT ON INSTAGRAM, TOO?
Kanthaka doesn't speak human language.
NO, IT WASN'T ON INSTAGRAM ...
HE'S ACTUALLY BEEN WEARING A DASHBOARD CAM LATELY.
WHA...
SOUNDS LIKE HIS DESIRE TO BE A CAR IS REALLY IN OVERDRIVE!
HE WANTS YOU TO FEEL SAFE AND SECURE WHEN RIDING HIM...
OHHH...
YOU SHOULD TAKE HIM ON A NICE, LONG RIDE!
ANY-WAY...
...THE VIDEOS GO RIGHT UP ONLINE ...
...SO YOU CAN SEE THEM FOR YOURSELF.
THAT'S A REALLY GREAT TOOL TO HAVE!

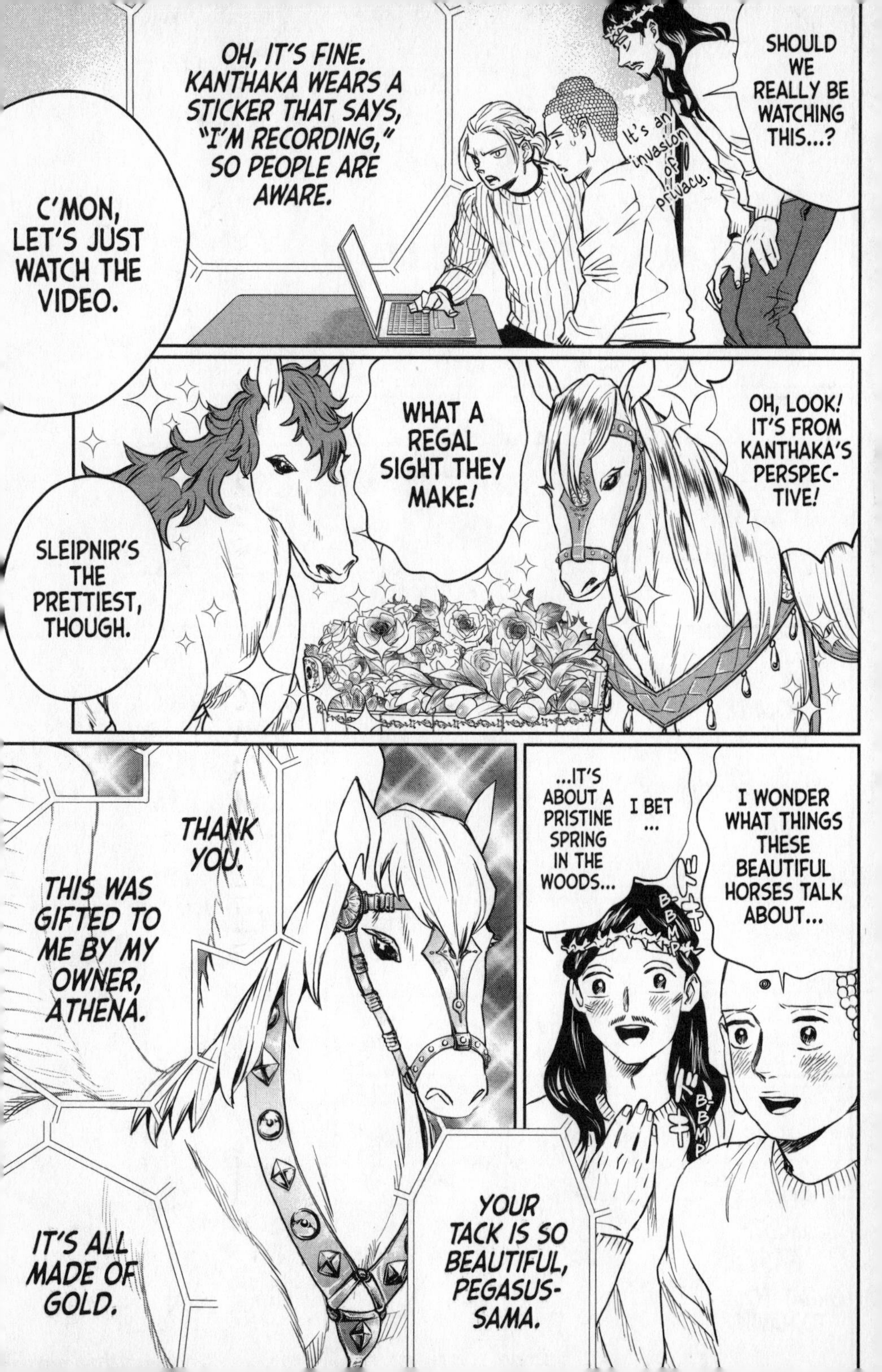
SHOULD WE REALLY BE WATCHING THIS...?
It's an invasion of privacy.
OH, IT'S FINE. KANTHAKA WEARS A STICKER THAT SAYS, "I'M RECORDING," SO PEOPLE ARE AWARE.
C'MON, LET'S JUST WATCH THE VIDEO.
OH, LOOK! IT'S FROM KANTHAKA'S PERSPEC-TIVE!
WHAT A REGAL SIGHT THEY MAKE!
SLEIPNIR'S THE PRETTIEST, THOUGH.
I WONDER WHAT THINGS THESE BEAUTIFUL HORSES TALK ABOUT...
I BET ...
...IT'S ABOUT A PRISTINE SPRING IN THE WOODS...
B-BMP
B-BMP
YOUR TACK IS SO BEAUTIFUL, PEGASUS-SAMA.
THANK YOU.
THIS WAS GIFTED TO ME BY MY OWNER, ATHENA.
IT'S ALL MADE OF GOLD.

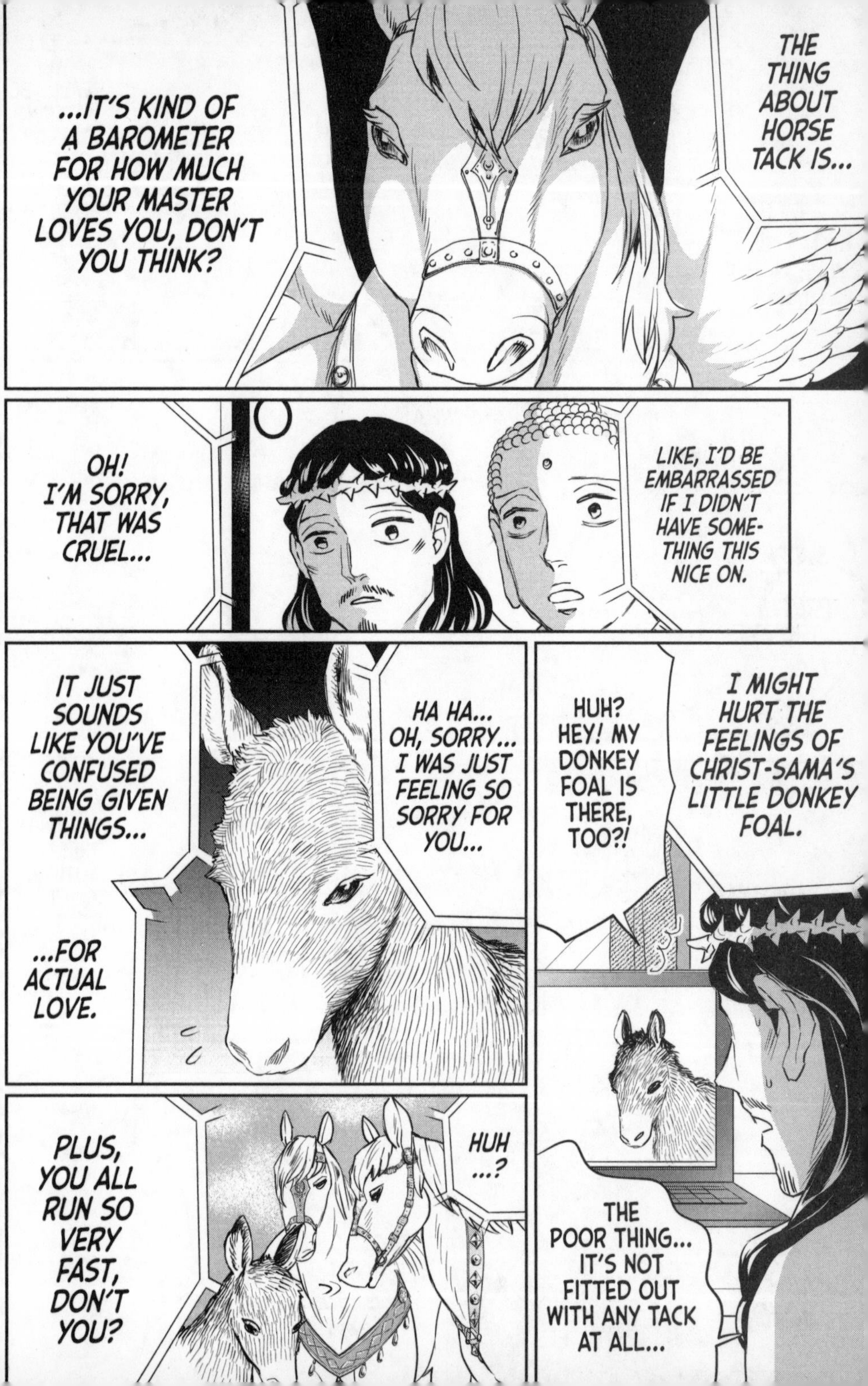
THE THING ABOUT HORSE TACK IS...
...IT'S KIND OF A BAROMETER FOR HOW MUCH YOUR MASTER LOVES YOU, DON'T YOU THINK?
LIKE, I'D BE EMBARRASSED IF I DIDN'T HAVE SOME-THING THIS NICE ON.
OH! I'M SORRY, THAT WAS CRUEL...
I MIGHT HURT THE FEELINGS OF CHRIST-SAMA'S LITTLE DONKEY FOAL.
HUH? HEY! MY DONKEY FOAL IS THERE, TOO?!
THE POOR THING... IT'S NOT FITTED OUT WITH ANY TACK AT ALL...
HA HA... OH, SORRY... I WAS JUST FEELING SO SORRY FOR YOU...
IT JUST SOUNDS LIKE YOU'VE CONFUSED BEING GIVEN THINGS...
...FOR ACTUAL LOVE.
HUH ...?
PLUS, YOU ALL RUN SO VERY FAST, DON'T YOU?

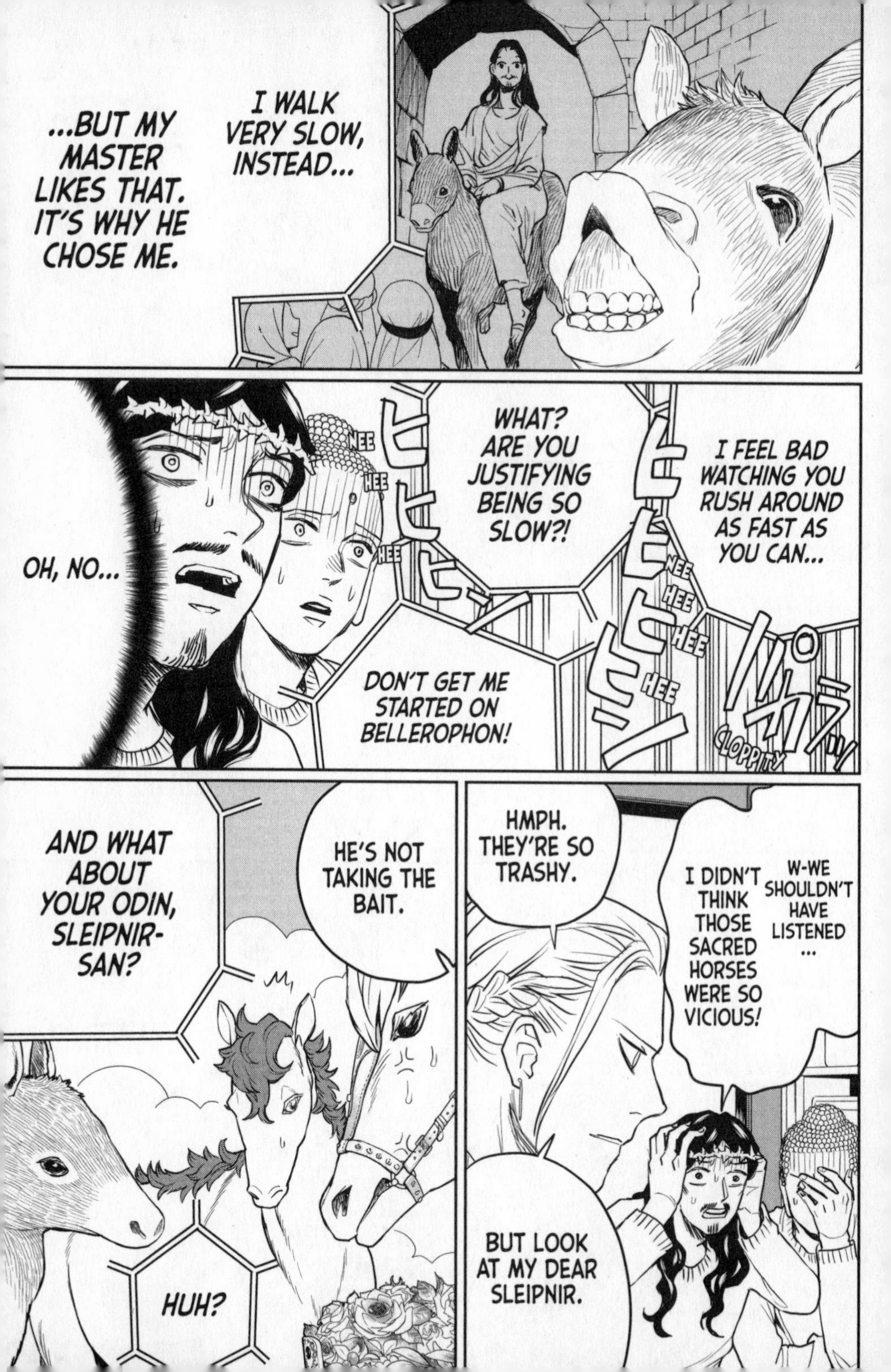

I WALK VERY SLOW, INSTEAD...
...BUT MY MASTER LIKES THAT. IT'S WHY HE CHOSE ME.
I FEEL BAD WATCHING YOU RUSH AROUND AS FAST AS YOU CAN...
パカラッ
CLOPPITY
ヒヒーン
NEE HEE HEE HEE
WHAT? ARE YOU JUSTIFYING BEING SO SLOW?!
DON'T GET ME STARTED ON BELLEROPHON!
ヒヒーン
NEE HEE HEE
OH, NO...
W-WE SHOULDN'T HAVE LISTENED ...
I DIDN'T THINK THOSE SACRED HORSES WERE SO VICIOUS!
HMPH. THEY'RE SO TRASHY.
BUT LOOK AT MY DEAR SLEIPNIR.
HE'S NOT TAKING THE BAIT.
AND WHAT ABOUT YOUR ODIN, SLEIPNIR-SAN?
HUH?

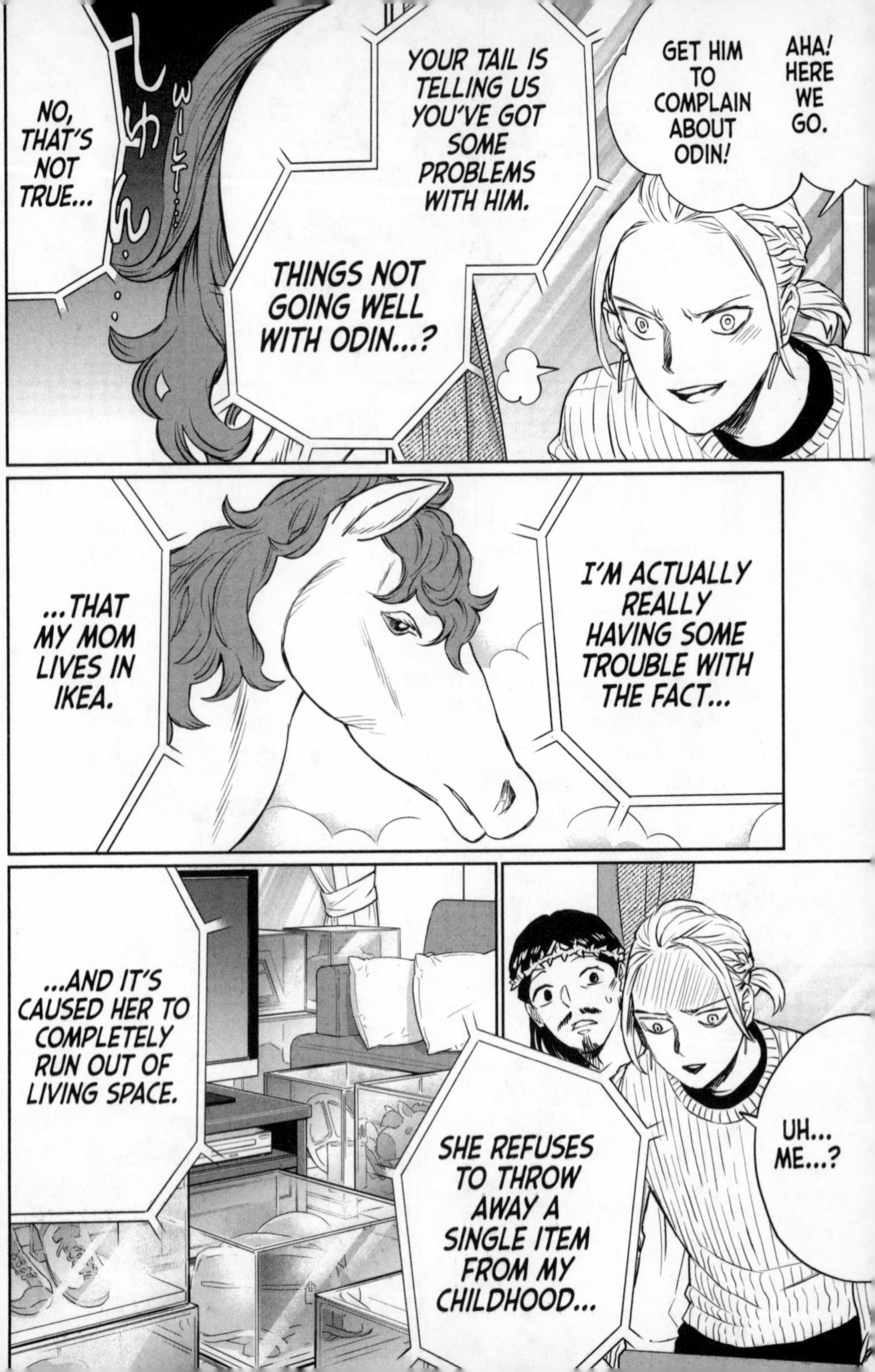
AHA! HERE WE GO.
GET HIM TO COMPLAIN ABOUT ODIN!
YOUR TAIL IS TELLING US YOU'VE GOT SOME PROBLEMS WITH HIM.
THINGS NOT GOING WELL WITH ODIN...?
しゅん
WILT...
NO, THAT'S NOT TRUE...
I'M ACTUALLY REALLY HAVING SOME TROUBLE WITH THE FACT...
...THAT MY MOM LIVES IN IKEA.
UH... ME...?
SHE REFUSES TO THROW AWAY A SINGLE ITEM FROM MY CHILDHOOD...
...AND IT'S CAUSED HER TO COMPLETELY RUN OUT OF LIVING SPACE.

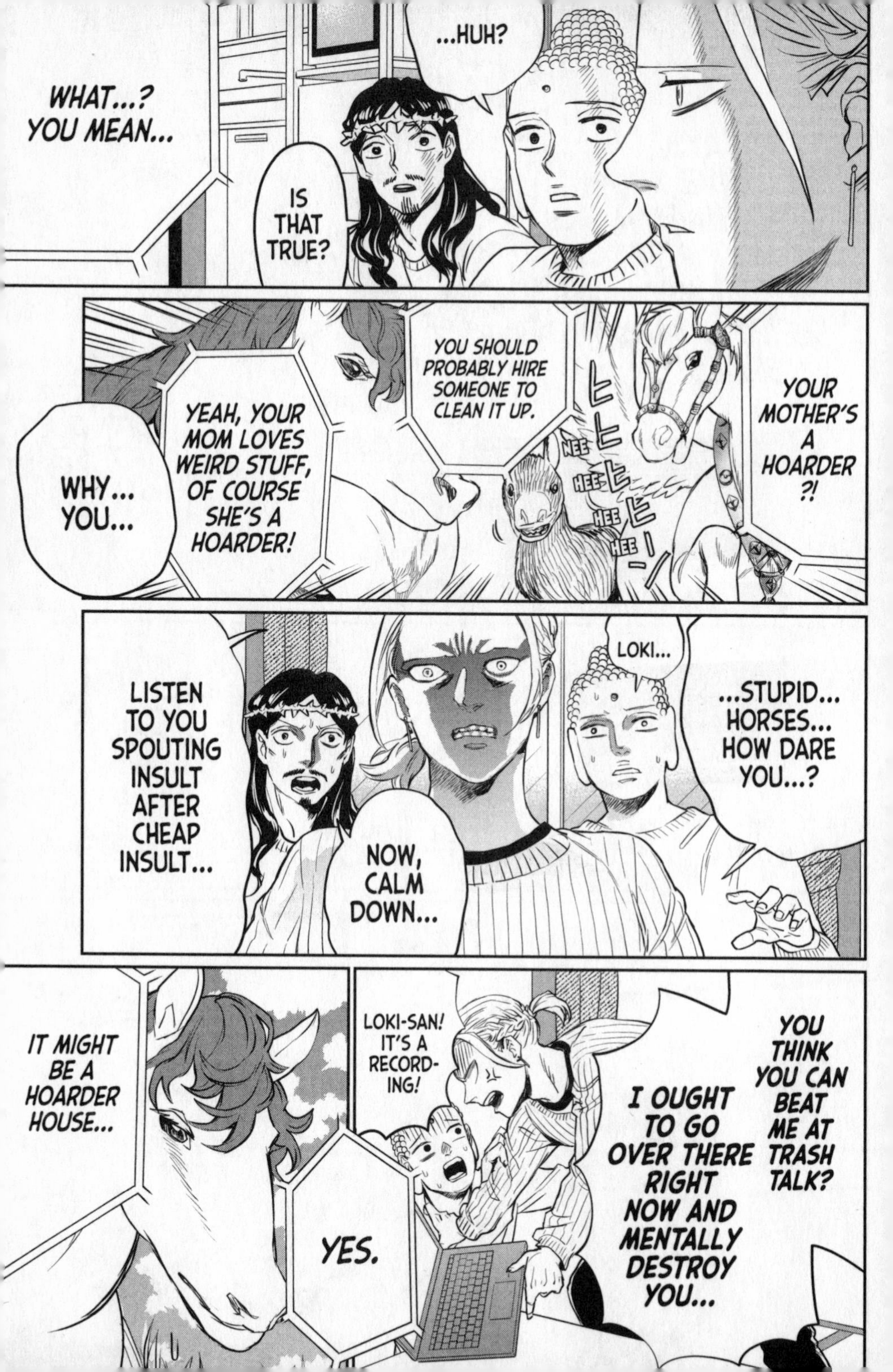
...HUH?
WHAT...? YOU MEAN...
IS THAT TRUE?
YOUR MOTHER'S A HOARDER?!
YOU SHOULD PROBABLY HIRE SOMEONE TO CLEAN IT UP.
ヒヒヒヒーン
NEE HEE HEE HEE
YEAH, YOUR MOM LOVES WEIRD STUFF, OF COURSE SHE'S A HOARDER!
WHY... YOU...
LOKI...
...STUPID... HORSES... HOW DARE YOU...?
NOW, CALM DOWN...
LISTEN TO YOU SPOUTING INSULT AFTER CHEAP INSULT...
YOU THINK YOU CAN BEAT ME AT TRASH TALK?
I OUGHT TO GO OVER THERE RIGHT NOW AND MENTALLY DESTROY YOU...
LOKI-SAN! IT'S A RECORDING!
YES.
IT MIGHT BE A HOARDER HOUSE...

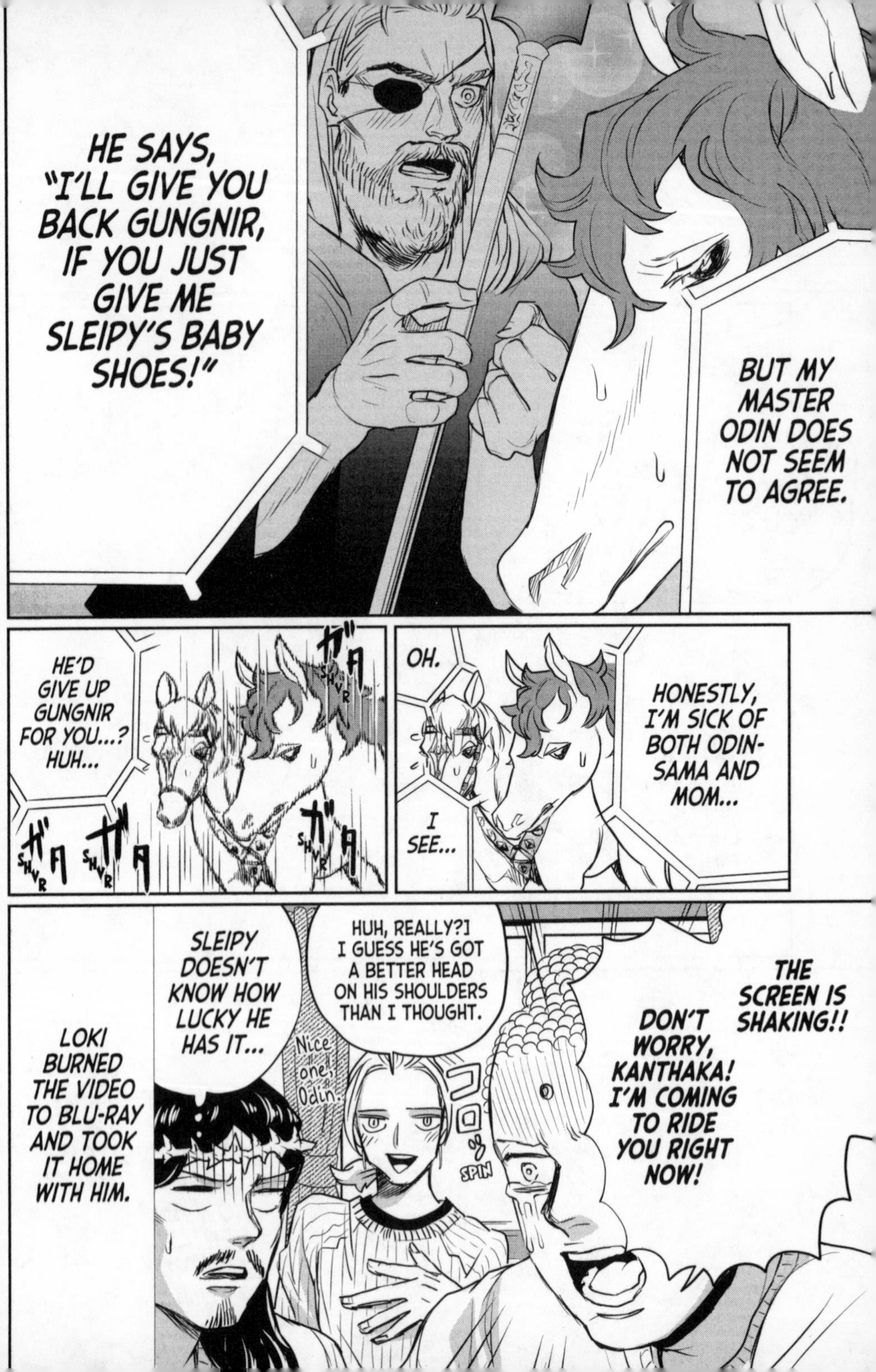
BUT MY MASTER ODIN DOES NOT SEEM TO AGREE.
HE SAYS, "I'LL GIVE YOU BACK GUNGNIR, IF YOU JUST GIVE ME SLEIPY'S BABY SHOES!"
HONESTLY, I'M SICK OF BOTH ODIN-SAMA AND MOM...
OH.
I SEE...
ガタ SHVR
HE'D GIVE UP GUNGNIR FOR YOU...? HUH...
ガタ SHVR
ガタ SHVR
ガタ SHVR
THE SCREEN IS SHAKING!!
DON'T WORRY, KANTHAKA! I'M COMING TO RIDE YOU RIGHT NOW!
コロ SPIN
HUH, REALLY?] I GUESS HE'S GOT A BETTER HEAD ON HIS SHOULDERS THAN I THOUGHT.
Nice one, Odin.
SLEIPY DOESN'T KNOW HOW LUCKY HE HAS IT...
LOKI BURNED THE VIDEO TO BLU-RAY AND TOOK IT HOME WITH HIM.

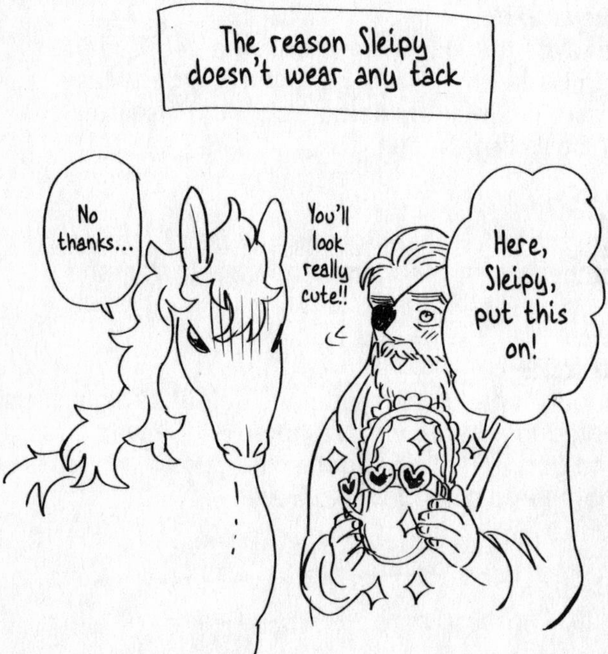
The reason Sleipy doesn't wear any tack
Here, Sleipy, put this on!
You'll look really cute!!
No thanks...

SAINT☆YOUNG MEN

CHAPTER 133 TRANSLATION NOTES

Horse saying, page 201
The aphorism mentioned in Buddha's profile comment translates to something like "all of humanity in the old man's horse," referring to a Chinese story about a prophetic old man. When his horse ran away, the man said, "Something good will happen eventually," and it returned with a speedy stallion in tow. As the village celebrated, he then said, "This will be the root of tragedy," and later his son fell off of that horse and broke his leg. But this time the man said, "This will be the foundation of good fortune." A year later, the village went to war and nearly all the young men died in battle, but because the man's son had a broken leg, he did not leave and was spared from that fate.

Sacred horses, page 201
The list of horses on Sleipnir's friends list are Kanthaka, the Buddha's horse; Gullfaxi, a horse in Norse mythology meaning "Golden Mane"; Pegasus, the winged horse of Greek mythology, child of Poseidon; and Xanthus, one of Achilles's two horses.

Pale horse, page 205
in the Book of Revelation, the pale horse is ridden by Death, the last of the Four Horsemen of the Apocalypse, after Conquest, War, and Famine.

Bellerophon, page 209
The Greek hero who caught Pegasus and rode it to defeat the Chimera. He also attempted to ride the winged horse all the way up to Mt. Olympus, home of the gods. But this angered the gods, and Zeus knocked him off of the horse and back down to Earth.

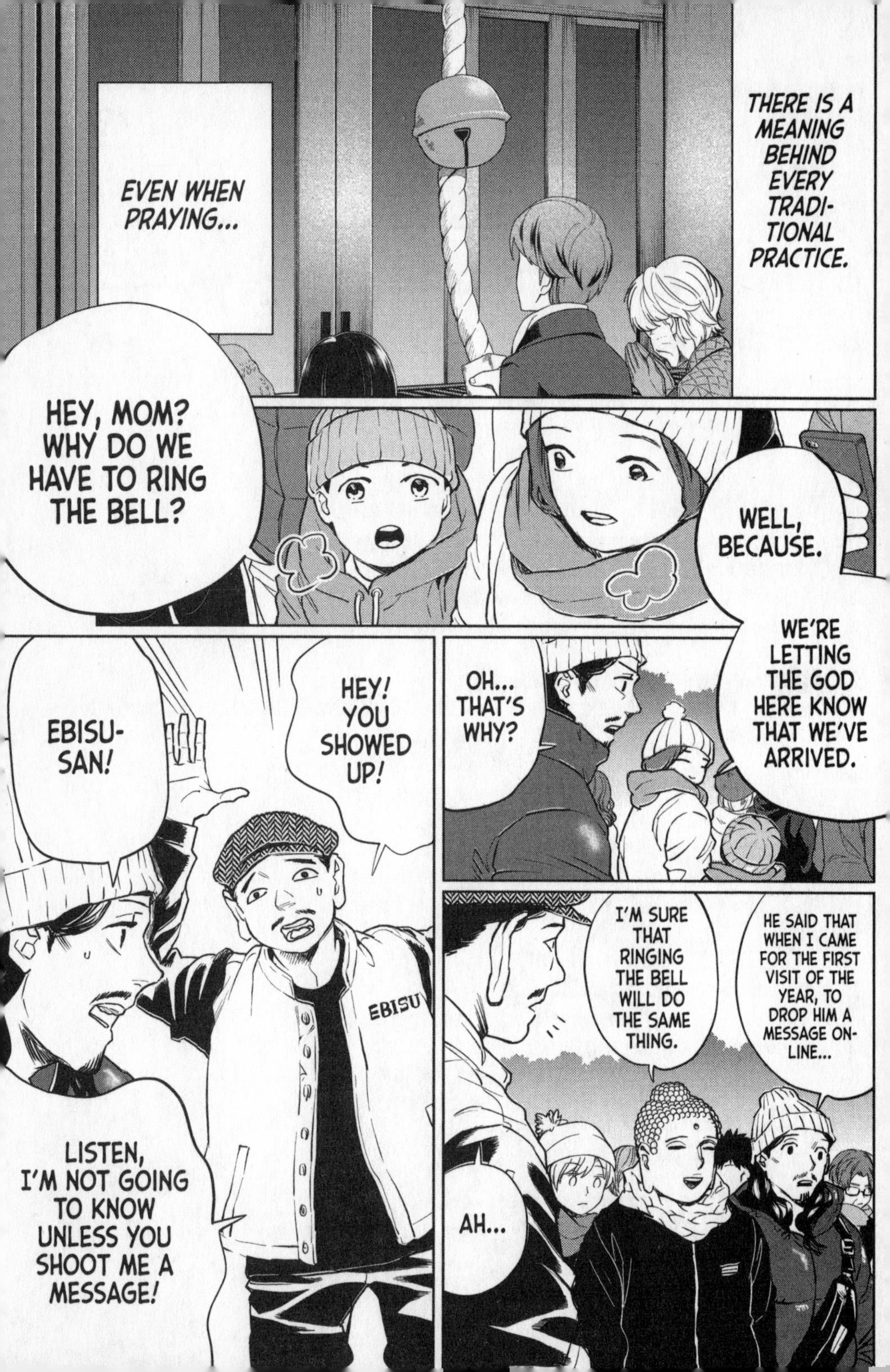
THERE IS A MEANING BEHIND EVERY TRADITIONAL PRACTICE.
EVEN WHEN PRAYING...
HEY, MOM? WHY DO WE HAVE TO RING THE BELL?
WELL, BECAUSE.
WE'RE LETTING THE GOD HERE KNOW THAT WE'VE ARRIVED.
OH... THAT'S WHY?
HE SAID THAT WHEN I CAME FOR THE FIRST VISIT OF THE YEAR, TO DROP HIM A MESSAGE ON-LINE...
I'M SURE THAT RINGING THE BELL WILL DO THE SAME THING.
AH...
EBISU-SAN!
HEY! YOU SHOWED UP!
EBISU
LISTEN, I'M NOT GOING TO KNOW UNLESS YOU SHOOT ME A MESSAGE!

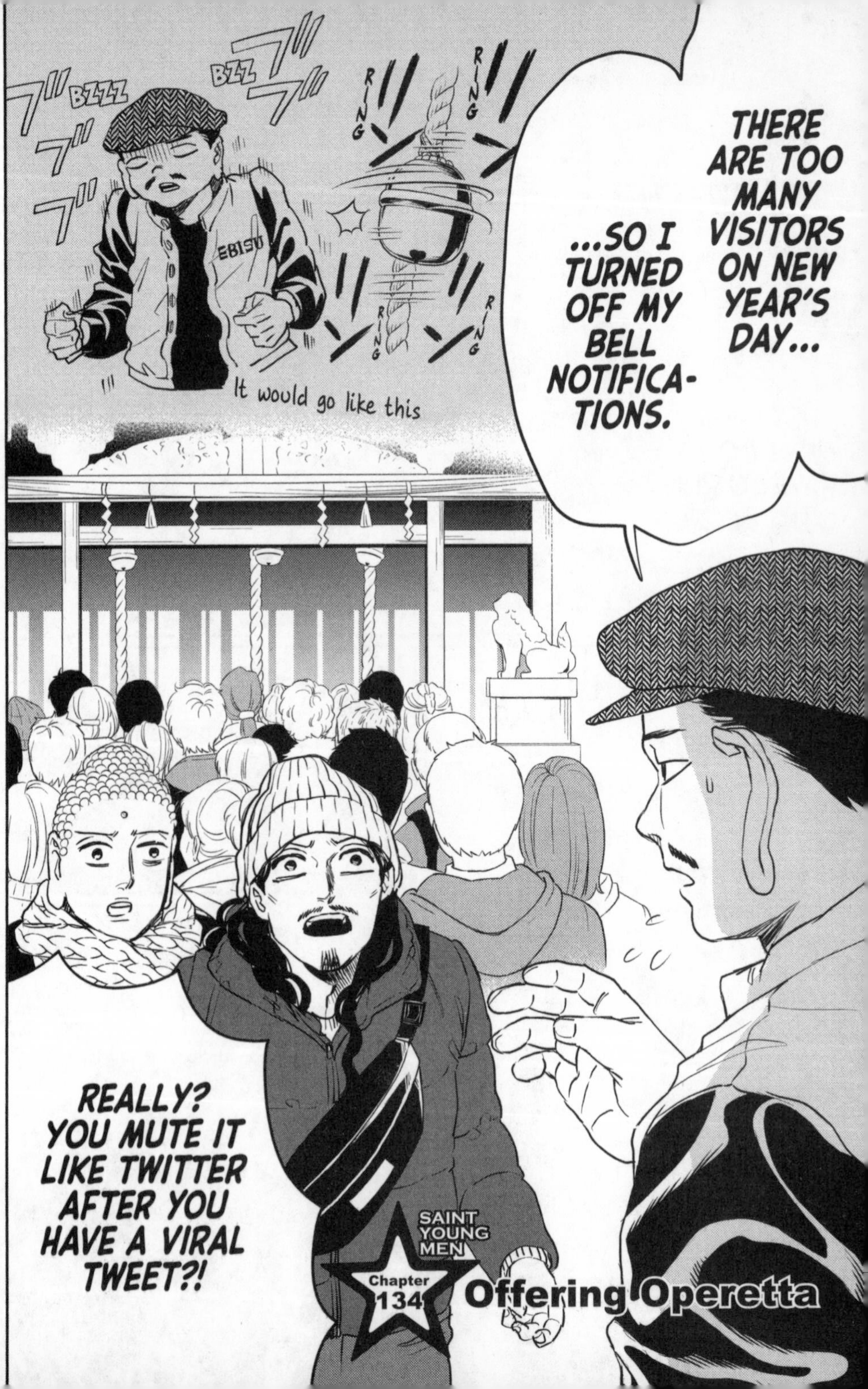
THERE ARE TOO MANY VISITORS ON NEW YEAR'S DAY...
...SO I TURNED OFF MY BELL NOTIFICA-TIONS.
BZZZ
BZZZ
RING
RING
RING
RING
It would go like this
REALLY? YOU MUTE IT LIKE TWITTER AFTER YOU HAVE A VIRAL TWEET?!
SAINT YOUNG MEN
Chapter 134
Offering Operetta

BUDDHA
THEY SHOULD HAVE OFFERING BOXES IN THE CONVENIENCE STORE BATHROOM. I FEEL BAD WHEN I'M NOT BUYING ANYTHING THERE.

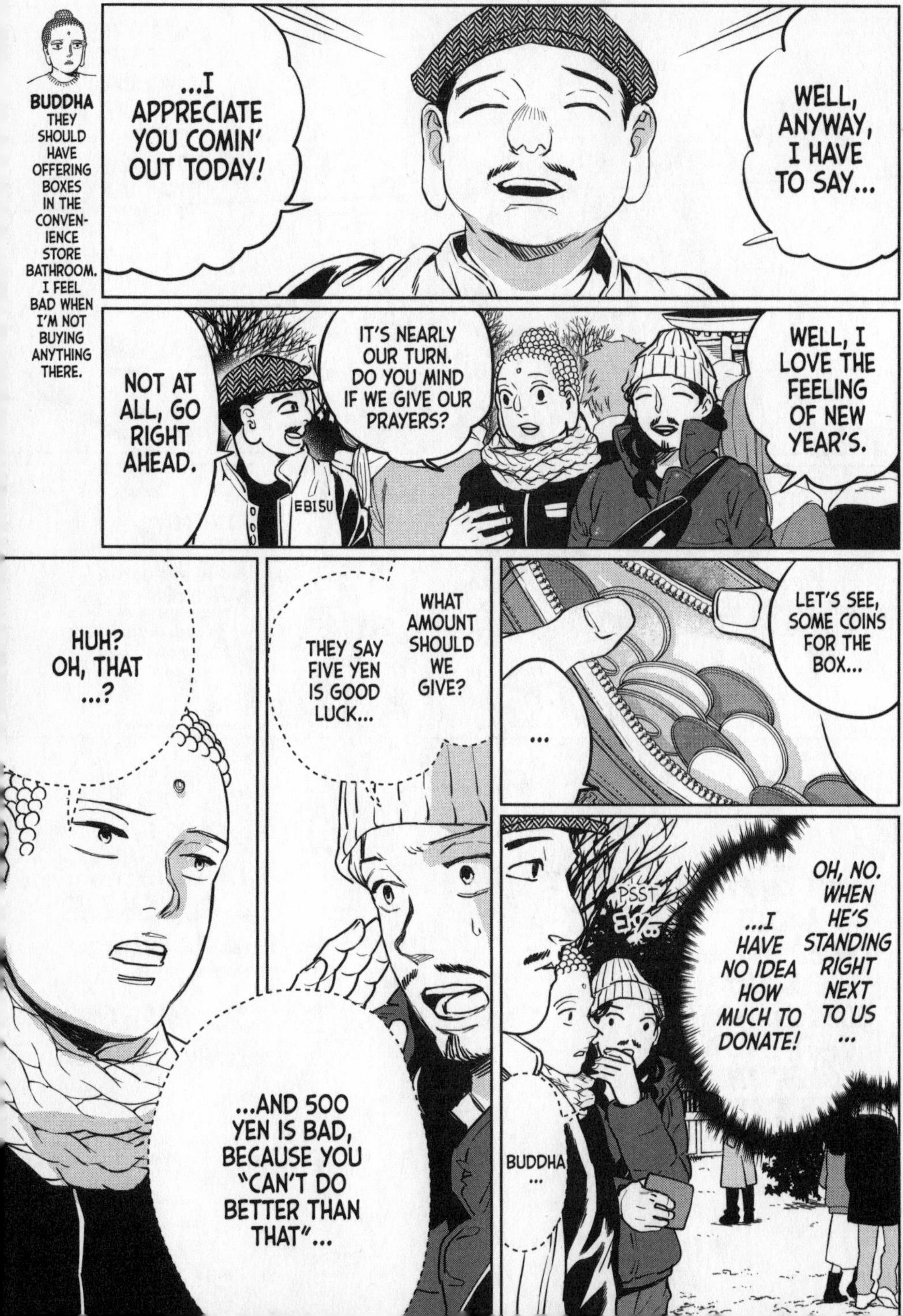

WELL, ANYWAY, I HAVE TO SAY...
...I APPRECIATE YOU COMIN' OUT TODAY!
WELL, I LOVE THE FEELING OF NEW YEAR'S.
IT'S NEARLY OUR TURN. DO YOU MIND IF WE GIVE OUR PRAYERS?
NOT AT ALL, GO RIGHT AHEAD.
EBISU
LET'S SEE, SOME COINS FOR THE BOX...
...
OH, NO. WHEN HE'S STANDING RIGHT NEXT TO US...
...I HAVE NO IDEA HOW MUCH TO DONATE!
PSST
BUDDHA...
WHAT AMOUNT SHOULD WE GIVE?
THEY SAY FIVE YEN IS GOOD LUCK...
...AND 500 YEN IS BAD, BECAUSE YOU "CAN'T DO BETTER THAN THAT"...
HUH? OH, THAT ...?

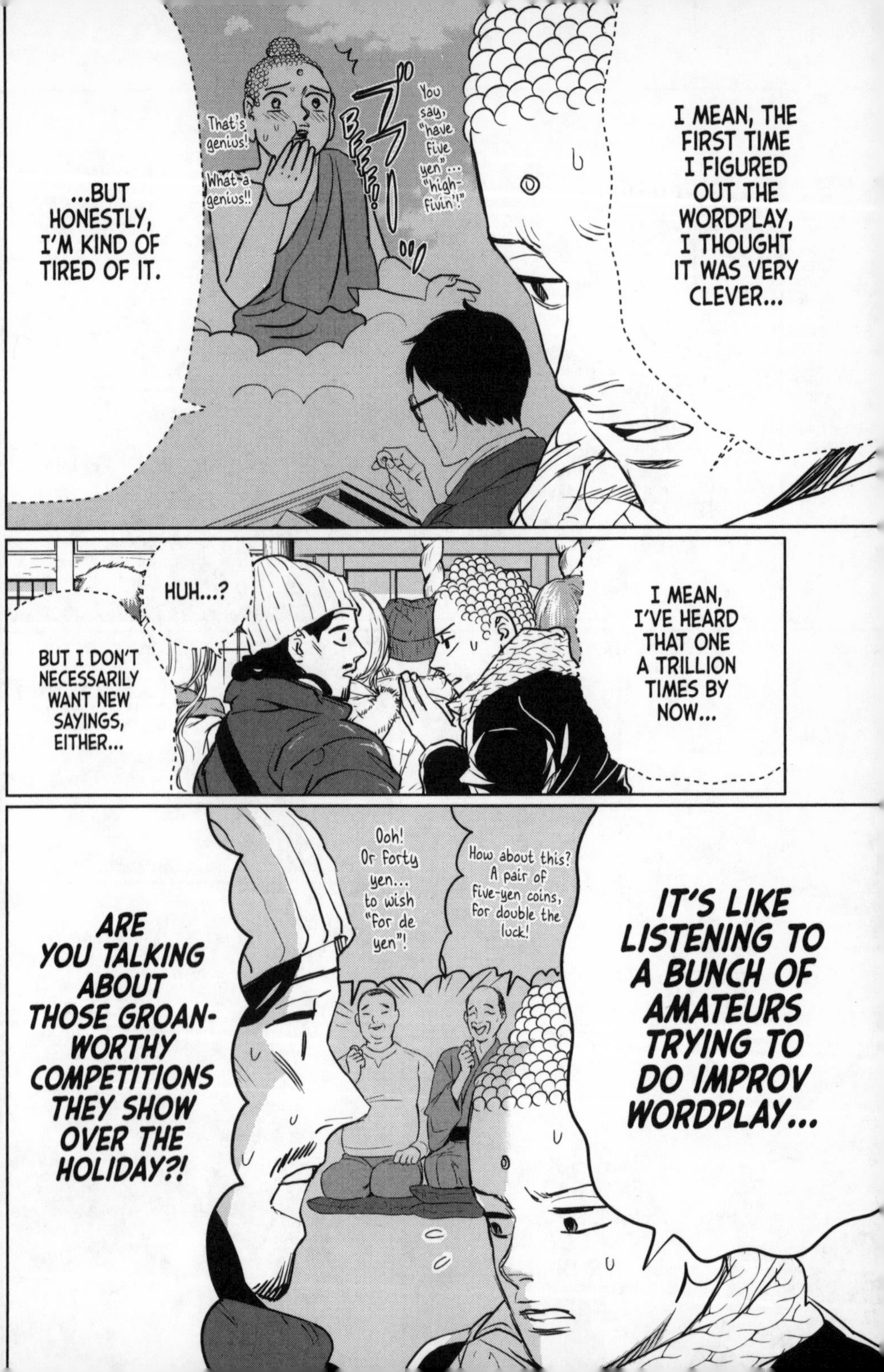
I MEAN, THE FIRST TIME I FIGURED OUT THE WORDPLAY, I THOUGHT IT WAS VERY CLEVER...
You say, "have five yen"... "high-fivin'!"
That's genius!
What a genius!!
...BUT HONESTLY, I'M KIND OF TIRED OF IT.
I MEAN, I'VE HEARD THAT ONE A TRILLION TIMES BY NOW...
HUH...?
BUT I DON'T NECESSARILY WANT NEW SAYINGS, EITHER...
IT'S LIKE LISTENING TO A BUNCH OF AMATEURS TRYING TO DO IMPROV WORDPLAY...
How about this? A pair of five-yen coins, for double the luck!
Ooh! Or forty yen... to wish "for de yen"!
ARE YOU TALKING ABOUT THOSE GROAN-WORTHY COMPETITIONS THEY SHOW OVER THE HOLIDAY?!

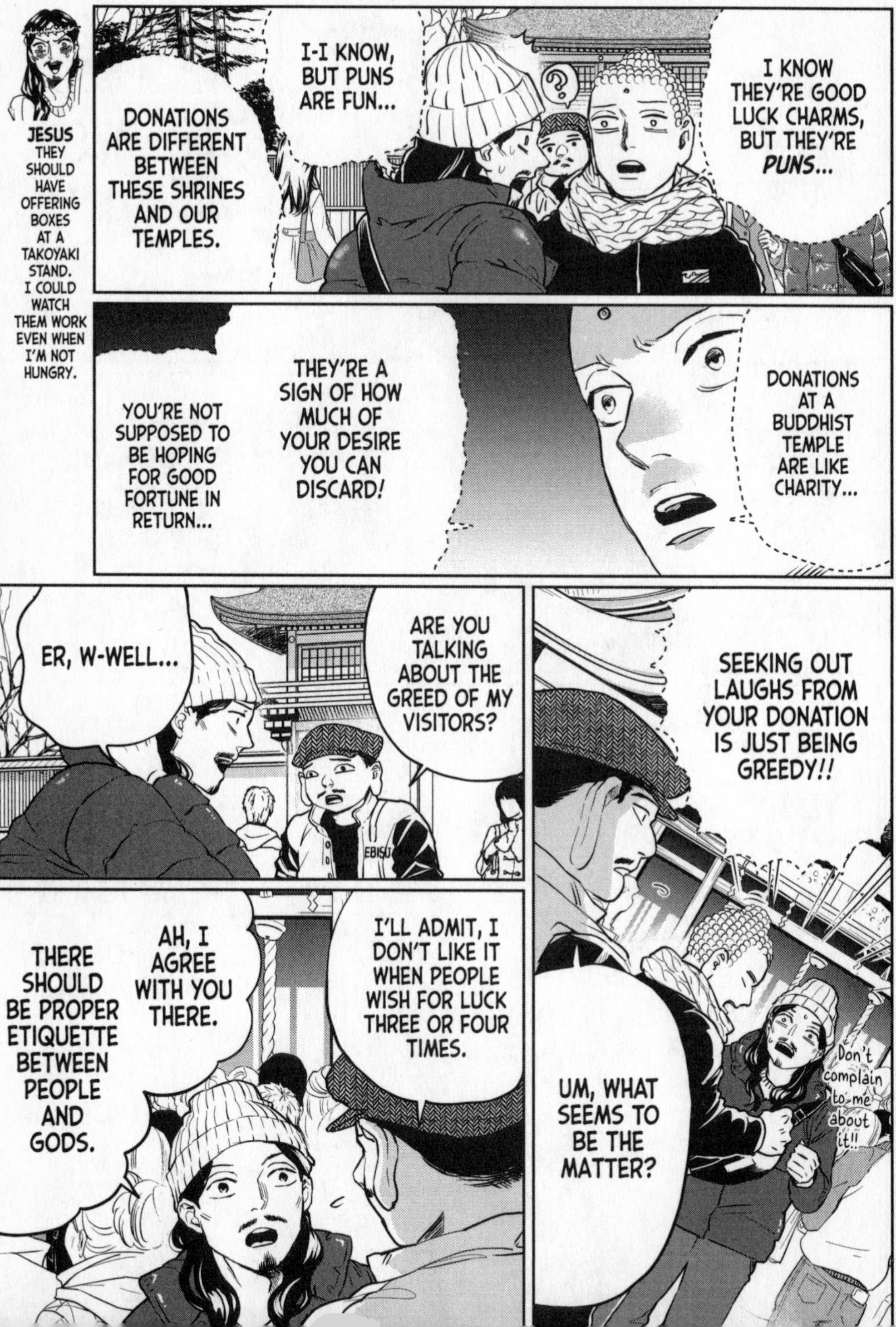
I KNOW THEY'RE GOOD LUCK CHARMS, BUT THEY'RE *PUNS*...
I-I KNOW, BUT PUNS ARE FUN...
DONATIONS ARE DIFFERENT BETWEEN THESE SHRINES AND OUR TEMPLES.
DONATIONS AT A BUDDHIST TEMPLE ARE LIKE CHARITY...
THEY'RE A SIGN OF HOW MUCH OF YOUR DESIRE YOU CAN DISCARD!
YOU'RE NOT SUPPOSED TO BE HOPING FOR GOOD FORTUNE IN RETURN...
SEEKING OUT LAUGHS FROM YOUR DONATION IS JUST BEING GREEDY!!
Don't complain to me about it!!
UM, WHAT SEEMS TO BE THE MATTER?
ARE YOU TALKING ABOUT THE GREED OF MY VISITORS?
ER, W-WELL...
I'LL ADMIT, I DON'T LIKE IT WHEN PEOPLE WISH FOR LUCK THREE OR FOUR TIMES.
AH, I AGREE WITH YOU THERE.
THERE SHOULD BE PROPER ETIQUETTE BETWEEN PEOPLE AND GODS.
JESUS THEY SHOULD HAVE OFFERING BOXES AT A TAKOYAKI STAND. I COULD WATCH THEM WORK EVEN WHEN I'M NOT HUNGRY.

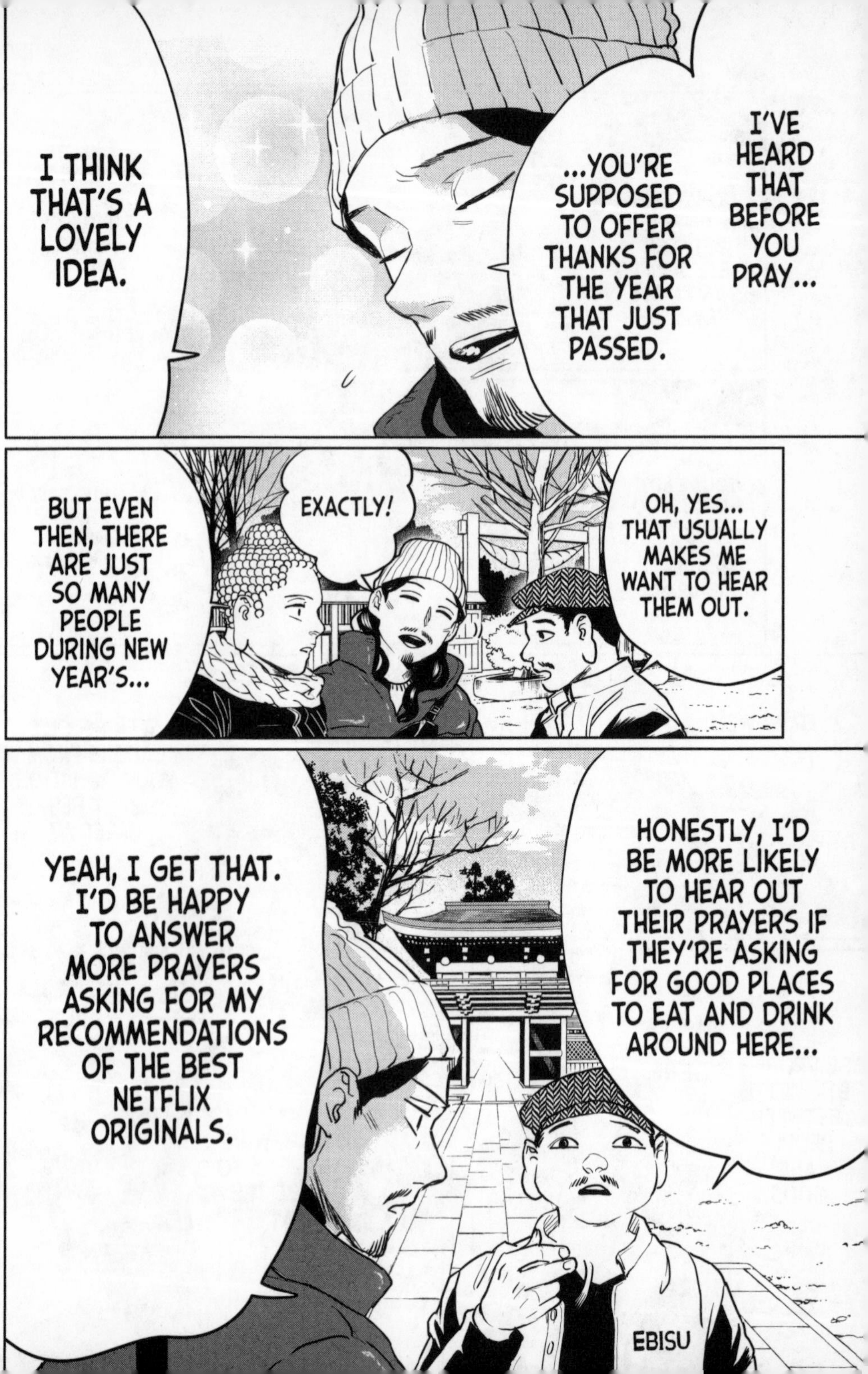
I'VE HEARD THAT BEFORE YOU PRAY...
...YOU'RE SUPPOSED TO OFFER THANKS FOR THE YEAR THAT JUST PASSED.
I THINK THAT'S A LOVELY IDEA.
OH, YES... THAT USUALLY MAKES ME WANT TO HEAR THEM OUT.
EXACTLY!
BUT EVEN THEN, THERE ARE JUST SO MANY PEOPLE DURING NEW YEAR'S...
HONESTLY, I'D BE MORE LIKELY TO HEAR OUT THEIR PRAYERS IF THEY'RE ASKING FOR GOOD PLACES TO EAT AND DRINK AROUND HERE...
YEAH, I GET THAT. I'D BE HAPPY TO ANSWER MORE PRAYERS ASKING FOR MY RECOMMENDATIONS OF THE BEST NETFLIX ORIGINALS.
EBISU

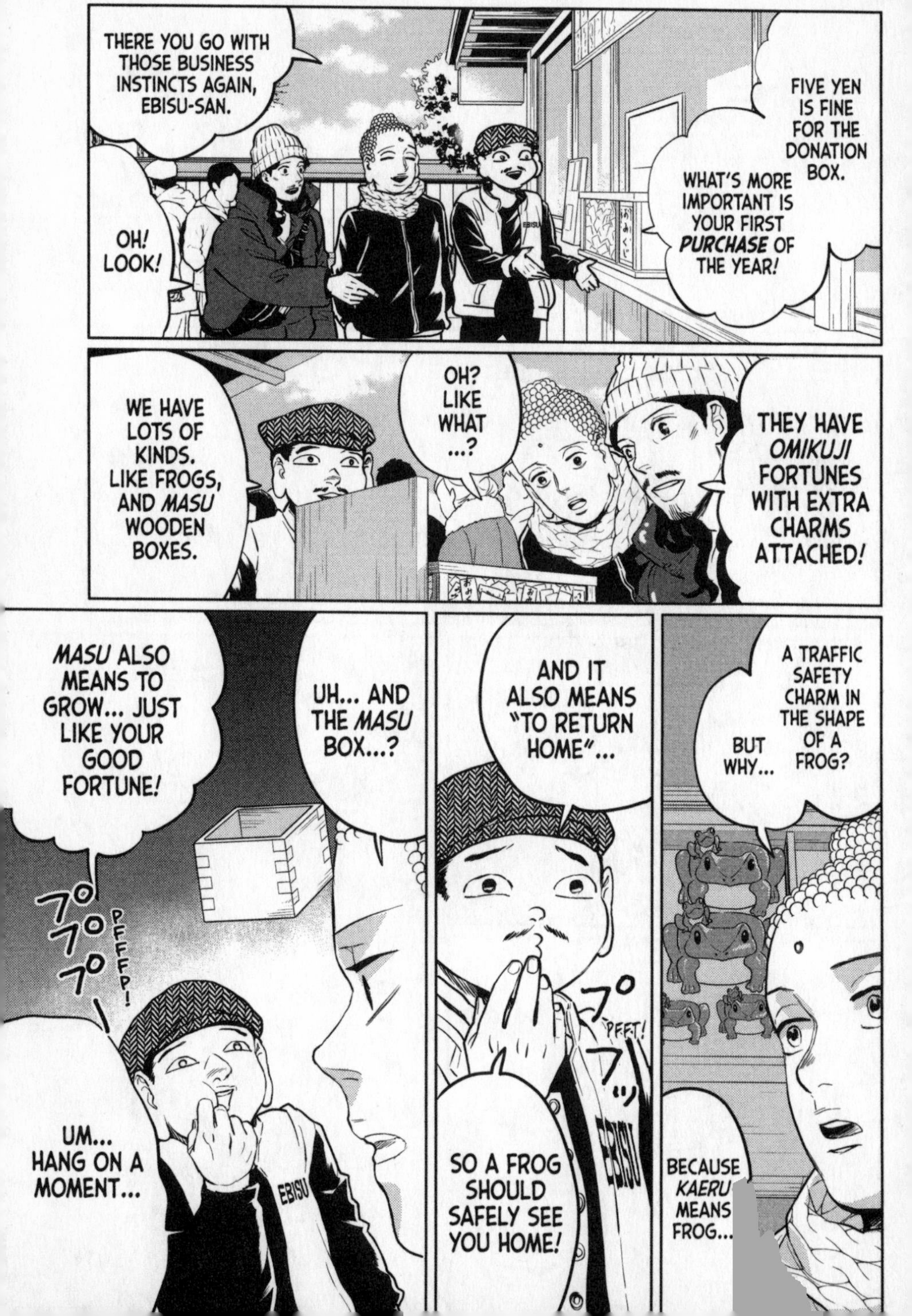
FIVE YEN IS FINE FOR THE DONATION BOX.
WHAT'S MORE IMPORTANT IS YOUR FIRST *PURCHASE* OF THE YEAR!
THERE YOU GO WITH THOSE BUSINESS INSTINCTS AGAIN, EBISU-SAN.
OH! LOOK!
THEY HAVE *OMIKUJI* FORTUNES WITH EXTRA CHARMS ATTACHED!
OH? LIKE WHAT ...?
WE HAVE LOTS OF KINDS. LIKE FROGS, AND *MASU* WOODEN BOXES.
A TRAFFIC SAFETY CHARM IN THE SHAPE OF A FROG?
BUT WHY...
BECAUSE *KAERU* MEANS FROG...
AND IT ALSO MEANS "TO RETURN HOME"...
PFFT!
SO A FROG SHOULD SAFELY SEE YOU HOME!
UH... AND THE *MASU* BOX...?
MASU ALSO MEANS TO GROW... JUST LIKE YOUR GOOD FORTUNE!
PFFFP!
UM... HANG ON A MOMENT...

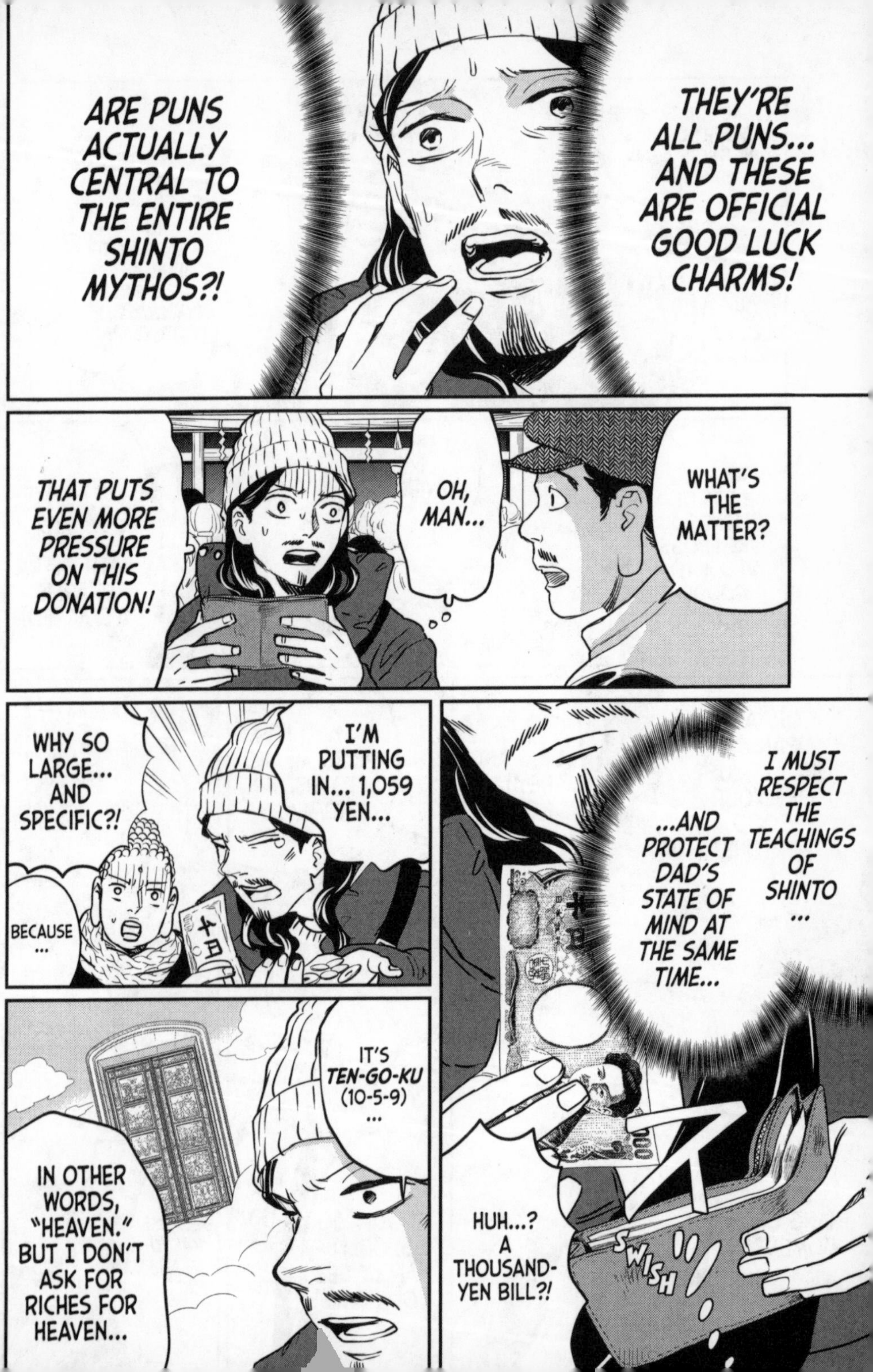
THEY'RE ALL PUNS... AND THESE ARE OFFICIAL GOOD LUCK CHARMS!
ARE PUNS ACTUALLY CENTRAL TO THE ENTIRE SHINTO MYTHOS?!
WHAT'S THE MATTER?
OH, MAN...
THAT PUTS EVEN MORE PRESSURE ON THIS DONATION!
I MUST RESPECT THE TEACHINGS OF SHINTO ...
...AND PROTECT DAD'S STATE OF MIND AT THE SAME TIME...
HUH...? A THOUSAND-YEN BILL?!
SWISH
I'M PUTTING IN... 1,059 YEN...
WHY SO LARGE... AND SPECIFIC?!
BECAUSE ...
IT'S TEN-GO-KU (10-5-9) ...
IN OTHER WORDS, "HEAVEN." BUT I DON'T ASK FOR RICHES FOR HEAVEN...

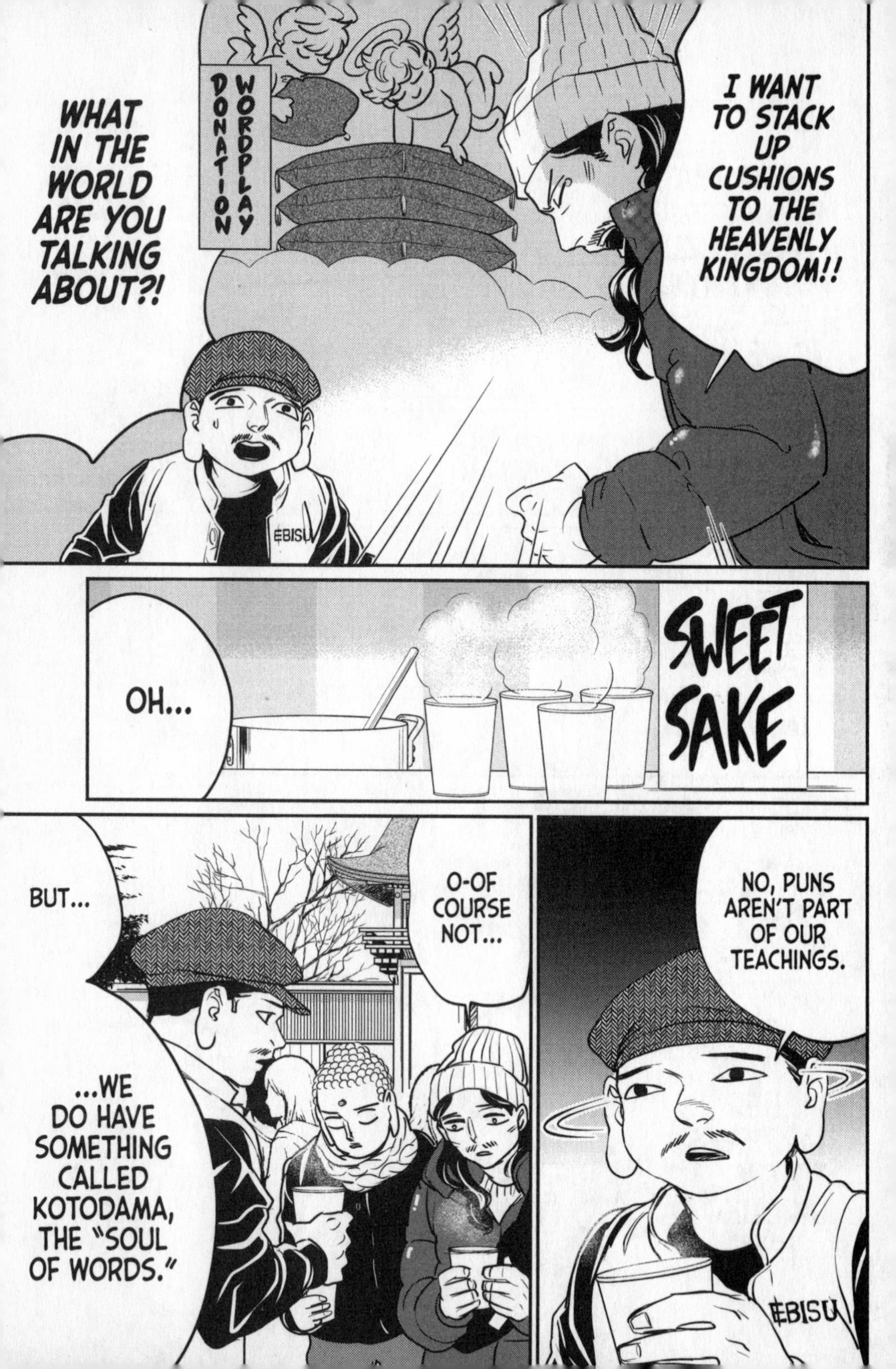
I WANT TO STACK UP CUSHIONS TO THE HEAVENLY KINGDOM!!
DONATION WORDPLAY
WHAT IN THE WORLD ARE YOU TALKING ABOUT?!
EBISU
SWEET SAKE
OH...
NO, PUNS AREN'T PART OF OUR TEACHINGS.
EBISU
O-OF COURSE NOT...
BUT...
...WE DO HAVE SOMETHING CALLED KOTODAMA, THE "SOUL OF WORDS."

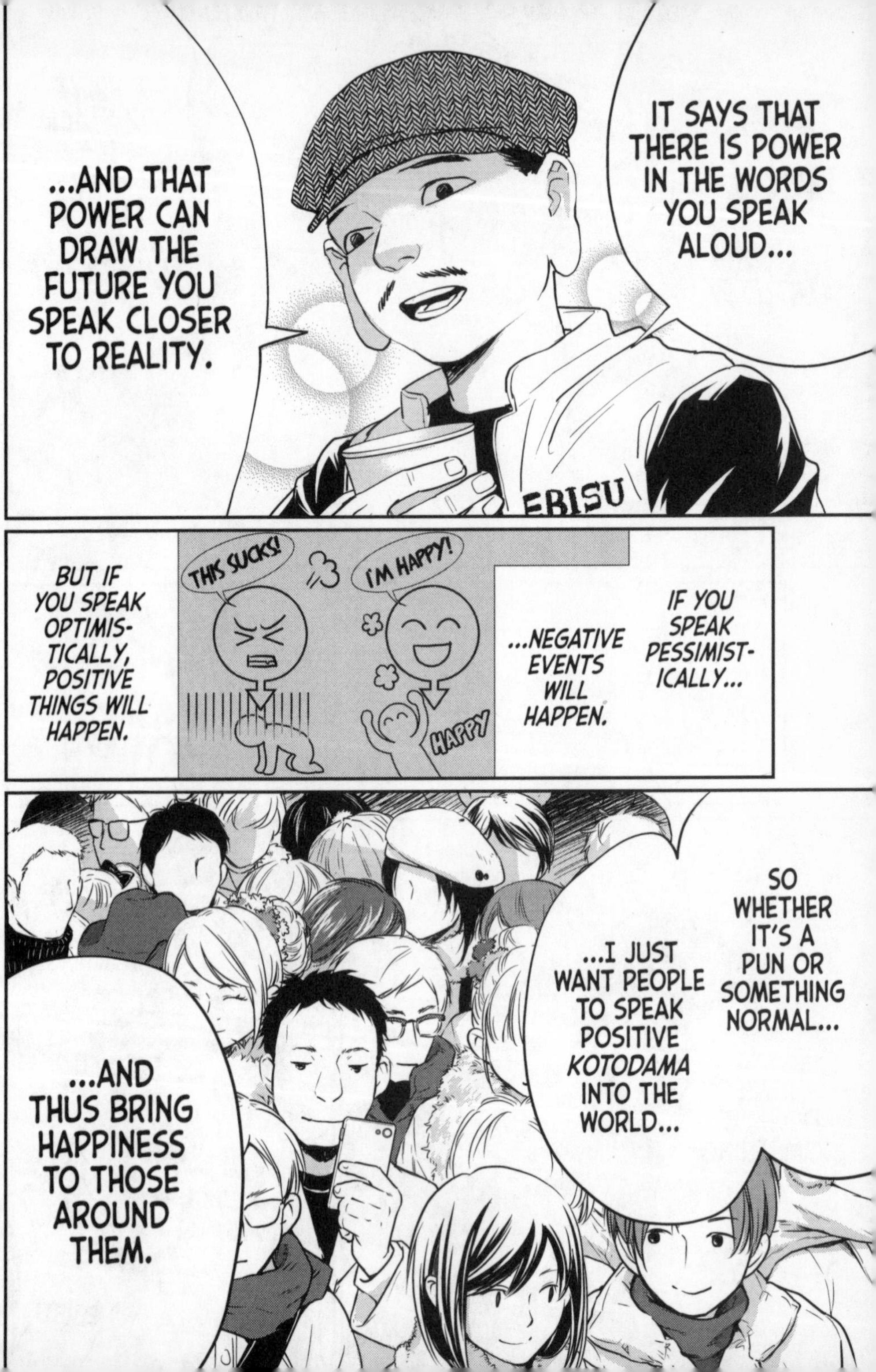
IT SAYS THAT THERE IS POWER IN THE WORDS YOU SPEAK ALOUD...
...AND THAT POWER CAN DRAW THE FUTURE YOU SPEAK CLOSER TO REALITY.
EBISU
IF YOU SPEAK PESSIMIST-ICALLY...
...NEGATIVE EVENTS WILL HAPPEN.
I'M HAPPY!
HAPPY
THIS SUCKS!
BUT IF YOU SPEAK OPTIMIS-TICALLY, POSITIVE THINGS WILL HAPPEN.
SO WHETHER IT'S A PUN OR SOMETHING NORMAL...
...I JUST WANT PEOPLE TO SPEAK POSITIVE *KOTODAMA* INTO THE WORLD...
...AND THUS BRING HAPPINESS TO THOSE AROUND THEM.

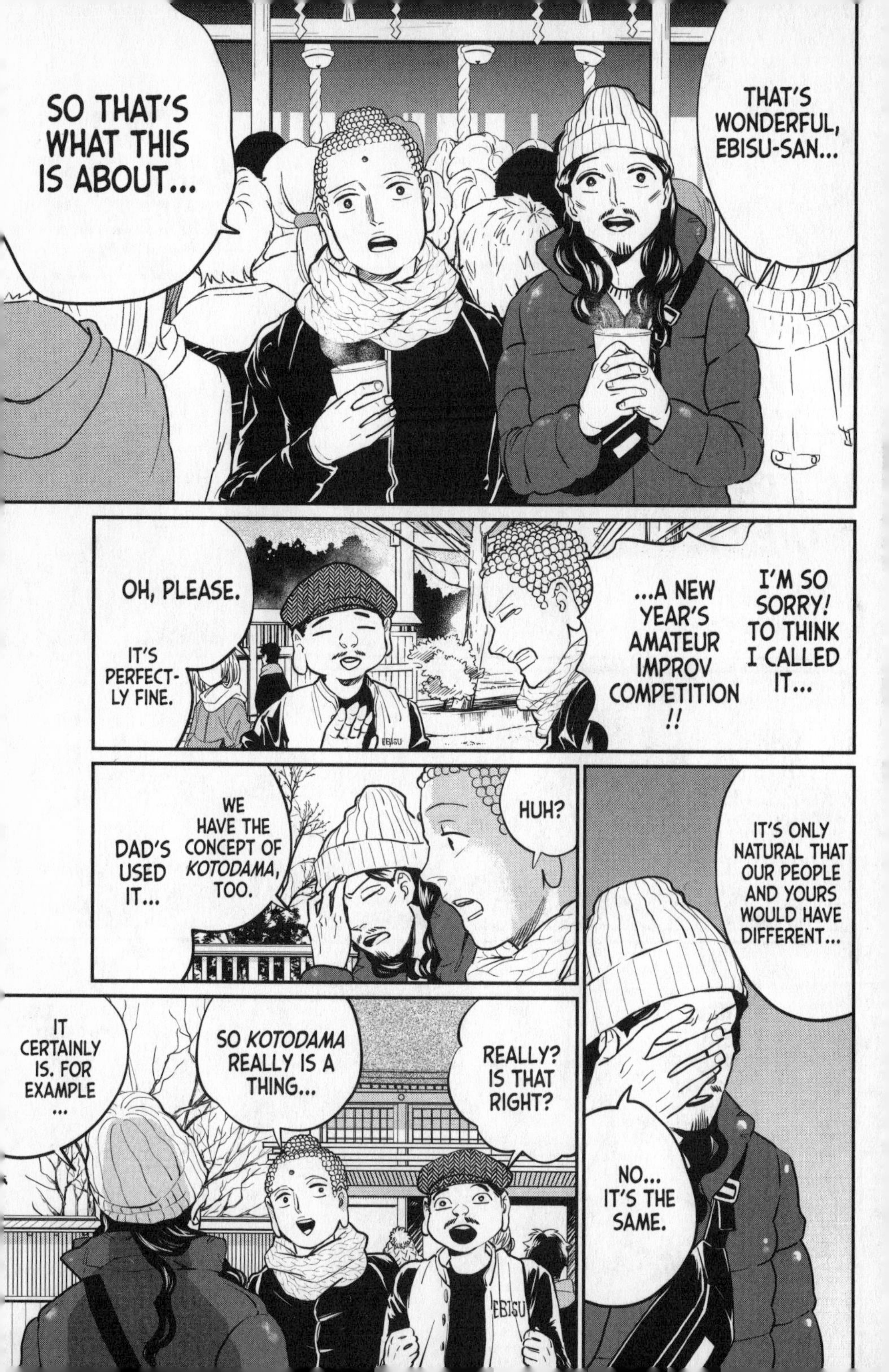
THAT'S WONDERFUL, EBISU-SAN...
SO THAT'S WHAT THIS IS ABOUT...
I'M SO SORRY! TO THINK I CALLED IT...
...A NEW YEAR'S AMATEUR IMPROV COMPETITION !!
OH, PLEASE.
IT'S PERFECT-LY FINE.
EBISU
IT'S ONLY NATURAL THAT OUR PEOPLE AND YOURS WOULD HAVE DIFFERENT...
NO... IT'S THE SAME.
HUH?
WE HAVE THE CONCEPT OF *KOTODAMA*, TOO.
DAD'S USED IT...
REALLY? IS THAT RIGHT?
SO *KOTODAMA* REALLY IS A THING...
IT CERTAINLY IS. FOR EXAMPLE ...
EBISU

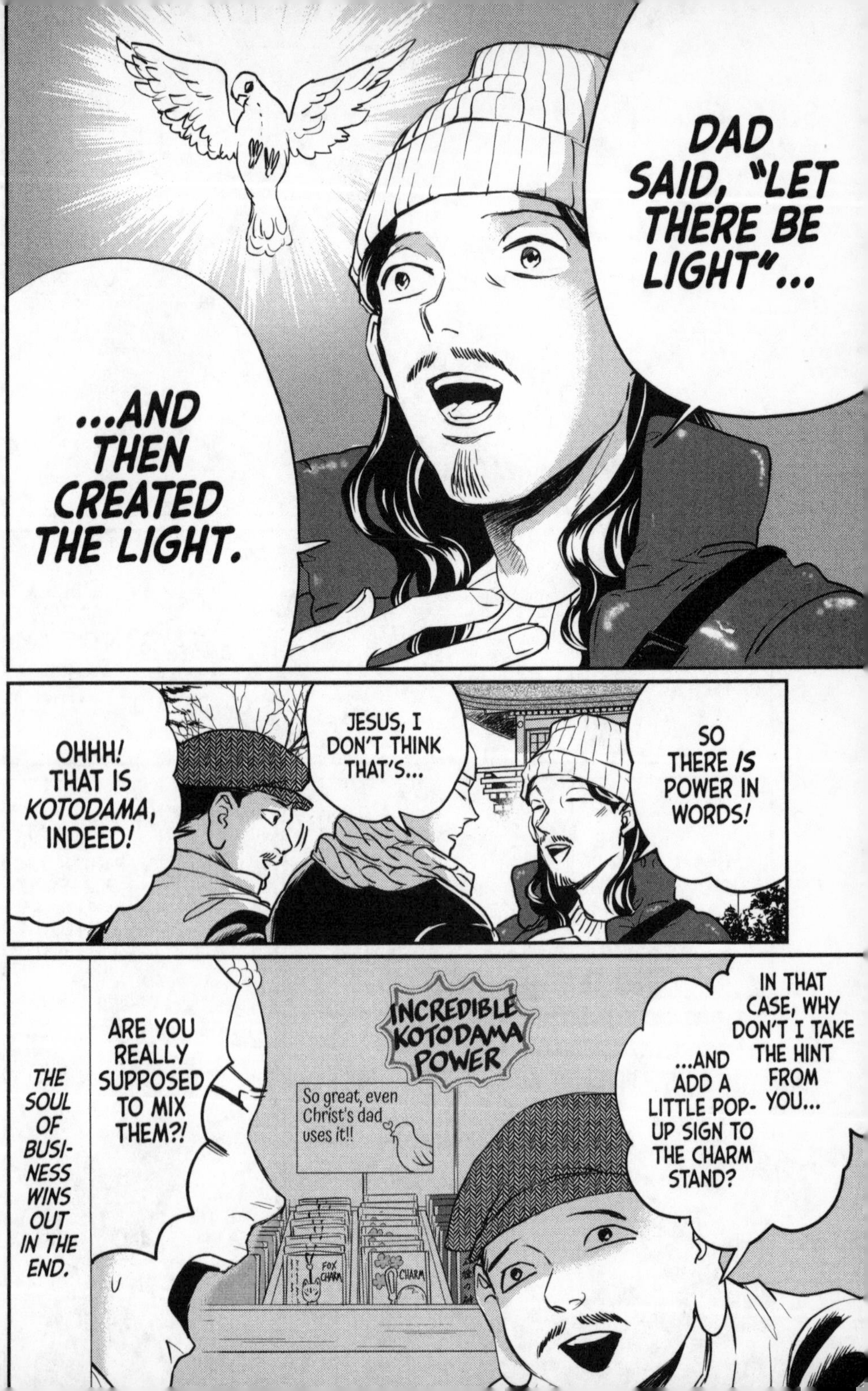
DAD SAID, "LET THERE BE LIGHT"...
...AND THEN CREATED THE LIGHT.
SO THERE *IS* POWER IN WORDS!
JESUS, I DON'T THINK THAT'S...
OHHH! THAT IS *KOTODAMA*, INDEED!
IN THAT CASE, WHY DON'T I TAKE THE HINT FROM YOU...
...AND ADD A LITTLE POP-UP SIGN TO THE CHARM STAND?
INCREDIBLE KOTODAMA POWER
So great, even Christ's dad uses it!!
FOX CHARM
CHARM
ARE YOU REALLY SUPPOSED TO MIX THEM?!
THE SOUL OF BUSINESS WINS OUT IN THE END.

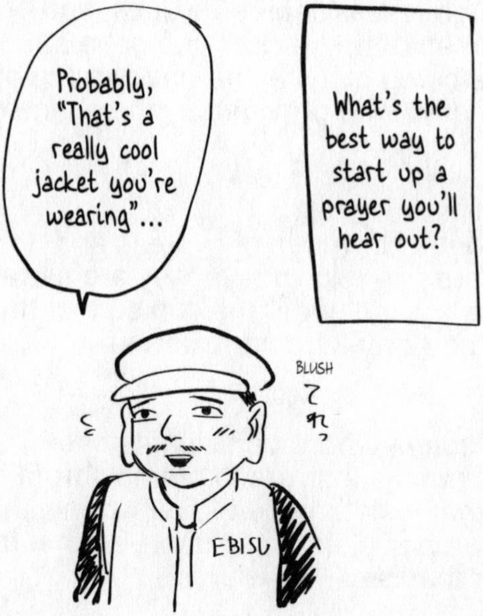
What's the best way to start up a prayer you'll hear out?
Probably, "That's a really cool jacket you're wearing"...
BLUSH
EBISU

SAINT☆YOUNG MEN

CHAPTER 134 TRANSLATION NOTES

Coins, page 217
Some punny sayings exist about donating coins at the shrine offering box. When Jesus mentions five yen being good luck, this is because "five yen" (*go-en*) is a homophone for "good karma" (*go-en*). The 500-yen coin is the most valuable coin (*kôka*) in circulation, so the saying goes that you won't get any further effect (*kôka*) after that.

Omikuji fortunes, page 221
An *omikuji* is a little strip of paper with a fortune written on it, kind of like what you find in a fortune cookie, obtained at Japanese Buddhist and Shinto shrines by making an offering and choosing one at random. Each strip lists the amount of luck the chooser is going to have, ranging from *dai-kichi* (great blessing, great luck), through lesser degrees of luck, and on through the degrees of curses or bad luck. if you get a bad luck fortune, you can dispel the curse by tying the *omikuji* strip of paper to a tree or a designated wire provided by the shrine or temple.

Masu, page 221
A small wooden box (without a lid) made of cypress and traditionally used to measure rice. Nowadays they are more often used to hold *sake*, as a base under the cup so that the overflow can be collected and drunk from the corner.

Cushions, page 223
A reference to the show *Shôten*, where participants offer quick-witted wordplay and punny answers to prompts from the judge. With each answer that is determined to be worthy, the contestant receives a *zabuton* cushion to sit upon, so that the better they do, they higher they sit.

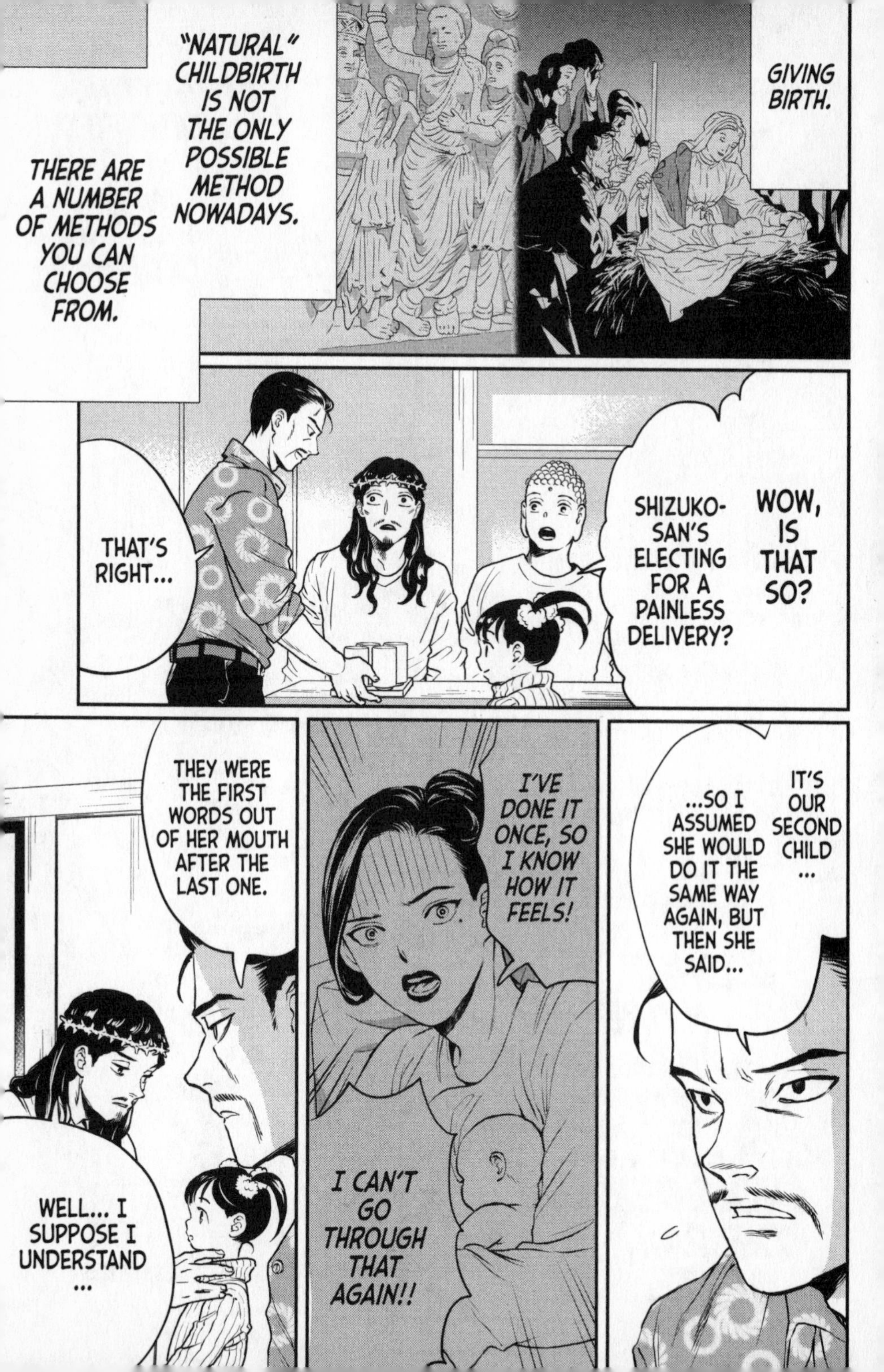
GIVING BIRTH.
"NATURAL" CHILDBIRTH IS NOT THE ONLY POSSIBLE METHOD NOWADAYS.
THERE ARE A NUMBER OF METHODS YOU CAN CHOOSE FROM.
WOW, IS THAT SO?
SHIZUKO-SAN'S ELECTING FOR A PAINLESS DELIVERY?
THAT'S RIGHT...
IT'S OUR SECOND CHILD ...
...SO I ASSUMED SHE WOULD DO IT THE SAME WAY AGAIN, BUT THEN SHE SAID...
I'VE DONE IT ONCE, SO I KNOW HOW IT FEELS!
I CAN'T GO THROUGH THAT AGAIN!!
THEY WERE THE FIRST WORDS OUT OF HER MOUTH AFTER THE LAST ONE.
WELL... I SUPPOSE I UNDERSTAND ...

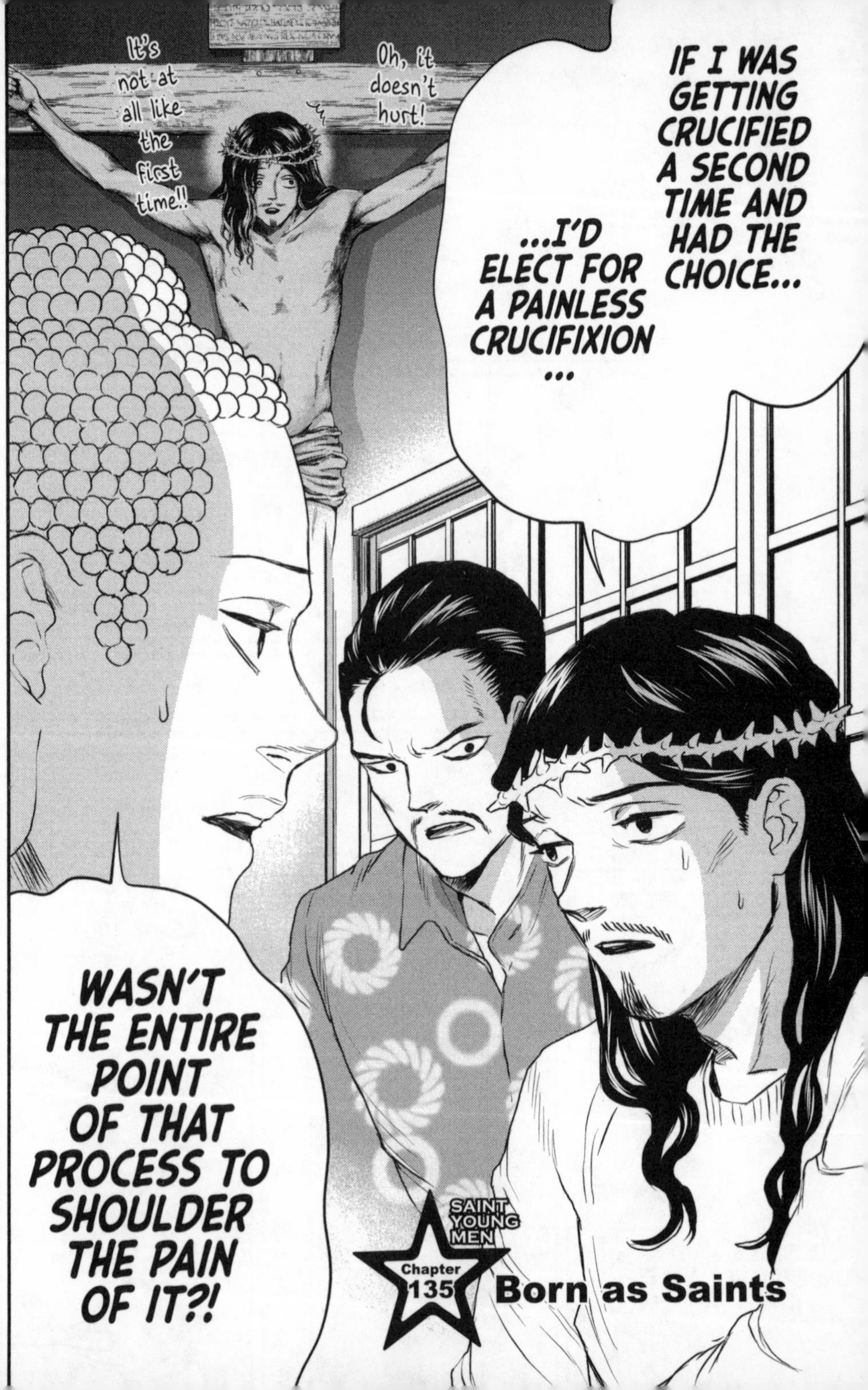
IF I WAS GETTING CRUCIFIED A SECOND TIME AND HAD THE CHOICE...
...I'D ELECT FOR A PAINLESS CRUCIFIXION ...
Oh, it doesn't hurt!
It's not at all like the first time!!
WASN'T THE ENTIRE POINT OF THAT PROCESS TO SHOULDER THE PAIN OF IT?!
SAINT YOUNG MEN
Chapter 135
Born as Saints

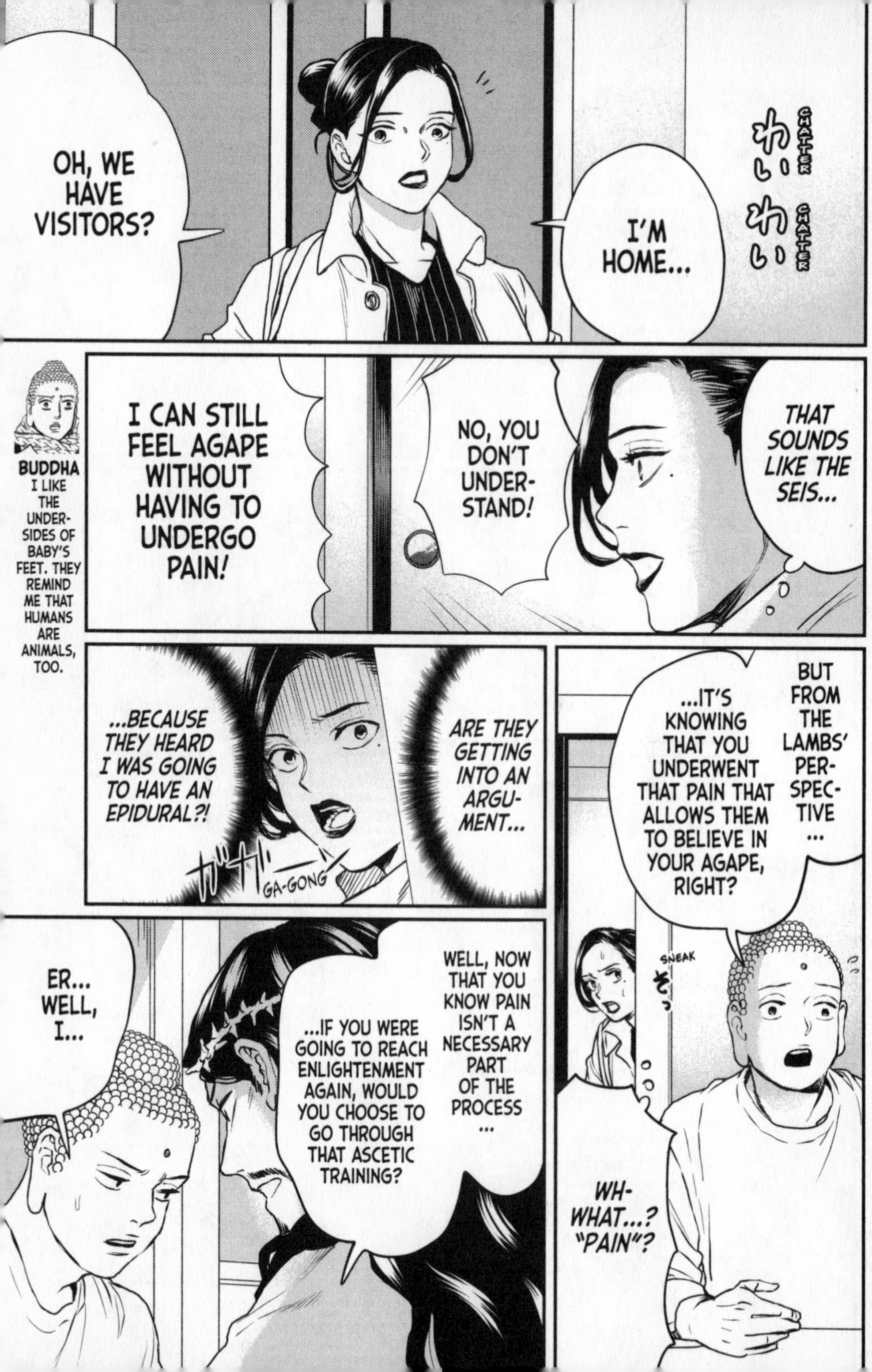
CHAPTER わいわい CHAPTER
I'M HOME...
OH, WE HAVE VISITORS?
THAT SOUNDS LIKE THE SEIS...
NO, YOU DON'T UNDER-STAND!
I CAN STILL FEEL AGAPE WITHOUT HAVING TO UNDERGO PAIN!
BUDDHA
I LIKE THE UNDER-SIDES OF BABY'S FEET. THEY REMIND ME THAT HUMANS ARE ANIMALS, TOO.
BUT FROM THE LAMBS' PER-SPEC-TIVE ...
...IT'S KNOWING THAT YOU UNDERWENT THAT PAIN THAT ALLOWS THEM TO BELIEVE IN YOUR AGAPE, RIGHT?
ARE THEY GETTING INTO AN ARGU-MENT...
...BECAUSE THEY HEARD I WAS GOING TO HAVE AN EPIDURAL?!
GA-GONG
SNEAK
WH-WHAT...? "PAIN"?
WELL, NOW THAT YOU KNOW PAIN ISN'T A NECESSARY PART OF THE PROCESS ...
...IF YOU WERE GOING TO REACH ENLIGHTENMENT AGAIN, WOULD YOU CHOOSE TO GO THROUGH THAT ASCETIC TRAINING?
ER... WELL, I...

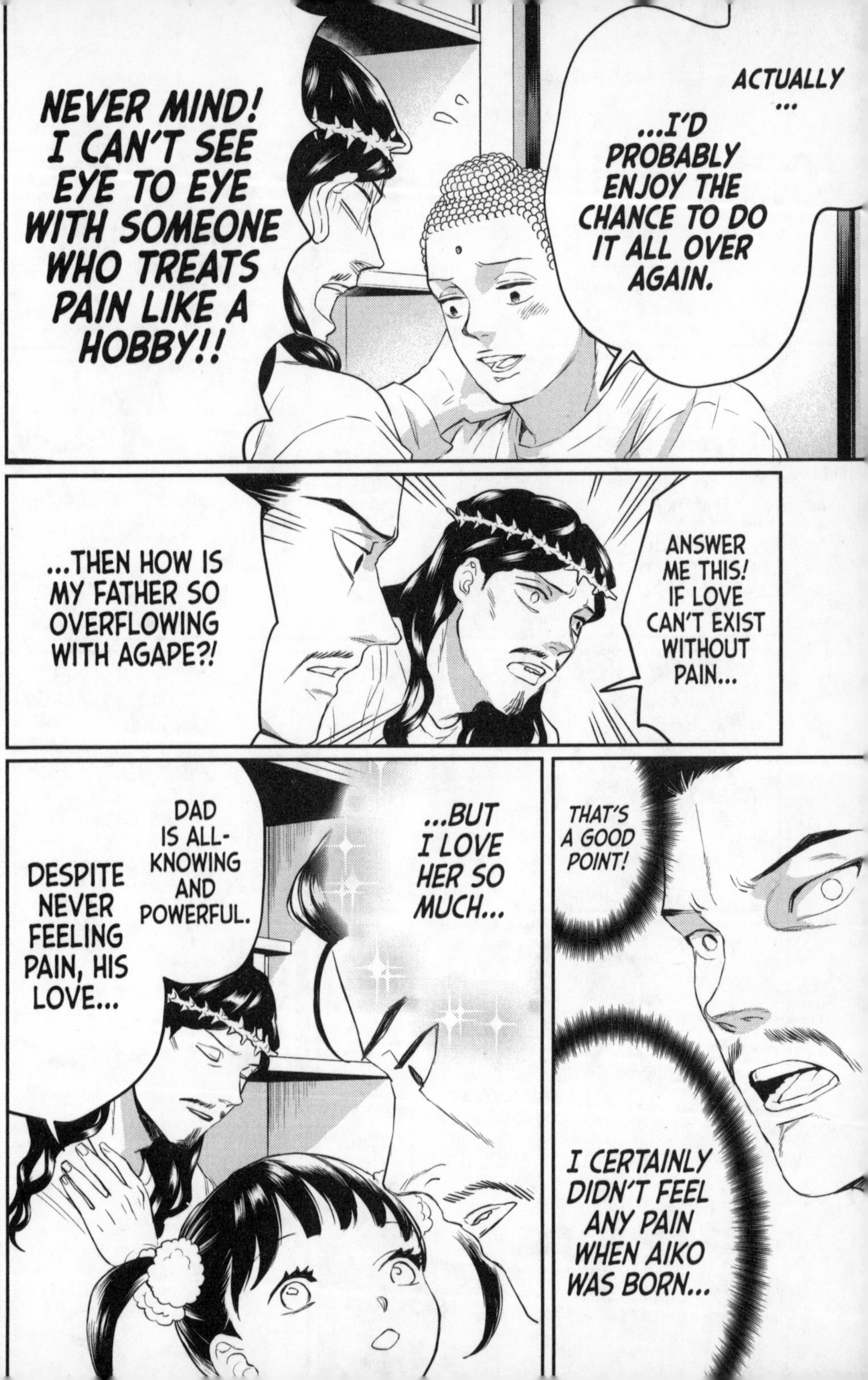
ACTUALLY ...
...I'D PROBABLY ENJOY THE CHANCE TO DO IT ALL OVER AGAIN.
NEVER MIND! I CAN'T SEE EYE TO EYE WITH SOMEONE WHO TREATS PAIN LIKE A HOBBY!!
ANSWER ME THIS! IF LOVE CAN'T EXIST WITHOUT PAIN...
...THEN HOW IS MY FATHER SO OVERFLOWING WITH AGAPE?!
THAT'S A GOOD POINT!
I CERTAINLY DIDN'T FEEL ANY PAIN WHEN AIKO WAS BORN...
...BUT I LOVE HER SO MUCH...
DAD IS ALL-KNOWING AND POWERFUL.
DESPITE NEVER FEELING PAIN, HIS LOVE...

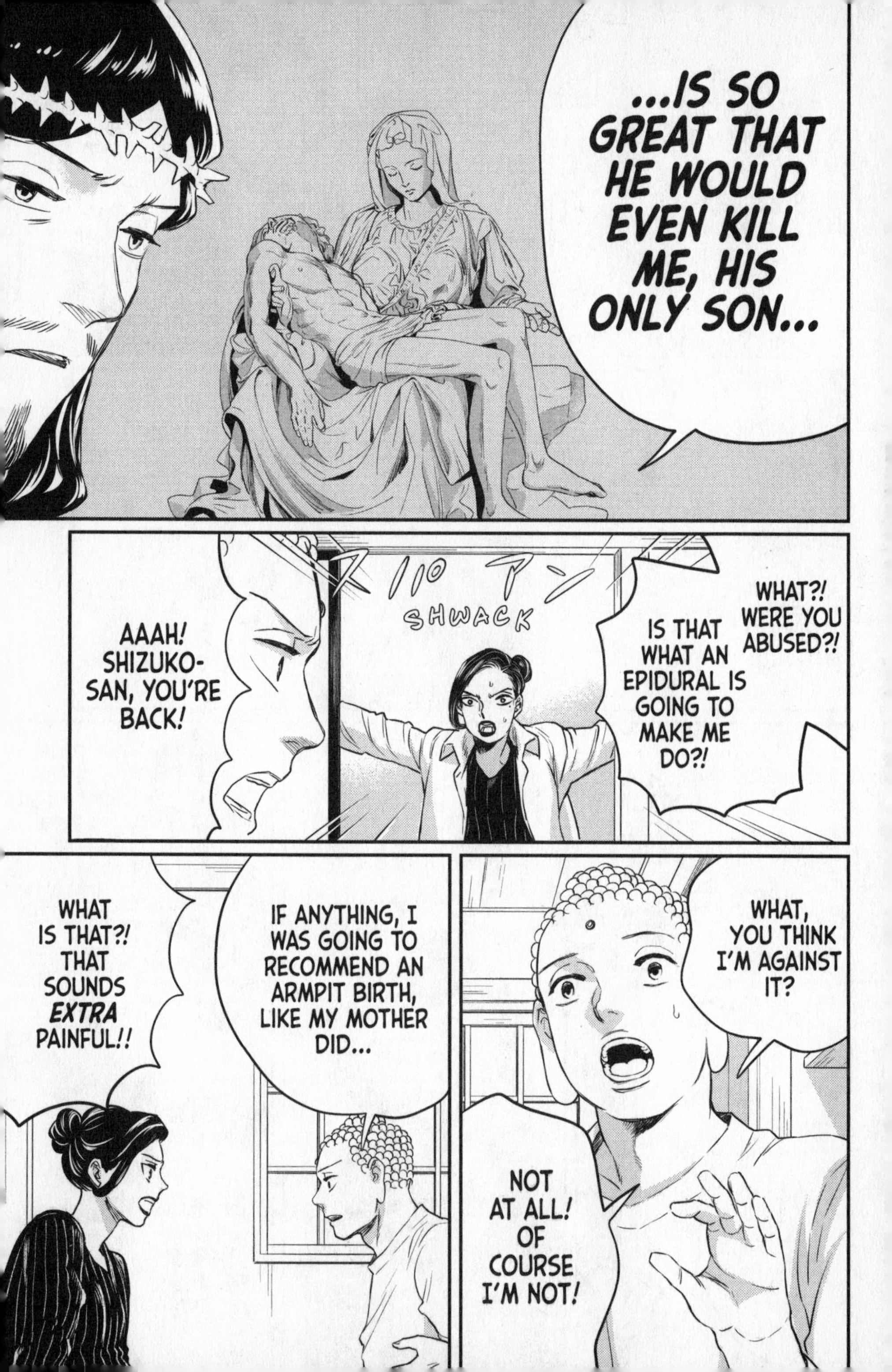
...IS SO GREAT THAT HE WOULD EVEN KILL ME, HIS ONLY SON...
WHAT?! WERE YOU ABUSED?!
IS THAT WHAT AN EPIDURAL IS GOING TO MAKE ME DO?!
SHWACK
AAAH! SHIZUKO-SAN, YOU'RE BACK!
WHAT, YOU THINK I'M AGAINST IT?
NOT AT ALL! OF COURSE I'M NOT!
IF ANYTHING, I WAS GOING TO RECOMMEND AN ARMPIT BIRTH, LIKE MY MOTHER DID...
WHAT IS THAT?! THAT SOUNDS EXTRA PAINFUL!!

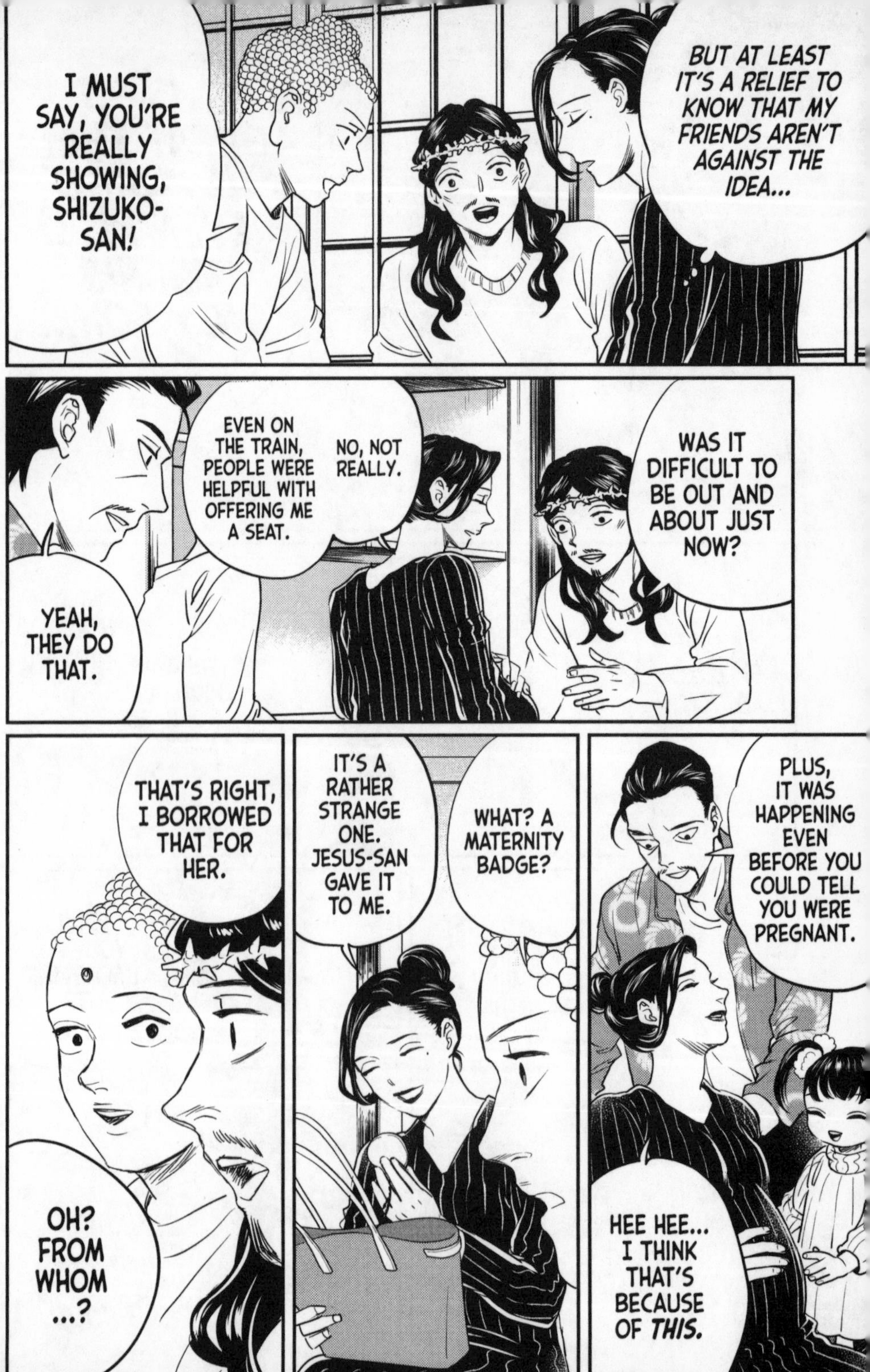
BUT AT LEAST IT'S A RELIEF TO KNOW THAT MY FRIENDS AREN'T AGAINST THE IDEA...
I MUST SAY, YOU'RE REALLY SHOWING, SHIZUKO-SAN!
WAS IT DIFFICULT TO BE OUT AND ABOUT JUST NOW?
NO, NOT REALLY.
EVEN ON THE TRAIN, PEOPLE WERE HELPFUL WITH OFFERING ME A SEAT.
YEAH, THEY DO THAT.
PLUS, IT WAS HAPPENING EVEN BEFORE YOU COULD TELL YOU WERE PREGNANT.
HEE HEE... I THINK THAT'S BECAUSE OF *THIS*.
WHAT? A MATERNITY BADGE?
IT'S A RATHER STRANGE ONE. JESUS-SAN GAVE IT TO ME.
THAT'S RIGHT, I BORROWED THAT FOR HER.
OH? FROM WHOM ...?

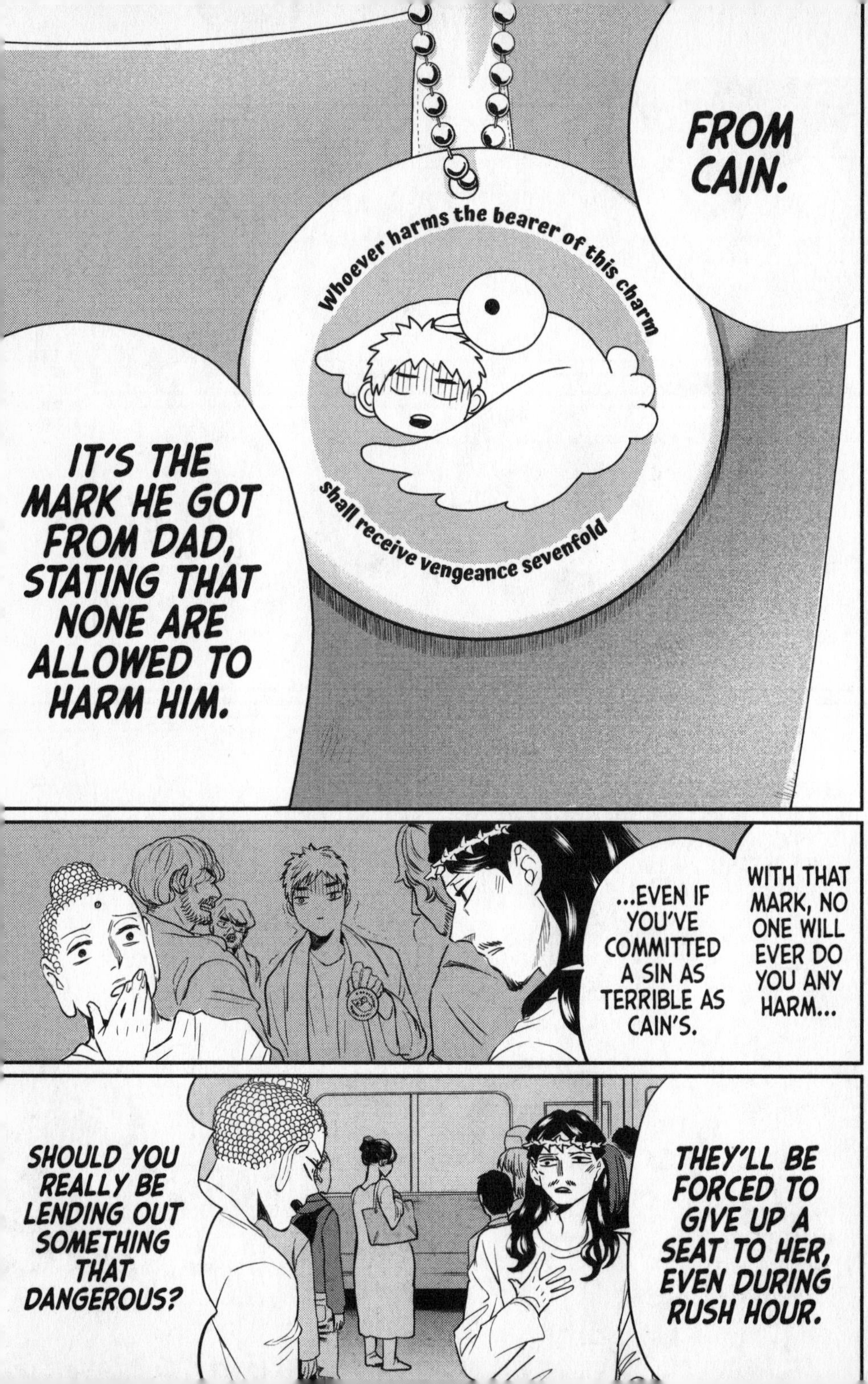
FROM CAIN.
Whoever harms the bearer of this charm
shall receive vengeance sevenfold
IT'S THE MARK HE GOT FROM DAD, STATING THAT NONE ARE ALLOWED TO HARM HIM.
WITH THAT MARK, NO ONE WILL EVER DO YOU ANY HARM...
...EVEN IF YOU'VE COMMITTED A SIN AS TERRIBLE AS CAIN'S.
THEY'LL BE FORCED TO GIVE UP A SEAT TO HER, EVEN DURING RUSH HOUR.
SHOULD YOU REALLY BE LENDING OUT SOMETHING THAT DANGEROUS?

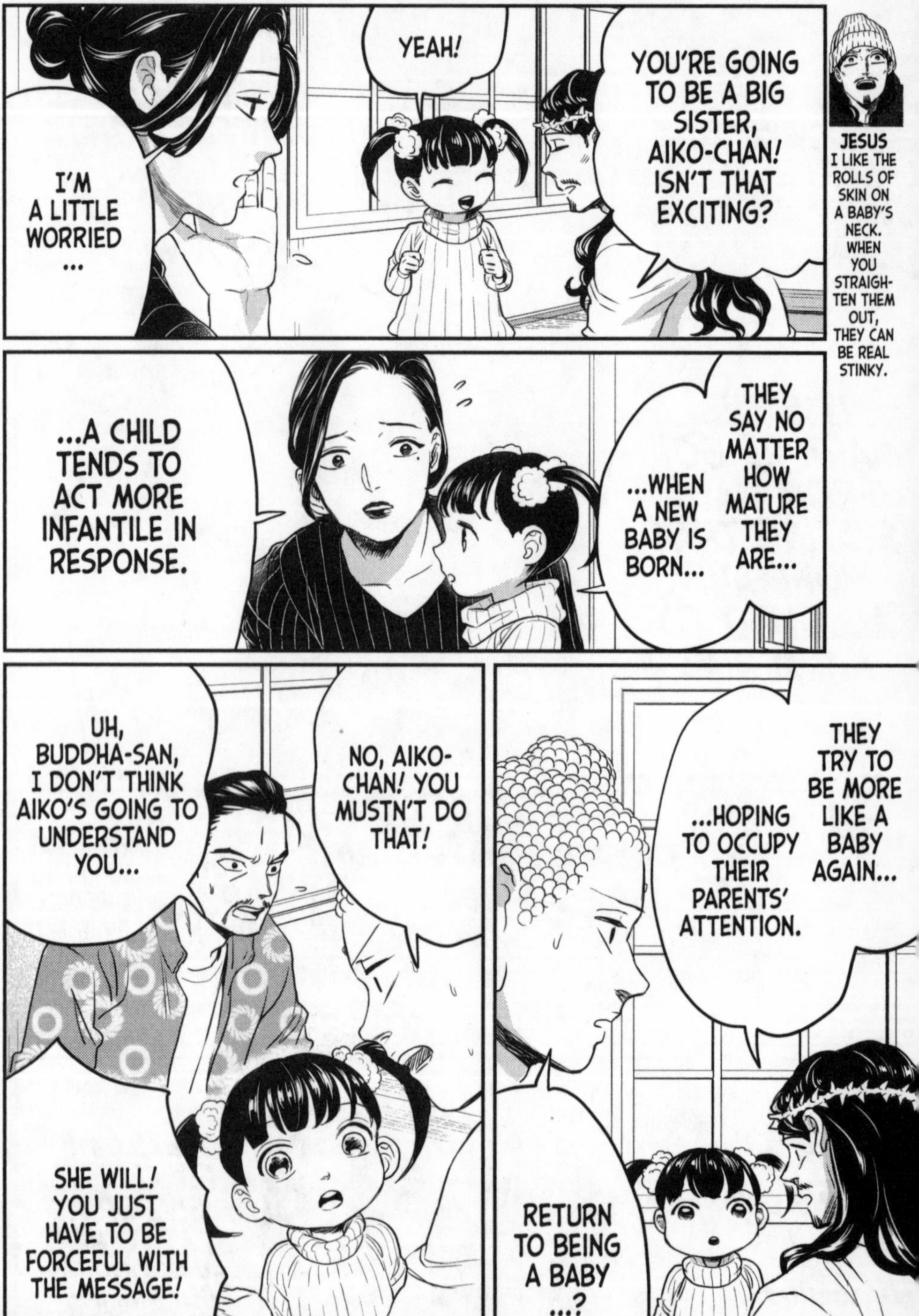
JESUS
I LIKE THE ROLLS OF SKIN ON A BABY'S NECK. WHEN YOU STRAIGHTEN THEM OUT, THEY CAN BE REAL STINKY.
YOU'RE GOING TO BE A BIG SISTER, AIKO-CHAN! ISN'T THAT EXCITING?
YEAH!
I'M A LITTLE WORRIED ...
THEY SAY NO MATTER HOW MATURE THEY ARE...
...WHEN A NEW BABY IS BORN...
...A CHILD TENDS TO ACT MORE INFANTILE IN RESPONSE.
THEY TRY TO BE MORE LIKE A BABY AGAIN...
...HOPING TO OCCUPY THEIR PARENTS' ATTENTION.
RETURN TO BEING A BABY ...?
NO, AIKO-CHAN! YOU MUSTN'T DO THAT!
UH, BUDDHA-SAN, I DON'T THINK AIKO'S GOING TO UNDERSTAND YOU...
SHE WILL! YOU JUST HAVE TO BE FORCEFUL WITH THE MESSAGE!

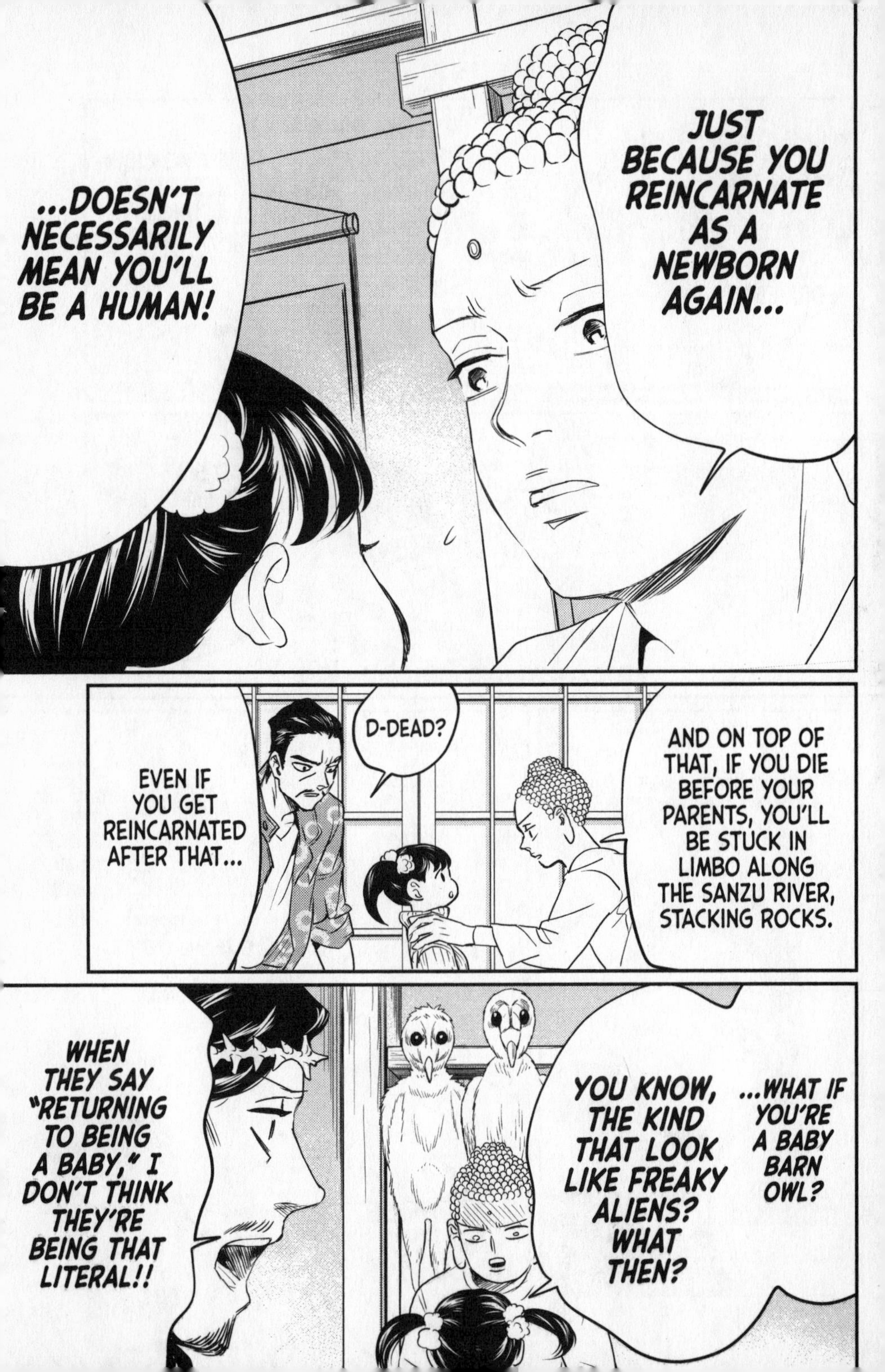
JUST BECAUSE YOU REINCARNATE AS A NEWBORN AGAIN...
...DOESN'T NECESSARILY MEAN YOU'LL BE A HUMAN!
AND ON TOP OF THAT, IF YOU DIE BEFORE YOUR PARENTS, YOU'LL BE STUCK IN LIMBO ALONG THE SANZU RIVER, STACKING ROCKS.
D-DEAD?
EVEN IF YOU GET REINCARNATED AFTER THAT...
...WHAT IF YOU'RE A BABY BARN OWL?
YOU KNOW, THE KIND THAT LOOK LIKE FREAKY ALIENS? WHAT THEN?
WHEN THEY SAY "RETURNING TO BEING A BABY," I DON'T THINK THEY'RE BEING THAT LITERAL!!

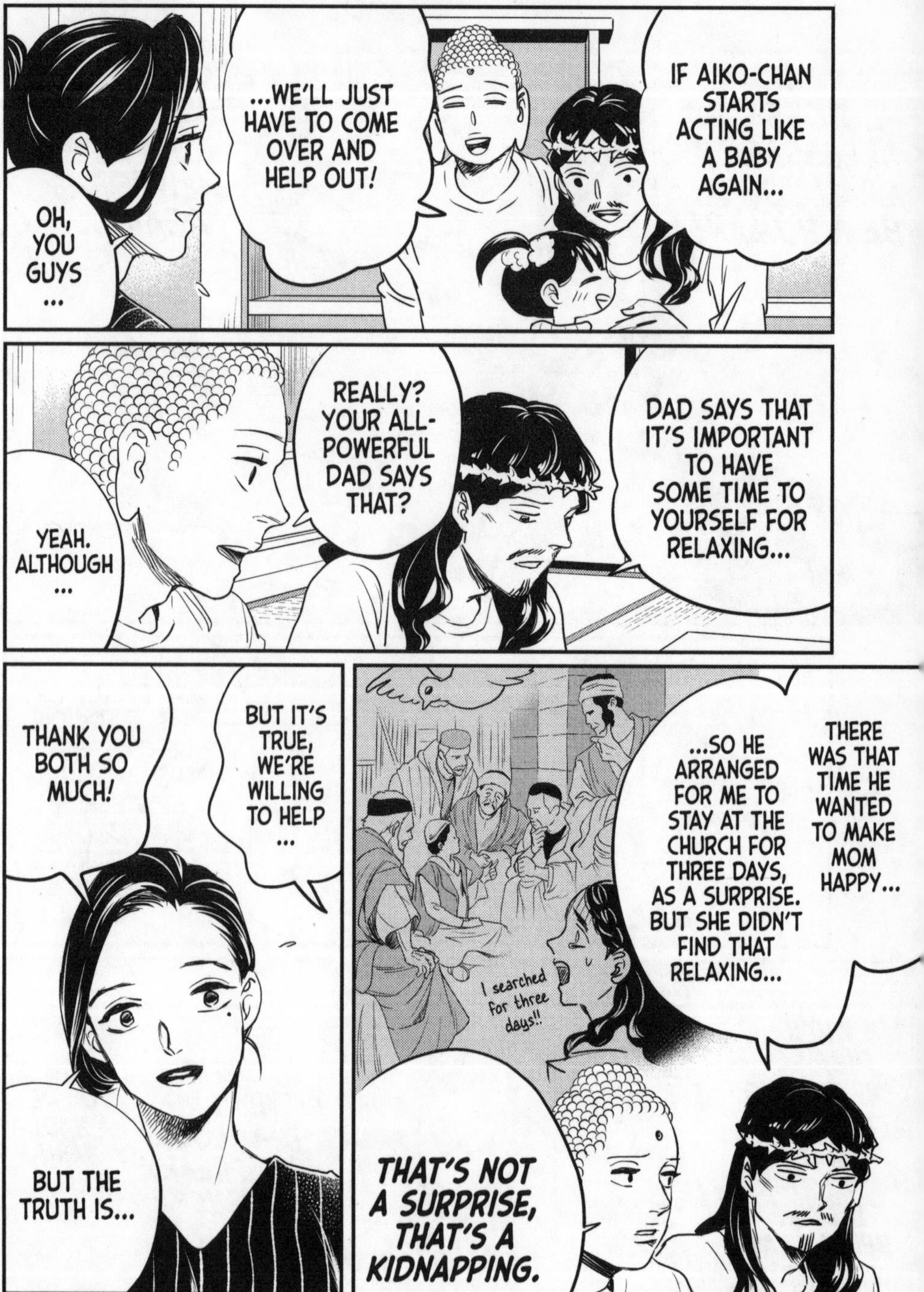
IF AIKO-CHAN STARTS ACTING LIKE A BABY AGAIN...
...WE'LL JUST HAVE TO COME OVER AND HELP OUT!
OH, YOU GUYS ...
DAD SAYS THAT IT'S IMPORTANT TO HAVE SOME TIME TO YOURSELF FOR RELAXING...
REALLY? YOUR ALL-POWERFUL DAD SAYS THAT?
YEAH. ALTHOUGH ...
THERE WAS THAT TIME HE WANTED TO MAKE MOM HAPPY...
...SO HE ARRANGED FOR ME TO STAY AT THE CHURCH FOR THREE DAYS, AS A SURPRISE. BUT SHE DIDN'T FIND THAT RELAXING...
I searched for three days!!
THAT'S NOT A SURPRISE, THAT'S A KIDNAPPING.
BUT IT'S TRUE, WE'RE WILLING TO HELP ...
THANK YOU BOTH SO MUCH!
BUT THE TRUTH IS...

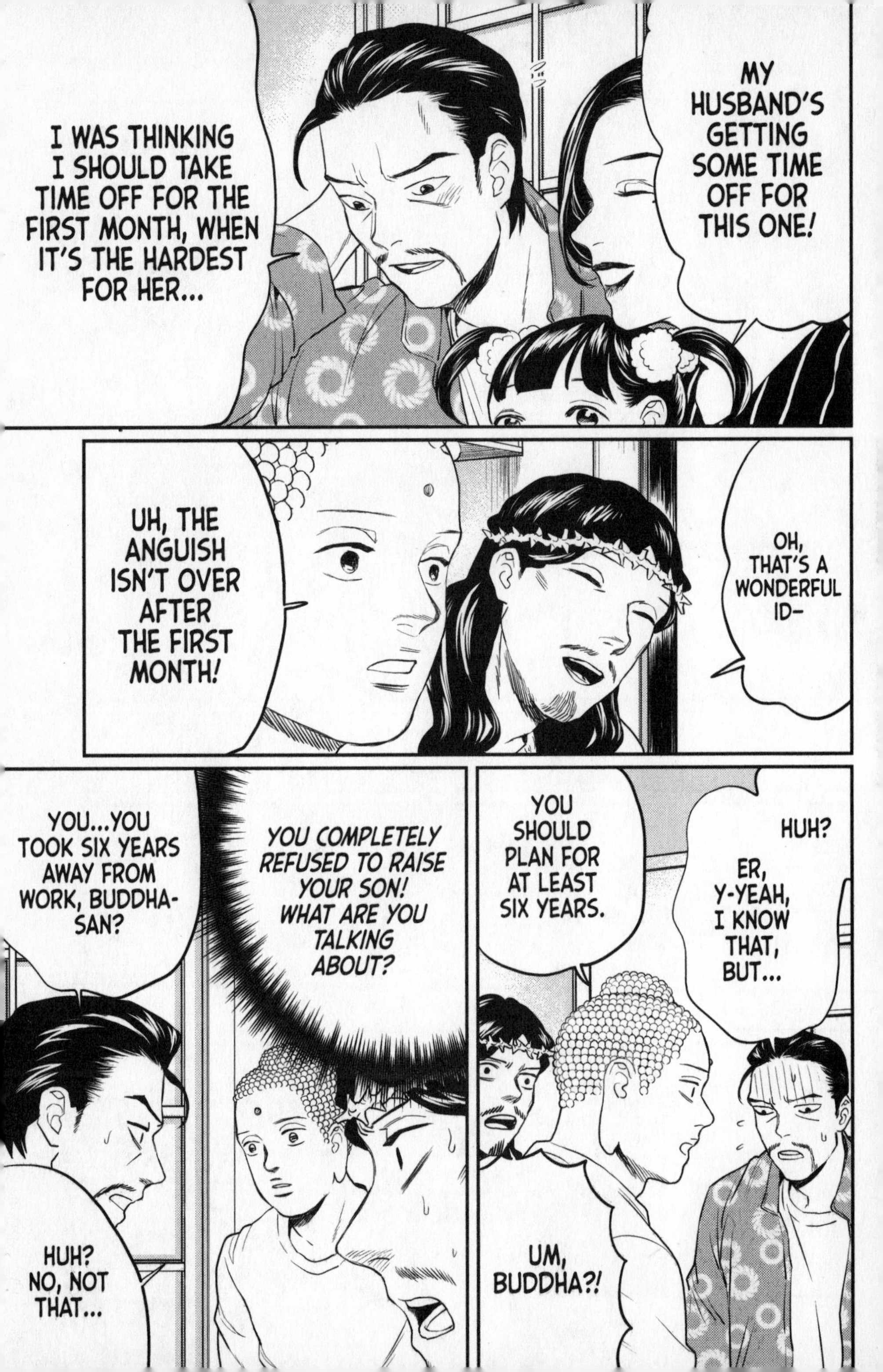
MY HUSBAND'S GETTING SOME TIME OFF FOR THIS ONE!
I WAS THINKING I SHOULD TAKE TIME OFF FOR THE FIRST MONTH, WHEN IT'S THE HARDEST FOR HER...
OH, THAT'S A WONDERFUL ID-
UH, THE ANGUISH ISN'T OVER AFTER THE FIRST MONTH!
HUH?
ER, Y-YEAH, I KNOW THAT, BUT...
YOU SHOULD PLAN FOR AT LEAST SIX YEARS.
UM, BUDDHA?!
YOU COMPLETELY REFUSED TO RAISE YOUR SON! WHAT ARE YOU TALKING ABOUT?
YOU...YOU TOOK SIX YEARS AWAY FROM WORK, BUDDHA-SAN?
HUH? NO, NOT THAT...

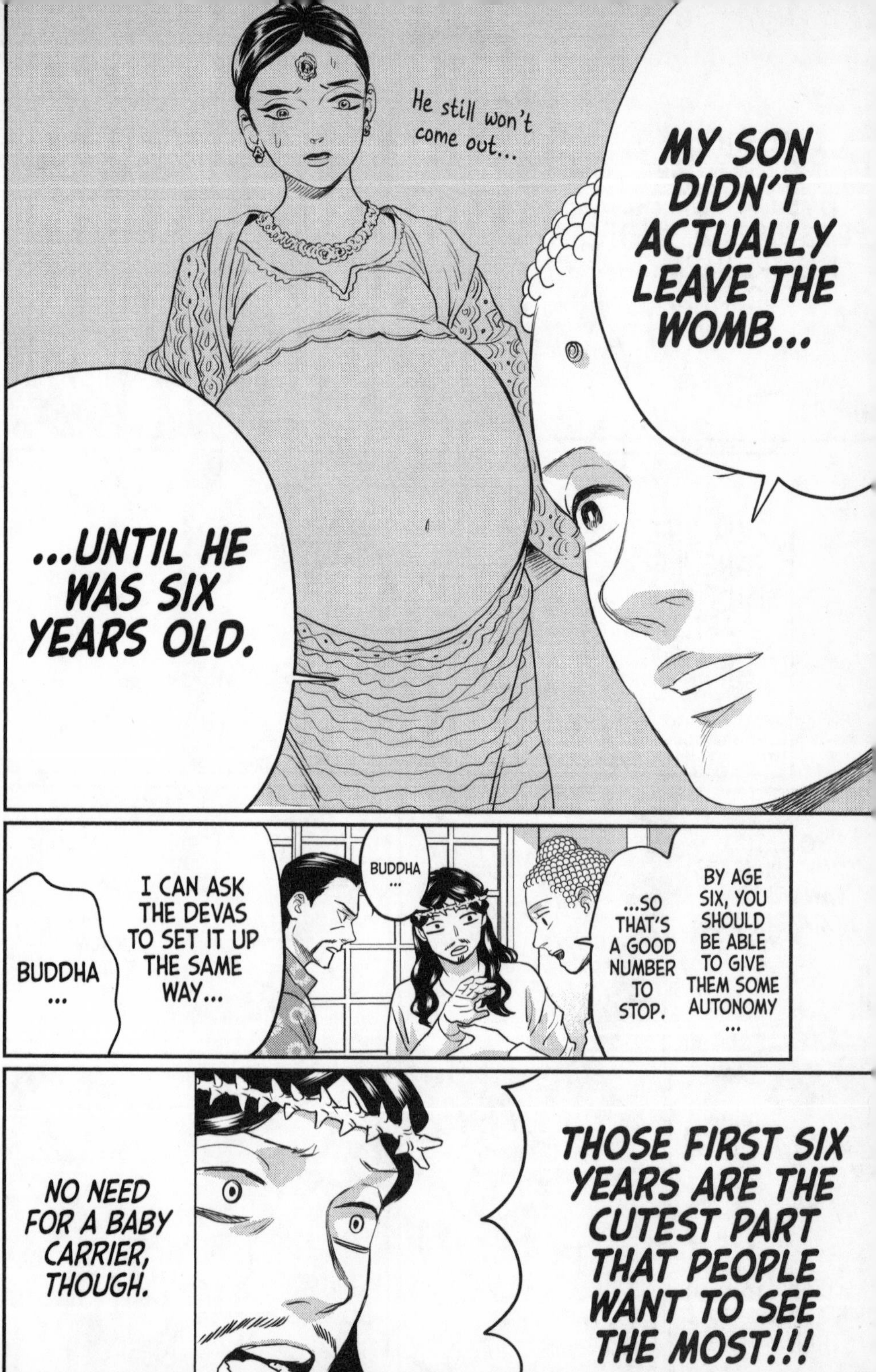
MY SON DIDN'T ACTUALLY LEAVE THE WOMB...
He still won't come out...
...UNTIL HE WAS SIX YEARS OLD.
BY AGE SIX, YOU SHOULD BE ABLE TO GIVE THEM SOME AUTONOMY ...
...SO THAT'S A GOOD NUMBER TO STOP.
BUDDHA ...
I CAN ASK THE DEVAS TO SET IT UP THE SAME WAY...
BUDDHA ...
THOSE FIRST SIX YEARS ARE THE CUTEST PART THAT PEOPLE WANT TO SEE THE MOST!!!
NO NEED FOR A BABY CARRIER, THOUGH.

She doesn't need an epidural.
I was going to make sure her birth was completely painless...

SAINT☆YOUNG MEN

CHAPTER 135 TRANSLATION NOTES

Young Jesus at the temple, page 238

A story of Jesus's childhood recorded in Luke. At age twelve, Jesus accompanied Joseph and Mary on a pilgrimage to Jerusalem, and lingered at the temple there. Joseph and Mary left for the return trip, believing Jesus was still among their traveling party, then realized they were wrong and went back to find him still in the temple after three days, conversing with the elders there. When they were shocked to see him, he said, "Did you not know that I must be in my Father's house?" referring to God.

Rahula, page 240

According to some traditions, Gautama Buddha's son Rahula was said to be conceived on the day of Gautama's renunciation of the world, but born six years later. (Others say Rahula was born on the day of the renunciation.) The delay between conception and birth is explained as the result of bad karma from previous lives.

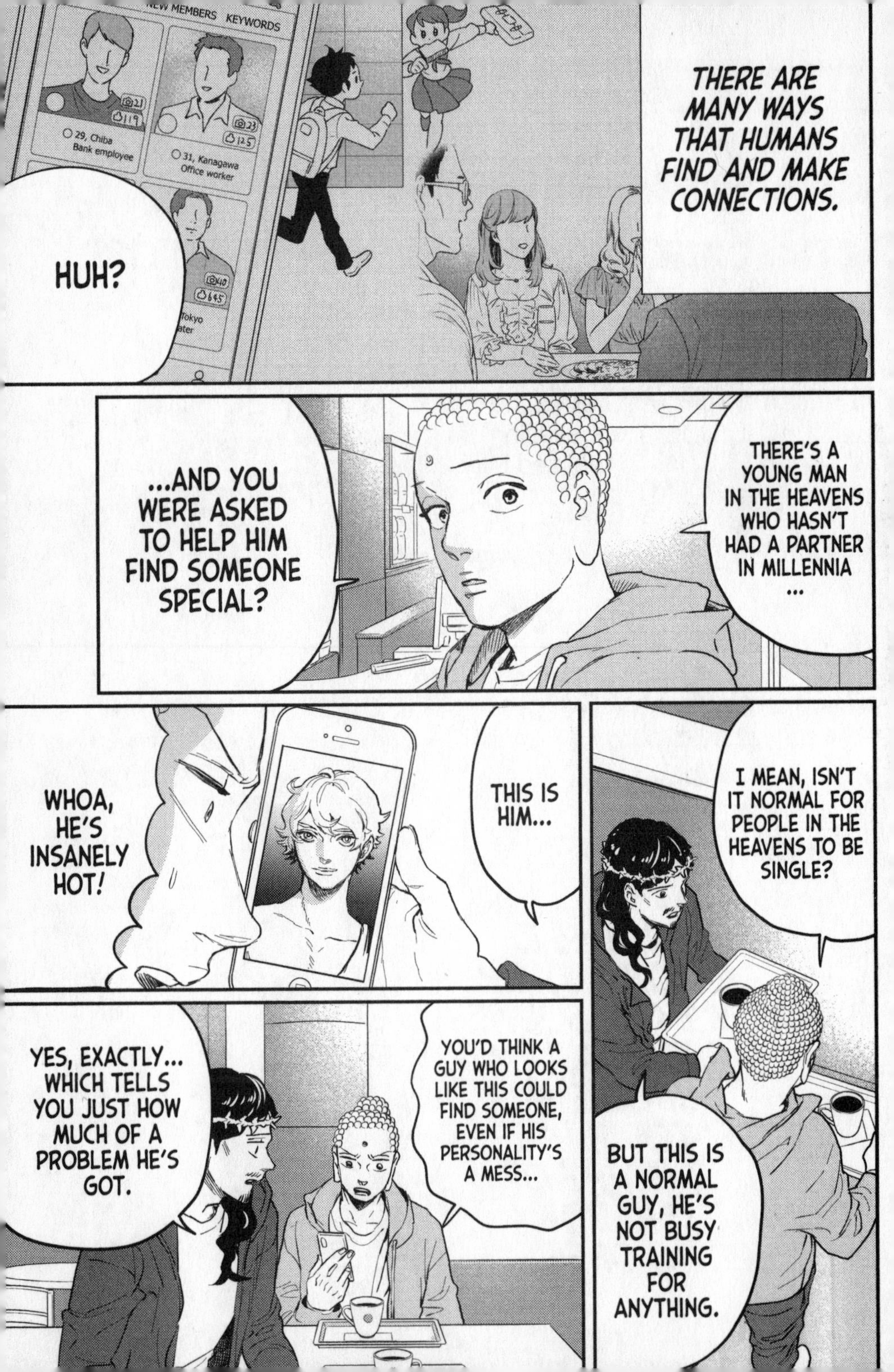
THERE ARE MANY WAYS THAT HUMANS FIND AND MAKE CONNECTIONS.
NEW MEMBERS KEYWORDS
29, Chiba Bank employee
31, Kanagawa Office worker
HUH?
THERE'S A YOUNG MAN IN THE HEAVENS WHO HASN'T HAD A PARTNER IN MILLENNIA ...
...AND YOU WERE ASKED TO HELP HIM FIND SOMEONE SPECIAL?
I MEAN, ISN'T IT NORMAL FOR PEOPLE IN THE HEAVENS TO BE SINGLE?
BUT THIS IS A NORMAL GUY, HE'S NOT BUSY TRAINING FOR ANYTHING.
THIS IS HIM...
WHOA, HE'S INSANELY HOT!
YOU'D THINK A GUY WHO LOOKS LIKE THIS COULD FIND SOMEONE, EVEN IF HIS PERSONALITY'S A MESS...
YES, EXACTLY... WHICH TELLS YOU JUST HOW MUCH OF A PROBLEM HE'S GOT.

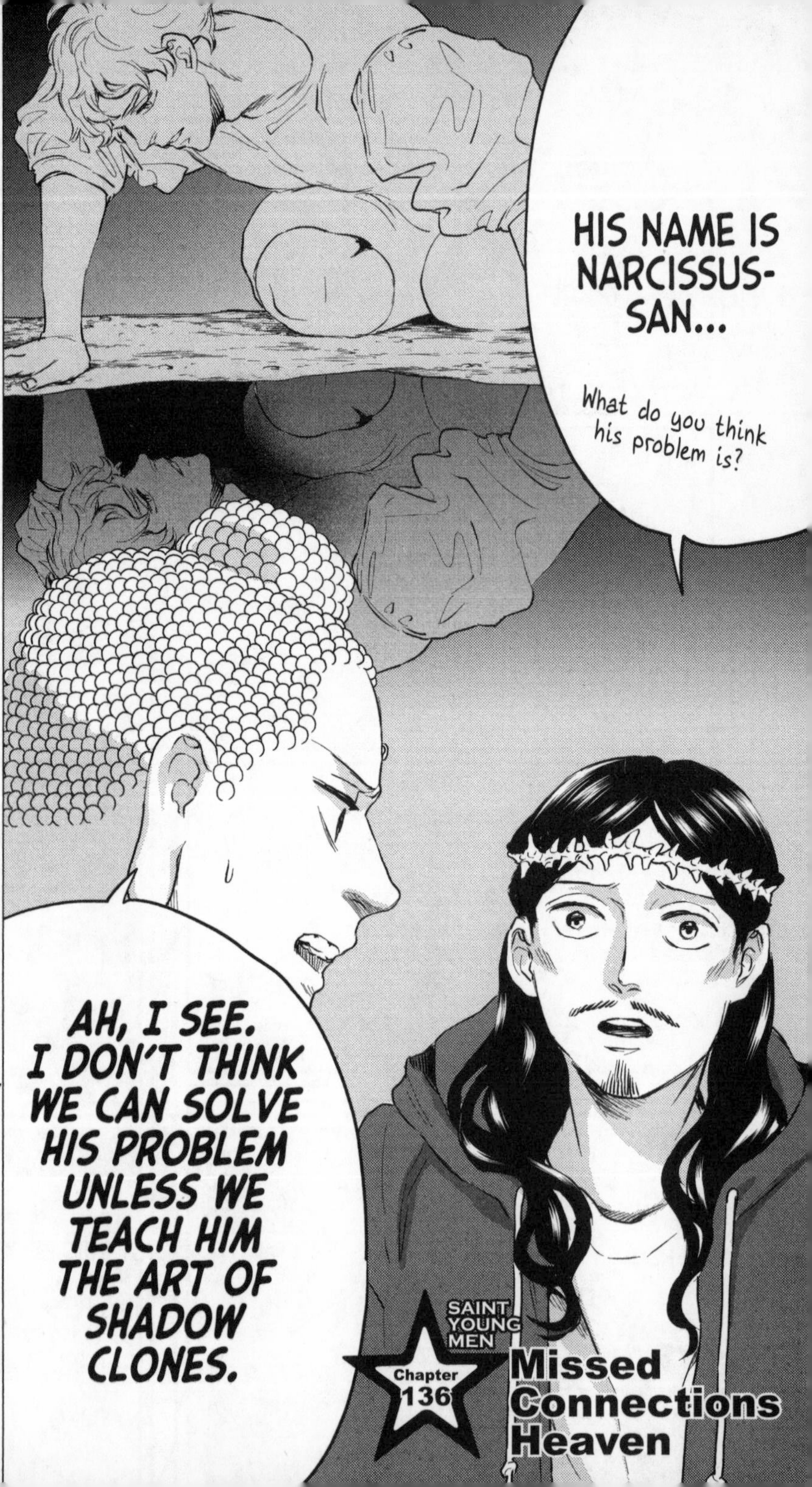
HIS NAME IS NARCISSUS-SAN...
What do you think his problem is?
AH, I SEE. I DON'T THINK WE CAN SOLVE HIS PROBLEM UNLESS WE TEACH HIM THE ART OF SHADOW CLONES.
SAINT YOUNG MEN
Chapter 136
Missed Connections Heaven

HE'S THE YOUNG MAN WHO FELL IN LOVE WITH HIS REFLECTION, THE ROOT OF THE WORD "NARCISSISM."

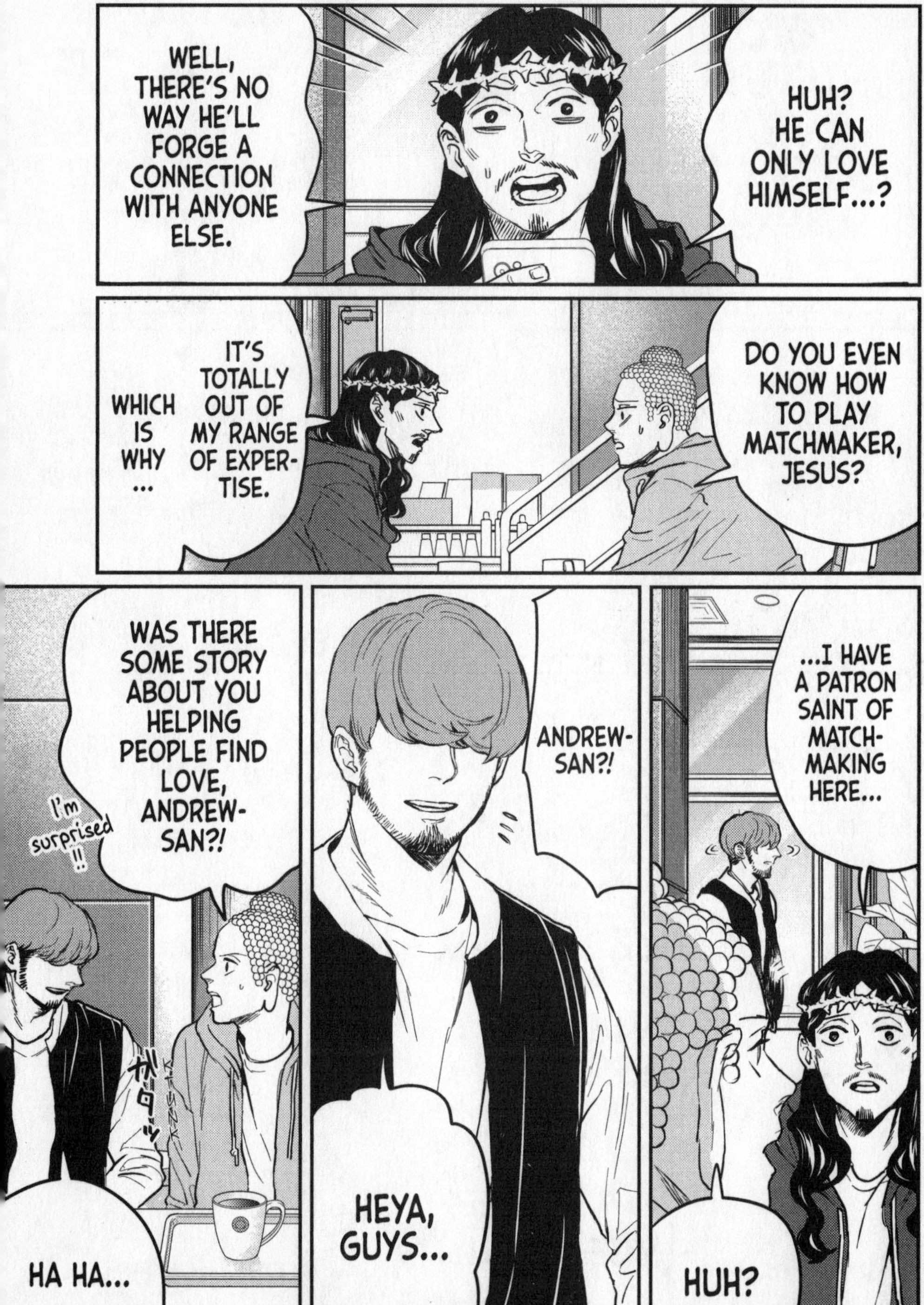
HUH? HE CAN ONLY LOVE HIMSELF...?
WELL, THERE'S NO WAY HE'LL FORGE A CONNECTION WITH ANYONE ELSE.
DO YOU EVEN KNOW HOW TO PLAY MATCHMAKER, JESUS?
IT'S TOTALLY OUT OF MY RANGE OF EXPERTISE.
WHICH IS WHY...
...I HAVE A PATRON SAINT OF MATCHMAKING HERE...
HUH?
ANDREW-SAN?!
HEYA, GUYS...
WAS THERE SOME STORY ABOUT YOU HELPING PEOPLE FIND LOVE, ANDREW-SAN?!
I'm surprised!!
HA HA...

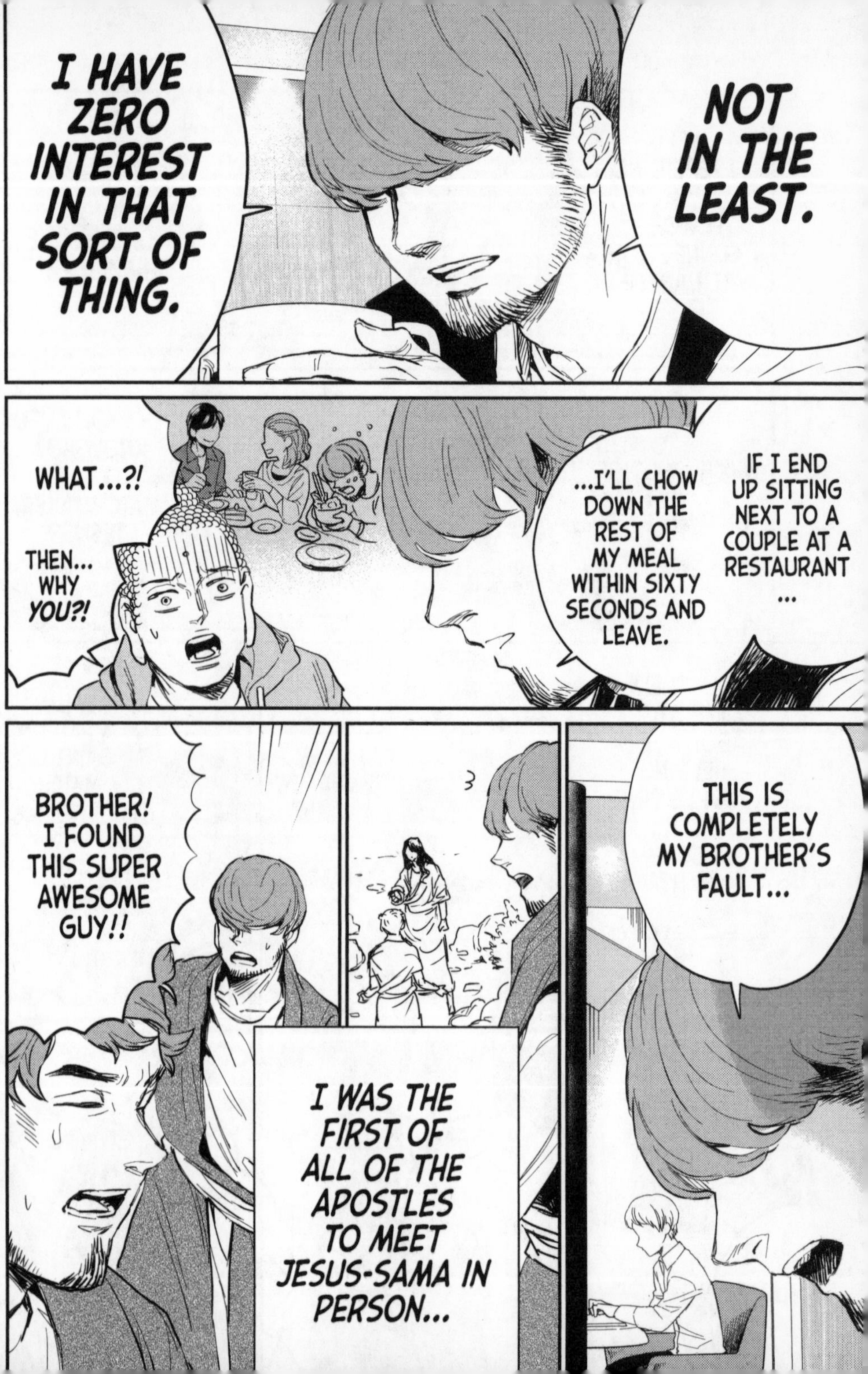
I HAVE ZERO INTEREST IN THAT SORT OF THING.
NOT IN THE LEAST.
IF I END UP SITTING NEXT TO A COUPLE AT A RESTAURANT ...
...I'LL CHOW DOWN THE REST OF MY MEAL WITHIN SIXTY SECONDS AND LEAVE.
WHAT...?!
THEN... WHY YOU?!
THIS IS COMPLETELY MY BROTHER'S FAULT...
I WAS THE FIRST OF ALL OF THE APOSTLES TO MEET JESUS-SAMA IN PERSON...
BROTHER! I FOUND THIS SUPER AWESOME GUY!!

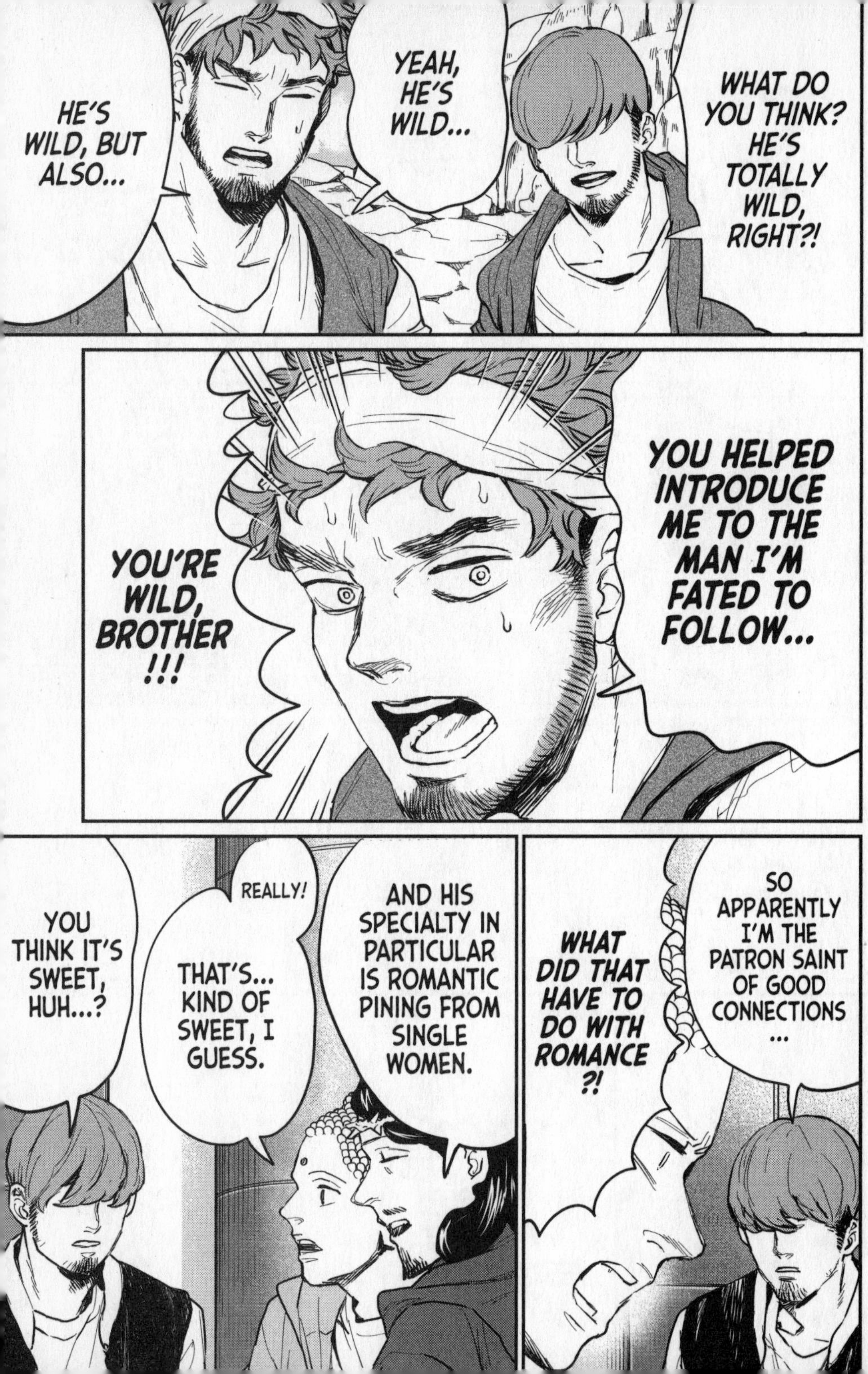
WHAT DO YOU THINK? HE'S TOTALLY WILD, RIGHT?!
YEAH, HE'S WILD...
HE'S WILD, BUT ALSO...
YOU HELPED INTRODUCE ME TO THE MAN I'M FATED TO FOLLOW...
YOU'RE WILD, BROTHER!!!
SO APPARENTLY I'M THE PATRON SAINT OF GOOD CONNECTIONS...
WHAT DID THAT HAVE TO DO WITH ROMANCE?!
AND HIS SPECIALTY IN PARTICULAR IS ROMANTIC PINING FROM SINGLE WOMEN.
REALLY!
THAT'S... KIND OF SWEET, I GUESS.
YOU THINK IT'S SWEET, HUH...?

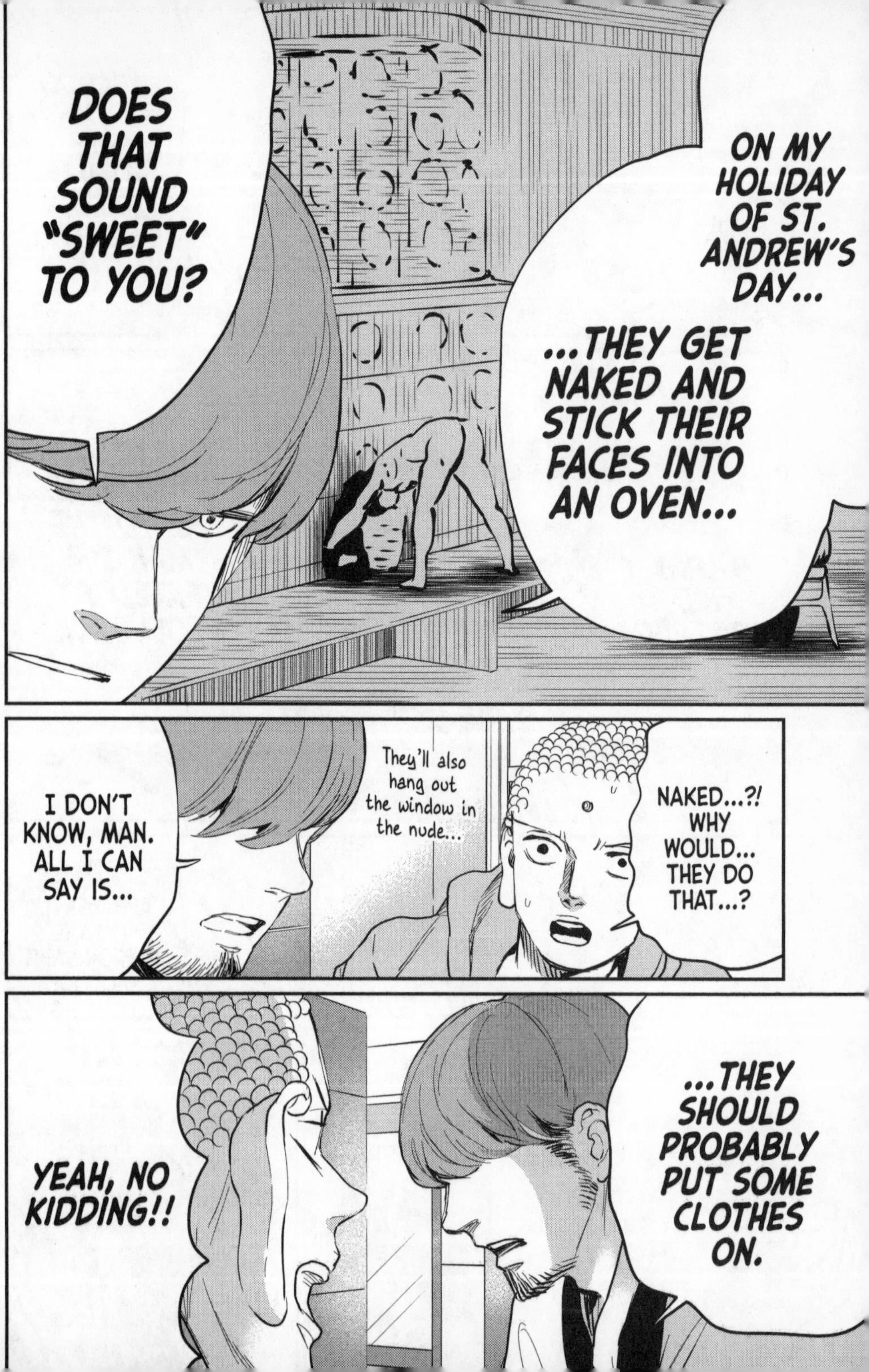
ON MY HOLIDAY OF ST. ANDREW'S DAY...
...THEY GET NAKED AND STICK THEIR FACES INTO AN OVEN...
DOES THAT SOUND "SWEET" TO YOU?
NAKED...?! WHY WOULD... THEY DO THAT...?
They'll also hang out the window in the nude...
I DON'T KNOW, MAN. ALL I CAN SAY IS...
...THEY SHOULD PROBABLY PUT SOME CLOTHES ON.
YEAH, NO KIDDING!!

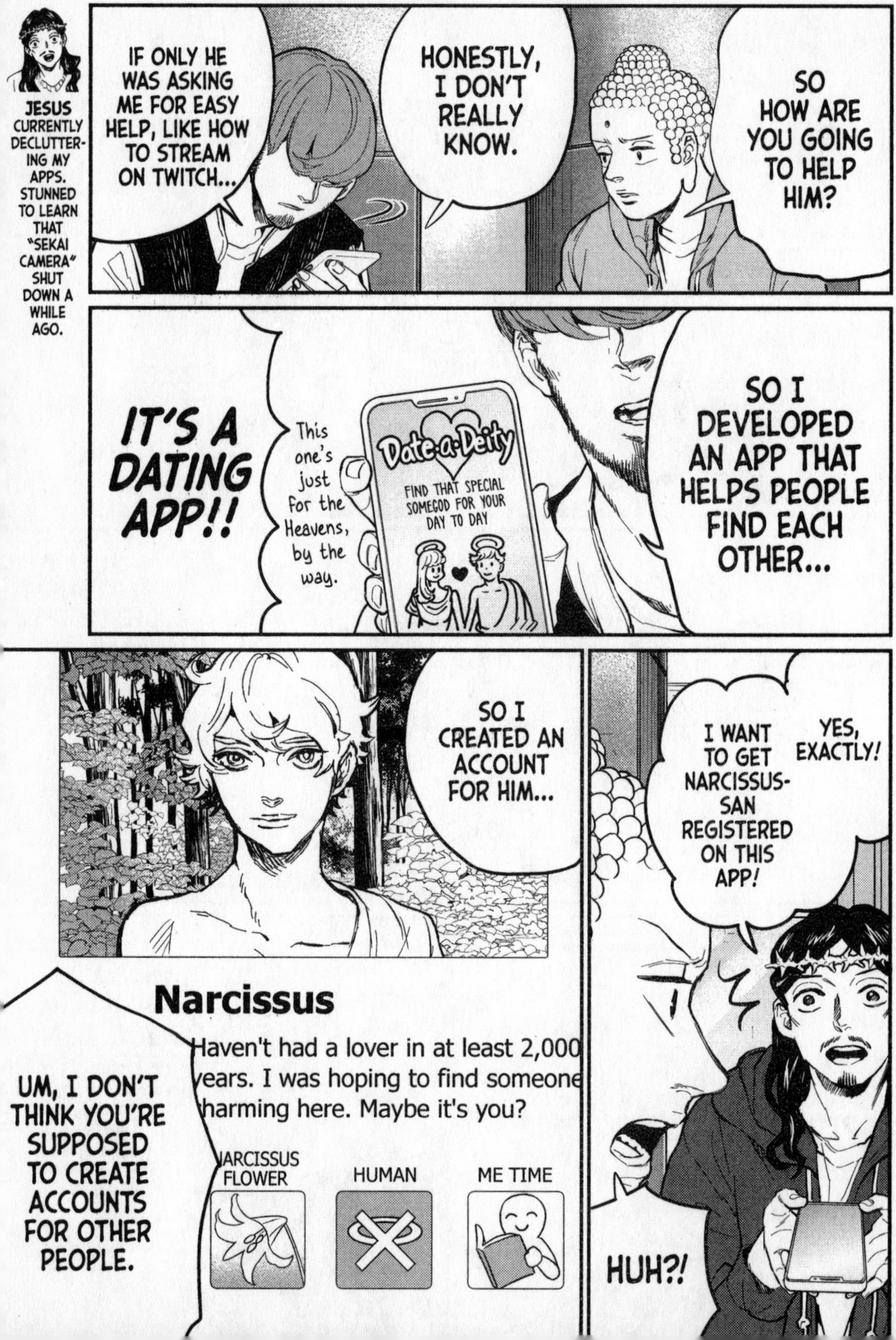
SO HOW ARE YOU GOING TO HELP HIM?
HONESTLY, I DON'T REALLY KNOW.
IF ONLY HE WAS ASKING ME FOR EASY HELP, LIKE HOW TO STREAM ON TWITCH...
JESUS CURRENTLY DECLUTTERING MY APPS. STUNNED TO LEARN THAT "SEKAI CAMERA" SHUT DOWN A WHILE AGO.
SO I DEVELOPED AN APP THAT HELPS PEOPLE FIND EACH OTHER...
Date-a-Deity
FIND THAT SPECIAL SOMEGOD FOR YOUR DAY TO DAY
IT'S A DATING APP!!
This one's just for the Heavens, by the way.
YES, EXACTLY!
I WANT TO GET NARCISSUS-SAN REGISTERED ON THIS APP!
HUH?!
SO I CREATED AN ACCOUNT FOR HIM...
Narcissus
Haven't had a lover in at least 2,000
years. I was hoping to find someone
harming here. Maybe it's you?
NARCISSUS FLOWER
HUMAN
ME TIME
UM, I DON'T THINK YOU'RE SUPPOSED TO CREATE ACCOUNTS FOR OTHER PEOPLE.

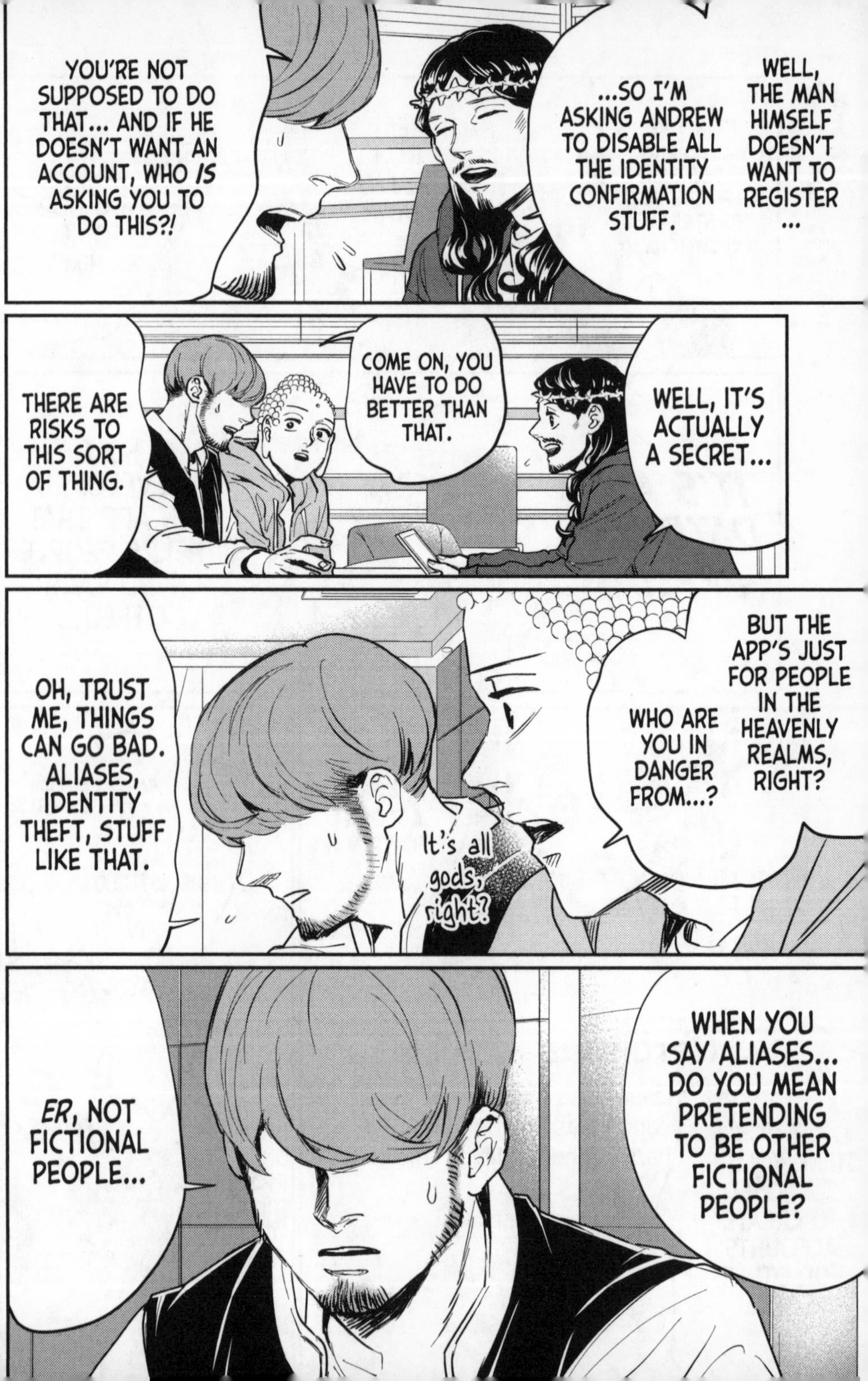
WELL, THE MAN HIMSELF DOESN'T WANT TO REGISTER ...
...SO I'M ASKING ANDREW TO DISABLE ALL THE IDENTITY CONFIRMATION STUFF.
YOU'RE NOT SUPPOSED TO DO THAT... AND IF HE DOESN'T WANT AN ACCOUNT, WHO *IS* ASKING YOU TO DO THIS?!
WELL, IT'S ACTUALLY A SECRET...
COME ON, YOU HAVE TO DO BETTER THAN THAT.
THERE ARE RISKS TO THIS SORT OF THING.
BUT THE APP'S JUST FOR PEOPLE IN THE HEAVENLY REALMS, RIGHT?
WHO ARE YOU IN DANGER FROM...?
It's all gods, right?
OH, TRUST ME, THINGS CAN GO BAD. ALIASES, IDENTITY THEFT, STUFF LIKE THAT.
WHEN YOU SAY ALIASES... DO YOU MEAN PRETENDING TO BE OTHER FICTIONAL PEOPLE?
ER, NOT FICTIONAL PEOPLE...

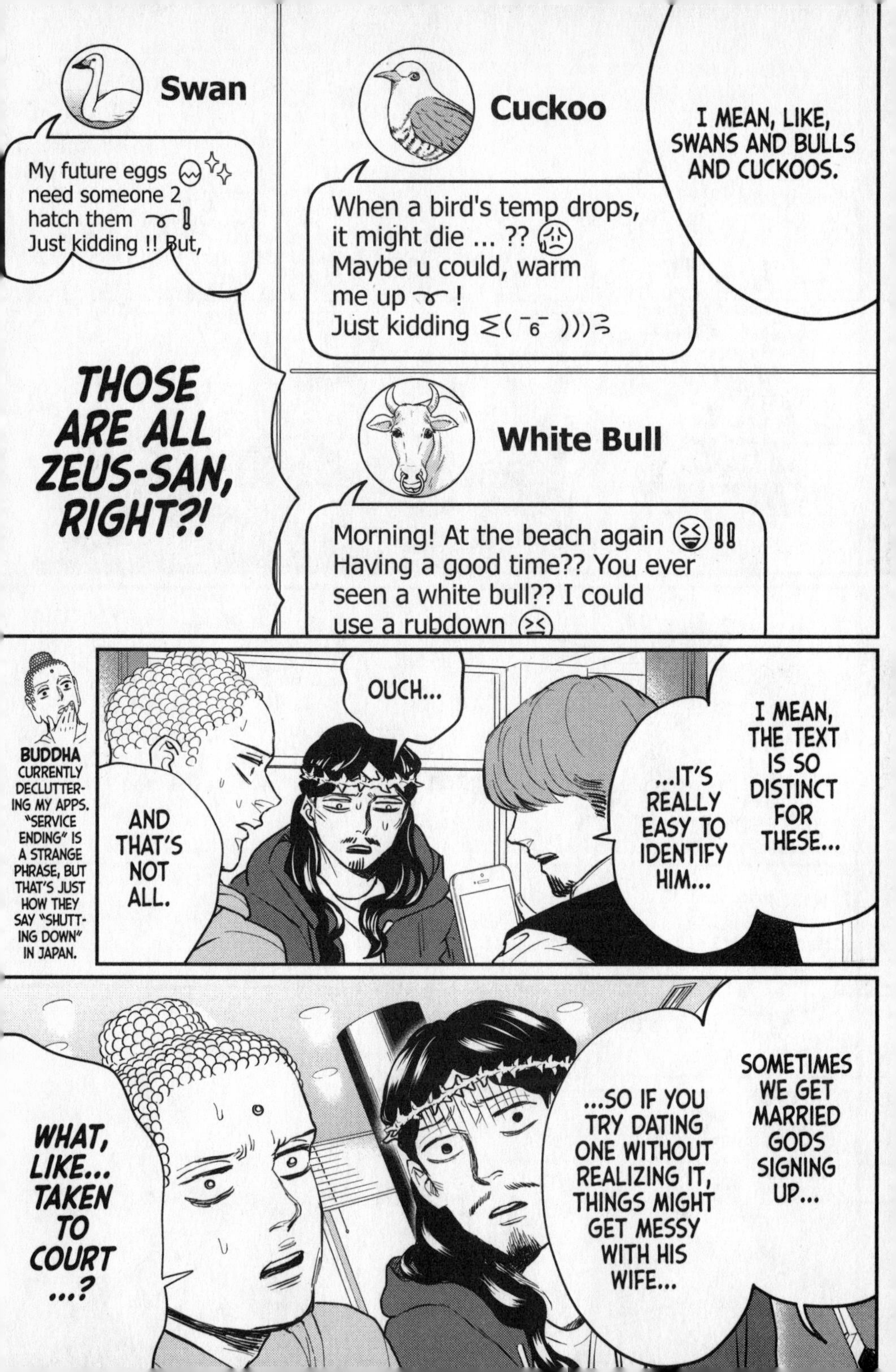
I MEAN, LIKE, SWANS AND BULLS AND CUCKOOS.
Cuckoo
When a bird's temp drops, it might die ... ?? Maybe u could, warm me up ! Just kidding
Swan
My future eggs need someone 2 hatch them ! Just kidding !! But,
White Bull
Morning! At the beach again !! Having a good time?? You ever seen a white bull?? I could use a rubdown
THOSE ARE ALL ZEUS-SAN, RIGHT?!
I MEAN, THE TEXT IS SO DISTINCT FOR THESE...
...IT'S REALLY EASY TO IDENTIFY HIM...
OUCH...
AND THAT'S NOT ALL.
BUDDHA CURRENTLY DECLUTTERING MY APPS. "SERVICE ENDING" IS A STRANGE PHRASE, BUT THAT'S JUST HOW THEY SAY "SHUTTING DOWN" IN JAPAN.
SOMETIMES WE GET MARRIED GODS SIGNING UP...
...SO IF YOU TRY DATING ONE WITHOUT REALIZING IT, THINGS MIGHT GET MESSY WITH HIS WIFE...
WHAT, LIKE... TAKEN TO COURT...?

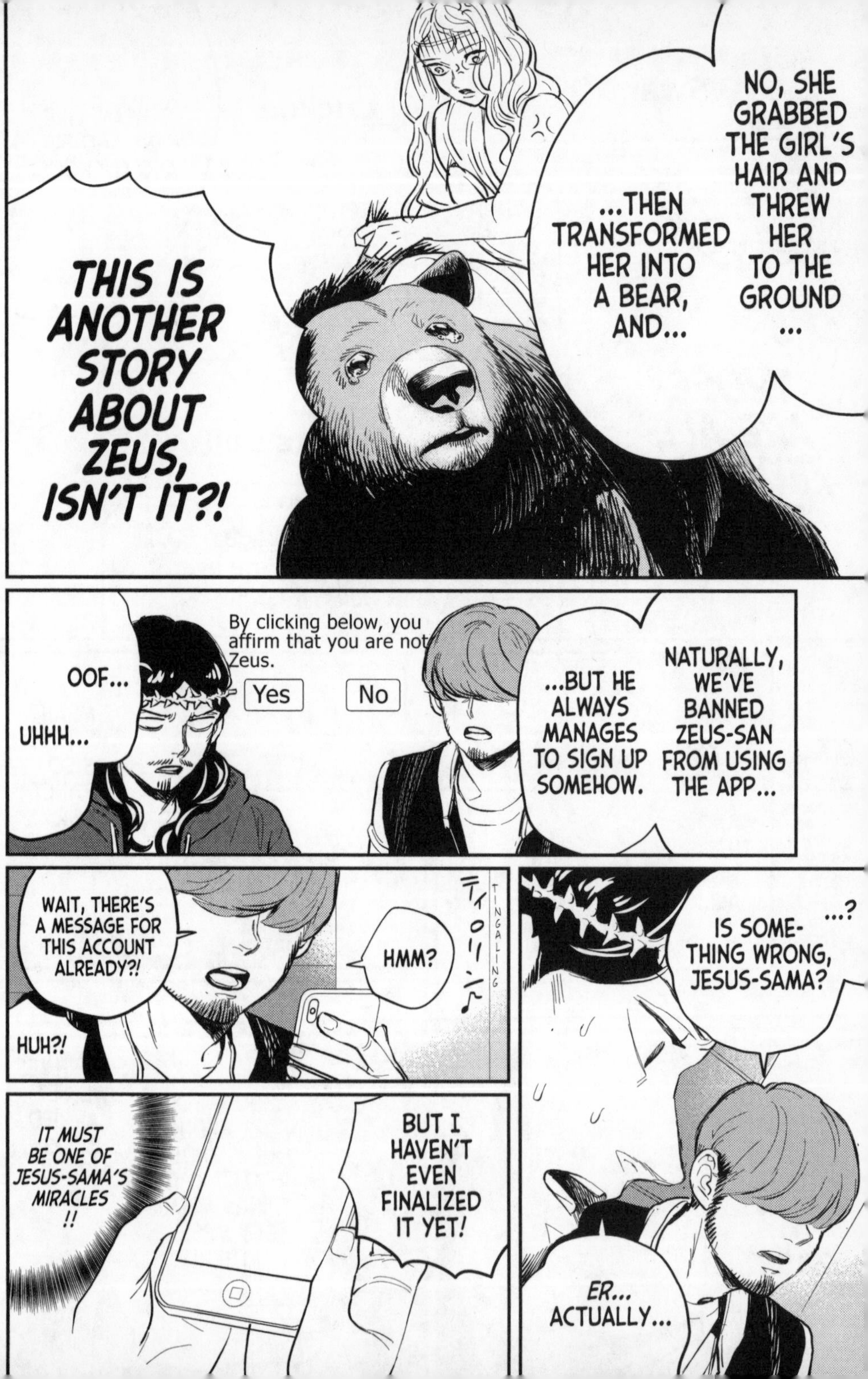
NO, SHE GRABBED THE GIRL'S HAIR AND THREW HER TO THE GROUND ...
...THEN TRANSFORMED HER INTO A BEAR, AND...
THIS IS ANOTHER STORY ABOUT ZEUS, ISN'T IT?!
NATURALLY, WE'VE BANNED ZEUS-SAN FROM USING THE APP...
...BUT HE ALWAYS MANAGES TO SIGN UP SOMEHOW.
By clicking below, you affirm that you are not Zeus.
Yes
No
OOF...
UHHH...
...?
IS SOME-THING WRONG, JESUS-SAMA?
ER... ACTUALLY...
TINGALING
HMM?
WAIT, THERE'S A MESSAGE FOR THIS ACCOUNT ALREADY?!
HUH?!
BUT I HAVEN'T EVEN FINALIZED IT YET!
IT MUST BE ONE OF JESUS-SAMA'S MIRACLES !!

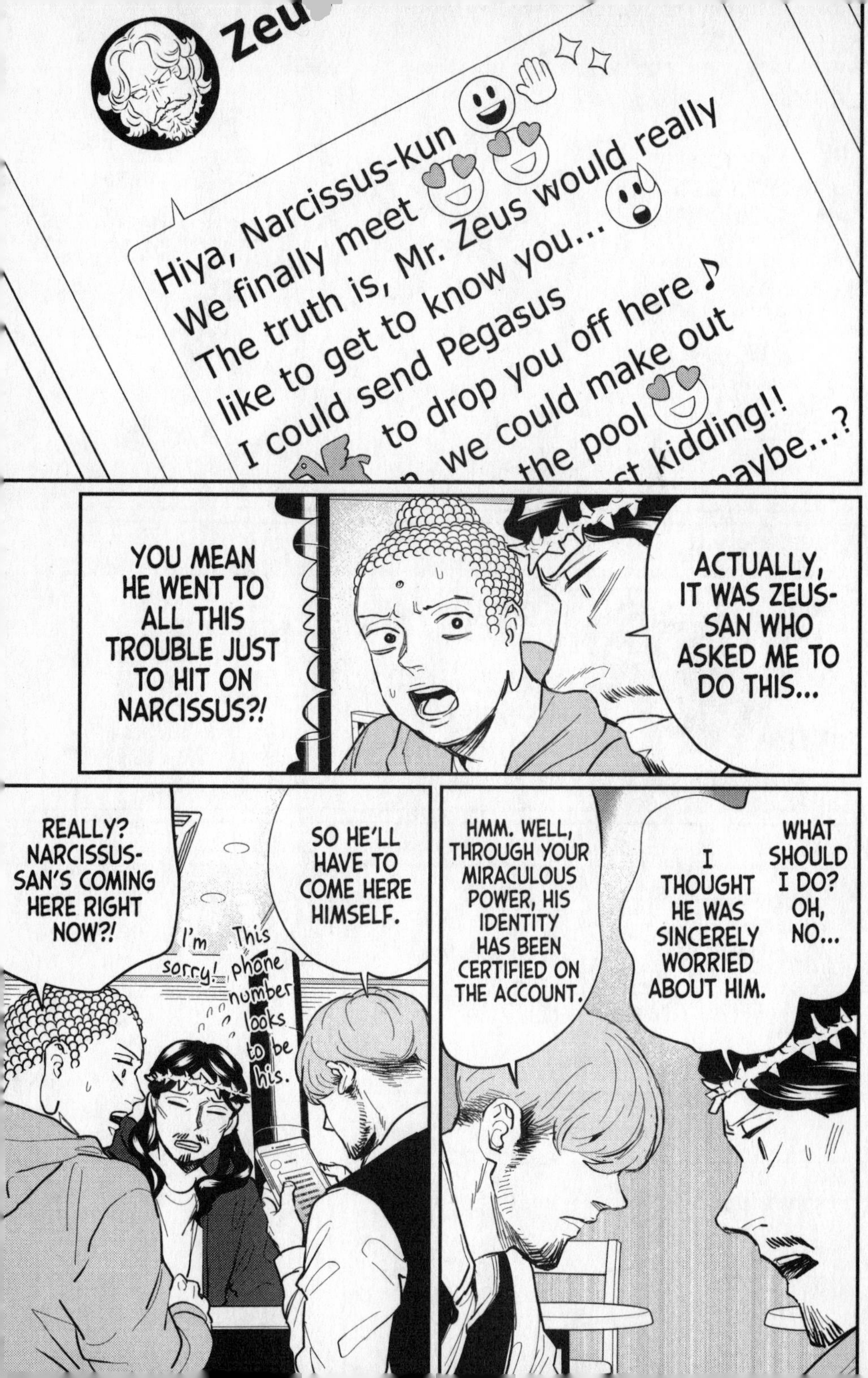
Hiya, Narcissus-kun
We finally meet
The truth is, Mr. Zeus would really
like to get to know you...
I could send Pegasus
to drop you off here ♪
we could make out
the pool
kidding!!
maybe...?
ACTUALLY, IT WAS ZEUS-SAN WHO ASKED ME TO DO THIS...
YOU MEAN HE WENT TO ALL THIS TROUBLE JUST TO HIT ON NARCISSUS?!
WHAT SHOULD I DO? OH, NO...
I THOUGHT HE WAS SINCERELY WORRIED ABOUT HIM.
HMM. WELL, THROUGH YOUR MIRACULOUS POWER, HIS IDENTITY HAS BEEN CERTIFIED ON THE ACCOUNT.
SO HE'LL HAVE TO COME HERE HIMSELF.
This phone number looks to be his.
I'm sorry!
REALLY? NARCISSUS-SAN'S COMING HERE RIGHT NOW?!

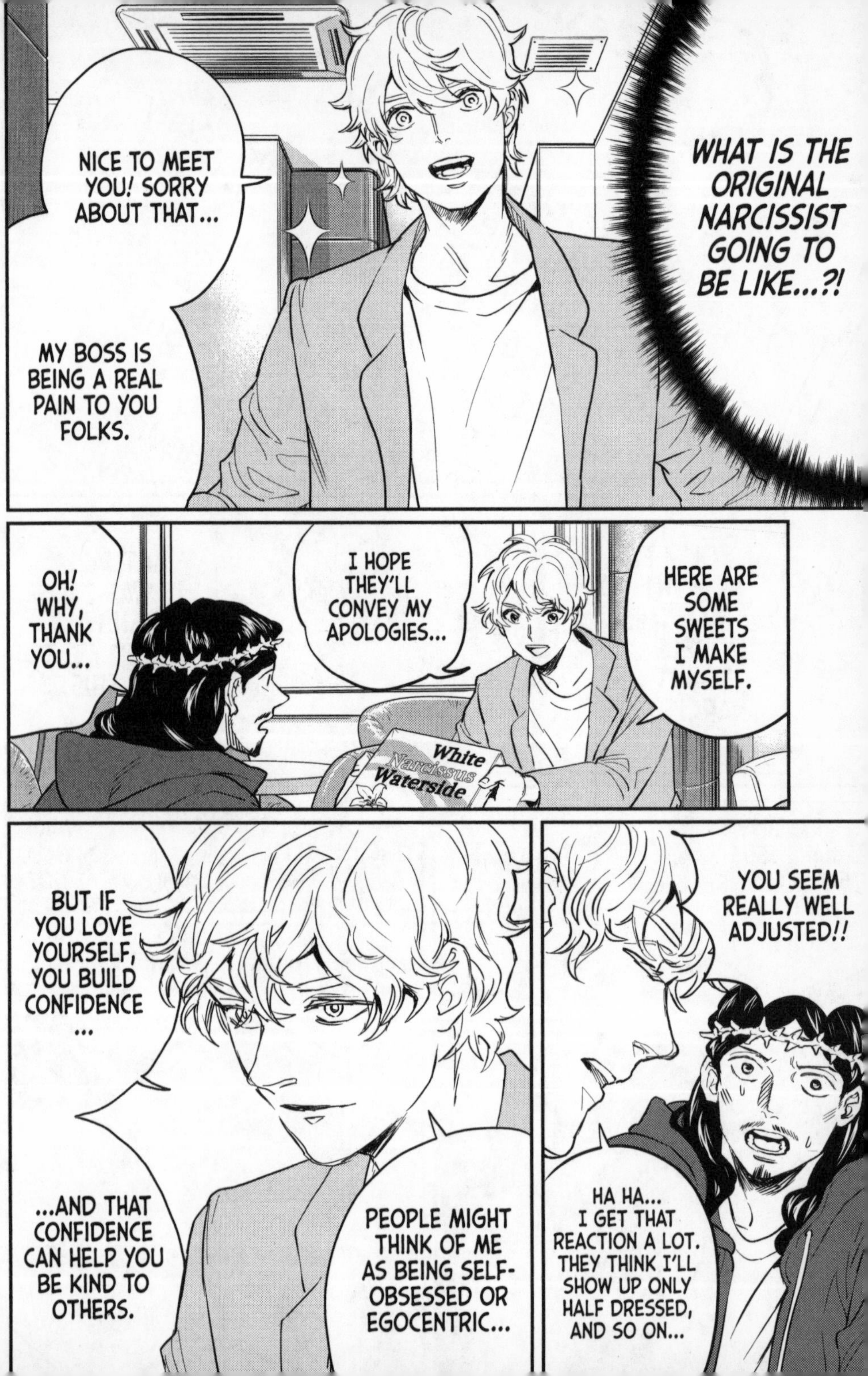

WHAT IS THE ORIGINAL NARCISSIST GOING TO BE LIKE...?!
NICE TO MEET YOU! SORRY ABOUT THAT...
MY BOSS IS BEING A REAL PAIN TO YOU FOLKS.
HERE ARE SOME SWEETS I MAKE MYSELF.
I HOPE THEY'LL CONVEY MY APOLOGIES...
OH! WHY, THANK YOU...
White Narcissus Waterside
YOU SEEM REALLY WELL ADJUSTED!!
HA HA... I GET THAT REACTION A LOT. THEY THINK I'LL SHOW UP ONLY HALF DRESSED, AND SO ON...
PEOPLE MIGHT THINK OF ME AS BEING SELF-OBSESSED OR EGOCENTRIC...
BUT IF YOU LOVE YOURSELF, YOU BUILD CONFIDENCE...
...AND THAT CONFIDENCE CAN HELP YOU BE KIND TO OTHERS.

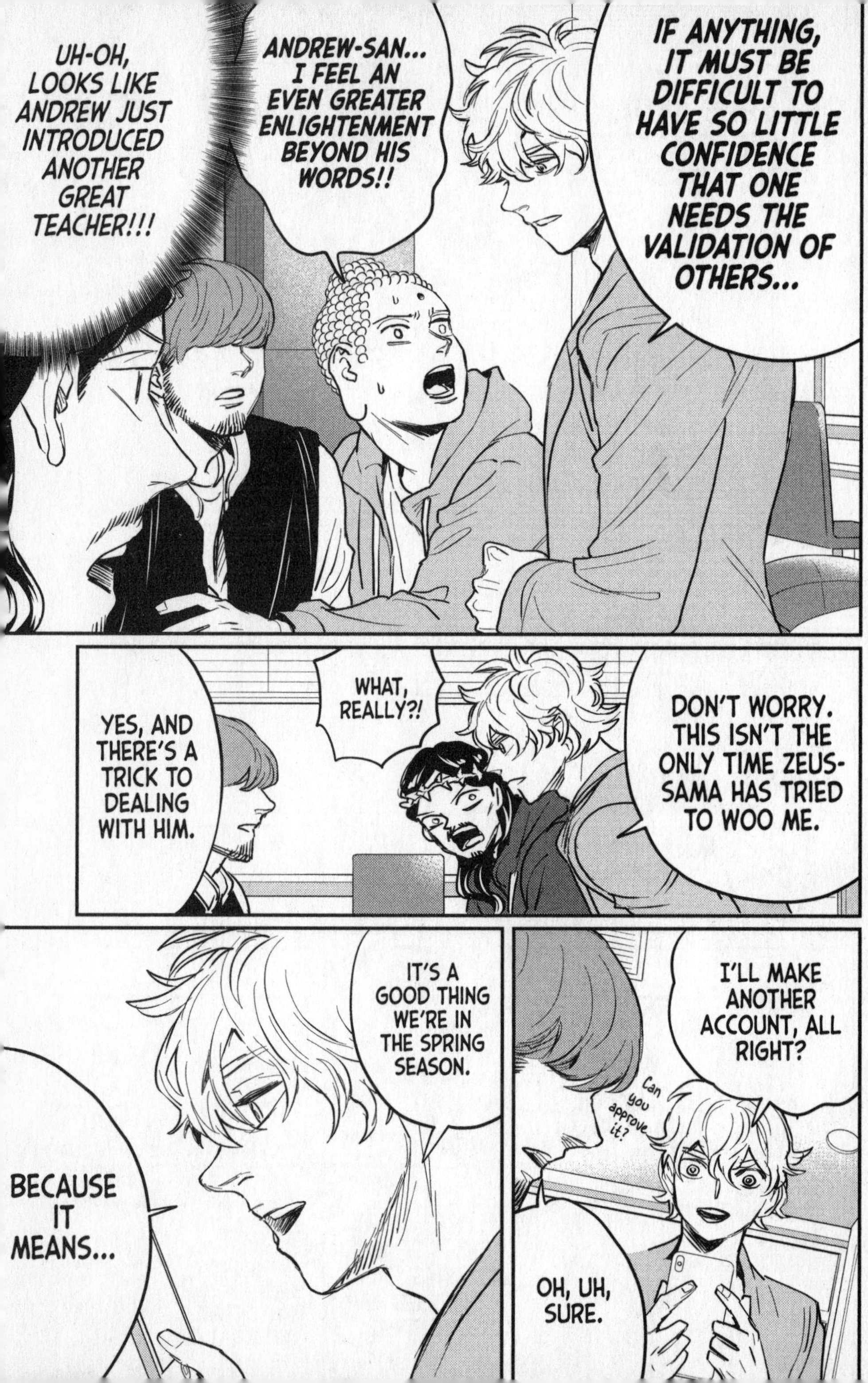
IF ANYTHING, IT MUST BE DIFFICULT TO HAVE SO LITTLE CONFIDENCE THAT ONE NEEDS THE VALIDATION OF OTHERS...
ANDREW-SAN... I FEEL AN EVEN GREATER ENLIGHTENMENT BEYOND HIS WORDS!!
UH-OH, LOOKS LIKE ANDREW JUST INTRODUCED ANOTHER GREAT TEACHER!!!
DON'T WORRY. THIS ISN'T THE ONLY TIME ZEUS-SAMA HAS TRIED TO WOO ME.
WHAT, REALLY?!
YES, AND THERE'S A TRICK TO DEALING WITH HIM.
I'LL MAKE ANOTHER ACCOUNT, ALL RIGHT?
Can you approve it?
OH, UH, SURE.
IT'S A GOOD THING WE'RE IN THE SPRING SEASON.
BECAUSE IT MEANS...

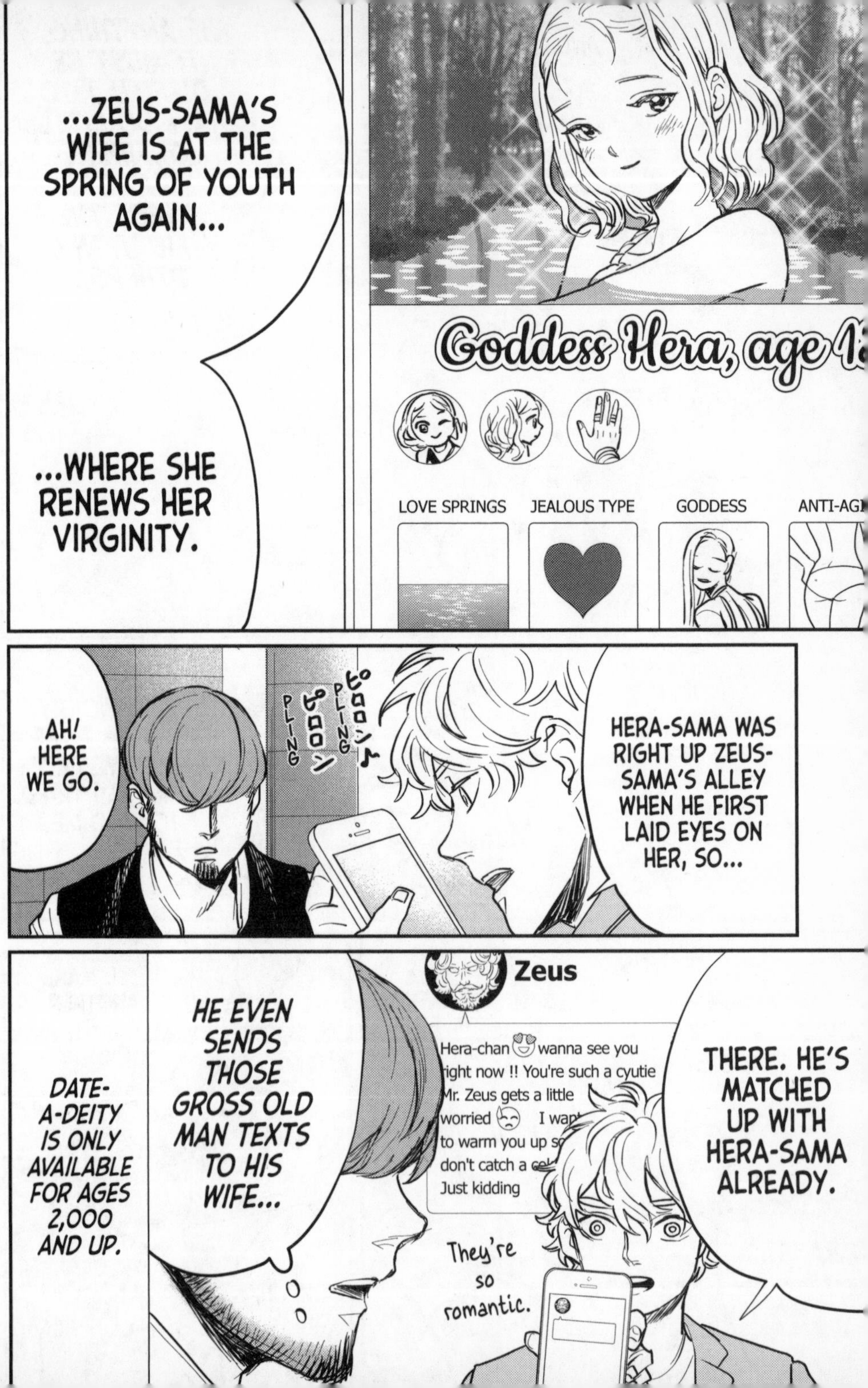

Goddess Hera, age 1
LOVE SPRINGS
JEALOUS TYPE
GODDESS
ANTI-AG
...ZEUS-SAMA'S WIFE IS AT THE SPRING OF YOUTH AGAIN...
...WHERE SHE RENEWS HER VIRGINITY.
HERA-SAMA WAS RIGHT UP ZEUS-SAMA'S ALLEY WHEN HE FIRST LAID EYES ON HER, SO...
ピロロン♪ PLING
ピロロン PLING
AH! HERE WE GO.
THERE. HE'S MATCHED UP WITH HERA-SAMA ALREADY.
Zeus
Hera-chan wanna see you
right now !! You're such a cyutie
Mr. Zeus gets a little
worried I wan
to warm you up s
don't catch a c
Just kidding
They're so romantic.
HE EVEN SENDS THOSE GROSS OLD MAN TEXTS TO HIS WIFE...
DATE-A-DEITY IS ONLY AVAILABLE FOR AGES 2,000 AND UP.

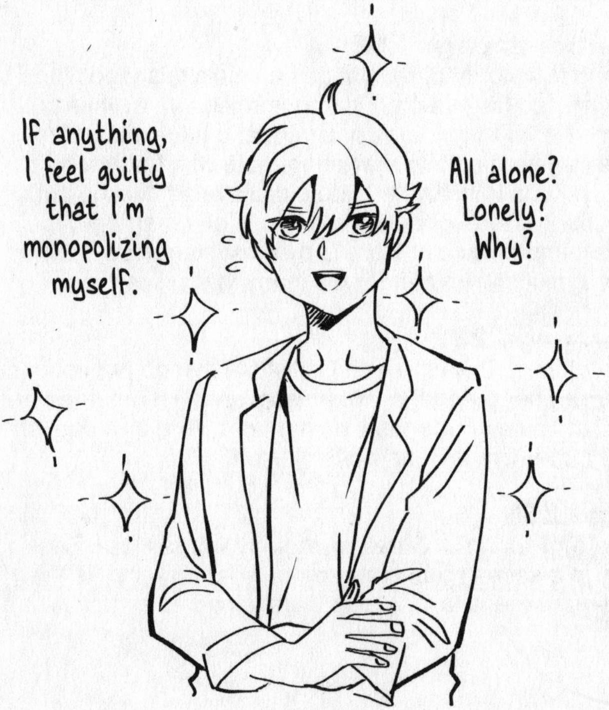
All alone? Lonely? Why?
If anything, I feel guilty that I'm monopolizing myself.

SAINT☆YOUNG MEN

CHAPTER 136 TRANSLATION NOTES

St. Andrew's Day, page 249
St. Andrew's Day is a holiday observed on November 30th in Scotland and other, mostly European countries. Depending on the country, there are many local customs and superstitions surrounding the holiday and the night before, many of which involve young women hoping for luck with getting married, or seeing their future husband in a vision.

Sekai Camera, page 251
A Japanese phone app and AR (augmented reality) tagging service. it allowed people to take photos and place shareable "tags" with messages and information inside of those photos, then upload to GPS so that the tags could appear when other people used their app camera in the same place. It shut down in 2014.

Zeus's transformations, page 252
Zeus is famous for having transformed into various animals to seduce the women and goddesses he had his eye on. He transformed into a white bull to abduct Europa, the mother of King Minos of Crete, and namesake of the continent of Europe. He transformed into a swan to mate with Leda, who later bore Helen (of Troy). Zeus transformed into a disheveled cuckoo during a storm to cause the stubborn Hera, goddess of women and marriage, to take the bird to her breast and nurture it. Hera is by most standards Zeus's "traditional" wife, and vengeful toward him for his many infidelities.

Hera and the bear, page 252
Another story of Zeus's adultery, this time with Callisto, a nymph or princess whom Zeus seduced. When her pregnancy was discovered, Hera turned her into a bear. Before Callisto could accidentally be hunted by her own son, she was added to Ursa Major, the "Great Bear" constellation.

Hera's spring, page 256
Kanathos was the name of a spring in Greek mythology where Hera, Zeus's wife, bathed every year, in a secret ritual that renewed her virginity. As the goddess of women and marriage, she was also worshipped as a virgin.

SAINT☆YOUNG MEN

SAINT☆YOUNG MEN

Saint Young Men 9 copyright © 2019-2020 Hikaru Nakamura
English translation copyright © 2021 Hikaru Nakamura

Published in the United States by Kodansha Comics, an imprint of Kodansha USA Publishing, LLC, New York.

Publication rights for this English edition arranged through Kodansha Ltd., Tokyo.

First published in Japan in 2019-2020 by Kodansha Ltd., Tokyo as *Seinto oniisan*, volumes 17 & 18.

ISBN 978-1-64651-281-2

Original cover design by Hiroshi Niigami (NARTI;S)

Printed in the United States of America.

www.kodansha.us

9 8 7 6 5 4 3 2 1
Translation: Stephen Paul
Lettering: E.K. Weaver
Editing: Nathaniel Gallant
Kodansha Comics edition cover design by Phil Balsman

Publisher: Kiichiro Sugawara

Director of publishing services: Ben Applegate
Associate director, publishing operations: Stephen Pakula
Publishing services managing editors: Madison Salters, Alanna Ruse
Production managers: Emi Lotto, Angela Zurlo